王杰 〔英〕斯宾塞 —— 主编

马克思主义与未来

第三届中英马克思主义美学双边论坛论文集

Marxism and The Future

The Third Sino-British Bilateral Forum on Marxist Aesthetics

中央编译出版社
CCTP Central Compilation & Translation Press

序 言

王 杰

公元1516年，在资本主义和现代化运动还仅仅有一些微小的因素和症候的时代，英国学者和社会主义者就出版了影响深远的《乌托邦》，它至今将近500年了。英国的社会主义思想后来成为马克思主义最重要的思想来源之一。追求一个符合人性的理想社会的愿望和设想，是所有文明都具有的，这与人性有关；另一方面，以对现实的深刻批评为基础，不满足于既有的现实，对一种更美好、更理想、更符合人性的社会的强烈情感驱动，在学术上称为"乌托邦冲动"的现象，却是工业化文明和现代化过程的一个伴生现象，也是工业文明和现代化过程的最重要的文化内驱动力。马克思主义的伟大贡献不在于指出这种现象的存在，而在于将这种现象的解释置于科学的理论——历史唯物主义的基础之上。

工业文明是建立在技术不断进步的基础上的，当技术成为一种技术至上主义，技术可以操纵和控制一切的时候，技术事实上就走向了人性的反面。在这种状况下，出现了反社会乌托邦的著作和思潮，人类的未来似乎不再美好，除了物质享受的高度发达以外，人类社会似乎正向着非人性和反人性的方向发展，因此，悲观主义的疑云一直在20世纪弥漫，在哲学、文学、艺术和社会科学研究的许多领域都有所体现。2012年4月，第二届中英马克思主义美学双边论坛在英国曼城的"工人阶级图书馆"落下帷幕，我与大卫·奥德尔森、麦克·桑德斯、罗伯特·斯宾塞、马海丽四人在曼城运河边上的一个餐馆里讨论下一届年会的主题，大家一致认为，美国和欧洲的经济危机还将持续，对现实和未来的思考应该重新提上议事日程，因此大家决定将2013年论坛的主题确定为"马克思主义与未来"。在当代社会不管欧洲、美洲还是亚洲，"未来"不再是一个清晰和明朗的概念，新自由主义所带来的社会严重不公平，生态危机急剧恶化，文化的批评性被市场经济严重腐蚀，社会伦理价值失范，等等，都需要我们正视现实的问题，勇敢地探讨其中的一系列重大理论问题，以便为社会的发展提供新的方向和动力。

论坛得到了国内外的广泛响应，15个国家与地区的100余名代表出席了会议，会议共收到81篇论文，围绕着"社会理想的文学艺术表达及其意义"、"'真实'的美学和社会意义"、"当代悲剧观念与马克思主义的解释"、"审美资本主义批评"、"马克思主义与当代大学教育改革"等议题发表了论文并展开了热烈的讨论。会议被《外国文学研究》、《文艺报》、《探索与争鸣》、《社会科学报》、《文艺理论与批评》等十余家媒体作了报道，国际美学学会网站、俄罗斯 TFRRA HUMANA 杂志、韩国《21世纪马克思主义》（Marxist 21）杂志也发表了会议综述。收录在这本文集中的，只是会议论文的一部分。在我看来，未来不是简单的"梦想"，不是物质生活水平的简单提高，未来也不惟是革命的激情和直接的"乌托邦冲动"的对象化，未来建立在技术进步的基础上，但技术进步不等于未来，未来是生态文明的时代，但也不仅仅是实现人与自然的协调统一。未来还涉及社会的合理、公正，涉及人的自由和解放，涉及符合于人性的生活。未来不是幻想而是可以达到的现实。在当今人文学科和社会科学中关于"未来"的思考林林总总，在这里我们发出马克思主义者的声音，希望激发出更多的"回声"，鼓舞那些善良和古道热肠的人们直面现实，并努力使它更加美好。

2013年10月20日
于上海交通大学美学与文化理论研究所

Preface

Wang Jie

In the year of 1516, the age when the feeble factor and symptom of capitalism and movement of modernization merely emerged, British scholars and socialists published the profoundly influenced masterpiece *Utopia*, which happened 500 years ago. British Socialism Ideology developed, in the sequel, as one of the most important thoughts of Marxism. The desire and presumption of a more ideal society, which is in accordance with humanism, inhere in every civilization, and it is related with the human nature. On the other hand, based on the profound critique of social reality, the disaffection to the existent real-life and the intense motional drive of a better, more ideal and more humanistic society, academically, can be named as the associated phenomenon of "Utopia Impulsion", which is the symbiosis of Industrialization and Modernization, and also as the most significant impetus of Industrialization and Modernization. The great contribution of Marxism not lied in indicating the existence of this phenomenon, but lied in placing the explanation of this phenomenon on the scientific theory: a theory based on the historical Materialism.

Industrial civilization is established on the foundation of the unceasing progress of technology. While the technology proves to be Technolatrialism and could control or dominate everything, technology, actually, heads to the opposition of humanity. Under this circumstance, writings and thoughts of anti-social Utopia arose and showed there was no more goodliness of human future. Except for the high development of material enjoyment, the human society seemed as if on the way of non-humanity or anti-humanity, hence, a haze of doubts and suspicions of pessimism permeated over through the entire twentieth Century and was embodied in various fields, such as the fields of Philosophy, Literature and Art.

In April of 2012, The Second Sino-British Bilateral Forum on Marxist Aesthetics lowered its curtain in the "Working Class Library" in Manchester of England. After the forum, David Alderson, Mike Sanders, Robert Spencer, Haili Ma and I sat in a restaurant near the Manchester Canal and discussed the theme for the next year's forum. We agreed, without dissidence, that the economic crisis in America and Europe would definitely continue, hence the deep consideration for the reality and the future should be put into agenda. Therefore, we decided to make "Marxism and the Future" as the theme of the coming 2013 year's forum. In the contemporary society, whether it is in Europe, in America or in Asia, the "future" is no longer a clear or familiar conception. The severe social inequity influenced by the Neo-liberalism, sharply-exacerbated ecological crisis, the acute depravation of critical reflections on culture brought by market-oriented economy, and the value of anomie of social ethics are all the realistic problems needed to be faced squarely. We must probe into these significant theoretical issues and try to find the new orientation and impetus of the social development.

The Forum was responded by not only domestic but also international scholars and more than one hundred delegates from 10 countries and regions attended in. The conference established the following topics such as "The Ideal Literature for Society", "Expression and Significance of Art", "Aesthetic and Social Content of Reality", "The Contemporary Conception of Tragedy and its Marxist Annotation", "Aesthetic Criticism to Capitalism", "Marxism and the Contemporary Educational Revolution in Universities", etc. The participants addressed their thesis, which was followed with enthusiastic discussion. More than ten media organization, such as *Foreign Literature Studies*, *Journal of Literature and Art*, *Exploration and Free Views*, *Social Sciences Weekly*, *Theory and Criticism of Literature and Art*, thoroughly reported this Forum, and the synthetic surveys published on the International Aesthetic Website, Russian academy journal *TFRRA HUMANA* and even Korean academic journal *Marxist 21*. Those treatises in this anthology are merely a portion presented during the Forum.

In my opinion, future is neither a simple dream nor a straightforward promotion of material subsistence. Future is neither the revolutionary passion nor the direct objectification of "Utopia Impulsion". It is admitted that the progress of technology is the partial basis for the stabilizations of "future", however, the progress of technology is not equivalent to the "future". The authentic future should be an age of ecological civilization; however, it is not only the achievement of harmony between human and nature. The future also involved the social fairness, justice, freedom, liberation of human, and, to sum up, a type of life in accordance with human nature. The future is not an illusion, but a reality which can be reached through unremitting endeavor. In the context of the contemporary disciplines of humanities or society, the thoughts of "future" varies and here we dispatch the voice of Marxism and expect to stimulate more "echoes", for the purpose of heartening those who are well-disposed and sympathetic and make our every efforts to create a better "future".

目　录

王杰

　　序言 …………………………………………………………………… 1

第一部分

凯文·安德森

　　结构主义和后结构主义之后的社会主义人道主义 …………………… 1

阿列西·艾尔雅维奇

　　"单刀直入！" ………………………………………………………… 16

大卫·马格列斯

　　辩证批评与具体分析 ………………………………………………… 32

巴得胜

　　马克思主义与新儒家的兴起 ………………………………………… 49

詹森·巴克

　　回归马克思：没有其他选择的革命 ………………………………… 72

大卫·奥尔德森

　　电视真人秀、性别的自我意识和资本的形式 ……………………… 82

奥尔顿·德格雷夫

　　幽灵障碍：神经—马克思主义与灵魂的状态 ……………………… 107

马修·博蒙特

　　乌托邦的幽灵：马克思主义与未来 ………………………………… 124

贾斯汀·奥康诺
　　"新唯物主义"抑或新自由主义资本主义的文化逻辑？ ………… 136
丁声镇
　　马克思未来社会的观念与21世纪诸种社会主义模式 ………… 145
亚历山大·维克多罗维奇·彼得罗夫
　　环境伦理、社会生态与可持续发展的经济障碍 ………… 168

第二部分

王杰，谢卓婷
　　中国悲剧观念：理论传统及其当代意义 ………… 174
朱立元，章文颖
　　马克思实践的唯物主义与现代美学革命 ………… 189
王元骧
　　对我国马克思主义文艺理论研究的哲学反思 ………… 210
冯宪光
　　后马克思主义文论的一个焦点问题 ………… 219
李志宏
　　马克思主义美学的科学化维度——"知觉模式说"概论 ………… 229
孙文宪
　　论马克思主义批评对文学思想内涵的诉求 ………… 240
杨杰
　　马克思主义与乌托邦精神 ………… 245
姚建彬
　　马克思主义同乌托邦究竟是什么关系——关于"空想社会主义"译名的检讨及其他 ………… 253
段吉方
　　文化研究与文化领导权——20世纪英国文化研究中的"葛兰西转向"问题 ………… 260

傅其林
　论东欧新马克思主义对反映论美学模式的批判 …………… 272
王 杰
　马克思主义美学可以再度成为公共话语吗？ ……………… 285
陈伯海
　马克思主义与中国美学的未来 ……………………………… 290
杨春时
　发掘和继承马克思美学思想的批判性，建设中国现代美学 …… 295
夏锦乾
　反思 20 世纪马克思主义美学的"主流现象"——兼谈马克思主义
　美学与中国传统美学精神的关系 …………………………… 302
王振复
　巫性美学：中国美学研究新路向 …………………………… 308
朱志荣
　论中国美学研究的当下性 …………………………………… 314
徐碧辉
　审美权利和审美伤害——马克思主义美学研究的一个新视阈 … 319
于 琦
　真实与现实：齐泽克式的一个考察 ………………………… 326
邵瑜莲
　左翼电影与马克思主义中国化 ……………………………… 339
贾 洁
　论特里·伊格尔顿美学批评的伦理学维度 ………………… 354
高建平
　什么样的生产主义 …………………………………………… 366
陆 扬
　大众文化的另一种解读 ……………………………………… 375

第三部分

杨荔斌
  肩起马克思主义美学理论的时代使命——第三届中英马克思主义
  美学双边论坛会议综述 ………………………………………… 385

张蕴艳
  马克思主义与中西美学的未来——第三届"中英马克思主义
  美学双边论坛"综述 …………………………………………… 399

Contents

Wang Jie

    Preface 1

I

Kevin B. Anderson

    Socialist Humanism after Structuralism and Poststructuralism:
    The Case For A Renewal 1

Aleš Erjavec

    "Beat the Whites with the Red Wedge!" 16

David Margolies

    Dialectical Criticism and Concrete Analysis 32

Bart Dessein

    "Marxism and the Rise of New Confucianism" 49

Jason Barker

    Marx Reloaded: Revolution Without Alternatives 72

David Alderson

    Acting Straight: Reality TV, Gender Self-Consciousness and
    Forms of Capital 82

Ortwin de Graef

    Spectre Disorder: Neuro-Marxism and the State of the Soul 107

Matthew Beaumont
　　The Spectre of Utopia: On Marxism and the Future ………………… 124
Justin O'Connor
　　What Kind of Materialism is the "New Materialism"? or,
　　The Cultural Logic of Neo-Liberal Capitalism ……………………… 136
Jeong Seongjin
　　Marx's Concepts of Future Society and Models of Socialism
　　for the 21st Century ……………………………………………… 145
Alexander V. Petrov
　　Environmental Ethics, Social Ecology and the Economic Barriers to the
　　Sustainable Development ………………………………………… 168

II

Wang Jie, Xie Zhuoting
　　Chinese Idea of the Tragic: Theoretical Tradition and Contemporary
　　Significance ……………………………………………………… 174
Zhu Liyuan, Zhang Wenying
　　Marx's Practical Materialism and the Revolution of Modern Aesthetics …… 189
Wang Yuanxiang
　　A Philosophic Reflection on the Chinese Research in Marxist Literary and
　　Artistic Theories ………………………………………………… 210
Feng Xianguang
　　The Focus Issue on Post-Marxism Literary Theories ……………… 219
Li Zhihong
　　How do General Things Become Beautiful? An Introduction to
　　"Perceptual Pattern Theory" …………………………………… 229
Sun Wenxian
　　On Marxist Ideological Content of Literary Criticism Demands ……… 240

Yang Jie

    Marxism and Utopian Spirit ··· 245

Yao Jianbin

    How on Earth Is Marxism Related with Utopia? ················· 253

Duan Jifang

    Cultural Studies and Cultural Leadership: On the Issue of "Turn to Gramsci" in the 20th Century British Cultural Studies ····················· 260

Fu Qilin

    On Eastern European Neo-Marxist Critique of Aesthetics of Reflection Paradigm ··· 272

Wang Jie

    Will Marxist Aesthetics Become Public Discourse Again? ··················· 285

Chen Bohai

    Marxism and the Future of Chinese Aesthetics ························· 290

Yang Chunshi

    Explore and Retain the Critical Spirit of Marxist Aesthetics and Construct Modern Chinese Aesthetics ··· 295

Xia Jinqian

    A Reflection on the "Maitstream Phenomenon" of Marxist Aesthetics of the 20th Century: Relation between Marxist Aesthetics and Traditional Chinese Aesthetics ··· 302

Wang Zhenfu

    Witchery Aesthetics: A New Direction of Chinese Aesthetic Studies ········· 308

Zhu Zhirong

    The Present of Chinese Aesthetics Research ···························· 314

Xu Bihui

    Aesthetic Rights and Aesthetic Injury ······································ 319

Yu Qi

    A Žižekian Study on the Real and Reality ······························· 326

Shao Yulian

    Left-wing Film and Sinicization of Marxism ·· 339

Jia Jie

    On Ethics of Terry Eagleton's Aesthetic Criticism ································· 354

Gao Jianping

    What kind of Productivism? ··· 366

Lu Yang

    Another Interpretation of Mass Culture ·· 375

III

Yang Libin

    Undertaking An Epochal Mission of the Development of Marxist Aesthetic Theory: A Summary of the Third Sino-British Bilateral Forum on Marxist Aesthetics ·· 385

Zhang Yunyan

    Marxism and the Future of Chinese and Western Aesthetics: A Summary of the Third Sino-British Bilateral Forum on Marxist Aesthetics ·············· 399

Socialist Humanism after Structuralism and Poststructuralism: The Case For A Renewal

Kevin B. Anderson

(University of California-Santa Barbara)

Abstract: Socialist Humanism after Structuralism and Poststructuralism will provide a renewal of the criticism to the global capitalism and it orients a refreshed free society where males and females wield their rights to self-determination in a way of social and individual as well. Jean-Paul Sartre, Erich Fromm and Eastern Europe Marxist Humanists offered considerable viewpoints on universal liberation and the Socialist Humanism also needs especially close attention, such as the thoughts of Raya Dunayevskaya, Frantz Fanon and Karel Kosik, for their humanism allowed universal value specialized. Simultaneously, some certain understandings of Poststructuralist Social critics needs critical application on Marxist Humanism in the 21th century, on matter in the fields of languages, prison, cultural heritage of imperialism and social gender or sexual orientation.

The Present Moment Exemplified: Bourdieu's Attack on Sartre

Since the 1970s, other forms of critical philosophy have largely displaced existential or Marxist forms of humanism. While radical thought has not for the most part returned to pre-1945 scientific rationalism, structuralist and post-structuralist theories that attack humanism and subjectivity as well as Hegel have become dominant among critical philosophers and social theorists. To illustrate the pervasiveness of these trends, consider the 1972 attack on Sartre by the sociologist Pierre Bourdieu, a thinker with only loose affinities to structuralism. Bourdieu's point of attack was a passage in

Sartre's *Being and Nothingness* of 1943, where he had written, in what I consider to be a fine dialectical passage:

> For it is necessary to reverse the common opinion and acknowledge that it is not the harshness of a situation or the sufferings it imposes that lead people to conceive of another state of affairs [*état de choses*] in which things would be better for everybody; instead, it is from the day that we are able to conceive of another state of affairs, that a new light is cast on our troubles and our suffering and we *decide* they are unbearable.

Here, Sartre is arguing for the crucial importance of the idea of freedom, and of thinking differently about the "given" world of capitalism—with its commodity fetishism, notion that there is no alternative, etc.—in order to overcome those conceptual barriers. Note that he is writing not so much of the individual subject as one involving "people" and "everybody." Sartre sees this kind of rethinking as the precondition for a genuinely revolutionary transformation, or even for a movement that is attempting to move in that direction.

Instead of grappling with these issues, Bourdieu simply dismisses Sartre's entire discussion of working class subjectivity as a form of idealism "devoid of objectivity":

> If the world of action is nothing other than this universe of interchangeable possibilities, entirely dependent upon the decrees of the consciousness which creates it, and hence totally devoid of objectivity, if it is moving because the subject chooses to be revolted, then emotions, passions, and actions are merely games of bad faith, sad farces in which one is both bad actor and good audience.

In carrying out this critique, Bourdieu proceeds to cite one of the most deterministic and positivistic texts of sociologist Émile Durkheim, *The Rules of Sociological Method*, published back in the 1890s.

The Althusserian Cul-de-Sac: Anti-Humanist Marxism

Althusser famously attacked both Hegelianism and humanism as bourgeois, if not reactionary. This was a departure from even orthodox, Engelsian Marxism. Although Engels had conceptualized idealism and materialism as a general dividing line between progressive and reactionary forms of philosophy, he made an exception for Hegel's idealism, which he regarded as definitely revolutionary. Thus, Engels had always acknowledged Hegel as an important antecedent of Marx's thought. Nor had Engels explicitly repudiated humanism, although he did not make a core category out of it either.

For his part, Althussser, reacting against both Marxist and existentialist humanism, went on the attack, writing of the "phantom" or "shade of Hegel." He called upon Marxists, as if exorcising a vampire, "to drive this phantom back into the night". Althusser was to continue this theme unabated throughout his intellectual career, rallying more orthodox Marxists against the threats posed by Hegelian and humanist versions of Marxism. He carried the debate into Lenin's work as well, attempting to separate Lenin from Hegel despite clear evidence to the contrary in Lenin's 1914—1915 Hegel notebooks.

In the early 1960s, Althusser famously dismissed the writings of the early Marx as pre-Marxist, imbued as he saw it with liberal and Hegelian notions of alienation and humanism. These writings were simply not Marxist, because they were humanist. Althusser "knew" what was true Marxism, even when confronted with writings by Marx that did not cooperate with his form of knowing.

Althusser goes further, however, placing antihumanism at the core of Marx's thought despite the lack of textual evidenced on this point: "One can and must speak openly of Marx's theoretical anti-humanism". In large part, this was because of Althusser's notion that Marx made an "epistemological break" in 1845 with his earlier writings, especially the 1844 *Manuscripts*.

A few years later, in his preface to a widely circulated paperback edition of *Capital*, published in French in 1969, Althusser complains that the entire first part of *Capital* is marked by "a method of presentation" imbued with "Hegelian prejudice". For these and other reasons, Althusser advises French readers to "leave Part I (Commodities and Money) deliberately on one side in a first reading".

By now, Althusser had modified his earlier notion of an 1845 "epistemological break" with Hegel on Marx's part, now lamenting "survivals in Marx's language and even in his thought of the influence of Hegel's thought" in *Capital* itself. Marx, it seems, did not become fully "Marxist" until a decade later, with "*Critique of the Gotha Program* (1875) as well as the *Marginal Notes on Wagner*" of 1881, texts finally free of the taint of Hegel and humanism. In other words, Marx remained a humanist until eight years before his death!

Here, Althusser's argument flirted with an open anti-Marxism, and in no small way anticipated the poststructuralist rejection of Marx *tout court* as an Hegelian humanist whose thought was supposedly marked by a concept of a fixed human essence.

Foucault's Anti-Marxist Anti-Humanism

Foucault attacked humanism even more forcefully, mocking its preoccupation with "man," with the human being in general. This was because human beings exhibited profound differences from each other that could not be captured within a humanist framework. Instead of Marx, it was Friedrich Nietzsche who anticipated the future, who "indicated the turning-point," that of "the death of man". In the bleak ending of *The Order of Things* (1966), Foucault wrote that while the Enlightenment "made it possible for the figure of man to appear," the era of humanism was "nearing its end" and by the 1960s "one can certainly wager that man would be erased, like a face drawn in sand at the edge of the sea".

At the same time, Foucault's hostility to the modern centralized state, and to modernity more generally, could lead in dangerous directions, as seen in his uncritical embrace of the Iranian Islamist movement. For the period 1978—1984 was a time when Foucault refused to criticize the outcome of the Iranian revolution in a thoroughgoing way, here similar to many other Western radical thinkers. But Foucault went further, becoming a quasi-follower of Khomeinism for a period in 1978—1979. (See Janet Afary and Kevin B. Anderson, *Foucault and the Iranian Revolution: Gender and the Seductions of Islamism*, 2005).

Until the mid-1970s, much of Foucault's work stressed the subjugation of the human subject under various institutions of power. This helped to give credence to the notion that his work was a variant of structuralism, despite his protests to the contrary.

In a remarkably original and distinctive manner, he focused his study of power not on the state but on less obvious institutions of power like the prison, the mental institution, and societal control over human sexuality. Through such a focus, he developed notions of the decentering of power.

In some respects, this decentering of power paralleled Marx's concept of capital, while at the same time diverging sharply from Marx in denying the centrality of the basic forces and relations of production. Foucault's world is one where modern forms of power are subtle in similar ways to capital's rule over the worker and society through the commodity fetish rather than the bullwhip or iron chains of old.

Also in contrast to Althusser, and to Bourdieu as well, there is more scope, especially in Foucault's later writings, for resistance to power. Resistance forms not so much within the modern working classes, which are seen by Foucault as integrated into the system, but from marginalized groups like mental patients, prisoners, sexual minorities, and religious fundamentalists.

Again in contrast to Althusser, who seemed to despise religion, there is a persistent nostalgia in Foucault's work for the religion-tinged past as an alternative to modern forms of power. As discussed below, this was seen most dramatically in his support for the Islamist wing of the 1978—1979 Iranian revolution.

A year after *Discipline and Punish*, Foucault sketches his notion of resistance at a conceptual level for the first time in the first volume of his *History of Sexuality* (1976):

> Where there is power, there is resistance, and yet, or rather consequently, this resistance is never in a position of exteriority in relation to power.... Their [power relationships'] very existence depends on a multiplicity of points of resistance.... Hence there is no single locus of Great Refusal[①], no soul of revolt, source of all rebellions, or pure law of the revolutionary. Instead there specific cases of resistance... They are the other in the relations of power; they inscribe themselves as irreducible in relation to it.

[①] The attack on the idea of a Great Refusal targeted Frankfurt School luminary Herbert Marcuse, whose writings had gained wide attention in France in the 1960s.

In the above sense, resistance is everywhere, without a fixed point, nor does it seem to be able to overcome power.

The Return of Marxist Humanism?

Thus, whether under the influence of structuralists like Althusser, or poststructuralists like Foucault, there was a turn away from humanism, from Hegel, and from the dialectic more generally in the 1970s and 1980s. In these milieus, Hegel had become a reactionary, pro-imperialist thinker, while Marx had become a Eurocentric thinker. Humanism in the socialist humanist sense was at best ignored and at worst maligned.

Nonetheless, the various poststructuralisms themselves reached an impasse by the end of the twentieth century. The work of Foucault had been too closely linked to identity politics, to the politics of difference. It fell short when younger intellectuals looked for sources from which to critique globalized capitalism.

Recently, many are returning to Marx, at least his critique of political economy. A number of others have advocated a return to Hegel and the dialectic, but very few are returning to socialist and Marxist humanism. This is unfortunate, for it is the humanist element that has helped to ground, at least philosophically, notions of a real alternative to the existing state of affairs, to the domination of capital and the state over the human being.

In the remainder of this paper, I will be calling for a return—albeit on 21st century ground—not only to Marx's humanism as seen in the 1844 *Manuscripts*, the *Grundrisse*, and *Capital*—but also to the writings of the post-World War II socialist humanists in the West, people like Sartre, Erich Fromm, and above all Raya Dunayevskaya; Eastern European dissident Marxist humanists like Karel Kosík; and finally, African socialist humanists like Frantz Fanon.

But let us start with the beginning, or one of the points of beginning for modern radical humanism, Sartrean existentialism.

The Moment of Sartrean Humanism

In his famous 1946 lecture, "Existentialism Is a Humanism," Sartre laid out his version of humanism, which he separated from liberal forms of humanism, which in his view naively admired human achievements and progress. Sartre also emphasized the processual side, that of "subjectivity": "Man is, indeed, a project which possesses a subjective life, instead of being a kind of moss, or a fungus or a cauliflower". While, to be sure, there were many expressions of subjectivity in a highly individualist form in Sartre's lecture, he also made room for "human universality," but again as something in process: "It is not something given; it is being perpetually made."

Much of the appeal of this radically subjectivist position rested upon two sets of issues: (1) a philosophical rejection of all forms of determinism, based in either religion or science; (2) a reproachful attitude toward those who had waited out the Nazi Occupation of France, not joining the Resistance until the Allied victory was assured, rather than making the choice to resist from the beginning.

Sartre's radical subjectivism was surely problematic from a Marxist standpoint. Another problem was his tendency to move from individual subjectivity toward abstract universalism, without sufficient mediation in terms of the ways in which the universal needed to particularize itself.

Erich Fromm's Socialist Humanism

By 1961, in his *Marx's Concept of Man*, Fromm foregrounded his Marxist humanist position, writing that "the very aim of Marx is to liberate man from the pressure of economic needs, so that he can be fully human; that Marx is primarily concerned with the emancipation of man as an individual, the overcoming of alienation, the restoration of his capacity to relate himself fully to man and to nature."

Fromm's (and Marx's) notion of human emancipation is markedly different from the Foucauldian notion of resistance. For Marxism the key is human emancipation, not only resistance to domination. Resistance to capital is predicated on a vision of a new society, not as a distant or imaginary utopia, but as a real possibility that exists as a tendency inside the very structures of capitalist society itself.

Unfortunately, in his introduction to *Marx's Concept of Man*, Fromm sometimes imposes his own more eclectic form of humanism on Marx himself, as for example when he writes that "Marx's philosophy constitutes a spiritual existentialism in secular language" and that Marx's concept of socialism is rooted in "prophetic Messianism". He also links it to Zen Buddhism.

Fromm followed up *Marx's Concept of Man* with an edited book, *Socialist Humanism: An International Symposium*, published in 1965 with one of America's largest publishing houses at the time, Doubleday. For several years afterwards, this volume was the only widely circulated book on socialism in the U. S. It comprised essays by some 35 noted intellectuals, among them over a dozen from within Eastern Europe, most of them philosophical dissidents, but also a few who hewed more toward the party line. The more dissident Marxist humanists included several who would become prominent in the upheavals of the 1960s in the Eastern bloc, most notably the Prague Spring of 1968. Among the intellectuals from Czechoslovakia was the Marxist humanist Karel Kosík.

In his introduction to *Socialist Humanism*, Fromm also spelled out more his notion of socialist humanism. Marxism also had to be differentiated along a humanist vs. crude materialist axis, with the latter not really Marxist in Fromm's eyes:

> Marx was misinterpreted both by those who felt threatened by his program, and by many socialists. The former accused him of caring only for the physical, not the spiritual, needs of man. The latter believed that his goal was exclusively material affluence for all, and that Marxism differed from capitalism only in its methods, which were economically more efficient and could be initiated by the working class. In actuality, Marx's ideal was a man productively related to other men and to nature, who would respond to the world in an alive manner, and who would be rich not because he had much but because he was much.

It was while putting together *Marx's Concept of Man* in 1959 that Fromm began his thirty-year correspondence with Dunayevskaya, which contains an interesting Marxist humanist discussion of gender.

In 1976, while working on her *Rosa Luxemburg, Women's Liberation, and Marx's Philosophy of Revolution* (1982), Dunayevskaya writes to Fromm concerning the "lack of camaraderie between Luxemburg, Lenin, and Trotsky." She asks: "Could there have been, if not outright male chauvinism, at least some looking down on her theoretical work, because she was a woman?" Fromm responds: "I feel that the male

Social Democrats never could understand Rosa Luxemburg, nor could she acquire the influence for which she had the potential because she was a woman; and the men could not become full revolutionaries because they did not emancipate themselves from their male, patriarchal, and hence dominating, character structure." (These letters can be found in Kevin B. Anderson and Russell Rockwell, eds., *The Dunayevskaya-Marcuse-Fromm Correspondence*, 1954—1979, published in 2012.)

Fromm's life and work centered on how human beings could realize their full humanity, not only in psychological terms, but also politically and philosophically. Always searching for a pathway out of the alienated world of capitalism, he played a major role in the discussions of Marx and of socialist humanism in the U. S. and internationally.

At the same time, his socialist humanism had something of an abstract character, often floating above the real social contradictions of modern capitalist society. This could sometimes lead him toward positions indistinguishable from ordinary liberalism.

Karel Kosík: Capitalism's World of the Pseudo-Concrete

Kosík's work was the finest flowering of that oppositional form of Marxist philosophy that arose in the 1950s in Eastern Europe, as seen in his greatest work, *Dialectics of the Concrete*, which originally appeared in Czech in the early 1960s. Its first chapter begins with the famous critique of the "pseudoconcrete" world of "fetishized praxis." In the world of the pseudoconcrete, i.e., the everyday world of capitalism, we are made to forget that we have the capacity to alter or even create our world, of course in Marxist terms within the given historical possibilities.

Kosík's attack on crude Marxist interpretations comes through when he writes that "even the totality of the base and superstructure is abstract" when it is forgotten that the human being "is the real historical subject" and actually forms "both the base and the superstructure" in the human "process of production and reproduction". In short, this is a most rigorous philosophical argument for a humanist position within Marxism.

In one remarkable passage, some brief allusions to Plato's cave are followed by the statements, "man is *walled in* in his socialness" and "man is a prisoner of socialness". This poignant image managed to evoke the Berlin Wall, which had gone up just two years before this book was published. What's more, it showed the possibility of a Marxist dialectical vision that did not fall either into the error of totalizing, or into that of reductionism to the social or the economic, while at the same time rooting itself in Marx's humanistic materialism.

Frantz Fanon and African Socialist Humanism

Let us move for a moment outside the sphere of North America and Europe, to the revolutionary African socialist humanism of Frantz Fanon, who was influenced by Hegel, Sartre, the Negritude School, and above all, Marx. Note Fanon's use, similar to Sartre, of the term "decide," this in a declaration about the future of an independent Africa in his *Wretched of the Earth* of 1961, the year so many new nations were being born, in many cases with aspirations toward socialist humanism: "Let us decide not to imitate Europe; let us combine our muscles and our brains in a new direction. Let us try to create the whole man, whom Europe has been incapable of bringing to triumphant birth."

While fighting in Algeria's war for independence from France, Fanon did not dismiss *tout court* the European humanist tradition. He said that the Europeans had not practiced it—whether under Nazism or in the colonies—but predicted that the emerging Third World would be able to do so: "This new humanity cannot do otherwise than define a new humanism both for itself and for others". Thus, it was both a humanism drawing from European revolutionary and democratic traditions to be sure, but at the same time it was a "new humanism," both critically appropriating and going beyond the limitations of those earlier forms of European humanism. As a theoretician of the newly forming Third World, Fanon also distanced himself from the Soviet bloc and its authoritarian and dehumanizing form of industrial "development," not only mentioning the Hungarian revolution of 1956, but also writing of the new Africa: "The pretext of catching up must not be used to push man around, to tear him away from himself or his privacy, to break and kill him". This was nothing short of a socialist humanist third way, neither Western style capitalism nor Eastern statist communism.

Fanon concluded *Wretched of the Earth* in a burst of dialectical insight. Given his universalizing humanist aims, he asked whether nationalism was obsolete. Shouldn't the new African nations drop nationalism entirely in favor of universal brotherhood and sisterhood of peoples across the world? No, he argued, one cannot "skip the national period," that of "national consciousness." Only through the particular, national consciousness, can one get to the universal, humanism: The consciousness of self is not the closing of a door to communication. Philosophic thought teaches us, on the contrary, that it is its guarantee. National consciousness, which is not nationalism, is the only thing that will give us an international dimension."

Thus, the new nations of the emergent Third World could not skip over the stage of national self-consciousness, as the road toward universal human emancipation passed of necessity through that particular, provided that that national consciousness did not solidify into a separatist type of narrow nationalism. Nor could the nations of Europe and North America skip over this either. They needed to recognize the fact that they had been complicit in systems of racist colonialism, not in order to wallow in guilt, but in order to make the kind of self-critique needed for a truly global human civilization.

Raya Dunayevskaya: Revolutionary Marxist-Humanism

Raya Dunayevskaya's Marxist-Humanism (hyphenated here as was her preference) had roots in Marx and Hegel, but also appropriated critically many of the other strands of socialist humanism discussed above. An emigrant to the U.S. from Russia, she came up through the U.S. anti-Stalinist left and then served as Leon Trotsky's Russian Secretary in 1937—1938 during his Mexican exile. Dunayevskaya also had strong ties to the U.S. Black, labor, and women's movements.

Dunayevskaya published *Marxism and Freedom* (1958), a book that placed humanism at the center of Marx's thought. In his preface to Dunayevskaya's book, Marcuse applauded her attempt "to recapture the integral unity of Marxian theory at its very foundation: the humanistic philosophy." Dunayevskaya's translation of two of the key essays in Marx's 1844 *Economic and Philosophical Manuscripts*, "Private Property and Communism" and "Critique of the Hegelian Dialectic," was appended to the original 1958 edition.

In *Marxism and Freedom*, Dunayevskaya addressed humanism in three contexts: the young Marx, the mature Marx of *Capital*, and the social movements of the period.

In her chapter on the young Marx, Dunayevskaya quotes and then uses as a point of departure the core passages on humanism in the 1844 *Manuscripts* that had not been addressed by Marcuse in *Reason and Revolution*, the only previous substantial discussion of these texts in English.

In so doing, she wove together in her trademark compressed form a number of issues, among them philosophical analysis of humanism in Marx, critique of the Soviet Union as an example of "vulgar communism," and present-day humanism in the sense of the striving of human beings to be free of capitalistic alienation:

> Marx drew the line so sharply between "vulgar communism" and even "positive communism," on the one hand, and his own philosophy of *humanism*, on the other hand, that it stands to this day as the dividing line between Marxism as the doctrine of liberation, and all who claim the name of "Marxism," "socialism," or "communism" while they pursue an entirely different course, both in thought and in practice, from all that Marx stood for. "Not until the transcendence of this mediation (abolition of private property) which is nevertheless a necessary presupposition does there arise positive Humanism beginning from itself," said Marx. In a word, another transcendence, *after* the abolition of private property is needed to achieve a truly new, *human* society which differs from private property not alone as an "economic system," but as a different way of *life* altogether. It is as free individuals developing all their natural and acquired talents that we first leap from what Marx called the pre-history of humanity into its true history, the "leap from necessity to freedom."

In this sense, Marx's humanism was itself the ground for a thoroughgoing critique of both statist communism in the East and formally democratic capitalism in the West.

A second humanist context was seen in the four chapters on *Capital* that formed the theoretical core of Dunayevskaya's book, with one of them entitled "The Humanism and Dialectic of *Capital*, Volume I, 1867 to 1883." She argued that the human being, the worker, remained at the center of his exposition and critique of capitalist value production. As she saw it, in *Capital*, each new objective development of this sort not only created an objective transformation in capitalist production, but it also re-formed the working class, leading to new forms of consciousness and of revolt.

This type of consideration formed the foundation of a third humanist element of *Marxism and Freedom*, the discussion—in a chapter entitled "Automation and the New

Humanism"—of a new stage of capitalist production in the 1950s, automation, and the resultant movements of rank-and-file labor and African Americans of the 1950s.

Dunayevskaya held that when one considered the human condition of the worker, the new stage of automated production, far from liberatory, was resulting in both mass unemployment and a deepening alienation on the part of those who still had jobs. Moreover, automated production led to new types of revolt, like the thousands of "wildcat" strikes that mushroomed from the rank and file, challenging not only capital but also a labor bureaucracy that had become a player in the system. She also took up the mass creativity of the Montgomery Bus Boycott of 1955—1956, carried out by African Americans against racial segregation.

In her *Philosophy and Revolution* (1973), Dunayevskaya analyzed critically, and drew into her own version of Marxist-Humanism, insights from a number of radical humanist theoretical strains that had appeared since 1945, among them Sartrean existentialism, African socialist humanism, and Eastern European Marxist humanism. Here I will concentrate on the latter.

Among the various strands of socialist humanism, with the possible exception of Fanon's version of African socialism, Dunayevskaya seemed to feel the greatest affinity for the Eastern European Marxist humanist philosophers, many of whom had appeared alongside her in Fromm's *Socialist Humanism* in 1965.

Among those whom Dunayevskaya saw as the most important thinkers of Marxist humanism was Karel Kosík of Czechoslovakia, who "had, in 1963 published an important philosophic work, *Dialectics of the Concrete*, which raised anew the question of the individual," and also spoken out, "although in abstract philosophic terms, against the 'dogmatic' Communist retrogressionism in life and thought". Soon after, in a 1974 critique of Adorno's *Negative Dialectics*, Dunayevskaya contrasted the German "ivory tower" philosopher Adorno with Kosík and Fanon, philosophers who had responded—and profoundly so—to the new liberatory impulses within their respective societies. (See Dunayevskaya, *The Power of Negativity* (2002), edited by Peter Hudis and Kevin B. Anderson.) Other Eastern European Marxist humanists also pointed to the problem of the individual within Marxist thought, while also rejecting Sartrean existentialism.

At the same time, however, there was a tendency toward the abstract universal in these Eastern European Marxist humanists.

Conclusion

Some forms of socialist and Marxist humanism have remained too often in the realm of the abstract universal. Only Fanon and Dunayevskaya succeeded in developing forms of socialist humanism that came down to earth in the sense of taking up issues like race and colonialism in ways that both held onto universalizing aspirations and acknowledged difference. Within socialist humanism, these strains were marginalized, however, relatively speaking, in the face of the towering influence of people like Fromm and Sartre.

All of this left the Marxist humanists open to the type of challenge the Foucauldians and other post-structuralists mounted after 1968 against Marxism, and particularly those Marxists in the humanist camp. Foucault could all too easily write that Marxists and humanists failed to address specific forms of resistance, that they were trapped in a generalized view of "man" that did not recognize specific human beings in all their variety. Under the influence of Foucault, radical philosophy was plunged into the politics of difference, as Marxism and humanism were swept aside completely.

That process has now run its course as well. It is high time that critical philosophers consider once again a radical humanism that will give their critique of global capitalism a type of content that points toward a new, liberated society in which women and men can exercise their self-determination in a way that is both social and individual. Much can be appropriated from the emancipatory universals of Sartre, Fromm, and the Eastern European Marxist humanists, provided that we don't fall into the trap of the abstract universal once again. In this regard, we need to look especially closely at those forms of socialist humanism, as found in Dunayevskaya, Fanon, and to a great extent, Kosík, forms that allow for the universal to particularize itself. At the same time, we need to critically appropriate into a 21st century Marxist humanism some of the insights from several decades of post-structuralist social critique, whether on language, prisons, the cultural legacies of imperialism, or gender and sexuality.

（本文责任编辑：安宁）

结构主义和后结构主义之后的社会主义人道主义

凯文·安德森

【内容摘要】结构主义和后结构主义之后的社会主义人道主义将对全球资本主义的批判提供一种新的内涵，它指向一个新的自由的社会，在那里，女人和男人能以一种既是社会的又是个体的方式行使他们的自决权。我们可以从萨特、弗洛姆和东欧马克思主义人道主义者的解放普世性中借鉴大量观点，我们需要特别密切关注那些社会主义的人道主义形式，比如杜纳耶夫斯卡娅、法农、科西克，因为他们的社会主义的人道主义允许将普世性进行特殊化。同时，我们需要批判性地将后结构主义社会批判家的一些见解运用到21世纪马克思主义人道主义中，无论是在语言、监狱、帝国主义的文化遗产或社会性别与性取向方面，都可以借鉴。

【作者简介】凯文·B.安德森，美国加州大学圣塔芭芭拉分校教授，国际马克思恩格斯著作 MEGA2 版和马克思晚年著作考证专家。

"Beat the Whites with the Red Wedge!"

Aleš Erjavec

(Scientific Research Center of the Slovenian Academy of
Sciences and Arts, Ljubljana, Slovenia)

Abstract: This paper is to take Soviet propaganda poster "Beat the Whites with the Red Wedge" for example, which was finished by artist Lazar Markovich Lissitzky in 1919, goes deeply into the subject of the autonomous of western modernist arts.

1.

What is considered today as "modern art" came into being in Europe after the French Revolution. In the century that followed this historic event museums developed—such as the Louvre already was—galleries, art criticism and the art market. These developments led to the special bourgeois high evaluation—or even mystification—of creativity and art in the second half of that century which resulted in aestheticism and symbolism, making art—very much under the influence of Nietzsche and Henri Bergson—into a sacred object, and the artist into a "genius."

In the nineteenth century art was political only rarely. The outstanding exception were those artists who supported the Paris Commune in 1870—1871 such as the poet Stéphane Mallarmé or Gustave Courbet. Courbet (1819—1877), was a realist painter who became in 1870—1871 a politician and, in his words, member of "four of the most important offices in Paris." After the fall of the Commune he was imprisoned during the political persecution of the Communards, and then returned to the life of an artist. His artistic and political activities were related to his political beliefs and were interdependent with them in a direct way—as in social and later socialist realism, i. e. via content. Nonetheless, his art was not "revolutionary" in a formal artistic sense—by its "style and technique"—nor avant-garde in the sense that his painterly work extended beyond the confines of autonomous art. In other words, "Courbet as an exemplary artist-revolutionary... does not exemplify the overlapping of art and revolution, but rather the rapid succession of the roles of artist and revolutionary politician."[①]

The crucial word here is the "avant-garde." The first relevant mention of it that we know of is in a writing by Gabriel-Désiré Laverdant from 1845, in which Laverdant observes that to ascertain "whether the artist is truly of the avant-garde, one must know where Humanity is going, know what the destiny of the human race is."[②] This means that an artist can be progressive, revolutionary or avant-gardist in a political sense only under the condition that he ascribes to a certain theory, philosophy, ideology or world view. It is the attachment to a certain vision, to "a certain image of the future—be it an image of paradise, Communist society, or permanent revolution"[③] that every ideology is based on, argues Boris Groys—and "this is what signals the fundamental difference between market commodities and political propaganda. The market operates by an 'invisible hand,' it is merely a dark suspicion; it circulates images, but it does not have its own image. By contrast the power of ideology is always ultimately the power of a vision. And this means that by serving any political or religious ideology the artist ultimately serves art."[④] Groys's argument is sound as long as we don't consider art to be a form of human emancipation—a position shared by most of the western aesthetic avant-gardes and presupposed by western art worlds. The opposition between the two interpretations of art is mirrored in their opposite stance toward modernity.

It is in the early twentieth century—between 1905 and 1930—that the dominant artistic trend become the avant-gardes, the main among the more radical ones being Italian and Russian Futurisms, Dadaism, Constructivism, the early Surrealism, and the

---

① Gerald Raunig, *Art and Revolution. Transversal Activism in the Long Twentieth Century*, Translated by Aileen Derieg (Los Angeles: Semiotext[e], 2007), p. 98.
② Quoted in Renato Poggioli, *The Theory of the Avant-Garde*. Translated by Gerald Fitzgerald (Cambridge: The Belknap Press of Harvard University Press, 1968), p. 9.
③ Boris Groys, *Art Power* (Cambridge, MA: MIT Press, 2008), p. 7.
④ Ibid, 7—8.

less radical Expressionism, Cubism, Bauhaus, De Stijl and so on. What distinguishes the radical ones from the rest is that the former programmatically demand "that art move from representing to transforming the world."① What this meant can be illustrated if we compare Cubism and Italian Futurism: both were in their time considered "revolutionary," but in different ways: the former concerned style and technique while the latter wanted to bridge the gap between art and life.

> Life was to be changed through art, and art to become a form of life. The Futurist project of innovation encompassed all aspects of human existence, and was conceived as a total and permanent revolution. What was [in 1915 in a manifesto by the same name] called "Futurist Reconstruction of the Universe" was aimed at a transformation of mankind in all its physiological and psychological aspects, of the social and political conditions in the modern metropolis. ②

Cubism was different. Consider the following description of Cubism given by the Mexican muralist painter Diego Rivera. Cubism, claims Rivera, was "a revolutionary movement, questioning everything that has previously been said and done in art. It held nothing sacred. As the new world would soon blow itself apart, never to be the same again, so Cubism broke down forms as they had been seen for centuries, and was creating out of the fragments new forms, new objects, new patterns, and—ultimately—new worlds."③ We see that Cubism too—at least according to Diego Rivera who was for some time himself a Cubist painter—signified the "creation of new worlds" but we of course also sense that these "worlds" are those of the mind and not of the material historical and social reality: they are limited to art and don't extend beyond it, into "life." Italian Futurism—to continue this parallel reading of two very different strands of avant-garde art from a century ago—in contradistinction to Cubism—fused art and life. To see how this Futurist perspective differed from that of Cubism, let me quote from an article by the Futurist Giovanni Papini that was published in the journal

---

① Boris Groys, *The Total Art of Stalinism*, Translated by Charles Rougle (Princeton: Princeton University Press, 1993), p. 14.
② Günter Berghaus, *Futurism and Politics* (Providence, RI: Berghahn Books, 1996), p. 47.
③ Quoted in David Craven, *Art and Revolution in Latin America 1910—1990* (New Haven: Yale University Press, 2002), p. 11.

Lacerba on December 1, 1913:

> I am a futurist because futurism signifies a total appropriation of the modern civilization with all its enormous wonders, its fantastic possibilities and its horrible beauties.... I am a futurist because I am tired of Byzantine tapestries, false intellectual profundity, ... of harmonious rhymes, pleasant music, pretty canvases, photographic painting, decorative, classical, antique and ambiguous painting.... I am a Futurist because futurism signifies love for risk-taking, for danger, for what didn't attract us for what we have not tried, for the summit that we didn't expect and for the abyss that we have not measured.... I am a futurist because futurism signifies a desire for a greater civilization, for a more personal art, for a richer sensibility and for a more heroic thinking. I am a futurist for futurism signifies Italy as it was in the past, more worthy of its future and its future place in the world, more modern, more developed, more avant-garde than other nations. The liveliest fire burns today among the futurists and I like and I am boasting that I am and remain among them. ①

We see that what distinguishes Futurism from Cubism is that Futurism is a complete worldview while Cubism remains limited to the domain of art in the sense that it is characterized by autonomy and the ensuing institution of art. To understand what that means suffices to remember the lesson of Marcel Duchamp's ready-mades: As we know, Duchamp's intention when introducing in 1915 the ready-mades was to subvert the institution of art—to show, by bringing a urinal or a bottle rack into an exhibition, that it is the context that makes a work into an artwork and not the other way around—an ambition in which he totally failed, for these objects, instead of serving as prime examples of non-art were swiftly assimilated into the realm of art. Or in the words of Duchamp himself: "I threw the bottle-rack and the urinal into the faces of [the public] as a challenge and now they admire them for their aesthetic beauty." ②

One would think that the two versions of avant-garde art—namely Futurism and Cubism—would cover the variety of artistic options developed by the early (also called "classical" or "historical") avant-gardes from a century ago, but this was not the

---

① Quoted in Giovanni Lista, *Le futurisme. Manifestes, Documents, Proclamations* (Lausanne: L'Age d'homme, 1973), pp. 91—92.

② Quoted in Edward Lucie-Smith, '*Movements in art since 1945* (London: Thames & Hudson, 1989), p. 11.

case, for even more radical varieties of art—that was and wasn't considered by their makers to be art—were soon developed. So let us take this story a step further, and quote the Russian Constructivist artist Aleksei Gan from 1922: "Our Constructivism has declared uncompromising war on art, because the means and properties of art are not powerful enough to systematize the feelings of the revolutionary milieu. It is cemented by the real success of the [October] Revolution and its feelings are expressed by intellectual and material production."① In other words, Constructivism wanted—independently of the events in New York triggered there at about the same time by Duchamp's ready-mades—to eliminate art as a bourgeois invention, believing that a new society, that of revolutionary communism required new expressive means, among which there was no place for art, for it was an obsolete part of an obsolete bourgeois society and of an obsolete period in human history. To replace such past art, the Constructivists went into two directions: one was the so-called "production art"— the making of useful everyday objects such as stoves and warm clothes—while the other was the continuation of the machine aesthetics elaborated already in the nineteenth century when industrial objects were often perceived as aesthetic—a tendency realized also in the Arts and Crafts movement (1860—1910) and later continued in Bauhaus.

In much Western scholarship, at least, Constructivism has become an integral part of the historiography of the October Revolution and tends to be appreciated almost exclusively as an immediate result of the new political order and to be granted an inordinate primacy in the development of early Soviet culture. All the more surprising, then, is the fact that Constructivism produced very little of permanence. It was a movement of built-in obsolescence, of ready-to-wear and throw-away, of designs often intended for multiple and mass consumption, of theories, statements, and projects which left behind a precious, but very scant, legacy of material objects. In other words, in remembering the icons of the Constructivist process, and Vladimir Tatlin's *Monument to the III International* is an obvious specimen, we realize that Constructivism is now celebrated more for what it did not create than for what it did.②

---

① Aleksei Gan, *Konstruktivizm* (Tver 1922), quoted in Christina Lodder, *Russian Constructivism* (New Haven: Yale University Press, 1983), p.338.
② John Bowlt, "5 x 5 = 25," unpublished manuscript.

In the opinion of the previously mentioned Aleksei Gan, Constructivism was both a Soviet and a Western invention, but they were not the same. The distinction between them

> hinges precisely on the concept of art. Gan argued that, for the West, Constructivism was merely the name given to the new artistic trend. "They [the West] simply call the new art Constructivism," he asserted. He particularly singled out [two of his fellow Constructivists] Erenburg and Lissitzky for blame. "The basic mistake," he stressed, "of comrade Erenburg and comrade Lissitzky consists in the fact that they cannot tear themselves from art." Gan stressed that the Russian Constructivists had dispensed with art and that it was the Revolution which ensured that this would happen. ①

In a society thoroughly permeated with political ideology, such as that of Russia of the twenties, art was no exception. What distinguished western notion of art from that of the former socialist countries was its social and political context in which there was no art market. "Art becomes politically effective only when it is made beyond or outside the art market—in the context of direct political propaganda. Such art was made in the former Socialist countries."②

Let us take two examples of art that could be called "propaganda" or political, but which could equally well be described as creating and erecting a new artistic paradigm which was inextricably linked with political purpose. The first is the mentioned *Monument to the III International* commissioned in early 1919 by the Department of Fine Arts and to be erected in the center of Moscow. "During 1919 and 1920 [Tatlin] worked on it and built models in metal and wood with three assistants in his studio in Moscow. One of these was exhibited at the Exhibition of the VIIIth Congress of the Soviets held in December 1920. 'A union of purely artistic forms (painting, sculpture and architecture) for a utilitarian purpose' was how Tatlin described it."③ The monument, resembling a leaning Eiffel Tower, was to be three times as high as the Empire State Building, with its glass body moving at different

---

① Lodder, op. cit., p. 237.
② Groys, *Art Power*, p. 7.
③ Camilla Gray, *The Russian Experiment in Art*: 1863—1922 (New York: Abrams, 1962), p. 225.

speeds: the cylinder once a year, the cone once a month and the cube on the top once a day with a continuous flood of political and propaganda activity going on inside it and emanating from it. "Unfortunately the project never got further than the models which Tatlin and his assistants built in wood and wire. These models came to be a symbol of the Utopian world which these artists had hoped to build. In many ways it is typical of their hopes: so ambitious, so romantic and so utterly impractical."①

Another such work was El Lissitzky's well-known poster "Beat the Whites with the Red Wedge" (1919—1920). It is this poster that will be the focus of this talk.

The poster as a whole, besides being a work o political propaganda, ... also exhibits an overt aesthetic function. Its simple graphisms convey an excess of signification. Pure ideological statement and pure aesthetic object never meet in a single space. ... In the case of the poster... the aesthetic effect engendered by pure geometric forms augments the ideological effect of the written statement, and vice versa. The image and the narrative exist in two distinct spaces. They merely intersect, producing in our perception not a unified effect, but a doubled or parallel impression—a binary effect.②

From the early twenties on, especially Lissitzky and Rodchenko discarded their previous artistic avant-garde modernist endeavors to turn to political education and state propaganda, with Rodchenko becoming the editor of the magazine *USSR in Construction*. It is from within this context that Benjamin Buchloh poses a question resembling that of Boris Groys: "Why did the Soviet avant-garde, after having evolved a modernist practice to its most radical stages in the postsynthetic cubist work of the suprematists, constructivists and Laboratory Period artists, apparently abandon the paradigm of modernism upon which its practices have been based? What paradigmatic changes occurred at that time, and which paradigm formation replaced the previous one?"③ In the West the answer to this question remained obscured by grouping much (or all) such later Soviet avant-garde work within political propaganda. "The problem with this criticism, is that criteria of judgment that were originally developed within the

---

① Camilla Gray, *The Russian Experiment in Art*: 1863—1922 (New York: Abrams, 1962), p. 226.
② Aleš Erjavec, "Introduction," in Aleš Erjavec (ed.), *Postmodernism and the Postsocialist Condition. Politicized Art under Late Socialism* (Berkeley: University of California Press, 2003), p. 44.
③ Benjamin Buchloh, "From *Faktura* to Factography," *October*, vol. 30 (Autumn 1984), p. 85.

framework of modernism are now applied to a practice of representation that had deliberately and systematically disassociated itself from that framework in order to lay the foundations of an art production that would correspond to the need of a newly industrialized collective society."①

The intent of these Russian avant-garde artists was to effect—or to take an active part in—a "'double revolution' by redefining revolutionary art practice so that it became revolutionary social practice as well."② As Victor Margolin claims, "The ambition of the artistic-social avant-garde ... was to close the gap between discursive acts, which were confined to postulation and speculation, and pragmatic ones, which involved participation in building a new society."③ It was for this reason that Lissitzky could write in his diary shortly before he died, in 1941, that "In 1926 my most important work as an artist began: the design of exhibitions."④

From the early twenties on some of the Russian avant-garde artists decided to take an active part in the building of the Soviet state. They considered such an endeavor to be a personal but not artistic continuation of their previous Constructivist or Suprematist artistic work: for them classical painting and traditional art forms have attained their final developmental form and had nothing more to offer to the future of society or art. This view coincided with Walter Benjamin's fascination with the Soviet revolutionary cinema and its technique of montage; cinema not only demolished aura, but offered a collective experience, with montage—a technique related to the earlier avant-garde practice of collage—offering an Adornian "resistance" when compared with the products of Hollywood film industry.

2.

In his book on public monuments Sergiusz Michalski discusses an unrealized "Project for a monument commemorating the victory over General Krasnov" from 1918, which was proposed by the Constructivist architect Nikolai Kolli (1894—1996). This

---

① Benjamin Buchloh, "From *Faktura* to Factography," *October*, vol. 30 (Autumn 1984), p. 108.
② Victor Margolin, *The Struggle for Utopia: Rodchenko, Lissitzky, Moholy Nagy. 1917—1946* (Chicago: University of Chicago Press, 1997), p. 3.
③ Ibid.
④ Buchloh, op. cit., p. 102.

"was," claims Michalski, "the first fully abstract political public monument in the world. This piece consists of a black pedestal from which rises a white stone, splintered at the top by a red wedge. A peculiar word play was intended here, since it had been by means of the red (*krasnij*) wedge that the 'bands of Krasnov' had been defeated."①

> Kolli's project," continues Michalski," was deftly plagiarized by El Lissitzky in his famous poster *Beat the Whites with the Red Wedge !* (1920), which showed a white circle (for the White Guards) being pierced by a red wedge, thus broadening Kolli's play on words. But the sequence of transformations and ripostes did not end here. In the fall of 1920, the famous avant-garde artist Malevich and his students erected a plywood monument to the October Revolution in Vitebsk which depicted a circular form splintered by a wedge. ②

In 1921 Walter Gropius developed what resembled an Expressionist monument that was to honor victims of the working-class in a putsch in Weimar. Later Kandinsky used the same motif and the image of the "wedge" to criticize Bolshevik symbolisms. These variations of the basic theme—white circle and the red wedge, supplemented with a few words to the same effect—witness that there must have been a reason why the whole composition met with such a widespread response.

The wedge and the circle started to reappear in Soviet Union and some other socialist countries also in the seventies, eighties and nineties of the previous century in works that were usually postmodern, namely ironic, referential or double-coded. In all instances these more recent versions of the circle and the wedge built upon what by now became the archetypal image associated with the October revolution.

It was Camilla Gray with her book *The Russian Experiment in Art*: 1863—1922 that in 1962 introduced Russian avant-garde to the Western public, including the work of El (for "Lazar") Lissitzky. In her view Lissitzky's 1919—1920 poster was linked to his abstract material bodies that he called "Prouns" (the first of which was also made in 1919). "A poster of his of 1919," muses Gray, "reading 'Beat the Whites with

---

① Sergiusz Michalski, *Public Monuments. Art in Political Bondage* 1870—1997 (London: Reaktion Books, 1998), p. 112.

② Ibid., p. 113.

the Red Wedge', is an amusing illustration of those 'leftish artists' contribution to Bolshevik propaganda."①

How did Lissitzky himself view the poster? Most certainly within the framework of his desire to partake in the avant-garde's attempt to redefine revolutionary art practice and to transgress the limits of art, moving into the territory of industrialism and constructivism. As Victor Margolin claims, "The ambition of the artistic-social avant-garde... was to close the gap between discursive acts, which were confined to postulation and speculation, and pragmatic ones, which involved participation in building a new society."② This also explains why Alfred Barr, the first director of the Museum of Modern Art in New York, was so surprised to discover during his 1927 visit to the Soviet Union that some of the best-known Soviet avant-gardists no longer painted: "'I asked [El Lissitzky] whether he painted. He replied that he painted only when he had nothing else to do, and as that was never, never.'"③ Benjamin Buchloh used this peculiarity of Lissitzky's "art" to point out the dividing line between Western modernism and Eastern avant-garde such as constructivism, a gap that even today continues to remain wide and unbreachable, in spite of now existing for almost a century. Hal Foster asks himself whether already then "Barr understood that Constructivist practices spoke to a historical rupture in the mode of production, not to the historicist logic of the institution of art. In any case,—continues Foster—MoMAist logic soon demanded the displacement of a heterogeneous, collectivist Constructivism by a Western Cubistic-constructive tradition."④

Why was Lissitzky problematic? "Like Heartfield, El Lissitzky transformed the legacies of collage and photomontage according to the needs of a newly industrialized collective."⑤

Lissitzky's 1919—1920 poster remained half way between Suprematism and Constructivism and even if it was an abstract work it nonetheless also contained explicit or

---

① Camilla Grey, *The Russian Experiment in Art*: 1863—1992 (New York: Harry N. Abrams Inc., 1971), p. 254.
② Ibid.
③ Ibid., p. 84.
④ Hal Foster, "Some Uses and Abuses of Russian Constructivism," in: *Art Into Life. Russian Constructivism 1914—1932* (Seattle: The Henry Art Gallery, University of Washington, 1990), p. 246.
⑤ Hal Foster et al (eds.), *Art Since 1900, Vol.* 1 (London: Thames and Hudson, 2004), p. 24.

implicit figurative representations as well as written text. In the opinion of Christina Kaier, Lissitzky's 1919—1920 poster contains also explicit sexual imagery: "The floating geometric forms of Lissitzky's Suprematist composition represent not only the penetration of the White Guard front by the Red Army, but the fantasy of the complete penetration of traditional Russian social life by the invigorating sharpness of Bolshevik ideology."①

It was to this motif that Lissitzky turned in 1929 when creating the stage design for the play *I Want a Child* by Sergei Tret'iakov. Here is the resume of the play:

> In *I Want a Child*, an unmarried party member named Milda, whose extensive public organizing work to benefit the collective leaves no time for marriage or children, suddenly realizes that she wants to have a child. As an agronomist well-versed in eugenics as well as Leninism, Milda decides that the prospective father must be of 100 percent healthy proletarian stock. Rationalist and antiromantic, she searches out an appropriate specimen.... She offers him a contract stating that after conception she will make no claims for his support of her or the child, nor will she ask him to play the roles of husband or father in any way.... Their son is raised communally in collective Soviet children's institutions.... In the play's conclusion, set four years later in 1930, [the father] catches a glimpse of his son when the child wins first prize in a 'Healthy Baby' contest—displayed as an object of collective consumption, rather than of traditional, individual parental pride. ②

For the stage design of the play *I Want Child* Lissitzky employed elements from his poster of ten years before—only now they functioned in a very different setting. On a 1929 photograph we thus see "Lissitzky leaning into the model of his stage set to adjust the fragile railing around a glass circle."③ Tret'iakov's play is suspended between a tragic existential human situation personified by the circumstantial father on the one hand and Milda's eternally one-dimensional world of satisfaction and contentment.

The continuous strength and persuasiveness of Lissitzky's work lie in the combination of the image and the text, that is, the narrative. Such creative gesture of

---

① Christina Kaier, *Imagine No Possessions. The Socialist Objects of Russian Constructivism* (Cambridge, MA: The MIT Press, 2005), p. 260.
② Kaier, op. cit., p. 245.
③ Ibid., pp. 263—264.

synthesizing the pictorial and the discursive elements which are simultaneously torn apart by an unbridgeable void, can be viewed both in Lissitzky's poster from 1919—1920 and in his 1929 stage design. There is something enigmatic in the white circle, the red wedge and the narrative that accompanies them, something that prevents us to regard the work from a single vantage point—the ideological, for example. The work offers what I have designated in 2003 as the "binary effect,"① comparing the nature of its impact to Fichte's dialectics, a dialectics that consists of thesis and anti-thesis without these two elements ever meeting in a common or shared space.

From this viewpoint Lissitzky's work seems to represent an instance of socialist modernism. Why? —Because it creates or builds upon an abstraction but one that at the same time possesses an excess of signification and one that carries an evident heteronomous content which is paradoxically revealed precisely through the use of abstract forms.

In his "Study of Ideologies and Philosophy of Language" from 1929 V. N. Voloshinov makes an important observation as regards the notion of ideology. In his view, "All manifestations of ideological creativity—all other nonverbal signs—are bathed by, suspended in, and cannot be entirely segregated or divorced from the element of speech."②

The prime location of ideology is the word. Or in Voloshinov's own words, "The word is the ideological phenomenon par excellence."③ It is this same notion of ideology that is so very present in Lissitzky's poster: political ideology does not hinder the artistic potential of the poster it instead enhances its aesthetic effect.

In the spring of 1968 Jean-François Lyotard held a seminar at Nanterre devoted to political posters. He was particularly interested in the work under discussion in this talk, namely in Lissitzky's "The Street Poster"—as the poster discussed in this talk is also known.

> The poster as a whole, besides being a work of political propaganda, also exhibits an overt aesthetic function. Its simple graphisms convey an excess of signification.

---

① See Erjavec, "Introduction," in Aleš Erjavec (ed.), *Postmodernism and the Postsocialist Condition. Politicized Art under Late Socialism* (Berkeley: University of California Press, 2003), pp. 44—46.

② V. N. Voloshinov, "The Study of Ideologies and Philosophy of Language," in: Alla Efimova and Lev Manovich (eds.), *Tekstura. Russian Essays on Visual Culture* (Chicago: The University of Chicago Press, 1993), p. 8.

③ Ibid., p. 6.

Pure ideological statement and pure aesthetic object never meet in a single space, for this would destroy the perception and reception of each of them. The effect produced by the poster resembles visual paradoxes where, by changing our inner perceptual vantage form, we see the same object in a different way, or as a different object. In the case of the poster (and in many other works by the same artist or by Malevich) the aesthetic effect engendered by pure geometric forms augments the ideological effect of the written statement, and vice versa. The image and the narrative exist in two distinct spaces. They merely intersect, producing in our perception not a unified effect, but a doubled or parallel impression—a binary effect. ①

If this is true, then we can claim that in the poster the image exists in one "reality" (or its dimension) and the discourse or narrative in another—in spite of both actually existing in a single visual space of the poster. It may thus be true, as Lyotard argued in his *Discourse, Figure* book,② that a letter is a figure and a discourse at the same time, but perhaps even more could be said: the discourse supplements and intensifies the effect of the image. This may be especially true when we are dealing with an image that is basically an abstract one. Already Camilla Gray noticed that after the introduction of "Prouns," "Lissitzky's interest in lettering was soon combined with these new abstract compositions." ③ Lissitzky was obviously aware that a picture that contains an abstract pictorial and a concrete discursive component achieves its maximum aesthetic effect when the two elements exist in a tension which is in his poster furthermore strengthened by the dynamic positioning of the red wedge. Perhaps we could even claim that Rodchenko's, Moholy-Nagy's and Lissitzky's later constructivist photographs (such as those presented in the twenties and thirties in the journal *USSR in Construction*), just as in the case of Lissitzky's work under consideration, built on the same principle of dynamism of geometrical forms which instantly evoked the aesthetic effect. It was probably this abstract aesthetic property of constructivism that attracted the attention of the post-war Western artists.

The textual or discursive ingredients of the image—the text, in short—thus offered an explicit statement but one that avoided the simple ideological effect of

---

① Erjavec, op. cit., p. 44.
② Jean-François Lyotard, *Discours, figure* (Paris: Klincksieck, 1971).
③ Gray, op. cit., p. 254.

ordinary political posters. Works such as these opened up a territory between the pure propaganda (be it ideological or commercial, as created in the twenties by Mayakovsky and Rodchenko) and autonomous western art. If then indeed, Barr wanted to promote and retain the global place for western art, he really had, as he put it during his winter 1927—1928 visit to Soviet Union, to "find some painters [in the USSR] if possible."①

In this way Barr partook in a dispute that has still not been resolved, although it is one of the primary instances of autonomization and heteronomization of art. Is, according to the western artistic standards art (or artwork) such as Lissitzky's 1919—1920 poster an instance of ideological or autonomous art? I would argue that it is an instance of both: On one level it represents a pure propaganda gesture, even in its first appearance, i.e., in Kolli's initial sculptural project. On the other it has today drifted into the institution of art and has lost its ideological potential, retaining only the aesthetic one. What used to be regarded in 1920 as a work of political propaganda which simultaneously possessed an aesthetic function and existed in a space opposite that of the artistic autonomy and the institution of art, was after decades of historical assimilation transformed into a yet another instance of institutional art thereby becoming assimilated, essentially abstract and "beautiful." Its textual component retains today only its visual aestheticized effect, this one being enhanced by the Cyrillic script. In this way the poster has undergone the processes that avant-garde art of the twentieth century underwent soon after its artistic and political successes and impacts. After World War II Lissitzky's poster turned from a specific avant-garde work of political propaganda into an assimilated modernist work more akin to western constructivism than to its original signification. Its context was gone so its ideological meaning was gone too.

I have mentioned that in the aftermath of the fall of the Berlin Wall in 1989 Eastern European artists have sometimes evoked Lissitzky's abstract geometric design from his 1919—1920 poster with the frequent postmodernist practice of quoting a well-known historical works. What probably attracted them in Lissitzky's poster was its binary nature: the dualism of the aesthetic and the ideological, the latter of them with the unfolding of time becoming increasingly aestheticized too.

---

① Quoted in Foster, op. cit., p. 246.

Such examples are not only to be found in Eastern Europe—in 1979 Huang Rui, a leading member of the Chinese "Stars" painterly movement, designed a logo of the Stars group. Nothing exceptional, you will say—except that it was (apart from the blue background) a copy of El Lissitzky's poster from more than half a century before, namely of the poster *Beat the Whites with the Red Wedge*.①

Let me end this talk by raising a few questions: First: How has an artist who was basically a "modernist" such as Huang Rui in the seventies stumbled upon Lissitzky's constructivist image? Second: Why did he think that a work that stood for the opposite of the autonomous art that he and his group were professing would suitably express and represent the nature or essence of the artistic orientation of the "Stars" groups? It would seem that such a question would have to be posed to Huang Rui. Nonetheless, perhaps we can venture and attempt to answer it by ourselves. I think it is important that in the "Stars" logo the political statement is gone. What remains is the abstract geometric image that incessantly reveals, expresses and confirms the aesthetic potential of geometric forms—just like in Lissitzky's "prouns." It is this gesture of removing the political and ideological statement that turns the poster into an empty shell of aesthetic form and allows the militant statement of the poster to be transformed into the aestheticized artwork that Huang Rui could employ to express the spirit of the "Stars" group. Put differently, the avant-garde and ideological signification of the street poster has with the removal of the ideological statement been transformed into a formalist work of art thereby confirming Voloshinov's statement about the ideological nature of discourse. Perhaps the incessant driftings of works such as Lissitzky's that lose their heteronomous nature and acquire (or retain) only their autonomous one, is what not only differentiates the original Lissitzky's work from that of Huang Rui's logo, but also separates western modernism form its eastern variety. At least the latter has already been incorporated into the art historical narrative.

（本文责任编辑：贾洁）

---

① Cf. Huang Rui, *The Stars' Time. 1977—1984* (Beijing: Thinking Hands + Guanyi Contemporary Art Archive, 2007), unpaginated.

"单刀直入!"

阿列西·艾尔雅维奇

【内容摘要】本文以苏联艺术家埃尔·利西茨基作于1919年的政治宣传海报"单刀直入"为例,条分缕析,深入探讨了西方现代主义艺术的艺术自主问题。

【作者简介】阿列西·艾尔雅维奇(Aleš Erjavec),国际著名哲学家、美学家,斯洛文尼亚科学与人文科学研究院哲学研究所所长,曾任国际美学协会主席。其学术兴趣集中在哲学美学,出版了多部具有广泛影响的美学著作,如《美学、艺术与意识形态》、《美学与认识论》、《意识形态与现代主义艺术》、《美学与批评理论》、《图像时代》、《爱在最后一瞥:先锋派、美学与艺术终结》、《美学与全球化》、《后现代主义、后社会主义及其他》等。其著作已经被译成了英文、法文、德文、西班牙文、波斯文、俄文、日文、中文等多种语言文字。

Dialectical Criticism and Concrete Analysis

David Margolies

(Goldsmiths College, University of London)

Abstract: Marx's statement from his preface to *A Contribution to the Critique of Political Economy* that social existence determines consciousness is fundamental to Marxist understanding of culture but it is not a formula; it offers context and direction for interpretation. Although it has been used typically to explain historical culture, Marxism, as its founders made clear, is also about changing the world.

The demand for change in the real world suggests that criticism of cultural products must pay attention not only to matters of objective political alignments but also to the construction of subjectivity and emotions. Criticism that ignores this complicated process while making political demands on literature tends to produce crude judgements. Christopher Caudwell, the English Marxist killed in the Spanish Civil War at the age of 29, showed that literature's power to encourage change comes primarily from emotional reorganisation rather than from rational political argument. The primacy of emotion has the important corollary for interpretation that analysis must be concrete. The power of emotion lies in the experience of an imagined reality. The emotion, because it is embodied in the experience, is concrete. Criticism must attend to this concreteness.

Rational/emotional and concrete/abstract distinctions can be illustrated by two pairs of proletarian novels—Lewis Jones, *Cwmardy* and *We Live*, and Walter Brierley, *Means Test Man* and *Sandwich Man*. Some reference is also made to Ang Lee's 2007 film *Lust, Caution* (*Sè, Jiè*). Finally, the prejudice in favour of abstraction is related to embedded class attitudes in the British education system.

Marxism has always involved abstraction. Abstraction is necessary in order to recognise patterns and, although practice is necessarily concrete (you can't do something in the abstract), abstraction is necessary to understand it. For Marxist theorising to offer a true understanding, and to be useful as a guide to practice, it has to be based on the concrete. This sounds terribly obvious but I want to examine two periods in Britain when the useful dialectical relation between concrete and abstract was seriously distorted. The first is the period following 1968, that year of extraordinary popular resistance in Paris, in Washington and in London. With exceptional speed, a generation of students and lecturers went through a process of radicalisation. They established for cultural and literary studies an approach and style in which theory assumed an unprecedented importance for at least the next decade. The second period is the 1930s, the period of the Popular Front or People's Front, as it was called in Britain, when radical criticism and theory flourished. The Spanish Civil War focused attitudes sharply and made neutrality impossible—you were either anti-fascist or fascist. Political criteria entered all fields. In such an environment, left criticism tended to treat explicit political perspective as the prime criterion and to devalue the importance of the aesthetic, emotional content of literature.

The problem of abstract criticism can probably be explained more clearly if I start with the post-1968 period and then deal with the 1930s. In British university literature departments one of the responses to the events of 1968 was a recognition that literature was ideological. But this was only half understood: "ideological" was not seen in its most general sense of embodying the perspective of the society that produced it, a principle fundamental to Marxist historical criticism in which ideology is recognised as something that changes from one social organisation to another; the newly radicalised lecturers saw ideology in its narrowest sense as false consciousness. Thus, because literature was ideological, it must display a false consciousness, which meant that teaching it would be spreading a corrupt view of the world. This was not just an intellectual change of understanding; students of literature felt they had been cheated, persuaded to honour false virtues; they seethed with resentment at those unreformed lecturers who continued to ignore or to disguise the dangers of literature by studying form, style and a humanistic vision. In the preceding decades F. R. Leavis, the most important influence on teachers of English, had given a generation of teachers a sense of mission by treating literature not as polite amusement or an accomplishment of a gentleman but as a bearer of social purpose. Although he was somewhat reactionary in his class perspective, he recognised that literature transmits values, which was a step toward a Marxist approach; yet he was seen as not just a purveyor of outmoded attitudes but in effect as a social traitor. The radical generation of 1968 concluded that there was something fundamentally wrong with teaching the texts of literature and studying them was corrupting.

Inevitably this posed problems. If the study of texts was potentially damaging because they were suffused with ideology, what were the radicalised teachers to teach? Eventually a shift to a sociological approach to texts (texts viewed as indicators of social attitudes) solved the problem, but the immediate answer in the wake of '68 was a turn to theory. Theory did not have the dangers present in texts; on the contrary, by its very nature theory was a corrective, something that could deconstruct, and thereby disarm, bourgeois ideology. However, there were two clear problems that theory-based literature education encountered. The first was that traditional scholars, an older generation that was unwilling to be displaced, often held positions of power in the universities and controlled the curriculum. The second problem was that English criticism was traditionally empiricist; there was little native theory. The Marxist theory that had blossomed in the 1930s did not gain many adherents in this period of radicalisation because the academic environment was still dominated by Cold War attitudes and thus Marxism was seen as tainted by association with the Soviet Union. However, French theory, which had entered the academy through linguistics and cinema studies, was acceptable and was taken up by literary studies. It was intellectually challenging, had a complex vision of human interaction, offered a Marxism with no Soviet tinge and was attractively daring in its departure from English tradition. It divided departments and generated some fierce conflicts.

Louis Althusser was probably the most-cited theorist of the period and one of his influences, paradoxically, was to treat criticism as scientific, parallel to the traditional Soviet stress on Marxism as a science. Terry Eagleton, the most influential of the '68 critics (and probably still today the world's most widely known literary critic), in his *Criticism and Ideology* of 1976, exhibited this "scientific" tendency in his use of mathematical-style formulas. This turned out to be a practice that he found not very relevant or useful and he did not use it again. But that did not stop many of his followers from adopting his statements mechanically; to his credit, he warned against this and explained clearly and concretely why making slogans out of theoretical principles was a false practice. (It was also strangely reminiscent of the warnings given at the 1934 Soviet Writers' Congress and Mao's 1942 speeches at the Yenan Forum on Art and Literature.)

This new radical perspective did not translate easily into the conventions literature students had traditionally been taught. The problem was exacerbated by the speed of radicalisation and by a suspicion of actual literary texts: examples that would have helped to explain the theory were invalidated even before they had been cited—because text was ideological. For instance, Shakespeare, the keystone of the British cultural edifice, was often rejected but any specific examination of the plays to justify that rejection was not thought necessary or acceptable. Many students were quite willing to reject works that were traditionally valued but were unable to give a reason for doing so beyond the fact that they were ideological. The lack of reasoning in no way inhibited the certainty of their conclusions. Concrete study was dismissed; they were willing to wave their little red books (we also had them in England) and look for no further truth.

* * *

I now want to move discussion back to the earlier period. The critical perspective of 1930s radicals in Britain suffered from abstraction in a manner less obvious than that of the post '68 generation. The Communist Party was a major force in left culture, even if the size of the membership did not make it dominant, and the rise of fascism in Europe gave importance to the communist integrated view of politics and culture. At the same time, the CP retained a strong element of the "class against class" attitudes of the preceding decade which encouraged in the party a hostility toward intellectuals and a perception of cultural activities as effete (in the sense that the serious issues were in politics). Culture was regarded as mere entertainment for those who lacked the strength of character to use their energies in political struggle. This downgrading of culture was considered good politics because it prioritised political struggle. But its narrow and non-dialectical understanding of politics was in fact bad politics because it misread the factors in life that drive action. Theory without practice, as Marx said, is useless, but he also said practice without theory is blind. Literature as a category was not rejected but the category was often narrowed to include little more than political pamphlets. The milder manifestations of this attitude did not reject imaginative culture outright but demanded relevance from it, relevance that was very narrowly conceived: the subject matter should be drawn from the working class and it should present positive models of behaviour. Narrative was of greatest interest, probably because what happens in the work could demonstrate the value of a course of action. Otherwise, information was what counted; anything of recognisable literary character served as no more than sugar on the pill of information. There was a single major criterion—political perspective.

There is nothing inherently wrong or necessarily abstract about political criteria, but to be useful and recognised as rational they have to be based on a dialectical understanding of what is involved in politics. The caricature version of political criteria, "Is it good for the workers?", is unreasonable if people attempt to apply it directly to texts; but as the ultimate concern from which the analytic criteria are derived (the motivation behind the criteria), it makes sense if detailed attention to all the stages of examination and argument necessary to arrive at a sound judgement are displayed. Without this it becomes irrational—a demonstration of feeling, not judgement. The inadequate understanding or perhaps unwillingness to take into consideration the concrete elements that generate political behaviour negated much of the usefulness of a political principle of criticism. An effective political criticism had to recognise the complexity of the body politic and of individuals. Political involvement is a matter of the heart as well as the head; people have to be motivated, not just made to grasp a rational argument. Such motivation is an essential element of political behaviour—it is *why* people do things. As has been shown by the advertising industry, the most successful mobiliser of behaviour in the West, emotional manipulation is clearly possible; and it is also possible for an emotional response to override reason.

The importance of concrete and specific factors in motivation was well understood by some of the radical theorists, notably C. Day Lewis, Alick West and Christopher Caudwell. Yet in book-reviewing and other critical writing their influence was limited;

simplistic criteria became the most widespread image of Marxist criticism. This was in part because simple criteria could easily be caricatured by the bourgeois cultural establishment, they were simpler to use for an audience with limited education, and they flattered a "workerist" view of the proletariat as the proper model for personal behaviour as well as the most important class because they were the bearers of revolution.

The most important year for British Marxist theory was 1937, the year that saw the publication of Ralph Fox's *The Novel and the People*, Alick West's *Crisis and Criticism* and Christopher Caudwell's *Illusion and Reality*. Fox was a very dynamic writer but his book did not progress beyond a rather simple socialist realism. West was a well-rounded, learned and subtle critic, who illustrated very well a Marxist interpretation of culture but whose style lacked the excitement of Fox's and whose brilliant perceptions were not made into an integrated theory. It was Caudwell who was the most complete and systematic of the theorists but, as an autodidact who left school before he was 15 years old, his work was in many ways idiosyncratic and did not have the ordered character that would be expected from academic theoretical writing. Like Fox, he had joined the British battalion of the International Brigades in the Spanish Civil War and was killed defending the Republic. He was 29; his major work, *Illusion and Reality*, was still in press when he died. The work of a young man, it displayed an immense knowledge of literary and scientific culture but it was also written at great speed and not all of it was entirely coherent.

The strength of Caudwell's approach was based on two elements. One was his grasp of the fundamental Marxist principle that, as Marx's Thesis XI on Feuerbach suggests, making change is the point of human activity. The second arises from his particular interest in poetry (the book is sub-titled *A Study of the Sources of Poetry*); it concerns the social function of poetry and how that function is carried out. He was perhaps stimulated by C. Day Lewis's "Revolutionaries and Poetry", published in *Left Review* in July 1935, and he drew on I. A. Richards's *Principles of Literary Criticism*, which stressed the importance of detailed examination of readers' actual responses to textual stimuli. Caudwell considered the emotional associations of a poem's words at a specific level and how they can be transferred to the real world in which the audience find themselves. He could then generalise about how poetry uses language to produce an emotional reorientation. In essence, it creates an imaginary, emotionally loaded picture of reality that enriches the audience's sense of the reality they know from real life experience and thus alters their response to it. The power of emotion lies in the audience's experiencing of the imagined reality; and because it is embodied in specific experience, it is necessarily concrete. The contrary of this specificity, abstract response, can be shown to be ridiculous in the way Dickens plays with it in the deathbed scene at the end of *Hard Times*: "I think there's a pain somewhere in the room," said Mrs Gradgrind, "but I couldn't positively say that I have got it."

"The poem", says Caudwell, "is what happens when it is read." Poetry *does* something. And because, through most of human history, poetry has existed in oral culture rather than in texts, its mode of existence has been public; and because it uses a language shared by its audience or readers it is in that sense public rather than private, capable of altering responses for a whole group. Thus poetry has not just a personal but a social effect. In a striking exercise of Marxist historical criticism, Caudwell traces the development of English poetry from the Renaissance to the modern period in some 50 pages, showing how it reflected but also helped to generate the spirit of the age. It is a brilliant attempt, yet also a superficial and sometimes erroneous survey. Not without reason, it attracted scorn and admiration in equal measure.

Caudwell says that the changes made in socially shared feeling are fundamental to art. "The sum of such changes, organised and made independent of men, is what art is, not in abstraction, but emerging in concrete living." Literature's relation to practical politics, as generalised by Caudwell's function of poetry, is to serve as a guide to action. It is not a guide because it argues rationally that we need to follow such and such a course of action. It is a guide in the sense that it organises emotion; it integrates and prioritises desires, which focuses attitudes in a way that is relevant to the choice of action. This should not be seen simply as encouragement, a call to arms, but as an organisation of values which helps to determine the direction of action. The reorientation comes not from rational consideration of the facts but emotionally, from the facts constructed by the author to give them a feeling of particular significance in people's lives. By the conclusion of his book Caudwell, with a political realism that may earlier have been suppressed by his enthusiasm, qualified his view of the current political possibilities for poetry and said that the large social function of poetry seen in earlier societies (e. g. , the Elizabethan age) could not really be carried out in the present situation because the audience for poetry had become too small and because the world was changing too quickly.

Some of the criticism of the 1930s displayed dialectical principles similar to those put forward by Caudwell. *Left Review* (a literary monthly which was published by the CP-dominated Writers' International between 1934 and 1938) published some excellent criticism but its wide perspective must have seemed too adventurous to the leadership of the Communist Party. Even though the party had no clear cultural line of its own, it leaned towards Comintern hard-liners. Dimitrov's speech to the Soviet Writers Association was published in *Left Review* in 1935 with the title "Georgi Dimitrov to Writers"; although he was a genuine hero in both personal and political aspects, Dimitrov was not an ideal person to pronounce on cultural values. The magazine, which had attracted to its pages and staff left-wing cultural figures both inside and outside the Communist Party, was becoming more closely controlled by the party, which organised its closure. "Workerist" criticism became the dominant CP approach, concerned with little more than class alignment, demanding models of revolutionary behaviour and scorning emotional aspects of literature as pandering to bourgeois individualism.

The problem of political response to imaginative writing can be clearly seen in the reception of two authors who wrote proletarian novels (i. e. , class-conscious novels by members of the working class) that reached an audience well beyond the radical left; they were praised but also subjected to workerist abstract criticism. Walter Brierley published *Means Test Man* in 1935 and Lewis Jones *Cwmardy* in 1937. Both then published second novels—Brierley, *Sandwich Man* (1937) and Jones, *We Live* (1939)— that showed they had responded to workerist demands: their content was more focused on immediate political struggle and they did not portray the complex motivation that had enriched the first novels[①]. They now seem in some respects contrived. They feel as if their authors were following an imposed agenda and their character-types often lack the

---

① Walter Brierley, *Means Test Man* (first published 1935; Nottingham: Spokesman Books, 1983);
Walter Brierley, *Sandwichman* (first published 1937; London: Merlin Press, 1980);
Lewis Jones, *Cwmardy* (first published 1937; London, Lawrence & Wishart, 1978);
Lewis Jones, *We Live* (first published 1939; London, Lawrence & Wishart, 1978).

individuation that marked the first books. Compared to the vitality of the first books they are rather wooden.

In terms of the narrative, very little happens in *Means Test Man*. The action covers a week in the life of a long-term unemployed miner and his wife and young son who are living on the "dole" (public assistance) as the Friday approaches when the Means Test investigator will make his monthly inspection. They live in grinding poverty. Each carefully considered purchase of their weekly shopping in the neighbouring town is described in detail, but what is emphasised by Brierley is not simply what they purchase and its cost but the psychological torment of having to weigh up every halfpenny of potential expenditure, making sure the week's dole money will last them to the end of the week. Any routine purchase—shirt buttons, potatoes for their dinner, a bus ride, etc. —demands careful consideration; every element of consumption causes a corresponding expenditure of emotional energy. When Jack (the miner) loses a threepenny piece through a hole in his pocket, he has destroyed the small flexibility they might have had in spending that tiny sum. He follows this emotional upset with the accidental breaking of one of their very few cups, causing a major domestic quarrel.

However, it is clear that they are not actually starving, nor are they homeless and having to live on the streets (like many people in Britain today). The greatest pain is psychological damage. In that society the sense of social validation, usefulness, positive connection with others and one's own humanity depend on being in work. Jane (his wife) suffers from feeling she has lost her respectability and is looked down upon by the local population because there is not enough money to do the things that proper working people do, such as having friends to tea, going on outings, shopping without having always to seek out the cheap clearance items. Jack's suffering has nothing to do with respectability, but his feeling of social uselessness is corrosive and makes him stay out of sight when the employed miners pass on their way to or from work. When he takes his son to the village cricket match he goes early enough to avoid other men seeing he pays the reduced unemployed entry charge. Jane's attitude toward Jack is accusatory; he does not fulfil his socially assigned role and she is not willing to see that he too is a victim. He understands her attitude but also resents it. Their having to spend most of the day in close proximity to each other destroys any pleasure in their marriage.

But worse than the poverty and the injured self-confidence is the monthly means test. The prospect of the Friday inspection makes tension build during the course of the week. There is nothing they can do about it; they face the humiliation of having their private lives measured unfeelingly by a petty bureaucrat—ungracious, unsympathetic and alert to anything that could be an excuse to reduce their meagre allowance.

> They were wanting him to get it over and go quickly. The master and mistress of a household-the two heads of a home-husband and wife in their castle-English. And this man sat here at the table where grace used to be said, where friends used to come and laugh over tea, always on the first Sunday in the year, that nearest John's birthday. And this man sat where those friends had sat, he was like a lord and they stood trembling before him. No, that wasn't the relation at all, there was something soulless in this, callous. Means Test. It was something else beside a means test, it tested one's soul, one's being, and the soul and the being were poorer every time. [1]

The elaboration of the picture suggests more than that things were better in the past; the table "where friends used to come" contrasts an image of social integration with the soulless interrogation in the present. Brierley makes the point through the contrast; there is no need for him to be more explicit. And he achieves a point that is both "informational"—giving knowledge of previous conditions—and emotional—the associations that give it significance. Whatever the sense of wrongs Brierley had developed earlier, the visit of the investigator gives them an objectivity; Jack and Jane are now "officially" non-persons.

Jane is very distraught after the visit.

> Oh, it was too much, it wasn't fair. She began speaking again to steady herself. "Why, it's shameful, no—no decent men and-and women would—would"—she was fast losing the battle with her emotions—"let them do this-this to you if only they—they realized—" [2]

---

[1] Walter Brierley, *Means Test Man* (first published 1935; Nottingham: Spokesman Books, 1983), p. 263.
[2] Ibid., p. 265.

Jack makes the same point more explicitly two pages later:

> "If all the women in England could feel for a minute what you've gone through this morning, there'd be no more of it, no more homes upset. Still no one could understand who hasn't gone through it ... " ①

Brierley has fulfilled his purpose; his readers have been taken through an image of the means test and they must now understand it. In Caudwell's terms, Brierley with very little "action" has done a stunning job of making readers grasp its significance. There are no explicit political demands, no call for "general strike now" or other summonses to immediate action. But by dealing concretely with the intricacies of the human effect of the means test, he has achieved a clarity about what values are important and an awareness of why, even if it is not fully articulated. In my view this book may have done more to lead people into action against the means test than volumes of statistics about nutritional deprivation or child development.

Yet the *Daily Worker* took a workerist line on the novel, demanding something that had more proletarian spirit:

> A book which brought out this fighting spirit of the unemployed would have a much greater use to the working-class, though the book does represent the sufferings of many, the ones who have never yet been on a mass demonstration, and has a great value for that alone.

And the image of the working class lacks the heroism it should have:

> The weakness of the book, recognisable, perhaps, only to those who have experienced long periods of unemployment, is that the unemployed worker who sits timidly at home waiting for the investigator is not the rule but the exception.

It is not considered to be without use, however: the book is good for "those who

---

① Walter Brierley, *Means Test Man* (first published 1935; Nottingham: Spokesman Books, 1983), p. 267.

want a detailed study of the agonies wrought on the more sensitive by the Means Test" (E. Woolley, "Tortured Under The Means Test", 22 May 1935). The tone is condescending, and the reference to "more sensitive" suggests that Brierley's hero and perhaps Brierley himself are not up to the rigours of real political struggle.

In *Sandwich Man* (1937) Brierley creates a hero he endows with more fighting spirit but he is unable to maintain the complex of emotional reactions that gave depth to *Means Test Man*. His hero moves through a wider landscape, has more varied experiences politically and personally (there is even a sexual interest) and finally rejects a settled life for the life of the road. The experiences relate to Brierley's own life but lack the excitement of personal discovery or the nuanced treatment of *Means Test Man*. There are more voices than in the first book but they are without distinctive personality and the narrative voice gives no colour to the events it presents, as in the following example:

> The world slowed suddenly for the young man; surgings he could not analyse flowed through him. He knew they were hung on to the violences of his life-stream— his mother, step-father, Nancy, the examination, the pit. These were real, the stuff of them was waiting for him in the real world. This place [the education institute] wasn't real at all, it was the falsest thing imaginable. Men were here, and none of them were their real selves, hadn't chance to be. [1]

The *Daily Worker* reviewer praised it as an informative work; there was no concern expressed for its emotional value:

> This book is a worthy successor to "Means Test Man."... It should inform those people who believe that the way from a working-class home to the Universities has been made easy. It is a social document that should interest the younger generation very much. (B. L. Coombes, 22—9—1937)

Lewis Jones's *Cwmardy*, which had appeared earlier in the same year, deservedly received a much warmer reception from the *Daily Worker*:

---

[1] Walter Brierley, *Means Test Man* (first published 1935; Nottingham: Spokesman Books, 1983), pp. 177—178.

> This story is a story that carries you along because you are interested in and, indeed, deeply moved by the characters who live it. And they are not conventional characters either. Once set upon the stage they do not just say what they are there to say, but a great deal more. They are rich in unexpectedness as people are in life, and in the book they do not represent an attitude, but grow before your eyes.... I think it is a find. (Ralph Wright, 23—6—1937)

The favourable response was probably a recognition of the book's integrating character-centred narrative into a political perspective. The novel is really a political *bildungsroman*-Lewis presents to us the life education of the hero, Len, as he goes from childhood in a Welsh mining village to radical maturity. The chapters follow the stages of his development through his own perceptions. The naivety of the child gives an excellent vision of the attitudes of the community and its social relations. We see the development of Len's hatred of school and authority when he is unjustly caned, and Lewis shows through the child's eyes his eager anticipation of starting work, joining the community of men, but having his rosy image dashed by the stark reality of mining. The mixing of the political with the personal response gives significance to the events. When the mature Len is involved in a strike across the whole coalfield, Lewis continues to offer mixed perspectives. The victory of the miners is the unquestioned goal but the choice of action is not simple; the personal perspective allows the presentation of contradictions and nuances, which gives an intensely real quality. For the reader, this encourages a complex response that is emotional as well as informative, something which could not be delivered by factual description alone.

The language of Lewis's characters is probably no less authentic than Brierley's passages of Derbyshire dialect but it is richer in images, more colourful and thus more interesting. For example, when Len's father comes home drunk in a bad mood, his mother tells him he should have come home "long ago instead of sitting on your backside in other people's place, then coming home here full of grunts" (p. 15). Lewis can give a reality to personal yet anonymous situations, as when a crowd of women await the identification of the dead following a mine explosion: "The name flew from mouth to mouth until it was stopped by a wild scream when it reached the ears of the widow. Willing and tender hands led her away" (p. 86). There are also a fair number of condensed expressions of political views that are appropriate to character and situation but which have a slogan quality that should satisfy a workerist interpretation. Thus when the mine owners try to make a cost-saving cut that would endanger the miners, Len's father says, "What do us men count? We be cheaper than chickens" (p. 89).

Lewis wrote a sequel to *Cwmardy*, *We Live*, that appeared in 1939. The book has attracted admirers who regard it more highly than *Cwmardy* for the intensity of political struggle in its pages. It is probably best characterised by David Smith in his introduction to the 1978 edition: "This eagerness to highlight each incident is the book's major weakness as a novel, since it causes Lewis Jones to turn almost all of his characters into automated abstractions whose fictional duty is only to spill the historical beans." The narrative, the political action, has a workerist appeal, but except for readers already persuaded of the book's argument, it would seem to have little political value. John Sommerfield, himself the author of a radical novel of considerable interest, *May Day* (1936), wrote to the *Daily Worker* in March 1937 to object to books being judged on the political activity of their authors. The *Daily Worker* is the only paper that "deals with books seriously from the point of view of the class struggle", he said, and "misleading and harmful 'revolutionary sentimentality' should not be encouraged".

Sandwich Man and *We Live* have a greater portion of the text occupied by political action or discussion than *Means Test Man* or *Cwmardy*, and this has led some critics to judge them to be superior politically. Their arguments that socialism is necessary to end the destructiveness of the capitalist system are intellectually sound and sufficiently illustrated in the text. On the other hand, *Means Test Man* and *Cwmardy* have a human intimacy that comes from the way their arguments are embedded in experience perceived by the protagonists; that gives them a greater emotional force. Although *Sandwich Man* and *We Live* may be convincing at a rational level in their argument for socialism, the emotional strength of *Means Test Man* and *Cwmardy* can better move readers to a commitment. *Sandwich Man* and *We Live* change understanding; *Means Test Man* and *Cwmardy* change attitude. Thus, if the criterion for judging novels is their political effect, *Means Test Man* and *Cwmardy* are superior to their sequels. The principle is illustrated by the success of Upton Sinclair's famous novel, *The Jungle*, set in the meat-packing industry of Chicago and written with the purpose of converting readers to socialism. The dispossessed hero is converted to socialism by long rational argument. But Sinclair hardly went beyond the rational argument; what stirred his readers most was the disgusting picture of the meat industry. This is said to have resulted in the passage of the US Pure Food and Drug Act of 1906, but it did not move the public to socialism.

The error of political judgement in regard to proletarian novels I would attribute to the abstract nature of the criticism: the narrative is used as the basis for judgement and the emotional effects are largely disregarded. This is a form of abstraction, one that distorts judgement. Probably more comprehensible and perhaps part of the experience of most people attending the Sino-British Bilateral Forum on Marxist Aesthetics is Ang Lee's film *Lust, Caution* (*Sè, Jiè*), where criticism that focuses primarily on the narrative at the expense of the emotion produces a notably different analysis from an emotionally attentive analysis. The publicity for the film in Britain emphasised its nature as an espionage thriller but also as an erotic thriller; the tension would justify the thriller designation (although the sex, I understand, was censored in China). But the film is organised and is shot in a way that emphasises the emotional aspects more than the espionage. The responses of Wong Chai Chi, the heroine, and Yee, the Chinese head of security in Shanghai for the Japanese occupiers, are visually the most important element in the film, and reveal the emotions on which the plot depends. It is because the members of the resistance cell, their leader, Kuang, and Lao Wu, the controller, do not or will not recognise Wong's emotional needs and the great stress she suffers in her role as Yee's mistress that their plot ultimately fails. Concentration on the narrative must be recognised as an abstraction when the concrete aspects of the film are the characters' emotions. And in this case, not to recognise the emotion is not simply bad criticism; it is also bad politics.

* * *

The problem of abstraction does not arise in a vacuum. A. A. Zhdanov, Secretary of the Soviet Central Committee, at the Soviet Writers' Congress of 1934, attributed the revolutionary power of Soviet literature to its depicting "reality in its revolutionary development" combined with "the ideological remoulding and education of the toiling people in the spirit of socialism"; "This method in *belles lettres* and literary criticism is what we call the method of socialist realism." If he had anchored these generalisations in any concrete reality or showed some understanding of "method" it might be acceptable, but as he stated it, it is an exhortation to something that is not at all clear; it is a bureaucrat's simplistic notion of literature. Ignoring or suppressing contradiction, Zhdanov was turning the weapon of Marxism into a blunt instrument, a bludgeon. The anti-aesthetic abstraction of England's political criticism in the 1930s had native roots but it was encouraged by Zhdanov's mechanistic views. The limited education of the working class made them more susceptible to sloganistic judgements and, at the same time, the Communist Party's emphasis on discipline discouraged independent thinking. Intellectuals, seen as inherently middle-class, were also distrusted, regarded as unreliable allies in making revolution, whereas workerist judgements had revolutionary credibility, though not throughout the whole movement.

The theoretical abstraction of the post-1960s period, while it was a response to rapid radicalism, also had roots in the education system that shaped the theorists. The system valued written work above any other means of displaying talent or intelligence, and individual performance above any group production. There was also a cultural preference for production that was purely intellectual (e.g. pure science over technology) and that which emphasised the qualitative judgement of the individual rather than the nature of the matter. In the massive expansion of universities in the 1960s many of the new students, although coming from backgrounds that would make them sympathetic to radical positions, won praise for their ability to handle abstractions and, unaware, found themselves co-opted into the insulated environment of the university with their radical edge blunted. The critical language, often borrowed from French and admired within the universities, was not comprehensible to the general public. There seemed to be two separate worlds. My favourite illustration of this kind of blindness was a remark my PhD supervisor made, frustrated by what I had written. He said, "Look, Margolies, let's get this theory and practice business straight: theory is thinking about things, right? And practice is writing it down."

Obviously without practice we have nothing, but we need theory to guide it. We must develop an education that encourages students to form their own judgements and asks that they support them concretely. In order to have a dialectic that is useful, that can work toward realising the humane vision of Marx as well as advancing Marxist aesthetics, we need to show a genuine respect for material practice and we need to value the concrete.

（本文责任编辑：于琦）

辩证批评与具体分析

大卫·马格列斯

【内容摘要】马克思在《政治经济学批判》的"前言"中提出社会存在决定社会意识，这是马克思主义基础性的文化解释方式，但并非唯一的公式；它所提供的是阐释背景和方向。尽管长期以来它被视为解释历史文化的典型方式，但正如马克思主义的首创者马克思所明确的，它也是改变世界的一种方式。

出于改变现实世界的需要，对文化产品的批判就不仅是客观的政治异化问题，也是主体性和情感的建构问题。忽视这一复杂进程的文学批评，出于政治需要往往会做出粗疏的判断。英国马克思主义者、29 岁时在西班牙内战中牺牲的克里斯托弗·考德威尔，已经向我们表明，文学推动世界改变的力量主要在于情感重组而非理性的政治性论辩。情感之重要性在解释方面的重要推论是：分析必须是具体的。情感的力量存在于有关想象性现实的经验之中。原因是体现在经验中的，情感是具体的。批评必须致力于这一具体性。

理性/情感与具体/抽象之间的区分，可由两对无产阶级小说来说明——路易斯·琼斯的《科沃马迪》与《我们的生活》，瓦尔特·布里尔利的《考验人的手段》与《三明治人》，有人还提到李安 2007 年的电影《色·戒》。最后需要指出，赞同抽象化的偏见与在英国教育系统中植入阶级态度有关。

【作者简介】大卫·马格列斯（David Margolies），伦敦大学戈德斯密斯学院荣休教授。在国际学术界享有较高知名度。他治学领域广泛，早年长期在英国和美国多所大学教授文艺复兴文学、莎士比亚戏剧和流行文化，后来又转向美学等研究领域。

"Marxism and the Rise of New Confucianism"

Bart Dessein

(Ghent University, Belgium)

Abstract: After, at the end of the 19th and the beginning of the 20th century, Chinese intellectuals had questioned the value of the Confucian tradition in its confrontation with European imperialism, the establishment of the People's Republic of China meant that imperial China's Confucianism was replaced by a Chinese variant of Marxism-Leninism as official ideology.

China's policies of opening up to the world that have started at the end of the 70s of the 20th century have transformed the country into a leading economic and increasingly also political power in the world. Growing social inequality as result of this economic development has led to an increase in social unrest, and has made one part of the Chinese population question the validity of the contemporary developmental model. Against this background, the similar economic growth of the so-called "Confucian" Asian tigers has given rise to the concept of an "Asian developmental model" of which traditional Confucianism is an important constituent. Such a revaluation of the ancient Confucian tradition in mainland China is inspired by the New Confucian movement in Taiwan, Hong Kong, and the US. Confucianism is, in this respect, seen as an instrument to alleviate social inequality and reinstall a "harmonious society".

It thus appears that the intellectual scene in contemporary China shows a variety of "ideological" trends: advocacy of capitalism and liberal democracy, continuation/redefinition of Chinese Marxism, return to/reinterpretation of the Confucian tradition, or a combination of some of these trends. As such, the contemporary situation is symptomatic for China's continuing "struggle for modernity".

This paper addresses this development, hereby focusing on the sociological divides in contemporary China, and tracing these divides back in history. It also evaluates this social division with respect to the issue of political participation in traditional and contemporary China.

1. Confucian China as a Peasant Society

The history of mankind is marked by the development of different paleotechnic ecotypes, i. e., systems that are marked by the employment of human and animal labor and that are the direct offspring of the first agricultural revolution that started about 7000—6000 BCE.① In the land we now know as "China,"② the knowledge to use bronze to make agricultural tools—a skill which most likely was learned from the northern Eurasian mobile pastoralists around 1700 BCE③—made it possible for its inhabitants to both enlarge the area of agricultural land that could be tilled and the efficiency with which this could be done. This major increase of agricultural output led to what Leon E. Stover (1974: 42 ff.) labeled "the era of regional development". This period of Chinese history stretched from roughly 1700 to 770 BCE. The possibility to nourish a larger number of people resulted in a population growth. After a primary phase of regional growth, however, the unremitting necessity for an ever-larger agricultural output to feed this growing population headed for a major crisis. Given the limited area of available farmland, "Chinese" civilization being concentrated in the fertile plains of the Yellow River and its tributaries, the point came where expansion of the farmland of one family was only possible to the detriment of another family, and expansion of the farmland of one of the many political unities—called "*guo*"—that constituted the "China" of that time, was only possible to the detriment of the

---

① These paleotechnic ecotypes are fundamentally different from neotechnic ecotypes that, especially in the 18th century, developed along with the industrial revolution and basically are the offspring of the second agricultural revolution. See Eric R. Wolf. *Peasants*. Foundations of Modern Anthropology Series Englewood Cliffs NJ: Prentice Hall, 1966, pp. 19—35.

② The name "China" is derived from "Cīna," a South Indian name for the region of the present-day Guangdong Province in Southern China, in use on the maritime route around 300 BCE. The name reached Europe from India. In most Western European languages, the name for China is derived from this "Cīna". The name "Seres" reached the West over the land route. Another group of names for China, among which "Cathay," is derived from "Khitai", a political union to the North-Northwest of the Chinese heartland in the 10th to 12th centuries CE. Contrary to what is generally accepted, the name "China" thus has no relation with the name "Qin," the name of the first Chinese empire, established in 221 BCE. See Berthold Laufer. "The Name China". *T'oung Pao* XIII, 1912.

③ See Louisa G. Fitzgerald-Huber. "Qijia and Erlitou: The Question of Contacts with Distant Cultures", *Early China* 20, 1995, p. 67.

neighboring "*guo*" (state).① This period has become known as the period of the "Warring States" (*Zhanguo*) in Chinese political history (435—221 BCE), and as the period of the "One Hundred Philosophical Schools" in Chinese intellectual history.② This context explains why Chinese philosophies are primarily concerned with the *Diesseits*, not with the *Jenseits*: their aim is to (re)-establish good order in society. This worldly orientation of Chinese philosophy also characterizes the preoccupation of Chinese (political) philosophy in the modern and contemporary era.

After the ruler of the Qin state—one of the Warring States—had become the final military victor, he successfully united the then Chinese territory, whereupon he established the first Chinese imperial dynasty—the Qin—in 221 BCE, and proclaimed himself the "First Emperor of the Qin" (*Qin shi huangdi*). The superior military force of the Qin state can basically be explained by its superior economic system. Being situated in an area stretching into the bend of the Yellow River to the northwest of Xianyang (Chang'an), the later capital of the Qin dynasty, and to the southwest of the same city, the region was less favorably situated for agriculture than the basin of the middle and lower ranges of the Yellow River was. It could only survive economically through irrigation works. A first canal with this aim was built in the 3rd century BCE. It ran in a line roughly parallel to and north of the Wei River (a tributary of the Yellow River), over a distance of approximately 120 kilometers.③ Commenting on this major technological achievement, the famous historian Sima Qian, in his *Shiji* (*Records of the Historian*) wrote the following:

> Thereupon the land within the passes became a fertile plain and there were no more bad years. Qin in this way became rich and powerful, and ended by conquering the various lords.④

---

① On the notion of "state" (*guo*) in this cultural period: see Bart Dessein. "Beyond Modernity: Chinese Self-identification in the Era of Globalisation", *Zhongguo Yanjiu / Revista de Estudos Chineses* 8, 2012, pp. 25—26.

② This period was coined the "*Achsenzeit*" by Jaspers 1949, as similar philosophical theories on the universe and mankind were proposed in the Western, Indian, and Chinese cultural contexts around this time. See in this respect also Bart Dessein. "Climbing a Tree to Catch Fish: Some Reflections on Plato, Aristotle, and China," in *La Rationalité en Asie / Rationality in Asia*, Johannes Bronkhorst (ed.), Études de Lettres 2001/3, Lausanne, 2001.

③ On the precise date of the building of this canal: see Derk Bodde. "The state and empire of Ch'in", in Denis Twitchett and Michael Loewe (eds.). *The Cambridge History of China. Volume I. The Ch'in and Han Empires*, 221 B.C. -A.D. 220. Cambridge: Cambridge University Press, 1986, p. 44, p. 46.

④ *Shiji* 1975: vol. 29, 1408. Translation see in Derk Bodde. "The state and empire of Ch'in", in Denis Twitchett and Michael Loewe (eds.). *The Cambridge History of China. Volume I. The Ch'in and Han Empires*, 221 B.C. -A.D. 220. Cambridge: Cambridge University Press, 1986, p. 46.

Sima Qian thus alludes to it that the surplus in agricultural output this developed production method yielded, must have made it possible for the state Qin to sustain a larger and more powerful army than the other "states" (*guo*) of the then China could.

Until the Han dynasty (206 BCE—AD 220), agriculture in the valleys of the Blue River (*Changjiang*) had been greatly inferior in productivity to that of north China. Both the *Shiji* and the *Han shu* (*History of the Han*) describe the type of agriculture in the south as "plowing with fire and weeding with water". ① According to this method, weeds were burnt off, after which water was poured and rice seeds were sown. As a result, both the surviving roots of the weeds and the rice would grow. Later on, the weeds were cut off again, and the rice would continue to grow. ② When the continued population growth in the north caused migration to the south, i.e., to the valleys of the Blue River, higher agricultural productivity was also needed in the south. With this aim, irrigation works such as the one mentioned above, and similar irrigation works that had been carried on in the delta of the Pearl River from the Qin dynasty onwards, were taken as examples. ③ As a result, hydraulic cultivation—one of the main types of paleotechnic ecotypes—matured in China. ④ Using the same agricultural areal, the hydraulic cultivation system could feed a larger population than the method of "plowing with fire and weeding with water"—a system that is typical for areas with

---

① *Shiji* 1975: vol. 30, 1437; *Han shu* 1975: vol. 6, 182.

② See Ying Shao, *Fengsu tongyi*, in *Sibu congkan*, vol. 6, p. 183.

③ Another famous example is the building of a network of irrigation canals in Sichuan in the 3rd century BCE. See Derk Bodde. "The state and empire of Ch'in", in Denis Twitchett and Michael Loewe (eds.). *The Cambridge History of China. Volume I. The Ch'in and Han Empires*, 221 B. C.—A. D. 220. Cambridge: Cambridge University Press, 1986, pp. 45—46.

④ See Michael Loewe. "The structure and practice of government", in Denis Twitchett and Michael Loewe (eds.). *The Cambridge History of China. Volume I. The Ch'in and Han Empires*, 221 B. C.—A. D. 220. Cambridge: Cambridge University Press, 1986, pp. 568—569. Through cutting forest and replacing it with a network of lakes and ponds, one continuously has a reservoir of water, used to flood the soil periodically. This technique avoids that the substances that are required to feed plants are washed away by excessive temporal rains on the either too permeable or not permeable enough soil. This technique makes the soil perfectly suitable for rice cultivation. Rice cultivation may further be complimented with work on land that cannot be irrigated. Here the peasant may grow oil-bearing seeds or perhaps cotton. Hill slopes may be planted to trees, such as mulberry, tea, or pepper trees. At the same time, fish can also be raised in the artificial ponds; sometimes in conjunction with irrigated rice fields, ducks are allowed to feed on aquatic plants, and the aquatic flora itself may be returned to the fields as fertilizer. The other types of paleotechnic ecotypes are (1) long-term fallowing systems, also called "swidden systems", (2) sectorial fallowing systems, (3) short-term fallowing systems, and (4) permanent cultivation of favored plots. All these ecotypes possessed their essential characteristics by about 3000 BCE. See Eric R. Wolf. *Peasants*. Foundations of Modern Anthropology Series Englewood Cliffs NJ: Prentice Hall, 1966, pp. 19—34.

few people and plenty of land—could. An important disadvantage of this system, however, is that the adaptation of the soil and cultivation of crops demands an enormous input of labor. In fact, in order to deliver economic output, the laborer consumes the largest part of his own produce. Put differently, this ecotype is characterized by high productivity per unit of land, but low productivity per unit of labor. ① Moreover, in areas where land was scarce and had to be used intensively—as is the case for China—competition developed between the use of land for human subsistence and for animal subsistence. The Chinese economic conditions could not sustain the breeding of an animal stock, nor the feeding of a large non-productive population.

It, therefore, does not come as a surprise that this type of hydraulic ecotype has been associated with the presence of a highly centralized political system that is capable of mobilizing men and directing goods towards the building of dikes and canals. The precise relation between cause and effect is, however, not fully clear. As shown by René Millon (1962: 87), autocratic systems may have greatly facilitated the construction of hydraulic ecotypes, but they are not a necessary condition. Ethnographic data rather suggest that "centralization of authority is an exceptional response to the problems of irrigation agriculture". ② This brings us to the particular role Confucianism has played in Chinese society, more precisely, the effect Confucianism has had on the creation and continuation of the Chinese agricultural system and on the perseverance of a Chinese "peasant society".

After having been in power for only 15 years, the Qin dynasty ended in 206 BCE and was followed by the Han dynasty. For the Confucian philosophers of the Han dynasty, the premature fall of the Qin proved that Legalism, the official philosophy of the first imperial dynasty, was unsuited as political philosophy. This made room for Confucianism to come to the foreground and to become the official orthodoxy in 136

---

① The comparison between hydraulic cultivation and more extensive ecotypes using moisture derived from rainfall alone is put in sharp relief when stated in terms of man-days—each involving 10 hours of work—devoted to the cultivation and care of a single acre. Thus, paleotechnic cultivators in Morocco and Algiers devote between 18 and 24 man-days of work to each acre. In Tepoztlán, Mexico, plow cultivation involves an average of 19.4 man-days per acre; the comparable figure for hoe cultivation is 57.9. But hydraulic cultivation of rice ascends to 90 man-days per acre in Japan and to 178.2 man-days per acre in Southwestern China. Figures: Dumont 1957: 181—190.

② See Eric R. Wolf. *Peasants*. Foundations of Modern Anthropology Series Englewood Cliffs NJ: Prentice Hall, 1966, pp. 25—26.

BCE. The Han Confucians did not emphasize law as fundamental value to safeguard social harmony and, by extension, political stability, but morality (*li*).① In his "*Chunqiu fanlu*" (*Abundant Dew of the Spring-and-Autumn Annals*) Dong Zhongshu (ca. 195—115 BCE), the most important exponent of political Confucianism in the Han dynasty, interprets this social and political harmony in terms of an intricate connection between earth, man, and heaven, whereby heaven is conceived as the collective of forefathers.② He thus presents a holistic worldview, labeled "cosmological Confucianism" by Joseph Needham (1958: 281—282),③ in which a change in one of the constituents naturally has its effect on all other constituents. It is the task of the Confucian ruler (*wang*) to safeguard the harmony between all constituent parts through his moral example, as exemplified in the wise words of the ancestors.④ This, combined with the fact that the time of Confucius was interpreted as the historical model to be followed, resulted in the Confucian cyclic time concept. The Confucian concept of moral virtue was further philosophically articulated in the concept *ren*: "humaneness,"⑤ and was ritually materialized in the rules of ancestor worship (*xiao*) that have become

---

① See Wing-tsit Chan. *A Source Book in Chinese Philosophy*. Princeton NJ: Princeton University Press, 1963, p. 271. The emphasis of morality is such that, for the Confucians, penal law is inferior, and serves to settle infringements on the moral standard. On the difficult balance between moral conduct (*li*) and penal law (*fa*) in imperial China: see Derk Bodde and Clarence Morris. *Law in Imperial China. Exemplified by 190 Ch'ing Dynasty Cases. Translated from the Hsing-an hui-lan. With Historical, Social, and Juridical Commentaries*. Cambridge MA: Harvard University Press, 1990, pp, 27—29.

② The "*Chunqiu fanlu*" is a commentary on the Confucian "*Chunqiu*" (*Spring-and-Autumn Annals*), a chronicle of the Lu state, birthplace of Confucius, between 722 and 481 BCE. For the relation between earth, man, and heaven according to Dong Zhongshu: see Wolfgang Bauer. *Geschichte der chinesischen Philosophie*. München: Verlag C. H. Beck, 2006, p. 122.

③ Benjamin I. Schwartz. *The World of Thought in Ancient China*. Cambridge MA and London: Harvard University Press, 1985, p. 364 defines this type of cosmology as "essentially a belief that political and social irregularities can invoke important disturbances in nature." See also Bart Dessein. "'Since Heaven has not yet destroyed this culture, what can the men of Kuang do to me?': Cosmological Confucianism and the Development of Science", *Philosophica* 83, 2008, pp. 25—49.

④ See Geoffrey Lloyd and Nathan Sivin. *The Way and the Word. Science and Medicine in Early China and Greece*. New Haven CN and London: Yale University Press, 2002, p. 193. It is a common characteristic of all Chinese philosophies that, in trying to re-establish a eulogized historical period, they are oriented towards the past, not towards the future. See Wolfgang Bauer. *Geschichte der chinesischen Philosophie*. München: Verlag C. H. Beck, 2006, p. 37. The latter, obviously, has its implications for China's "struggle for modernity".

⑤ For a discussion of *ren*: see Benjamin I. Schwartz. *The World of Thought in Ancient China*. Cambridge MA and London: Harvard University Press, 1985, pp. 75—85.

identified with Confucianism. The continued potential of the ancestors to interfere in this world make heaven (the collective of forefathers) not only the last example of the ruler, but also his last judge: it is from heaven that the ruler, the son of heaven (*tianzi*) obtains his mandate to rule (*tianming*), and it therefore also is heaven that can, ultimately, withdraw this mandate. ① Interpreted in this way, the concept of the "Mandate of Heaven" makes government a sacred institution, and any disruption in the social and political harmony is seen as an infringement of a sacred order. The concept of "moral virtue" to govern was expanded to all who aspire to an official function. All functionaries of the Han bureaucracy—as this would also be the case in later dynasties—were to be recruited on grounds of their Confucian moral conduct, verified through the Confucian examination system. ②

This emphasis on "harmony" does not imply that the Confucian society was an egalitarian one. Confucian state ideology philosophized social and political distinctions in terms of primary (literati and farmers) and secondary (craftsmen and merchants) professions. ③ As is evident from the above, farmers were unable to take part in the Confucian examinations because of economical restraints, and people who belonged to the secondary professions were, until the Mongolian Yuan Dynasty (1279—1368), excluded from doing so. ④ The traditional Chinese state thus became one in which public life was dominated by a Confucian political elite, and in which membership of this elite depended on knowledge of the Confucian ideology.

Economic and politico-philosophical developments thus made China to a typical peasant society. A peasant has to sustain himself economically, and he is part of a cultural tradition. In order to comply with the customs and to be able to perform the

---

① See Benjamin I. Schwartz. *The World of Thought in Ancient China*. Cambridge MA and London: Harvard University Press, 1985, p. 23.

② Jack L. Dull. "Determining Orthodoxy: Imperial Roles," in *Imperial Rulership and Cultural Change in Traditional China*. Frederick P. Brandauer and Chün-chieh Huang (eds.). Seattle WA: University of Washington Press, 1994, p. 3, remarks that the reign of Emperor Wu (140—87 BCE) is the period in which Confucianism for the first time was recognized as the "*ism*," "to the exclusion of all others, that was to be acceptable to the state and was to become the object of study for those who hoped for official careers".

③ See Derk Bodde and Clarence Morris. *Law in Imperial China. Exemplified by 190 Ch'ing Dynasty Cases. Translated from the Hsing-an hui-lan. With Historical, Social, and Juridical Commentaries*. Cambridge MA: Harvard University Press, 1990, pp. 26—41.

④ See on this Benjamin A. Elman. *A cultural history of civil examinations in late imperial China*. Berkeley CA: University of California Press, 2000, pp. 240—247.

rituals this cultural tradition imposes on him—as for the ruler, also for the peasant, rituals are part of holistic world concept—he has to produce surplus beyond the sustainment level. This economic position of a peasant translates in terms of his "replacement fund" and his "ceremonial fund" respectively. This, the peasant shares with the primitive cultivator and the farmer. What distinguishes the peasant from the latter two however, is that he also has to produce a "rent fund". In a situation with asymmetrical power relations, this rent charge—to be paid in money, in produce, or in labor—has to be paid to a superior as the result of the latter's claim to the peasant's labor on the land. That the peasant has a "rent fund" is the result of a state's social order—a social differentiation between producers and power-holders, in which cultivators have become subject to the demands and sanctions of power-holders outside of their own social stratum. Such a social division is typical for the Chinese Confucian state, and can be illustrated with the following quotation from the Confucian *Mengzi*, a work attributed to Mengzi (Mencius) (371—289 BCE), pupil of Zisi and grandson of Kong Fuzi (Confucius) (552—479 BCE), founder of Confucianism:

> Great men have their proper business, and little men have their proper business [...] Hence, there is the saying: "Some labor with their minds, and some labor with their strength. Those who labor with their minds govern others; those who labor with their strength are governed by others. Those who are governed by others support them; those who govern others are supported by them." This is a universally recognized principle.
> (*Mengzi*, book III, part I, chapter 4) (own translation B. D.)

In economic terms, the "support" mentioned in this quotation is the peasant's "rent fund," paid out to the Confucian overlords. Rules of "moral conduct" in the Confucian hierarchy further also determine the amount of areal land a Confucian noblemen has rights on as his "rent fund". This is evident from the following quotation from the *Mengzi*:

> The most important ministers of the son-of-heaven (*tianzi*) received a territory that was equal in size to that of a *hou* (marquis), a *daifu* (great officer) received as much as a *bo* (earl), a noble of higher class received as much as a *zi* (vicount) or a

nan (baron). In a great areal community (*guo*), where the territory was one hundred square *li* , the ruler [...]. (*Mengzi* , book V, part II, chapter 2) (own translation B. D.)①

This dual structure of the Confucian society—ossified through, among others, the examination system—did not create a forum for political participation by the peasant. In political terms, the "support" mentioned in the quotation above therefore basically translates negatively, i. e. , as an ultimate non-interference by the peasant in the world of the Confucian elite.

2. Max Weber and the Potential for the Development of a Chinese Nation-state

It may be evident that the hydraulic ecotype that developed in China fostered feelings of solidarity between the members of one nuclear family, one extended family, or one clan, but was not favorable to the development of feelings of "national" solidarity. ② To the peasant, his caloric minimum and his replacement fund are primary, and are complemented with the expenses he has to make—within the limits allotted to him by the Confucian code of moral behavior—to keep up his ceremonial duties. ③ This explains why, the Confucian road of upward mobility being virtually closed for the peasant, a variety of popular beliefs, Daoism, and Buddhism developed as the traditional alternative for the peasant's religious aspirations. ④

---

① The translations of ranks of nobility in this quotation follow the traditional practice. The precise content of them, however, does not correspond with the content of the same terms in the European feudal system.

② In China, extended families were largely found among so-called middle peasants, well-to-do peasants, and landlords, but lacking among farm laborers and poor peasants. The extended family could guarantee the concentration of resources and labor within a kinship group, was a defense against fragmentation of the economic basis through the law of inheritance, and could, possibly, guarantee that enough means were collected to let one member of the extended family take the Confucian examinations and thus create the possibility for upward social mobility for the extended family. See Eric R. Wolf. *Peasants*. Foundations of Modern Anthropology Series Englewood Cliffs NJ: Prentice Hall, 1966, pp. 66—67.

③ While, e. g. , noblemen had the right to erect ancestral temples, for the petty farmer, only a house altar was allowed, and ceremonial expenses were likewise regulated.

④ Also members of the Confucian elite were, in private, not seldom adherents of Daoism or Buddhism. See on this Jack L. Dull. "Determining Orthodoxy: Imperial Roles," in *Imperial Rulership and Cultural Change in Traditional China*. Frederick P. Brandauer and Chün-chieh Huang (eds.). Seattle WA: University of Washington Press, 1994, p. 12, pp. 14—15, p. 19. Tu Weiming (杜维明) *Confucian Ethics Today: The Singapore Challenge*. Singapore: Federal Publications, 1984, p. 5, remarks that, in traditional China, the boundary between private and public has never been clear.

Given the economic system—the fact that the laborer consumes the largest part of his own produce in the process of food production—a tension exists between the resources needed to sustain himself and his family, and the resources needed to fulfill his ceremonial duties on the one hand, and the resources demanded by outsiders—be it another family or clan, or a power-holder as representative of the "state" at large on the other hand. For the latter, the peasant is his means to sustain and possibly to increase his power position. ① In the constant struggle to balance his own needs and the requirements of the power-holder, the peasant basically has two options: curtailing his own consumption so as to fulfill the demands of the power-holder, or increasing his production. Given the difficulty of the latter, he, in the short run, most likely will pursue the first option. This behavior is also given in by the fact that the peasant—through his illiteracy—will remain loyal to tradition and prefers the uneasiness of tradition to the uncertainty of innovation. This affirms Antonio Gramsci's remark that:

> In acquiring one's conception of the world one always belongs to a particular grouping which is that of all the social elements which share the same mode of thinking and acting. We are all conformists of some conformism or other, always man-in-the-mass or collective man. ②

When, however, the power of the power-holder weakens, the peasant may go for the second option, i.e., filling the power vacuum that is created. ③ In practice, the Chinese peasant's discontent with the ruling elite was then channeled through messianic movements, peasant rebellions and secret societies that, not seldom, fell back on the popular beliefs, and Daoist and Buddhist premises that were shared by the members of

---

① See Eric R. Wolf. *Peasants. Foundations of Modern Anthropology Series* Englewood Cliffs NJ: Prentice Hall, 1966, p. 13.

② Antonio Gramsci. *Selections from the Prison Notebooks*. New York NY: International Publishers, 1971, p. 324. See also *op. cit.*: 419—420.

③ See Eric R. Wolf. *Peasants. Foundations of Modern Anthropology Series* Englewood Cliffs NJ: Prentice Hall, 1966, p. 15.

the concerned social sub-group. ①

Confucian society thus developed into an organization (the Weberian *Gesellschaft*) consisting of different communities (the Weberian *Gemeinschaften*)—families, clans and tribes—that each had their own sentiments of solidarity, ② i. e. Confucianism created different sub-cultures in society, each forming a separate "epistemic community," articulated in terms of a uniform Confucian state ideology and a variety of self-centered popular cultures respectively. ③ This social stratification was culturalized to such extent that once merchants could take part in the Confucian examinations, the result was that the successful examination candidates identified themselves with the ruling Confucian elite and merged with them, and thus did not change the social stratification. ④ Put differently, the Confucian road to upward mobility being closed for the masses of the people, and the absence of an institutionalized political opposition, made the "Confucian harmony" one of an ultimate mutual non-interference of the different sub-cultures, and of a non-interference of the individual sub-cultures with the overarching class of the Confucian elite, which, for them, could be perceived as an external political force. ⑤

According to Max Weber, also a *nation* is a form of *Gemeinschaft*. In this sense, a *Gemeinschaft* is not different from other communities that are characterized by a high

---

① Given the philosophical background of Chinese law, the formation of secret societies was interpreted as a criminal fact. See Oskar Weggel. *Chinesische Rechtsgeschichte*. Handbuch der Orientalistik. 4. Abteilung, China. 6. Leiden-Köln: E. J. Brill, 1980, pp. 127—128. See also Ownby 1996; Perry 2001.

② See Max Weber. *Economy and Society*, Guenther Roth and Claus Wittich, eds. Berkeley and Los Angeles CA: UCLA Press, 1978, pp. 40—41.

③ See Kenneth Thompson. *Beliefs and Ideology*. Chichester: Ellis Horwood, 1986, pp. 113—114.

④ Jack L. Dull. "Determining Orthodoxy: Imperial Roles," in *Imperial Rulership and Cultural Change in Traditional China*. Frederick P. Brandauer and Chün-chieh Huang (eds.). Seattle WA: University of Washington Press, 1994, p. 23 meaningfully characterizes the changes in the Confucian orthodoxy during the Yuan as an issue not of "an *ism*, but of a culture".

⑤ This also explains why law in imperial China was only in second instance interested in the defense of an individual or a group against another individual or another group, and was not at all interested in the defense of one individual or a group against the state. Traditional Chinese law focused on activities against morality and criminal infringements that according to traditional Chinese interpretation were actions against the cosmological harmony, and therefore were subject to juridical outcome. See Bodde and Morris 1967: 4. An important consequence of this concept is that traditional Chinese law does not regard citizens as juridical subjects. Only those individuals who infringe on morality have—through their very criminal act—a juridical position *vis-à-vis* the state. See Oskar Weggel. *Chinesische Rechtsgeschichte*. Handbuch der Orientalistik. 4. Abteilung, China. 6. Leiden-Köln: E. J. Brill, 1980, p. 228.

degree of solidarity. What makes a *nation* different from such other communities, however, is its close relation to statehood. A *state*, according to Max Weber, is an association (*Gesellschaft*) that, through "political nationalism," is created for specific purposes: a *nation* is, by political nationalists, thought to be better able to secure the well-being of its constituent members if it has its own *state*, as a *state* essentially has its own administrative system, fiscal system, juridical system, army and police. In these fields, it does not tolerate interference by other states.① On the other hand, a *state* needs the *nation*, because the *state* can best survive when its inhabitants share a common feeling of national community. These feelings are typically based on such attributes as common race, territory, history, language, religion, and customs.② It thus appears that the conditions were not favorable to create a modern Chinese nation-state from the existing peasant society.

A dramatic change came in the middle of the 19th century, when the Confucian "state" was confronted with Western imperialism. It was obvious that the traditional Confucian state could no longer guarantee the well-being of its members. This was especially felt by the intellectual elite of China. It has, in this respect, been suggested that it, indeed, are typically intellectuals who are most susceptible to feelings of humiliation of national proud, as the illiterate masses, through their illiteracy, remain more insulated from the full psychological impact of imperialism. It is the intellectual who, outraged by imperialism and appalled by the great discrepancies in standards of

---

① See Jaap Kruith. *Het neoliberalisme*. Berchem: EPO, 2000, pp. 233—234.

② Anthony D. Smith. *National Identity*. Reno, Las Vegas and London: University of Nevada Press, 1993, p. 14 defines "nation" as: "a named human population sharing a historic territory, common myths and historical memories, a mass, public culture, a common economy and common legal rights and duties for all members". Because the existence of a *nation*, for which, at some point, a *state* might be created, depends on sentiment, it is a highly subjective and volatile concept. This also makes the connection between a *nation* and a *state* a volatile one. Even elements that, at first sight, might seem to be objective—e. g. a common language-are subjective in the sense that they are not necessarily seen as a criterion in nation building by the members of a given group of people. Likewise, the lack of a common language does not prevent the rise of the concept of a common nation. It are the members of a given nation who—through contact with others—define themselves as a "nation". It further needs to be remarked that the members of a given nation do not always identify themselves with the (nation) state, and that a nation does not always correspond to the territorial boundaries in which a (nation) state has the juridical power to operate. On the tension between nation and state: see Émile Durkheim. *Textes*. Edited by Victor Karady. vol. 3, Paris: Editions de Minuit, 1950, pp. 179—180 and John Breuilly. *Nationalism and the State*. Manchester: Manchester University Press, 1993, pp. 8—9. On the subjectivity of feelings of nationalism: see Peter Mentzel. "Nationalism", *Humane Studies Review* 8/1, 1992, p. 9.

living and culture between his people and the West, feels the need for action. ① The gravity of this awareness is also evident from Karl Marx's comment on the Chinese situation in his article "Revolution in China and in Europe", published in the *New York Daily Tribune* of 14 June 1853:

> It is almost needless to observe that, in the same measure in which opium has obtained the sovereignty over the Chinese, the Emperor and his staff of pedantic mandarins have become dispossessed of their own sovereignty. It would seem as though history had first to make this whole people drunk before it could rise them out of their hereditary stupidity. ②

In their struggle for modernity, Marxists treated the peasantry and the workers as allies. It has, in this respect, been observed (Ulam, 1956—1957) that Marxism has particular appeal for uprooted peasants and those caught in transition between tradition and modernity, as Marxism gives them the promise of an idealized future in which the coercive institutions of state and factory have both withered away. In the Chinese situation, the Chinese Communist Party (hereafter CCP) that portrayed itself as the modernist vanguard, was seen as the force that could remove the traditional Confucian overlord. The Marxist class struggle gave the peasants and the workers a historical mission. History, however, has proven that, rooted in their economic and cultural tradition, the peasantry wants autonomy and will see coalitions only as temporary. ③ Once they have obtained areal land through revolution, they will become conservative again. The peasantry therefore is an ally that must be organized from without, and it is task to transform the peasantry into a new kind of social grouping. ④ Industrialization has the force to rationalize agriculture and transform it into an economic enterprise

---

① See Edward Shils. "The Intellectuals in the Political Development of New States," in *Political Development and Social Change*. Jason L. Finkle and Richard W. Gable (eds.). New York NY: John Wiley & Sons, 1971, pp. 258—260.

② See also Avineri, Shlomo (ed.). *Karl Marx on Colonialism and Modernisation*. New York NY: Anchor Books 1968, p. 68.

③ See Eric R. Wolf. *Peasants*. Foundations of Modern Anthropology Series Englewood Cliffs NJ: Prentice Hall, 1966, p. 91. This is also evident from the history of peasant uprisings in China.

④ See Eric R. Wolf. *Peasants*. Foundations of Modern Anthropology Series Englewood Cliffs NJ: Prentice Hall, 1966, p. 92 and p. 109.

which primarily aims at maximal output and only secondarily takes account of the subsistence, replacement, and ceremonial needs of the peasantry. Put differently, industrialization has the ability to transform the peasant into an "agricultural worker," a producer as any other, who can be paid a salary according to the same system also factory workers are paid. ①

3. The Creation of a Chinese Nation-state

Through the May 4th Movement of 1919 and World War II, support for the CCP in different social layers of society increased. It needs to be remarked that this support was largely given in by nationalist feelings, as the Guomindang led Republic did not succeed in resisting foreign dominance in China. It might therefore appear as remarkable that the CCP propagated that *class struggle* was the inevitable instrument in China's *national* revolution. With this claim, however, the CCP was in line with Marx and Engels (2009: 17) who had argued that:

> Though not in substance, yet in form, the struggle of the proletariat with the bourgeoisie is at first a national struggle. The proletariat of each country must, of course, first of all settle matters with its own bourgeoisie. ②

The emphasis on class-struggle can also be explained by the following: Just as the liberal thinkers of the 19th century, Marx was of the opinion that the future of mankind is connected to great nations that are characterized by highly centralized political and economic structures, because it are such structures that make the development of a bourgeois class, and thus of a capitalist society, possible. According to Marx, further, smaller nations cannot play an independent role in the historical development of building up their own national state. Their only option is therefore to assimilate with a

---

① See Eric R. Wolf. *Peasants*. Foundations of Modern Anthropology Series Englewood Cliffs NJ: Prentice Hall, 1966, p. 36.

② Also Vladimir I. Lenin had claimed that "[...] every revolution, by destroying the state apparatus, shows us the naked class struggle". See Vladimir I. Lenin. *The State and Revolution*. Resistance Marxist Library. ResistanceBooks: Chippendale NSW, 1999, p. 19.

greater nation that, by definition, is more vital. ① In a later phase of historical development, a proletarian revolution (not a peasant revolution) is predicted to occur in these nations, after which wealth will be evenly distributed, and both the nation and the state will have become historically outdated. ② In the era of socialism, the equalization of wealth would be the primary occupation, not dealing with the problem of production. ③ As, in 1949, China was far from being a capitalist industrialized nation, the class struggle could prove to be the appropriate instrument to bring the different non-Han peoples of the former Qing Empire (1644—1911) into one nation-state: in the class struggle, not the opposition between the various ethnic groups and the Han is highlighted as the most fundamental opposition, but the class differences within each of these individual ethnic groups. The concept of the class struggle thus makes all ethnic groups identical, and gives the working class, the agents of the industrialization process and, thus, the vanguards of modernization, a historical mission and a prominent place. ④ Already in 1920, Chen Duxiu (1880—1942), one of the founders of the CCP, had written:

> I recognize the existence of only two nations: that of the capitalists and that of the workers [...] At present, the "nation" of the workers exists only in the Soviet Union; everywhere else we have the "nation" of the capitalists. ⑤

The Marxist class struggle could thus overcome the threat that non-Han people

---

① See Will Kymlicka. "Introduction," in *The Rights of Minority Cultures*. Will Kymlicka (ed.). Oxford: Oxford University Press, 1995, pp. 5—6. See also Ephraim Nimni. "Marx, Engels, and the National Question," in *The Rights of Minority Cultures*. Will Kymlicka (ed.). Oxford: Oxford University Press, 1995, p. 63; Marie H. Chang. *Return of the Dragon. China's Wounded Nationalism*. Boulder CO: Westview Press. 2001, pp. 23—24; Peter Mentzel. "Nationalism", *Humane Studies Review* 8/1, 1992, p. 10.

② See Ephraim Nimni. "Marx, Engels, and the National Question," in *The Rights of Minority Cultures*. Will Kymlicka (ed.). Oxford: Oxford University Press, 1995, pp. 66—67 and 71—72.

③ Marie H. Chang. *Return of the Dragon. China's Wounded Nationalism*. Boulder CO: Westview Press. 2001, pp. 142—143.

④ Also the Guomindang had given the working class a prominent place. However, while the CCP stressed their role in the class struggle, the Guomindang saw their role as one of cooperation with the capitalist class to develop the economy of the Chinese nation. See on this Elizabeth J. Perry. *Challenging the Mandate of Heaven: Social Protest and State Power in China*. Armonk, NY: M. E. Sharpe, 2001, p. 172.

⑤ Quoted through, Benjamin I. Schwartz. *Chinese Communism and the Rise of Mao*. New York, Evanston, and London: Harper & Row, 1968, p. 28.

would break away from the newly established Chinese nation-state, i. e. , it was instrumental in creating a great nation. With respect to political institutionalization, further, it has been proven that building one single political party is more efficient than immediately proceed to a multiparty system is. In Samuel P. Huntington's words (1971: 478):

> Where traditional political institutions are weak or non-existent, the prerequisite of stability is at least one highly institutionalized political party. States with one such party are markedly more stable than states which lack such a party. States with no parties or many weak parties are the least stable. ①

In practice, however, the attempt to create a "classless harmony" to a more or lesser extent, and at different moments, resurfaced the borderlines between the traditional social and ethnic sub-cultures that had constituted Confucian China. Where, in imperial China, Confucianism had been the uniform ideology of the ruling elite, the political class of New China shared the Marxist-Leninist ideology as indisputable truth. The class struggle, further, builds on social class, not on "individual" properties. As individuals, citizens are subject to the state, and the state incarnates the nation. ②

During the land reform movement of the 1950s, "popular" protest against the implementation of the new economic policy centered around those persons who were the focus of CCP policies, such as landlords or rich farmers and who developed to be the leaders of protest movements that appealed to their recruits on the basis of popular religion. ③ When some of the mutual aid teams (*huhuzhu*) put their community

---

① John Fitzgerald. *Awakening China. Politics, Culture, and Class in the Nationalist Revolution*. Stanford CA: Stanford University Press, 1996, p. 348: "The question at issue was how to essentialize the national self, which was to be represented by the state and awakened as a mass community". It should, in this respect, also be remarked that tolerance and mutual security are more likely to develop among a small elite sharing similar perspectives than among a large and heterogeneous collection of leaders representing social strata with widely varying goals, interests, and outlooks. See for the latter Dahl 1971: 36.

② Marie H. Chang. *Return of the Dragon. China's Wounded Nationalism*. Boulder CO: Westview Press. 2001, pp. 23—24, see also in p. 103.

③ See Elizabeth J. Perry. *Challenging the Mandate of Heaven: Social Protest and State Power in China*. Armonk, NY: M. E. Sharpe, 2001, pp. 285—286.

interests above those of the state, such movements were seen as contra-revolutionary, in the same way as they had been seen as movements that challenged the "Mandate of Heaven" in imperial times. ① This resurfacing of traditional loyalty to kinship groups and communities was further strengthened by the imposition of migration restrictions through the *hukou* system in 1958. ② This again affirms Antonio Gramsci's observation quoted above. Also the Great Leap Forward (1958—1959) strengthened the old kinship groups and community loyalties. It has been shown that many people reverted to such old pre-revolutionary religious activities as worshipping deities, divination, or fortune-telling, and that violence between enemy lineages and communities was often accompanied by religious rituals that served to express kinship and community solidarity. ③ The main difference with the imperial period in this, however, was that the leaders of the new communities in the aftermath of the Great Leap Forward were no longer lineage elders, but rural cadres. All in all, popular resistance remained much smaller than this had been in the imperial period or in the Republic. This on the one hand testifies the strength of the CCP state in the 1950s, but on the other hand also shows that the great majority of poor peasants were satisfied with CCP policy. ④ The era of the Cultural Revolution can, in some respects, be seen as an attempt to prevent peasants and workers to re-install their old community kinship, i.e., to transform them to "new citizens". That China had, at that moment, not yet developed into a fully industrialized nation, made this undertaking a precarious one.

4. The Era of Globalization and the Rise of New Confucianism

In 1976, the failure of class struggle to create a modern nation had become visible, and the country was in dire need of economic progress. According to Deng Xiaoping (1904—1993), not class struggle but industrial development had to make

---

① See Elizabeth J. Perry. *Challenging the Mandate of Heaven: Social Protest and State Power in China*. Armonk, NY: M. E. Sharpe, 2001, pp. 277—281.

② John W. Lewis. "The Leadership Doctrine of the Chinese Communist Party: The Lesson of the People's Commune", *Asian Survey* 3, 1963, p. 463.

③ Elizabeth J. Perry. *Challenging the Mandate of Heaven: Social Protest and State Power in China*. Armonk, NY: M. E. Sharpe, 2001, pp. 288—294.

④ Ibid., 286.

China into a modern nation state. He therefore appealed to another Marxist concept than Mao Zedong had done. He emphasized the concept of "productive forces," and thus managed to bring economic reforms into a Marxist framework, as "productive forces" encompasses more than only the working class, and gives room for the introduction of capitalist instruments. This new emphasis redefined Marxism as a "developmental nationalism".

As mentioned, Marxism claims that it is the historical fate of a nation that it develops to a phase of fully developed capitalism, after which a proletarian revolution will follow. It therefore appears as a paradox that, in China, it is the CCP that introduces capitalist elements. More importantly, as the state and its institutions have increasingly become perceived as providers and facilitators of the production of consumer goods and services,① for the growing number of consumer-citizens who aspire a steady increase in their general sense of well-being, the legitimacy of the CCP has thus become the extension of its success to cater to these needs. Or, as observed by Max Weber, the state can only survive in so far as it harnesses the feelings of solidarity of the national community in support of its power.②

Dengist policies, further, have led to an increased economic and social inequality in Chinese society. In these circumstances, the socialist identity of the CCP has become rather meaningless for a part of the population. It is not without importance that those citizens who have suffered the most from economic reforms and social inequality in the new era—farmers and workers—are not seldom precisely those citizens who had been the greatest advocates of CCP rule in the Maoist era.

Social disharmony and the fact that both the capitalist production model and Marxism-Leninism are Western political theories, have strengthened New Confucianism in China. This movement that started in circles of overseas Chinese and in Taiwan in the transition period from the Empire to the Republic, recently also gains momentum among academics in the PRC. They feel supported by the fact that Confucianism was seen as an obstacle for development in the Republican period and in the first decades of the PRC, but that history has proven otherwise: in much of South-East Asia, the presence of elements of traditional Chinese culture, often labeled Confucianism, has

---

① See Gianfranco Poggi, *The Development of the Modern State*, London: Hutchingson, 1978, p.134.
② See Kenneth Thompson, *Beliefs and Ideology*, Chichester: Ellis Horwood. Thompson, 1986, p.59.

not hindered economic progress. On the contrary, for New Confucians, it precisely are these traditional elements—the organization of production in these communities in many respects parallels the structures of the traditional Chinese peasant society—that explain the success of business and commerce within the Chinese communities in this region. ①
It is, in this respect remarkable that, although in the not too far past, Confucius was condemned as a reactionary enemy, Confucian concepts are now re-emerging. The term "*Xiaokang shehui*" which refers to the economic policy of the Hu Jintao era, e. g., already appears in the Han Dynasty Confucian Classic *Liji* (*Records of Ritual*). The passage concerned (Chapter VII, Liyun) runs as follows:

> This is why Yu, [Cheng] Tang, [King] Wen, [King] Wu, king Cheng, and the Duke of Zhou were selected. Of these six gentlemen (*junzi*), there is none who does not obey the rituals (*li*). They have manifested their justice, tested their trustworthiness, manifested those who had done mistakes, executed benevolence, made [people] give way to each other, and have instructed the people to constantly do so. Those who did not do so were chased away by those having power and position, and they were regarded as unfortunate by the masses of the people. [Then came] what is said to be a "peaceful era" (*xiaokang*). (own translation B. D.)

In fact, the term "*xiaokang*" can be traced back to the Confucian classic *Shijing* (*Classic of Poetry*). In the section "Min lao" of the part *Daya* of the *Shijing*, we read:②

> The people indeed are heavily burdened,
> But perhaps a little ease (*xiaokang*) may be got for them.

The message the "*Xiaokang shehui*" conveys thus is that the masses of the people resort to a moral leadership that will guide them to a peaceful era through economic

---

① See Henrietta Harrison, *China. Inventing the Nation*, London: Arnold, 2001, p. 262.
② Translation: Legge, James Legge. *The She King or The Book of Poetry*. The Chinese Classics. Hong Kong: Hong Kong University Press, [1960] 1970, p. 495. The first stanza of the ode goes on as follows (in the translation of Legge): "Let us cherish this centre of the kingdom, To secure the repose of the four quarters of it. Let us give no indulgence to the wily and obsequious, In order to make the unconscientious careful, And to repress robbers and oppressors, Who Have no fear of the clear will [of Heaven]. Then let us show kindness to those who are distant, And help those who are near; -Thus establishing [the throne of] our king."

development and social redistribution. Confucian concepts are thus reinterpreted in a Marxist framework. The same type of fusion of Confucian doctrine and Marxist dogma is also evident in the concept: "*Hexie shehui*", translated as "harmonious society". Although there is no direct reference to this concept in the Confucian literature, it is generally accepted to be related to the concept "brotherhood" (*datong*) of the same chapter VII, Liyun, of the *Liji*:

> When the big road of virtue was followed, all under heaven (*tianxia*) was public good (*gong*). Functionaries were selected according to their abilities. Their words were trustworthy, and they cultivated harmony. Therefore, people did not only treat their own relatives as relatives, did not only treat their own children as children, and made sure that elder people had all they needed until the end of their days, that grown-ups had all they needed, that children had all they need to grow, that widowers and widows, orphans, and sick ones all had what they needed to sustain themselves. They made sure that men had a job, and women had a place where they belong to. They disliked that the harvest was left in the field; but neither did they want to store it for themselves. They disliked that their power was not made useful for others; but neither did they want to use it for themselves. Therefore, bad plans were not put into practice, there were no robbers, thieves, nor traitors. Therefore, outer doors were not closed. This is what is called the universal brotherhood (*datong*). (own translation B. D.)

In terms of New Confucian thinkers, further, the concept of the "harmonious society" is interpreted as a counterweight to the Marxist class struggle, Confucianism being depicted as an ideology of harmony.

5. A Future for Marxism in China

Despite existing discontent with social inequality, it is important to observe that the CCP continues to enjoy the patriotic feelings of most of its citizens.[1] Chinese

---

[1] On a scale of 10, China comes at 8.5. See Wang Shaoguang. "Is the Way of the Humane Authority a Good Thing? An Assessment of Confucian Constitutionalism," in Jiang Qing. *A Confucian Constitutional Order. How China's Ancient Past Can Shape Its Political Future.* Daniel A. Bell (ed.). Princeton NJ and Oxford: Princeton University Press, 2013, pp. 143.

citizens thus continue to identify the Chinese nation-state with the CCP. Data of the World Value Survey, most recently carried out in China in 2007, show that an average of 34.9 percent of the Chinese value "maintaining order in the nation" as the most important task of the government. More importantly, "maintaining order in the nation" was valued higher (47.5 percent) by people aged 15—29 than by people of 50 and more years (31.7 percent). The higher educated one is, further, the more highly "maintaining order" is rated, with 50.0 percent of the Chinese having enjoyed higher education seeing "maintaining order" as the most important task of the government. Developing towards a knowledge economy and implementing sustainable economic policies (the *kexue fazhan guan*) that will enhance the possibilities for alleviating social inequality—a potential threat to national harmony—through social redistribution, will therefore be an increasingly important issue. Social redistribution is also important to (re-)establish trust in the CCP by those groups that, as mentioned above, were the first advocators of CCP policy, but have suffered most under the economic reforms. In this respect, also a further development of modern agriculture (as addressed in the policies with respect to the *san nong wenti*) is an important instrument to capitalize the trust of the farmers in the CCP. ① As is evident from the above given historical outline, Marxism definitely provides better possibilities to attain this aim than a renewed emphasis of Confucian thought does. Establishing trust in the CCP through sustainable economic policies can also build on the following: the East-Asian Barometer Survey (most recent data 2002) shows that, in China, economic development is generally valued higher than a multi-party democracy is, with those who are better off, more educated and younger giving greater priority to economic development over multi-party democracy. ②

Although contemporary China has seen a major increase in incidents of "social unrest," ③ this social unrest is not the result of an economic downturn, but the result of

---

① The history of industrialization shows that it are peasant nucleus families—an important category in traditional China—that remain in agriculture and become a vulnerable social group. See Eric R. Wolf *Peasants. Foundations of Modern Anthropology Series* Englewood Cliffs NJ: Prentice Hall, pp. 72—73.

② See Freeman and Geeraerts. BICCS Asia Paper, Vol. 5 (1), pp. 22—26.

③ 8,700 "mass incidents" were recorded in 1993; 87,000 in 2005; estimates for 2010 range between 180,000 and 230,000. See Christian Göbel and Lynette H. Ong, *Social Unrest in China*. Europe China Research and Advice Network, London 2012, pp. 8—12.

specific issues such as land disputes (65% of all cases of social unrest), environmental degradation, labor conflicts, and ethnic strife. This explains why social protests are usually outbreaks of discontent from within a specific homogenous group, such as peasants, or migrant workers. As such, contemporary social unrest follows the lines of social unrest in traditional China. Most important, though, is that contemporary social unrest does not seem to have a negative impact on the legitimacy of the CCP. Rather, protestors stress that they abide by the laws, as they are eager to enlist the support of the media and higher-level governments. Social unrest should therefore rather be interpreted as a form of participation.① In order to avoid that social unrest turns itself against the Chinese nation-state, it is therefore increasingly important that Chinese leadership engages in deepening public debate, and that Marxism in China increasingly takes up its role as source of inspiration for the political vanguard. China's return to Confucianism may, theoretically, be an interesting symptom of its "struggle for modernity", in practice, however, the future never lies in in a (partly) reconstructed past.

（本文责任编辑：于琦）

马克思主义与新儒家的兴起

巴得胜

【内容摘要】自 19 世纪末和 20 世纪初，中国知识界在遭遇欧洲帝国主义的同时，开始质疑儒家传统的价值。中华人民共和国的建立即是这样一个标志：中华帝国的儒家传统被马列主义的中国变体这一官方意识形态所取代。始于 20 世纪 70 年代末的中国对外开放，已使这个国家变成了世界主要的经济体，其政

---

① 8,700 "mass incidents" were recorded in 1993; 87,000 in 2005; estimates for 2010 range between 180,000 and 230,000. See Christian Göbel and Lynette H. Ong, *Social Unrest in China*. Europe China Research and Advice Network, London 2012, p. 9.

治影响力也与日俱增。经济发展引发的日益严重的社会不公正日渐成为社会动荡的原因，而且使部分中国人质疑当前发展模式的正当性。在此背景下，一种与之类似的经济模式，即具有浓厚儒家思想传统的所谓亚洲四小龙发展模式逐渐兴起。中国大陆重估儒家传统的价值，得益于中国台湾地区、香港地区和美国"新儒家"的推动，在新儒家视野中，儒学被视为可减轻社会不公并重建"和谐社会"的工具。

于是在当今中国知识界，存在各种各样的意识形态倾向：或赞同资本主义和自由民主制；或主张延续/发展中国式马克思主义；或回归儒家传统或对之加以再解释；或上述某些倾向的组合。同样地，当前局面对中国继续"实现现代性的奋斗目标"也是症候式的。本文讨论上述方面的理论进展，并把焦点置于当代中国的社会分化方面，再追溯这些分化的历史根源。我们还将就中国古今的政治参与情况对社会分化做出估价。

【作者简介】 Bart Dessein，中文名巴得胜，比利时根特大学教授，现任根特大学汉学系系主任，同时任教于根特大学佛学研究中心。曾在中国辽宁大学学习，他对中国传统思想的研究在国际上享有重要学术地位。

Marx Reloaded: Revolution Without Alternatives[1]

Jason Barker

(Professor in Film and Moving Image, European Graduate School, Sass-Fee, Switzerland)

Abstract: Today everybody agrees that "Marx was right". In fact, for several years the observation that Marx is "relevant" has been widespread even among "opponents" of his ideas or at least among those who would never dare to call themselves Marxists. This is the context in which I came to write and direct the documentary *Marx Reloaded* , which was filmed in 2010 and first broadcast on Arte TV in April 2011.[2] The film was intended to address an alleged "cultural phenomenon" known as the "idea of communism", which was the name given to a symposium organized by Slavoj Žižek and held at Birkbeck College in London in March 2009.[3] A second symposium took place in Berlin in July 2010, again organized by Žižek, and some of which appears in the film. To what extent does this "idea of communism" enable us to make sense of the Great Recession (as it's now called)? Or: what possible relations exist between, on one hand, global capitalism, its seemingly endemic and immanent crises; and, on the other, the idea of communism, whether it be as a possible "solution" to capitalism or as some kind of "alternative" to it: a philosophical, political, or social alternative? This is an interesting question. Because today it seems there is only one "alternative" to capitalism: revolution. Of course, I do not pretend for a single

---

[1] This is a slightly edited version of a paper which was presented at "Marxism and the Future": The Third Sino-British Bilateral Forum on Marxist Aesthetics, held at Shanghai Jiao Tong University, Shanghai, China, 6—8 April 2013. I would like to thank Dr. Qinghong Yin, the conference organizer, and Dr. Haili Ma of Leeds University, who read the paper in my absence.

[2] *Marx Reloaded*. DVD. Written and directed by Jason Barker. UK, Films Noirs / Medea Film, 2012. Available at: http://www.filmsnoirs.com/

[3] The proceedings of this conference are published as *The Idea of Communism*, eds. Costas Douzinas and Slavoj Žižek, London, Verso, 2010.

moment that "revolution" is possible. On the contrary: "revolution" no longer has any meaning, at least not in the way that Marx envisaged revolution as the global transformation of the economic forces and relations of production leading to the overthrow of capitalism. But the "idea" of revolution, which is sometimes synonymous with "communism" in the work of the philosophers Slavoj Žižek, Michael Hardt, Antonio Negri and others, seems to have a great future ahead of it. In fact, so widespread is their kind of revolutionary thinking today that the question we need to be asking ourselves is not "Is there no alternative to capitalism?" but instead "Is there no alternative to communism?", or "Is there no alternative to revolution?"

This paper will consider this question by drawing on *Marx Reloaded* and the arguments of its central protagonists.

Today I want to consider this revolutionary thinking and some of its implications. Žižek, Hardt, Negri, Alain Badiou and others—to whom I will refer to collectively as neo-Marxists—publish books which are inspired by Karl Marx. However, none of them claims to be a faithful follower of Marx. Let's take two brief examples. First, in the *Empire* trilogy, Negri and Hardt talk about the "immaterial labour" of the "informational revolution" which heralds a qualitative change in global capitalism and what they call "the potential for a kind of spontaneous and elementary communism". [1] Second, Slavoj Žižek often criticizes Marx's "classical theory of exploitation", arguing that surplus value is no longer extracted from labour but from "rent" in the form of personal subscriptions to all manner of essential services (in *Marx Reloaded* he singles out Bill Gates and the "means of communication"). Hence the title of my film: *Marx Reloaded*. What's at stake in "reloading" Marx—or at least this would be my hypothesis—is not merely whether Marx is still socially or conceptually "relevant", but instead the extent to which his ideas can endure such re-readings.

Is it possible to generate new meanings from old Marxist concepts? Is it possible, using Marx's ideas, to shake the dominant conceptions of the social world to its foundations? In 1843, in a letter to Arnold Ruge, Marx defined his thinking in these terms: "I am referring to ruthless criticism of all that exists, ruthless both in the sense of not being afraid of the results it arrives at, and in the sense of being just as little

---

[1] Michael Hardt and Antonio Negri, *Empire*, Cambridge, Harvard University Press, 2000, p. 294.

afraid of conflict with the powers that be."① Perhaps by reloading Marx we might travel back in time to 1843, or to the type of social conditions which were ripe for his revolutionary thinking. Or perhaps we might transport Marx forward in time.

Obviously something happens to Marx's ideas in the years between his death, in 1883, and the Russian Revolution of 1917. A new political sequence emerges based on a quite different set of priorities. Socialism becomes a really existing social reality. ② According to the neo-Marxists socialism is politically outdated and has nothing more to offer us. As Antonio Negri says in *Marx Reloaded*, "The Russian Soviets always said: 'We're in socialism'. And socialism is a way of managing capital. Just like liberalism is, too."③ In *Marx Reloaded* Žižek also dismisses a long list of political ideologies including "social democracy" and "communism in its 20th century form". Pure communism, by contrast, is the idea which transcends all specific social formations. As Alain Badiou puts it elsewhere, communism is historically "invariant"④ and therefore not the ultimate stage in a historical process passing through capitalism and then socialism. As Marx and Engels themselves put it in *The Communist Manifesto*, "the history of all hitherto existing societies is the history of class struggle." In other words, on this reading, the allegation of Marx's bad influence on the 20th century and his "responsibility" for its communist disasters and crimes is incorrect, since what that century proves is not Marx's all-controlling influence but the innate and spontaneous desire of the oppressed to break the chains of their oppression. The very essence of life, as Marx himself observed—what both defines *and* escapes life—is *struggle*. ⑤ Marx's influence or "responsibility" for the way in which that struggle evolved in the 20th century is at the very most only one side of history's dialectical movement.

This, then, is the neo-Marxist argument: communism is a political ontology. But

---

① Marx letter to Ruge, September 1843, available at: http://www.marxists.org/archive/marx/works/1843/letters/43_09.htm.

② The importance of the idea of socialism and precisely how it differs from communism in Marx's work need not detain us, although it is important to recognise that these rival ideas are in fact different, and refer to different forms of society. For example, Marx defined socialist society as still being dominated by class struggle, whereas communism would be a "classless society".

③ See also Antonio Negri and Raf Scelsi, *Goodbye Mr. Socialism*, trans. Peter Thomas, New York, Seven Stories Press, 2008.

④ See Alain Badiou, *The Communist Hypothesis*, London, Verso, 2010.

⑤ Marx's interview with John Swinton in *The New York Sun*, 6th September 1880.

this ontology is not just given to our experience. If Marx defines history as class struggle then everything which forms part of that history—not just the objective facts of life under capitalism, but even our subjective thoughts and philosophy itself—forms part of that struggle. Today capitalism is the name not merely for an economic and social system; capitalism is the name for the very limits of our world. Is it really easier to imagine the end of the world than the end of capitalism when capitalism has itself become the world in its totality? Antonio Negri says, "We are always 'inside' capital. There is no 'outside'." But then in this case how can we "struggle against it"? What is the "it"? What does it mean to struggle against a system which is part of us in its very being?

This is, perhaps, where the matrix of Marx's thought becomes philosophical. Or the point where the identity of the world we think we know is placed in question. For Žižek (again speaking in *Marx Reloaded*) thinking with Marx involves "rethinking our notion of the most basic naive questions-objective reality, the world, the nature of the world, and so on." The risk of course, as Marx himself was well aware, is that by peeling away the layers of reality we uncover a brutal and uncompromising truth. Marx's famous "ruthless criticism of all that exists" risks revealing things about reality that may even prove damaging for our survival as well as for society in general. As Alberto Toscano says in *Marx Reloaded*, Marx's personal life was a case study in a kind of fanatical thinking that was completely and yet compulsively irresponsible. Although of course this is not to say that such thinking will *necessarily* change anything, radically or superficially, about capitalism as such.

Marx Reloaded presents a resurrected Marx—and ultimately the viewer of the film as well—with a choice between taking a blue or a red pill. But as seductive as it might seem, can we really distinguish capitalism with a blue pill (a conservative choice) and communism with a red pill (a revolutionary choice)? One need only read Marx in *The Communist Manifesto* in order to confirm that capitalist society is itself revolutionary. For instance, when Marx and Engels speak of "Constant revolutionising of production, uninterrupted disturbance of all social conditions, everlasting uncertainty and agitation" they are saluting capitalism's egalitarian transformation of "All fixed, fast-frozen relations, with their train of ancient and venerable prejudices and opinions."[①]

[①] Marx and Engels, *The Communist Manifesto*, Part 1.

Given such dynamism why would a self-confessed revolutionary need to take a red pill at all? Elsewhere in Marx's relatively early works it's clear that the spectre of communism is no alien force threatening the "stability" of capitalism from the outside. When Marx and Engels write, "We call communism the real movement which abolishes the present state of things"[①] it is clear they harbour no abstract or utopian visions for a better world. Indeed, in the true spirit of Marx's ruthless materialist philosophy we might even go so far as to say that "the world" is the entire problem when trying to build a "better" world. In other words, capitalism and communism are, for better or worse, part of the same world.

So what might it mean to frame today's relentless global economic and financial crisis in terms of a choice between two pills? If the choice between a blue and a red pill cannot offer a solution to capitalist exploitation, especially that of our planet's natural resources, then what purpose does it serve to promote such a stereotype of liberation? The answer is: in order to try to expose the deadlock which Marxist discourse itself runs up against time and again.

Today we are firmly stuck in this deadlock which has Marx, like a figure of the Eternal Return, reliving the historical defeats of Marxism in every conceivable configuration. It's as if by mentioning his name enough times Marx can will us toward some ultimate victory or shift in the balance of political forces. A "blue or red pill" offers us no real choice. Instead, what the "choice' may expose is the facetiousness of such binary choices: capitalism "or" communism; capitalism "or" socialism; democracy "or" dictatorship; socialism "or" barbarism. In this sense there really is no way out of capitalism, and in accepting as much we may begin to grasp the true insidiousness of what Marx called the "religion of everyday life".[②]

Marx Reloaded is a sketch of the economic crisis which began in 2007. But what the film could hardly have predicted was the political evolution of this crisis. What we seem to be experiencing in its aftermath is a partial collapse of neoliberal ideology. The measure of political power in the liberal democratic tradition is parliamentary democracy, where the largest political party or bloc holds power on behalf of the

---

① In Part I of *The German Ideology*, available at: http://www.marxists.org/archive/marx/works/1845/german-ideology/ch01a.htm

② This phrase is found in Chapter 48 of Marx's *Capital*, Vol. 3.

dominant social and economic class. Representative democracy at least depends on the principle of the majority share, in terms of votes cast, assuming that all votes are "equal". This is the measure of political consent which translates the will of the majority into the decision-making power of government. In the parlance of the American liberal and revolutionary tradition of the 18th century the key slogan was once, "No taxation without representation." But in the wake of the US and now global Occupy movement(s) this myth has finally been dispelled. It had already been profoundly shaken with the TARP agreement, the US government's $700 billion bailout of private banks and institutions passed by George W. Bush in 2008. The mobilisations which began in New York in September 2011 could be seen as delayed mass expressions of opposition, not just to the privileges of private enterprise during a global recession, but to the financing of private enterprise from the public purse. What Occupy exposed, albeit briefly, with its simple slogan "We are the 99%" was the fact that liberal democracy is founded not on the principle of equality (this much was already clear prior to the crisis) nor even on the principle of the majority (where the largest political party holds power on behalf of the dominant social and economic class) but on the principle of *minority rule*. Of course the idea that this minority comprises 1% of the global population need not be strictly accurate. What Occupy succeeded in doing was dissolving the myth, perhaps once and for all, that liberal democracy expresses the interests of the majority. But it has also done more than that. For in opening up the question of who rules in whose interests such movements explode the myth of political power itself.

  Marx is rather vague when it comes to explaining how the overthrow of capitalism—or at least its "democratic management"[1]—will come about. We know that the point is to change the world, not to interpret it. But how? What will be the trigger for this fundamental change in consciousness where cynical disdain for capitalism is transformed into *active consent* for a completely different economic and political system? Let me venture a straightforward, albeit simplistic, hypothesis: the fact that mass politics in modernity has never succeeded in transforming so-called "proletarian dictatorship" into a durable, viable and consensual system of mass

---

[1] Whether the overthrow of capitalism should lead to its democratic management is often answered in the affirmative by socialists, and in the negative by neo-Marxists and communists.

democracy suggests that it will never achieve such a feat. Let me put it simply: there is no possible transition from socialism to communism. Isn't this the parody in Trotsky's imaginary encounter with Marx in the opening scene of *Marx Reloaded*? Despite Trotsky's dream of leading global proletarian revolution, in this scene he merely succeeds in introducing himself as the leader of half a dozen social misfits. We might say that Trotsky's marginality is precisely the point. For if we accept that, in Negri's words, "we are capital", and that the limits of capitalism are the limits of our world, being and consciousness, then what sense is there in fighting for some imaginary liberation from capitalism, especially if the only alternative on offer is socialism, which for the neo-Marxists is politically outdated? This is where the idea of communism comes into its own; a communism no longer aimed at the liberation from capitalism; but what Alberto Toscano describes as communism as "a separation of and from reality".[①]

Does the idea of communism as separation inform the politics of Occupy? Not explicitly or intentionally. But through its mass occupations of what the neo-Marxists call "the commons" the behaviour of Occupy does suggest the kind of "dysfunction of representation" which characterises the political situation we find ourselves in today. Obviously the 99% will no more take over the world than Trotsky, in his day, could have formed a world government. It seems to me that the real political aim here is not about amassing power. The real political aim is about exposing the extent to which the amassing of power itself relies on a corrupt and dysfunctional system of political representation. When we say communism as "separation of reality" we are not talking about the retreat into a fantasy world which renounces all responsibility, in the way we might imagine disenfranchised youth retreating to their bedrooms to play computer games. Communism as separation is the deactivation of the power which *defines* reality.

Finally we can see how the "blue or red pill" conundrum is more than a merely rhetorical device. The choice on offer no longer simply *exposes* its own deceitfulness as a choice. The choice also *affirms* that communism—or what Alain Badiou calls the egalitarian principle[②]—has already arrived. Communism is the freedom to choose the pill which will always be "red". This is what I mean by "revolution without alternatives".

---

① See Alberto Toscano, "Communism as Separation" in ed. Peter Hallward, *Think Again. Alain Badiou and the Future of Philosophy*, London, Continuum, 2004.

② See Badiou, *The Communist Hypothesis*.

It's the equality of choice. In Spinoza it is the proposition according to which true freedom coincides with necessity. ① To be free is to be free from external causes or constraints, to be a true individual, and so free to choose. As such communism is the name for the society in which no one rules—where multiplicity reigns②—and therefore where no one can determine the choice you make, or induce you to make the "correct" choice. Under such conditions the allegation that communism equals totalitarianism seems disingenuous. Of course, the critics of communism are right in pointing to the disastrous human rights legacy of the 20th century's communist experiments. John Gray—one of several opponents of the idea of communism to appear in *Marx Reloaded*—often insists that the idea of communism cannot be separated from its tyrannical reality. But this is to restrict one's understanding of communism to specific instances of state violence and incompetent central planning more characteristic of state socialism than communism. The idea of communism confidently demonstrates that there is no central power. The global crisis proves it. At international summit after international summit the politicians reach the same conclusion. Nothing can be done because no one is in charge. Power is absent. Capitalism, like a runaway train, is finally seen to be working all by itself.

Is this utopian thinking and a utopian idea of power? It could be labelled as such, according to a certain Cold War, western liberal conception of freedom, such as we find in the work of the political philosopher Isaiah Berlin. By contrast the neo-Marxists put forward an idea of communism which dares to be positive and speculative. The idea of communism as separation works at transforming the dominant perceptions of power. As such it is a *subjective* process both simultaneously *for* and *from* freedom. ③ The objective fact of capitalism and its extraction of profit from surplus value as the true

---

① See Spinoza, *Ethics*, trans. Andrew Boyle, London, Everyman Library, 1993. Part 1, Proposition XXIX states: "In the universe there exists nothing contingent, but all things are determined by the necessity of the divine nature to exist and operate in a certain way."

② For Badiou mathematical ontology presents the idea that "being" (*l'être*) is pure multiplicity without unity. We might equate such multiplicity with the adequate intuition of Spinoza's third type of knowledge. However, for Badiou pure multiplicity is a feature of discourse, rather than of what can be proved about empirical reality or "the world". See Alain Badiou, Being and Event, trans. Oliver Feltham, London, Continuum, 2005.

③ And this is why the idea of communism undermines the distinction which Berlin makes between positive liberty and negative liberty in his 1958 essay "Two Concepts of Liberty". See Berlin, *Liberty: Incorporating Four Essays on Liberty*, Oxford, Oxford University Press, 2002.

cause of global inequality—which I assume for the sake of my argument to be indisputable—is something else. The revolution of the communist idea takes place in the political system, not in the economic forces and relations of production. It is what we might call (e. g. in thinking of Mao Tse-tung) a *cultural* revolution.

This is clearly the kind of abstract utopian thinking that Marx himself, like Berlin, would also have firmly rejected—although of course for completely different reasons. For Marx capitalism is a historical phenomenon, it evolves as part of society and continues to adapt to it. "There is a continual movement of growth in productive forces," Marx says, "of destruction in social relations, of formation in ideas; the only immutable thing is the abstraction of movement—*mors immortalis*."① Nothing, Marx insists, not even capitalism, lasts forever. Then again, perhaps a reloaded Marx might be inclined to see things differently. If we accept that capitalism is self-regulating in the sense of being a free entity (causa sui in Spinoza's terms), then no amount of revolution will ever overthrow it. The capitalist system "works" because we invest our faith in it. Remove that faith and its subjective hold on us collapses.

（本文责任编辑：安宁）

回归马克思：没有其他选择的革命

詹森·巴克

【内容摘要】今天，每个人都会同意这个判断："马克思曾经是对的。"事实上，近年来马克思依然与生活"相关"这个论断，在马克思主义的所谓"反对者"或者那些从不敢自称马克思主义者的人群中广泛流传。这就是吸引我写作"回归马克思"这篇论文的语境所在，"回归马克思"这个话题我曾在 2010 年录制过短片，并在 2011 年 4 月在艺术（Arte）电视台首次播放。这个短片意

---

① See Marx, *The Poverty of Philosophy*, Chapter 2.

在阐明一个"文化现象",这个文化现象被认知为"共产主义思想",而此命名来自于一次由斯拉沃热·齐泽克(Slavoj Žižek)组织、于2009年3月在伦敦博贝克(Birkbeck)学院召开的一次专题讨论会。齐泽克随后又于2010年7月在柏林召开了第二次专题讨论会,有关这次讨论会的情况会部分地出现在短片中。那么,共产主义的思想在多大程度上使我们能够将经济大萧条(这是一个当代的命名)解释得通?或者是这样一个问题:共产主义思想与当代经济大萧条有着什么可能的关联?一方面是全球性资本主义和它明显的局部甚至普遍的危机;另一方面是共产主义思想究竟是不是资本主义一个可能的解决途径,或者某种可以选择的一条出路:哲学的、政治的或者社会性的选择。今天,对资本主义来说,或许只有一条"可能的"途径:革命。当然,我并不是故作深沉地认为"革命"在某一个特定时刻会发生。相反,我认为,"革命"不再有任何意义,至少它不是如马克思所设想的、作为全球化经济力量和产品关系的变革、并最终推翻资本主义这样意义上的革命。然而,这个革命的"思想",有时在哲学家斯拉沃热·齐泽克、麦克·哈德(Michael Hardt)、安东尼奥·聂格里(Antonio Negri)和其他人的著作里与"共产主义"是同义的,而且似乎前景远大。实际上,革命的思想在当今传播如此广泛以至于我们不得不反躬自问的不是"在资本主义有没有别的出路?",而是"在共产主义有没有别的出路?",或者是"在革命自身有没有别的出路?"。此篇论文将引入《回归马克思》及其主要的支持者的观点,并予以讨论。

【作者简介】詹森·巴克教授,任职于瑞士萨斯费市的欧洲研究院,是研究电影与移动影像方面的教授。

Acting Straight: Reality TV, Gender Self-Consciousness and Forms of Capital

David Alderson

(University of Manchester)

Summary: 'Straight acting' is a recent coinage to describe men who have sex with other men, but are not considered effeminate. This paper looks at the significance of this term in relation to the increased social self-consciousness of gender, especially in relation to sexuality, by focusing on the reality TV series, *Playing It Straight*. While ultimately straight acting is regarded as socially conservative in its appeal to various kinds of norm, it may in some respects also be critical of the kind of 'postmodern' gender consciousness promoted under neoliberal conditions.

My principal interest here is in the category 'straight acting' and what it signifies. It is a recent coinage invoked, obviously enough, to describe a man who appears not to be gay, but is sexually attracted to other men (and the term does seem to be used exclusively of men). However, it doesn't suggest any precise set of characteristics. It's not necessarily about being especially or self-consciously masculine, though that might be intended; often, it refers to someone who is simply unexceptional, 'ordinary' or 'normal', and therefore lacking in what is considered to be affectation or ostentation.[1] And yet, of course, 'straight acting' is not a free-floating term. It can't mean just anything, and must therefore cohere in relation to certain pervasive

---

[1] Connell, for instance, highlights the cases of three gay men who 'reject hyper-masculinity, but also express their distaste for queens.' One describes himself as 'a very straight gay'. Connell, R. W. (1995). *Masculinities*, Cambridge, Polity, p. 156.

assumptions about the relations between gender and sexuality. Principally, it highlights the absence of 'effeminacy', and may suggest a fairly powerful disidentification with the category 'gay' insofar as it is taken to connote this. Equally, though, the term gets applied to those hardly conscious of themselves as such.

I am only concerned with straight acting as an identity, then, to the extent that I am interested in the ideological work the category performs in the ensemble of gender terms that govern contemporary understandings of sexuality, as well as more general relations between men, and between men and women. Beyond this, I shall also explore the ways in which these categories are bound up with configurations of class in relation to commodification, cultural capital and capital as such. This is a large project for one paper, and its ambition in this respect is made more of a challenge when one considers the relatively informal way in which the category circulates: there are no substantial straight acting subcultures, organizations or manifestos to study, for instance. There is a website, straightacting.com, and some work has been done on this,[1] but analysis of such essentially privatized interactions, divorced from the testing ground of broader social interaction and scrutiny, is not part of my purpose here. I propose therefore to focus for the most part on a particular, highly formalized, context, from which I think it is nonetheless possible to draw more general conclusions, in the form of the Channel Four reality TV series, *Playing It Straight*.

Before turning to the series, though, it is important to establish whether consciousness of straight acting marks an historical shift in perceptions of gender and sexuality, or is merely a new name for an established phenomenon. To the extent that the category has been discussed elsewhere, there seems to be agreement that the period following gay liberation was key. Alan Sinfield suggests that, in the 1970s, 'it [was] the straight-acting types who had a new opportunity: to come out'.[2] In other words, prior to this, it was effeminate men who were marked and identifiable, as they intended themselves to be. Their particular mode of defiance, however, always invited popular notoriety, and was repudiated by those who sought to prove that male

---

[1] Clarkson, Jay (2006). ' "Everyday Joe" versus "Pissy, Bitchy, Queens": Gay Masculinity on Straightacting.com', *The Journal of Men's Studies*, vol. 14, no. 2, pp. 191—207.

[2] Sinfield, Alan (2004). *On Sexuality and Power*, New York, Columbia University Press, p. 95. See also Sinfield, Alan (1999). *Out on Stage: Lesbian and Gay Theatre in the Twentieth Century*, New Haven, Yale University Press, p. 154.

homosexuals might, and ideally should, be decent and respectable. In *Against the Law*, written after his conviction in the 1953 'Montagu Case', Peter Wildeblood claimed to be speaking out 'not for the corrupters of youth, not even the effeminate creatures who love to make an exhibition of themselves', but only for those who 'behave more conventionally in public than the "normal" men I know'. ①

We might have expected gay liberation's disdain for apologia and discretion to have prompted a break with such normativity, but David Halperin has recently argued that 'in at least some of its later manifestations [it] encouraged lesbians and gay men to act out new, positive, non-deviant sex and gender roles in everyday life'. We should be careful to note the nuance in Halperin's argument, though: gay liberation facilitated divers things, including 'forms of androgyny',② and even radical, purposeful rejections of gender norms in the form of sloppy drag and genderfuck strategies. Nonetheless, for many gay men, an identification with masculinity became the means of expressing dignity. This is because, even today, effeminacy appears inherently trivial, even abject, not something anyone could possibly be proud of, as a number of recent vituperative and uncomprehending reviews of Halperin's book in the British press indicate. Written by gay men who no doubt reckon they are thereby insulated from accusations of homophobia, what these reviews suggest above all is that you can't possibly take camp seriously, as Halperin does, and expect to be taken seriously yourself. Peter Conrad, for instance, complains of Halperin's 'nostalgia for the heyday of giddy effeminacy', and even remarks of his argument that camp offers a challenge to US imperialist masculinity that 'this swishing makes me wonder whether al-Qaida's fanatics may have a point about the decadence of the west'. ③ The positive image agenda that emerged out of gay liberation identified the effeminate man as *the* stereotype, the figure to be repudiated and eradicated from cultural representation. Halperin's project, to be clear, is not to prescribe camp, but rather to explain its cultural transmission among, and appeal to, gay men, though it is also true that he

---

① Wildeblood, Peter (1955). *Against the Law*, London, Weidenfeld and Nicolson, p. 7.
② Halperin, David (2012). *How To Be Gay*, Cambridge Mass., Belknap Press, pp. 47—48.
③ Conrad, Peter (2012). '*How to Be Gay* by David Halperin-a review', *The Guardian: New Review*, 16 August: 33. The other reviews along similar lines included Philip Hensher, '*How to Be Gay* by David M. Halperin-review', *Guardian Review*, 1st Semptember 2012, 8, and Richard Davenport-Hines, 'How Best to Be Gay', *Times Literary Supplement*, 17th October 2012.

credits it with a certain critical—even democratic—value in relation to socially valorized masculinity.①

Even so, while 'straight acting' seems to describe the logic underpinning the masculinization adopted by many gay men in the seventies, the term functions in ways that would surely have been discountenanced at that time. This is because it consolidates the presumed relation between masculinity and straightness that gay men were then attempting to challenge through their embodiment of masculinity. We might imagine that 'straight acting' serves to differentiate a person from those who are considered 'gay acting'. In fact, however, since it registers an apparent contradiction in the person described, the differentiation straight acting proposes is between that person and those who are quite simply gay—those, that is, whose gender and sexuality conform in such a way as to preclude the need for further clarification. From just about any perspective generated by gay liberation, in other words, straight acting can only be regarded as a reactionary category that presumes a perhaps natural, but in any case typical, correspondence between masculinity and heterosexuality, as well as effeminacy and homosexuality.

It is surely this that highlights not only the term's recent provenance, but its specifically contemporary significance: it represents a particular mode of conformism through an acceptance that 'the stereotype' is both true and to be personally repudiated. But even this does not quite capture the particular structure of feeling highlighted by the category, since it often suggests a dissident response to an apparent consolidation of the relations between gay and effeminate, even through its very bid for normalcy. Straightacting.com, for instance, claims to advocate plurality, but also to be 'masculinely politically correct'.② The bid to be unremarkable, or even aggressively a man's man, is therefore formed by contrast with a perceived institutionalization—and especially, I shall suggest, commodification—of what it means to be 'gay'. Mark Simpson, who has made a career of attacking what he perceives as the gay establishment, opens his edited collection, *Anti-Gay*, with a parodic enthusiasm for Pride:

---

① Halperin, David (2012). *How To Be Gay*, Cambridge Mass., Belknap Press, pp. 201—202.
② http://www.straightacting.com [accessed 05/01/2013]

we have everything you could ask for, and if, by some strange delusion you feel you're missing something in your life, thoughtful niche marketeers will think of it for you. The gay press, courtesy of kind telephone sex operators and their lovely sex-positive ads featuring buffed men in some really stunning underwear is free and never stops telling us how marvellous we and the products aimed at us are. ①

The reference to 'buffed men' here does not necessarily contradict the feminizing ambience evoked through unthinking consumerism, hyperbole, and self-congratulation: the muscle Mary is also part of the scene.

It would be a mistake, then, to regard the category straight acting as itself fundamentally unserious or playful on the grounds that it appears to suggest a postmodern self-consciousness about performance. A straight acting identification is for some an important subjective commitment, possibly extending so far as a phobic response to the effeminate. Indeed, Joseph Bristow has traced a tradition of 'effeminophobia' in relation to twentieth century literary traditions (Bristow, 1995). Beyond those contexts, and connecting them with the dominant, effeminophobia may often be a more precise and appropriate term for what is called 'homophobia', since the latter tends to gloss over the specific gendered dynamics at work. As an identity, straight acting is at least implicitly contemptuous: I might have sex with men, it suggests, but I'm not *one of those*. Moreover, the belief in one's own straight acting-ness often goes hand-in-hand with a desire for other, similarly masculine men. 'I'm gay because I like *men*' is one typical expression of contempt for both women and effeminacy, and in this there is as powerful an investment in the ideological correspondence between sex and appropriate gender as one is likely to find anywhere. Thus, while some earlier twentieth century same-sex relations were marked by a cross-class desire that idealized the supposedly raw, uncultivated features of working class men②, contemporary notions may more frequently be predicated on an egalitarianism③ that simultaneously presumes the

---

① Simpson, Mark(1996). 'Gay Dream Believer: Inside the Gay Underwear Cult', *Anti-Gay*, ed. Mark Simpson, London, Cassell, pp. 1—12.

② E. M. Forster's *Maurice* (1971) is the most celebrated literary expression of such cross-class desire. David Leavitt's *While England Sleeps* (1995) represents a modern attempt to capture its dynamics.

③ This may be facilitated by the category of homosexuality itself, since 'homosexual relations cease to be compulsorily structured by a polarization of identities and roles (active/passive, insertive/receptive, masculine/feminine, or man/boy)' (2002, 133).

masculinity of both parties. We should therefore be cautious about claiming that there is anything even unintentionally destabilizing or subversive about the straight actor. Rather, the term may be one sign among many of an increasingly reconfigured male homosocial continuum① in which being masculine in terms of conduct and appearance is more significant than being heterosexual as the basis for joining the club. Another sign of this, defined by a different dynamic, is the emergence of metrosexuality, to which I return below.

'Straight acting', then, testifies to a remarkable contemporary popular alertness to gender that is not in the least bit denaturalizing or demystifying for all its apparent recognition that conduct may be conventional or even performative. Nonetheless, I am reluctant simply to assume that the category is straightforwardly reactionary on the basis that it is intolerant of greater gender plurality, since the problem with advocacy of the latter as such is that it continues to identify particular traits as either masculine or feminine in the first place, and thereby to collude, however transgressively, with these forms of reification. While it is undoubtedly politically important to demasculinize men, the conviction that this may be achieved through their greater feminization remains in thrall to the ideological terms that feminism has traditionally sought to displace altogether. One of the ironies of theories of gender performativity is that they have assisted in establishing the category of gender as ubiquitous to both analysis and perception by assuming its discursive primacy: if we believe gender, as a Foucaultian form of power, is everywhere, then we will undoubtedly *see* it everywhere precisely because its traditional ideological work has been to divide a common world according to a once prevailing, and still persistent, division of labour, value and subjectivity. ② In a brilliant, but mostly overlooked, critique of postmodern/ poststructuralist gender theory, Toril Moi asks why we should feel compelled to see abstract qualities through the lens of gender, rather than in terms of their value in relation to particular

---

① The term is Eve Sedgwick's, but she presumed that this continuum was also characterized by an abrupt break between male bonding in general and sexual activity between men specifically (see Sedgwick, 1985, 1—5).

② Judith Butler, however, sees utopian possibilities in gender plurality: 'The task is not to repeat, but how to repeat or, indeed, to repeat and, through a radical proliferation of gender, to *displace* the very gender norms that enable the repetition itself' (Butler 1990, 148).

situations, a category she understands in a sense indebted to de Beauvoir. ①

The issues raised by this term are not trivial, then, but raising them through a consideration of *Playing It Straight* may be a viewed as a means of trivializing them. Indeed, this was the point put to me by some of those students with whom I have discussed the show in seminars. The show is, they suggested, 'trash TV', and therefore unworthy of serious consideration. I'm not wholly unsympathetic to that view, as this discussion will no doubt indicate. Still, 'trash TV' is a paradoxical form of dismissal, since it is not only a judgement offered up by those contemptuous of it, but also one used by others to justify watching something in the first place. This stuff is watched *because* it is trash, because it requires little of us and helps us 'relax', because it is not high-minded or serious or particularly challenging. It answers therefore to the demand highlighted by Adorno that our 'free time' should be qualitatively contradistinguished from work, commodified and reified as all that work is not ②: purged of concentration, effort and difficulty, it should be a form of endless distraction, or, in a word, fun. Hence, though *Playing It Straight* evinces certain purposes that I shall come on to shortly, it doesn't want to make anyone think too much. It is therefore continuous with a relatively uncritical, everyday (self) consciousness of gender, even as it foregrounds that consciousness by giving it a particular form to which I want to turn first.

Straight realities

> 'The most gayest person there could in fact be straight.'
> George, *Playing It Straight* contestant

> 'At the end of the day, there's such a fine line between heterosexuality and homosexuality these days.'
> Marco, *Playing It Straight* contestant

---

① Moi, Toril (1999). *What is a Woman? And Other Essays*, Oxford, Oxford University Press, esp. 99—112.

② Adorno, Theodor (1991). 'Free Time', in *The Culture Industry: Selected Essays on Mass Culture*, ed. J. M. Bernstein, London, Routledge, pp. 162—170.

The reality TV format of *Playing It Straight* was developed for a US version of the series. This, however, was unsuccessful in attracting viewers and was dropped after only a few episodes.① The first British series, by contrast, was broadcast in 2005, repeated on Four Music in 2010, and is still available on Four On Demand. A new series was broadcast in 2012, and a third is rumoured to be under consideration, suggesting that neither the format nor its concerns have dated, though, for reasons that will become clear, I here focus on the far more compelling first series, not least as its significance may be considered to have increased over time for reasons I have already begun to touch on.

This is set on a Mexican ranch, and brings together twelve men to compete in 'seducing' the sole woman, Zoe, and persuade her to pick one of them. However, some of the men are straight, and some are gay. None are bisexual or in any other sense queer: such disruptive possibilities simply aren't broached. Indeed, they couldn't be without undermining the very logic of the competition, which is that if Zoe chooses a straight man she shares the £ 100,000 prize money with him, but if she chooses a gay man he takes *all* the money. Zoe therefore not only doesn't know which men are straight and which are gay, but she doesn't know how many of each there are (and nor do the audience or the presenter). The men are made to take on various tasks over the course of the series and get to socialize together as Zoe looks on in order to pick up clues about their 'true sexuality'. They also have various opportunities to spend time alone with Zoe, often in intimate or stock romantic contexts, though this intimacy is obviously compromised by the presence of the camera. Following a familiar reality TV convention, two contestants are selected for eviction at the end of each episode, but by Zoe herself rather than the audience.② Whereas other reality TV shows place great emphasis on the abstract value of individuals to an audience, *Playing It Straight* emphasizes contestants' value to Zoe as mediated by her sense of her value as a woman to them. This establishes Zoe's perspective as the privileged one within the more general system of valuation and evaluation that regulates gender 'performance' in

---

① Fox pulled the series in 2004 after only a few episodes because of disappointing audience figures. An Australian version was also made. See Tropiano (2010), whose analysis focuses on the deployment of the effeminate stereotype as evidence of the series' homophobia.

② In this sense, the series eschews the faux-democracy of reality TV, as focused on in Andrejevic, Mark (2004). *Reality TV: The Work of Being Watched*, Lanham, Rowmand and Littlefield.

the series according to criteria that are simultaneously social and sexual, as we shall see.

The difficulty of Zoe's task, however, is self-consciously highlighted by the series itself in a way that makes explicit the contradiction at the heart of the project. The title draws our attention to the fact that some contestants must be pretending to be what they are not, and the only way to do so is to act in a way that is not tainted by effeminacy. Nonetheless, the opening voiceover to each episode suggests that in order 'to win the money and find true love, Zoe must see beyond gay stereotypes and turn some of these guys' Mexican excursion into a full-blown outing.' Hence, the setup implicitly lays claim to a certain educative purpose in a way that establishes its Channel Four-ness: its supposed experimentalism and appeal to minority audiences.① Thus, the show encourages Zoe and viewers to look out for signs of fakery, while nonetheless treating sceptically the assumption that being straight is a totalizing force that produces the kind of subjective coherence we can all recognise.

This contradiction, then, is central to what I shall refer to as the show's 'setup', by which I mean not only its rules and scenarios (the ranch and the various tasks set for the contestants), but also its careful selection of participants, and its organising assumptions and intentions (insofar as these are clear or can plausibly be inferred). It is through the setup that 'good television' may be secured 'spontaneously', despite the risks and chance that inevitably attend reality TV, since it is in this way that the desired tensions can be established, prolonged and managed. In the case of *Playing It Straight*, which eschews any element of live transmission, it is important that both stylized framing and careful editing of all the footage shape viewers' experiences in order to intensify these tensions and highlight the specific questions and issues that the programme makers consider most important.

The setup of *Playing It Straight* draws on at least four social phenomena or dynamics that I want to consider in some detail. First, there is the central value placed on what I call heterosacramentalism: the principle that privileges cross-sex over same-sex relations through the superior, redemptive love that supposedly characterizes it. Governed by a logic of complementarity, it presumes that a nurturing and sensitive,

---

① On the appeal of reality TV to Channel Four in this respect, see Bignell, Jonathan (2005). *Big Brother: Reality TV in the Twenty-First Century*, Houndmills, Palgrave Macmillan, p. 122.

and therefore vulnerable, femininity will tame an otherwise (sexually) errant and aggressive masculinity whose spontaneous recognition of femininity's value will lead to the chivalrous protection of it. This is what we continue to mean by 'romance', and its logic also determines perceptions of same-sex relations. Sex between men, for instance, tends to be considered more bodily than spiritual. Henning Bech, for instance, has argued that this is one characteristic of the modernity of gay sex, determining its negative evaluation as frequently alienated and instrumental (Bech, 1997, 119—120). Lesbians, by contrast, have traditionally been desexualized by being rendered ethereal .[1] These perceptions are persistent, despite the egalitarian intentions of those advocating gay marriage to spread the sacramentalism around a bit.

The logic of heterosacramentalism structures the series, then, though not without being subjected to certain forms of ironic scrutiny and complication. At the start of each episode, the voiceover claims that 'some of these men represent every modern girl's dating dilemma'. 'Modern girl' here effectively designates a particular kind of sensibility: liberal, post-feminist, heterosexual. It presumes that she is at least likely to mix in the same circles as gay men, whom she is likely to find especially sympathetic and attractive. She is, however, still happy to define herself as a girl and enjoy 'girlie' things, possibly with an irony that doesn't preclude compliance. She consequently regards herself as obviously different from boys, who have their own legitimate interests and preoccupations. Hence, the masculine-feminine, opposites attract presumption is still in place, though troubled both by the sense that heteromasculinity might be excessive, and that gay men are not necessarily so sensitive as to be effeminate.

The sense that masculinity may be threatening to women is nothing new, of course. What is distinctive about the setup, however, is that it significantly displaces the danger presented by men in general onto gay men specifically, even though they would not normally figure as a sexual threat to women, since they are tasked with undermining the romance logic of the series. Hence, a highly charged moral language impinges on the contest right from the start, complicating its status as a game, as *fun*, and thus making it more real, more consequential. In this language, gay men are

---

[1] Castle, Terry (1993). *The Apparitional Lesbian: Female Homosexuality and Modern Culture*, New York, Columbia University Press.

regarded not merely as playing it straight, but also, in consequence, as deceivers and liars.

The extent to which this is the case is illustrated over the course of the first series by the relationship that Zoe pursues with one contestant, Danny B. The setup makes likely the possibility that Zoe will fall for one of the men, and perhaps have a kind of relationship with him (which appears not to be against the rules). Zoe nonetheless comes to doubt Danny B's sincerity, but, crucially, her worry is that he is deceiving her *because* gay, not that he may be straight and deceiving her out of some combination of cynical motives to get the money *and* prove his masculinity to the other contestants and viewers by bedding the girl. Of him specifically, she says 'I will actually be physically sick if I find out he's been lying to me. Because the stuff he's been saying is full on. And if he's lying, then I'll never speak to him again'. Interestingly, some of the other contestants appear to doubt Danny B's romantic sincerity, though not necessarily his (hetero)sexuality.

The possibility that Danny B might be lying is raised not so much by a complication to the heterosacramental logic of the setup as a potentially contradictory structuring of it: the financial reward attendant on success. If, as the voiceover suggests, Zoe's aim must be to find love *and* money, this establishes a potentially ideal, because satisfying, complementarity between moral and financial value emphasized in the symbolic sharing of the prize money (reward *and* mutuality), should Zoe choose rightly. But the possibility that this will not be the case plays on a larger social anxiety within capitalism that financial and moral value do not coincide, and may even be at odds with each other, given the general self-interest that prevails. Romance and marriage supposedly provide the alternative to all that, hence the value accorded privacy and intimacy as the epitome of a human truth and constancy absent from relations more generally.① The possibility that a gay man will walk off with everything further consolidates his associations with the selfishness and egotism of the commercial public sphere with which the true feeling of heterosacramentalism is contrasted.

---

① As Michèle Barrett and Mary MacIntosh put it, 'Marx's "from each according to his ability, to each according to his needs" is an ideal to which the nearest approximation we can imagine is a caring family where the contribution of each is not subjected to exact calculation' (1982, 18).

The second social phenomenon drawn on by the series, necessarily brought into sharp relief by the first, is the one I began by discussing: that gay men might not only become accomplished at temporarily acting straight, but that they might even be 'straight acting' to begin with. This is exemplified half way through the series when one contestant, Alex, while having a romantic dinner with Zoe, takes the opportunity of an intimacy that clearly makes him uncomfortable to confess that he is gay. Explaining his decision afterwards, he says: 'I've worked out everything gay in my life, that I've realised I just don't actually want to lie any more [sic]. Well, I just don't wanna do this, and I just thought I have to tell her this. So I did. ' Lying, then, is experienced as incompatible with his integrity as a gay man, and the other gay contestants similarly express relief at being able to 'be themselves' when evicted, though he is the only one to take the step of confessing. He is also the first to equate dignity with gender: 'We're not all fairies,' he says, 'We're actually, genuinely men. ' The insistence here is in one sense typical of a kind of middle class overemphasis that characterizes the speech of many of the contestants, but it also indicates that the one thing that *must* be predicated of manhood is that it is authentic, even if the nature of that authenticity becomes less clear, and necessarily more questionable, the more desperately it is insisted on.

If gay men can act straight, the third dynamic is provided by a complementary phenomenon: the metrosexual. This figure's defining characteristic is a narcissism fed by consumerism. Since such traits are presumed to have once been characteristic of gay men specifically, but to have subsequently extended to men more generally, the result is an erosion of visible distinctions and a liberalization of attitudes .[①] Given that, in *Playing It Straight*, the men are described by the voiceover as metrosexuals right from the start, there is a further implicit acknowledgement that the series' constant scrutiny of the men is pointless.

It is not only Zoe, though, who is encouraged to evaluate the men in this way. At various points, the shifting relations among the men ensure that suspicions converge on particular individuals. One of these is George, and, possibly because of this, his eviction clearly rankles with him. The contestant evicted just prior to him, Demetrius,

---

[①] Simpson, Mark (2002). 'Meet the Metrosexual', Salon. com, 22 July, reproduced at http://www. marksimpson. com/meet-the-metrosexual/ [accessed 19/10/2012]

confirms that he is gay with the words 'Congratulations, you've just increased your chances of winning.' When George is evicted, though, his response is almost hostile:

> [Shouting to the other men looking on] I hope you're listening fellas. Zoe, you have just increased your chances [pause] of going home with nothing. I am in fact straight.

'I'm sorry,' Zoe responds, presumably for having given offence. George's statement is interesting for the way in which it exploits the dramatic style of reality TV itself to express an evidently deeply felt resentment at being singled out. He unnecessarily, and solemnly, addresses her by name, and teases her by delaying the knockout line that announces the *factuality* of his straightness. This, however, comes across as not only unchivalric but also absurd, because the fact is not self-evident.

The speculation that George is so impatient to dispel leads me to the fourth dynamic. This complicates the rest, and is associated not with Zoe or the male contestants, but rather with the setup itself. Richard Kilborn comments on 'the extensive use of humour and self-deprecating irony in the narrational commentaries that are an integral feature of [reality tv] formats' (Kilborn, 2003, 60). The scrutiny that is directed at the boys' masculinity by the voiceover in this series, however, consists in a specifically campy scepticism directed at their conduct. Model Danny K, for instance, is often ridiculed for an injury he sustains to his arm and the various visits to the hospital he insists on to treat it, the implication being that he is a bit soft. But typically things aren't left at that: after an injection he receives on one of these visits, the (usually unheard) interviewer's voice off camera asks 'Is that the first time you've taken a shot up the bum?' Moreover, some of the tasks are themselves parodic of the conventions of romantic love, as when the boys have to deliver chocolates to Zoe after the fashion of the Milk Tray man, leaping from a helicopter into the sea while wearing evening dress, and swimming to a boat. Other tasks are less symbolically freighted tests of masculine nerve or strength, but are exploited for the wordplay they offer and the potential for inverting meanings: 'Please señor, I want a good bucking,' the voiceover intones as Peter prepares to straddle a bronco. In the first series, the bisexual actor, Alan Cumming, provides the voiceover; in the second, it is gay comedian, Alan Carr.

As the bronco instance indicates, the ranch—El Rancho Macho—also conduces to the general campiness of the presentation, and simultaneously attests to the continuing Anglophone tendency to regard Hispanic cultures generally, and Mexico in particular, as unserious, essentially comedic and self-parodic. It is a perception that can tip over into explicit racism. ① The setting and presentation of *Playing It Straight* converge in particular in the figure of 'Brian', a sombrero-wearing guitarist and singer. Towards the end of each episode, he presents a song about the contestants, casting doubt on the masculinity of the men and therefore their heterosexuality. Thus, within the symbolic economy of the series, any sense of ethnic or cultural difference from white, Anglo-Saxon norms may connect a connotative logic that leads from artifice to gayness, and it perhaps isn't coincidental that the choices about eviction made by Zoe ultimately resolve a fairly diverse bunch into the three white men featured in the final episode (a similar tendency is clear in the second series). At the end of the first episode, the Greek Versace sales assistant, Raphael—who is suspected by all the men—and the British Asian, Pritesh—whose hair straighteners are particularly focused on by Zoe—are eliminated. Both are straight, and both are indignant about being targeted for what seem to them arbitrary associations of specific vanities with effeminacy and sexual identity. The norms to which straight acting appeals may also determine forms of cultural chauvinism in a way that I return to.

By further exemplifying in the framing of events the very stereotype the series claims to want to challenge, its central contradiction is intensified, of course, and the fact that the series is so utterly contradictory effectively renders irrelevant any speculation about whether this means of framing things on the whole undermines the seriousness assumed by straight masculinity or serves to underscore the incompatibility of masculinity with being gay. Clearly, it does both in a way that is designed to ensure broad appeal—to men and women, gay or straight—compatible with Channel Four's consciousness of its 'demographic', and in the process further highlights that irony is not necessarily critique, but can be more or less sustained alongside a commitment to

---

① Recently, the BBC had to apologise for comments made on its *Top Gear* programme, suggesting Mexicans were 'lazy, feckless, flatulent, overweight, leaning against a fence asleep looking at a cactus with a blanket with a hole in the middle on as a coat' (*sic*). Mexican food was described as 'refried sick. ' See http://www.bbc.co.uk/news/world-latin-america-12361790

the very principles being ironized. Indeed, the lack of a consistent purpose attests to the unlikelihood of anyone learning anything at all from the series, and its experimentalism goes hand in hand with a very powerful drive towards containment and reassurance through the shaping of the narrative that emerges, as we shall see.

Raphael and Pritesh experience the suspicion that they might be gay as a kind of accusation, as does George, and it is difficult to see how it might be otherwise, given the setup. Some of the gay men try to resist feminization, but, on finally coming out, end up whooping, or camping it up, in a way that suggests release, the ability to be themselves at last (even Alex does this). They thus confirm that their inauthenticity has been discovered. One contestant, however, consistently notes their conduct from the sidelines with contempt.

The Salience of Class

More needs to be said about the term 'metrosexual'. Clearly, it alludes to metropolitanism, and therefore not merely urban styles, but the international and interchangeable ones that travel, and, for that reason, can be found anywhere in the world, along with the commodities that make them possible. Its 'iconic' representatives are celebrities, and metrosexuality is therefore also bound up with the kind of aspirationalism that seeks fame for nothing in particular. Beckham—Mark Simpson's favoured example—is celebrated by people who have absolutely no interest in football; his 'lifestyle' was regarded with suspicion as a distraction by his first manager at Manchester United, the almost definitively non-metrosexual Alex Ferguson. Metrosexual style is therefore global in the sense that it disavows and can be highly judgmental towards specificities of class, culture, place, and belonging, even while it acknowledges the forms of diversity necessarily attendant on aspiration and geographical mobility. It is, quite literally, the embodiment through stylization, commodification and reification of a certain kind of liberalism. Metrosexuality may be the object of imitations more or less inadequate because insufficiently grounded in privilege, but it may also become the focus of non-metropolitan resentment, often expressed through gender or sexuality—including 'straightness'. Metrosexuality is not about taste in the sense that Bourdieu suggests—of being 'bound up with the systems of dispositions (habitus) characteristic of the different classes and class fractions'①-since this relates to stability achieved through reproduction. Rather, metrosexuality is predicated on the universal, 'democratic' appeal of advertising and celebrity, such that it exists in a complicated dialectical relation with taste passed down through familial or educational contexts. Metrosexuality instils taste, certainly, but through centripetal pressures, and has lent its name to style and conduct books aimed at those who would like to get on. ②

One interesting feature of this dynamic was exemplified by the US series, *Queer Eye for the Straight Guy*, which sought to disseminate new standards for heterosexual compatibility based on middle class norms that, through their 'critique' of masculinity, appear also to complement rather timid gay and feminist social agendas. In fact, though, the Fab Five's missionary zeal confirmed their relative depreciation according to the values and standards of taste they assist in consolidating: they were hardly taste*ful* themselves. Katherine Sender argues that the series assumes 'that after seeing themselves through borrowed queer eyes [...] reformed heterosexuals will have had just enough training in romantic, female-friendly, hygienic living to function effectively in the straight world' ③. 'Just enough' is exactly right, and highlights the extent to which 'gay' figures as ostentation or meretricious excess, and the error of apparently seeing style as an end in itself.

As we have already seen, there is a limited diversity among the middle class male contestants, but even within this one, Ben, stands out. He is unique in being a manual labourer, a builder, though his comments at various points suggest he now runs a business. At the outset, he is pointedly described as being from *East* London, a fact his accent and linguistic habits confirm. The others describe him as a 'geezer', which marks him out as *culturally* working class, though his relative wealth enables him to mix in circles beyond that class. He is the least obviously self-conscious about his appearance, in one sense, though he equally obviously spends a lot of time in the

---

① Bourdieu, Pierre (1984). *Distinction: A Social Critique of the Judgement of Taste*, London, Routledge & Kegan Paul, p. 6.

② Flocker, Michael (2004). *The Metrosexual Guide to Style: A Handbook for the Modern Man*, Cambridge, Mass., Da Capo Press.

③ Sender Katherine (2006). 'Queens for a Day: *Queer Eye for the Straight Guy* and the Neoliberal Project,' *Critical Studies in Media Communication*, vol. 23, no. 2, pp. 131—151.

gym, as builders paradoxically often do. At one point, he says his biggest regret in life is having left school at 15. Ben's behaviour towards the other men in the series is distant, at times becoming aggressive and threatening. In the very first episode, he threatens to hit Danny K after a night of drinking. Moreover, differences between the men tend to be mediated by their attitudes towards Ben, establishing him as a central, even in some ways defining, presence physically and symbolically. After his eviction, Danny K offers video advice to Zoe about whom she should choose, saying of Ben: he's 'too ignorant to be gay. And I don't think it's a double bluff… he's just too… straight.'

Education in its broadest sense, then, is both a marker of class and at stake in the definition of gender and sexuality. To assist in understanding why, it may be helpful to reflect on the debates on language and education between Basil Bernstein and William Labov in the 1960s and '70s. Bernstein sought to explain educational underperformance as determined by class. He posited two different speech codes, restricted and elaborated, as tending to characterize working class and middle class speech respectively. The former evinces a strong identification with community that leaves norms implicit, ensuring speech is habitually directed to others from the same community, but is more or less opaque to those outside it. The elaborated code, by contrast, makes assumptions explicit and is therefore directed at universalizing understanding, having the effect also of individualizing by differentiating the speaker and what s/he has to say [1]. Labov responded by arguing that middle class speech was rather characterized by specific stylistic features that often rendered it 'turgid, redundant, bombastic and empty',[2] evincing more the kind of confidence borne of privilege than greater rationality as such.

Labov's real aim was to defend black ghetto speech specifically from racist attributions of primitivism through 'linguistic deprivation' made by right-wing educationalists who drew on Bernstein's arguments (Bernstein, by contrast, considered himself and his arguments as progressive). In arguing that such speech does operate according to

---

[1] Bernstein, Basil (1971). 'Social Class, Language and Socialization' in Basil Bernstein, *Class, Codes and Control*, vol. 1, London, Routledge and Kegan Paul, pp. 170—189.

[2] Labov, William (1972). 'The Logic of Nonstandard English', in *Language in the Inner City: Studies in the Black English Vernacular*, Philadelphia, University of Pennsylvania Press, p. 213.

specific norms, however, Labov effectively confirmed Bernstein's claims that restricted codes are community focused. So, while Labov rightly drew attention to Bernstein's failure to recognize that supposedly 'elaborated codes' were not culturally neutral, he was less successful in addressing Bernstein's concern over the extent to which restrictive codes serve to confirm integration into a specific community in ways that explain a certain resistance to education (and, presumably, especially the kind of education that teaches 'aspiration', i. e. *separation*). A dialectical grasp of these debates would suggest that the codes of the disadvantaged are both the consequence of limitations imposed on their experience by that disadvantage, and result from differences in class milieux that accord different values to different cultural markers. For these reasons, working class speech—and, by extension, the perspectives and sensibilities it evinces—often demonstrates a keen eye for middle class snobbery and pretension, even though it may also demonstrate chauvinism through an attachment to the way the world is and understood in a specific portion of it. Sometimes the difference is a fine one.

A case in point takes place in the final episode of *Playing It Straight*, when the three remaining contestants and Zoe enter a temescal (a Native American sweat lodge). 'The idea,' according to the ironic voiceover, 'is that their souls are reborn and purified, the result of which is total honesty.' All except Ben claim to enjoy the ritual of the visit, evaluating it in the vague experiential language of middle class ethnotourism that necessarily annuls cultural specificity through the commodification of it and the abstraction of its meaning as mere 'experience'. 'I came out peaceful, chilled out,' says Danny B; 'I did get clarity. I really, really did,' Zoe insists overmphatically. Ben, though, is sceptical:

> For some people that might work, I'm not sure, I don't know. I didn't feel like I'd been reborn. I got bloody 'ot at one point. And she kept 'itting me over the 'ead with this fuckin' 'olly bush, soaked me with it. But that was alright, that was good. You know, you gotta respect it cos they been doin' it for 'undreds of years. Why they've been doin' that for 'undreds of years I don't know, but... some people find themselves. Wherever they've been, they find themselves. Those two [Danny B and Marco] they were right into it. They were levitatin' I think at one point, you know. They had their eyes shut, they were fuckin', you know, they got the old glockenspiel

out, and eyes closed and sing along, not that they knew the words. But they were getting right into it…I thought it was alright, I mean, I wouldn't do it again. ①

It's significant that Ben's extended comedic riff is granted the amount of time it is, constituting one of the lengthiest continuous speeches to camera anyone is permitted in the series. Even the programme makers accord him a peculiar respect. The faux tolerance and self-effacement with which this begins ('For some people that might work… I don't know') leads into an assertion of Ben's distinction from and mild contempt for the others through a parody of their behaviour that translates it into absurd, yet familiar, terms ('glockenspiel' and 'sing along'). There is a knowingness to this way of speaking; it is improvisation using familiar techniques. The masculinity of Danny B and Marco, meanwhile, is challenged by highlighting their willingness to participate in and be seduced by all this hokus pokus. It is precisely their inauthentic claims to have discovered authenticity that Ben targets by invoking a despised countercultural reference ('they find themselves. Wherever they've been, they find themselves') in a way that simultaneously evinces incuriosity towards Mexican traditions, however repackaged. Indeed, there is a consistent, barely concealed *in*tolerance behind all the apparently 'live and let live' rhetoric. ② The defining characteristic of Ben's masculine response is that he remains unchanged, untransported, even though away from home. Indeed, speaking to the camera perhaps allows him to take his audience with him.

Ben's straightforwardness/intolerance is one of the qualities that ultimately conditions Zoe's '100%' trust in him by the end of the series: she ultimately chooses him. And she gets it wrong, spectacularly so, since this means she fails to win the money and has rejected Danny B, who turns out to be straight after all. Ben, then, is gay, but his victory is certainly not made to feel like one. As he apologises for winning, and shamefacedly looks at the ground, the congratulations from the presenter

---

① I indicate the dropped aitches here not to indicate linguistic 'inferiority', of course, but rather that accent is important to the overall effect of Ben's speech, in a way that may even be wholly or partially calculated.

② Richard Hoggart once pointed out that, in working class life, 'such tolerance exists along with conservatism and conformity… they clash only rarely. They co-exist, are drawn upon at different times and for different purposes, and people know instinctively which is relevant at any time. Far from contradicting, they thus mutually reinforce each other' (1990, 93).

and Zoe range from flat to reproachfully ironic: 'Congratulations, Ben. Well done, mate, you played us all,' says Zoe, struggling with tears, before being led away by a sympathetic presenter. Of course, this is an intolerable conclusion and the series cannot end with it: there is discord, a woman has been wronged, and the setup itself looks vulnerable-its very educative purpose now looks rather vindictive.

Happily, though, Ben understands what he must do. Earlier in the series, In one of the speeches each contestant is permitted to make before Zoe discloses their fate, Ben has told Zoe that if she finally picks him, he will give her his half of the money—an offer that is in keeping with the pretence that he is straight, but that also suggests a suspicious sense of guilt on his part. At the end, he is shown remorseful before resolving to fulfil more than this promise. His words to Zoe are significant:

> I come on 'ere to prove a little point... but sort of like quite an important point, erm, and I think I've proved that for me... I think the world of you, and I feel like I wanna cuddle you and hold you all the time... almost like my little sister ... and I'm sorry... and I feel like I've let you down big time, and I'm sorry... Oh, I don't want to start crying. Look, I'm a man of my word and, erm, and I will 'elp you out, and I want you to 'ave all the money.

This is effectively a plea from Ben for the restoration of his value as it is bound up with his masculine authenticity. Some justification for his conduct is offered by the fact he was making a point, which is what men do if they feel even abstractly denigrated. But in the process he has let down Zoe, who, as his appropriately desexualized and patronizing familial analogy indicates, represents for him virtuous girlhood in general. And so he must demonstrate that he is 'a man of his word'—a phrase that mingles connotations of bourgeois probity with those of chivalry, restoring the link between financial and moral value. Zoe, in turn, appreciates what is required of *her* and insists they share the money. In the general emotional incontinence that passes for sincerity in of all of this, Ben repeatedly expresses his desire not to appear 'a cissy' by crying, and Zoe even manages to tell him 'I'm so pleased I picked you. I'm so pleased from the bottom of my heart.' Thus, romance of a sort flourishes. 'Brian' then sings about having found a (very US-looking, and therefore macho) cowboy himself, and fireworks light up the sky in abstract recognition that someone, somewhere might be having an orgasm.

It only remains for Ben further to justify what he was doing participating in this series in the first place. He is given the very final say, spoken direct to camera, with no campy ironization:

> I ain't the airy fairy bloke that fuckin' goes to Abba concerts and waves 'is arms about, you know. I'm glad that I am a pouf, but I just don't think I need to let everyone know it, you know. So I'm trying to prove…a bit of a point. We're not all the same.

The multiple paradoxes here—a coming-out on national TV justified as discretion, an intolerant appeal to the value of diversity, the backward-looking identification with an insult ('pouf') that no-one else is trying to appropriate as radical chic—all place Ben as the embodiment himself of the ideal to whom this address is made: *we're* not all the same, because I'm the same as *you* (the fact that this is made to a Channel Four audience specifically merely highlights its fantasmatic qualities).

This 'you', however, is itself a complex phenomenon. It is the 'you' of restrictive codes and communal values, including continuing patriarchal ones, all expressed in a reassuringly familiar accent. But it is also the narcissistic 'you' of the mirror-lined gym, a site of aestheticized male bonding predicated on a desire to be whose distinction from the desire for has become increasingly problematized, as gym-going as a means of defining masculinity has extended beyond working class circles to become integral to metrosexual and gay lifestyles. This has generated forms of differentiation that sustain the distinction—gyms that are recognized as gay or straight, for instance—as well as to varying degrees of tension or liberalization within particular gym spaces. Thus, there is in one sense a contradiction, and in another a powerful continuity, between Ben's culturally working class, masculine persona on *Playing It Straight*, and his earlier competitive success as Mr GayUK 1998 (a fact never mentioned as part of the series, even after he'd won).

Our sense that Ben's two achievements indicate something contradictory about him says something in turn about the extent to which being gay has indeed remained persistently associated with effeminacy, despite the efforts of all those who have sought to challenge 'the stereotype'. In fact, 'gay' was always an odd choice of term for an egalitarian political movement, originating as it did as a designation of sexuality in the class-based metropolitanism of Coward and his circles.① It thereby also reminds us that effeminacy designates not merely an abstractly 'inappropriate' gender in men, but also, quite specifically, an affiliation with extravagance and decadence② that is connotatively elitist, even when expressed in such non-elite and 'vulgar' modes as drag often is. It is one consequence of this dynamic that masculine heterosexuality is most emphatically signalled through working class codes, authenticated by their distance from 'culture'.

What distinguishes Ben's project on the series, of course, is a purposefulness that is itself significant. As we have seen, this both converges with the educative project of the series, and departs from its playful liberalism, which is why his final speech is both wholly consistent with the rest and strikes a disturbingly aggressive tone that appears *generically* out of place. Jonathan Bignell has argued that, by contrast with the documentary forms it helped to displace, reality TV both feeds and feeds off a *post*modern sensibility that is consumerist, passive and therefore coded as feminine: it is to be enjoyed for the spectacle, not intended to stimulate action or social change, as documentaries did, and is therefore playful in form and tone rather than earnest.③ What Bignell's comments also help to highlight, then, is the problematic potential in this context of valuing the feminine over the masculine in whatever combination with sexual difference or sexuality: it may well be that *this* is complicit with culturally dominant, consumerist postmodernity and the neoliberalism that sponsors it.

In a curious kind of way, then, I find myself returning to Adorno's comments on free time. Being against camp is very much like being against fun. It's not merely that no-one could bear to live without some form of play, but rather that the advocacy of play may itself be one appropriate, even utopian, response to the grim morality—including the masculine work ethic—imposed by repressive societies, as Adorno's colleague, Marcuse, knew well.④ Nonetheless, Marcuse also argued that we increasingly live, not

---

① Sinfield, Alan (1999). *Out on Stage: Lesbian and Gay Theatre in the Twentieth Century*, New Haven, Yale University Press, p. 109.

② Sinfield (1994), argues that the Wilde trials were crucial in consolidating the class-based, effeminate, decadent stereotype of the queer.

③ Bignell, Jonathan (2005). *Big Brother: Reality TV in the Twenty-First Century*, Houndmills, Palgrave Macmillan, p. 27.

④ Marcuse takes the category of play (and display) from Schiller's aesthetics. Marcuse, Herbert (2005). *Eros and Civilization: A Philosophical Inquiry Into Freud*, London, Routledge, pp. 185—196.

in sexually repressive societies, but in ones characterized by repressive desublimation and other forms of deprivatization through the commodification of pleasure that thereby binds it to the insatiable capitalist demand for growth and the exploitation entailed by this.[①] Fun in that context becomes compulsory, the heteronomous demand of the system that we pursue it. And if these concerns sound archaic, quite out of keeping with our supposedly consumerist present, listen to the arguments being advanced by one influential group of Tory polemicists looking to the future: Britain, they claim, is falling behind other nations, and needs to rediscover its work ethic, abandon welfare 'dependency', and embrace further deregulation of the market, including—even especially—the labour market.[②] This is not a sectarian view on the right, but accurately captures the common, global direction of travel, and the tone set by national governments the world over. Its patriotic veneer acquires its ideological distinction from the fact that it seeks to galvanize workers in the name of national competition, when the neoliberal project pursued through national and supra-national institutions has all along been ' a *universal* project aimed at maximizing the level of capitalist hegemony, capitalist development and capitalist competitiveness throughout the global capitalist economy'.[③] The end of the age of expansive credit for virtually everyone, if that is what we are facing, is ushering in an age of austerity that will be far from temporary, even if growth is more generally restored, and will bring more and more people face to face with realities they thought had been superseded: play is already becoming increasingly a sign of privilege, as well as the focus of resentment—all over again. In this context, it is worth recalling Peter Conrad's approving nod towards Al Quaida and its perception of the decadence of the West.

It is necessary, then, to assert that Ben's masculine, straight acting identifications are reactionary, patriarchal, and chauvinistic, but, even for those of us who despise these things, he nonetheless brings to the first series a seriousness that feels somehow

---

[①] On 'repressive desublimation', see Marcuse, 1991, 59—86. Marcuse's influence never quite disappears, thankfully. For a recent defence of the category of repressive desublimation, see Bowring, Finn (2012). 'Repressive Desublimation and Consumer Culture: Re-evaluating Herbert Marcuse', *new formations*, vol. 75, pp. 8—24.

[②] Kwarteng, Kwasi, Priti Patel, Dominic Raab, Chris Skidmore, Elizabeth Truss (2012). *Britannia Unchained: Global Lessons for Growth and Prosperity*, Houndmills, Palgrave Macmillan.

[③] Cammack, Paul (2009). 'The Shape of Capitalism to Come', *Antipode*, vol. 41, p. 273.

refreshing because of its aggressive impatience with privilege, pseudo-individualism, and commodity fetishistic consciousness. After all, the reason the second series was ultimately so dull is that it was so utterly inconsequential. Nothing mattered very much to anyone, and everyone was quite proficient in recognizing and appropriating gender codes, at least within the boundaries determined by metrosexuality. I doubt anyone will be motivated to write an academic paper about it.

The category of 'straight acting' may therefore have something of critical significance to say about what 'gay' has come to mean, not through some autonomous evolution of the subculture and its traditions, but in neoliberal conditions. Needless to say, asserting this is not a matter of advocating a return to disapproval of 'the stereotype', and privileging the masculine over the effeminate. To be clear, my own view of camp is that, while it may be 'about deflating pretension, dismantling hierarchy, and remembering that all queers are stigmatized and no one deserves the kind of dignity that comes at the expense of someone else's shame',[1] it should not be essentialized as either subversive or conservative, since its potential in those respects will always depend on the context in which it is deployed as a mode capable of various effects. It may be hilariously liberating and exhilarating, or obnoxiously puerile, snobbish, and, in its own way, normative, as well as lots of other things too (most of us can supply our own instances). There is no necessary reason to defer to it. Straight acting, which should not be essentialized either, is a further permutation of the well-worn reifications of gender and sexuality—masculine, feminine, effeminate—inseparably relational categories determined by complex social divisions and dynamics that have not disappeared, even if they are being reconfigured. If the aspiration of gay liberation at its most ambitious was to contribute towards a univerally libertarian, rather than narrowly workerist, left, the emergence of a subculturally divisive distinction between the straight acting and effeminate gay man testifies to the failure of that ambition and the triumph instead of marketized liberties.[2]

(本文责任编辑: 尹庆红)

---

[1] Halperin, David (2012). *How To Be Gay*, Cambridge Mass., Belknap Press, p.207.

[2] Again, I should stress Halperin's care here, precisely because he has been spectacularly misrepresented: 'it is unreasonable to expect gay male culture to dismantle the dominant social and symbolic system of which it is merely the lucid and faithful reflection' (Halperin, 2012, 208). If we differ, this is mostly a question of emphasis and purpose.

电视真人秀、性别的自我意识和资本的形式

大卫·奥尔德森

【内容摘要】"做个直男"近年来被用来描述男人与男人之间的性行为,且不被看作是伪娘行为。本文试图探寻这个术语与社会性的性别自我意识相关联的意义。通过对"做个直男"这一电视真人秀系列的分析,尤其探讨其与性取向相关的意义。由于其不同的表现形式,这一术语最终被看作是社会的过于保守,在某些方面,也被批评为是在新自由主义条件下,"后现代人"的性别意识被激发出来。

【作者简介】大卫·奥尔德森(David Alderson),英国曼彻斯特大学艺术、语言与文化学院教授、性别研究中心主任,现为上海交通大学人文学院访问特聘讲授。主要研究性别理论、马克思主义文学理论和文化唯物主义。

Spectre Disorder: Neuro-Marxism and the State of the Soul

Ortwin de Graef

(University of Leuven, Leuven, Belgium)

Abstract: This paper proves that we live in the era of neuro-ideology. One spirit of Marx stresses the forces of alienation that facilitate human inhumanity, then putting its faith in human nature or just use value, as the last resort. Another spirit of Marx questions the former opinion, and embraces findings of neuroscience on human nature, since neuroscience could restore natural harmony, it could make us finding the real problems of human society. The autor called the latter thought as neuro-marxism.

Any reflection on Marxism and the future must engage with its past. Depending on the processing of the pronoun, that may mean either the past of Marxism, or the past of the reflection on Marxism and the future. It should always mean both, but life is short and discursive regimes differ, so as a philologist rather than a philosopher or political scientist I am drawn to the latter option.

Twenty years ago, in April 1993, at a conference called *Whither Marxism?*, Jacques Derrida called for a commemoration of the radically unprecedented event of the advent of Marxism. For the first time in the history of the world, a philosophico-scientific discourse resolutely renouncing any appeal to myth, religion, or nation, called for the formation of global social organisations in the name of new concepts of the human, of society, economy, nation and State.[1] Inheriting that event, or that

---

[1] Jacques Derrida, *Spectres de Marx: L'État de la dette, le travail du deuil et la nouvelle Internationale* (Paris: Galilée, 1993), 149—150.

promise, Derrida argues, requires a double interpretation of the world and all of its wrongs, a twofold interpretation faithful to at least two spirits of Marx—and, it's worth underscoring, two spirits of Derrida, since this double programme echoes the set-up already announced in *De la grammatologie* in 1967 and rehearsed in "Structure, signe et jeu dans le discours des sciences humaines" in the same year.① Uncharacteristically straightforward, Derrida list ten things that plague the world in 1993. They're still with us: unemployment, homelessness, global economic war, freaks of the free market, foreign debt, the arms industry in general, nuclear arms in particular, inter-ethnic war, crime syndicates and crises of international law. Ten indices of badness, out-of-jointness or evil requiring double interpretation. The first interpretation consists in the denunciation of the gap between what is the case in the world and what should be the case in the name of the measures of justice—minimally liberty, equality and dignity. Here, interpretation is the name of a praxis that seeks to efface itself: the point is to change the world so that it may finally coincide with the proposed ideal and render all critical interpretation superfluous. The second interpretation "obeys a different logic"②: it targets the concept of the ideal itself—liberty, equality, dignity, and inevitably also the very notion of the human—inspired in this activity by Marx's own insistence on the inevitable obsolescence of his theses in the face of the future.③ The point is precisely not to choose between these two approaches: both are necessary in their incompatibility, and this necessary incompatibility challenges the Eleventh Thesis on Feuerbach by advocating the defiant oxymoron of a performative or transformative interpretation.④

One form of our question today is how to inherit this programme—not as philosophers, as Derrida does in the second half of *Spectres*, which mounts meticulous analyses of Marx's acerbic dealings with the spectres haunting Max Stirner and of the celebrated turning table in the opening pages of *Capital*—but, speaking for myself, as philologists, doing the scholarly work of our trade, reading literary texts and the history they inherit and transmit. My comments here will involve the representation of

---

① For a suggestive inflection of this double programme in the inheritance of Derrida's thought, see the concluding speculations in Richard Beardsworth, *Derrida & the Political* (1996).
② Derrida, *Spectres*, 143.
③ Derrida, *Spectres*, 35.
④ Derrida, *Spectres*, 89.

collective agency and the ideology of sympathy.

In the wake of the Napoleonic Wars, the English establishment's fear of revolutionary unrest fostered a climate of harsh repression, as evident most notably in the brutal attack on reform protesters known as the Peterloo Massacre on August 16, 1819. The event infuriated the poet Percy Bysshe Shelley and inspired him to write a series of political poems venting his indignation. But sharing indignation is easy. These poems are worth reading again for what seems much harder to share—the voice of the people they would represent, and therefore also the agency such voice might voice.

The song "To the Men of England" is a good case in point, moving as it does from insurrectionary interpellation and exhortation to a sense of semi-cynical resignation. The first half of the poem consists of a series of questions addressed to the working classes, asking them why they slave away for the tyrants that exploit them. In the fifth quatrain, the speaker summarises the basic condition Marx would soon diagnose as "alienation," and in the sixth quatrain he calls on the workers to take control of their own labour. But then, in the two closing quatrains, the poem takes a strange turn, ordering the workers to "shrink" back to their holes and to dig their own grave:

> With plough and spade and hoe and loom
> Trace your grave and build your tomb
> And weave your winding-sheet—till fair
> England be your Sepulchre. (ll. 29—32)①

While this closing injunction asks to be understood as at least in some sense ironic, it does conclude the poem on a doubtful note, indicating a lack of confidence in the potential for agency in the workers whose liberation the poem sets out to preach. ② Importantly, the men of England addressed in the poem remain silent throughout, and

---

① Percy Bysshe Shelley, "Song: To the Men of England," *The Poems of Shelley*, Volume 3: 1818—1920. Ed. Jack Donovan, Cian Duffy, Kelvin Everest & Michael Rossington (London: Pearson, 2011), 278—280.

② For a vivid account of the questions raised by the conclusion of "Men of England", see William Keach, "Rise Like Lions? Shelley and the Revolutionary Left," *International Socialism*, *quarterly journal of the Socialist Workers Party*, July 1997. http://pubs.socialistreviewindex.org.uk/isj75/keach.htm. Last accessed February 13, 2013.

the only actions positively ascribed to them are their acts of servitude.

The sepulchral trope closing the poem also marks the end of another poem written around the same time, the sonnet "England in 1819."① In sharp contrast to the short straigthforward sentences in "Men of England," this text consists of one extended sentence only: twelve lines listing all that is ill in England form the subject; verb and predicate make up the concluding couplet. The litany of ills here also mentions the Peterloo Massacre, but apart from that the diagnosis of the condition of England is delivered in a discourse destined for the politically literate rather than the labouring poor. The sonnet's *volta* twists that dark diagnosis into a conditional prognosis of redemption: all the ills of England in 1819

> Are graves from which a glorious Phantom may
> Burst, to illumine our tempestuous day. (ll. 13—14)②

While at first sight this trope might seem to harbour more hope than "Men of England," it is important to note that here, too, positive collective agency is bracketed and release is featured only as a miraculous spectral intervention from beyond the grave. As for the lower classes, if anything they appear even more impotent here, unrepresented in most of the text, featuring only in one verse of Shelley's catastrophe catalogue: "A people starved and stabbed on th' untilled field" (l. 7).

"Ode to the West Wind," one of Shelley's more canonical works, while also written in 1819, at first reading seems very far removed from the "tempestuous" political unrest informing the two previous pieces. It, too, deploys sepulchral tropology, but this at first appears to be a more speculative formulaic matter, an invocation of the regenerative cycle of nature in which the—here literally—tempestuous autumn wind scatters seeds into the "grave" (l. 8) from which the spring will release them.③ In the fourth stanza, however, in line with its overall structure as a sequence of five sonnets, the Ode takes a turn and begins to draft an overarching analogy

---

① The richest reading of this sonnet remains James Chandler, *England in 1819: The Politics of Literary Culture and the Case of Romantic Historicism* (Chicago: U of Chicago P, 1998), esp. 23—33.
② Shelley, "England in 1819," *Poems*, 189—192.
③ Shelley, "Ode to the West Wind," *Poems*, 200—212.

between the speaker and the natural objects subject to the wind's workings in the three preceding stanzas. In the final stanza, this analogy reaches a climax in the image of the wind scattering the poet's "words among mankind," thus delivering "a prophecy" "to unawakened Earth." (ll. 67—69) While the substance of that prophecy remains undisclosed, what demands attention is the complexity of its transmission which the initial analogy tends to naturalise away. Imagining the wind scattering seeds or leaves across the universe, it is tempting to anthropomorphise or indeed spectralise it as a purposive agent serving a focussed intention. What makes Shelley's rhetoric so complex—most obviously perhaps in the slightly earlier "Mont Blanc"—is its struggle against the theist or pantheist fantasies it also always harbours, a struggle which often requires a resistance to the teleological charge informing grammar itself. Giving in to this teleological temptation facilitates the seductive fantasy of an analogous power intelligently servicing the distribution and preservation of words and thoughts, and "Ode to the West Wind" certainly flirts with such fantasy. But ultimately Shelley's rigour scrambles the analogy of agency the Ode entertains: the interjection "by the incantation of this verse" (l. 65) puts the wind in its place and insists it won't just blow where it lists—"Be through my lips to unawakened Earth / The trumpet of a prophecy." (ll. 68—69)[1] The performative power of the poem's verse defies the natural force it simultaneously seeks to model itself on.

Abandoning the teleological temptation of natural analogism comes at a price, though: the homonomic indifference of metabolic transmission served by fortuitous physical conditions (or not, as the case may be: seed will land on barren rock) finds its other in the radical heteronomy of symbolic transmission, requiring responsibilities of reception that exceed the logic of life alone. Yet the infusion of sheer force in the practice of "incantation" offers surrogate seductions for the temptations of natural analogism. Returning to "Men of England," we should at least register that this text was not primarily destined for reading but rather for singing—and indeed it has become a popular number at socialist gatherings. I have tried to test this power of incantation myself when teaching this poem, first doing a solo attempt at hymnody, which didn't

---

[1] For more extended alternative readings of Shelley's poetics of transmission in the Ode, see Chandler, *England in 1819*, 531—554, and Andrew Franta, "Shelley and the Poetics of Political Indirection." *Poetics Today* 22. 4 (2001): 765—793; 789—791.

work, but then trying out punk and gangsta style remixes, and that did seem to fan the flame. But the question remains whether that flame burns for pleasure or business—or how its burning for both affects justice. If the semantics of the poem's closing couplet play a sardonic pun on "fair" England as a pleasing substitute for a just society, thereby deconstructing the aesthetic ideology subtending business as the purveyor of pleasure at the expense of justice, the somatic charge released in chanting "fair" to rhyme with "sepulchre" risks rewiring the singing subjects into a scenario that perpetuates the confusion of business-cum-pleasure with justice. While there is no doubt communal chanting releases sensations of power that may enable collective agency in response to discontent, the aesthetic quality of the experience always also (but especially perhaps in the absence of articulated alternative interests) translates this potential as the disinterested pleasure of purposiveness without purpose—or the disabling sense of awe in the face of what Marx calls the "indefinite colossalness" of the goals of the proletarian revolution. ①

First as tragedy, then as farce. Just under half a century after the Peterloo Massacre, a massive Reform League demonstration demanding the franchise for men is denied access to Hyde Park. The crowd bring the railings down, invade the park, and the planned meeting proceeds. Soon after, in the lectures later published as *Culture and Anarchy*, Matthew Arnold holds up "the Hyde Park rioter" for ironical ridicule

> Just as the rest of us,—as the country squires in the aristocratic class, as the political dissenters in the middle-class,—he has no idea of a *State* , of the nation in its collective and corporate character controlling, as government, the free swing of this or that one of its members in the name of the higher reason of all of them, his own as well as that of others. He sees the rich, the aristocratic class, in occupation of the executive government, and so if he is stopped from making Hyde Park a bear-garden or the streets impassable, he says he is being butchered by the aristocracy.
>
> His apparition is somewhat embarrassing, because too many cooks spoil the broth; because, while the aristocratic and middle classes have long been doing as they like with great vigour, he has been too undeveloped and submissive hitherto to join in the game; and now, when he does come, he comes in immense numbers,

---

① Karl Marx, *The Eighteenth Brumaire of Louis Bonaparte* (1852), chapter 1. Online at http://www.marxists.org/archive/marx/works/1852/18th-brumaire/ch01.htm. Last accessed Febrary 14, 2013.

and is rather raw and rough.①

If for Shelley the challenge seemed primarily to imagine working-class agency, for Arnold such agency is all too apparent: like the agency of the other classes, the Barbarians and the Philistines, it is the loose-cannon agency of anarchy, of doing as one likes. Arnold's alternative is the agency of culture, driven by the spirit of perfection, and established in the structures of the State.② Arnold's challenge, then, is the imagination of a state serving not self-interest or class-interest but the interest of what he calls our best self and higher reason.

It is more fun to imagine the contempt such thinking would have met with from Marx than to entertain the prospect of what such a State of Perfection might look like. Yet precisely the spirit of Marx can be critical here—at least that spirit of Marx that is ready to reconsider the dynamics of alienation and to take seriously Arnold's claim that the State he seeks to think as the structure of our best self is in essence the State of the Aliens: "persons who are mainly led, not by their class spirit, but by a general *humane* spirit, by the love of human perfection."③ To call these lovers of human perfection "aliens" invites a reflection on the human as an unfamiliar animal—a *Gattungswesen* concerned in all it produces with its own species—or rather its species as never quite its own, not just more of the same but precisely the species of difference. For instance the difference between the "bright powers of sympathy and ready powers of action" which the Reform League's Frederic Harrison singles out as distinctive working-class virtues and the "increased sympathy" Arnold holds up as distinctive of human perfection.④ For the difference between "bright powers of sympathy" and "increased sympathy" to be critically meaningful, it must make more difference than increase itself can cover and must also affect the very idea of sympathy.

I want to return once more to 1819, and another Shelley poem responding to Peterloo.

---

① Matthew Arnold, *Culture and Anarchy and other writings*, ed. Stefan Collini (Cambridge: CUP, 1993), 88.

② For Arnold's conception of the State, see Ortwin de Graef & Anke Gilleir, "'The Stigma of Its Present Name': Matthew Arnold's Scripts of State ." *Occasion: Interdisciplinary Studies in the Humanities* v. 2 (December 20, 2010), http://occasion.stanford.edu/node/48.

③ Arnold, *Culture*, 110.

④ Arnold, *Culture*, 97, 76.

"The Mask of Anarchy" is a much more ambitious work than the other occasional pieces mentioned before, but it, too, has been the subject of critical debate regarding Shelley's representation of working-class agency.① A substantial part of the 91—quattrain-long text offers an alternative address to the "Men of England," and as in that other poem, the addressees are not given direct access to speech—though their imagined repetition of the speech urged on them by the address's speaker is explicitly figured as a powerfully performative force of attack and protection:

> 'Let a vast assembly be,
> And with great solemnity
> Declare with measured words that ye
> Are, as God has made ye, free—
>
> 'Be your strong and simple words
> Keen to wound as sharpened swords,
> And wide as targes let them be,
> With their shade to cover ye. (ll. 299—306)②

That these words should be sanctioned by God complicates the freedom they proclaim, and the people's potential for self-assertion is further qualified when they are urged to "Let the laws of [their] own land, / Good or ill, between [them] stand" as "Arbiters of the dispute." (ll. 327—330) Represented as still determined by nation and God rather than justice, the working class appears to remain destined for England fair's sepulchre. But the poem also imagines an alternative power for the people, a force beyond or beneath speech representing an alternative authority in the face of Anarchy:

> 'Stand ye calm and resolute,
> Like a forest close and mute,

---

① For a recent state of the art account, see Kir Kuiken, "Shelley's 'Mask of Anarchy' and the Problem of Modern Sovereignty." *Literature Compass* 8/2 (2011): 95—106.
② Shelley, "The Mask of Anarchy: Written on the Occasion of the Massacre at Manchester," *Poems*, 27—63.

> With folded arms and looks which are
> Weapons of an unvanquished war (ll. 323—326)

It is this image of resolute mute resistance frankly facing the forces of oppression that has made this poem an important moment in the history of pacifist protest—and indeed a direct source of inspiration for Ghandi.① The authority imagined here derives from neither God nor nation, nor even from abstract enlightenment principles like liberty, but from the naked human face:

> And if then the tyrants dare
> Let them ride among you there,
> Slash, and stab, and maim, and hew,—
> What they like, that let them do.
>
> With folded arms and steady eyes,
> And little fear, and less surprise
> Look upon them as they slay
> Till their rage has died away.
>
> Then they will return with shame
> To the place from which they came,
> And the blood thus shed will speak
> In hot blushes on their cheek. (ll. 344—355)

Shelley's imagination of the force of the naked human face is powerful and just—though just not just enough. Not because it demands the impossible but because it doesn't. The combination of ruthlessness and defiant trust informing the command to offer defenceless bodies up for slaughter as a test of shared humanity is both appalling and appealing and exerts an ultimately aesthetic fascination which risks obscuring just how low the standard is set. Slashing and stabbing and maiming and hewing other

---

① Susan Wolfson presents a powerful reading of these stanza's as a "fantasy of political performance" in which political action is translated into "static aesthetic spectacle." Susan J. Wolfson, *Formal Charges: The Shaping of Poetry in British Romanticism* (Stanford: Stanford UP, 1997), 200.

humans is wrong. Not that that standard does not need constant reinforcement—as the occasion of the poem and the two centuries since make all too depressingly clear. But to ground that standard in the face-to-face of singular human beings, victims and perpetrators, is to give human nature too much credit. Yes, human animals are singularly subject to upsurges of sympathy which foster compassion and hinder the infliction of pain; yes, sympathy is easily overruled in the service of self-interest or the vicarious self-interest of subservience to force, leading to indifference to suffering or (but it may be the same thing) direct denial of the humanity of the victims of suffering. The increasingly complex and interconnected networks of human interaction characterising our modern condition, of which Shelley witnessed but the first real manifestations, only make such overruling, indifference and denial easier still. But trusting the bright powers of sympathy to redress this just by reminding us of the human nature so easily overruled in the first place is to sentimentalise a predicament that requires not more feeling, not a deeper, but a different shade of shame—a passionate indifference, an acute disinterest, a more alien sentiment of discontent desiring a justice that exceeds the prevention of human inhumanity to man, a sober anger that dismisses aestheticisations of human sympathy which only serve to strengthen the invisible-hand fantasies that give capitalism its all too human face. In sum, a willingness to entertain alienation as what it has come to for us humans as we begin to live the posthuman, and the species-being we are demands to differ. ①

Shelley's uneasy explorations of the aesthetic ideology of sympathy deserve a better reading than I intend here. This would minimally require an engament with the ghost of Wordsworth, who haunts *The Mask of Anarchy* in various guises and will always remain Shelley's unfinished business. ② And indeed ours, for the ideology of sympathy Wordsworth inherited from Adam Smith and naturalised as our common humanity still

---

① For some further thoughts on the right to alienation, see Pieter Vermeulen, Stef Craps, Richard Crownshaw, Ortwin de Graef, Andreas Huyssen, Vivian Liska & David Miller, "Dispersal and redemption: The future dynamics of memory studies-A roundtable." Memory Studies 5:2, 2012, 223—239; 232—234.

② For a direct allusion to Wordsworth's "The Thorn" in *The Mask*, see Morton D. Paley, "Apocapolitics: Allusion and Structure in Shelley's 'Mask of Anarchy'," Huntington Library Quarterly 54: 2, 1991, 91—109; 96. Chandler's *England in* 1819 offers an excellent exploration of Shelley's "sublime casuistry" (511) as a critical and genuinely historical alternative to both the natural/national ideology of sympathy associated with Wordsworth and the insufficiently dialectical programmes of utilitarian reform.

informs us—though now, as indeed Wordsworth anticipated in the Preface to *Lyrical Ballads*, it has morphed into science:

> If the labours of men of Science should ever create any material revolution, direct or indirect, in our condition, and in the impressions which we habitually receive, the Poet will sleep then no more than at present, but he will be ready to follow the steps of the man of Science, not only in those general indirect effects, but he will be at his side, carrying sensation into the midst of the objects of the Science itself. The remotest discoveries of the Chemist, the Botanist, or Mineralogist, will be as proper objects of the Poet's art as any upon which it can be employed, if the time should ever come when these things shall be familiar to us, and the relations under which they are contemplated by the followers of the respective Sciences shall be manifestly and palpably material to us as enjoying and suffering beings. If the time should ever come when what is now called Science, thus familiarized to men, shall be ready to put on, as it were, a form of flesh and blood, the Poet will lend his divine spirit to aid the transfiguration, and will welcome the Being thus produced, as a dear and genuine inmate of the household of man. ①

The curious narrative inversion and the imagery in this projected alliance of science and poetry rehearse the domestication of revolution that is the dominant trope in Wordsworth's aesthetic ideology: just as Wordsworth's initial fervent support for the French Revolution suffered a sea change in the course of the 1790s which he himself retrospectively diagnosed as a gradual recognition—catalysed by the horrors of the September Massacres—that whatever enthused him in the Revolution was really only ever its imitation of the domestic natural liberty England was always already blessed with,② so the challenge of science the poet vows to follow is recuperated in its projected integration in the "household of man" thanks to the theotropic hospitality of poetry. Science "now", in 1802, is something of a spectral force, which may work a revolution that will change our "condition"; yet the effect of that revolution will be an

---

① William Wordsworth, "Preface to *Lyrical Ballads* (1802)," *Lyrical Ballads and Other Poems*, 1797—1800, *The Cornell Wordsworth*, ed. James Butler and Karen Green (Ithaca: Cornell UP, 1992), 740—760; 753.

② For a concise account of this tropological pattern in Wordsworth's 1805 *Prelude*, see Ortwin de Graef, "Nothing out of Hermeneutics' certain course". *Image & Narrative: On-Line Magazine of the Visual Narrative*, 3 (2001) http://www.imageandnarrative.be/inarchive/illustrations/ortwindegraef.htm.

aesthetic de-spectralisation, transfiguring science into comforting confirmation. The poet, Wordsworth writes, "is the rock of defence of human nature; an upholder and preserver, carrying everywhere with him relationship and love"; "bind[ing] together by passion and knowledge the vast empire of human society, as it is spread over the whole earth, and over all time."① Aided by poetry, the revolution worked by science ends up in a reconfiguration of this vast empire into a family by the fireside.

We live in the era of neuro-ideology. The trust in human nature as a secret resource whose disclosure by science will truly bring the new millennium that failed to materialise along with the Y2K bug has never run so high. A recent instance is Simon Baron-Cohen's *Zero Degrees of Empathy: A New Theory of Human Cruelty and Kindness* (2011), presented by the author as a sequel to two of his earlier books, *Mindblindness: An Essay on Autism and Theory of Mind* (1995) and *The Essential Difference: Men, Women and the Extreme Male Brain* (2003).②

It is not insignificant that in presenting *Zero Degrees* as third in a trilogy, Baron-Cohen glosses over his other single-authored book, *Autism and Asperger Syndrome: The Facts* (2008)—for as its subtitle suggests, that volume, in all its helpfully informative expert modesty, interrupts the increase in ideological ambition driving the trilogy. Baron-Cohen's first book, *Mindblindness*, was a revision of his doctorate thesis aimed at fellow scientists but also at "the general reader," and has been rightly recognised as an important contribution to the wider understanding of what is now usually called autism spectrum disorder.③ The subtitle mentions "theory of mind," but the book does not pretend to be a theory of the mind—rather, it advances the hypothesis, backed up by empirical observations and experiments, that typically developing humans learn to detect intentionality and eye direction in others, can process this information into the construction of shared attention between themselves and others, and can thereby richly represent the mental state of other human beings—imaging or imagining their inner life, so to speak; theorising, effectively, that they, too, have a mind. Autism, from this perspective, amounts to a defect in this set of mechanisms: humans suffering from

---

① Wordsworth, "Preface," 752.
② Simon Baron-Cohen, *Zero Degrees of Empathy: A New Theory of Human Cruelty and Kindness* (London: Penguin, 2012), xi.
③ Simon Baron-Cohen, *Mindblindness: An Essay on Autism and Theory of Mind* (Cambridge, Mass.: MIT Press, 1997), xix

spectrum disorders have trouble reading other minds because they don't feel they know there are minds to be read there in the first place. *Mindblindness* does not focus in any great detail on the distinction between knowing and feeling. Only towards the end, in a section on "Individual Differences in 'Empathy'," does Baron-Cohen briefly signal the importance of emotion in mindreading, suggesting this is an avenue for further research and indicating there may be gender differences involved here too.① *The Essential Difference* is Baron-Cohen's answer to his own question, but it is essentially different from the previous book in that it is explicitly conceived as an exercise in "toe"—"dip [ping]" into "politically dangerous waters"② and self-consciously eschews "tiptoe [ing]" around what it's about: "*The female brain is predominantly hard-wired for empathy. The male brain is predominantly hard-wired for understanding and building systems.*"③ I am not concerned here with the substance of Baron-Cohen's contribution to gender trouble, questionable though it remains;④ rather, what demands notice here is the scientist's forceful performance as a popular public intellectual who emerges from the laboratory to bring much-needed truth to current ideological debates. Much of the evidence presented to back up the book's central claims is still rooted in autism research, but the cautious explication characterising *Mindblindness* now gives way to audacious extrapolation. In *Zero Degrees of Empathy* that trend comes to a climax as Baron-Cohen proposes "a new theory of human cruelty and kindness"—or even, as the title of the American edition has it, invents *The Science of Evil: On Empathy and the Origins of Cruelty*.

The basic proposition of the book is straightforward enough: "the unscientific term 'evil'" should be replaced with "the term 'empathy' erosion."⑤ The assumption is that the brain has an empathy circuit or Empathizing Mechanism whose performance is, like all brain events, in principle open to measurement and ultimately manipulation.

---

① Baron-Cohen, *Mindblindness*, 135—136.
② Simon Baron-Cohen, *The Essential Difference* (London: Penguin, 2004), xi.
③ Baron-Cohen, *Essential Difference*, 1.
④ For a critique of the evidence base of Baron-Cohen's construction of gender difference, see Alison Nash and Giordana Grossi, "Picking Barbie's [MT] Brain: Inherent Sex Differences in Scientific Ability?", *Journal of Interdisciplinary Feminist Thought* 2:1, 2007, article 5 (available at http://digitalcommons.salve.edu/jift/vol2/iss1/5) and Cordelia Fine, *Delusions of Gender: The Real Science Behind Sex Differences* (Icon Books, 2010).
⑤ Baron-Cohen, *Zero Degrees*, xi.

This brings the advantage that rather than having to worry in speculative, religious or crypto-religious terms about human inhumanity to humans, we can now see nastiness obstructing the circuit when we run fMRi scans of the brains of the bad, and perhaps even wash them nice with the help of oxytocin nasal spray.① The question is of course how these advantages travel, if at all, outside the controlled conditions of the laboratory, but Baron-Cohen is clearly confident that focusing on empathy will bring peace:

> By the end of our journey, there should be less of a nagging need for answers to the big question of understanding human cruelty. The mind should be quieted if the answers are beginning to feel satisfying.②

And not just peace of mind either: in the final pages of the book, Baron-Cohen talks about empathy between Israeli and Palestinian parents of children killed in the Intifada and, while admitting that "this is just a tiny step," adds that "each drop of empathy waters the flower of peace," for "Empathy is like a universal solvent. Any problem immersed in empathy becomes soluble."③

Baron-Cohen does not discount the importance of environmental, historical, and cultural contingencies, but fundamentally, identifying obstructions in the empathy circuit as the necessary condition for human cruelty does in effect suggest that if only we were more true to neuro-typical human bio-being, universal peace would come at last. If only we were nicer to each other. Do we really need scientists to tell us this? Judging by the popular success of books like *Zero Degrees*, yes, apparently we do: we do need "if only"—"just so"—stories to forget about all those problems empathy cannot solve—including empathy itself. Just like we need a hole in the head to house what religion calls our soul. Baron-Cohen takes pains to distinguish his scientific answer to the question of cruelty from the answers of religion, but the distinction breaks down the moment his hyperbolic extrapolation drive kicks in. It is one thing to identify a circuit in the human brain that lights up when humans feel kindness; it is a second

---

① Baron-Cohen, *Zero Degrees*, 105.
② Baron-Cohen, *Zero Degrees*, 6—7.
③ Baron-Cohen, *Zero Degrees*, 132.

thing to argue that this is in all likelihood an evolutionary adaptation reflecting the ultra-social comportment of human animals when compared to other primates; but it makes little sense to conclude from this that empathy is therefore "effective as a way of anticipating and resolving interpersonal problems, whether this is a marital conflict, an international conflict, a problem at work, difficulties in a friendship, political deadlocks, a family dispute, or a problem with the neighbour."① If empathy could achieve all this, it would have done so already. After all, empathy is already at work in human conflict as a matter of course and damage control: if it weren't, it wouldn't be the hardwired adaptation the scientist uncovers; but to the extent that it is, it obviously doesn't deliver the universal solvent the ideologue imagines. There is no doubt more can be done to unlock the positive potential of empathy in all manner of situations, but to advance it as an answer to the challenges of 21st-century life on this planet is to commit a category mistake. Just as religion masks the real contradictions of human life by appealing to an alternative order of ultimate reality and meaning, so neuroscience as ideology denies real time disorder by gesturing towards a deep time source of truth that will restore natural harmony.

None of this is to suggest that empathy is not an important faculty, and rigorous scientific investigation of all human mental labour is clearly to be applauded. But if what such science delivers in response to suffering and injustice is only a souped-up version of what ideologies of sympathy have been piously proposing for the past three centuries or so, the science does not make the difference we need and instead of solving real problems threatens to obscure them. Evidently, not all neuroscientists succumb to the temptation of extrapolation so spectacularly as Baron-Cohen does as he takes up his seat by the fireside in Wordsworth's household of man to join in the mind-quietening. And in itself extrapolation is a risk science must take if it is to develop the new hypotheses it needs to work. But for a risk to be worth taking it should be critical: the hypothesis should respond to the problem it proposes to address in terms that are adequate to it. If neuroscience wants to matter in the diagnosis of global injustice and suffering, it will have to engage with the historical nature of the human animal, not just its natural history, and with the record of such engagement in other disciplines. Most

---

① Baron-Cohen, 132.

importantly it will have to engage with itself: with the vast gulf between its reach and its grasp (science is nowhere near determining the real complexity of the relation between human conduct, let alone discursively negotiated collective conduct, and the megabillions of neuronsparks firing away in the brain), and with the conceptual incongruities riddling its self-understanding as superscience.

For even if neuroscience could comprehensively and exhaustively articulate activity in the brain with complex human behaviour, the question would still have to be: so what? That there *is* a relation between human behaviour and brain fireworks seems to be a surprise primarily to neuroscientists themselves. The rest of us tend to take this as read. After all, where else would sparks fly if not in the brain? But while it is interesting to learn how and where they fly, it is not clear how exactly that knowledge is supposed to matter in addressing global suffering and injustice. Given the current state of human life on the planet, we already know that our hardwired or wetwired routines are not responding very well to the challenges of the 7 billion and counting. To see them fully imaged in action, however unlikely that prospect is at present, may be satisfying for science and aesthetically pleasing for all, but will not in itself change anything. If the further goal would be to manipulate these fireworks to bring about world peace, assuming for the moment that any manipulation as such would be at alll possible (Welcome to the Matrix), the question would have to be precisely which mental states need to be suppressed and which require boosting to favour the kind of comportment that would bring the Millennium. And for those questions to be answered, the neuro-engineer would have to turn to all humans who have been investigating versions of these questions throughout human history. All humans. And then the surprise would be that quite a few of them have had pretty sound ideas about this already and actually succeeded translating them in beta-applications using the human animal's arch digital imaging technology: the transmission of information through time and space between dead and unborn brains we call writing. Not that those efforts have achieved all that much, but they comfortably outstrip the workings of oxytocine nasal spray.

Marx promised a non-religious resolutely internationalist philosophico-scientific account of human species-beings organising a State that would approximate something like justice. One spirit of Marx scans the world and finds it wanting and decries the forces of alienation that facilitate human inhumanity, putting its faith, like Shelley and Baron-Cohen, in human nature, or just use value, as the last resort. Another spirit questions the adequacy of notions of human nature, and use value, to the challenges of 21st-century human being on this planet. It, too, embraces findings of neuroscience on human nature but reads them not as solutions but as problems indicating that humans are not wetwired for the life we have produced: default empathy routines just won't do. Let neuro-marxism be one name for the science that sees this.

(本文责任编辑：贾洁)

幽灵障碍：神经—马克思主义与灵魂的状态

奥尔顿·德格雷夫

【内容摘要】 本文提出人类正生活在一个神经意识形态的时代。马克思主义的一种观点是强调异化造成了人的非人化，从而将一线希望寄存于人性或使用价值中；另一种观点则对此表示质疑，同时利用神经科学来解读人性，鉴于神经科学有能力恢复自然的和谐，从而可能真正找出人类社会问题的症结所在。笔者将后一种思想称为神经—马克思主义。

【作者简介】 奥尔顿·德格雷夫（Ortwin de Graef），比利时鲁汶大学艺术系教授。其研究领域包括审美意识形态、神经意识形态、创伤理论、后结构主义的理论等方面。

The Spectre of Utopia: On Marxism and the Future

Matthew Beaumont

(Unversity College London)

Abstract: This talk explores the dialectics of possibility and practicability that have shaped the history of utopian thought. It argues that it is the figure of the ghost that best enables us to articulate the unsettling ways in which utopia unsettles neat epistemological or ontological distinctions between the actual and the imaginary, the present and the absent: the specter of utopianism. The talk teases out the philosophical and political implications of this conception of utopianism, discussing some of the ways in which, historically, this specter has haunted Europe and North America; and examining its current invocations.

I

One of the effects of T. J. Clark's attempt, twelve months ago, to foreclose discussion of utopia on the Left, in his theses 'For a Left with No Future', published in the *New Left Review*, was precisely to provide an opportunity to reopen the ongoing discussion of the political significance of utopia. In this strange collage of ideas, a series of unpredictable, and highly unsystematic, lucubrations on A. C. Bradley and Nietzsche, among others, Clark argued for an 'anti-utopian politics', and concluded that '*there will be no future*'. There is no such thing as futurity, he seemed to be announcing, as if provocatively echoing Margaret Thatcher, who in 1987 famously asserted that 'there is no such thing as society'. Dismissing the tradition of utopian thought as an 'invention of early Modern civil servants', a caricature which implied that Thomas

More, in spite of his critical and satirical inventiveness, had no more imagination than a primitive bureaucrat, Clark declared that 'utopias reassure modernity as to its infinite potential'. ①

There is of course some truth to this claim. Like the gleaming, transparent forms of architects' three-dimensional models, utopias have often presented an image of the future that is merely a clean, socially harmonious, and technologistic projection of the present. In the period in which, at least in Europe and the US, utopian fiction was produced in the greatest quantity, the late nineteenth century, most utopias were reformist fantasies that, in spite of their criticisms of the depredations of capitalism, were principally concerned to modify society just enough to allay the more serious threat to contemporary civilization, as they perceived it, which was the prospect of an insurgent proletariat, the spectre of communism. Utopias in this period, as in others before and since, were on the one hand a recognition that 'there is something rotten in the State of Things', and on the other an attempt to conjure away the excess or disharmonious remainder that, in symptomatic form, testified to this social rottenness. If serious thinkers in the nineteenth century in particular, according to Alenka Zupancic, in a commentary on Alain Badiou, were preoccupied with the problem of thinking this 'spectre of excess', of 'tarrying with the excess', then 'utopias, designed to eliminate social and other injustice, mostly proposed to achieve this by eliminating this very excess'. ②

The most popular and politically influential utopia of the late nineteenth century, Edward Bellamy's *Looking Backward* (1888), illustrates this point, in that, in spite of its spirited attack on capitalist competition, and its vision of a state-socialist solution to the problem of social and other kinds of injustice, its politics are driven by a fear of revolution. If Bellamy attacked capitalism, he also feared socialism, which, as he put it in a letter, 'smells to the average American of petroleum, suggests the red flag, with all manner of sexual novelties, and an abusive tone about God and religion.'

The mechanisms *Looking Backward* identifies as the motor of utopian society,

---

① T. J. Clark, 'For a Left with No Future,' *New Left Review* 74 (March/April 2012), 68, 69, 73, 75. Susan Watkins offers a wide-ranging and effective critique in 'Presentism?' *New Left Review* 74 (March/April 2012), 77—102—but not one that gives any space to the question of utopia.

② Alenka Zupancic, 'The Fifth Condition,' in *Think Again: Alain Badiou and the Future of Philosophy*, ed. Peter Hallward (London: Continuum, 2004), 196—197.

state monopolies, protectionism, consumerism, the so-called 'industrial army', are finally idealized adaptations of contemporary capitalism's own solution to the successive recessions of the so-called Great Depression. As Ernst Bloch put it, Bellamy's utopia 'lies flawlessly in the line of extension of the modern world; it is fundamentally satisfied with the disposition of capitalist civilization'.

Clark is correct, then, that many utopias have precisely reassured modernity as to its infinite potential. But here I want to argue for a reconception of utopia that emphasizes its persistent capacity for unsettling modernity, discomposing it, haunting it, and for drawing attention not to its infinite potential but its contingency and vulnerability to change and transformation. This involves thinking of it not as a utopian text or even idea so much as a fragment of the future in the present. There will be no future, Clark writes. But there will be a future. Indeed, there is a future.

II

In *The Story of Utopias: Ideal Commonwealths and Social Myths*, published ninety years ago, in 1923, the great American sociologist of the city and technology, Lewis Mumford, pleaded with his readers to 'be convinced about the reality of utopia'. This was probably the first monograph on utopianism to be published, at least in English, in an epoch increasingly defined by dystopianism (Yevgeny Zamyatin's *We*, banned in the Soviet Union in 1921, appeared in England in 1924). In his book, Mumford insisted that, despite inhabiting the 'pseudo-environment' of ideas, or 'idolum', utopia is every bit as real as history. He ended, in an appealing polemic, by affirming the importance of utopian thinking at the present time, emphasizing that 'if our eutopias spring out of the realities of our environment, it will be easy enough to place foundations under them'. 'When that which is perfect has come,' he announced in the book's final sentence, 'that which is imperfect will pass away.'[1] A generation later, in the grimly titled *Values for Survival* (1946), where he grieved for the death of his son in the Second World War, and deplored the devastation caused by the atom bomb, Mumford felt less inclined to celebrate utopia's reality for the collective

---

[1] Lewis Mumford, *The Story of Utopias: Ideal Commonwealths and Social Myths* (London: George C. Harrap, 1923), 15, 24, 307, 308.

imagination. In the 1930s and 1940s, the social myth of the nation state had been violently realized, and the results of this, visible above all in the rise of Fascism, didn't exactly resemble an ideal commonwealth. In this book, in contrast, Mumford lamented that 'the spirit of utopianism has not yet been exorcised'. ①

So if 'in its ghostly way, utopia continues to haunt mankind,' as Chad Walsh claimed in *From Utopia to Nightmare* (1962), it is not simply 'a good ghost that won't go away', as he maintained. ② At times, it is manifestly a bad ghost that won't go away. In the course of the last century, in particular, utopia is generally thought to have been benign when it hasn't exceeded the ideational sphere and malign when it has; benign when it hasn't impinged on history, malign when it has. The prevailing assumption is that if utopia remains utopian, in the dismissive colloquial sense of the term, it is perfectly acceptable; and that if it acquires an ideological force, and can no longer be dismissed as hopelessly unrealistic, because it is deemed to have encroached on politics, it is unacceptable. ③ In order to sidestep this assumption, then, perhaps it is productive to identify utopia as occupying a shifting, often contradictory space between the utopian and the ideological, between fantasy and reality. For heuristic purposes, this is my initial supposition.

Krishan Kumar has claimed that utopia articulates the 'tension between possibility and practicability'. ④ This formulation is as useful as it is neat, but I prefer to embroider its dialectic slightly and summarize utopia instead as a form that articulates the tension between impossibility and practicability. Its solutions to those social

---

① Lewis Mumford, *Values for Survival* (New York: Harcourt, Brace, 1946), 74.

② Chad Walsh, *From Utopia to Nightmare* (London: Geoffrey Bles, 1962), 16.

③ Of course, there have also been people, on both the left and right of the political spectrum, who conflated all forms of utopianism with totalitarianism in the second half of the twentieth century, and hence dismissed utopian thought *tout court*. A statement made by Michel Foucault, in the course of a conversation in 1971 about the way in which, 'as a result of [its] Utopian tendencies,' the Soviet Union 'returned to the standards of bourgeois society in the nineteenth century', can stand as representative of this libertarian critique of Utopia: 'I think that to imagine another system is to extend our participation in the present system.' See 'Revolutionary Action: "Until Now"', in *Language, Counter-Memory, Practice: Selected Essays and Interviews*, ed. and trans. Donald F. Bouchard and Sherry Simon (Oxford: Blackwell, 1977), 230—231.

④ Krishan Kumar, *Utopianism* (Milton Keynes: Open University Press, 1991), 3. The immediate context for this statement might be helpful: '[Utopia] is more than a social or political tract aiming at reform, however comprehensive. It always goes beyond the immediately practicable, and it may go so far as to be in most realistic senses wholly impracticable. But it is never simple dreaming. It always has one foot in reality' (2).

contradictions that it overtly or covertly critiques are imaginable but, in the prevailing circumstances, unrealizable. Utopia, it could be said, inhabits a region that is at the same time possible and impracticable. Of course, the boundaries of this region are defined historically rather than absolutely, for the political imagination is contingent on the ideological conditions that predominate at a given time. But in general, utopia occupies a liminal space between the impossible and the practicable.

It is the figure of the ghost, I propose, that most productively enables us to conceptualize this dialectic of utopia. Terry Castle has explained that, since the eighteenth century, in the Enlightenment and post-Enlightenment culture of Europe, ghosts have existed 'tantalizingly on the edge of possibility, somewhere just beyond the boundary of the real'.① They therefore unsettle neat epistemological distinctions between the actual and the imaginary, the present and the absent. The same might be claimed about utopia, which isn't exactly ideal or material, spiritual or physical, impossible or practicable. Furthermore, if a spectre represents the intrusion into the present of a repressed historical past, utopia could be said to represent the intrusion into the present of a future whose historical possibility has been suppressed by the ideological limits that shape the political imagination. 'The Future as Disruption,' Fredric Jameson calls it.② Utopia, then, insinuates a troubling sense of absence into the present, and so reveals that reality is not complete, that it is not identical to itself. Like ghosts, utopias momentarily make the unreal seem real, and at the same time make the real seem unreal. They are not real or unreal but fantastic; and 'like the ghost which is neither dead nor alive', as Rosemary Jackson once suggested, 'the fantastic is a spectral presence, suspended between being and nothingness.'③ This is the ontology of utopia.

More precisely, perhaps, this is utopia's 'hauntology'. The term 'hauntology',

---

① Terry Castle, *The Female Thermometer: Eighteenth-Century Culture and the Invention of the Uncanny* (Oxford: Oxford University Press, 1995), 159.

② This is the title of the final chapter of Fredric Jameson's *Archaeologies of the Future: The Desire Called Utopia and Other Science Fictions* (London: Verso, 2005).

③ Rosemary Jackson, *Fantasy: The Literature of Subversion* (London: Methuen, 1981), 20. If utopias constitute a mode of the fantastic, then, in contrast to 'much mimetic art', they too can be said to evince what Mark Bould has called 'a frankly self-referential consciousness (an embedded, textual self-consciousness, whatever the consciousness of the particular author or reader) of the impossibility of "real life", or Real life'. See 'The Dreadful Credibility of Absurd Things: A Tendency in Fantasy Theory', *Historical Materialism* 10: 4 (2002), 83.

which critics of deconstruction tend to regard as an absurd neologism, but which I believe is deeply suggestive, is the one Jacques Derrida devised in order to explore the dialectics of the ghost in *Specters of Marx* (1994). It is an ambitious attempt to think the 'logic of haunting' rather than of being. ① 'Ontology speaks only of what is present or what is absent,' as Warren Montag has commented; 'it cannot conceive of what is neither.' ② Hauntology thinks and speaks of this neither, and this both, that is the spectre: 'neither soul nor body, and both one and the other' (6). The ghost, as Derrida describes it, is 'a paradoxical incorporation, the becoming-body, a certain phenomenal and carnal form of the spirit' (6). It is a liminal entity, or non-entity, neither living nor dead, suspended between being and nothingness.

In the present context, I am not especially interested in Derrida's 'spectropolitics' (107), as he calls it at one point, and not least because the historical moment in which his book intervened has passed, along with much of its political urgency. ③ I am interested instead in its possibilities for a 'spectropoetic' account of utopia (45). I propose to treat Derrida's book 'primarily as a *literary* text'; like Aijaz Ahmad, I believe it is most productive to interpret it as 'essentially a *performative* text in a distinctly literary mode'. ④ Derrida's book is not, it must be admitted, a meditation on the idea of utopia. He does at one point allude to utopia in passing, affirming that Marx thought 'that the dividing line between the ghost and actuality ought to be crossed, like utopia itself, by a realization, that is, by a revolution' (39)—but he doesn't develop the point, or even attempt to clarify the ambiguities that this analogy rather unhelpfully generates. So it is of course important to resist falling into the trap of translating his term 'messianic' as 'utopian', as he

---

① Jacques Derrida, *Specters of Marx: The State of the Debt, the Work of Mourning, and the New International*, trans. Peggy Kamuf (London: Routledge,1994), 10. Hereafter references to this edition are cited in the text.

② Warren Montag, 'Spirits Armed and Unarmed: Derrida's *Specters of Marx*', in *Ghostly Demarcations: A Symposium on Jacques Derrida's Specters of Marx*, ed. Michael Sprinker (London: Verso, 1999), 71.

③ For a brisk critical account of the relationship of *Specters* to this moment, the aftermath of the collapse of communism in Eastern Europe, see Terry Eagleton, 'Marxism without Marxism', in *Ghostly Demarcations: A Symposium on Jacques Derrida's Specters of Marx*, ed. Michael Sprinker (London: Verso, 1999), 83—87—a response to the book that infuriated Derrida!

④ Aijaz Ahmad, 'Reconciling Derrida: "Specters of Marx" and Deconstructive Politics', in *Ghostly Demarcations: A Symposium on Jacques Derrida's Specters of Marx*, ed. Michael Sprinker (London: Verso, 1999), 90—91.

accuses Jameson of consistently doing.① But Jameson is surely right to notice the relevance of the term, even if Derrida didn't concede this, and I believe it is highly productive to rethink aspects of what *Specters of Marx* has to say about ghosts, and 'hauntology' more generally, in relation to utopia.

III

Derrida's poetics of the *revenant*, the remnant from the past that reappears and disrupts the present, is predicated on a conception of the present that, as one might expect of the architect of deconstructionism, emphasizes that it cannot be completely present to itself. He refers in the book's exordium, for example, to the '*non-contemporaneity with itself of the living present*' (xix). Then, in the first chapter, he points again to 'the disjointure in the very presence of the present, this sort of non-contemporaneity of present time with itself', which he immediately identifies as 'this radical untimeliness or this anachrony on the basis of which we are trying here to *think the ghost*' (25). Derrida derives this formulation from Heidegger, his old interrogator; but in light of the book's title he might also have had recourse to the Marxist tradition in excavating the non-identities of the present.② For it is through the idea of the non-synchronous present that Ernst Bloch, who regarded Heidegger as one of his principal intellectual antagonists, tries to think utopia. According to him, the present contains an '*objectively* non-contemporaneous element as a continuing influence of older circumstances and forms of production, however they may have been crossed through, as well as of older superstructures'. Bloch establishes that the present is not

---

① Jacques Derrida, 'Marx and Sons', in *Ghostly Demarcations: A Symposium on Jacques Derrida's Specters of Marx*, ed. Michael Sprinker (London: Verso, 1999), 248—249. Part of the problem, predictably enough, is that Jameson and Derrida, in spite of their mutual admiration, are here deploying quite different definitions of 'utopia' and 'utopian'. The latter has no sense of the former's ambitious attempt, throughout the last three or four decades, to restore not simply respectability but philosophical complexity, and political valence, to the term 'Utopian'.

② Although he isn't mentioned in this context, it seems plausible, given their relationship, which Derrida himself has commemorated, that Louis Althusser is also a spectral presence at this point. I am thinking in particular of his insistence, in *Reading Capital*, that 'the co-existence of the different structured levels, the economic, the political, the ideological etc. […] can no longer be thought in the co-existence of the Hegelian *present*, of the ideological present in which temporal presence coincides with the presence of the essence with its phenomena'. See Louis Althusser and Etienne Balibar, *Reading Capital*, trans. Ben Brewster (New York: Pantheon, 1970), 99. In contrast to Bloch, Derrida's discourse on the present in *Specters of Marx* doesn't press beyond the philosophical to the historical; it doesn't rise, as Marx might have phrased it, from the abstract to the concrete.

identical with itself because capitalist society contains residues of pre-capitalist economic and social forms; that is, for historical and material reasons. ①

But Bloch also insists that, for reasons that are no less historical and material, the present is non-contemporaneous with itself because it contains intimations of post-capitalist relations—in the shape of participatory forms of democratic association for example. His conviction, to appropriate Terry Eagleton's comments on Bloch's friend Georg Lukács, is that 'the outline of [a] desirable future can already be detected in certain potentialities stirring within the present'. 'The present is thus not identical with itself,' either for Bloch or Lukács: 'there is that within it which points beyond it, as indeed the shape of every historical present is structured by the anticipation of a possible future.' ② The future, like the past, shapes the present from the inside. Those elements of the present that are 'distant from and alien to the present', as Bloch puts it, are comprised not only of the '*unrefurbished past*' but of the '*prevented future*'. ③ This repressed utopian impulse, the prevented future, threatens to irrupt into the present. It is not simply a 'radical untimeliness', in Derrida's abstract sense, but a potentially revolutionary untimeliness, in some more concrete sense. ④

If Derrida overlooks the philosophical and political significance of the 'non-present present' for the Marxist tradition that he so carefully, self-consciously filters in *Specters of Marx* (6), he nonetheless offers a fertile metaphorical reconception of the idea. The book's epigraph is taken from Shakespeare's *Hamlet*: 'The time is out of joint'. For Hamlet himself, Derrida explains, 'time is *disarticulated*, dislocated, dislodged, time is run down, on the run and run down, deranged, both out of order and mad' (18). And the ghost of the protagonist's father, according to Derrida, is the figure generated by this disadjustment of time. In deconstructive terms, it is a supplement, which exposes a constitutive lack in that which hitherto seemed complete

---

① Ernst Bloch, *Heritage of Our Times*, trans. Neville and Stephen Plaice (Cambridge: Polity, 1991),108.
② Terry Eagleton, *Ideology: An Introduction* (London: Verso, 1991), 106.
③ Bloch, *Heritage of Our Times*, 108, 110.
④ On the dialectical relationship between what Bloch refers to as the 'unrefurbished past' and the 'prevented future', see Pierre Macherey's statement that, in affirming the spirit of Marx, a Marxist 'inherits from that which, in the past, remains yet to come, by taking part in a present which is not only present in the fleeting sense of actuality, but which undertakes to reestablish a dynamic connection between past and future'. See 'Marx Dematerialized, or the Spirit of Derrida', in *Ghostly Demarcations: A Symposium on Jacques Derrida's Specters of Marx*, ed. Michael Sprinker (London: Verso, 1999), 19.

and self-contained. So Derrida goes on to explore the disconcerting effect that old Hamlet's spectral presence has, in the opening scenes of the play, on Horatio, on Marcellus, and on his son. These scenes dramatize the disruptive impact the past has on the present, in part because it reveals that this present is always-already inadequate to itself. Derrida's interpretation of the armed apparition's gaze, which is uncanny in the precise Freudian sense, is especially suggestive:

> This Thing meanwhile looks at us and sees us not see it even when it is there. A spectral asymmetry interrupts here all specularity. It de-synchronizes it, recalls us to anachrony. We will call this the *visor effect*: we do not see who looks at us. (7)

This 'visor effect', which evokes a protective helmet into which 'slits are cut' so as to permit Hamlet's father 'to see without being seen' (8), is a brilliant conceptual innovation (Derrida, incidentally, derives the term 'visor' from Yves Bonnefoy, whose version of *Hamlet* translates Shakespeare's term 'beaver', which signifies the lower portion of the face-guard of a knight's helmet, as 'visière'; Derrida also, incidentally, slightly misreads *Hamlet*, since Shakespeare's ghost actually wears his beaver up, as Horatio testifies, and constantly fixes his eyes on those who encounter him). Disappointingly, Derrida immediately notes that he 'will probably not speak of this *visor effect* any more, at least not by that name' (7). But, in fact, he does refer to it again explicitly, on one occasion. The visor-effect, he adds there, is what makes us 'feel ourselves seen by a look which it will always be impossible to cross' (7). Hamlet's father's unhomelike look therefore concentrates the sense of uncanniness that is structural to 'the logic of the ghost', as Derrida will subsequently characterize it (63).①

---

① Note that Jameson domesticates and neutralizes the uncanny otherness that Derrida identifies with the concept of spectrality when he claims that 'all it says, if it can be thought to speak, is that the living present is scarcely as self-sufficient as it claims to be; that we would do well not to count on its density and solidity, which might under exceptional circumstances betray us'. Postmodernism, according to Jameson, provides these exceptional circumstances: 'Derrida's ghosts are those moments in which the present-and above all our current present, the wealthy, sunny, gleaming world of the postmodern and the end of history-unexpectedly betrays us' (see 'Marx's Purloined Letter', 39). For Derrida, in contrast, the living present implicitly betrays us under ordinary as opposed to exceptional circumstances: it is ontologically self-divided, so to speak; and it is for this reason that it is necessary to speak about it in the language of hauntology. In effect, my position mediates between those of Derrida and Jameson, since I presuppose that it is in the specific historical conditions of capitalism, which creates circumstances that are permanently both ordinary and exceptional, that the present is constitutively non-contemporaneous.

'This spectral *someone other looks at us*,' Derrida continues, italicizing his reference to the other in order to reinforce its uncanny associations; 'we feel ourselves being looked at by it, outside of any synchrony [⋯]' (7). Derrida doesn't mention Brecht in *Specters of Marx*, but the former's 'visor effect' irresistibly evokes the so-called 'alienation effect', that is, the *Verfremdungseffekt*, or 'V-effect', that is central to the latter's aesthetic. 'A representation that alienates is one which allows us to recognize its subject,' Brecht writes in his 'Short Organum for the Theatre' (1948), 'but at the same time makes it seem unfamiliar.'[①] Instantiated in the concealed gaze of old Hamlet's ghost, the 'visor-effect' is a V-effect because, like Brecht's celebrated device for distancing or alienating the spectator from the action on stage in epic theatre, which he compares to a 'detached eye', it effects a subtle transformation of its object, unsettling it, disadjusting it, rendering it unfamiliar. The past, in the form of the look embodied by this *revenant*, or half-embodied by it perhaps, thus interrupts the present; it 'diarticulates it, dislodges it, displaces it out of its natural lodging' (31). The future also interrupts the present and disjoints it, as Bloch and Lukács among others recognized. So my claim is that utopia too activates a visor-effect, a V-effect that uses a fantastical future to displace and upset the synchronicity of the present. It institutes a 'spectral asymmetry' that 'de-synchronizes' and 'recalls us to anachrony' (6—7).

Utopia is not a future that can be prophesied or predicted; it is a displacement of the present, a desynchronization of it. It reveals the incompleteness of the present and points to alternative presents, different futures, secreted in its interstices. In terms that can be appropriated from Jameson, it is 'a wandering signifier capable of keeping any number of conspiratorial futures alive'.[②] Utopia shadows the movements of history but never fully materializes. It is doomed to be no more than a becoming-body. It remains Not Yet, in Bloch's formulation.

[①] Bertolt Brecht, 'A Short Organum for the Theatre', in *Brecht on Theatre: The Development of an Aesthetic*, ed. and trans. John Willett (London: Methuen, 1974), 192.

[②] This is Jameson's final description, in his response to Derrida's *Specters*, of what he calls 'Marx's purloined letter' (see 'Marx's Purloined Letter', 65).

VII

So a fragment of the future materializes in the present, defamiliarizing it, and transforming it, in the fragmentary form of an unsettling or uncanny gaze the meaning of which cannot fully be comprehended. This is the spectre of utopia. Where is it to be located today? I'd like to propose in conclusion that, in contrast to the utopia identified by Zupancic, which is designed to eliminate what she calls, after Badiou, the excess, the spectre of utopia that I have invoked should be identified precisely with this spectre of excess. This is a utopia that, instead of conjuring away the spectre of excess, constitutes an uncanny concrete instance of it

In emblematic terms, this spectre of utopia that is the at the same time the spectre of excess, and which embodies the visor-effect I have described, can perhaps be identified in images of the masked faces of the protesters, rioters and strikers who have figured in the class struggles of the last few years. In such images, we confront both the presence and the otherness of what Bloch calls the prevented future. We confront both its blankness and its unsettling, hieroglyphic promise of a different social order. Here the protestor, or indeed the riot policeman, issues an enigmatic challenge. His or her masked or visored face ensures, when we encounter it, that we feel ourselves being looked at outside of any synchrony. It is as if we are being looked at from the future. The visored face is a sign without an immediate referent, for its meaning lies in the future, whether that future entails socialism or barbarism.

（本文责任编辑：安宁）

乌托邦的幽灵：马克思主义与未来

马修·博蒙特

【内容摘要】 这篇讲稿试图在辩证法的基础上探索曾经建构历史形态的乌托邦思想的可能性与可行性。有观点认为，有一个比喻使我们能最好地把乌托邦将现实与想象、存在与缺席之间本来毫不拖泥带水的认识论和本体论之间的区别搅乱的这样一种状态表达出来,那就是:乌托邦主义者的幽灵。此篇讲稿将指出乌托邦这个概念在哲学与政治上的隐晦之处,讨论在历史层面上这个幽灵是如何在欧洲与北美世界出没,并指出它在当今的时代诉求。

【作者简介】马修·博蒙特,任职于伦敦大学学院,致力于乌托邦问题的研究,著有《有限的乌托邦:1870—1900年间的英国社会空想理论》(*Utopia, Ltd.: Ideologies of Social Dreaming in England 1870—1900*)、《乌托邦的幽灵:世纪末的乌托邦与科幻小说》(*The Spectre of Utopia: Utopian and Science Fictions at the Fin de Siècle*) 等作品。

What Kind of Materialism is the 'New Materialism'? or, *The Cultural Logic of Neo-Liberal Capitalism*

Justin O'Connor

(Monash University, Melbourne, Australia; Shanghai Jiaotong University, Chian)

Abstract: This paper is an attempt to think through the 'turn to materialities' in Cultural Studies and its implications for a progressive politics. The paper will be a little provocative; not dismissing 'materialities' but suggesting that it has some ambiguities for cultural studies and, in certain aspects, some clear dangers.

This paper is an attempt to think through the 'turn to materialities' in Cultural Studies and its implications for a progressive politics. The paper will be a little provocative; not dismissing 'materialities' but suggesting that it has some ambiguities for cultural studies and, in certain aspects, some clear dangers.

At a recent Cultural Studies Association conference in Sydney the conference theme was advertised thus:

> Cultural studies has a long history of investigating material practices—indeed it was a founding tenet of British cultural studies—but recently a new turn or return to materialism seems to be emerging in the field. What this materiality now means is still open, but we suggest that it flags a renewed interest in questions of how to study cultural objects, institutions and practices (methods), what constitutes matter and materiality (empiricism), and how things (humans and non-humans) are being reworked at a time of global economic, environmental and cultural flux.

This seems to raise many questions.

First, 'material practices': I take to refer to Williams' 'whole way of life' and Hoggart's rooted working class communities. These material practices were signifying, they were cultural, they aimed to give meaning to, or express, or inform a particular 'form of life'—and one that had more than local consequences but were part of a 'national-popular'. That is, these 'material practices' were also cultural practices, and they were more or less situated in a broader historical narrative of change and the dangers and possibilities of that change.

Second, there has been 'recently a new turn or return to materialism'. The first observation is to ask where cultural studies has been in the interim—idealism? The second is to suggest that materialism and materiality are not the same things; and whatever this return is it seems highly unlikely that it marks some neo-classical return to cultural materialism of the Williams/ Hoggart variety.

Third, where does this materiality/ materialism/ material practices lead us:

1) a renewed interest in questions of how to study cultural objects, institutions and practices—again, what have we been doing in the last 30 years. However, this is classified as 'method' so perhaps we have been studying these, but using the wrong methods. It might be that these previous methods have not been materialist enough.

2) A renewed interest in what constitutes matter and materiality (empiricism). I don't recall Williams and Hoggart being particularly interested in 'what constitutes matter'. They were certainly critical—or at least Williams was—of 'dialectical materialism' in the metaphysical-Stalinist fashion. But one thing they were surely clear about was that empiricism was not materialism; indeed, one might say that whilst intensely engaged with contemporary culture in all its institutional and economic materiality they were not empiricist—which was a method they rejected not an account of matter but because it accepted the real as a given rather than trying to explain the process of its construction.

3) A renewed interest in 'how things (humans and non-humans) are being reworked at a time of global economic, environmental and cultural flux'. The reduction of human and non-human to 'things' capable of being 'reworked' is absolutely not something early cultural studies would subscribe to—unless as an effect of alienation. //// In any event, this is clearly not a renewed interest as this post/ more-than-human and matter-that-thinks is a very new set of concepts and, I would suggest, provides the real context for this whole question of materiality. //// Finally

the flux in question is less a moment of crisis and change but one of endless change. What Zizek calls 'mobilism'.

Let me go over some of these points in more detail.

What is does this new or renewed concern with materialism/ materiality mean? Are we witnessing a wholesale shift to empirical research; a turn away from theoretical work to engagement with data-collection, in-depth ethnographies, extended case studies? I do not think so.

Has it sparked a new kind of policy engagement, 'useful' social research? The questions would be: first, has this been driven by a renewed interest in material practices or an institutional/ economic pressure to conduct useful research with defined social and economic benefit. Second: if the latter is the case, is presenting this as a return to 'materiality' not ideology (in the old sense the word).

On perhaps this comes after a period of idealism, some corrective to an over-conceptual, over theoretical period. Or some ultra-radical critique which cannot accommodate the real world. I will come back to the question of idealism in a moment, though I don't think anyone knows anyone who claims to be an 'idealist' anymore. Perhaps more pertinent has been the de-constructivist, highly conceptual work of the 1990s, whose disengagement from 'the real' (note the scare quotes) is usually associated with postmodernism and indeed ivory tower cultural studies. So perhaps this is what we are returning from?

But alongside deconstructionism was the 'cultural turn' which, at the time, was deemed a moment of triumph for cultural studies, as well as the point where its disciplinary uniqueness was threatened—'we all do cultural studies now'. One of the things the cultural turn did—across many disciplines—was to loosen up the empirically given. Social constructivism suggested that this empirical given was a complex socio-cultural creation. However, it would be surely incorrect to see materiality as some sort of corrective here. Social constructivism introduced many elements that have come to be associated with materialities: the material weight of technologies and institutions but also the performative function of language—not only describing the world but acting to bring people and things into particular configurations. So materialities was already there in the hey day of the cultural turn.

So, it seems to me that 'materialities' is being used in a very particular way—

even though it is covered in claims about pragmatism, empirical studies etc. I would suggest we have a crisis of signification—of the real limits to discursive communication (argument, deliberation, even ideology) and of the ability to assign significance, meaning to the world. **Finally, the unavailability of any historical project of transformation of the sort early cultural studies set out to investigate.**

Let me justify this by looking at three elements of 'materialities'.

First, empiricism. This is increasingly being used in a philosophical rather than a social scientific or methodological sense (as indicated in the conference blurb). On the one hand it is a rejection of sociological accounts of causality and of meaning. This is exemplified by actor-network theory as elaborated by Bruno Latour. It can be (badly) summarized as the claim that the social does not exist, it is merely a term that emerges from the complex interaction of people and things in specific configurations. Latour rejects Durkheim and Marx and Weber (in favour of Hyppolyte Taine): social explanations elaborate a 'context' which inhibit our ability to actually see what is going on, and identify who is actually carrying out the work sociologists ascribe to social causality.

A second element of empiricism is its return to a pre-Kantian empiricism. Delueze is highly influential here in his adaption of Spinoza's monism into a new vitalism (on which more below); it can be found in crass form in Manuel De Landa's *A New Philosophy of Society: Assemblage Theory and Social Complexity*. In it he devotes a chapter to rehabilitating David Hume, via Delueze. There are only individual entities which interact externally; there is no totality within which an entity finds its place; rather a series of potentialities which are assembled.

He reads Braudel's account of capitalism in this light. Capitalism is built up block by block from local markets, to the regional, the national and the international—it has no inherent logic but is the outcome of these small markets expanding into a complex assemblage. The result to my mind is an appalling piece of simplistic narrative which undoes decades of serious historical work.

Nevertheless, whatever one thinks of it this new empiricism is not a materialism as understood in any philosophy or social science since Kant. Which can be good or bad but needs to be confronted.

A second area is the notion of bodies subject to 'affect': I think this has had profound consequences for cultural studies in the last few years. Affect is a preconscious hard-wired response to the world. The body is the site of 'meaning' that runs through the brain as a neural-circuitry but not through consciousness. We are in a world of 'intensities' which operate before and outside consciousness. This is our true 'being in the world' which we misrepresent as intentionality (Hume). As Ruth Leys has shown, this leads in two directions though the assumptions are the same (and, I would say the consequences). The shift to the neuro-biological across the social sciences which is going on apace (neuro-aethetics). On the other hand we have a Deleuzian radicalism—exemplified by Brian Massumi: because there is a radical bifurcation (emotions are pale, tamed echoes of affect) we can expect change from affect whereas emotions are already corralled by consciousness. This is clearly based on Deleuze and Guatarri's 'nomad thought' operating outside 'civilisation' or 'state philosophy' or 'representational thinking' or 'the logos'. The prevalence of 'affect' over 'emotions', intensity over meaning, of bodies over minds has become de rigour in cultural studies—but what kind of cultural politics does it put into play?

Third the notion of matter and mass itself has come under great scrutiny. In part it comes from the recognition of the role of things and technologies in actor-network theory. It comes from research into interspecies communications and of course neurobiology which locates us firmly with the animals and with the matter out of which our bodies are constructed and with which we constantly interact. The permeability of the body and its connections with animals is at one with the collapse of the solid I, the identical subject, the subject of the logos. Post-human, more than human. If the subject becomes more like a thing-in-the-world then why can't thing aspire to thought?

Writing on the latest Documenta 13 Julian Stallabrass:

> Christov-Bakargiev is led to ask, not just what she wanted or what the rock's custodians—the indigenous Moqoit people in Argentina—wanted, but what it wanted:
> It had travelled through vertiginous space before landing on Earth and settling. Would it have wished to go on this further journey? Does it have any rights, and if so, how can they be exercised? Can it ask to be buried again, as some of the Moqoit argue, or would it have enjoyed a short trip to an art exhibition, rather than a science or world's fair?

Thinking of this type is used to prop up a series of gestures towards radical positions: environmental, activist, participatory, anti-war, minority. In all this, it is paramount that there be no 'closure', no settling and no agreement: rather a dissonant dance of beings and objects in which all perspectives are acknowledged in an 'anti-logocentric' frame.

The last paragraph indicates what Stallabrass thinks of much of this. Let me say that I am not dismissing the body of this research. Working in cultural economy (both senses) I welcome the attention to detail, the recognition of the performative work of language and the interaction of people and things, institutions, practices, and technologies. Much of this work is debt to actor-network theory, as it is to some detailed, conceptually inform historical work on things such as the electricity industry, stock exchanges, shopping trolleys—all those thing we once thought we knew were about 'technology', 'capitalism' and 'consumerism'.

But there are more ambiguous aspects. My sub-title is a reference Frederick Jameson's 1984 *Postmodernism: or, the cultural logic of late capitalism*. He pointed to a moment when 'the cultural' had been annexed by the 'economic'. This was clearly not a bemoaning of culture being reduced to the 'material' in Adorno's sense (at least not in the cultural studies version of Adorno⋯.); it suggested a closing of historical horizons, a permanent 'now' in which the critical stance associated with culture was no longer available. This was exemplified for Jameson in a series of postmodern texts characterized by flatness, pastiche, affectlessness (in the older sense); but equally certain texts responded to the 'all space and no time' element of global capitalism—Michael Herr's choppers that moved around the space of Vietnam in *Dispatches*, for example

For a contemporary image we might think about Facebook and Google through the eyes of *The Matrix*. Here we are talking to our friends, posting our baby photos, telling everyone what we have read. Underneath huge data-milking machines take our preferences and likes, our contacts and purchases and construct powerful data streams generating revenue, excess 'big data' and feed back into the Facebook 'liking machines' to complete the circuit.

It seems to me something similar is going on in the following:

> Although humanized intentionality, as expressed through negotiation and advocacy,

also appears and reappears and disseminates throughout the social fabric, it does not characterize the system as a whole. Like life itself, human intentionality has become an internal variable of capitalist power.... Mediation-based strategies, whether of reform or of dialectical struggle, are now bit players on the global scene of power ...
If the human disappears and reappears locally and primarily affectively, globally it is relegated to the status of a reflex machinic relay. For example, instant opinion polling elicits human reflex responses that are relayed via the autonomic apparatus of the mass media to other apparatuses, where they legitimate or enable certain autonomic operations. In such autonomic surroundings, it is vain to mourn the passing of moral reasoning and philosophies of right. Our social existence is affective and reflexive, and it serves little purpose to deny it (Massumi, 'Requiem for Our Prospective Dead [Toward a Participatory Critique of Capitalist Power],' in Deleuze and Guattari: New Mappings in Politics, Philosophy, and Culture, ed. Eleanor Kauffman and Kevin John Heller [Minneapolis, 1998], p. 58)

Affect—the transhuman, the inhuman—is now directly related to the lines of force produced by capitalism—but, though there are echoes of Hardt and Negri in the above there can be no intentional response, or at least such is minimal, secondary. As Nigel Thrift puts it: 'individuals are generally understood as effects of the events to which their body parts (broadly understood) respond and in which they participate'.

As Eric Shuse says: 'Affect is not a personal feeling. Feelings are personal and biographical, emotions are social, ... and affects are pre-personal.... An affect is a nonconscious experience of intensity; it is a moment of unformed and unstructured potential.... Affect cannot be fully realised in language ... because affect is always prior to and/or outside consciousness.... Affect is the body's way of preparing itself for action in a given circumstance by adding a quantitative dimension of intensity to the quality of an experience. The body has a grammar of its own that cannot be fully captured in language'.

This is much more than the return to 'material practices' of British Cultural Studies. It is a materialism radically distinct from that of the historical materialism that informed this project. I might also add that it is certainly not a manifesto for doing 'cultural policy studies' or other useful forms of research.

What is this materialism in an age when, as Jameson wrote recently, everybody is materialist? At the end of the 1980s, what Althusser called, the three bastards of the

19th century—Marx, Freud, and Nietzsche—came under sustained attack. The first two were traditionally known as 'materialists'; only Nietzsche, who was never described thus, survived this turn to materiality. Perhaps because only he believed that the subject was an illusion based on a vitalist pre-conscious will-to-power.

The question is what kind of cultural politics does it put into play. In Deleuze and Guatarri the nomadism of affect is presumed to carry the weight of a radical politics—Larry Grossberg's repeated statement that nobody is going to die for fluxity says a lot about this.

I suggest that we have here a vitiation of the concept of culture as it operated in cultural studies (and not just that of course), a radical disinvestment from the idea that a project of culture can realistically aim to shape life—ones self and ones communities. That this new materialities claims to be a monism but frequently works its own mind/body distinction such that the two remain separated. The work of Merleau-Ponty—much revived these days-indicates how the body and meaning are not exclusive to one another—where sens (meaning) and sens (path, direction) go together.

When they set up Les Temps Moderns in 1945 Merleau-Ponty and Sartre set out to be 'hunters after meaning' in a new, uncertain world. Their optimism was that meaning could be found in a world that radically challenged it at all points. It was an act of courage. Cultural studies is set for its own bi-furcation between the pragmatics of 'cultural research' which increasingly abandons the critical moment of the negation; and the false radicalism of a vitalism which looks for change in those aspects of our lives which least respond to our sense of meaning. That change is an historical-biological flux which refuses all connection with a telos or intentionality, and cannot be captured in language so is outside of any possible tradition. With no past and no future there is no culture.

（本文责任编辑：贾洁）

"新唯物主义"抑或新自由主义资本主义的文化逻辑?

贾斯汀·奥康诺

(澳大利亚莫纳什大学、上海交通大学)

【内容摘要】 本文试图深入思考文化研究中的"物质性转向"及其对于进步政治而言所蕴藉的内涵。本文提出的具有讨论价值的观点是,"物质性"这个概念在文化研究中有些意义不明,甚至在某些方面对文化研究构成危险。值得注意的是本观点的提出并非要摒弃"物质性"。

【作者简介】 贾斯汀·奥康诺(Justin O'Connor),创意产业(Creative Industries)的首位提出者,多年来致力于文化和创意产业的研究与推广。现任澳大利亚莫纳什大学文化经济学教授,上海交通大学人文学院访问讲席教授。

Marx's Concepts of Future Society and Models of Socialism for the 21st Century

Jeong Seongjin

(Institute for Social Sciences at Gyeongsang National University in South Korea)

Introduction Since the explosion of the global economic crisis of 2007—2009, the ideology of 'TINA' (There is no alternative to market economy or capitalist globalization), which has dominated the world since the collapse of Soviet and Eastern bloc, has been totally discredited, and now seems to be a thing of the past. As the unemployment, poverty, polarization, ecological crisis exacerbate with the deepening crisis of global capitalism, anti-capitalist sentiments and movements are reviving all over the world, as was recently seen in Occupy movements. However, the experiences of the crumbling of Soviet and Eastern bloc, combined with the lack of confidence on whether we can get a better society than capitalism after we get rid of it, are deterring people from anti-capitalist socialist politics and stopping them at various kinds of reformism, such as left-Keynesianism, Autonomism etc. [1]

Therefore, establishing the case for socialism, in terms of its superiority compared to capitalism as well as its feasibility in the changing condition of the 21st century, not just in terms of its necessity, considering the disastrous reality of today's capitalism, is becoming a urgent task for the radical left, far from a futile utopian socialist mongering. Before proceeding this project, it is necessary to confirm that the crumbling

---

[1] According to R. Hahnel, *Economic Justice and Democracy: From Competition to Cooperation*, Routledge, 2005, pp. 168—169, after the demise of the Soviet and Eastern Europe bloc, alternatives to the capitalism sought by the left can be classified as following three types: market socialism, community-based economics, and democratic or participatory planning.

of Soviet and Eastern bloc shows just a failure of special kind of planning, that is, 'administrative command economy' (Gregory, 2004). It cannot be taken as a proof of the infeasibility of Marxian socialism in the original meaning of Marx. Of course, we need to make it clear what is meant by Marxian socialism, and establish the feasibility of Marxian socialism, considering the changing conditions of the 21st century, especially, globalization and information technology (IT) revolution. Repeating the slogan of 'imminent breakdown of capitalism' or limiting ourselves to 'movementism' ('struggle is everything, final goal is nothing'), would be insufficient to attract the intelligent mass of the 21st century towards anti-capitalist socialist politics.

In this paper, I will explain Marx's concept of socialism, focusing on his *Critique of the Gotha Programme*, and discuss the recent works on participatory planning which have been proposed as models for Marxian socialism in the 21st century. This paper will compare three recent models of participatory planning and discuss their merits and demerits: 'parecon' [1] model of Michael Albert and Robin Hahnelp; 'negotiated coordination' model of Pat Devine and Fikret Adaman; 'labor-time calculation' model of W. Paul Cockshott and Allin Cottrell.

Marxian Concept of Socialism
Marxian Concept of Planning

The essence of Marx's concept of communism can best be summarized as '*association of free individuals*', as is illustrated in his mature work, *Capital*, Volume One: 'Let us now picture to ourselves, by way of change, an *association of free individuals*, carrying on their work with the means of production in common, in which the labor power of all the different individuals is consciously applied as the combined labor power of the community' [2].

As is clear from above quotation, Marx's concept of 'association of free individuals' is composed of three core elements, 'free,' 'individuals,' and

---

[1] Parecon is the abbreviated word of 'particpatory economy'. Recently R. Hahnel. *Economic Justice and Democracy: From Competition to Cooperation*, Routledge, 2005, renamed their model as equitable cooperation model.

[2] K. Marx. *Capital*, Vol. 1, Vintage Books, 1981, p. 171, my emphasis.

'association', which are coordinated by 'conscious' application of 'the combined labor power of the community', in other words, 'participatory planning'. According to Marx, 'association of free individuals' is impossible in market economy, and feasible only by 'participatory planning', as following quote from *Capital* Volume Three shows: 'Freedom in this field can only consist in socialized man, the *associated producers*, *rationally regulating* their interchanges with Nature, bringing it under their common control, instead of being ruled by it as by the blind forces of Nature; and achieving this with the least expenditure of energy and under conditions most favorable to, and worthy of, their human nature.'[①]

Marx meant planning as democratic participatory economy where the economic life of human being, including production, distribution, and consumption, etc., is controlled by human being's own autonomous will, not by any kind of external forces, such as market or state. In *Capital*, Marx specified the meaning of planning in contrast to capitalist market economy as follows.[②] While, in the capitalist market economy, 'the interconnection of production as a whole... forces itself on the agents of production as a blind law', and 'the process of production has mastery over man, instead of the opposite', in the planned socialism, it is 'grasped and therefore mastered by their combined reason', and 'brings the productive process under their common control'. In Marxian planning, direct producers themselves become the planners of the economy. As Ticktin said, Marxian socialism can be defined by 'the degree to which the society is planned. Planning here is understood as the conscious regulation of society by the associated producers themselves'.

In short, Marxian socialism is 'socialism from below' and 'the self-emancipation of working class,' the essential economic component of which is the participatory planning by 'freely associated producers.' In this respect, so-called 'actually existing socialism,' including former Soviet Union, has nothing common with Marxian socialism.

---

① K. Marx. *Capital*, Vol. 3, Vintage Books, 1981, p. 959, my emphasis.
② On recent discussion of Marxian concept of socialism, refer to Teinosuke Otani, *Marx on Association*, Sakuraishoten, 2011, (In Japanese), P. Hudis, *Marx's Concept of the Alternative to Capitalism*, Brill. 2012, and A. Campbell, ed. Designing Socialism: Vision, Projections, Models, *Science and Society*, Vol. 76, No. 2. 2012, Special Issue.

Rereading *Critique of the Gotha Programme*

Marx's *Critique of the Gotha Programme* should be the starting point for the project of designing socialism for the 21st century. Dunayevskaya regarded it as the 'New Ground for Organization,' and urged all the Marxist organizations to adopt it as the basis of their actual politics. However, most socialist organizations tend to regard Marx's *Critique of the Gotha Programme* as the description of 'kingdom of freedom' of far distant future, ('from each according to his ability, to each according to his needs'), and assume that it has no direct relevance to day-to-day strategies and tactics for the struggle for socialism. However, the picture of communist society delineated in Marx's *Critique of the Gotha Programme*—especially, the transparent society where all the categories of commodities and money and all the products are basically distributed according to labor-time, etc. —is worth careful rereading for the project of socialism for the 21st century. 'Within the cooperative society based on common ownership of the means of production the producers do not exchange their products; similarly, the labor spent on the products no longer appears as *the value* of these products, possessed by them as a material characteristic, for now, in contrast to capitalist society, individual pieces of labor are no longer merely indirectly, but directly, a component part of the total labor. The phrase "proceeds of labor" (Arbietsertrag), which even today is too ambiguous to be of any value, thus loses any meaning whatsoever. We are dealing here with a communist society, not as it has *developed* on its own foundations, but on the contrary, just as it *emerges* from capitalist society. In every respect, economically, morally, intellectually, it is thus still stamped with the birth-marks of the old society from whose womb it has emerged. Accordingly, the individual producer gets back from society—after the deductions— exactly what he has given it. What he has given it is his individual quantum of labor. For instance, the social working day consists of the sum of the individual hours of work. The individual labor-time of the individual producer thus constitutes his contribution to the social working day, his share of it. Society gives him a certificate stating that he has done such and such an amount of work (after the labor done for the communal fund has been deducted), and with this certificate he can withdraw from the social supply of means of consumption as much as costs an equivalent amount of labor. The same amount of labor he has given to society in one form, he receives back in another'[①]

In above paragraphs of *Critique of the Gotha Programme*, Marx clearly states that labor appears directly, while categories of commodity, money and value disappears, and labor products are distributed according to labor-time, even in the first phase of communism. But, in *State and Revolution*, Lenin equated socialism with 'first phase of communism,' or with the transition period from capitalism to communism, sometimes even with the state ownership of means of production. Problem is that Lenin's formulation provides the room for separating socialism from communism, thereby leading to Stalinist theory of 'socialist mode of production,' which asserts that the categories of commodity, money, market and value will exist in the socialism as the transition period from capitalism to communism. Moreover, Stalinist theory of 'socialist mode of production' makes the specific feature of Marx's first phase of communism—coordination of economy in terms of labor-time—invisible, and postpones any programmatic concept of achieving the first phase of communism to a distant task, justifying the long-term coexistence of the market with socialism. Indeed, despite the apparent opposition between Stalinism and market socialism, they are simply the two obverse sides of the same coin. However, in *Critique of Gotha Programme*, Marx clearly states that the planning in terms of labor-time in the first phase of communism should be the urgent programmatic task of German Social Democratic Party rather than a goal of distant future. What differentiates the first phase of communism from its developed phase is that the former still needs the coordination of the economy by labor-time due to still existing scarcity, rather than that it can only be achieved in the latter.

Therefore, it lacks textual evidence for Nishibe or Karatani to interpret Marx's thesis of labor certificate in *Critique of the Gotha Programme* as the renunciation of his early critique of Proudhon's or Gray's theory of labor money, or try to discover in it the origin of 'local exchange trading system' (LETS) or 'new association

---

[①] K. Marx, *Collected Works*, Vol. 24, Progress Publishers, 1989, pp. 85—86.

movement' (*NAM*). ① It is also incorrect to read Marx's thesis of labor certificate in *Critique of the Gotha Programme* as the thesis of distribution according to the performance of labor, rather than the thesis of distribution in terms of labor-time. ②

Indeed, the idea that labor-time replaces value as the economic coordinator even in the first phase of communism, which is fully developed in *Critique of the Gotha Programme*, is constantly and consistently recurring theme of Marx, as can be evidenced in various pages of *Grundrisse*, *Theories of Surplus Value*, and *Capital*. For example, following paragraph of *Grundrisse* is lucid enough. 'If we presuppose communal production, the time factor naturally remains essential … Ultimately, all economy is a matter of economy of time … Economy of time, as well as the planned distribution of labor-time over the various branches of production, therefore, remains the first economic law if communal production is taken as the basis'.

Common Features of Models of Participatory Planning

During the recent revival of the debate on the models of post-capitalist society,

---

① The heart of Marx's criticisms of the thesis of labor money, expounded especially in *Poverty of Philosophy* and *Grundrisse*, is debunking the fantasy of the 19th century market socialists, like, Proudhon and Gray, who imagined that the capitalist exploitation could be abolished by the realization of the equal exchange through the introduction of labor money without abolishing the commodity economy itself. For more discussion of Marx's critique of Proudhon, refer to McNally. Therefore, Marx's critique of the thesis of labor money does not run counter to his project of communism based on labor certificate as is proposed in *Critique of the Gotha Programme*. In other words, 'What Marx and Engels are rejecting is the notion of fixing prices according to actual labor content *in the context of a commodity producing economy* where production is private. In an economy where the means of production are under communal control, on the other hand, labor *does* become "directly social," in the sense that it is subordinated to a pre-established central plan. Here the calculation of the labor content of goods is an important element in the planning process' (W. Cockshott and A. Cottrell, 'Reflections on Economic Democracy', *Research in Political Economy*, Vol. 22, 2005, p. 254. Emphasis in original).

② It is true that Marx admits the 'differential distribution according to differential quality of labor' in *Critique of the Gotha Programme*. However, it is not same as the 'distribution according to the performance of labor.' Differential performance of labor has more to do with the differential labor productivity owing to differential objective conditions of labor, such as production equipment and technology, which workers have no control of, rather than with the 'differential quality of labor,' such as skill and intensity of labor, which workers do have some control of. It is unbelievable that Marx regarded the differential performance of labor due to differential objective conditions of labor as the distribution principle even in the first phase of communism. Indeed, Marx himself explicitly writes in *Critique of the Gotha Programme* that 'the phrase "proceeds of labor" (Arbietsertrag. Roughly the same meaning of "performance of labor"—My emphasis and comments), which even today is too ambiguous to be of any value, thus loses any meaning whatsoever,' because the individual labor no longer directly appears as the value of the products, but as a component part of the total labor in an indirect way. In other words, Marx argues that the 'distribution according to the performance of labor,' or, 'proceeds of labor,' becomes obsolete even in the first phase of communism.

following three models for participatory planning stand out: Albert and Hahnel's parecon; Devine and Adaman's 'negotiated coordination'; Cockshott and Cottrell's 'labor-time calculation' model. Despite the differences and disputes among themselves, ① they are in concert to reject all forms of market economy, including the market socialism, and in pursuing the participatory planned society based on direct democracy.

Theorists of participatory planning are very critical of market socialism. For example, Adaman and Devine classifies Oscar Lange, who is usually regarded as the father of theory of market socialism and believed to prove the possibility of economic calculation in socialism against the critique of Hayek, as just 'neoclassical socialism', in that he embraces neoclassical economic theory of general equilibrium and fails to recognize the importance of 'tacit' knowledge, role of uncertainty and democratic participation. ② Devine also argues that 'market socialism, interpreted as a system in which efficiency is sought through decentralization of economic decision-making to more or less fully independent enterprises, is a blind alley. It ignores the characteristic feature of the modern world—interdependence'. The weakest point of market socialism is its internal contradiction of its constituent parts. For example, the workers self-management and market mechanism, the two principles of market socialism, cannot co-exist in the long term. ③ If market mechanism is allowed to operate even within the framework of workers' self-management, it is only a matter of time for workers to give up self-management and elect or hire professional managers for the survival of their

---

① For example, Adaman and Devine argue that only their model qualifies as a participatory planning model, while parecon or Cockshott and Cottrell's model should be classified as a 'direct calculation' model (F. Adaman and P. Devine, 'On the Economic Theory of Socialism', *New Left Review*, No. 221, 1997, p. 78).

② For reviews of the socialist calculation debate in the 1930s by the theorists of participatory planning, refer to Adaman and Devine ('On the Economic Theory of Socialism', *New Left Review*, No. 221, 1997) and W. Cockshott and A. Cottrell, *Towards a New Socialism*, Spokesman, 1993).

③ While Nove (1983) or Schweickart (2002) tries to prove the feasibility of market socialism, those who tried to apply the market socialist model to actual economies, like Brus or Kornai had admitted the impracticability of market socialism long before. (W. Brus, and K. Laski, *From Marx to the Market*, Clarendon Press, 1989, p. 149) once tried to apply the market socialist model in its true sense of the word by allowing even the capital market, besides product and labor markets, retaining only the state property of the means of production, only to face the hard fact that the conditions necessary for the model to function necessitated the replication of capitalism and rendered the state property itself redundant. Indeed, 'the pure logic of the fully fledged market mechanism seems to indicate the non-state (private) enterprise as the more natural constituent of the enterprise sector'.

firms in the competitive struggle necessitated by the market mechanism. 'Market socialism by itself reinforces and extends the power of enterprise management, at the expense of ordinary workers'. The experiences of Yugoslavia evidence that the market socialist project of workers' self-management within the environment of market is unworkable in reality, and inescapably leads to full-fledged market capitalism. As Konings indicates, the regulation of social interaction by markets will set market socialism 'on a slippery slope of marketization. ... If it is assumed that human interactions need to be regulated by markets as the exclusive alternative to hierarchic planning, an inexorable logic of marketization is encountered.' Indeed, for many market socialists, the importance of self-organization of grass roots producers, such as workers' self-management or labor unions, are only the hindrances to the economic reform. Considering this, it is not surprising that all the actually existing market socialist societies were nothing else than new class societies, ruled by so-called 'coordinator class.'

Another feature shared by recent formulations of participatory planning is their common emphasis on the importance of mass participation and the role of direct democracy. Some theorists, for example Cockshott and Cottrell even advocate lottery, that is, far beyond the experiences of radical form of representative democracy in Paris Commune of 1871 or soviets of 1917, where officials are elected and recalled by the people with their remuneration limited by the levels of workers' wages.

Parecon

In parecon, all workplaces are owned by workers' council. Parecon economy is coordinated from below by the participation of workers' council and consumers' council.

Parecon introduces the principle of balanced job complex (BJC) which balances the empowering jobs and disempowering jobs for every workers within and across the workplaces in order to abolish the social division of labor. Contrary to common criticisms, parecon does not mean that everybody does everything. In parecon, 'Each person will still perform a very small number of tasks in his/her BJC. Some will still specialize in brain surgery, others in electronical engineering, others in high voltage welding, and so on. But those who perform these specialized tasks if they are more empowering than average tasks will also perform some less empowering tasks as well, and if they are more desirable than average, will also perform some less desirable tasks—unless they wish to work more hours or accept a lower effort rating'. Contrary to the conventional wisdom, the introduction of BJC would not hurt the specialization and efficiency. Because, 'while efficiency requires an important role for experts in determining complicated consequences, efficiency also requires that those who will be affected determine which consequences they prefer'.

Albert and Hahnel think that the mass participation and equity can only be guaranteed by the abolition of social division of labor through the introduction of BJC. If only a few monopolize empowering jobs, and the rest of the members of society do only tedious and repetitive jobs, the former group eventually dominate and dictate the latter group, even if the society has perfect formal democratic decision making procedures. In this respect, the introduction of BJC is essential for avoiding the emergence of so-called coordinator class which monopolize the empowering jobs.

As to the income distribution, while capitalism rewards both the property and the contribution to production, market socialism rewards only the contribution to production, because it is assumed to abolish the private ownership of means of production. On the contrary, parecon rewards neither the property nor the contribution to production, on the ground that workers have no or little control of them. Parecon rewards only the effort for which workers are responsible. If we are rewarded or punished for which we have no control of, it is against the principle of justice. But, in market socialism, peoples are remunerated according to their contribution to production, in other words, their 'performance of labor,' which are in large part independent of peoples' own efforts, because it is closely related with differential talent or production facilities of which people have no control. Therefore, if the distribution according to property in capitalism violates the principle of justice, distribution according to the performance of labor in market socialism does no less so. Rewarding only the efforts, as in parecon, fits with the principle of justice.

Moreover, only if workers are rewarded according to the efforts of which they have control, they would be motivated to work hard and the performance would be enhanced too. In parecon, effort levels of each worker, which provide the basis of his or her income, are rated by 'effort rating committee' composed of peer workers. Therefore, the common criticism that, without performance based payment, parecon will soon face the lack of motivation to work or deterioration of performance is groundless.

The macroeconomic coordination of parecon is accomplished through the specific participatory planning mechanism. First, Iteration Facilitation Board (IFB), a sort of central planning board, announces the estimated opportunity costs, or indicative prices, of all the goods, resources, labor, and capital stock, etc. Based on the announced indicative prices, consumer councils submit their consumption plans, and workers councils submit their production plans and required inputs. The consumption plans submitted by the consumers councils should, of course, be substantiated by their respective effort ratings. In other words, any member of consumers councils with more than average effort rating can submit more than average consumption plan. On the other hand, workers councils are required to show that the social benefits of their production plans are above their social costs, when they submit their production plans to the IFB. Of course, social costs and benefits are also compared in capitalist market economy, but they are seldom done correctly, due to market failure, like public goods, external effects etc.① Contrary to capitalism, social costs and benefits can be correctly calculated and compared in parecon, thanks to the participation of all the workers and consumers affected by them.② After comparing the production plans and consumption plans submitted by workers and consumers councils, IFS determines the degrees of excess demand or excess supply by every product, and re-announce their new indicative prices: increase the indicative prices of the products with excess demands, and reduces those with excess supplies. Now, based on the revised indicative prices,

---

① 'Markets are biased against provision of goods with greater than average positive external effects and biased in favor of goods with greater than average negative external effects. But what is not readily admitted is that external effects are the *rule*, not the exception, because this implies that market prices generally *mis*estimate social benefits and costs, and that markets generally *mis*allocate resources' (M. Albert and R. Hahnel, 'Participatory Planning', *Science and Society*, Spring, Vol. 56, No. 1, 1992, p. 42. Emphasis in original). In other words, 'Markets bias consumer choice by overcharging for goods whose production or consumption entails positive external effects, undercharging for goods with negative external effects, and by oversupplying private goods relative to public goods'(R. Hahnel, 'In Defense of Democratic Planning', 2000, p. 331).

② However, D. M. Kotz ('Socialism and Innovation', *Science and Society*. Vol. 66, No. 1, 2002, p. 115) qualifies that the social costs and benefits cannot be calculated or compared as a 'scalar,' as is asserted by parecon model. He argues that the social costs and benefits, as the qualitative and multi-dimensional entities, can better be determined through the discussion and negotiation by all the stakeholders affected, like in Devine's 'negotiated coordination.'

consumers and workers councils adjust their consumption and production plans and submit them again to IFS. These processes are repeated several times until the production and consumption plans matches with each other, and excess demands and supplies diminishes reasonably, and at that point, after referendum, if necessary, production and consumption are executed actually. Of course, most procedures of the participatory planning in parecon are electronically done through Internet and computer.

Negotiated Coordination

In 'negotiated coordination' model of Devine and Adaman, companies are socially owned by those affected by their activities. "Social ownership is neither private ownership nor state ownership, but rather ownership by those who are affected by the use of the assets involved". The owners would include the companies' workers, other companies in the same industry, major suppliers and users, the local communities where the company is based, and interested NGOs, like environmentalists and equal opportunity groups, etc. The social owners are represented on the Board of Directors of the company.

The abolition of the social division of labor is as much crucial to 'negotiated coordination' model as to parecon model. In 'negotiated coordination' model, all social activities are classified as following five categories: ①planning and running, ② creative, ③nurturing, ④skilled, ⑤unskilled and repetitive. According to Devine, 'Abolition of the social division of labor means ending the social stratification that arises when people spend their lives performing primarily just one category of activity'. ① The reason why the abolition of the social division of labor is essential is that people who spend all their time being told what to do, rather than learning how to decide what to do for themselves, develop subaltern consciousness, and 'people with partial subaltern consciousness cannot take an overall view and share the responsibility

---

① However, according to P. Devine, 'Participatory Planning Through Negotiated Coordination,' *Science and Society*. Vol. 66, No. 1, 2002, p. 73, the abolition of the social division of labor 'does not mean ending the functional division of labor.' Moreover, Devine's idea of abolition of the social division of labor is less radical, in comparison with parecon's BJC, in that it assumes the process over a lifetime course, rather than over a short term horizon.

of running things'. In this respect, socialism is 'the social transformation that is needed if people are to gain control over their lives.' In other words, 'Socialism should be reconceptualized as a society in which the social division of labor has been abolished'.

Devine distinguishes 'market exchange' from 'market forces.' According to Devine(1992: 79—80), 'Market exchange involves transactions between buyers and sellers, where what is being exchanged consists of either stocks (inventories) or goods and services produced by enterprises using their existing capacity. Market forces refer to the process whereby changes are brought about in the underlying allocation of resources, the relative size of different industries, the geographical distribution of economic activity, through the interaction of decisions on investment and disinvestment that are taken independently of one another, with coordination occurring *ex post*'. In other words, market exchanges become uncontrollable and unpredictable market forces once market coordination is extended to investment decision. Devine argues that, in his model, 'market forces,' which is intrinsic to capitalism with its permanent drive for accumulation dictated by cut-throat competitive struggles, is extinct and replaced by 'negotiated coordination.' According to Devine, not only market exchange but also market forces operate in market socialism model. However, in negotiated coordination model, while market forces are disabled, market exchange still exists and operates in the realm of production using existing capacities. But the changes in capacities, that is, new investment or disinvestment, are executed through negotiated coordination not by market exchange. In other words, all the new (or dis) investments are adjusted by *ex ante* negotiation by all the groups affected. However, 'negotiated coordination' covers only some part of the whole economic activities, especially new (or dis) investment. So, the common criticism of 'negotiated coordination' model that it would degenerate into a 'monstrous apparatus of unlimited interferences and endless deliberation' is groundless.

'Negotiated coordination' model emphasizes the importance of negotiation through the participation of all the groups affected by the activities of the companies. Devine argues that the reason why the economic activity must be based on the active participation of the direct producers in decision on what and how to produce is that 'knowledge can only be drawn upon, made use of, by those who have acquired and possess it. ' In other words, 'local' and 'tacit' nature of knowledge necessitates the 'negotiated coordination' based on the participation of all the social owners. Participatory negotiated coordination is 'a process through which tacit knowledge is socially mobilized'.

'Negotiated coordination' model emphasizes very much the qualitative aspect of the information, or the 'local' and 'tacit' nature of the knowledge, unlike parecon or 'labor-time calculation' model. For example, when the decision on new (or dis) investment should be made, the qualitative information such as how the workers or local community would be affected by it is brought on the table of 'negotiated coordination.' According to Adaman and Devine, 'negotiated coordination' process is 'deliberative democratic process' in which all the participants discuss with each other, rather than the automatic aggregation process of existing preferences by parecon's IFB or Cockshott and Cottrell's supercomputer. ① Devine emphasizes that 'negotiated coordination' is the transformative process by which the cognitions and preferences of the participants could be changed.

In 'negotiated coordination' model, prices are set by the company at the social average cost of production, which includes the cost of primary inputs, such as labor, capital, and natural resources, and various intermediate inputs. The price should include the capital costs or expected average returns to capital, calculated at the level of whole economy, besides primary and intermediate input costs. ② Therefore, it can be said that in 'negotiated coordination' model, companies are 'price makers,' On the contrary, in parecon or 'labor-time calculation' model of Cockshott and Cottrell, companies are 'price takers' who should accept the prices determined by the iterative

---

① P. Devine('Book Review: Economic Justice and Democracy,' *Science and Society*, Vol. 71, No. 2, 2007, p. 258) criticizes parecon or 'labor-time calculation' model, in that they do not 'address the impossibility of codifying and transmitting tacit knowledge: knowledge acquired through action and experience, which can not be transmitted electronically'.

② Price determination in Devine's 'negotiated coordination' model draws upon Sraffa's model of production price. 'National decisions about the distribution of available output between personal or household consumption, on the one hand, and social consumption and social and economic investment, on the other, have implications for the average level of real wages. At a formal level, abstracting from rent, once the real wage is determined, the rate of return and the structure of relative prices are also determined; alternatively, once the rate of return is determined, the pattern of relative prices and the real wage are also determined (Refer to Sraffa's *Production of Commodities by Means of Commodities*[1960])' (P. Devine, *Democracy and Economic Planning*, Westview Pres, 1988, p. 198).

adjustment process (parecon) or by the central calculation agency ('labor-time calculation' model). Because companies are 'price makers' in 'negotiated coordination' model, price of the product will vary between different companies in the same industry, according to the difference of productivities of the companies. As a result, realized actual returns to capital will be different from expected average returns to capital. Based on the differential actual returns to capital, companies will adjust their production level through the adjustment of existing capacity utilization in the short run, that is, market exchange, or through new (or dis) investment determined by 'negotiated coordination' in the medium or long run.

Labor-time calculation

In 'labor-time calculation' model of Cockshott and Cottrell, 'the means of production are in unitary public ownership'.

Cockshott and Cottrell argue that thanks to the development of IT and computing technology, it is perfectly possible to compute the balanced central plan in terms of the labor-time embodied in the products, despite the enormous size and complexities of the modern economy.① Cockshott and Cottrell show that it takes only a few minutes to compute the labor-time embodied in each product, which is the sum of directly

---

① However, Devine argues that even with the help of state-of-art IT and computer, it is not possible to calculate a balanced central plan, for much of the knowledge that is relevant for economic decision making cannot be centralized due to its 'local' and 'tacit' nature. Especially, 'the tacit nature of much of this knowledge prevents it from being codified and transmitted to the center' (P. Devine, 'Participatory Planning Through Negotiated Coordination,' *Science and Society*. Vol. 66, No. 1, 2002, p. 66). Adaman and Devine also argues that Cockshott and Cottrell's 'labor-time calculation' model formally embraces neoclassical assumption of a complete knowledge of all production functions. 'Models of direct calculation are able to deal with the technical problem of calculation, but not with the actual problem of discovery that confronts real economies. They operate within the neoclassical epistemological paradigm in which knowledge is assumed to be objectively given and readily codified and transmitted. While they are in principle able to deal with the imperfections of knowledge arising from atomized decision making, they are unable to deal with the imperfections arising within the Austrian epistemological paradigm, in which knowledge is tacit and has to be discovered through a process of social mobilization' (F. Adaman and P. Devine, 'On the Economic Theory of Socialism', *New Left Review*, No. 221, 1997, p. 75). Hodgson(G. Hodgson, 'Socialism Against Markets? A Critique of Two Recent Proposals', *Economy and Society*, Vol. 27, No. 4, 1998, p. 425) also argues that Cockshott and Cottrell 'have a technocratic and empiricist conception of information, and are most incautious concerning the limits of artificial intelligence and computing technology'. However, against these criticism, Cocckshott and Cottrell retort in an Althusserrian way, arguing that such a 'emphasis on the irreducibly human nature of tacit knowledge' is 'deriving from a philosophical humanism'.

expended present labor to produce the product and indirectly expended past labor to produce the intermediate inputs for the product, for a whole economy composed of about as many as 20,000,000 products, by calculating the inverse matrix of input coefficients, using supercomputer.

Based on the data of the labor-time embodied in the product calculated by super computer, Cockshott and Cottrell suggest exactly the same kind of distribution principle, described in Marx's *Critique of the Gotha Programme*: remuneration of workers by the labor certificate which shows how long and how hard they work, and the exchange of the labor certificate with the products, tagged by the labor-time embodied in them. Cockshott and Cottrell think that only through the application of Marxian labor certificate distribution principle can the egalitarianism in its true sense of the word be realized. ① Marxian labor certificate is in no sense the money, because it is thrown out once it is used to exchange with the products, like movie thicket. In this sense, the exchange of labor certificate with labor products cannot be conceived as market exchange.

In 'labor-time calculation' model, the level of production of each product is adjusted based on the ratio of the amount of labor certificate offered to purchase the products to the amount of labor-time embodied in the product. For example, ' production is expanded for those products showing an above-average ratio of market-clearing price (expressed in labor tokens) to labor values (sic), and reduced for those products showing a below average ratio'. To emphasize this aspect, Cottrell and Cockshott call their model as 'Marx plus Lange plus Strumilin' model. ②

As for the decision making procedure, Cockshott and Cottrell reject the representative

---

① One of the reasons why the distribution based on the labor-time calculation has never seriously been applied in the former Soviet Union is its radical egalitarian implications (W. Cockshott and A. Cottrell, *Towards a New Socialism*, Spokesman, 1993, p. 13). Indeed, the ruling class in the former Soviet Union was afraid that their privileged income would have been threatened, if the distribution based on the labor-time calculation would be literally, not just rhetorically, introduced.

② 'From Marx, we take the idea of the payment of labor in "labor certificate," and the notion that consumers may withdraw from the social fund goods having a labor content equal to their labor contribution. ... From Lange we take up a modified version of the "trial and error" process, whereby market prices for consumer goods are used to guide the reallocation of social labor among the various consumer goods. From the Soviet economist Strumilin we take the idea that in a socialist equilibrium the use value created in each line of production should be in a common proportion to the social albor time expended' (W. Cockshott and A. Cottrell, *Towards a New Socialism*, Spokesman, 1993, p. 105).

democracy, and advocate for direct democracy and loterry. According to them, 'Elections are aristocratic, not democratic: they introduce the element of deliberate choice, of selection of the 'best' people, the aristoi, in place of government by all the people. A system of election always favors the upper strata of society, those who are best educated, have the greatest access to money and means of communication'. They do not think that Leninist 'council-state' would be the answer, because 'grass-roots representative bodies will either be dominated by the Communist Party or by representatives of reaction'. Instead, they suggest lottery as the ideal democratic procedure. 'If soviet states are to survive in the long term, they will have to rediscover lot, the *ur*-principle of democracy'.

Considering the great emphasis given on the role of the participation and direct democracy by the theorists of participatory planning, common objections to socialism that it inevitably represses individual freedom and democracy, or the related argument that only the introduction of market mechanism is the cure for it, are groundless.

However, Cockshott and Cottrell do not mention about the abolition of the social division of labor or BJC, which is central to Devine's or Albert's model. Moreover, they do not seem to put any importance to Marx's crucial idea of 'association of free individuals'. For this reason, their plea for radical direct democracy sometime sound like empty slogan. In this regard, following critiques are relevant: 'Cockshott and Cottrell's institutional proposals contain no transformatory dynamic towards classless, or stateless, society based on participatory self-government. ···*In their model, politics is strangely absent*. ... There is no room for different views of the good life. ... As with their model of central planning, Cockshott and Cottrell's model of the "political" level is in fact technocratic and managerial rather than political'. In their model, there is 'no provision for face-to-face social interaction and negotiation' (Adaman & Devine, 1997: 74)①.

---

① P. Devine, 'Book Review: Economic Justice and Democracy,' *Science and Society*, Vol. 71, No. 2, p. 257 and p. 259, directs the same critique to parecon as well: In parecon, 'Social interaction, in the sense of face-to-face contact and discussion, takes place only within councils; interaction between councils is mediated by computer-transmitted data in the course of the iterative process. ... There is no room in this vision for people acting as citizens in the public domain in relation to collective choices over economic priorities and the sort of society they wish to live in'. In a similar vein, M. Löwy, 'Eco-socialism and Democratic Planning,' *Socialist Register*. 2007, p. 302, criticize parecon: 'Albert's model mirrors the existing technological and productive structure, and is too "economistic"... He leaves out not only the state as an institution-a respectable option-but also politics as the confrontation, of different economic, social, political, ecological, cultural and civilizational options, locally, nationally and globally'.

Table 1 summarizes and compares main characteristics of three models of participatory planning.

Table 1: Comparison of Participatory Planning Models

	Parecon	Negotiated Coordination	Labor-time calculation
Theoreticians and Main Works	Albert & Hahnel (1991)	Devine (1988)	Cockshott & Cottrell (1993)
Ownership of Means of Production	Workers' council ownership	Social ownership	State ownership
Abolition of Division of Labor	Balanced job complex	Life-time job rotation	—
Distribution Principle	Efforts	Negotiated coordination	Labor-time certificate
Determination of Prices of Consumption Goods	Iteratively adjusted indicative prices	Sraffian price equation (= social average costs of production + expected rate of return)	Labor-time calculation by central planning agency
Determination of Investment	Negotiation between workers council and consumers council	Negotiated coordination	Central planning agency
Market	No market	Market forces no, but market exchange yes	No market
Decision Making	Direct and representative democracy	Direct and representative democracy	Direct democracy and lottery
On USSR	Coordinator class rule	Statism	Socialism

Feasibility of Participatory Planning

In recent debates on participatory planning models, some important issues are prompted, which need to be addressed more seriously. I will first focus on the issues of feasibility and innovation, and argue that they are short of raising any serious doubt on the project of participatory planning. Then, I evaluate the existing models of participatory planning, focusing on their attitudes to Marxian labor theory of value and the former Soviet Union.

Most common objection to the participatory planning is that it is simply not possible to coordinate the modern complex economy without market mechanism. Indeed, the impossibility of market abolition, or the infeasibility of planned economy in the 21st century conditions is received almost as an axiom by most progressives today. For example, left-Keynesians or market socialists argue that the abolition of market is not only impossible, considering the changed conditions in the 21st century, especially globalization and IT revolution etc., but also undesirable, considering the efficiency issues.

But, these assertions are questionable. Of course, it is true that globalization tends to render Stalinist 'socialism in one country' nothing but a fantasy. However, Stalinist 'socialism in one country' has nothing to do with Marxian socialism which can be achieved only through revolution on a world scale. Globalization acts to deepen the interconnection between national capitalisms and mature the objective conditions for Marxian socialism as world revolution.

However, Schweickart repeats that the idea of parecon or participatory planning is just utopian pipe-dream in complex modern economy, and asserts that market socialism is the only feasible model for the progressives. But, it is evident that market socialism as well as participatory planning needs enormous surge of mass anti-capitalist struggles before it can be initiated. Indeed, state ownership of means of production, the essential prerequisite of market socialism, can only be achieved in the revolutionary conjunctures, because it will seriously threaten the private property. Then, it will be helpful to approach the issue from strategic point of view, and determine which vision, market socialism or participatory planning, is more effective to build the collective struggle for post-capitalist future. Like Albert, I think that participatory planning is far more effective than market socialist oxymoron. Paradoxically, market socialism, which is usually advocated and received in the name of realism, is actually more unrealistic and utopian than the radicalism of participatory planning.①

Also, rapid development of technology should not be the reason to reject the planning, because new technology, especially IT, enables the application of very

---

① D. Elson, 'Market Socialism or Socialization of the Market,' *New Left Review*, No. 172, Nov/Dec, 1988, p.9, also notes that 'Nove's "feasible socialism" is more utopian than at first sight it appears,' owing to its superficial understanding of the contradictory dynamics of market competition.

detailed planning on a whole economy scale, which was unthinkable in early 20th century. For example, using 'bar code' that enables every single product to have a unique identification number, we can construct a planning system that can control whole process of distribution from production to consumption and its feedback for almost all the products on a national and even global scale. Indeed, for many large companies, the process of production and distribution has already been highly planned at the company level. What is problematic with capitalism is that the planning is limited to the company level, and anarchy of production is the rule in the whole economy. However, if all the companies are required to upload regularly their detailed financial statements, including balance sheet, profit and loss account, and factory cost report, etc, on the standardized web page, then the information could easily be captured by systems analogous to Google and integrated and calculated to construct a production and investment planning on a national or global scale.

Marx's project of building non-market planned economy in terms of labor-time, as is delineated in his *Critique of the Gotha Programme*, is literally feasible today. Of course, for this, the calculation of labor-time embodied for millions of goods interrelated with each other through input-output relations is needed, which requires solving the same number of simultaneous equations. Common criticism raised in the socialist calculation debate of the 1930s is that even if it is theoretically possible it is practically irrelevant because it would take more than ten years to compute just one-year planning. However, Cockshott exemplifies an experiments with a modest computer costing about 5,000 pounds which found that 'the equations of an economy roughly the size of the Swedish economy' could be solved 'in about a two minutes.' ① In addition, thanks to the dazzling development of internet and network technology and internet, Marxian concept of socialism from below, in other words, participatory planning, becomes an actuality nowadays. For example, on-line discussion combined with internet voting can provide effective tools for realizing the principle of direct democracy of Athens in the 21st century economy and politics. ②

---

① Indeed, the estimation of the labor-time embodied in the goods in capitalist economies is one of the common research topics in the empirical Marxian economics. As for the estimation for the US and Korea, refer to Shaikh and Tonak(1994) and Tsoulfidis and Rieu(2006) respectively.

② While the democracy of Athens is generally criticized for its material basis on the slavery mode of production, Cockshott and Cottrell emphasize the aspect of direct and peoples' democracy, following Wood(1995).

In contrast, even in the former Soviet Union, the most advanced 'actually existing socialism,' the input-output tables, the essential basic technical requirement for central planning, had never been compiled. Indeed, calculation of necessary level of 'gross output' from the target level of 'final output' by using input-output analysis, including inversion of input coefficient matrix, could not be done in the former Soviet Union. The Soviet Union did compile the material balance, the elementary primitive equivalent of input-output tables. But they could do it only for about 2,000 products as late as in 1980s. Moreover, the level of computing and telecommunication facilities, essential infrastructure for any economic planning, was very poor, compared to that of Western market economies. For example, only 23 percent of urban families had phones as of 1985. Then, so-called the most developed 'actually existing socialism,' had never been planned, even in its technical sense of the term.

Innovation of Participatory Planning

Another common objection against the idea of participatory planned economy is that it will be poor in dynamic efficiency compared to capitalism, because it does not have Schumpeterian 'creative destruction' through technological innovation, though it may succeed in guaranteeing the static efficiency in resource allocation. However, it is groundless too. Because the alienation and division of labor are abolished in participatory planned economy, work motivation and productivity can be greatly enhanced. Moreover, if the mobilization of 'local' and 'tacit' knowledge of direct producers is maximized through their democratic participation in the company management, technological innovation will be more dynamic than in capitalism. [1] In contrast, it is very difficult for capitalists to snatch the 'local' and 'tacit' knowledge of direct producers at the

---

[1] Indeed, 'local' and 'tacit' knowledge of direct producers play crucial roles in technological innovation, as was argued by Austrian School in the socialist calculation debate in the 1930s.

workplace in capitalism, where capitalists monopolize the management rights.① Under the hierarchical decision making structure of capitalism, workers and consumers tend to become passive and have no interests in innovative thinking. Since the hierarchical management of capitalism robs people of control of their lives, capitalism cannot mobilize creative economic potentials, and absence of innovation is its corollary.

Advocates of market economy argue that, because the extra profit, or technological rent, which accrues to the innovator, provides the incentive for technological innovation, there will not be any significant innovation without the expected technological rent for the innovator, which can only be secured by capitalist property system. However, extra profits are not the only incentive for innovation. As Elson argues, "more leisure time, less arduous work, social esteem, the sheer pleasure of producing new knowledge and solving problems are all powerful incentives".

Contrary to capitalism where the public goods, such as investment for R&D, tend to be under-supplied due to market failure, participatory planned economy, free from the problem of market failure, can allocate more resources for R&D and innovation. Eeven in capitalism, some phase of technological innovation, like invention and development, are largely carried out by non-profit public institutions, like government or universities. Also, because there is no intellectual property right in participatory planned economy, innovation of one economic unit can be easily and rapidly generalized to all the other units. Unlike capitalism where the lion share of the fruits of innovation accrues to the profits of capital, it will be shared by entire human race for their well-being in participatory planned economy. Hayek's accusation that planned economy is prone to lack of innovation, though somewhat relevant regarding the Soviet

---

① According to F. Adaman and P. Devine, 'The Promise of Participatory Planning: A Rejoinder to Hodgson', *Economy and Society*, Vol. 35, No. 1, 2006, p. 145, 'The question is whose tacit knowledge is drawn on and in whose interest. In our model, participation in key economic decision making is generalized to representatives of all the social owners, not just of shareholders'. But, M. Albert and R. Hahnel, 'In Defense of Participatory Economics', *Science and Society*, Spring, Vol. 66, No. 1, 2002, pp. 112—113, think that their model, parecon, is superior to 'negotiated coordination' model in terms of innovation, arguing that, in 'negotiated coordination' model, any innovation must be arranged for all those affected by enterprise decision, and 'workers must convince representatives of numerous groups who do not work at the enterprise that an innovation is worthy before they can go ahead with it. … But this particular way of representing those legitimate interests has the drawback of creating the possibility of considerable bureaucratic inertia, which might discourage innovation'.

style planned economy, cannot be applied to participatory planned economy.

Contrary to conventional wisdom, there exist serious limits and bias in the technical change in capitalism. As Cockshott and Cottrell argue, 'The real criticism that can be levied at capitalist economies in this regard is that they are too slow to adopt labor-saving devices, because labor is artificially cheap.'[①] In this regard, Marx's classic discussion about the conditions of introducing machinery is still valid. In *Capital* Volume One, Marx argues that it is more difficult to introduce machinery in capitalism than in communism, because in capitalism it is introduced only for economizing the necessary labor, that is, only for maximizing the surplus value, while in communism it is introduced for economizing labor in general.[②] Last but not least, capitalist innovation, which is motivated by profit-seeking and fear of extinction by ruthless competitive struggles, and proceeded in an anarchic unregulated way, is inevitably wasteful and destructive of environment as well as of human being.

5. Concluding Remarks

Three models stand out in the recent debates on the participatory planning. They are Albert's 'parecon' model, Devine's 'negotiated coordination' model, and Cockshott and Cottrell's 'labor-time calculation' model. Despite their important differences with each other, they all contribute to revitalize the discussion and activities for anti-and post-capitalist alternatives. Their common critique of market socialism, theorization of the role of participation from below, emphasis on the role of abolition of division of labor and direct democracy, focusing on the 'local' and 'tacit' nature of knowledge and information, making workable planning model based on labor-time

---

① In capitalism, labor is always cheap in the sense that capitalist pays worker only for the part of the labor he or she worked, that is, for the 'necessary labor.'

② 'The use of machinery for the exclusive purpose of cheapening the product is limited by the requirement that less labor must be expended in producing the machinery than is displaced by the employment of that machinery. For the capitalist, however, there is a further limit on its use. Instead of paying for the labor, he pays only the value of the labor-power employed; the limit to his using a machine is therefore fixed by the difference between the value of the machine and the value of the labor-power replaced by it. ···The field of application for machinery would therefore be entirely different in a communist society from what it is in bourgeois society' (K. Marx. *Capital*, Vol. 1, Vintage Books, 1981, p. 515). It is also remarkable that Marx proves the superiority of communism regarding the adoption of new technology with the help of labor-time calculation in above paragraph.

calculation, etc., are all noble and precious contributions to the development of Marxian concept of socialism. With these new contributions by participatory planning models, Marxian vision of socialism proves to be feasible, far from being a bankrupted utopian project in the 21st century of globalization and IT revolution. Indeed, only by participatory planning, 'self-management (decision making input in proportion to degree affected), equity (to each according to effort), efficiency (maximizing benefits from scarce productive resources), solidarity (concern for others), and ecological restoration' can be assured, Progressives should embrace Marxian participatory planning as the alternative to neoliberal market economy, instead of outdated Keynesian social economy or self-contradictory market socialism. Of course, recent attempts to theorize participatory planning still contain some limitations and biases which need to be addressed from the standpoint of classical Marxism. Developing the theory of participatory planning and allying it with the mass movement for the anti-and post-capitalist alternative must be one of urgent tasks of the progressives.

（本文责任编辑：于琦）

马克思未来社会的观念与 21 世纪诸种社会主义模式

丁声镇

【中文摘要】本文基于马克思关于未来社会的设想，尤其是"共产主义"、"联合"与"计划"等，并对 21 世纪各种社会主义或共产主义模式做出评价，包括参与性计划模式，如迈克尔·阿尔波特所提出的"参与型经济"，迪瓦恩的"协商式调和"，柯克肖特的"劳动时间核算"，以及诸种共产主义模式，如巴丢的"共产主义假设"、奈格里的"共有主义"等。

【作者简介】Jeong Seongjin，丁声镇，韩国庆尚国立大学经济系教授，庆尚大学社会科学研究所所长，主编马克思主义美学研究领域的一种杂志 *Marxism 21st Century*，近年来有多部马克思主义政治经济学论著发表，产生了较大学术反响。

Environmental Ethics, Social Ecology and the Economic Barriers to the Sustainable Development

Alexander V. Petrov

(Saint-Petersburg State University, Russia)

Summary: This report focuses on the analysis of contradictions in the development of environmental ethics in the contemporary social and economic conditions. The report discusses the issues of environmental ethics for sustainable development.

Key words: sustainable development, neoliberal capitalism, environmental ethics, social ecology, Marxist economic sociology

The concept of sustainable development is perhaps the most popular concept of social development amongst politicians and scientists in the late 20th—early 21st centuries. This concept is opposed to the concept of neo-liberal capitalism. The concept of sustainable development implies economic development of society in harmony with nature. This type of social and economic development requires the effective use the limited resources in the modern (post)industrial system and preserve natural resources for future generations. Sustainable development is such type of development that involves maintaining natural environment, because the destruction of nature means the destruction of society.

The concept of neo-liberal capitalism implies the social development through the creation of the opportunities for stable economic growth and rapid capital accumulation. According to the concept of neo-liberal capitalism only unlimited economic growth and capital accumulation can solve all social problems, including environmental issues. Only free economic growth creates the wealth of nations. And only rich nations can successfully solve the problems of social development. But for successful economic growth is necessary to use more and more natural resources. Therefore, nature becomes a hostage to the economic success of modern societies.

Both concepts recognize the possibility and necessity of environmental ethics. No one denies the need for environmental ethics. Environmental ethics has become an integral part of modern political discourse and the discourse of social sciences. Moreover, environmental ethics has become a fashionable ideology. But there are different interpretations of the ethics in the framework of these two concepts, and fundamentally different views on the possibilities of solving modern global and local environmental problems.

What is the environmental ethics? There are many scientific approaches and definitions of environmental ethics. According to the sociology and social ecology *environmental ethics* can be defined (in general, because the sociologists and social ecologists have different points of view like other social scientists) as a special spiritual environment of the everyday human life or, specifically, an element of the structure of social consciousness consisting of values, norms, rules of social actions. These values and norms determine the attitude of different modern societies and social groups to nature, to the possibility of careful use of its resources under existing economic, political and cultural constraints.

The concept of sustainable development requires an environmental ethic based on the idea of the harmony of economic growth, technological changes, institutional changes and transformation of social consciousness. Harmony is achieved through the unity of economic development (accumulation of investment capital for the creation of environmental technologies), technological progress (accumulation of intellectual capital for creating energy and resource efficient technologies) and artificial institutional limitations of human intervention in nature (to save the consumption possibilities of future generations). Environmental ethics is becoming a most important part of the socio-institutional framework for implementing policy of sustainable development in various modern states and societies. Nature is the primary ethical value, and the human will always be a part of it.

The neo-liberal concept of socio-economic development is focused on ensuring the conditions for capital accumulation, efficient (profitable) work of all branches of modern industry, unlimited consumption and comfortable life. The successful economic development is possible with the implementation of externalization of environmental costs. Environmental degradation is only a temporary phenomenon, which can easily be changed. But these changes are needed financial resources. Only the investment resources and new technologies will be able to save nature. In this case, environmental ethics is an element of neo-liberal ideology of nature preservation by strengthening its exploitation. Nature is the primary ethical value too, but the nature during two hundred years of rapid industrial development has long since become a part of the human comfortable life. And nature will stay a part of it.

Thus we have in the new century at least two types of environmental ethics, two systems regarding the role of nature in human life and two ways of organizing social life and activity in natural environments. Of course it's very nice to have a choice between different ways of social development and understanding of reality. People have a choice. But has nature such possibility to make a choice?

It is very difficult to predict the choices made by different societies in the new century. Hopefully, most politicians and ordinary people from different states will choose the concept of sustainable development and the appropriate type of environmental ethics. But now we can definitely say that the environmental ethic of sustainable development has significant barriers for the implementation. And these barriers are related primarily to economic factors determining the attitude of modern societies to nature.

The first barrier is a modern anti-environmental economic ethics. Typically, social scientists (especially neoliberal economists) do not regard this factor as a major. Modern economic ethics is the ethics of economic efficiency and unlimited success. Economic efficiency is determined only by low costs and high profit. Moreover, thanks to classical and neoclassical economic theory, economic efficiency is considered identical with social efficiency. The logic is simple: low costs mean big profit, big profit means a rich and prosperous society. The modern production system based on this logic. But the question arises: who needs the unnecessary economic costs of such system? Unnecessary costs do not need anyone. Most unnecessary costs for this system are the environmental costs of economic activity.

In principle, the whole history of humanity might well be interpreted as a set of adaptation processes of different societies at different times to the natural environment due to degradation of nature. The efficiency of this adaptation is directly proportional to the degree of the destructive influence of human activities on the environment. The first environmental laws have appeared in the era of ancient Babylon (the code of Hammurabi) and ancient China. But no laws could change the human attitudes to nature as a limitless source of economic possibilities, possibilities for unlimited consumption. A successful industrial growth is only possible while maintaining the principle of externalization of environmental costs. But we've long since learned that industrial growth is the foundation of social progress.

Next barrier is growing geoeconomic differentiation between countries and societies. More and more experts come to this conclusion. Inequality between countries is widening. The U. S., Western European countries are 100 times richer than Ethiopia, Haiti, Nepal and many other countries now. If we abandon preconceived approaches to the study of poverty, one finds that in reality in the world live more than 4 billion poor people. The global economic crisis of the late-2000s only exacerbated this differentiation.

The global industrial development is often proclaimed one of the main ways to solve all the contradictions between rich and poor countries. But the price of this development is the increase in environmental costs. Any restrictions on economic growth will be perceived as a barrier for the social development of poor countries. Rich countries will accept environmental restrictions as an obstacle to technological progress. Moreover, according to popular concept of neo-liberal capitalism, almost all environmental problems have only a technological answer.

Another barrier is the spread of the global consumer society. Reducing total costs in developed and developing countries due to the externalization of environmental costs stimulates further growth of global consumption. Values of the global consumer society orientate to the total subjection of nature to the interests of comfortable life. Mass culture of the consumer society is opposed to national cultures. The national cultures oriented people to the harmonious interaction with the environment during thousands years. But the mass culture of consumer society suppresses the national cultures and forces the majority of people around the world to follow in their consumer behavior the universal strategy of personal comfort at any cost. And this cost is the degradation of nature.

The concept of sustainable development implies the creation of conditions for moderate consumption. But this idea comes into clear conflict with the desire of transnational producers of goods and services to obtain excessive profits at the expense of the global spread of the industry and the expansion of consumption. There is another problem with mass culture of consumer society. This problem is a demonstration effect, which manifests itself in increasing the imitational consumption. The imitational consumption is determined by the fashion trends from rich countries. And environmental ethics is becoming a fashionable trend or ideology. Environmental ethics has also become an object of consumption within the social communications of the modern consumer society.

Another barrier is the process of transnationalization. Most experts believe that it would be impossible to solve environmental problems without the investments and high technologies of the transnational corporations. The transnational corporations are developing around the world new energy-saving and resource-efficient productions, new environmental standards, creating new jobs in poor countries, contribute to increase the financial capacity of such countries in solving environmental problems. Dissemination of environmental standards promotes environmental ethics among national producers and consumers in all countries.

The process of transnationalization hides a set of environmental hazards. There are problem of global placement of polluting industries, problem of hazardous waste, problem of international environmental standards, which eliminate economic competition in the different domestic markets. There is also a danger of freezing of environmental regulation, especially in poor countries. Perhaps it is the most difficult problem.

Of course, there are a lot of barriers to the development of environmental ethics for sustainable development. But the economic barriers are the most important under modern conditions. Researches of the possibilities of overcoming these barriers should be the subject of contemporary Marxist economic sociology.

（本文责任编辑：尹庆红）

环境伦理、社会生态与可持续发展的经济障碍

亚历山大·维克多罗维奇·彼得罗夫

【内容摘要】 本文主要分析在当代社会和经济条件下环境伦理发展的困境，以及讨论环境伦理对可持续发展的重要性等相关问题。

【作者简介】 亚历山大·维克多罗维奇·彼得罗夫（Petrov V. Alexander）俄罗斯圣彼得堡大学社会学系俄中比较社会、经济与政治研究中心主任，教授。

中国悲剧观念：理论传统及其当代意义

王杰，谢卓婷*

（上海交通大学人文学院）

【内容摘要】 马克思主义美学要想重返公共话语空间，最重要的是在历史悲剧的理论框架下对现代性悲剧存在作出批判与反思。马克思主义悲剧美学虽然是一种外来的理论模式，却与中国文化传统和现实审美经验存在着内在的精神契合点，中国文化的悲剧观念与马克思主义现代悲剧美学中的"革命悲剧"、"日常生活悲剧"以及"尘世的崇高"等悲剧观念息息相通。作为中国文化传统与中国现代化过程中各种悲剧性现象相结合的结果，中国悲剧观念已成为中国式审美现代性的核心概念之一。在审美现代性、悲剧观念、世俗性崇高等成为全球性现象和全球性问题的条件下，马克思主义美学有可能对此种陷于深刻伦理危机和价值危机的现象作出理论的阐释，并将获得自身理论的进一步发展。

在中国美学百余年来的发展地形图中，马克思主义美学是其中最引人注目，也是最复杂多元的一条主脉。自 20 世纪二三十年代以来，由瞿秋白、鲁迅、冯雪峰等人对苏联现实主义文论的引入，再经 1942 年毛泽东《在延安文艺座谈会上的讲话》对新民主主义革命中"文化领导权"问题的确立，从而标志着具有中国特殊风格的中国马克思主义美学的正式形成，中国马克思主义美学一路经过了新民主主义革命、新中国成立、文化大革命、改革开放等四个重要的历史阶段，并形成了颇具影响力的实践美学、审美意识形态理论、人民美学等重要的美学流派。进入 90 年代后，马克思主义美学又进一步拓展到中国社会文化生

---

* 王杰，1957 年生，男，江苏无锡人，文学博士，上海交通大学人文学院特聘教授，博士生导师，主要从事马克思主义美学研究和文学人类学研究；谢卓婷，1974 年生，女，湖南益阳人，上海交通大学文艺媒介管理专业 2011 级博士研究生，长沙理工大学文法学院讲师。

活的更多领域,形成后实践美学、审美文化研究、生态美学、审美人类学、文学人类学等诸多分支。此外,更重要的是,作为一种审美意识形态话语理论,在近一个世纪以来,马克思主义美学在中国整个现代化进程中都扮演着重要的角色,它不仅直接参与了社会革命和中国社会主义进程,更是在时代转型和思想震荡变革之际,为改革的深入与主流意识形态的价值重构提供了丰富的思想文化资源,一度成为现代"启蒙"和历史批判的公共话语。

但是,进入20世纪90年代以来,马克思主义美学以及整个中国美学,事实上也是所有人文学科领域的这种社会参与和现实介入的公共话语热情都仿佛一去不复返了。在充满"主义"之争的喧嚣和表面繁荣之下,美学话语更多地成为了消隐于书斋的学者们的喃喃自语。马克思主义美学研究,则要么自囿于理论科学主义的教条故步自封,要么纷纷远离传统意义上的马克思主义,成为"没有马克思的马克思主义美学"以及以各种文化理论形式出现的美学。与此同时,我们也看到,正是自上个世纪末以来,伴随着全球技术时代到来的日常生活审美化的潮流,不仅带来了艺术和审美方式的深刻变化,也在某种程度上加深、加剧了社会整体的后现代和全球资本化的历史进程。已有学者指出,一个"审美资本主义"①的时代正在悄悄来临。因此,在物质丰盈与精神虚无的后现代生存图景中,传统的人性和文化正经历着怎样丰富而深刻的痛苦?艺术该如何表征现代性的悲剧现实及其复杂矛盾?"美"作为一种文化内驱力,是否依然具有形而上超越的意义?以上种种现象和问题都表明,事实上,我们身处的这个时代比以往任何一个时代都更急切地需要真正意义上的美学,特别是作为一种历史文化批判的马克思主义美学对现实作出理论的阐释与回应。

一、马克思主义美学与中国文化传统

马克思主义美学要走出纯学术的象牙塔,重返文化批判与现实反思的公共话语空间,在现有的历史条件下,该怎样既忠实于马克思主义的思想原则,同时又能真正切入到中国当下复杂的悲剧性现实之中?作为一种"舶来"的理论,马克思美学在中国的发展足以表明其自身强劲的理论生命力,以至于一部中国当代美学史,几乎就是一部中国化的马克思主义美学史。马克思主义美学与中国美学原本是建立在两种不同文明之上的美学传统,但凡一种外来理论,

---

① [法]奥利维耶·阿苏利:《审美资本主义》,黄琰译,上海:华东师范大学出版社,2013年。

如若找不到与中国文化传统和现实审美经验之间内在的精神契合点和哲学表达的学理依据,那么就很容易成为东西方美学术语与概念的简单比附或拼合,或者,仅仅会是如很多人比较褊狭地认为的那样,将马克思主义美学的中国化视为只是主流意识形态简单表达的结果。

事实上,如果回溯到中国马克思主义美学产生的具体的历史语境,会发现,马克思主义美学的中国化并不是马克思美学理论的中国化,而是自1942年毛泽东在《讲话》中就已经确立了的模式:马克思主义基本原理与中国的民间文化模式和中国人具体的审美经验的结合。① 这种审美经验和艺术实践不是来自于远离工人运动实践的书斋案头,而是来自活生生的具体革命实践;不是个体的自由情感的表达,而是社会和大众的共同经验和普遍情感的表征;不是偶然的个体性的撕裂与对抗,而是一般性的"历史的必然要求"的传达。所以,正是在这个意义上,有人将马克思主义美学称为是一种"人民美学",但和那种民粹主义的身份立场认同和对抗模式不一样,《讲话》所确立的美学模式不是以边缘对抗主流,而是以对底层审美经验的认同来服务于主流意识形态的改造,服务于社会变迁和社会变革的需求。正是这种既不同于苏联本质主义反映论、认识论美学模式,又不同于以文化、意识形态、政治批判为中心的西方马克思主义美学模式的马克思主义美学中国化,为我们提供了一个思考马克思主义美学与现实之间关系的新途径,那就是,中国的文化传统和审美经验与马克思主义思想之间的本质关联。

现在回过头来看马克思主义美学中国化的路程。不难看出,实际上无论是早期马克思主义者救亡图存的理论引入,还是"左联"时期的美学"革命",毛泽东的意识形态改造,甚至到解放初期"美学大讨论"以及80年代"美学热"中学院派知识分子对"实践美学"和重读《手稿》的热情,尽管时代各异,具体的情形也十分不同,但对于革命、政治与文学艺术之间的现实关联的热情,其实都是与中国人"经世致用"的文化传统分不开的。马克思主义,以及马克思主义美学的中国化实际上就是经典马克思主义理论中的"实践"原则与中国文化中的现实精神以及"载道"、"通变"的知识传统内在契合的结果。循此思路,我们可以接下去思考的是:在一个"后革命"、"后启蒙"的时代,在历史行进到现代化进程已高速发展的21世纪,中国有没有既表征着"历史意识",又属于我们自己文化传统的"地方性知识"或"共同文化"可以成为马

---

① 王杰:《中国马克思主义美学的基本问题与理论模式》,《文艺研究》,2008年第1期。

克思主义美学的现实根基呢？特别是，有没有可以与马克思主义自身的理论基础和阐释机制产生内在联系的文化传统？

按照刘纲纪先生的理解，马克思主义美学的理论基础有两个直接相关联的特点："第一，它是以马克思主义哲学所讲的实践（首先是物质生产实践）为理论基础的……第二，马克思主义美学是和马克思主义的科学社会主义共产主义理论及其实现不能分离的。"① 这正是马克思主义及马克思主义美学理论最大的魅力所在，即，它是在实践的过程中，对现有文明不断作出批判性的"扬弃"，并指向新文明类型之可能的面向未来的理论体系。这种建立在批判基础之上的未来，本身也包含着对既存现实关系的破坏与颠覆。因此，从政治经济学与历史唯物主义出发，马克思把资本主义理解为是一种流动的现代性，并指出资本主义总是处于革命和动荡之中，并最终走向灭亡的宿命。历史的阶段性或过程性的悲剧无可避免，而且总会在不断自我"异化"的过程中螺旋向前。这种历史的悲剧意识也决定了人们与现实之间的局限性关系，但最终却指向一种超越现实的努力。

马克思主义思想中这种历史悲剧的内在超越理念对于中国文化的"情感结构"来说是有说服力和亲和力的。中国是一个没有宗教传统的国度，但却不乏内在超越（宗教的超越是外在超越，即在自身和现世之外悬设一个神主）的信念。在传统的文化心理结构中，一方面是中庸、乐生、忧患的现实精神，一方面则是"生生之谓易"的发展理念和"天人合一"的时空宇宙模式。如果说，马克思主义最初被引入国门时是伴随着"十月革命"的背景，因而自然地突出了其摧毁旧世界的革命"暴力"，而在被主流意识形态化的过程中又不断地被强调了其政治功利性的"权力"，以及一种天真的革命浪漫主义式的未来承诺的话，那么，在一个"后革命"、"后启蒙"的时代，如果能够吸收并重新激活那些在中国现代化进程中日益消失了的传统形而上理念，或者结合中国文化传统中的某些因素来进行文化批判与建设，马克思主义美学话语的公共空间将会开阔很多，对现实的接应能力也会强大很多。譬如说，除却那种既肯定"此岸世界"、又强调以"修身养性"和"自强不息"来提升自我并兼济天下的儒家精英理念，在中国民间文化传统中更具有草根性，同时在当下也更具现实活力的佛教文化思想也不容忽视。佛教哲学的两极正是处于否定与肯定之间，以"苦谛"为基础的现世观似乎是一种彻底的悲观主义，但另一方面，在"缘起"、"业报"、"轮回"等理念中又将宇

---

① 刘纲纪：《马克思主义美学在当代》，《马克思主义美学研究》，2007年第1期。

宙万物置于现实世界错综复杂的各种相关条件之中，生、住、异、灭，形成一个不断变异、流转、运动、发展的过程。故此，有学者把佛学之美归结为是一种"生成的动力学"（dynamics of becoming）①。至于大乘佛教借鉴"般若无知"的知识论，讲求"不畏生死"、"不求解脱"，积极入世的人生观，以及万物皆有佛性、"众生平等"的共同理想，则更是直接予人以一种道德形而上的力量。中国民间佛教理念的这种现实的悲剧感与超越性无疑和马克思主义富于内在超越性的历史悲剧意识是存在着某种内在的精神契合的。

近些年来，学术界其实已有不少呼声，认为中国化的马克思主义不仅要"切中中国的现实"，而且要结合中国的传统思想，特别是中国传统思想中"以儒道禅为主体的智慧"②。确实，马克思主义美学思想要想真正成为与中国当代社会的文化心理、情感结构内外兼容的思想和文化资源，就要更多地与中国民间性、大众性的情感形式，与日常的共同文化和审美经验相结合。这种"化合"的过程，对于马克思主义美学自身理论建设而言也将是一种丰富和发展。

二、关于中国悲剧观念

以马克思主义美学的历史悲剧理论切入中国文化艺术的现实，其中一个必然会遭遇的问题就是关于中国的悲剧观念的问题。无须讳言的是，这里似乎有一个公认的前提，那就是，中国不仅文艺中少有悲剧这种艺术形式，中国文化和中国人的精神结构里也缺乏悲剧性和悲剧感，因此，关于中国的悲剧观念问题似乎最终只会是一个"伪命题"。关于中国没有悲剧的提法，早在王国维、朱光潜、鲁迅等学者那里就已有过充分的论述。西方学者雅斯贝尔斯更是在他的《悲剧的超越》中认为中国人只具有一种"悲剧前知识"，因为在中国文化里，"所有的痛苦、不幸和罪恶都只是暂时的、毫无必要出现的扰乱。世界的运行没有恐怖、拒绝或辩护——没有控诉，只有哀叹。人们不会因绝望而精神分裂：他安详宁静地忍受折磨，甚至对死亡也毫无惊惧；没有无望的郁结，没有阴郁的受挫感，一切都基本上是明朗、美好和真实的。"③苏珊·朗格在其《情感与形式》中也有类似的说法："悲剧是一种成熟的艺术形式，这种形式不是

---

① 彭彤：《佛教与中国美学之特征》，《宗教学研究》，2003年第12期。
② 彭富春：《论中国化的马克思主义哲学和美学》，《湖北大学学报》（哲学社会科学版），2010年第7期。
③ [德]卡尔·雅斯贝尔斯：《悲剧的超越》，亦春译，北京：工人出版社，1988年，第13页。

世界各地都有的。悲剧概念要求一种个性感（A sense of individuality），这是某些宗教和某些文化——甚至是高度文化——所未曾孕育的。"① 确实，作为艺术之"冠冕"的悲剧，不仅是西方艺术的最高艺术形式，也往往是人们掌握世界、思考人生的重要方式和范畴。因此，在西方，无论是作为艺术形式的悲剧创作，还是有关悲剧的哲学与美学论述都特别发达。虽然，从古希腊的神人一体，到亚里士多德对伟人或高尚之人的行动的摹仿，再至自文艺复兴以后越来越多地面向大众和普通人的悲剧，直至19世纪、20世纪以来，以对整个人类的生命、存在、意义等内在冲突发问的现代悲剧的产生，悲剧在西方的演进和发展也经历了诸多的变化，但是，受形而上学哲学传统的影响，尽管悲剧的形式以及关于悲剧的思考都发生了重大的改变，悲剧对精神的高贵性和人的神性方面的强调却从未改变。相比之下，中国虽也有"苦戏"、"怨戏"、"悲情戏"的传统，而且，中国文化中也具有浓郁的悲剧意识和悲哀的底色，但常常被认为这只是建立在现实匮乏或对生活不满的客观基础之上的悲剧意识，尚未上升到对人类存在的整体追问和自我主体性价值的严肃思考，所谓"有悲剧意识，但少悲剧精神"②，故此，还算不上是真正的悲剧观念。

然而，事实是否果真如此呢？究竟何谓悲剧？使悲剧成其为悲剧的到底是什么？我们这个时代是否还有悲剧观念？和中国无悲剧论相关的另一个命题是西方的"悲剧衰亡论"，它也许可以从反面为我们提供理解中国悲剧的新路径。"悲剧衰亡论"最早是尼采1872年在《悲剧的诞生》中提出来的，他认为欧里庇得斯将酒神从悲剧中赶走从而导致了古希腊悲剧的衰亡，因为支撑着整个悲剧大厦的神秘主义非理性基础被理性主义所代替。事实上，这种衰亡在黑格尔的"终结论"中就已经开始了。围绕着黑格尔和尼采的这种"悲剧衰亡论"，西方整个20世纪长期以来展开了热烈的讨论。其中最著名的两次分别是20世纪60年代在斯坦纳的《悲剧之死》（1961）和威廉斯的《现代悲剧》（1966）之间，以及90年代以后，围绕着《悲剧之死》第三次出版（1996）与伊格尔顿的《甜蜜的暴力》（2003）之间的争论。

威廉斯最大的贡献在于提出"革命悲剧"的理念，从而将那种被视为是真理系统和永恒抽象的神学或悲剧哲学推至具体的历史文化变迁的"情感结构"之中，并将之拉平至日常生活活生生的经验层面。在他看来，首先，悲剧意

---

① ［美］苏珊·朗格：《情感与形式》，刘大基、傅志强译，北京：中国社会科学出版社，1986年，第386—387页。
② 王富仁：《悲剧意识与悲剧精神》（上），《江苏社会科学》，2001年第1期。

总是受到文化和历史的双重限定，因而悲剧不是先前那种特殊的、永久的既存事实，而是不断变化的"一系列经验、习俗和制度"①，是一种我们每一个人都正感受和经历着的"经验形式"②。其次，任何"革命"，无论是资产阶级革命，还是社会主义革命，都是"深层的悲剧性无序状况必不可少的运动"。革命是一个复杂的过程，不是进步的直线上升与必胜信念的宏大叙事。正是沿着威廉斯"革命悲剧"的思路，伊格尔顿在《甜蜜的暴力——悲剧的观念》中进一步揭示现代性的悲剧性，即在于现代性是一个悲剧性与进步性张力共存的进程，是一个复杂的有机混合体，而不是那种单线发展的"斯坦纳主义的最纯粹本质"③。

此外，也是沿着威廉斯的悲剧世俗化的思路，并出于对斯坦纳的现代性令悲剧走向没落的观点的反驳，伊格尔顿提出了一个全新的悲剧概念：悲剧的观念。这是与传统的严格"以许多种区别而定"的悲剧概念不同的审视现代性的新视点，是根据维特根斯坦的"家族相似"原理，对传统的悲剧概念的一种更为灵活宽泛的理解。在日益流动、无序、日常的现代社会，悲剧观念不再是案头剧和舞台表演的形式，而是成为了"现代主义"，成为了"一种成熟哲学"，"一种形而上的人道主义"④，以及反思现代性的"文化批判形式"。但是，和传统悲剧一定要涉及灾难性的逆转，悲剧英雄一定要是贵族，悲剧一定要有毁灭性的结局，一定要涉及命运、净化、道德缺陷、众神等等理念不一样，在伊格尔顿这里，悲剧所呈现出来的深度和严肃性并不是来自绝对纯粹的精神性和价值抽象，不光是"文化价值观和历史主体性"，而恰好是来自"最名副其实的唯物论"⑤——身体，一个自然与文化、善与恶共存的混合物。通过耶稣受难时"痛苦的身体"和担负着共同体的罪恶却被人们所排斥的神圣又可怕的"替罪羊"形象，悲剧产生意义的机制被描绘为这样一种积极的苦难方式：痛苦的身体以自然性、肉体性的生命之力抵抗着苦难的束缚，在经历一场类似于人类学通过仪式般的"象征性的死亡"之后重新激发出主体性，并最终获取绝对的自由。因此，悲剧的美学效果是崇高，但这种崇高和康德式的主客体撕裂，最

---

① ［英］雷蒙·威廉斯：《现代悲剧》，丁尔苏译，上海：译林出版社，2007年，第37页。
② 同上，第24页。
③ ［英］特里·伊格尔顿：《悲剧、希望与乐观主义》，许娇娜译，《马克思主义美学研究》，2008年第2期。
④ ［英］特里·伊格尔顿：《甜蜜的暴力——悲剧的观念》，方杰、方宸译，南京：南京大学出版社，2007年，第21页。
⑤ 同上，第9页。

终统一于想象性的自由意志不一样,崇高不是来自于理性道德的框架,而是始终与自然的肉身欲望扭结在一起。因此,悲剧的崇高,不仅是主体意志的伟大,更是作为感性生命的卑微的展现,是一种"尘世的崇高"。

从威廉斯作为不断变化的"习俗、制度"和"一场经验"的悲剧观念,到伊格尔顿伦理学意义上的"尘世的崇高"的悲剧观念,回过头来反观中国的悲剧观念,会发现关于中国有无悲剧观念的很多争端是并不成立的,因为在很大程度上,他们用以评判的标准正是左派批评家们所极力反驳的那个带有意识形态色彩的纯粹抽象的悲剧传统。这些观点的基本判断不外乎这样几种:1. 悲剧是人类绝对精神的体现,现实人生的悲剧性感受是不构成悲剧的;2. 构成悲剧的行为必须是伟大的行为,通过英雄式的抗争甚至是个体的毁灭,将人的主体性力量发挥到极致;3. 悲剧的快感源于最高级的崇高感,即所谓"悲剧是崇高最高最深刻的一种"[1],这种崇高一方面是人的最高意志或理性的体现,另一方面又要求我们能抛弃意志的利害关系,以便成为纯粹的审美知觉。这样的标准之下,中国的悲剧观念就荡然无存了,因为无论是老子哲学的顺应天然,还是儒家的礼乐秩序、佛教的去执忘我,以及中国文化里过于直接的道德教化意识,过于现实的人生态度,过于稳态的人伦色彩,都会成为消弭苦难和矛盾的力量,使中国的悲剧最终指向平静、安稳、圆满。但是,威廉斯和伊格尔顿关于日常生活的悲剧观念却提醒我们,悲剧往往就是我们人人都可能身处其中的感官化、肉体化的苦难,无视这种悲剧性苦难,就是对历史内容的抽空。

另外,伊格尔顿的"尘世的崇高"更要求我们不得不重新去审视那些由小人物、失败者组成的,也许还充满了玩笑、幽默、宽恕、隐忍的人生。中国式的悲剧里,少有力与力的冲突,少有一悲到底、知其不可而为之的英雄,以及如同真理探寻一般对命运的好奇与求索。例如,和西方悲剧中的"命运"不同,在中国的悲剧观念里起着支配作用的更多的是"命"。虽然,这两种似乎都是被外加于人身上的关于世界的最后的原因或理由,但"命运"更像是一种不可逆违的,外界强制的必然性。而对于中国人来说,虽然"命"是"善则予之吉,恶则加之凶"的天道,但又有"天难谌,命靡常"的另一种开脱。正如前所述,中国人的时空观念里,存在着一种生生不已的圆形循环的运动模式。事实上这也是为什么佛教的轮回说可以和中国人的文化心理立刻契合的原因所在。这一可变(所谓"时来运转")但又始终能维系整体意义上的循环稳定的

---

[1] [俄]车尔尼雪夫斯基:《艺术与现实的审美关系》,周扬译,北京:人民文学出版社,1979年,第21页。

"命",使得中国人将"安"作为人生幸福的栖所,因此重人伦礼序,知天乐命。这一点伊格尔顿也感受到了,他认为在中国的悲剧观念里,"有一种与受到某种权力控制的普遍和谐有关的幻想,虽然这种权力的配置往往高深莫测,但是却可以证明其使得人类社会秩序合法化的合理性"。①

不过,这种似乎安然、稳态,世俗的"合理性",往往恰是以对人生苦难的深切体验和感知为基础的,其内里常常暗涌或奔突着一种黑色精灵一般的生命之力和情感之力。这种悲剧形态在中国的文学艺术作品中有着丰富的表现。如鲁迅的《野草》,所谓绝望之虚妄,正与希望相同,生命之力并不在于惨淡淋漓的鲜血,而是在"明暗之间"的徘徊,在"无物之阵"的荷戟独彷徨,但最终的精神指向却是绝望之中的希望,黑暗之中的光明。再如一个非常有意思的当代作品——陈继明的中篇小说《北京和尚》。在这里,物欲横流的现代大都市"北京"与一心向佛,但事实上却在俗世中"处处染尘埃"的年青和尚可乘,小说标题中这两个"异质"形象的组合,自身就如同一道禅语,表明日常人生的混杂丰富。可乘经历了剃度出家、还俗娶妻、开"般若素食"饭馆、断指忏悔等诸多尘世的"劫场",他并不是清心寡欲的圣僧,而是一个凡俗卑微的"肉体"之人。然而,其内心念念不忘的信仰却又总使他的生命始终散发着一种淡淡的人性光芒。作为僧人的可乘打坐时的感受奇特而又真切,他觉得"打坐其实是一种战斗的姿态,入静是向混乱无序的思想宣战。进一步说,出家人其实是战士,软弱的战士,静的战士,空的战士,自取失败的战士"②,正是这融合了丰富的"肉身性"的体验提醒我们,其实芸芸众生每一个人都是这样的"战士",都是默默承受生活艰难和精神之痛,但又指向生活和希望之意义的"尘世的悲剧"。这种悲剧依旧呈现出一种人性的崇高感,但不是"最高最深刻"的那种崇高,而是世俗化、优美化崇高的混合体。

三、马克思主义美学成为公共话语的可能性

21世纪,美学何为?实际上,在西方,早自上个世纪60年代后期以来,随着后现代主义、解构主义思潮,以及文化研究的兴起,美学研究渐渐从对现代主义艺术的"纯粹性"的研究,转向了广泛社会参与和批判的政治社会美学

---

① [英]特里·伊格尔顿:《甜蜜的暴力——悲剧的观念》,方杰、方宸译,南京:南京大学出版社,2007年版,第76页。
② 陈继明:《有些羞愧》,《小说选刊》,2011年第11期。

研究。阶级、身份、性别、族裔，以及艺术生产与消费等问题，逐渐代替了昔日关于美的形式、审美经验、美的普遍性等问题而成为美学研究的主要论域。在这场由学院书斋的纯粹艺术研究延伸到社会政治公共话语领域的美学研究的历史性转向中，以审美意识形态研究见长的马克思主义美学研究可谓是其先锋和主力。但是，随着"审美资本主义"成为一种全球化的现象，美学与消费主义、大众文化、文化产业的兴起紧密关联起来，艺术和审美日趋走向消费化、商品化、资本化的道路。对于很多"后学"研究者们来说，这种消费时代或全球化时代的审美"奇观"是令人欢欣鼓舞的。这里有一段对这样一种"美学设计时代"的到来的赞词：

"不管传统美学的持守者们姿态如何，经济领域的美学设计都一定会成长壮大成另一种与时代相互应的'美学'。与传统美学仅止于'思辨的美学'不同，这种美学不仅是思想的、诗意的，尤其是实战的。它所成长的空间不仅是思想的空间、文化的空间，尤其是经济的空间。"①

这种把美学直接当作了资本驱动力，或者是与科学技术一样的"生产力"的经济主义美学，不仅是对传统审美主义的威胁，实际上也是对所有作为哲学反思和文化批判的美学传统的解构。与这种赤裸裸的市场主义美学或者说审美资本主义并行的，是日渐成为显学的文化研究对美学阵地的占领与僭越，它们以政治实用主义和社会功能主义的方式形成与这个时代同构的风景，而思辨的、审美救赎的美学则逐渐淡出公众视野，这其中自然也包括马克思主义美学。尽管西方有布鲁姆和美学"右翼"对后现代主义、文化研究等"非美学"表示义愤，斥责文学批评如今已被"文化批评"所取代："这是一种由伪马克思主义、伪女性主义以及各种法国/海德格尔式的时髦东西所组成的奇观。西方经典已被各种诸如此类的十字军运动所代替，如后殖民主义、多元文化主义、族裔研究，以及各种关于性倾向的奇谈怪论"。② 但是，确确实实，无论是西方，还是在中国，美学都正面临着自身的问题。这些年来，无论是"回到康德"③的主张，还是呼吁建构一种无差异的"全球美学"④，事实上都表明美学在这样一个多变的时代，对自身所面临的问题和困境正努力作出回答和探索。当然，也有学者直接呼吁，要回到马克思主义，因为只有它才是既面对艺术，又面对全社会发

---

① 吴兴明：《消费时代或全球化重振美学的一线生机》，《当代文坛》，2004年第6期。
② ［美］哈罗德·布鲁姆：《西方正典——伟大作家和不朽作品》，江宁康译，南京：译林出版社，2005年，第2页。
③ 周宪：《美学的危机或复兴？》，《文艺研究》，2011年第11期。
④ 陈望衡：《"全球美学"与中国美学———中国美学如何与世界接轨》，《学术月刊》，2011年第8期。

展的，无论是对于艺术还是社会，马克思主义都具有极好的批判性反思能力。[①] 还有类似的观念认为，中国美学要寻求发展，就需要马克思主义为其奠立哲学基础，因为，没有哪一种哲学像马克思主义哲学那样，"不仅为科学地探讨感性与理性、人和自然的关系，审美活动与其他生命活动的关系提供了基本的理论依据，而且为这些关系的实际解决开辟了道路。"[②]

马克思主义思想确实是一个丰富的矿藏，马克思主义美学也确实可以为社会和艺术提供一种批判性反思。但它绝不是万能的，也不是唯一的。特别是对于我们身处的这个时代和我们自身的文化传统而言，马克思主义美学最有意义的补充恰恰是我们人人都可以感同身受的那一部分价值，而不是外在于我们的生活、传统、情感的抽象绝对的理性，以及对于现实和芸芸众生审视的、抽离的目光。因此，如果一定要思考马克思主义美学在未来能给我们带来什么，或者，要探讨马克思主义美学重返公共话语空间的可能性，本人觉得，最值得关注的依然来自构成马克思主义历史悲剧哲学的相反相成的两个方面：

其一：从伦理精神的维度，对悲剧信仰的强调。马克思、恩格斯对悲剧的阐释主要来自两处。一是《〈黑格尔法哲学批判〉导言》，认为"当旧制度还是有史以来就存在的世界权力，自由反而是个人突然产生的想法的时候，简言之，当旧制度本身还相信而且也应当相信自己的合理性的时候，它的历史是悲剧性的。当旧制度作为现存的世界制度同新生的世界斗争的时候，旧制度犯的是世界历史性错误，而不是个人的错误。因而旧制度的灭亡也是悲剧性的"。[③] 另一处是源于和剧作家拉萨尔讨论济金根的悲剧性，恩格斯明确地将悲剧因素视为"历史的必然要求和这个要求实际上不可能实现之间的悲剧性的冲突"[④]，而不是作为骑士起义领导人的济金根在智力上和伦理上存有"过失"，或者"在实现目的的方法上实行了狡诈"。[⑤] 在这里，一方面是关于历史的悲剧。历史的悲剧在于历史自身就是合理与不合理的两面之间的同一体，是新与旧，进步与落后二律背反的自身批判。另外，"历史不过是追求着自己的目的的人的活动而已"[⑥]，人作为历史的主体，正是历史悲剧性的承担者。因此，在马克思主义的历史悲剧里并不只是某种革命和历史的抽象，而恰恰是饱含人性和人生的伦理

---

① 高建平：《后文化研究时代的美学》，《美育学刊》，2011 年第 4 期。
② 阎国忠：《中国美学缺少什么》，《学术月刊》，2010 年第 1 期。
③ 《马克思恩格斯选集》第 1 卷，北京：人民出版社，1995 年，第 5 页。
④ 《马克思恩格斯选集》第 4 卷，北京：人民出版社，1995 年，第 560 页。
⑤ 《马克思恩格斯选集》第 1 卷，第 23—24 页。
⑥ 《马克思恩格斯选集》第 2 卷，北京：人民出版社，1995 年，第 118 页。

价值意义的。历史不是神秘的命运,也不是高高在上的理性和上帝,而是相互交错互为作用的多重现实关系,它规定了历史和主体的有限性。但悲剧之所以是悲剧,还在于它是一种"必然",它总是指向合理、进步、肯定的一方。历史总是从"恶"的一面前进,人性也总是在否定性的、有限性的一面得以超越。事实上,威廉斯和伊格尔顿的悲剧观也正是在马克思、恩格斯的历史悲剧理论框架下加以展开的。马克思主义的历史悲剧意识可以予人以彻底的现实清醒感,它使得任何单向的价值判断都成为一种肤浅。此外,现实中的苦难与超越又分明是人的主体性的明证,对于物质时代人的"溃败",特别是对于后现代时代里过于浅表的"快乐主义"来说,这无疑是一种反省与批判。但是,始终值得强调的是,马克思主义美学的批判不是高屋建瓴的道德批判,而是人伦意义上的"尘世"的悲悯,因为悲剧的苦难与超越是历史人群中每一个人的恶与善。

其二,从发展的角度,提供未来的价值指向。马克思主义之前的哲学,从柏拉图到费尔巴哈,都是指向一种理性的沉思,而马克思主义却引入了一个未来的尺度。历史不是某种抽象,而是可以经由主体的实践不断改变的具体过程。所以马克思有精辟的名言:"哲学家们只是用不同的方式解释世界,问题在于改变世界"①。然而,以"人的解放和自由全面发展"为理想目标和价值尺度,并指向"每个人的自由全面的发展"的共产主义理想既是对有限性的超越,又没有落入简单的审美乌托邦。它始终是一个在现实世界里实践和"改变世界"的过程。这个过程包括相反相成的两个路向,一是向前的未来的维度,一是向后的批判的维度。因此,马克思主义在未来的维度里并没有像他们所批判的空想社会主义家们那样,"替未来设计公共厨房",确立一个精确的"蓝图"式的预言,而是以现实为基础,并积极地、有意识地参加到对社会进行革命改造的历史进程中来,从而与旧的、抽象的乌托邦幻想区别开来。正是在这种意义上,布洛赫曾将这一过程称之为"具体的乌托邦";詹姆逊也认为马克思主义是一种"乌托邦计划",在把对"未来"的信仰肯定为"事物本身的性质"与"深层存在的可能性和潜力"②的前提下,詹姆逊还创造性地继承马克思主义的历史辩证法,发展出了一套批判地与现实保持距离的否定的乌托邦意识形态理论。同样是出于对未来意义的积极肯定,伊格尔顿则更明确地指出,马克思主义与其说是发展了一种"唯物主义",还不如说是发展了一种"伦理的"或者"乌

---

① 《马克思恩格斯选集》第1卷,第17页。
② [美]弗雷德里克·詹姆逊:《乌托邦作为方法或未来的用途》,王逢振译,《马克思主义与现实》,2007年第5期。

托邦"的社会主义理论。①

雅斯贝尔斯20世纪30年代的作品《时代的精神状况》中对现代人的非精神化的生活样态曾做了如下描述:"终于这样的时代到了:个人直接的现实的周围世界中不再有任何东西是由这个个人为了他自己的目的而制造、规划或形成的了。每一样东西都应一时的需要而来,然后被用完,然后被扔掉。就连住所本身也是机器的产物。环境变得非精神化了。白天的工作自行其是,不再组合到工人的生活要素中去——所有这一切,可以说,使人失去了他自己的世界。人就是这样地被抛入了漂流不定的状态之中,失去了对于连接过去与未来的历史延续性的一切感觉,人不能保持其为人。这种生活秩序的普遍化将导致这样的后果,即把现实世界中的现实的人的生活变成单纯的履行能力。"② 雅斯贝尔斯所描述的30年代的情景也是今天我们每一个人正在身经感受的悲剧性情景。马克思主义,或者马克思主义美学对于未来的贡献就在于,它指出这种悲剧性,并指向了一个可能的更好的世界。而这也正是在一个对未来普遍充满焦虑感的时代,马克思主义美学重新成为公共话语的可能性所在。

结　语

在中国迅速"全球化"的具体语境中,我认为"中国悲剧观念"对于马克思主义与未来的关系的思考是可以做出自己的贡献的。"中国悲剧观念"首先是建立在中国社会现代化过程的审美经验基础上的。正如特里·伊格尔顿指出的,这是20世纪最大的悲剧性现象和悲剧性事件。这种悲剧观念在鲁迅的作品中得到了很好的表征,是一种绝望中的希望,是放弃中的坚守,是世俗中的崇高,或者以优美的形式而体现出来的崇高。在陈凯歌的电影《霸王别姬》,在莫言的小说《蛙》和《酒国》等作品中,我们都能够感受到这种东方风格的悲剧性,或者说,中国的悲剧观念。令人遗憾的是,中国的理论家们一直没有对"中国悲剧观念"作出系统的理论说明和美学论证。

在中国文化传统中,儒家文化的悲剧性观念得到了学术界的认识和重视,值得注意的是,佛教文化与现代日常生活的结合正在形成一种重要的文化力量。去年11月,我到台湾成功大学出席第十届亚洲新人文联网会议,会议期间访问

---

① [英]特里·伊格尔顿:《马克思主义与社会主义》,王朝元译,《马克思主义美学研究》第6辑。
② [德]卡尔·雅斯贝尔斯:《时代的精神状况》,王德峰译,上海:上海译文出版社,2005年,第11页。

了"佛光山",看到了世俗化的宗教文化对现代化过程中的中国的巨大影响力。这种影响成了中国现代化的一个重要特征。我曾经用"优美化的崇高"来概括本文所讨论的这种不同于西方悲剧观念的中国式悲剧观念。① 中国悲剧观念是中国文化传统与中国现代化过程中的悲剧性现象相结合的结果,它本身就是一个十分矛盾的现象。对这个复杂现象的审美经验,是我们在似乎令人绝望的现实生活中仍然保持住善良、正义和良知的现实基础;而对这个复杂现象的理论说明,也许是中国马克思主义美学走出"阿尔都塞学派"的阴影,重新成为公共话语的一个契机。

2011年《人民文学》发表的小说《北京和尚》,也许可以成为我们较全面地理解"中国悲剧观念"的一个例证。小说以现代化中国的过度商业化和社会生活的道德危机为背景,以一个年青和尚与一个妓女的爱情故事为线索,叙述了一个中国式的"浮士德"的情感漂泊和精神寄托"现实化"的过程。在这个故事中,悲剧性的冲突不在于主体世界的分裂,也不根源于魔鬼的巨大创造力和对纯粹美的追求之间的巨大张力。《北京和尚》的悲剧性在于:"好人"和"神圣者"在物欲横流的现实生活中处处碰壁,在"失败"和退让的过程中达到平静与和谐的生存状态的悲悯和悲壮。小说通过隐喻告诉我们,未来或彼岸不是神圣化的"永恒的女性",而是带着缺陷和世俗性的"麻脸观音"。而这也表明,现实的具体性和人类学意义上的人性的相结合,不仅是可能的,而且是必然的。马克思主义美学的重要性就在于,在审美现代性、悲剧观念、世俗性崇高等成为全球性现象和全球性问题的条件下,马克思主义美学有可能对这种陷于深刻伦理危机和价值危机的现象作出理论的阐释。

与中国迅速地现代化的过程相联系,中国悲剧观念已成为中国式审美现代性的核心概念之一,这个概念的物质基础是当代中国的审美经验和审美关系,它的文化表达机制是一种以"音像"特征为基础的"回旋",而不是以"视像"为特征的距离感和神圣化。在西方当代艺术碎片化的后现代场景中,当代中国文学艺术最优秀的作品仍然是"余音绕梁,三日不绝",这就是我们可以对未来抱有信心的根据。我相信,通过对"中国悲剧观念"的深入研究和阐释,中国的马克思主义美学将得到进一步的发展。

(本文责任编辑:于琦)

---

① 王杰:《审美幻象研究:现代美学导论》,北京:北京大学出版社,2012年,第229—239页。

Chinese Idea of the Tragic: Theoretical Tradition and Contemporary Significance

Wang Jie, Xie Zhuoting

Abstract: Critical reflection on the tragedy of modernity within the theoretical framework of historical tragedy is the most important for Marxist aesthetics to return the public discourse space. Although Marxist aesthetics of tragedy is one of the foreign theories, it keeps internal correspondence with Chinese cultural tradition and the reality of aesthetic experience. There is congeniality between the idea of tragedy in Chinese culture and the views of "tragedy of revolution", "tragedy of daily life" and "sublime of the mortal" in Marxist aesthetics of modern tragedy. As a result of the mixture of Chinese cultural tradition and the tragic phenomenon during the process of modernization, the idea of the tragic has become one of the corn concepts about China's aesthetic modernity. Under the condition that aesthetic modernity, the idea of the tragic and sublime of the mortal have become the global phenomenon and problems, Marxist aesthetics is likely to bring out theoretical interpretation of the severe crises of values and ethics, and it will achieve its self-development of theory further.

马克思实践的唯物主义与现代美学革命

朱立元,章文颖

(复旦大学中文系)

【内容摘要】 马克思实践的唯物主义是对绝对唯心主义和直观唯物主义的双重扬弃和超越。它颠覆了近代西方形而上学的传统,在哲学史上掀起了一场革命:确立了现代存在论的根基,超越了主客二分的认识论思维模式;打破了形而上学的现成论,形成了动态生成的世界观;在"实践"的基础上建立了新的人本主义思想,关注人的自由本质的全面实现。这场深刻的哲学革命也为现代美学带来了革命性的转变,启发了现代美学在研究对象、研究内容和研究方式等方面进行学科建构的突破性的变革,同时也为当代中国美学走向中西融会、古今传承的历史性发展提供了多种可能。

在西方近代哲学史上,马克思以"实践"为核心建构的唯物史观掀起了一场影响深远的哲学革命。唯物史观是对费尔巴哈直观唯物主义和以黑格尔为代表的绝对唯心主义历史观的全面批判和扬弃。马克思既克服了黑格尔精神产生物质、意识决定存在的、头足倒置的唯心史观,吸收了其历史辩证发展的合理内核,又批判了费尔巴哈的直观唯物主义的直观性和非历史性,创建了实践的唯物主义,即历史唯物主义。因此,唯物史观既纠正了旧唯物主义忽视人的实践、片面、直观、被动地单纯从客体方面理解世界的错误方式,也指出了唯心主义观念论者脱离物质生活和实践,单纯地从精神方面理解和解释世界的形而上学谬误。从更长的历史视野观照,马克思的唯物史观还对整个西方传统的形而上学,特别是笛卡尔开启和确立的西方近代哲学即主体性认识论哲学,做了颠覆性的批判和反思,确立了以人的现实生活即实践活动作为新哲学的理论基础,完成了一次从近代认识论到现代本体论(存在论)的重大转移和超越,从而革命性地开启了现代哲学发展的新方向。

这场深刻的哲学革命也为现代美学带来了革命性的转变,启发了现代美学在研究对象、研究内容、研究思路、思维方式、逻辑构架等各个方面的突破和变革,同时也为当代中国美学的发展,提供了中西互鉴、古今对话、综合创新等多种契机和可能。本文试从三个密切联系又各有侧重的方面——实践概念的存在论根基、动态的生成观以及人本主义视野——来论述马克思给现代美学带来的革命性影响。

一、实践的唯物主义是绝对唯心主义和直观唯物主义的双重扬弃和超越

马克思实践的唯物主义(唯物史观)既是马克思扬弃费尔巴哈直观唯物主义和黑格尔唯心史观的理论基石,也是马克思主义引发现代哲学革命的逻辑起点,为现代哲学、美学奠定了存在论的根基。

马克思认为,包括费尔巴哈在内的旧唯物主义虽然将哲学的视点从抽象的理性的形而上学重新引回了直观的感性世界,对德国古典哲学唯心主义的形而上学传统进行了某种纠偏,有着积极的意义;但在理论基础上却存在着严重的缺陷:一方面,费尔巴哈直观的唯物主义看待现实世界的方式只能"从客体的或直观的形式去理解"[1],忽略了主体的能动性和主体的对象化(客体化)建构和实现,即忽略了人的实践;另一方面,虽然费尔巴哈的唯物主义不同于一般的唯物主义,是"人本学"的唯物主义,也就是马克思所说的"和人道主义相吻合的唯物主义"[2],但是,作为这种唯物主义核心和基础的"人",却主要是一个自然的、肉体的、生理意义上的直观感性的人;由于不懂得乃至撇开了实践活动,这种"人"被抽离了鲜活生动的经验世界和物质生活的内容,终归只能是抽象的、非现实、非历史、非社会的人。这个空洞的主体只能用感性直观的方式被动地认识客体,而非能动地、真实地在实践中认识客体、改变客体,因而造成主体与客体、自然与人类社会相互割裂、相互孤立,失却了历史发展的内在动力。所以,费尔巴哈的唯物主义在历史观上仍然是唯心主义的,正如马克思切中肯綮地指出的那样,"当费尔巴哈是一个唯物主义者的时候,历史在他的视野之外;当他去探讨历史的时候,他决不是一个唯物主义者。在他那里,

---

[1] 《马克思恩格斯选集》(第1卷),北京:人民出版社,1995年,第54页。
[2] 《马克思恩格斯选集》(第2卷),北京:人民出版社,1957年,第160页。

唯物主义和历史是彼此完全脱离的"①。

与旧唯物主义相反，黑格尔的唯心主义观念论"抽象"地发展了主体的能动性，却将这种能动性只是集中在主体的精神活动层面，而脱离了现实的物质实践层面，片面夸大了主体精神的作用，导致其历史观只能依托"关于精神和怪影的神话"②，用抽象的观念集合或某种抽象的精神实体作为历史运动的原动力，抽离了感性物质世界和感性主体的实践参与，最终造成其历史观的头足倒置，即认为"观念、想法、概念一直统治和决定着人们的现实世界，现实的世界是观念世界的产物"③，而不承认人们的现实生活决定着他们的观念、意识，从而陷入历史唯心主义。

费尔巴哈的直观唯物主义和黑格尔的绝对唯心主义虽然看似截然相反，但在历史观上却都陷入了唯心主义。马克思实践的唯物主义即历史唯物主义的世界观正是对二者的双重扬弃和超越，这种扬弃和超越的关节点恰恰都在"实践"上。

费尔巴哈直观唯物主义的要害就在于不懂得并忽视人的实践。马克思明确地批评道，"费尔巴哈不满意抽象的思维而喜欢直观；但是他把感性不是看作实践的、人的感性的活动"，这种"直观的唯物主义，即不是把感性理解为实践活动的唯物主义至多也只能达到对单个人和市民社会的直观"④，而不可能正确解释社会历史现象及其发展，所以，在历史观上只能停留于唯心主义。

黑格尔的绝对唯心主义，首先和主要是历史的唯心主义而不是一般的唯心主义。马克思对黑格尔唯心主义的批判也集中在其唯心主义的历史观方面。这同马克思创建唯物史观是从批判黑格尔的法哲学和现象学入手这一点密切相关。马克思在《巴黎手稿》中在对黑格尔的《精神现象学》的历史辩证法内核给予高度评价，指出其"作为推动原则和创造原则的否定性的辩证法——的伟大之处首先在于，黑格尔把人的自我产生看作一个过程，把对象化看作失去对象，看作外化和这种外化的扬弃；因而他抓住了劳动的本质，把对象性的人、现实的因而是真正的人理解为他自己的劳动的结果"，就是说，黑格尔已经看到并肯定了人是自己劳动实践的产物，这一点远比费尔巴哈高明。但马克思同时又批

---

① 《马克思恩格斯选集》（第3卷），北京：人民出版社，1960年，第51页。
② 同上，第132页。
③ 同上，第16页。
④ 《马克思恩格斯选集》（第1卷），北京：人民出版社，1995年，第56—57页。

评他只看到人的"精神劳动"①（或者"精神实践"），而忽视了人的物质劳动实践。马克思说，"由于《现象学》紧紧地抓住人的异化，——尽管人只是以精神的形式出现的——其中仍然隐藏着批判的一切要素，而且这些要素往往已经以远远超过黑格尔观点的方式准备好和加过工了"，其中"包含着对宗教、国家、市民生活等整个领域的批判的要素，但还是通过异化的形式"。这段话与前面那段话的内涵完全一致，既肯定了黑格尔"紧紧地抓住人的异化"的辩证运动来解释历史，实际上已经包含着"远远超过"其绝对唯心主义的历史辩证法因素；但同样也批评黑格尔的"人只是以精神的形式出现的"，而不是实践的人、现实的人，诚如马克思所说，"对象仅仅表现为抽象的意识，而人仅仅表现为自我意识"，因而"这一运动的结果表现为自我意识和意识的同一，绝对知识，那种已经不是向外部而是仅仅在自身内部进行的抽象思维活动，也就是说，其结果是纯思想的辩证法"②。换言之，黑格尔所肯定的人的精神劳动（实践），归根结底只是在意识内部的"抽象思维活动"即"纯思想的辩证法"而已。概而言之，黑格尔的实践只是精神劳动、精神实践，而不是马克思强调的以物质实践为基础的实践（包含精神实践）。这正是黑格尔历史观的唯心主义实质所在。

马克思正是在对黑格尔绝对唯心主义和费尔巴哈直观唯物主义（历史观上仍然是唯心主义）的实践观双重批判和扬弃的基础上，创立和建构起实践的唯物主义即唯物史观的。

二、实践的唯物主义为美学确立了现代存在论的哲学根基

需要指出的是，马克思实践的唯物主义，不能局限于仅仅从近代认识论角度加以把握，而首先或者主要应当从存在论（Ontology，亦译本体论）视角来理解。实践的唯物主义的哲学根基不是认识论，而是存在论。它是对近代西方由笛卡尔开启的主客二分的认识论形而上学传统的批判和超越。因为，按照这种二元对立的认识论思维模式，世界被分为现成存在的主体与客体两部分，同时，具有独立性的主体自身也被分成感性与理性对立二元。如此一来，人与世界之间的无限复杂多样的存在关系就被简化为现成主体对现成客体的单纯认识关系，全部哲学则围绕"我是怎样思维和认识世界"这样一个

---

① 《马克思恩格斯选集》（第42卷），北京：人民出版社，1979年，第163页。
② 同上，第162—163页。

单纯认识论问题来展开思考。在这种主客二分的单纯认识论思维模式下，真正的存在论问题却被有意无意地遮蔽、甚至取消了。这正是近代理性主义和经验主义哲学的失足之处，也是包括费尔巴哈在内的一切旧唯物主义的失足之处。

在我们看来，马克思实践的唯物主义突破的就是近代哲学这种将主、客体现成两分的单纯认识论的思维模式，而将之转移到以实践为核心的存在论（本体论）的根基之上。在马克思看来，人和自然本来就是同为一体，不可分割的，他明确指出"人不是抽象的蛰居于世界之外的存在物。人就是人的世界"①，又说"自然界，就它本身不是人的身体而言，是人的无机的身体。人靠自然界生活。这就是说，自然界是人为了不致死亡而必须与之不断交往的、人的身体。所谓人的肉体生活和精神生活同自然界相联系，也就等于说自然界同自身相联系，因为人是自然界的一部分。"② 就是说，人是在世界中存在的人，没有世界也就没有人；同样，世界是人的世界，因为有人的存在，世界才有意义。所以，"人就是人的世界"这个命题，在原初的意义上，即人与世界同为一体。这实际上已经体现了现代存在论的思想。后来海德格尔对存在的意义的追问，也是从存在论（本体论）的高度对西方形而上学传统中主客二分的单纯认识论进行深刻的批判。海德格尔批判笛卡尔开启的"知识形而上学"是建立在一种"不证自明"的现成的主客对立的关系上的，而在主体存在的独立性的逻辑的开端，却恰恰回避了"我在"的存在的方式和意义，缺乏了存在论的根基。而对一切存在问题的探寻，必须从"此在"（Dasein）的生存领会中获得，海德格尔说"一切存在论所源出的基础存在论必须在对此在的生存论分析中来寻找"③。海德格尔将"此在在世"（人生在世）看作人的存在，看作此在的基本结构，世界因人而有意义，世界在人之中；人是世界的一部分，人在世界中存在，人与世界原初是合为一体的。海德格尔就是在"此在"的生存论的探讨中，奠定了此在的基础本体论（存在论）的地位。

实际上，马克思早在海德格尔之前，就已经提出了现代存在论的思想，不同的是马克思的现代存在论思想是在"实践"的基础上建立的，而非此在的"生存论的分析"。"实践"是唯物史观的核心和理论基石。在《关于费尔巴哈

---

① 《马克思恩格斯选集》（第1卷），北京：人民出版社，1995年，第1页。
② 《马克思恩格斯选集》（第42卷），北京：人民出版社，1979年，第95页。
③ 海德格尔：《存在与时间》，陈嘉映、王庆节合译，北京：三联书店，2012年，第16页。

的提纲》中，马克思将"实践"界定为"现实的"、"感性的人的活动"①，而对"对象、现实、感性"等一切人、社会、历史和自然界，必须从人的"实践"出发去理解。人的"实践"活动是人与世界的一种对象性关系中展开的，也就是说在实践中，人实现了本质力量的对象化和自然的人化，从而真正占有了对象，同时人在与事物的对象性关系中也生成并确立了自身的存在。当然人与感性世界的对象性关系是丰富的，包括"视觉、听觉、嗅觉、味觉、触觉、思维、直观、感觉、愿望、活动、爱"②，不仅仅是物质的、生理的关系，还有情感、精神上对象性关系。因此，"不仅五官感觉，而且所谓精神感觉、实践感觉（意志、爱等等），一句话，人的感觉、感觉的人性都只是由于它的对象的存在，由于人化的自然界，才产生出来"，"因此，一方面为了使人的感觉成为人的，另一方面为了创造同人的本质和自然界的本质全部丰富性相适应的人的感觉，无论从理论还是从实践方面来说，人的本质的对象化都是必要的。"③ 显然，马克思的实践不仅是物质生产活动（虽然物质生产是最基础的实践），还包括政治、道德、艺术、审美、爱等精神实践活动，是广义的人生"实践"。马克思用"实践"的概念沟通了主体与客体间的丰富的对象性关系，只有在实践中人才成为人，自然才成为人的自然。也就是说，所谓的主体和客体只有在实践中才现实地相互生成。马克思说"感觉为了物而同物发生关系，但物本身却是对自身和对人的一种对象性的、人的关系"，也就是说"只有物按人的方式同人发生关系时，我才能在实践上按人的方式同物发生关系。"④ 只有在与人的实践关系中才有物的存在，也只有在与物的对象性实践关系中才有真正的人的存在，即在实践中，主客体回归了同一。

再者，"实践"是人的最基本的在世或存在的方式。"人们生产自己的生活资料，同时间接地生产着自己的物质生活本身。"⑤ 物质生产劳动是"实践"的基础和根本，与此同时人们开展着与之相关的其他丰富的包括精神生活在内的人生实践，形成了现实生活的广阔图景，同时也展开了社会历史发展的壮丽画

---

① 马克思在《关于费尔巴哈的提纲》批判费尔巴哈的直观唯物主义，说"从前的一切唯物主义（包括费尔巴哈的唯物主义）的主要缺点是：对象、现实、感性，只是从客体的或者直观的形式去理解，而不是把它们当作感性的人的活动，当作实践去理解，不是从主体方面去理解。因此，和唯物主义相反，能动的方面却被唯心主义抽象地发展了，当然唯心主义是不知道现实的、感性的活动本身的。"（《马克思恩格斯选集》[第1卷]，北京：人民出版社，1995年，第54页。）

② 《马克思恩格斯选集》（第42卷），北京：人民出版社，1979年，第123页。

③ 同上，第126页。

④ 同上，第124页。

⑤ 同上，第67页。

卷,在这个意义上,马克思说"人们的存在就是他们的现实生活过程"①,而"全部生活在本质上是实践的"②。在实践中的"主体","不是他们自己或别人想象中的那种个人,而是现实中的个人,也就是说,这些个人是从事活动的,进行物质生产的,因而是在一定的物质的、不受他们任意支配的界限、前提和条件下活动着的"③,就是在现实生活中从事各种实践活动的个人,而非费尔巴哈感性生理意义上的抽象的人。"因此,正是在改造对象世界中,人才真正地证明自己是类存在物。这种生产是人的能动的类生活。通过这种生产,自然界才表现为他的作品和他的现实。因此,劳动的对象是人的类生活的对象化:人不仅像在意识中那样理智地复现自己,而且能动地、现实地复现自己,从而在他所创造的世界中直观自身。"④ 自然通过实践对人而言成为现实的存在,人通过实践将精神与肉体统一,在自然中现实地"复现自己""直观"自己。在这里,人和自然、主体与客体的自明的现成性被取消,代之以"实践"为"整个现存的感性世界的基础"⑤。这样,实践就成为马克思存在论思想的核心,实践的唯物主义即唯物史观就获得了存在论的现实根基。

更进一步的,"实践"不仅是马克思哲学理解世界的出发点,也是整个人类历史、现实世界存在和发展的能动性原则和总根基。既然人与自然是在实践中相互生成的,那么我们完全可以理解,"整个所谓世界历史不外是人通过人的劳动而诞生的过程,是自然界对人来说生成的过程"⑥。而实践作为自然与自由统一的哲学范畴,是整个感性的现实世界的不断生成的基础,也是世界发生发展的动力源泉。因此,马克思说"这种活动、这种连续不断的感性劳动和创造、这种生产,正是整个现存的感性世界的基础,它哪怕只中断一年,费尔巴哈就会看到,不仅在自然界将发生巨大的变化,而且整个人类世界以及他自己的直观能力,甚至他本身的存在也会很快就没有了"⑦。世界在人的感性活动即实践中生成、统一、发展,生生不息、循环不止,世界须臾离不开人的感性实践活动,感性实践活动也必须在现实世界中不断地进行。

马克思已经明确意识到他的实践观包含着存在论(本体论)维度。他在

---

① 《马克思恩格斯选集》(第42卷),北京:人民出版社,1979年,第72页。
② 《马克思恩格斯选集》(第1卷),北京:人民出版社,1995年,第56页。
③ 同上,第71—72页。
④ 《马克思恩格斯选集》(第42卷),北京:人民出版社,1979年,第97页。
⑤ 《马克思恩格斯选集》(第1卷),北京:人民出版社,1995年,第77页。
⑥ 《马克思恩格斯选集》(第42卷),北京:人民出版社,1979年,第131页。
⑦ 《马克思恩格斯选集》(第1卷),北京:人民出版社,1995年,第77页。

《巴黎手稿》中，曾经直接谈论到人的感觉、情欲等对象化即实践的存在论（ontologisch）意义：

> 如果人的感觉、激情等等不仅是［狭隘］意义上的人类学的规定，而且是真正本体论的（ontologisch）本质（自然）肯定；如果感觉、激情等等仅仅通过它们的对象对它们来说是感性地存在这一事实而真正肯定自己，那么，……只有通过发达的工业，也就是以私有财产为中介，人的激情的本体论的（ontologisch）本质才在总体上、合乎人性地实现；因此，关于人的科学本身是人在实践上的自我实现的产物。①

由此可见，马克思的实践观是与存在论紧密结合的，他对存在论问题的探讨，是以实践为核心展开的，这就为实践论、进而为实践的唯物主义即唯物史观确立了存在论的根基。这不仅仅超越了近代主客二分的单纯认识论传统，而且为现代哲学开启了存在论的新路径。同样，马克思实践的唯物主义的革命意义也主要不在于认识论上的革命，而正是在于通过"实践"范畴的提出，不仅改变了旧唯物主义对世界的直观、片面的理解方式，代之以用实践解释世界、解释历史的全新观念，即从主体现实的感性活动、现实生活着眼来谈历史、社会和世界万物的存在，跳出了唯心史观的形而上学怪圈；而且更重要的，它是从本体论（存在论）高度开启了通过实践活动现实地改变世界的历史唯物主义的全新视野。确立实践唯物主义的存在论根基，将近代形而上学的单纯认识论传统转移到以实践为核心的存在论根基上，这才是马克思哲学革命最重要的意义。这一哲学观念的革命性转变，宣告了在西方形而上学统治的终结，直接开启了现代西方思想界向存在论研究视点的转移，把哲学变革做到了极致，正如海德格尔所说"纵观整个哲学史，柏拉图的思想以有所变化的形态始终起着决定性作用。形而上学就是柏拉图主义。尼采把他自己的哲学标示为颠倒了的柏拉图主义。随着这一已经由卡尔·马克思完成了的对形而上学的颠倒，哲学达到了最极端的可能性"。②

实践的唯物主义的存在论根基为现代美学的学科建设和研究带来了深刻的启示。首先，为美学研究开辟了从单纯认识论向现代存在论转移的新路向，特

---

① 《马克思恩格斯选集》（第42卷），北京：人民出版社，1979年，第150页。
② 海德格尔：《海德格尔选集》（下册），孙周兴等译，上海：上海三联书店，1996年，第1244页。

别是为美学奠定以实践为核心的存在论的马克思主义哲学根基。中国现当代美学，长期以来局限于认识论范围，包括20世纪五六十年代美学大讨论，对于美的本质问题的争论，基本上也没有超出认识论的范围。实际上，美学的基本问题决不仅仅限于认识论，或者更确切地说，主要不是认识论问题，只有把重点转移到存在论（本体论）层面，美学研究的论域和视野才能得到新的拓展。其次，使美学研究跳出了主客体二元对立的认识论思维框架，取消了本质主义追问的美学研究方式。从而可以在生生不息的、活的生活实践、审美实践的过程中，揭示出审美活动的无限丰富复杂性。再次，把人与世界在审美实践中生成的具体的审美关系作为美学研究的逻辑起点，而非孤立、现成、静止的审美对象或审美主体。因此改变了在单纯认识论框架下形成的现成审美主体对现成审美客体（美的实体）的再现和反映的传统认识论美学的思路，而把现实的审美活动及其展开作为美学研究的主要对象和内容。

马克思实践的唯物主义也为中国当代美学的突破和发展开启了综合中西、古今的新思路，即尝试发掘中国古典美学与西方美学相互参照和融会贯通的新的可能性。笔者提出的实践存在论美学关于实践是一种人生实践、审美活动是人生实践的重要方式之一、审美对象和审美主体都是在审美活动过程中现实地生成的、审美境界是人生境界的高级层次等观点，都是尝试将马克思的实践唯物主义存在论与中西传统美学思想相互对话、融通而产生的。实践唯物主义使中国美学的发展有可能在继承传统的基础上形成新的历史性突破。

三、实践的唯物主义的动态生成观念对现代美学变革的影响

实践的唯物主义存在论根基的确立，使人与世界的关系不再处于二元对立的状态，而是统一于不断交互作用、相互生成、不断更新创造的实践过程中，这生生不息的实践活动正是"人生在世"的基本方式。马克思关于"整个所谓世界历史不外是人通过人的劳动而诞生的过程，是自然界对人来说生成的过程"[①]的经典论断有力地证明，实践的唯物主义存在论包含着深刻的"动态生成"的辩证观念和思维方法。按照"动态生成"观，既没有现成存在的、永恒不变的主体，也没有现成存在的、永恒不变的客体，所谓的主体与客体都是在实践活动中现实地生成的，并继续处在变化的过程中，相对于主体和客体，实

---

① 《马克思恩格斯选集》（第42卷），北京：人民出版社，1979年，第131页。

践在存在论上是更加本源的存在。更进一步,只有在实践活动的对象性关系中,世界才是人的世界,而人也才成为在世界中存在的人。换言之,客体因与主体的发生实践的对象性关系而成为现实的客体,主体也同样因为与客体发生实践关系,才现实地成为与客体相对的主体。如果没有实践活动,也就根本不存在所谓的主体与客体。这种双向生成的"动态生成"观,不仅是实践的唯物主义存在论的必然推论,也是其突破西方传统认识论哲学主客二分的现成论思维的禁锢,向现代哲学转变的又一革命性贡献。正如恩格斯所说:"认为事物是既成的东西的旧形而上学,是从那种把非生物和生物当作既成事物来研究的自然科学中产生的。而当这种研究已经进展到可以向前迈出决定性的一步,即可以过渡到系统地研究这些事物在自然界本身中所发生的变化的时候,在哲学领域内也就敲响了旧形而上学的丧钟。"①

按照实践的唯物主义的观点,任何所谓客体,都不是像旧唯物主义所认为的那样是处在主体之外的纯粹的客观实体,而应该"从主观方面去理解",看作是有主体能动参与的"感性活动"即"实践"的结果。主体"周围的感性世界绝不是某种开天辟地以来就直接存在的、始终如一的东西,而是工业和社会状况的产物,是历史的产物,是世世代代活动的结果"。② 这个结果既是以往人们生活实践的积累,也是新的生活实践的起点,是与主体在实践过程中共同建构生成的存在,因而始终处在不断变化更新的过程中,而非现成存在、静止不变的"实体"。旧唯物主义的这种将现成客体存在作为理论前提的思路,最终不可避免地导致主客体的分离,非但不能保证人之外的客体的纯客观性,反而使客体与主体渐行渐远直至走向人的对立面,使"唯物主义变得敌视人了"③。而失去了与人的实践活动的联系,客体实际上也不能成为真正现实的客体。我们已经说过,在实践的唯物主义存在论看来,主体和客体只有在实践活动中才能相互形成,彼此赋予意义,在"人的世界"中根本不存在完全脱离主体的孤立的客体,因为"物本身是对自身和对人的一种对象性的、人的关系"④,是人的本质力量的对象化,对象能在多大程度上实现主体自身,取决于"对象的性质以及与之相适应的本质力量的性质"⑤,而这种对象化活动本质上就是实践。

---

① 恩格斯:《路德维希·费尔巴哈和德国古典哲学的终结》,北京:人民出版社,1997年,第37页。
② 《马克思恩格斯选集》(第1卷),北京:人民出版社,1995年,第76页。
③ 《马克思恩格斯选集》(第2卷),北京:人民出版社,1957年,第164页。
④ 《马克思恩格斯选集》(第42卷),北京:人民出版社,1979年,第124页。
⑤ 同上,第125页。

对象（客体）只有在人的实践活动中与主体一起现实地生成。因此，马克思说，只有"在历史中即在人类社会的生产过程中形成的自然界是人的现实的自然界"才"是真正的、人类学的自然界"。①

同样，人作为主体，也是在生成"过程"中的人。他不是与对象分离的单独的精神个体，或是离群索居与世隔绝的个体，而是就生活在不断变动的现实世界之中，与世界互动生成的主体性存在。人们接触世界、与世界打交道的主体"五官感觉的形成是以往全部世界历史的产物"②，都是在人与自然的对象化的实践活动中逐渐形成并发展起来的，而不是人生来就有的现成的生理能力。人自身的本质力量在不断对象化的同时，获得了自我提升，与自然界各个方面相对应的主体感觉能力才变得愈来愈丰富。甚至"不仅是五官感觉"，而且"所谓精神感觉、实践感觉（意志、爱等等）"都是在人与对象世界的对象性实践关系中形成并发展起来的，是人的"本质力量的确证"③。因此，"只有当对象对人来说成为人的对象或者说成为对象性的人的时候，人才不致在自己的对象里面丧失自身"。④ 任何个体都存在于具体的历史、社会环境，和与他人的交往关系之中，是受动与能动的统一。他既受外部世界（包括物质自然规律）的制约和作用，同时也将自己的精神和意志付诸实践改变着外部世界。因此，作为主体的人是与外部世界不断进行着实践沟通的现实的人，他改变着世界，世界也改变着他。人类历史就是在有生命的人的现实生活中不断延伸、展开、变动、发展的。在这个意义上，马克思说，"社会结构和国家经常是从一定个人的生活过程中产生的"。⑤ 也就是说，有生命的人是历史形成的前提和逻辑起点，而人必须在延绵不断的现实生活的过程中不断地与现实生活世界进行着生产和交换才获得真正的现实存在的。主体正是在全部的感性实践活动中，实现着自己的本质力量，同时也展开着自己的存在，也就是说"人不仅通过思维，而且以全部的感觉在对象世界中肯定自己。"⑥

所以不论是"客体"还是"主体"都只有在双向互动的实践过程中才得以生成并不断变动发展着。在此意义上，任何脱离实践过程而孤立地处于人或自然界之外的物质或精神的实体都不可能现实地存在，都不具有实在性，"因为人

---

① 《马克思恩格斯选集》（第 42 卷），北京：人民出版社，1979 年，第 128 页。
② 同上，第 126 页。
③ 同上，第 126 页。
④ 同上，第 125 页。
⑤ 同上，第 29 页。
⑥ 同上，第 125 页。

和自然界的实在性，即对人来说作为自然界的存在以及自然界对人来说作为人的存在，已经变成实践的、可以通过感觉直观的，所以，关于某种异己的存在物、关于凌驾于自然界和人之上的存在物的问题……在实践上已经成为不可能的了"。① 而实践本身就是一个动态的过程，因此，"整个所谓世界历史不外是人通过人的劳动而诞生的过程，是自然界对人来说的生成过程"。② 历史在变动中产生、在变动中发展，世界是"过程的集合体"③，它本身就是一个不断发展和运动着的过程，而不是既定的种种现成的事物的集合。

动态生成观是实践的唯物主义存在论必然的、革命性的逻辑推演，它取消了现成的主客体存在的自明性，同时跳出了二元对立的思维方式，使哲学理论不再停留于主体与客体、感性与理性、思维与存在、物质与精神等简单、僵硬的非此即彼的二分法的问题模式之中，与辩证法具有精神上的一致性。它用双向互动的实践生成观代替了单向性的认识论或决定论的思维，在实践的高度上打破了形而上学的本质主义，将哲学研究的视点从形而上学转向了现实的人生存在，使人与世界丰富多样的关系得以全方位地展开。

唯物史观所引发的美学的实践生成论的观点，对以往以主客体二分为基础的认识论美学产生了巨大的冲击，改换了新的提问方式，为现代美学的革命提供了新的方法论和新的研究思路和视野。

首先，按照实践的动态生成观，作为审美主体的人和作为审美客体的对象，都不是孤立的、既定的现成个体或实体，而是在审美实践中双向互动、相互生成的。美本身是一个生成的过程，而不是一个现成的结果，根本不存在一种先在的、现成的"美"的实体、客体等待着现成的审美主体去发现和认识。所以，既不能单向地从审美客体的角度理解"美"，在客体上寻找现成的"美"的本质和规律；也不能单向地从审美主体的角度出发去理解"美感"，预设一个固定不变的审美主体去反映、认识、感受、理解美而形成美感。离开审美实践的动态生成观，将审美主体和客体割裂开来、对立起来（主客二分），抽象地追问"美"和"美感"在主体精神世界中产生的普遍原则，是不可取的。

第二，人与世界之间在审美活动中形成、建立起来的审美关系也不是现成的，因为根本不存在固定不变的现成的审美客体（美）和同样固定不变的现成的审美主体，也就根本不存在由这二者建立起来的审美关系。审美关系也是在

---

① 《马克思恩格斯选集》（第42卷），北京：人民出版社，1979年，第131页。
② 同上。
③ 恩格斯：《路德维希·费尔巴哈和德国古典哲学的终结》，北京：人民出版社，1997年，第36页。

实践中动态生成的，它在逻辑上先于审美主体和客体的形成。这个逻辑上"关系在先"原则，正是由动态生成观确立的。

第三，据此，根不不存在孤立于人与世界之外的永恒不变的美或美的本质。美是在人与世界审美关系中现实地生成，并不断变动着的，脱离了在现实生活中的生命个体即人的存在，美也就根本不存在了。"美"有着鲜明的属人的性质。如果不结合人的具体的生活实践来理解，"美"只是一个抽象的、空泛的概念。"美"从宏观上讲是人类的实践活动、特别是艺术和审美实践的历史、总体积累生成、发展的，在微观上则是在审美活动中通过与特定主体（个体）的交互作用现实地生成的，所以"美"无论在纵向还是横向上都不存在终极的现成性。

第四，同样，"美感"也不是现成的、固定不变的。不是一切人，也不是个人的一切时间、场所都作为现成的审美主体而存在。任何一个审美主体只有在审美实践活动中通过与对象的互动才得以现实地生成，"美感"也就同时产生。审美主体也是受动与能动的统一，他既受制于审美对象的属性和自身感官性能的条件限制，同时也能调动和发挥自身的主体能动性，对对象进行创造性的审美实践。同时，主体的本质力量也就在这种对象性的审美活动中得到实现，并在与对象交互动态的审美实践过程中自身的审美能力得到发展和提升。正如马克思所说："只是由于人的本质的客观地展开的丰富性，主体的、人的感性的丰富性，如有音乐感的耳朵、能感受形式美的眼睛，总之，那些能成为人的享受的感觉，即确证自己是人的本质力量的感觉，才一部分发展起来，一部分产生出来。"①

总之，美和美感都不是什么现成存在的现象或实体，它们是在现实的审美关系中，通过主客体间对象性活动生成并发展的，它是历史的、现实的、具体的。

对于中国当代美学来说，实践的唯物主义存在论为我们破除机械化、教条化、僵化地解读马克思美学思想提供了可靠的理论支持。使我们能够跳出在主客二分的单纯认识论框架内打转的僵化的思维方式，在动态生成观的基础上，重新审视审美活动。打破本质主义的思维定势，把美学研究的主要对象和论域从对探寻固定不变的所谓"美的本质"转移到现实生动的人生的丰富审美实践活动上来。由此，我们看到了现实的审美关系对于审美主、客体现实生成的逻

---

① 《马克思恩格斯选集》（第42卷），北京：人民出版社，1979年，第126页。

辑上的优先性，看到只有在审美活动和审美关系建立的前提之下，才能现实地建构起审美主体和客体并在它们二者之间展开双向建构；从而进一步看到了审美客体和主体、"美"和"美感"甚至审美关系本身的过程性和生成性，因此也看到了美的恒变恒新以及人的审美感觉和能力在审美关系中不断自我发展和更新的可能性。

四、实践的唯物主义为现代美学确立了人本主义的基本尺度

马克思实践的唯物主义思想中还蕴含着深刻的人本主义精神。人本主义是实践唯物主义即唯物史观的主要价值尺度，是唯物史观的题中应有之义。现实的、实践的人，是实践唯物主义存在论的出发点、核心和归宿。马克思从生活在实践中的真实的人出发，关注个体存在的真实性和现实性，引导人们扬弃异化的存在方式，最终"消灭"异化，从而在自由自觉的劳动实践的基础上全面实现人的本质力量，最终达到人的自由全面发展和人性的复归这一终极目标。

首先，实践唯物主义的出发点是现实的人的存在。唯物史观所说的历史，不是精神主体的主观想象或抽象的观念的集合，也不是"僵死的事实的汇集"①，而是始终着眼于人的现实生活，把人的现实生活、实践活动作为历史形成、发展的出发点和前提，"从直接生活的物质生产出发阐述现实的生产过程"②，"从这些自然基础以及它们在历史进程中由于人们的活动而发生的变更出发"③，通过考察生产力以及与之相对应的生产关系和交往关系的总和，进而阐发在生活实践的基础、前提和条件下，所形成的意识形态的各种形式及变化，从而科学地解释历史的发展。就此而言，世界历史本质上是一部现实的人的实践活动史。正是人的这种能动的生活实践活动，源源不断地更新、发展、前进，形成了整部活的、具体的、过程中的人类史。可见，与实践的唯物主义存在论根基和动态生成观一样，马克思的人本主义思想也与他的实践观紧密结合。马克思所关注的"人"处在与对象世界不断交互生成的实践活动过程中，是在现实生活中真实存在的、具有社会性的人。因为马克思存在论的基础——实践——必须落实在现实的、具体的、在感性世界中活动着的人身上，"全部人类

---

① 《马克思恩格斯选集》（第1卷），北京：人民出版社，1995年，第73页。
② 同上，第92页。
③ 同上，第67页。

历史的第一个前提无疑是有生命的个人的存在"①。这个"个人"不是孤立、没有具体生活内容的抽象的"人"或"人类",而是在现实生活中能动地进行着实践活动的具体的个人,"不是处在某种虚幻的离群索居和固定不变状态中的人,而是处在现实的、可以通过经验观察到的、在一定条件下进行的发展过程中的人"②。人的实践是感性世界存在的基础。这个"人"既不是纯粹受自然本能支配的动物性的感性肉体,也不是纯粹由主观意志决定的精神实体,而是在生活实践中受到自然物质一定的限定、制约却能发挥主观能动性的现实的、社会的人。现实的"人"的基本点切入点又是具体的、当下的"个人","不过当然是处于既有的历史条件和关系范围之内的自己,而不是玄想家们所理解的'纯粹的'个人"③。总之马克思实践的唯物主义即唯物史观建构的基础和出发点是在实践活动中展开的各个维度上得到关怀的现实的、具体的个人的存在。

第二,马克思实践的唯物主义主张扬弃异化劳动,实现真正的自由劳动(实践),全面体现人的自由本质。马克思认为,异化劳动把人降低到了动物的存在水平,阻碍了人的自由自觉的本质力量的全面实现。他指出,人与动物最直接的区别在于其生命活动是"自由自觉"的、"有意识的生命活动",而且"仅仅由于这个缘故,人是类的存在物。换言之,正是由于他是类的存在物,他才是有意识的存在物,也就是说,他本身的生活对他来说才是对象,只是由于这个缘故,他的活动才是自由的活动。"④ 这就是说,人之区别于动物之"类本质"的人的"类特性",是"自由自觉的活动"⑤。在马克思看来,人正是在自由自觉的生命活动中,在对象化的实践活动中才成为有意识的主体;此时的实践主体的肉体与精神是统一的,他的劳动实践就是他的本质力量的对象化或在对象中的实现。在此,劳动本身就是劳动的目的,"而生活本身"应该"仅仅表现为生活的手段"⑥。此时的劳动是自由自觉的劳动,是人全面的本质力量的对象化。但是资本主义私有制下的异化劳动将这个关系完全颠倒过来了:劳动的目的与手段分离,以至于"人正因为是有意识的存在物,才把自己的生命活动,自己的本质变成仅仅维持自己生存的手段"⑦。这样一来,主客体站在了对

---

① 《马克思恩格斯选集》(第1卷),北京:人民出版社,1995年,第67页。
② 同上,第73页。
③ 同上,第119页。
④ 《马克思恩格斯选集》(第42卷),北京:人民出版社,1979年,第96页。
⑤ 同上。
⑥ 同上。
⑦ 同上。

立的位置上，肉体与精神在劳动实践中相分离，实践不再是人的全部本质力量的对象化活动，而是仅仅作为肉体生存需求的一种手段。这种片面、异化的劳动是不自由的劳动，它使人的存在降低为动物性的生存。总之，马克思站在对人的价值关怀立场上，对资产阶级国民经济学及其所辩护的异化劳动，进行了深刻的批判。这种看似冷静客观的实践唯物主义的政治经济学批判，贯穿着极其鲜明的人本主义价值立场。

第三，实现人的全面自由的发展，是马克思的人本主义关怀的终极指向。在马克思看来，私有制和异化劳动使人与自身对立，自身生命成为外化的生命，人成为自身的异己力量，这样的"人"是不完整的，片面的；真正意义上的完整的人，是积极扬弃了私有财产和异化劳动，将一切感性能力和本质特性彻底解放之后的人，"也就是说，为了人并通过人对人的本质和人的生命、对象性的人和人的产品的感性的占有，……以一种全面的方式，也就是说，作为一个完整的人，占有自己的全面的本质"。① 马克思用异化劳动理论解剖了资本主义市民社会，并指出了一条消除异化劳动的途径，即通过共产主义运动实现人的全面自由的发展。他说，"共产主义是私有财产即人的自我异化的积极的扬弃，因而是通过人并且为了人而对人的本质的真正占有；因此，它是人向自身、向社会的（即人的）人的复归，这种复归是完全的、自觉的而且保存了以往发展的全部财富的。"② 我们看到，马克思共产主义理论的终极关怀，仍然是人和人的自由。不过历史唯物主义的人的自由，不是"在一定条件下不受阻碍地利用偶然性的权利"的"个人自由"③，而是"个人才能获得全面发展其才能的手段"，并"在自己的联合中并通过这种联合获得自己的自由"④。也就是通过共产主义，消除私有制、特别是资本主义私有制造成的劳动异化，使主体与客体重新在实践中同一，复归到自由、自觉劳动的人的类本质。实践活动本身成为主体意识的对象成就着主体的意识，而不是主体意识用来实现功利目的的手段。在自由自觉的劳动中，人与自然肉体与精神，人与产品，人与生产实践，人与社会都本然同一，因而实现了真正的自由，在更高层次上实现人对人的本质的重新占有，获得真正的自由，回归了人的本性，成为全面发展的、真正的"完整的人"。

---

① 《马克思恩格斯选集》（第42卷），北京：人民出版社，1979年，第123页。
② 同上，第120页。
③ 《马克思恩格斯选集》（第1卷），北京：人民出版社，1995年，第122页。
④ 同上，第119页。

马克思还为我们描绘了消除异化劳动的共产主义条件下每个人的自由的生活状态:"在共产主义社会里,任何人都没有特殊的活动范围,而是都可以在任何部门内发展,社会调节着整个生产,因而使我有可能随自己的兴趣今天干这事,明天干那事,上午打猎,下午捕鱼,傍晚从事畜牧,晚饭后从事批判,这样就不会使我老是一个猎人、渔夫、牧人或批判者。"① 人不再禁锢于某一社会分工和有限的生活活动,而是完全根据自己的个性、能力、兴趣从事自己的自由自觉的劳动,个体完全从自然和社会的强力压迫下解放了出来,物质生活与精神自由不再分离对立,人类可以自由自觉地创造自己的历史。这将是怎样的一幅散发着人性光辉的诗性人生的画卷啊!总之,马克思实践的唯物主义即唯物史观,最终所要达到的目标仍然是现实的人的价值和人性本质在最高层面上的全面实现。因此,"完整的人"的实现是马克思唯物史观的价值核心和最终归宿,为马克思的人本主义思想完成了一个圆满的理论建构。

马克思建立在实践基础上的人本主义思想有别于传统的人道主义、人本主义。马克思所说的"人"既不是脱离时代和社会的抽象意义上的人,也不是纯粹受生理本性支配的生物学意义上的人,更不是被宗教性的"爱"所填充的抽象的精神个体,而是就生活在现实、当下的人生实践中的具体的个人。这一思想是对西方传统人本主义思想批判地继承和创造性的发展;它不同于种种依附于唯心史观的人本主义学说、理论,而是立足于唯物史观的基石上、关注人们的现实人生、把人文关怀指向每个个人的自由全面的发展,进而达到全人类的自由和解放。这不仅拓展了哲学研究思路,同时也为美学开启了现代人本主义的新视野。

第一,马克思的人本主义思想启发我们将美学研究的中心定位为现实"人",使美学的研究视角、贯穿思路、理论展开回归到实践中的"人"本身,确立了现代美学的人本主义主线。

首先,马克思的人本主义使我们认识到,"美"的产生、形成和发展与处在实践过程中的"人"息息相关,"美"因人而存在,只对人有意义;反之"人"的存在、发展和自我实现也与审美实践密不可分。如果说文学是人学,那么,美学更是一门真正意义上全面关怀人的存在的"人学"。

其次,马克思从实践的唯物主义出发,深刻解释了美之所以产生的人类学

---

① 《马克思恩格斯选集》(第1卷),北京:人民出版社,1995年,第85页。

原因。马克思指出，人的自由自觉的劳动是人的类本质，使人区别于动物。也正是由于人能自由自觉的劳动，使人具有按照美的规律造型的能力，而美就根源于自由自觉的劳动过程中。他说：

> 通过实践创造对象世界，即改造无机界，证明了人是有意识的类存在物，也就是这样一种存在物，它把类看作自己的本质，或者说把自身看作类存在物。诚然，动物也生产。它也为自己营造巢穴或住所，如蜜蜂、海狸、蚂蚁等。但是动物只生产它自己或它的幼仔所直接需要的东西；动物的生产是片面的，而人的生产是全面的；动物只是在直接的肉体需要的支配下生产，而人甚至不受肉体需要的支配也进行生产，并且只有不受这种需要的支配时才进行真正的生产；动物只生产自身，而人再生产整个自然界；动物的产品直接同它的肉体相联系，而人则自由地对待自己的产品。动物只是按照它所属的那个种的尺度和需要来建造，而人却懂得按照任何一个种的尺度来进行生产，并且懂得怎样处处都把内在的尺度运用到对象上去；因此，人也按照美的规律来建造。①

马克思这段话，一是突出了人的生产实践（创造对象世界）的四大特点即全面性、超越性、创造性、自由性，核心是人的自觉性与自由性，体现了人的自觉的目的性通过对象化的活动在对象世界中的实现，也体现了人对自然界的能动性（在受动性之中）。可见马克思是将实践看成人之为人、人形成为类存在物即社会的人的本源和原动力，实践于是就具有了存在论和人类学的双重意义。二是正是在这样的上下文特定语境中，马克思通过三个"尺度"（动物所属的物种的尺度、自然对象所属的物种的尺度，人自身的"内在的尺度"）及其关系的论述提出了美的规律问题：动物只能按其所属的物种的尺度在本物种自然尺度规定的范围内进行"生产"，而人却不但能超越自身族类的自然尺度，懂得（意识到）按照一切动物种的尺度来进行生产，而且能把由自身需要和目的出发形成的"内在的尺度"自由自觉地运用到对象上去，实际地改造对象世界。所以，第三个尺度即"内在的尺度"是属人的，依属于以自由自觉的实践活动为本质的人。三是美的规律因此也应该是属人的规律，应该体现人的自由、自觉的类本质，它只对人有意义，因为只有人能认识和应用美的规律，动物是

---

① 《马克思恩格斯选集》（第42卷），北京：人民出版社，1979年，第97页。

不能按照美的规律造型的，动物的产品本身无所谓美与不美。四是美的规律应该体现主客体两种尺度的辩证统一，这种统一是合目的性与合规律性、自由和必然、人和自然的统一，集中体现了人的生产的自由自觉性。这正是"美的规律"在人的全部劳动实践活动中均得以成立的最深刻的基础。五是美的规律应该是对象事物（包括人）何以成为美的事物、何以具有审美特性和价值、何以成为审美对象并能引起人们审美愉快的规律，在这个意义上，美的规律实际上也就是审美的规律，是人通过实践活动与现实（对象）世界建构起审美关系的规律。

以上几点，是马克思在实践论与人类学的结合上对审美和美的规律深度阐发。

第二，马克思的人本主义思想为我们在人与世界的现实的审美实践关系中展开美学研究开辟了全新的视域。既然实践是现实的人的基本存在方式，既然审美活动也是人生实践的基本方式之一，那么美学研究的基本出发点，也应该着眼于具体审美活动中的现实的人，以及人与现实在实践中生成的无限丰富多样的具体的审美关系。因此，美学研究的视角也应转向关注人们日常生活的审美实践，关注具体的、现实的、丰富的、动态生成的生活中的审美活动。这一研究视点的转变，不但对于扭转美学仅在狭隘的学术圈内作形而上学理论探讨的风气有正面的促进作用，也与国外"生活美学"转向的新趋势相呼应，而且使美学回归更加广阔的现实生活，回归更加丰富的大众审美实践，接上地气，从而获得新的生机和活力。

尤其需要强调，当前的现实是，我们进入了全球化的时代，以信息化为标志的现代高科技迅猛发展，从各个方面挤压人的自由、全面发展的空间；同时，消费主义已经开始在中国蔓延、泛滥，一切都商品化、市场化了，如同伊格尔顿所说，"文化和社会生活再一次紧密地结成联盟，但这时则是表现为商品的美学形态、政治的壮观化、生活方式的消费主义、形象的集中性，以及最终将文化变成一般商品生产的综合。"[①] 金钱和商品拜物教严重地侵袭、腐蚀人的心灵。在这样一种人本主义底线被不断击破的现实语境下，马克思关于"完整的人"的理想追求和现实关怀，无疑给当代美学的复苏和建设提供了强大的思想武器和最终的价值标杆。

第三，马克思建立在实践的唯物主义基础上的人本主义，启发了现代美学

[①] 伊格尔顿：《文化的观念》，南京：南京大学出版社，2003年，第33页。

超越主客二分的僵化思维，同时突破了自然中心主义或人类中心主义的狭隘视野，站在人与自然平等、同一的立场上，全面思考世界和谐发展的美学新课题，为现代生态美学的建构和发展提供了坚实的理论基础。从实践的唯物主义存在论出发，人与世界在"实践中"互动生成，本然同一，自然界构成为人的世界，成为人的身体的延伸，人则成为自然界内在的组成部分。人与自然界不再是传统认识论框架下的两分状态，自然界不仅仅是被认识、被改造的对象，而是与人类血脉相连、生息相关的和谐整体。无数的经验事实已经证明，认识论观念指导下人们对自然的过度开发和利用，造成日益严重的环境污染和生态破坏，最终换来的是大自然对人类生存的无情报复甚至巨大灾害，这正证明了人与自然本然平等、同一的现代人本主义思想的合理性和必要性。而主张人对环境、自然尊重、友好、亲近，追求人与环境、自然的和谐统一、协调发展，这也正是生态美学研究的最高宗旨。

综上所述，马克思实践的唯物主义给现代美学的发展带来了巨大变革的动力和极为深远的影响，它颠覆了传统形而上学二元对立的思维模式，其犀利的思想锋芒直指当代哲学、美学存在的根本问题，引导我们对传统美学研究进行深刻的反思并尝试重建新的范式。这场美学革命将是一个漫长的探索过程，但在当代中国，必然为我们推动美学理论的多元发展提供多维的研究视野和源源不断的动力。

（本文责任编辑：张永禄）

Marx's Practical Materialism and the Revolution of Modern Aesthetics

Zhu Liyuan, Zhang Wenying

Abstract: Marx's Practical Materialism sublated and transcended both absolute idealism and intuitive materialism. It subverted the tradition of modern western metaphysics and set off a revolution in the history of philosophy; it established the foundation of modern ontology so that the epistemological thinking mode of subject—object dichotomy was transcended; it broke the subsistent metaphysics so that the dynamically generative view of the world was formed; it based the new humanism thoughts on "Practice" and focused on the comprehensively implementation of the nature of human freedom. The profound philosophy revolution also brought a revolutionary change of modern aesthetics. At the same time, it provides many possibilities for modern Chinese aesthetics which will develop into the combining of west and east, inheriting the past for the present.

对我国马克思主义文艺理论研究的哲学反思

王元骧

（浙江大学，浙江杭州）

【内容摘要】 本文就以往我国马克思主义文艺理论研究中所存在的直观论、纯认识论和教条主义倾向作了简略的评论，并认为造成这些倾向的思想根源从哲学上来看，是由于一方面把"思维与存在的关系"混同于"精神与物质的关系"，视马克思主义文艺观为仅仅是在总结现实主义文学经验基础上形成的"认识论文艺观"而未能深入发掘它的"人学"内涵。另一方面，由于不理解"思维与存在的关系"是在实践基础上所形成的动态的对立统一的关系，因而也不理解任何理论的真理性都是相对的，它只有借助一定的方法在实际运用过程中才能转化为具体的真理。

一

文艺理论总是以一定的哲学为基础的，马克思主义文艺理论也不例外。以往我国的马克思主义哲学按恩格斯的"全部哲学，特别是近代哲学的重大的基础问题，是思维和存在的关系问题"① 这一原则来探讨哲学问题时，一般都把"思维与存在的关系"，亦即"意识与存在的关系"等同于"精神与物质的关系"，按物质第一性精神第二性的观点，引申出文艺是社会生活的反映并据此来说明文艺理论中的一系列的问题。这对于引导作家深入生活，从现实生活中提取创作题材来进行创作虽然有一定的意义，但从理论上说是不够准确而全面的，

---

① 《马克思恩格斯选集》第2版第4卷，第219页。

从而导致我国马克思主义文艺理论研究中长期存在的直观论的倾向、纯认识论的倾向以及教条主义化的倾向。

要从根本上改变情况，我觉得首先需要对"精神与物质"和"思维与存在"的关系有一个正确的认识。这两者之间的关系虽然十分密切，但却不能彼此混淆、互相等同和取代的。因为物质与精神的关系是一个"本体论"的问题，物质第一性，精神第二性这两者的关系是不容颠倒的，否则就分不清唯物主义与唯心主义的区别。而思维与存在的关系则是一个"认识论"的命题，就"存在"来说，它作为思维的对象是指世界上一切客观存在着的东西，不仅是指物质的东西，而且也包括精神的东西；不仅是指社会的精神现象，而且也包括认识主体自身的精神活动在内。因为当主体的内心活动作为思维的对象的时候，它就意味着被"二重化"了，就像黑格尔所比的"心灵就在它的主位变成自己的对象"①，它与物质的、外界存在的东西一样都成了客观存在着的。就"意识"来说，它作为现实世界在人类头脑中反映的产物，总是在主客体之间的交互作用中产生的。因为人的头脑不像亚里士多德所比喻的是"蜡块"或洛克所说的"白板"，它储存着由以往大量经验积累所形成的认知结构和思维定势，这决定了人们对客观事物的反映总是受着这些认识结构和思维定势的选择和建构；从知识论的观点来看，它必然受着实践发展所达到的认识水平所制约，如同恩格斯所说，在人的思维活动中，"世界体系的每一个思想映象，总是在客观上被历史状况所限制，在主观上被得出该思想映象的人的肉体状况和精神状况所限制"。② 这就使得一切真理都是相对的、有条件的，它只能在一定的条件下才能成为真理。从价值论的观点来看，人的一切意识活动总是在一定的需要的驱使下进行的。由于需要的不同，所获得意识也可以分为两种形式，即"事实意识"和"价值意识"，前者是出于认识世界的需要，按存在本身的样子来反映存在，所要揭示的是"是什么"，是事物的客观规律性；后者是按照人的意志和愿望的要求来反映存在，是经由主观愿望的评价和选择而作出的，是为了向人指明"应如此"，是人的活动的主观目的性。它是人的活动的内在尺度，正是由于目的的驱使，才使得人的活动与动物的活动从根本上区别开来，使世界朝着人类所追求的目的得以发展。而这种目的性以前往往被直观的、机械的反映论排斥在认识的活动之外，错误地视之为是一种反科学社会学的唯心主义的意识观，这就等于把人的活动的主观能动性彻底地否定了，就像恩格斯当年

---

① 黑格尔：《美学》第3卷（下），北京：商务印书馆，1981年，第10页。
② 《马克思恩格斯选集》第2版第3卷，第76页。

在批判施达克"把对理想和目的的追求也叫做唯心主义"时指出说:"如果一个人只是由于他追求'理想的意图'并承认'理想的力量'对他的影响,就成了唯心主义者,那么任何一个发育得稍稍正常的人都成了唯心主义者了,这样怎么还有唯物主义者呢?"①

文学艺术是以作家的审美情感为心理中介对于现实人生所作的评价性反映的产物,它的对象是人,它把作家的主观目的体现在对自己笔下所描写的现实人生的抑扬和褒贬之中,通过艺术形象的塑造,让读者意识到什么是应该追求的,而什么是应该鄙弃的。所以在上述两种意识形式中,它的性质无疑是属于价值意识的范围。它的目的不只是为了让人们看到现实人生是怎样的,而更在于通过对应是人生的、愿景的描写来凝聚和团结社会集团的成员的力量,为着这一共同的理想去进行奋斗,就像马克思在谈到哲学的功能时所说的"不在于用不同的方式解释世界,而问题在于改变世界"。② 否定了文艺作品审美属性的这种价值内涵,把它仅仅视为一种娱乐的方式和牟利的工具,也就等于放弃了我们自己的尺度去迁就别人之所好,也就等于在文艺领域中放弃了马克思主义思想的指导地位。

如果以上的分析是符合马克思主义的基本精神的话,那么我认为文艺在马克思主义视野中就不能仅仅看作是一种认识现实的形式,而更应该被看作是一种变革现实的力量,它的目的就是为了人,为了促进个人的全面发展和人类的自由解放来推动社会的进步和发展。

二

但是在我国以往的马克思主义文艺理论研究中,一般都按认识论的观点,把文艺看作是一种知识的形式,它的目的只是为了让人认识社会,并往往引用马克思在谈到19世纪中叶英国现实主义小说家时说的:"他们以那明白晓畅和令人感动的描写,向世界揭示了政治的和社会的真理,比起政治家、政论家和道德家合起来所作的还多"③,以及恩格斯谈到巴尔扎克的小说时所说的"他汇集了法国社会的全部历史,我从这里,甚至在经济细节方面(如革命以后动产

---

① 恩格斯:《路德维希·费尔巴哈和德国古典哲学的终结》,第228页。
② 《马克思恩格斯选集》第2版第1卷,第18页。
③ 马克思:《1854年8月1日〈纽约论坛〉上的论文》,《马克思恩格斯论艺术》(二),北京:人民文学出版社,1963年,第402页。

和不动产的重新分配）所学到的东西，也要比从当时所有职业的历史学家、经济学家和统计学家那里学到的全部东西还要多"① 等论述，视真实性、典型性等为马克思主义文艺学的基本命题。这虽然都是马克思、恩格斯所关注的文艺问题，但如果脱离了他们谈话的具体语境把它无限放大，视马克思主义的文艺观为仅仅是在总结现实主义文学经验基础上所形成的"认识论的文艺观"，那就必然背离马克思主义哲学的基本精神而使认识陷于片面。

那么，马克思是怎样把人的自由和社会的发展和进步统一起来来理解文艺的性质和阐述文艺的价值的呢？联系马克思所处的历史年代的人的生活处境，我认为马克思就是通过对文艺审美原属性的揭示表示它可以抵制人的"异化"而维护人的整体存在，实现人性的"复归"而达到人类社会发展最终的目的。因为人类史不同于自然史，它是"我们自己创造的"②，所以历史就是"追求一定目的的人的活动"③。要是离开了人和人的活动也就无所谓社会和历史。这样，就把人的问题与社会的问题统一起来，把社会的问题当作一个人的问题，从人的问题切入来加以研究，同时也决定了马克思在从事理论活动一开始就对人的问题给予极大的关注。早在《1844年经济学哲学手稿》中，就从人的活动与动物活动的比较分析中提出："人类的特性恰恰是自由的有意识的活动"，这使得人的产品不是像"动物的产品那样直接同它的肉体相联系"，以"占有"的方式满足于"直接的片面的享受"；而认为真正的人的活动应该是摆脱了物欲的强制，以"一种全面的方式，也就是说，作为一个完整的人，占有自己的全面的本质"，所以"社会人的感觉不同于非社会人的感觉"，就在于他的"需要和享受失去了自己的利己主义性质，而使自然界失去了纯粹的有用性"，超越功利目的限制，本着一种自由的态度来予以对待，而使效用成了一种"人的效用"，从而表明"按照美的规律"来从事生产活动的④乃是人的本质特性之所在。而人的活动的这一特性在马克思看来在中世纪的手工业者那里还是存在的。因为那时劳动者之间还没有什么分工，"每一个劳动者都必须熟悉全部工序，凡是他的工具能够做的一切他都应当会做"，"所以中世纪的手工业者对于本行专业和熟练技巧还有一定的兴趣"，这不仅使得他们"对自己为工作都是兢兢业业、奴隶般的忠心耿耿"，"对工作的屈从程度远远超过对本身工作漠不关心的

---

① 《马克思恩格斯选集》第2版第4卷，北京：人民出版社，1972年，第463页。
② 《马克思恩格斯全集》第23卷，北京：人民出版社，1972年，第409—410页。
③ 《马克思恩格斯全集》第2卷，北京：人民出版社，1957年，第150页。
④ 马克思：《1844年经济学哲学手稿》，北京：人民出版社，1985年，第53—54页。

现代工人"，而且"这种兴趣还能使他们在工作中产生有限的艺术感"①。只是到了资本主义社会，"异化劳动把这种关系颠倒过来"而使劳动"变成仅仅维持自己生存的手段"，使"动物的东西成为人的东西，而人的东西成为动物的东西"②，从而使得工人的活动与审美分离，失去了自主和自由而成为苦役，不能再从中得到劳动本身所固有的享受和乐趣了。

马克思的这一思想明显地可以看出是受了席勒的影响。席勒在《美育书简》中把"现代人"与"希腊人"加以比较，认为在古希腊，人是作为一个整体而存在的，而现代社会的生活方式把人"束缚在整体中一个孤零零的断片上，人也就把自己变成一个断片了"，这实际上就是一个人的"异化"的问题。但另一方面我们又应该看到，由于席勒对人的理解是抽象的，他把人的异化看作纯粹是一个心理的问题，所以试图以康德的美学思想为指导，求助于通过审美来使人获得自由和解放，这样就陷入了"审美救世主义"。与席勒等人不同，马克思不是把人的"异化"仅仅当作一个抽象的人性问题，而认为根本上是一个社会的问题，从而把它与资本主义"异化劳动"联系起来，作为批判资本主义"异化劳动"的现实依据来进行论述。他之所以强调人是"按照美的规律"来从事生产活动的，就是因为在他看来对于一个真正的人来说，劳动应该是一种"体力和智力的游戏来享受"③，这是作为一个完整的人实现全面地占有自己本质的标志。所以他提出这个问题目的是为了借批判"异化劳动"来否定资本主义私有制的合理性，说明唯有"私有财产的扬弃"，才能使"人的一切感觉和特性彻底解放"，把"以往发展的全部财富"还给了人，而实现"对人的本质的真正占有"，"它是人向自身、向社会的（即人的）人的复归"④。这样就从根本上克服席勒美学所带有的"审美救世主义"倾向。所以尽管《1844年经济学哲学手稿》作为马克思的早期著作，还带有某种人本主义的印记，但就其精神而言，它与成熟时期的著作是完全一致的。

正是从人是"按照美的规律"来从事生产活动的，人应该把劳动"作为体力和智力的游戏来享受"这一认识出发，所以马克思认为人的"异化"根本上是情感的欲望化，它使得人在活动中所本应具有的精神享受都为"占有"的欲望所剥夺。因此在马克思看来，要实现人性的"复归"，也就是要使人的情感

---

① 《马克思恩格斯选集》第2版第1卷，第58—59页。
② 马克思：《1844年经济学哲学手稿》，第53、55页。
③ 马克思：《资本论》，《马克思恩格斯论艺术》（一），北京：人民出版社，1960年，第369页。
④ 马克思：《1844年经济学哲学手稿》，第77—81页。

从欲望的统治下解放出来,把被"异化劳动"所剥夺了的人在活动中所应有的美的享受还给人,在审美活动中使人达到心灵的自由和解放。我觉得马克思就是以抵制人的异化,实现人的自由解放这一大目标为指导思想来理解文艺的性质的,他强调"作家绝不把自己的作品看作手段,作品就是目的本身","诗一旦变成诗人的手段,诗人也就不成其为诗人了"①,这"目的"我认为也就是为了人。这思想既是对康德、席勒美学思想的继承,又为后来的法兰克福学派理论家如马尔库塞等人所发展。但是与康德、席勒以及马尔库塞等人不同的是,马克思不是脱离社会现实抽象地谈论这个问题,而始终把人的解放与社会的变革、与私有制的扬弃结合在一起来进行分析。这里就涉及对于"人的复归"的理解的问题。这个作为"复归"的目标的理想人显然只是存在于马克思头脑之中的,是历史上未曾有过的,因而也被有些学人视为是一种乌托邦。这理解我认为需要作进一步的分析,因为自近代以来,西方哲学研究中有这样一个传统,即为了阐述自己的学说首先设置一个思想前提,就像卡西尔在谈到卢梭"自然人"时所说的:"卢梭试图把伽利略在研究自然现象中所采取的假设法引入到道德科学的领域中来",认为"只有靠这种假设的和有条件的推理方法,我们才能达到对人本性的真正理解"②。这种研究方法也不可避免地会对马克思产生一定的影响;但是与卢梭的"现在已不复存在、过去也许从来没有存在过、将来也许永远不会存在的一种状态"的这样一种"纯粹的假设"③ 不同,在马克思那里,它同时也是作为历史追求的目的,而放到与对私有制的扬弃这一现实变革前提条件上来说的。所以尽管他后期转向从物质领域、从生产力和生产关系的方面来研究社会的变革和历史的发展,但是总的目的都汇归到人的自由解放那里,即把人的自由解放看作是历史发展的最终目的,认为"共产主义是私有财产即人的自我异化的积极的扬弃,因而是通过人并且为了人而对人的本质的真正占有,因此,它是人向自身、向社会的(即人的)人的复归"④。表明都是把"人的复归"与"私有制的扬弃"作统一的理解的。这不仅是对康德与席勒的超越,也是法兰克福学派所不能望其项背的。因为法兰克福学派在论述文艺的解放功能方面虽然有不少创造性的发挥,但是他们不仅把精神的解放与物质解放分离开来甚至对立起来,而且对解放的论述也仅仅局限于感性层面而无

---

① 《马克思恩格斯全集》第 1 卷,北京:人民出版社,1956 年,第 87 页。
② 卡西尔:《人论》,上海:上海译文出版社,1985 年,第 78 页。
③ 卢梭:《论人类不平等的起源和基础》,北京:商务印书馆,1962 年,第 63—64 页。
④ 马克思:《1844 年经济学哲学手稿》,第 77 页。

视理性层面,这样也就背离了马克思主义和现实主义而重新回到了浪漫主义的梦想之中,这才真正是"审美的乌托邦"。

三

由于以往我们在马克思主义研究中把"思维与存在的关系"混同于"精神与物质的关系",并以直观的思维方式来看待思维与存在,不理解它们是在实践的基础上历史地形成的一种动态的对立统一的关系,因而也不理解任何理论的真理性都是相对的,它只是在一定条件下才是真理;而往往把马克思的理论加以绝对化,看作是脱离具体关系而抽象存在的万古不变的准则,不作具体分析拿到丰富多彩的文学现象上来加以简单套用,以致教条主义和庸俗社会学的批评在我国猖獗一时。这种情况现在虽然并不存在,但认为当今文艺的发展趋向消费化的现状已使马克思的理论丧失了"阐释的有效性"而予以放弃甚至否定又成了当今马克思主义理论界看待马克思主义的另一种倾向。这同样是一种以教条主义的观点来看待真理,而不理解理论的反思批判功能所造成的误判。

怎么来看待这个问题?在我看来与其说马克思主义文艺理论对当今的文艺现状丧失了阐释的能力,不如说当今的文艺已没有能力来承担马克思提出的在促进人的自由解放现实"人性复归"方面的历史重任。所以需要我们放弃的不是马克思主义,而正是坚守在马克思主义指导下对现状的反思和批判的精神。这涉及我们对理论包括马克思主义文艺理论的意义和作用的理解的问题。卡西尔在对欧洲18世纪哲学与17世纪哲学作比较研究中得出:在17世纪"理性是'永恒真理'的王国",是"通往超感觉的绝对世界的大门"。与之不同,到了18世纪,它就不再被看作只是一座"储存真理的宝库","而是引导我们去发现真理,建立真理和确定真理的独创性的理智力量",即"把它视为一种能力,一种力量,这种能力和力量只有通过它的作用和效力才能充分理解"[①]。表明理论作为以原则的形式所承载的真理,它的内涵需要联系具体的客观实际并借助一定的方法在实际运用中才能得到激活,因为一切原则的东西总是绝对性与相对性的统一,它只有在一定条件下,在实际运用过程中才能使普遍的原则转化为具体的真理。这就需要借助一定的方法。所以在马克思主义哲学包括文艺理论中,观点与方法总是统一的。

---

① 卡西尔:《启蒙哲学》,济南:山东人民出版社,1996年,第11页。

正是基于这样的认识，恩格斯在谈到马克思主义时特别强调"马克思的整个世界观不是教义而是方法"，它提供的"不是现成的教条，而是进一步研究的出发点和供这种研究使用的方法"①。并对"官方的黑格尔学派"视"黑格尔的全部遗产不过是可以用来套在任何论题上的刻板的公式，不过是可以用来在缺乏思想和实证知识时搪塞一下的词汇语录"②的见解作了尖锐的批判。全部马克思主义著作，就是在历史唯物主义的观点指导下按照唯物辩证的思维方法在分析、解决问题上的具体演示，所以不懂得唯物辩证法也就不可能真正理解马克思主义。"辩证法的基本原理是：没有抽象的真理，真理总是具体的"③。因而我们在学习马克思主义时，就不能仅仅只看它的结论，还应该关注这结论是怎样答出的，还应该同时把它当作是一种认识问题、分析问题和解决问题的方法来进行学习。这样我们对于问题的理解才能避免抽象而会有具体的领会。唯此，马克思主义在我们意识中才是鲜活的，它是在具体的解决实际问题的过程中不断丰富而发展的。只要当时马克思所面临的现实问题在今天仍然存在，马克思主义就不会过时。这同样也应该是我们研究马克思主义美学和文艺理论所必须贯彻的思想原则。

比如对于"人的复归"这个命题，虽然马克思当初是针对人在活动中由于受物质所驱使而丧失了"作为一个完整的人，占有自己的全面的本质"而提出的，但并不表明这种情况现在已不存在，只是造成这种情况的原因已与当年不完全相同。如果说在马克思写作《1844 年经济学哲学手稿》当年，它主要是由外部原因，是由于资本主义异化劳动使得人把自己的劳动"变成仅仅维持自己生存的手段"所造成的，所以马克思构想了一个"作为人的人"主要是用来作为批判资本主义"异化劳动"的假设；那么，在经历了 170 年历史的今天，虽然"异化劳动"的现象在社会上并没有完全消失，但是由于人的内部原因所造成的人的"异化"现象，即随着物质产品的不断丰富而带来人的物欲的不断膨胀，使人沉溺于一种"片面的享受"，而导致的"人自身的丧失"，正在成为当今社会的一种主导的"异化"倾向。但由于这种"异化"是由人的内部原因即欲望的膨胀所造成的，所以审美作为一种"无利害关系的自由愉快"在抵制欲望对人的统治，实现向作为"人的复归"的目标来说，就显得更有意义。它在

---

① 《马克思恩格斯全集》第 1 版第 39 卷，北京：人民出版社，1975 年，第 406 页。
② 恩格斯：《卡尔·马克思：政治经济学批判》，《马克思恩格斯选集》第 2 版第 2 卷，北京：人民出版社，1972 年，第 119 页。
③ 《列宁选集》第 1 版第 1 卷，北京：人民出版社，1960 年，第 507 页。

肯定人的自由解放是一个现实的问题，从根本上是需要通过社会的变革和发展来实现的前提下，更凸显了文学艺术在引导着人走向回归自身之路过程中所应有的精神承担。

为在上海交通大学召开的"中英马克思主义美学双边论坛"而作

2013年3月下旬初稿、6月下旬修改

（本文责任编辑：任天）

A Philosophic Reflection on the Chinese Research in Marxist Literary and Artistic Theories

Wang Yuanxiang

(Zhejiang University)

Abstract: On the basis of criticising some of the defects in the past practice of China's Marxist literary theory research like intuitivism, pure epistemology and dogmatism, the author points out that, for the philosophical point of view, the ideological roots of these tendencies are equating the relationship between thinking and existence with the relationship between spirit and matter, and distinguishing Marxism from Non-Marxism simply by the standard of idealism-materialism

后马克思主义文论的一个焦点问题

冯宪光[*]

(四川大学文学与新闻学院)

【内容摘要】后马克思主义理论的译介和研究在国内文学理论研究中尚属未开拓的领域。关于世界文学的研究和辩论是后马克思主义文论的一个焦点问题。卡萨诺瓦的《文学作为一个世界》集中地论述了她的世界文学观,从中可以看到后马克思主义文论的一些显著特色。这种理论突显了后现代思想改变现代思想重视的时间维度,在空间维度上展开理论思考的特色,同时它回到马克思的世界文学话题,表明后马克思主义文论,在面对当下文学问题,整合当代思想资源时,十分注意与经典马克思主义保持一种实际联系。卡萨诺瓦的理论对中国当代文学和文论建设都有一定的借鉴意义。

国内关于后马克思主义理论的译介和研究主要在哲学、政治学领域展开,在文学理论研究中尚属未开拓的领域。2011年年底,人民出版社推出了张永清、马元龙主编的《后马克思主义读本》两册。一册是"理论批评",泛论当代文化、政治的核心问题,展现后马克思主义作为"理论之后"时代的一种"理论"风采。另一册为"文学批评",围绕"后马克思主义文学批评视域中的世界文学争论"与"后马克思主义文学批评的阅读实践"两个主题,选编了19篇第一次以中文翻译问世的文章。这是后马克思主义文论在中国译介的重要读本,也是选编者对后马克思主义文论研究的重要贡献。这几乎可以作为在国内开拓后马克思主义文论研究的一个新的开端。

---

[*] 冯宪光,男,1945年生,四川大学文学与新闻学院教授,主要从事西方马克思主义美学与文艺学研究。

后马克思主义一语，有许多歧义。而现今无论国内外都以拉克劳和墨菲作为后马克思主义的主要代表，也基本上以他们关于后马克思主义的论断作为一种对后马克思主义的一种界说。他们在1985年出版的《领导权与社会主义的策略》中提出，"现在我们正处于后马克思主义领域，不再可能去主张马克思主义阐述的主体性和阶级概念，也不可能继续那种关于资本主义发展历史过程的幻象，当然也不能再继续没有对抗的共产主义透明社会这个概念，如果本书的认识主题是后马克思主义的（post-Marxist）的，它显然也是后马克思主义的（post-*Marxist*）。"据翻译者介绍，拉克劳、墨菲与中译者通信说，这句话的英文斜体字（中文用楷体字）强调的是，如果本书一方面是后马克思主义的（post-Marxist），另一方面，它确实仍然把马克思主义（Marxist）作为出发点。① 拉克劳等的后马克思主义与我们过去介绍过的"西方马克思主义"不同，它认为，在当下不可能继续只用阶级、阶级斗争的思路去认识晚期资本主义，不可能用人本主义的主体性思想批判资本主义，但是仍然要用诸如女性、有色人种等边缘人口的抵抗主义、生态环境保护主义等激进、自由和多元的民主斗争形式，开展反对资本主义的社会主义运动。国内外许多研究者认为，这种后马克思主义根本否定马克思对资本主义社会的总体性论断，将马克思主义的基本论断视之为本质主义，是后现代主义的一种理论，不是马克思主义。这种观点不是完全没有道理。但是后现代主义正是晚期资本主义的文化表征，它反映了晚期资本主义的社会现实和社会心理，后马克思主义在吸收后现代主义文化时，并没有断然抛弃马克思思想的出发点，这与一些曾经信奉马克思主义而后来又明确地抛弃马克思主义的后现代主义理论家不同，不能简单地把后马克思主义完全纳入西方后现代主义，视为资本主义文化。后现代社会是晚期资本主义社会，这个时代特色使当代资本主义社会的形态与马克思在世时的资本主义形态有很大区别。立足于西方的国外马克思主义可以有一种切合当代资本主义的理论形态，正如中国自身在实践中认识到社会主义有初级阶段，以后可能还有高级形态等，目前根据社会主义初级阶段的现实，建构了中国特色社会主义理论。马克思主义的每一次重要发展阶段都是对当时资本主义社会变化发展特色的捕捉，研究新情况，发现新问题，提出新观点。后马克思主义是否是马克思主义的争论，可能还会持续。对于这个问题可以再观察一段时间，不必匆匆定论。但这并不影响我们应该而且可以具体地研究后马克思主义的一些在当代有价值的观

---

① ［英］拉克劳、墨菲：《领导权与社会主义的策略》，尹树广等译，哈尔滨：黑龙江人民出版社，2003年，第4页。

点。后马克思主义也有自身的文学理论思想,后马克思主义文论也具有与以前的马克思主义文论不同的思路、问题和视域。对于后马克思主义文论,中国学者不能不做认真研究。

张永清、马元龙主编的《后马克思主义读本:文学批评》一书,集中译介了后马克思主义文论关于世界文学的争论文章,这是后马克思主义文论的一个焦点问题。后马克思主义有一个特点,就是始终关注现实问题而不空谈理论,而且确实是以马克思的思想作为出发点来讨论现实问题。关于世界文学的论题即是一个例子。

在西方文学史上首先提出"世界文学"概念的是19世纪的歌德。1827年歌德在谈到他正在读法文译本的中国清代小说《好逑传》时说,"中国人有成千上万这类作品,而且在我们的远祖还生活在野森林的时代就有这类作品了。""我愈来愈深信,诗是人类的共同财产。""我们德国人如果不跳开周围环境的小圈子朝外面看一看,我们就会陷入上面说的那种学究气的昏头昏脑。所以我喜欢环视四周的外国民族情况,我也劝每个人都这么办,民族文学在现代算不了很大的一回事,世界文学(Weltliteratur)的时代已快来临了。现在每个人都应该出力促使它早日来临。不过我们一方面这样重视外国文学,另一方面也不应拘守某一种特殊的文学,奉它为模范。"[①] 20年后,马克思和恩格斯在《共产党宣言》中又提出"世界文学"的概念:"资产阶级,由于开拓了世界市场,使一切国家的生产和消费都成为世界性的了。""物质的生产是如此,精神的生产也是如此。各民族的精神产品成了公共的财产。民族的片面性和局限性日益成为不可能,于是由许多种民族的和地方的文学形成了一种世界的文学。"[②]

无论是歌德的、还是《共产党宣言》的世界文学的概念和问题,从19世纪以来都没有成为文学理论家专门研究的问题。在20世纪后期,随着通讯技术的发展,全世界范围的信息交流变得快捷、简单,1960年加拿大传媒理论家麦克卢汉在《交往的探索》中提出的地球村(global village)的概念。麦克卢汉关于传媒改变世界结构关系的地球村说法,受到社会学家的普遍重视,在20世纪80年代后期到90年代形成全球化(globolization)的社会理论。此后,关于世界范围的文学问题的研究和思考往往冠之以"全球化"概念,而成为文学全球化问题,一时文学的全球化与本土化关系成为文学理论研究的一个热点。在20世纪行将结束之时,后马克思主义文论家帕斯卡尔·卡萨诺瓦出版了《文学的世界

---

① 《歌德谈话录》,朱光潜译,北京:人民文学出版社,1978年,第113页。
② 《马克思恩格斯文集》第2卷,北京:人民出版社,2009年,第35页。

共和国》一书，在左翼文学理论领域引起强烈反响。卡萨诺瓦竭力回避或破除文学全球化这个命题，意在表明，所谓文学全球化的概念将全球文学置于一种一体化、同质化的状态中，全球化强调世界文学在文学流通、出版发行中各个国家文学市场壁垒的消解，强势出版国家、地区和集团统一全球文学传播、交流的趋势不可阻挡，如果只从全球化角度认识当下全球文学格局，则有巩固和扩大西方文学霸权主义，维护世界文学的不平等格局之嫌。然而，文学的世界性又确实是这个世界文学存在的现实问题。所以，她要回到歌德和马克思的世界文学概念上，重新提出世界文学问题。文学全球化问题是中心地区文学向边缘地区传播、流动、影响，引起边缘地区本土文学的变化，突出的是中心对边缘的占领和征服。而卡萨诺瓦拒绝用文学全球化概念来描述当下全球文学的格局，转而研究目前无论是文学创作或是阅读都离不开的一种世界文学的观念，这种世界文学的概念不是在政治、经济主宰、统辖的一种文学运行结构，而是文学自身存在和发展的世界空间。世界文学这个观念的焦点问题不是全球化与本土化的关系问题，而是民族文学与世界文学的关系问题。这个问题不仅是歌德的超越民族边界的一种世界文学形成，扩展各民族间文学的广泛对话的殷切期望，而且是马克思和恩格斯对资本主义时代民族文学与世界文学关系的深刻认识。卡萨诺瓦拒斥文学全球化观念，回到《共产党宣言》来认识、描述当代世界文学现状，重新提出世界文学问题，表明了后马克思主义文论在研究当代文学新格局时，不落入当代资本主义文化窠臼，坚持回到马克思的出发点，这对于当代国外左翼文学理论以及国外马克思主义文论的建树，都有不可忽视的重要意义。

《后马克思主义读本：文学批评》所载卡萨诺瓦的《文学作为一个世界》集中地论述了她的世界文学观。从这篇论文，我们可以看到后马克思主义文论的一些显著特色。

值得关注的是，后马克思主义文论开拓了一种侧重于从空间性审视文学的新视野，来超越文学的外部研究与内部研究的划分，力图有效地解释文学的具体现象。20世纪文论在批判了19世纪以黑格尔为代表的形而上学中心主义、本质主义的文学观之后，先后出现了语言论转折和社会学转向，这两种转折分别使文学研究走向片面、单纯的内部研究和外部研究两个极端。它们都在各自的聚焦点上，深度地挖掘了文学在内部和外部的许多逻辑网节点，是有一定成效的。但是，文学的实际存在不可能只建基于它的内部元素，也不可能只与外部世界的若干因素连接，文学的结构性存在只能是若干内部因素与外部因素的有机、整体的组构。卡萨诺瓦提出的世界文学观，则要突破20世纪文论的单纯踩踏上内部或外部一只脚的片面的深刻化或深刻的片面化，超越文学的内部研究和外部研究划分，既与西方当代脱离社会性研究文学的内部研究划清界限，又超越了传统马克思主义、西方马克思主义和后殖民主义等专注于意识形态批判的文学理论。她认为，"在文学与世界之间存在着一个中介空间：一个平行版图，相对自治于政治领域，这个地方因而专属于某种特定文学性质的相关问题、争论和创新。在这里政治的、社会的、民族的、性别的、伦理的各类斗争最终依照某种文学逻辑，并且通过文学形式而得到折射、变形或改造。从这个假设出发来思考，并努力构想这一假设的全部理论和实践后果，我们便能沿着既是内部的又是外部的一种批评路线开始工作"。①

毋庸讳言，任何严肃的马克思主义文学批评都在力图将外部批评与内部批评联系起来或者结合起来，反对把二者割裂开来或对立起来。西方马克思主义理论家在这方面做了很多努力，詹姆逊在《政治无意识》中，把历史唯物主义的生产方式的分析与精神分析理论和语言学、符号学方法结合起来，形成马克思主义关于文学历史性的新的阐释方法，成为当今马克思主义文学批评的经典范例。但是，詹姆逊的历史主义阐释学是把历史理解为时间性概念，在时间的演进中把文学与社会联系起来。而像卡萨诺瓦这样的后马克思主义理论家则试图不通过共时性的流行理论方法的整合，不在时间性维度上把握文学的社会性，而直接从空间理论入手，寻找整合文学、历史和世界的整体思维方法。卡萨诺瓦认为，福柯在《词与物》中提供了对物的空间布局整体性的观看方式，只有把握物的各个部分在整体空间中的配置，物的各个部分的形状与颜色的规律、变化和复现便能被人所把握；其连贯性和内在的关系也才能得到理解。只有从每个部分构成为空间图形在整体中所占据的位置出发，只有从每个空间图形与其他空间图形的相互关系出发，才能理解每个作为空间的图形。而文学的社会性不仅是文学的历史性（时间性），还是文学的空间性。这样，似乎只有把文学不仅理解为时间性的历史，而且理解为空间性的世界，才有可能真正实现外部研究与内部研究的有机统一。

按照卡萨诺瓦的逻辑，马克思讲的在资本建立世界市场之后开拓出的世界的文学，并不是一种外部研究的视野，而是从文学实际存在的空间场域，对在现代资本主义生产方式中文学空间性的解释。这是社会存在对社会意识的决定作用在文学存在的空间性上引起的变化，文学存在的空间场域从民族文学走向

---

① ［意］卡萨诺瓦：《文学作为一个世界》，张永清、马元龙主编：《后马克思主义读本：文学批评》，北京：人民出版社，2011年，第1—2页。

了世界文学。这不是一种外部研究的结论，而是一种对在一定历史条件下，文学的外部因素与内部因素紧密结合的内在结构的深刻阐释。

  文学可以作为一个空间世界来观看和分析，就是卡萨诺瓦给我们提供的一种新视野，这就是她试图把文学的外部研究与内部研究有机地结合而不是使二者割裂的分析方法。客观而论，这种视野和方法，无论在当代西方文论中，还是马克思主义文论中，都是独树一帜的。现代性思想强调现代社会与前现代社会的不同时代性，因此建立和发展了以时间性作为根据的历史主义思维方法。而后现代思想则打破线性时间在思维中的必然联系，要求人们直接地面对自身生存的现实，而这个现实往往并不是以时间性来运行，而是以空间性面貌突显在人们面前。在后现代感受中，人们处身于特定时空之下，人类生存的空间性问题扑面而来，即以2013年伊始，中国广大地域空间普遍经历雾霾引起的严重环境污染为例，其空间性感受比时间性感受倍加强烈。海德格尔作为现代思想大师，其代表作书名为《存在与时间》，而后现代思想大师福柯则把人的存在用语言表述中的空间关系来作《词与物》的分析。像卡萨诺瓦这样的后马克思主义理论家，提出用空间性来分析文学，以解决20世纪在西方文论中外部研究与内部研究分立的局面，不能不说俨然摆出一副后现代姿态。

  当然，卡萨诺瓦的世界文学空间的概念也受到法国社会学家布尔迪厄思想的重要影响。她说，"构想一个世界空间，它通过一种主导结构而发挥作用，在某种程度上，这种主导结构独立于政治、经济语言和社会形式。这种设想显然受惠于皮埃尔·布尔迪厄的'场'的概念，并且更其明显的是，受惠于其'文学场'的概念。但是，后者迄今都是在一个民族国家框架内而进行构想的，这个框架受到了某个特定民族国家的疆界、历史传统和资本积累过程的局限。我在费尔南德·布罗代尔的著作中，并且特别是在其'世界经济体系'当中发现了将这些机制扩展至国际范围的思想和可能性。"① 布尔迪厄的"文学场"的概念，不是一个文学与外部其他因素关联的一般性概念，而是由于文学处于外在世界的各种关系之中而形成的文学自身的内部场域，就不能仅仅只有艺术的审美因素，而是内部的艺术审美核心因素与实际上影响文学存在的各种外部因素，在文学自身的内在场域中的整体性结合。这个思想是相当精彩的。文学的外部因素影响文学不是外在发生的，而是通过影响内部特质，使纯粹的审美因素发生具体改变的过程与结果，这个过程改变文学自身的内在结构，从而形成文学

---

① ［意］卡萨诺瓦：《文学作为一个世界》，张永清、马元龙主编：《后马克思主义读本：文学批评》，北京：人民出版社，2011年，第10页。

自身存在的场域。其实，康德关于美的分析的经典论述就包含了这一层思想。康德把美分为纯粹美和依存美两种。纯粹美的特质是无功利、无目的、形式的美感，这是审美之为审美最根本的因素，舍此则无所谓审美。艺术的内在因素是审美的，但是艺术根据康德的看法并不是纯粹美，而是依存美，即艺术不是也不能以纯粹美的方式存在，它是有功利、有目的、有内容的，而这种与外在世界关联的功利、目的、内容则只有通过无功利、无目的、形式的纯粹美的形态显现出来，才成为艺术。这就是说，外在的社会因素使内在的审美因素发生改变，使纯粹美成为依存美，才有艺术的存在。纯粹美与依存美的整合就是文学场。文学场并不存在于文学与外部世界的关系中，而是存在于文学自身之中。但是在许多借鉴布尔迪厄文学场观念的研究者那里，文学场基本上成为文学与外部世界关系的一种解读，而卡萨诺瓦则是深刻地理解了布尔迪厄这个重要概念的要义，把文学场理解为文学自身存在的内在空间，在这空间之中，文学的民族性和世界性都与文学之为文学的艺术审美特质结合起来。在她看来，文学作为一个世界就是文学有一个内在特质与外在关系整合在一起的文学场。这是对布尔迪厄文学场理论的最好理解和运用。

　　文学作为一个世界而存在是说文学的内部因素与外在世界的关系不要在外在世界中去寻找，它已经独立地存在于文学自身之中。由于资本主义社会的出现强化了文学与世界的关系，作为一种马克思主义的文学批评必须从文学场的角度去认识和理解文学，受到费尔南德·布罗代尔的"世界经济体系"理论启发，卡萨诺瓦则把文学场的疆域从民族文学扩展到世界文学，就与《共产党宣言》中的世界文学论相契合。这样几种概念、观念、思想的结合就成为卡萨诺瓦的文学的世界共和国的思想。这是对马克思"世界文学"思想在当代的实际运用。从这一点我们可以看出后马克思主义文论，在面对当下文学问题，整合当代思想资源时，十分注意与经典马克思主义保持一种实际联系。这应该是后马克思主义文论的一个明显特点。是不是凭借这一点，我们就可以说后马克思主义就是马克思主义的，可能还有待于继续观察。

　　卡萨诺瓦指出，当前在世界文学的这个既有格局中，其结构是不平等的。"世界文学空间的基本特征在于其等级结构和不平等性。商品和价值的不平衡分配一直以来是这个结构的构成性规律之一，因为出于历史原因，该结构的资源是在民族国家疆界范围之内积累起来的。"[①] 欧洲国家率先进入资本主义，利用

---

① [意]卡萨诺瓦：《文学作为一个世界》，张永清、马元龙主编：《后马克思主义读本：文学批评》，北京：人民出版社，2011年，第12页。

现代化概念把这些民族文学装扮成为主题、形式、语言和故事类型规范化和标准化的文学样板，而且通过文学商品市场化途径，以实现该类商品的"非民族化"快速流通，占据其他民族国家的文学市场，形成所谓文学的全球化。文学全球化是一个以西方文学，特别是以"权威英语作家"作品作为规范和样板树立起来，以市场商品化方式推销到世界各地的试图建立一种规范和价值一体化的文学趋势。世界文学空间概念之所以优越于文学全球化概念就在于，它一方面承认由于文学全球化造成了世界文学空间在结构上的不平等，它作为世界文学空间的第一个构成性特点而存在，是十分重要的。但是，世界文学空间作为文学场还有文学自身的内在因素顽强地存在。因此，"文学世界第二个构成性特征就是它的相对自治性"。① 世界文学空间中既有政治统治，也有语言统治和文学统治，这三者互相交叠、渗透、遮蔽。"文学不平等极其复杂的统治关系激起了文学自身的斗争、反抗和竞争形式。这个空间中的被压迫者也形成了特有的反抗策略，这些策略虽然也会引发政治后果，但只能在文学框架内得到理解。叙事秩序中的形式、创新、运动与革命在尝试着推翻现有文学权力关系的过程中也会被利用、被俘虏、被盗用、被收编。"② 作为一个后马克思主义理论家，卡萨诺瓦是赞成和支持非欧美国家作家进行改变世界文学空间不平等结构的斗争。但是，她认为，这种斗争虽然具有政治意义，但它不是政治斗争，而是文学革命。有许多"伟大的文学革命都是发生在边缘和受压迫地区的，乔伊斯、卡夫卡、易卜生、贝克特、达里奥等人就是见证。正是由于这一原因，认为中心的文学形式及体裁是强加于被压迫地区作家身上的殖民遗产的说法忽略了这样一个事实，即文学本身作为这个空间内的共有价值，也是一种工具，如果对之加以再一征用，那么它就能使作家——特别是那些掌握最少资源的作家——获得某种自由，并在其内部获得承认与存在。"③ 文学的相对自治性一方面指世界文学空间中的文学统治是超越政治统治的重要因素，政治统治不能起最终决定作用，另一方面指文学现象有一种自身独立的标准。比如当今世界的诺贝尔文学奖"正是一个世界文学空间存在的最好的客观的指标"。④ 拉丁美洲作家获得诺贝尔文学奖没有依赖于政治优势，也没有依附语英语权威文学的样板，正是世界文学空间相对自治性的表现。而欧美文学中也有超越政治统治的文学性

---

① [意] 卡萨诺瓦：《文学作为一个世界》，张永清、马元龙主编：《后马克思主义读本：文学批评》，北京：人民出版社，2011年，第14页。
② 同上，第18页。
③ 同上，第19页。
④ 同上，第5页。

自治因素，边缘地区的乔伊斯、卡夫卡、易卜生、贝克特、达里奥等人的成功，也证实了学习英语权威文学形式本身也可以使文学资源积累较少地区的文学得到迅速提升，在世界文学空间中享有盛誉。这个观点值得在改革开放中发展的中国当代文学思考和借鉴。

2012年诺贝尔文学奖授予中国作家莫言，诺贝尔文学评奖委员会主席韦斯特伯格的颁奖词指出，"莫言的想象力穿越了人类的历史，他是一位杰出的写实主义者，作品描述了20世纪中国的历史"，"他比拉伯雷和斯威夫特以及当代的加西亚·马尔克斯以来多数作家更滑稽和震撼人心。他语言辛辣，在他描述的中国近100年的画卷中，令人亲临其境"。① 按照卡萨诺瓦关于拉丁美洲文学崛起的说法，也可以说，莫言是在世界文学边缘向世界文学空间不平等格局发起冲击，又一个引起文学革命的作家。莫言作为第一位中国籍作家获诺贝尔文学奖，在世界文学空间中提升了中国文学的地位，表明中国文学在莫言等作家的长期努力中达到了世界文学的最高水准。改革开放的中国广大公众对莫言的获奖表示了祝贺和欣慰，中国文学事实上以莫言的获奖进入了世界文学的殿堂。中国文学将越来越受到世界的关注和评价，也必然从中获得进一步深化发展的支持。从这样的角度来看，面对中国文学进一步发展的需求，我们还应当更加深入地研究卡萨诺瓦的世界文学空间理论。当前中国对西方文论的译介和研究已经较为全面，但是这种译介和研究不能是为译介而译介，为研究而研究，依然应该秉持洋为中用的要旨，把西方文论的译介和研究与中国当代文学发展和当代文学理论的建设更加密切地结合起来。正是因为如此，我觉得应该重视后马克思主义文论关于世界文学这个焦点话题的研究成果。

（本文责任编辑：张永禄）

---

① 转引自李枚忆、刘华：《莫言瑞典领奖纪行》，《文艺报》2012年12月24日。

The Focus Issue on Post-Marxism Literary Theories

Feng Xianguang

(school of Literature and journalism, Sichuan University)

Abstract: The translation, introduction and study of Post-Marxism theories are fields not being developed in our domestic literary theories study. The focus of Post-Marxism literary theories is study and debates of World Literature. Pascale Casanova has discussed intensively on her concept of *World Literature In Literature as a World*, in which we can capture some outstanding features of Post-Marxism literary theories. The theories underline character that Post-modernism theories start theoretical thinking from the view of space dimension rather than temporal dimension as modernism did. Moreover, they return to the topic of Marx's World Literature that indicates Post-Marxism literary theories pay close attention to keep actual connection with classic Marxism when they are facing current literary issues and integrating contemporary thought resources. Pascale Casanova's theories have certain reference value for contemporary Chinese literature and literary theories.

马克思主义美学的科学化维度

——"知觉模式说"概论

李志宏[*]

(吉林大学文学院)

【内容摘要】 马克思美学思想的光辉之处是以唯物史观看待审美中人的因素;要透彻地了解人,必须引入科学维度。美学研究不能在事物及其形式中寻找美或美属性,而应解释人怎样把一般事物看成美的事物。审美的关键环节是认知结构中的知觉模式。知觉模式是在认知经验中形成的神经结构,对外连接着客观事物的形式信息,对内连接着身体的情感体验。由此,特定形式与特定情感之间建立起稳定的联系;人一见到对应的形式就直觉地产生美感。美感不是被"美"所引发,而是被与知觉模式相匹配的形式所引发。引发美感的一般事物被称为美的事物,从而被人为地赋予审美属性和审美价值,又被误以为是"美"。

马克思主义的特点是具有实践的品格,要回答实践中的问题。美学研究的目标是解释审美现象,解决审美实践中的问题。长久以来,令人百思不得其解的现象是:为什么人一看到某些事物的形式就产生出美感。似乎这些事物在人产生美感之前已经先在地具有审美属性和审美价值,已经是美的事物。其实,所有美的事物本来是一般事物。那么,一般事物怎样成为美的事物?或者说,一般事物中的审美属性及审美价值从何而来?对此,要在马克思主义世界观和

---

[*] 李志宏,1953年生,男,山东淄博人,文学博士,现任吉林大学文学院教授,主要从事美学原理研究。本文系国家社科基金重大项目(12&ZD013)和教育部人文社会科学规划基金项目(11YJA751042)阶段性成果。

方法论的基础上，借助现代科学的成果加以认识。

一、美学的合理路径是探寻主体的认知过程

近代美学研究的一大进展是形成了"审美关系说"，既看到了审美客体又看到了审美主体。不过，对于审美关系中主体和客体的地位和作用，人们的见解各不相同，大致形成了两类理论主张和两种不同的研究路径。一类理论认为：是客体事物中的美或美属性引起了主体的美感，美学研究要在作为客体的对象事物上寻找到"美"。这种理论可称为"客体主导论"。另一类理论认为，不存在一个客体性的、抽象的"美"，当审美主体产生美感时，就把引发美感的客体事物叫做"美的"，美的事物就是所谓的"美"；因此，美学研究要揭示审美主体的构成和过程。这种理论可称为"主体主导论"。

客体主导论的路径以对"美是什么"问题的回答为最终目标，已被证明是不可靠的、不能成立的；① 相关研究必定陷于困境之中，再也没有可发展的空间了。

主体主导论的路径由康德所开创。康德说："一种'离开任何利害关心'的愉悦之对象便被名曰'美'"。② 即，人在非利害鉴赏中形成了愉悦感，一个这样的愉悦的对象就叫做美的。③ 这一思想的价值在于：不认为对象事物中存在着"美"，不在客体事物中寻找抽象的"美"或"美属性"；而是看到，被人们称作"美"的事物实际上是"美的事物"；当人形成美感的时候，就把对象事物称作"美的"。因此，美学的重要目标是揭示主体进行审美判断的过程和规定。不过，康德美学建基于唯心史观之上，无法回答人的认识、观念从何而来的问题，当然也不能回答审美观念从何而来的问题，只能以"先验"等人为的规定、假说不了了之。

尽管如此，康德的美学思想仍具有相当的合理之处，在美学史上具有重要的变革意义。在这一路径上，马克思引入了唯物史观，认为，社会存在决定社会意识；"五官感觉的形成是迄今为止全部世界历史的产物"，"不仅五官感觉，

---

① 张法：《为什么美的本质是一个伪命题——从分析哲学的观点看美学基本问题》，《东吴学刊》2012年第4期；王峰：《美，一个被毁弃的盟约》，《文艺争鸣》2012年第11期；李志宏：《认知美学原理》（第一章），北京：光明日报出版社，2011年。

② 牟宗三：《康德：判断力之批判》，西安：西北大学出版社，2008年，第130页。

③ 邓晓芒：《康德〈判断力批判〉释义》，北京：生活·读书·新知三联书店，2008年，第214页。

而且连所谓精神感觉、实践感觉（意志、爱等等），一句话，人的感觉、感觉的人性，都是由于它的对象的存在，由于人化的自然界，才出来的。"① 由此，才可能在科学基础上说明人的意识的形成；人的感觉、观念，一定是以客观世界为本源，不是先验的存在，不是上帝的赐予；审美意识也一定是在客观社会中形成、发展的。

还要看到，虽然审美活动既依赖客体的因素又依赖主体的因素，但相对说来，客体事物是稳定的、静态的，主体则是变化的、动态的。因此，审美关系中，主体的作用更为重要。马克思说："对象如何对他来说成为他的对象，这取决于对象的性质以及与之相适应的本质力量的性质；因为正是这种关系的规定性形成一种特殊的、现实的肯定方式"；"对于没有音乐感的耳朵来说，最美的音乐也毫无意义，不是对象……因为任何一个对象对我的意义（它只是对那个与它相适应的感觉来说才有意义）恰好都以我的感觉所及的程度为限"。② 马克思充分看到主客体关系中的实际状况，反对机械的、形而上学的思想方法，对我们深有启发。我们不能套用存在与意识关系的原理，以为美感来自于"美"。但美感一定来自于客观物。问题是，这个客观物是怎样的物，人怎样形成审美感觉。对这种问题，马克思并没有直接地加以研究，正需要我们在马克思主义原理基础上加以扩展丰富，而不是照搬某些现成的结论。

对审美主体的构成和状态进行研究，首先看到的一个现象是，美感具有直觉性，表明主体的认知结构同客体事物形式之间具有合谐对应关系，即马克思所说对象物与主体感觉之间的相适应。阿恩海姆的格式塔心理学美学曾经试图解释其中的原委，提出"异质同构说"，有相当的合理性。但他以为，人脑中同事物形式对应的结构是先天的、固定的，这就不免流于机械、生硬和武断，不能解释审美时由时代、文化、意识造成的动态性和差异性。

理论的缺点往往昭示着理论发展的增长点。如果能够克服格式塔心理学美学机械而僵化的缺陷，发现审美主体认知结构的动态形成机制，就可能合理地解释审美主客体之间何以能够结成合谐对应关系的问题，在审美基本原理方面取得深入的进展。客观地说，在格式塔心理学美学的时代，神经科学及心理学的发展还没能达到清晰揭示主体认知结构的水平，其局限是时代造成的，并不是研究路径错误。今天的情况大为改观。现代认知科学对大脑、对神经系统和心理的研究已经提供了足够多的材料，可以较清晰地揭示审美主体的认知结构

---

① 《马克思恩格斯文集》第 1 卷，北京：人民出版社，2009 年，第 191 页。
② 同上。

和过程。由此形成的认知美学理论提出了"知觉模式说",冀图开启美学研究的新进展。

二、知觉模式是将事物形式与美感相连接的枢纽结构

审美是从知觉开始,以情感体验结束的;知觉和情感都是主体认知过程的表现,应该是美学研究最直接的切入点。

所谓知觉,既指知觉认识活动,又指知觉认识的结果。知觉活动是认知系统对客观事物的整体特征和属性加以反映的过程,也是大脑对知觉信息进行加工计算的过程;其结果就是我们获得的知觉认识。大脑的信息加工过程是脑内神经细胞按照一定方式组织起来的活动。其大致过程是:事物的外在形式信息对感知觉系统形成刺激,激起神经系统的反应;具有不同特征的刺激信息首先在感觉器官和脑的初级部位被分解编码,尔后逐级向脑的高级部位传导;经过逐级加工,最终被整合为完整的知觉。

人的实践活动都要通过认识过程而进行。以视知觉为例,每见到一个事物,对这一事物外形的知觉和对这一事物内在价值的认识都会同时在大脑中形成。如果视觉经验足够深刻,就能保持在长时程记忆之中。外在信息刺激与大脑内部反应之间有对应关系。每一事物都有独特的外形表现,对主体的认知结构形成为样态独特的信息刺激,相当于对大脑神经系统进行着专门化的刻画。大脑神经反应方式的形成是神经细胞及其连接方式生物性化学变化的结果,即在外界刺激信息作用下形成的有特定方式的神经联系结构。事物的外形是何种样式,认知结构中的神经反应就是何种样式。对牛马的知觉经验会在大脑中形成关于牛马外形的神经细胞连接结构,对草木的知觉经验会形成关于草木的神经细胞连接结构。知觉经验中这样形成的特定神经联系结构,我们称之为"知觉模式",大致相当于皮亚杰所说的认知"图式"。

知觉模式形成之后,成为脑内认知的框架根据,以后再知觉到与知觉模式相类似的事物或其外形显现,已经建立起来的神经联系结构就会在信息加工时表现出"易化"现象,形成我们所说的"直觉",有利于迅速地对外界事物加以识别并作出反应。

每一事物都是内质与外形的统一体。因此,知觉模式中不仅包含对事物外形的识别,还包含对事物内在价值的认识。事物外形一般不对人的需要有利害价值,事物内质才对人的生存需要有利害价值。只要是同生存需要相关的信息,

都能引起主体的情感反应。

所谓情感，是生命体从生存目的出发对身体内外多方面信息加以评估而产生的反应性体验。人类的生存不仅是低级进化过程中的生物性、生理性活动，还发展出高级的社会性、精神性活动，形成高等智能。按照进化的规律，发生在大脑高级部位的认知活动可以支配大脑低级部位的情绪中枢，形成受到认知和观念影响的情感反应。"对意义或者重要性的认知评价是基础，也是所有情绪状态的基本特征。"[①] 这种高级认知活动的出现及同情感状态的连接，使得人的所有情感体验都以机体状态和认知状态为前提，有什么样的认知就会有什么样的情感。所以，世上没有无缘无故的爱，也没有无缘无故的恨；爱恨情感都建基于认识之上。

事物的外在形式本身不具有引发情感反应的作用。但由于事物的内质和外形是不可分离的，外形成了内质及其价值的表征。当外形成为内质的信号、表征时，这种信号、表征作用就通过认知过程形成了类似于内质的作用，可以像内质一样引发一定的利害性反应。例如，训练实验鼠将声音与电击刺激相关联，就使实验鼠对特定声音产生恐惧性的情感记忆。[②] 对实验鼠造成伤害的是电击，不是作为形式知觉的声音。但当有害的电击感觉同对声音的感觉在时间上非常接近时，实验鼠会把两个事件联系在一起，对特定声音也形成造成恐惧感的知觉。

人类与此相似。所谓"一朝被蛇咬，三年怕草绳"，就是这种情形的一个表现。人之所以关注事物外形，目的在于把握事物内在的利害价值。在事物利害性的中介作用之下，事物外在形式同人的情感反应之间建立起了稳定的联系。这种情形使得人的情感态度可以全方位地同事物相连接，就好像粘着于事物整体之上——既粘着于事物的内在功用之上，又粘着于事物的外形之上。不仅事物的内质可以由于直接的利害性而引发情感，没有利害性的事物外形也可以经由知觉即形式认知而间接地引起情感。事物内质与其外形的联系是稳固的，事物内质功用性同情感反应的联系也是稳固的，由此造成的事物外形同情感的联系同样是稳固的。在这一意义上，可以说知觉模式中还包含着特定的情感。

在人们的生活中，许多具体事物的外形与人的知觉和情感之间有较为稳定

[①] ［英］艾森克、［爱尔兰］基恩：《认知心理学》第4版，高定国、肖晓云译，上海：华东师范大学出版社，2003年，第750页。

[②] 《感官与情感捆绑被大脑储存》，中国脑科学网，http://www.pai314.com/news.asp?/5160.html。

的联系。例如，花草、牛羊、山水的外形普遍地与好感相联系，白骨、老鼠、粪便的外形普遍地与厌恶感相联系。在人的感觉中，似乎是事物形式直接地引发了人的情感，表现为"事物形式——情感反应"序列。其实，在事物形式与情感反应之间还存有一个重要的中间环节，即知觉活动过程。知觉活动是人类认知的一般机能，其具体实施或实现，需要通过一定的结构，即知觉模式。其表现是："事物形式——知觉（知觉模式）——情感反应"序列。在这种序列关系中，首先是事物外形同人的知觉模式形成主客体之间的知觉关系，然后是知觉模式同情感相联系。知觉模式作为知觉活动的具体结构组织，具有枢纽的地位和作用，对外连接着客观事物的形式信息，对内连接着身体的情感体验。知觉模式建立起来之后，一当事物外形同主体的知觉模式相契合、相匹配，就可以引发直觉性的情感。

三、美感即非利害状态下的形式愉悦感

将事物外形、价值和情感连接在一起的知觉模式是人一般性认知活动的通用结构；不论在利害性的一般认识活动中还是在非利害性的审美认识活动中，知觉模式都存在，都在发挥着作用。就具有肯定性情感的知觉模式来说，既可能引发利害性的愉悦感即好感，又可能引发非利害性的愉悦感即美感。那么，知觉模式所引发的究竟是好感还是美感，由什么来决定呢？

美感作为非利害性的愉悦感，应该来自于对事物形式的知觉，不能来自于对事物利害性价值的把握。人们常举例说："矿石商人仅仅看到矿石的货币价值，而看不见矿石的美的性质"。[①] 当人只关注矿石的货币价值时，自然不会关注矿石外在形式中的审美价值。矿石的货币价值是内在的，要在具有商业意识的前提下被思维所把握，不是凭感官可以看到的；矿石的美的性质即矿石的外在形式表现，则要通过对矿石形象的知觉而把握。那么，具有商业意识的矿石商人还能不能把矿石当作审美对象来欣赏呢？

事物都是内质价值和外形表现的统一体。人在面对一个事物时，例如矿石商人在面对矿石时，应该是既能看到事物的外形又能意识到事物的内在价值。人所关注的究竟是事物的内质功利价值还是外形审美价值，怎样做出选择呢？西方审美知觉理论曾经做出一种阐述：是否具有审美态度决定了怎样做出选择；

---

① 宗白华：《美学散步》，上海：上海人民出版社，1981年，第16页。

而审美态度来自于审美注意。那么,审美注意又来自何处?人们或者把它归于偶然,① 这将陷入神秘论;或者归于事物特殊性质的刺激,② 这将倒向客观论。因此,审美知觉理论不彻底,不成功。不过,审美知觉理论的不足也具有积极的意义,它凸显出美学研究需要集中力量加以攻克的一个关卡——解决审美注意的来源问题。

"知觉模式说"认为,是否形成审美注意的决定性因素是人的身体需求状态,即与生存相关的利害性需要状态。在利害状态下,人自然地形成利害性注意,不能审美;在非利害状态下,没有利害性注意,这时才能形成对事物形式的注意,进入审美状态。利害状态主要受到两方面因素的制约,一是自然因素,一是观念因素。自然因素即身体的自然性需求状态,例如饥渴需求状态。观念因素主要是社会性的意愿、要求,如对经济地位、社会地位、社会理想的要求。利害状态关乎人的生存,是人的第一需求,居于优势主导地位。人在极度饥饿时,如果面对一块蛋糕,不论是看在眼里还是吃到肚里,情感反应都是利害性的。人在商业意识强烈、急于赚钱时,看到什么都会首先想到它的货币价值,不会关注可能的审美价值,不会形成审美情感。这时,尽管事物外形能够同知觉模式相匹配,能够引发形式愉悦感,但由于功利价值优先,占据了意识和情感的主导地位,致使人只能体验到由功利价值引发的利害性愉悦感,体验不到由形式刺激而来的非利害性愉悦感。当人没有急切而强烈的利害性需求时,就是处于非利害状态。此时,不形成利害性需求,身体的情感体验中心不被利害性的情感所笼罩,人才能明显地体验到由事物形式刺激所引发的形式愉悦感。这时的形式愉悦感就是美感,审美关系只在这时才能结成。

还以矿石商人为例。当他一心想着利用矿石赚取利润时,是利害性意识占据主导地位,处于利害状态;当事业进入正常轨道,矿石可以按部就班地带来滚滚利润时,矿石的货币价值作为既定事实已经被解决,不必再操心;即,不需要对矿石怀有强烈的利害性意识。这时再面对矿石,就可以是"平常心",处于非利害状态,矿石的外形可以引发他的美感。非利害状态相当于审美的待机状态。人在这种状态下,随时可以进行形式认知活动,即形成审美活动,产生非利害性的形式愉悦感即美感。

---

① 朱狄:《当代西方美学》,北京:人民出版社,1984年,第265页。
② [美] M. 李普曼:《当代美学》,邓鹏译,北京:光明日报出版社,1986年,第289页。

四、类化的知觉模式大于具体的知觉模式

知觉模式的形成机制表明,只有于人有利的事物才能建立起同肯定性情感相连接的知觉模式,只有同肯定性情感相连接的知觉模式才能引发美感。这一规则在审美中的表现是,只有于人有利的事物才能是美的事物,于人有害的事物不能是美的。在生活中,蜜蜂是好的而苍蝇是不好的;表现在审美中,蜜蜂可以被审美而苍蝇不能被审美。仅从这两种昆虫的外形上看,没有什么本质的不同,人们甚至难以看清二者外形上的细致差别。决定二者美与不美的关键性因素在于:蜜蜂对人有利而苍蝇对人有害。说明,事物内在的有利性决定了事物外形可以具有审美性,事物形式的美与不美是以事物自身的有利性为基础的。

但是,实际生活中确实有一些事物虽然于人有利却不美,或者虽然于人有害却可以很美。如,农民种田所需要的粪肥是于人有利的,但人们一般不以之为美。这是人们曾经问过实践美学的问题。按照实践美学的理论,粪肥是既合规律性又合目的性的,是真与善的统一,充分具有自由的性质,因而具有美的本质,粪肥应该是非常美的。与此相反,罂粟花是毒品的原材料,毒品于人有害,罂粟花应该是不美的。但是,那些生活中根本不沾染毒品、反对吸毒并且也知道罂粟花是毒品原料的人,也很欣赏罂粟花。这样看来,以有利性为知觉模式得以形成的基础是否可以成立?

"知觉模式说"认为:知觉模式的形成既然是对事物外形的反映,事物的存在样态就可以对知觉模式的形成样态产生作用。事物的存在样态多种多样,有些事物以种类的方式存在,同一种类中有多种不同但却相似的存在表现。当许多于人有利的事物因其特征的相似而形成类群时,相应的知觉模式也可以形成类群,即形成"知觉模式类"。例如,一般的植物都是于人有利的,都以开花为突出而明显的外部表现形式。在植物有利性的中介作用下,植物的花朵为人所喜爱,并且在人的知觉结构中刻画出与肯定性情感相连接的知觉模式。即,许许多多植物共同组成花朵的类群;人对花朵类群的知觉被类群化,形成有关花朵的形式知觉模式类。

物理世界中存有引力。引力作用的规律是,质量大的事物对质量小的事物有吸引力。知觉的规律是,知觉模式类的作用大于个别的知觉模式。好像是知觉模式类的质量重于个别的知觉模式,因此可以吸引或涵盖个别的知觉模式。罂粟花是花朵种类中的一个。罂粟花作为具体的事物可能是于人有害的;但对

于大多数人来说，罂粟花的有害性仅只是理论上的、概念上的，并不是亲身感受到了罂粟花的毒性。概念性的知识总不如切身感受那样生动、鲜明、强烈，对情感体验的影响也很有限。在人的知觉经验中，罂粟花的有害性并不明显而强烈；与这种有害性相比，罂粟花的外形与花朵知觉模式类的一致性反倒更为明显而突出。就是说，在罂粟花的有害性不被人所关注的条件下，罂粟花的外形被类化进入人有利的花朵的知觉模式类中，因而可以被人所欣赏，成为美的。农用粪肥就其自身而言是于人有利的，但粪便作为种类事物，在人们的日常生活中是肮脏的、有害的、令人厌恶的，使人形成了否定性的知觉模式类。日常生活的普遍性使得人们对粪便的不利性感觉很强烈，对粪肥的有利性感觉不强烈。因而，个别的、本来于人有利的粪肥被类化到否定性的知觉模式类之中，不能被审美。

知觉模式与事物利害性之间的关系可以称之为纵向的联系；知觉模式的类化关系可以称之为由形式到形式的横向联系。纵向联系是更为根本的、具有决定性作用的。只有当纵向联系不紧密、不明显、不强烈时，事物外形才可以被横向地类化进具有相反利害价值的知觉模式之中。一旦事物本来的利害价值突出而强烈，纵向联系将显现出来，事物外形的价值和意义将与自身的利害性质相一致，不能被利害价值相反的知觉模式所类化。假如某个人被由罂粟花制成的毒品害得家破人亡，明显地感觉到罂粟花的有害性，罂粟花的外形将同有害性建立起纵向联系，形成同厌恶感相联系的罂粟花知觉模式。在这个人眼中，罂粟花就不能是美的。

五、知觉模式是自动形成的内隐式存在

生活中的审美现象是，一个事物一出现，美感随即产生，不需要经过分析思考，甚至也不需要以往的知觉经验。例如，有的花草、鸟雀人们从来没有见过，一看见就感觉到美；有的地方人们从来没有去过，一到这个地方就会觉得当地的景色非常美。这些情形常常使人们以为，是客观事物中的美引发了人的美感，自然界中客观地存在着美。人们还可能会说，只有在知觉到事物之后才能建立起相应的知觉模式；在第一次见到事物就产生美感时，还没有知觉模式存在；因此，"知觉模式说"不能成立。

这其实同知觉模式类相关。知觉模式是建构出的、动态发展的，有一定的弹性，有一定的容纳宽度；凡是处于这个容纳宽度内的事物形式都可与知觉模

式构成契合一致的关系。我们没见过这种鸟,但见过其他种类的鸟,见过同鸟羽毛相似的艳丽颜色;我们没有见过这座山,但见过其他的山,见过同山势类似的形式。这些类化的知觉模式已经存在于我们的认知结构中,可以容纳第一次知觉到的类似事物。

按照神经活动的规律,知觉模式的建立,包括在知觉到事物外形时知觉结构的内化过程、对事物价值的领悟和与情感的连接,都是大脑神经活动自动完成的,不为人的意识所觉察。因此,现实生活中,人们完全意识不到自己的知觉模式是怎样形成的。例如,对蜘蛛恐惧症的研究发现:大多数蜘蛛恐惧症源于幼儿时的经历。对于成年的蜘蛛恐惧症者来说,看到蜘蛛就会立即感到害怕,而让他们说出害怕什么,他们倒什么也说不出。① 从"知觉模式说"的角度看,这种情形是因为在幼年时已经将对蜘蛛外形的知觉同恐惧感紧密相连,建立起稳定的知觉模式;以后再看到蜘蛛,会形成自动的情感反应;而幼年的经历已经被忘却。因此,尽管人的所有知觉模式必有形成的过程和具体的原因,但人们未必都能清醒地认识到、觉察到;人对自己喜欢什么、不喜欢什么的知觉偏好,有的能找出原因,更多的是找不出原因。

由于不了解自己知觉模式的形成过程,也觉察不到知觉模式的存在,人们往往只能注意到事物与情感反应之间当下的因果关系,发觉不到事物与知觉模式之间的关系,也发觉不到知觉模式与情感反应之间的联系。在对事物产生美感的过程中,表面上看似乎是新出现的客观事物引发了人的美感,实际上是新发现了与知觉模式相契合的个别客体对象,或者说是凭借已有的知觉模式识别了事物从而激活了情感。美感不是由"美"所引发,而是由与既有知觉模式相匹配的形式所引发;某一事物及形式之所以能引发美感,不是由于含有"美属性"或"美本质",而是由于同主体认知结构中的知觉模式相契合。

总起来说,美学研究的主体主导论路径由康德所开辟;马克思为这条路径奠定了唯物史观基础;阿恩海姆的格式塔美学引入了自然科学的方向;认知美学的知觉模式说进一步应用现代认知科学成果初步形成了完整的阐述。

知觉模式是指认知结构中与特定的客观形式信息相对应、与特定价值认定和情感倾向相联系的较稳定的神经活动方式。事物及其形式中并不含有美或审美价值,而是含有功利性或功利价值;功利价值决定了形式和知觉模式同怎样的情感相联系。知觉模式在审美中的表现就是审美眼光。以知觉模式为枢纽,

---

① [英] 艾森克:《心理学——一条整合的途径》下册,阎巩固译,上海:华东师范大学出版社,2000年,第775页。

事物形式与美感形成了稳定的联系，可以在非利害状态下经由知觉过程而直觉性地产生美感。引发美感的一般事物被叫做"美的"，从而由一般事物转变成美的事物；美的事物又被叫做"美"。这一过程不能被理解为"美感决定了美"，而应是"有没有美感决定了事物是不是美的"。世上并不真实地存在一个独立的"美"事物，真实存在的是"美"字。"美"字指代美的事物、审美属性、审美价值。当事物引起美感时，就被叫做美的事物，美的事物的自然属性和社会属性被叫做审美属性，美的事物引发美感的作用被叫做审美价值。所谓的"美"由此而来。

（本文责任编辑：张永禄）

How do General Things Become Beautiful?
An Introduction to "Perceptual Pattern Theory"

Li Zhihong

(College of Humanities, Jilin University)

Abstract: The appropriate approach of aesthetics research is not to look for attributes of "beauty" or "beauty" perse, but to investigate how people perceive general things as "beautiful". The key element of aesthetics is the perceptual pattern of cognitive structure. Perceptual pattern is a neural structure formed by people's cognitive experience that associates information of external objects with people's emotional experience. Due to the function of perceptual patterns, each emotion would be associated with certain material forms. Things matching people's perceptual patterns will automatically cause one's aesthetic perception. Therefore, aesthetic perception is not triggered by the actual "beauty", but by forms that match the perceptual patterns. If something causes people's aesthetic perception, people will artificially attribute aesthetic value to it, and perceive it as "beautiful" even if it is not.

论马克思主义批评对文学思想内涵的诉求

孙文宪[*]

(华中师范大学文学院)

【内容摘要】 马克思主义批评是一种有别于现代文学理论的、自成系统文学研究范式。作为一种文学研究范式，其特质主要体现在四个方面：以马克思主义的基本原理、知识系统作为研讨文学问题的学理基础；具有不同于一般文学理论的问题意识和研究对象；有自己阐释文学问题的理论、范畴和命题；在马克思主义的问题域中展开文学研究。马克思的文学批评反思和批判"资本现代性"对文学活动、审美活动乃至整个精神生产的影响，构成了马克思文学批评的思想基础和主要对象，并由此形成了马克思主义文学批评的"问题域"。

与现代文学批评执著于读解文本的审美意义不同，马克思主义批评更关注文学艺术作品审美取向的社会价值及其思想内涵，并由此形成了与之相关的读解文本的另一种视域，那就是在阐释文本思想内涵的同时，还要探究这种思想生成的历史语境，甚至还会更进一步追问，文本的创造与接受实际上要受制于什么样的意识形态，又与怎样的社会体制和文化运作模式相关联。在韦勒克看来，这种与现代文学批评旨趣相异的做法虽然也有助于理解文学作品，但只能算是关于文学的"外部研究"，而"文学研究的合情合理的出发点是解释和分析作品本身"。据此他断言，外部研究的如是操作"显然决不可能解决对文学艺术作品这一对象的描述、分析和评价等问题"。[①] 关于文学批评取向的这一界

---

[*] 孙文宪，男，1947年生，华中师范大学文学院教授，博士生导师，全国马列文论研究会副秘书长，《华中学术》杂志副主编，从事文学理论和文学批评学研究。

[①] 韦勒克、沃伦：《文学理论》，刘象愚等译，南京：江苏教育出版社，2005年，第73、155页。

说不仅对文学研究产生了深远的影响，而且更通过大学的文学理论教育成为关于文学和文学批评的一种"知识"乃至"常识"。文学研究于是有了所谓的"内部"与"外部"的区分，文学批评也因此身不由己地陷入了一种二元对立的思维方式——在阐释各种文学现象时，批评必须在审美性/思想性、艺术/政治、自律/他律等说是处于矛盾或对立关系的两项中，做出非此即彼的抉择。在这样的知识语境中讨论马克思主义批评，不要说其文本阐释的文学价值会遭到质疑，就连马克思主义批评的文学身份似乎都成了问题。

倘若上述看法只是表达了韦勒克们的认识，倒可以说是情有可原，不足为虑，因为他们原本就和马克思主义批评持有不同的文学观念。现在的问题是，似乎许多认同马克思主义批评的人也认为马克思主义批评有忽略文学审美性的缺陷，主张要用"内部研究"来弥补马克思主义批评的不足。这就引出了一个必须认真思考的问题：当我们认可了文学批评存在着"内部研究"与"外部研究"之别的时候，我们是否忽略了这种认识实质上是以现代文学理论知识为依据的，而马克思主义批评则是建立在另一种文学知识基础之上的。也就是说，我们是否忽略了，马克思主义批评所以要坚持所谓的"外部研究"，是因为马克思主义批评原本就是一种有别于现代文学理论的、自成系统文学研究范式。

人们似乎已经习惯了把马克思主义文学批评理解为一种运用马克思主义的社会历史方法去解决各种文学问题的阐释活动，却忽略了作为一种有别于其他文学理论的研究范式，马克思主义文学批评的规定性实质上应取决于其特有的文学观念、问题意识和由此形成的研究对象，而不是仅仅取决于批评方法的不同。正像贝尼特曾尖锐指出的那样，如果认为马克思主义批评的特质仅在方法上，"这样做的代价是，马克思主义批评只是在方法层面上与资产阶级批评有区别（用不同的分析原则处理同一类问题），而在批评对象的理论构形这一关键层面上却丝毫没有区别"，并认为这是造成"马克思主义批评构成了马克思主义理论中最缺乏马克思主义"的重要原因。① 就是说，马克思主义的研究方法是从属于马克思主义理论体系的，把方法从理论体系中剥离出来，无视理论系统对批评方法和批评对象的规定性，会从根本上模糊马克思主义批评的特质，忽略马克思主义文学理论特有的问题意识，所以贝尼特说这种马克思主义批评最缺乏马克思主义。

我们说马克思主义文学批评是一种自成系统的文学研究范式，首先是因为

---

① 贝尼特：《马克思主义与通俗小说》，见马尔赫恩编：《当代马克思主义文学批评》，北京：北京大学出版社，2002年，第206页。

马克思主义的理论体系对其批评方法的规定性。从结构上讲，马克思主义文学批评范式由两个基本系统构成。其一是方法系统，体现为作为方法的马克思主义文学批评具有某种阐释模式的特征，这一特征通常被解释为从社会历史的角度对文学的审视。其二是知识系统，体现为马克思主义的理论知识系统对其文学研究的概念范畴、阐释对象和研究方法的规定性和制约性；马克思主义的基本理论构成了文学研究的学理基础和批评展开的论域架构。作为"模式"的方法只有在马克思主义的理论知识系统中才能充分实现。强调这一点是想说明，马克思主义的文学研究并不是在既定的或一般的文学理论框架中、去思考和回答由这种理论所提出的文学问题；马克思主义批评是以自己的问题意识和由此形成的研究对象，在马克思主义的知识系统中来阐释文学活动的。所以，我们应该把在马克思主义理论范式中展开的文学研究，和用马克思主义的理论观点去回答其他文学理论所提出的问题的文学研究区别开来，前者是严格意义上的马克思主义文学批评，后者只是运用马克思主义的理论方法去研讨一般文学理论所关注的文学问题，二者有根本的不同。

作为一种具有自身特点的文学研究范式，马克思主义文学批评的特质主要体现在四个方面：①以马克思主义的基本原理、知识系统作为研讨文学问题的学理基础；②具有不同于一般文学理论的问题意识和研究对象；③有自己阐释文学问题的理论、范畴和命题；④在马克思主义的问题域中展开文学研究。正是相互关联的这四个方面，体现了马克思主义文学批评和一般文学批评的不同。强调二者之间存在的这种差异是为了指出这样一个事实：把马克思主义文学批评泛化，使之成为一个几乎无所不包的概念，只能淡化、模糊、甚至消解马克思主义文学批评的特质，这实际上已成为阻碍中国马克思主义批评的发展和创新的重要原因之一。

用既定的文学理论框架读解马克思主义的文学批评理论，不仅模糊了对马克思主义文学批评理论特质的认识，而且会导致理论研究上的许多"盲点"，例如忽视马克思主义文学批评有自己的文学问题和研究对象。也就是说，我们必须从"问题域"上思考马克思主义文学研究的特点与特质，以及马克思主义的文学研究与一般文学理论的不同。自从阿尔都塞提出，只有把握了马克思理论研究的"问题域"，我们才能准确理解马克思的思想理论这一具有方法论意义的观点之后，确认马克思理论研究的"问题域"已成为众多学者阐释什么是马克思主义的要义势必涉及的一个话题。那么，马克思主义及其文学研究的问题域是什么呢？伊格尔顿指出："马克思主义的典型特征是特别注意资本主义的矛盾：它无法自禁地同时生产财富和贫困，二者互为物质条件。这反过来使马克思主义对现代性问题表现出一种特有的立场。"① 美国学者劳洛也认为："对于资本主义的发展变化的分析，才是马克思的真正遗产和他的研究工作的旨趣所在。"② 英国著名的社会学家吉登斯则通过比较马克思的社会学思想与韦伯、涂尔干的区别，指出马克思的"首要兴趣是资产阶级社会的动力学。……《资本论》的首要目标就是要考察资产阶级社会生产基础的动力，揭示资产阶级社会的'经济运动法则'。"③ 从这些论述中可以看出，认为马克思理论研究的"问题域"是"资本与现代性的关系"已成为许多人的共识。从马克思的理论研究中我们也确实可以看到，他把资本主义生产方式的出现视为现代性的标志，指出"资本一出现，就标志着社会生产过程的一个新时代。"④ 强调现代性发展的动力来自资本对剩余价值的追求，资本主义社会的矛盾、危机、异化和阶级斗争都是资本现代性问题的表现。为此，马克思把现代性批判的基本任务，定位于揭示和反思资本作为现代性原则的普遍贯彻，从而更深刻地揭示了现代性的二重性。一方面，马克思指出只有经过资本主义这个历史阶段，人类社会才能走出愚昧落后，获得巨大发展；另一方面，马克思又对资本现代性作了深刻的批判，指出资本现代性的历史"只不过是现代生产力反抗现代生产关系、反抗作为资产阶级及其统治的存在条件的所有制关系的历史"。⑤ 马克思的文学批评就是在上述"问题域"中展开的，反思和批判"资本现代性"对文学活动、审美活动乃至整个精神生产的影响，构成了马克思文学批评的思想基础和主要对象，并由此形成了马克思主义文学批评的"问题域"，形成了不同于一般文学理论的、马克思主义文学批评范式特有的问题意识、研究对象和理论范畴。其集中体现在两个方面：

第一，在批判"资本现代性"的语境中，马克思主义文学批评没有简单地接受现代文学理论以审美性界说文学的性质与功能的观点，而是揭示资本主义私有制所造成的异化对文学审美活动的影响，致力于研讨现代社会中的文学审美活动

---

① 伊格尔顿：《马克思主义文学理论》，见《历史中的政治、哲学、爱欲》，北京：中国社会科学出版社，1999年，第108页。
② 詹姆斯·劳洛：《马克思主义哲学和共产主义》，见欧阳康主编：《当代英美哲学地图》，北京：人民出版社，2005年，第628页。
③ 吉登斯：《资本主义与现代社会理论——对马克思、涂尔干和韦伯著作的分析》，上海：上海译文出版社，2007年，第54页。
④ 《马克思恩格斯文集》第5卷，北京：人民出版社，2009年，第198页。
⑤ 《马克思恩格斯文集》第2卷，北京：人民出版社，2009年，第37页。

与意识形态之间的复杂关系，关注现实社会的运作机制对文学活动的影响，关注社会的政治、经济体制和文化制度对文学生产的制约和干预，在文学艺术与政治、经济和文化的关联性中研讨文学的"自律"与"他律"，强调现实生活中的文学活动所具有的多重价值与功能，尤其重视文学活动对社会变革的介入和参与。

第二，在反思"资本现代性"的基础上，马克思主义文学批评拓展了现代文学理论的研究领域和知识结构，在马克思主义批评的论域中发现和提出了新的文学问题，为文学批评引入新的研究对象，如艺术生产问题、艺术生产与物质生产的不平衡关系、现代科学技术的发展对文学艺术的影响、文学艺术在商品生产及市场经济条件下的生存与发展、以"两种生产"的唯物史观诠释文学活动的价值，等等。

可以说，正是上述的内在规定，决定了马克思主义批评对文学思想内涵的诉求。

（本文责任编辑：张永禄）

On Marxist Ideological Content of Literary Criticism Demands

Sun Wenxian

Abstract: Marxist literary criticism is different from the modern literary theory, which is of a system paradigm. As a literary research paradigm, there are four characteristics in it: the basic principles of Marxism, knowledge systems as a theoretical discussion based on literary issues; literary theory is different from the general awareness of the problem and the object of study; it has their own interpretation of literary theory problem, scope and propositions; problems in the domain of Marxist literary studies commenced. Marx's critique of modernity basic task, located in the capital as a modern reveal and reflect the principle of universal implementation, and thus more profoundly reveals the duality of modernity. Marxist literary criticism and critical reflection "Capital modernity" of literary activities, and the whole spirit of the production of aesthetic activity influence of Marxist literary criticism constitutes the ideological foundation and the main object, and the formation of the Marxist literary criticism of the "problem domain".

马克思主义与乌托邦精神

杨 杰

【内容摘要】 物质文明与精神文明的不断和谐提升的历程构成人类社会历史，二者的发展相辅相成、互为前提。作为人类文明的乌托邦精神的产生与存在不仅依赖于所处的社会现实物质文明，同时它又具有批评现实社会、超越社会物质现实而引导人类社会面向未来发展的特征和作用，集中体现了人类精神主体性、超越性、前瞻性特征，这正是马克思所说的人的自由自觉的类的特征。

物质文明与精神文明的共同发展构成了人类社会历史演进的滚滚洪流。物质文明是精神文明产生与存在的基础。作为人类精神文明表现形式的乌托邦精神具有批判现实、超越现实物质条件而面向未来的前瞻性，这是主体"合目的性"的表现，乌托邦精神正是人的主体精神超越性的集中体现的载体。

一

在《巴黎手稿》中，马克思提出了著名的"美的规律"命题，即"合规律性"与"合目的性"的统一。社会实践是人现实存在与发展的基础和前提条件，正是在社会实践中，主体的人与客体的自然形成了性质各异的对象性关系。人的生存、繁衍的前提是必须要解决最基本的物质需求，于是，人与自然之间形成的物质实践关系成为最基本的对象性关系，即狭义的实践关系，为了更好地改造客观自然界，人们就要尽可能地掌握自然规律以便于驾驭、运用自然规律为人类服务，即马克思所说的"合规律性"，改造客观世界的结果就是物质文明，反映到主体意识方面就形成了人的科学意识；在人们进行物质生产实践活动中,"趋利避害"不仅是一切生物的本能,更是人类活动的出发点与终点,是人类意志目的的表现,即"合目的性"。

　　自由、自觉是人的类的本质特征,自觉能动性是为实践主体的特性,如果说动物更多地表现为被动适应环境,那么,人的社会实践活动则是主体主动地按照人的主观意愿与自身需求去征服、改造自然的活动,在主体的人与客体的自然形成对象性关系结构的过程中,人的主动选择性接受可以将客体的自然属性内化为主体的本质力量,实践的能动性更为集中地体现为人在改造自然之前就已经主观地创造性地构建了实践结果的"宏伟蓝图",并通过实践将主观的"蓝图"对象化为客观现实物质世界,使人的本质力量外化为物质性的存在,使自在之物转化为"为我之物"。"合规律性"要求主体的社会实践符合自然规律,也就是说,主体要受动于客体的制约,主体表现为受动性;"合目的性"要求客体为主体所支配,客体服务于主体,如此一来,主体与客体、主动性与受动性、支配与制约之间就形成了对立、矛盾,如何解决这种矛盾对立?那就是"合规律性"与"合目的性"的统一,就是马克思说的"美的规律",当然,这是一种理想的状态,也是人类为之奋斗的目标。

　　然而,现实世界总与人的主观理想世界存在相当大的距离,人类只能是由"必然王国"部分地、逐渐地向着理想的"自由王国"发展而趋向无限接近。正是对现实社会的不满足,对未来美好前景的憧憬和坚持不懈的追求才化作人类不断发展进步的不竭动力。也正是从这个角度上讲,乌托邦精神具有不可忽视的作用和积极意义,它是"对超越价值理想的不懈追求精神,乃是人之为人、人区别于动物的重大标志,正是它体现了人的高贵、尊严和勇气,表现了人在宇宙中不同凡响的地位","人无时无刻不在为超越动物地位、超越其生存的偶然性和受动性以及成为一个'创造者'的愿望所驱使,无时无刻不在内心激荡着一种趋向自由的力量,热情与憧憬。……人能够通过自身创造性的实践活动打破肉体存在束缚,使自己的存在获得开放的、应然的和生成的性质,从而彻底超越了自然物那种预成的、单调的、封闭的和宿命的存在方式。……人是一种必然通过自身创造性活动,不断向未来开辟可能性并塑造自我的自由存在物。"[①]

二

　　马克思主义哲学是关于人的哲学,十分关注人的精神世界状况,包含着积

---

① 贺来:《现实生活——乌托邦精神的真实根基》,长春:吉林教育出版社,2004年,第6页。

极的乌托邦精神维度。从表面上看，"乌托邦"一词出现较晚，来源于英国思想家托马斯·莫尔的同名著作，但乌托邦思想由来已久，从古希腊肇始。通常，人们习惯将其视作为"不切实际的空想"，带有较强的贬义色彩，但对其积极意义的一面相对缺乏足够的认识，今天，我们应该为其正名，客观地对待"乌托邦精神"。

客观说，自"乌托邦"一词诞生，对其评价褒贬不一，见仁见智。否定者认为，"乌托邦"不过是"空想"、"不切实际"、"非科学"、"子虚乌有"的代名词而已，因此，其贬义的、讽刺的、否定的色彩浓厚。在一些自由主义思想者看来，马克思主义理论是乌托邦主义的典型代表之一，必将随着意识形态时代的终结而走向终结。尽管自由主义对马克思主义否定的观点存在明显的谬误，但至少从反面揭示出了"片面的真理"——马克思主义思想包含着人类对未来社会美好理想的憧憬的乌托邦精神维度，这恰恰是乌托邦精神否定现实、满怀希望地向往未来理想的批评精神。我们认为，正是乌托邦精神所具有的积极性的一面，是对人主体的能动性、精神性的充分肯定与展示，必将伴随人类解放、历史发展的历程而不断向前推进，从这个意义上讲，乌托邦精神成为马克思主义哲学的重要组成因素有其深厚的逻辑必然性。

因此，"乌托邦"是人类精神家园，它严肃地对待现实社会中存在的各种局限性，激励着一代又一代人不断改造现实社会，向着光明的未来努力，它是人类文明前进的指航灯。通览学界的有关研究成果，学者们通常认为，乌托邦精神源远流长，历史悠久，其"家族相似性"特征在于，它以批判的眼光审视现实社会，并试图超越现实社会的局限，对未来理想社会充满希望、充满信心，凝聚着深厚的人文终极关怀，它是"一种普世情怀，一种人类共有的精神财富"[1]。乔多柯夫曾说："乌托邦冲动是对现存社会状态的反映并试图超越现实改变那些状态以达到理想状态的尝试。它总是包含着两个相互关联的因素：对现存状态的批评与一个新社会的远景或更新的方案。"[2] 退一步讲，即使乌托邦难以成为明天的现实，但它至少可以使我们获得对美好未来的憧憬，这种情怀能够不断驱使我们为改变现实社会而不懈去奋斗，这本身就具有重要的意义。与那些轻视乌托邦的学者的观点截然不同，赫茨勒给予了高度赞扬，"乌托邦思

---

[1] ［美］拉塞尔·雅各比：《乌托邦之死——冷漠时代的政治与文化》，姚建彬译，北京：新星出版社，2007年，第3页。

[2] Daniel Chodorkoff, "The Utopian Impulse: Reflection on a Tradition", *The Jounal of Social Ecology*, 1.1 Winter 83.

想家在他们各自所处的时代,都毫无例外地表现为思想上富于创新性和建设性思想力的人……他们是面对着一片荒野却看到了一座乐园的人"①。

我们之所以肯定乌托邦精神的原因在于,它的"重大使命不在于对未来世界做出面面俱到细节上的设计与规划,而在于克服人的自然惰性对现存事实的消极默认,为人和社会走向新境界提供新的可能性。它启示人们不要放弃这一种希望——去寻找一个先前不曾有过的世界,在那里'最有可能找到正义'。因此,乌托邦精神总是涉及人之为人,社会之为社会的最基本的原则和律令的追问,所要探究的是人之所以为人的可能性,即'人的价值'这一根本性的大问题"②。

马克思主义与以往的乌托邦既有逻辑沿承关系,又有着革命性的突破。马克思主义批评地继承了人类社会历史上的乌托邦精神的合理内核,既扎根于现实物质基础,又将其从精神领域拓展到社会实践层面,成为改造现实世界的真正动力,可见,乌托邦与幻想有着本质的区别,幻想建立在无根据的想象之上,是永远无法实现的,而乌托邦则蕴含着希望,体现了对一个与现实完全不同的未来的向往,为开辟未来提供了精神动力。马克思主义是汲取了乌托邦精神的③。由此可见,乌托邦精神对于人类的重要性并不是在现实的今天能有多少可以得到实证检验,而是在于面向未来的精神慰藉,是精神的家园;但是,另一方面,这种精神的希望又不是虚无缥缈的,它是以现实物质基础为逻辑起点而向未来开放的,否则只能变成"空想"、"幻想",永远滞留于精神的层面。至少在这一点上,马克思主义批评地继承了乌托邦精神的合理性因素。

人类自诞生之时就赋予生命以价值和意义,走向美好和谐的未来社会是人类历史的必然选择。自从人类历史揭开了文明的篇章,柏拉图的"理想国"、陶渊明的"世外桃源"、康帕内拉的"太阳城"、培根的"新大西岛"、莫尔的"乌托邦"、傅立叶的"全世界和谐"、圣西门的"新基督主义"、欧文的"新和谐公社"、魏特琳的"民主共产主义家庭联盟"、威尔斯的"现代乌托邦"、米切尔的"伊托邦",到《共产党宣言》,一页又一页的历史篇章无不闪耀着人类探寻人生价值、追求幸福生活、实现社会理想的足迹。在中国传统文化中,"大同"世界就表现了乌托邦美好蓝图:"大道之行也,天下为公。选贤与能,

---

① [美]乔·奥·赫茨勒:《乌托邦思想史》,张兆麟等译,北京:商务印书馆,1990年,第251—252页。
② 贺来:《现实生活——乌托邦精神的真实根基》,第6页。
③ [德]尤尔根·哈贝马斯、米夏埃尔·哈勒:《作为未来的过去》,章国锋译,杭州:浙江人民出版社,2001年,第122—123页。

讲信修睦，故人不独亲其亲，不独子其子，使老有所终，壮有所用，幼有所长，矜寡孤独废弃者皆有所养。男有女，女有归。货恶其弃于地也，不必藏于己；力恶其不出于身也不必为己，是故谋闭而不兴，盗窃乱贼而不作，故外户不闭，是谓大同。"①

不同的历史时期都有自己时代的理想——乌托邦精神。曼海姆认为，任何时代必然要有自己的意识形态，一方面，它要立足于现实的利益基础，另一方面，又要担负起引导人们为之奋斗的作为这个历史时期社会发展驱动力的社会集体无意识，乌托邦精神中总是蕴含着积极的变革现实社会的否定性的革命因素，"反映了政治斗争中……某些受压迫的群体在理智上如何强烈地对破坏和改变既定的社会状况感兴趣，以至于他们不知不觉地紧紧看到局势中那些倾向于否定它的因素"②，"当这种否定性因素通过一定的方式成为物质现实时，之前的乌托邦（理想性）的某些成分就会转化为托邦（现实性），新的乌托邦继而又会以此为基础产生并成为继续为之奋斗的动力，直至实现其理想，人类社会就是这样不断地往复运动中向前发展的"，"每个历史事件都是由于乌托邦而从托邦（现存秩序）中产生的一种不断更新的解放。……历史的道路总是从一个托邦经过一个乌托邦而导向下一个托邦"③。可见，人类历史就是这样一个不断适应着已经改变的社会前提条件，并以此前提条件为自身发展新起点继续提升主体改造现实世界能力的过程，只要有人类的存在，乌托邦精神就不会消失，"历史的动力（而且的确是一种历史必然的动力），不在于乌托邦的实现，而是对它的奋力追求"。它正像韦伯曾经指出的，人们必须一再为不可能的东西奋斗，否则他就不可能得到可能的东西了。

三

当代中国，我们之所以再次谈及"马克思主义与乌托邦精神"这一命题的根本原因在于，面对社会现实中存在各种问题，仅仅满足于"物质文明"不仅是远远不够的，而且是极其危险的，必须有"精神文明"的引航，人类的生存需要"乌托邦精神"家园的慰藉和引航。

伴随着我国改革开放政策的不断深化，中国社会的政治、经济、文化等诸

---

① 《礼记·礼运》，阮元：《十三经注疏》，北京：中华书局，1979年。
② [德] 卡尔·曼海姆：《意识形态与乌托邦》，黎鸣译，北京：九州出版社，2007年，第83页。
③ [美] 拉塞尔·雅各比：《乌托邦之死——冷漠时代的政治与文化》，第407页。

方面实现了跨越式发展，取得的成绩令世人瞩目，这是不容置疑的。同时，随之而来的是一些值得引起注意的问题，突出表现为精神文明与物质文明发展的失衡。一言以蔽之，就是现代人精神家园的迷失。究其原因，主要有两个方面：一是社会历史的"转型"带来的系列问题，一是主体自身面对如此"转型"的"心理失调"。从客观社会方面讲，"文革"结束，人们由以往的"政治斗争为纲"转向了以经济建设为核心，社会话语由政治化、军事化的术语转向了经济化就可窥见一斑。譬如，由"先锋队"、"坚强的战斗堡垒"、"攻坚战"、"突击队"转向"形象工程"、"希望工程"、"菜篮子工程"、"阳光工程"等等的系列"工程"，一向羞于谈钱的中国人终于揭掉这层"遮羞布"，振聋发聩地喊出了"时间就是效益"、"时间就是金钱"的口号，成为一个旗帜鲜明的时代里程碑式表征。然而，"发展是硬道理"被主观地、想当然地解读为狭隘的"经济发展才是硬道理"，于是，经济指标不自觉地就上升为社会各行各业的"风向标"和最高评价尺度，有人概括为"一切向钱看"，此语难免夹杂一些情绪化成分，或许略显极端，但在一定层面反映了这种社会倾向，"房子、票子、车子"成为衡量人们日常生活质量的标尺，GDP成为各级政府追逐和被考量的唯一目标，"拜物教"成为人们的至上信仰。如此的社会转型与人们心目中原有的价值观念体系发生了激烈的碰撞，以往的建立于农业经济基础之上的文明与工业文明相呼应的价值观形成对立，固有的价值体系面对现代经济社会遇到了前所未有的挑战，人们如何应对社会现实，实现传统价值观的现代转换成为国人的困惑。于是，从主体角度讲，人们的心理必然出现失衡。当人们都处于相对平衡的物质条件时，宣传的各种精神慰藉是有效的，但这种物质条件的均衡一旦被打破，过去我们常常用来形容资本主义的"物欲横流"也残酷地发生在我们的眼前，面对物质利诱，精神的力量显得那样柔弱而不堪一击。

正如布洛赫所忧心忡忡的慨叹："我们已沦落为最可怜的脊椎动物地步；我们中的所有人或者崇拜自己的肚子，或者崇拜国家，除此之外，其他的都降到了要么可笑要么玩乐的境地。"① 然而，就是在人类如此迫切需要乌托邦精神的时刻，有人却提出了反乌托邦和乌托邦终结的声音。的确，乌托邦精神正面临严峻的生存挑战。詹姆逊认为，因为我们今天处于一个尴尬的境地，一方面，社会充满了诸如苦难、贫穷、失业、饥饿、腐败、暴力以及死亡等等的危机，相比之下，那些执著于建构美好社会计划的乌托邦思想的研究者们的努力却显

---

① Ernst Bloch, *The spirit of Utopia*, trans., Anthony Nassar, meridian, 2000.

得如此苍白无义而多此一举；另一方面，社会又表现出前所未有的繁荣——社会财富剧增、数字化的生产，科学与医学的惊人飞速发展更是上个世纪难以想象的，人们从事着遍及全球的商业交往活动，尽情地享受各种文化带来的"盛宴"，在如此令人耳目一新的时代，所有的乌托邦幻想与构建的幻象都显得相形见绌与不合时宜①。前者使得乌托邦的存在虚无缥缈而不切实际，后者又令乌托邦的存在显得多余。伽达默尔不无忧心地叹息："当今的时代是一个乌托邦精神已经死去的时代。过去的乌托邦一个个失去了他们的神秘的光环，而新的、能鼓励人们为之奋斗的乌托邦再也不会产生。这正是我们这个时代的悲剧。"②

难道说乌托邦精神在今天就该退出历史舞台？其实不然。即使将马克思主义列入乌托邦主义行列，认为伴随意识形态时代终结而"寿终正寝"的丹尼尔·贝尔也不得不承认"今天比任何时候都更加需要乌托邦"，因为"人们需要——像他们一直需要的那样——得到其关于可能性的前景，关于把激情和理智结合起来的方式"③。对于一个国家来说，"如果没有乌托邦冲动，政治就会变得苍白无力，机械粗暴，而且往往会沦为西西弗式的神话；尽管它是一个接一个地堵塞漏洞，船舱却垮漏了，船也就沉默了。自然，水漏是应该被堵塞。但是，我们也许需要一艘新船，需要一种理想。"④ 杜塞尔·雅各比的话是有一定道理的。

人类的本性需要精神寄托，尤其是在社会急剧变革的今天，面对技术理性的恶性膨胀，乌托邦精神蕴含着人类对理想世界的追求，并为人类历史指引航向，可以肯定地说，"如果没有预示未来乌托邦展现的可能性，我们可能只会看到一个颓废的存在，人类的可能性的自我实现都受到了窒息。没有乌托邦的人总是沉浸于现实之中，没有乌托邦的文化总是被束缚于现实之中，而且会迅速地倒退到过去，因为现在只有处于过去和未来的张力之中才会充满活力。"⑤

今天，当我们坚持马克思主义中国化的思想原则时，不要忽视其乌托邦精神的维度。随着现代化进程的推进，世界不断理智化和理性化，工具理性主导一切，功利型的经济社会极易塑造"精于算计"的人格，利益的最大化驱使人

---

① See Fredric Jameson, *The Politics of Utopia*, *New Left Review* 25, Jan Feb 2004, p.35.
② 章国锋：《伽达默尔谈后现代主义》，《世界文学》，1991年第2期。
③ [美] 丹尼尔·贝尔：《意识形态的终结》，张国清译，南京：江苏人民出版社，2001年，第465页。
④ [美] 拉塞尔·雅各比：《乌托邦之死——冷漠时代的政治与文化》，第196页。
⑤ [德] 保罗·蒂里希：《政治期望》，何光沪译，成都：四川人民出版社，1989年，第6、215—216页。

类的贪婪攫取，乌托邦精神有利于我们丰富本已异常贫乏精神生活，重新扬起追求美好理想的风帆。

温家宝在同济大学百年校庆时语重心长地说："一个民族有一些关注天空的人，他们才有希望，一个民族只是关心脚下的事情，那是没有未来的。"① 乌托邦精神的价值或许至少如此。

（本文责任编辑：任天）

Marxism and Utopian Spirit

Yang Jie

Abstract：Human history is one of continual harmonization of material and spiritual civilization, which supplement and anticipate each other. Utopian spirit, as part of human civilization, is subject to a society's material civilization. At the same time, it evaluates social reality and guides a society towards a higher stage of development. Utopian spirit embodies the subjectivity, transcendence, and foresight od human spirit, which Marx called human autonomy and self-awareness.

---

① 邵龙宝：《我们应该怎样"仰望天空"》，《中国教育报》2007年10月11日。

马克思主义同乌托邦究竟是什么关系

——关于"空想社会主义"译名的检讨及其他

姚建彬*

(北京师范大学文学院)

【内容摘要】 从源头出发,厘清马克思主义同乌托邦之间的关系,就会发现,马克思与乌托邦之间并不是截然对立的,即便是粗糙的列宁的现实主义偶尔也具有乌托邦主义的味道。把马克思主义同乌托邦联系起来,决不是丢脸或背叛的事情,称马克思主义者为乌托邦主义者,决不意味着批判与否定!相反,在一定意义范围内,马克思主义者可以而且应该自豪地宣传,我们就是乌托邦主义者!共产主义理想就具有乌托邦的成分。

国内对马克思主义著作,尤其是马克思主义经典著作的译介与研究,已经有了将近百来的历史,但是对于涉及马克思主义思想三大来源之一的"空想社会主义"的认识和理解仍然存在不能忽视的误区。尽管笔者深知,在跨文化的交流与理解上,"误解"和"误读"其实是一种常态,但是,当我们意识到"误解"和"误读"已经发生了之后该怎么办?是听任"误解"和"误读"继续持存,还是在可能的情况下对其予以矫正呢?我想,对于大多数理智健全的人来说,合适的选择当是后者。最近几年来,笔者在研究西方乌托邦思想史及乌托邦文学的过程中,注意到了我们在理解和阐释乌托邦社会主义、空想社会主义和乌托邦等重要概念上所存在的一些误区。这样的误区同"空想社会主义"这个译名中存在的误会、扭曲和错误的价值判断联系在一起的。这样的误

---

* 姚建彬,1972 年生,男,湖南汉寿人,文学博士、博士后,北京师范大学副教授,研究方向为西方马克思主义文艺美学、中西比较文学、欧美文学、乌托邦文学、乌托邦思想史。

会、扭曲和错误的价值判断，直接涉及我们如何理解和评价马克思主义同乌托邦之间的关系。

在我们国内所有的马克思主义教科书，所有政治经济学，所有马克思主义哲学原理的相关著述中，都无一例外地承认，"空想社会主义"是马克思主义的三大来源之一。颇为奇怪的是，从总体上看，对于马克思主义的其他两大来源，我们都能够以辩证的观点来把握它们同马克思主义之间的关系，但是唯独对于同马克思主义关系或许更加密切的"空想社会主义"却从来没有放松过警惕。"空想社会主义"一直就是作为反面教员出现在马克思主义的视野之中的。但是，对于二者之间关系的这种近乎一厢情愿似的维护，并没有太多的实际意义，除了束缚马克思主义者对于马克思主义的认识与理解之外，也丧失了马克思主义论战中的一些主动权，丧失了一些得分机会。

按照笔者的理解，当初之所以把 utopian socialism 译作"空想社会主义"，大致有三个方面的理由：其一，强调马克思主义思想体系中的社会主义思想的科学性，正统性乃至权威性。其二，"五四"精神的影响。在那场深刻影响了中国现代化进程的"五四"运动中，"德先生"与"赛先生"这两面大旗曾经激发了无数的梦想与思考，同时也招致了无可否认的争议，从而影响了当时及后世对于乌托邦等重要外来思想范畴的理解。其三，对"西方乌托邦思想"的肤浅了解所致。

当然，如果认真地予以考证，马克思、恩格斯之后的马克思主义者之所以对于"乌托邦"、"乌托邦的"、"乌托邦主义者"，或者"乌托邦主义"抱有反感或抵触情绪，并且将其作为具有明显倾向性的政治范畴加以运用，与马克思、恩格斯当初对乌托邦的批评有着较为密切的关系。任何对马克思主义略有了解的人都知道，马克思的确是在贬义（pejorative）上运用"乌托邦主义者"（utopian）这一字眼的，在使用乌托邦主义者这一术语时，马克思严格地将其限制在指称那些非科学的社会主义者（the non-scientific socialists）。在马克思看来，这些人都是做白日梦的人和不切实际的浪漫主义者（day-dreamers and impractical romantics）。

马克思的这种批评无疑是非常犀利、富有洞见的。从乌托邦思想史来看，有些乌托邦主义者的确就是"做白日梦的人和不切实际的浪漫主义者"。毫无疑问，如果听任这样的人来主导人们的观念，则只会把社会引向无序和混乱，因而必须对其予以坚决否定。也正因如此，马克思的这种态度，成为了后来的马克思主义者对于乌托邦的标准态度。恩格斯、列宁以及中国的马克思主义者也都是在这一标准态度的指引下来处理与乌托邦相关的所有问题的。

众所周知,"马克思的反乌托邦主义的标准来源是弗雷德里希·恩格斯的《乌托邦社会主义和科学社会主义》"①。作为马克思思想与学说的最权威阐释者,恩格斯在这一重要文献中对于"科学的"与"乌托邦的"所作的划分,以及他对科学社会主义所做的论述,成为了后世关于科学社会主义表述的唯一根据。恩格斯的这一褒贬鲜明、对比强烈的划分,堪称社会主义思想史上的历史性转折,它不仅标志着马克思主义的社会主义学说的根本确立,也标志着马克思主义同所有非科学的社会主义学说的彻底断交。

恩格斯之所以拥护"科学社会主义",反对"理想社会主义",主要原因在于后者"无法理解历史的矢量与工人阶级的向量"。

令人颇为遗憾的是,马克思和恩格斯,尤其是马克思对于乌托邦所做的非常具体,而且也具有直接针对性的批评,却被后来的马克思主义者不适当地扩大到了对于所有乌托邦的批评与否定,以致形成了一个怪圈:凡属乌托邦的,就是"无事实根据的、模糊不清的以及转移注意力的"。简言之,乌托邦就是坏的、要不得的,而凡属科学的,就是"切实可行的、清楚明白的以及凝聚意志的"。简言之,科学的就是好的、该拥护的。更加庸俗化的推理就是:既然"马克思主义是科学的",那么"科学 = 马克思主义",或者"马克思主义 = 科学";反过来,既然"马克思主义是科学的",那么就不可能同乌托邦有任何关系。在马克思主义的实践中,这种绝对主义、庸俗化的倾向大有独揽话语权的趋势。很长一段时间以来,在马克思主义成为指导思想的国家,比如中国,任何将马克思主义同乌托邦联系起来的做法,都是要遭到质疑或者批判的。1988年,曲彪出版了《毛泽东思想、社会主义、乌托邦主义》一书。同年,《毛泽东思想研究》上刊登了一篇措辞严厉的书评,质问作者为什么把毛泽东思想称为"乌托邦主义"。受这种影响,我们长期以来形成了这样一种共识,任何把社会主义思想与实践以及共产主义思想与实践同乌托邦相联系的做法,都是别有用心的,都是对马克思主义的背叛。问题果真有如此严重吗?马克思主义果真同乌托邦没有任何血缘关系吗?

如果我们认真去追溯马克思主义的形成轨迹,去重读马克思主义的著作,尤其是经典马克思主义的著作,就不难发现我们或许难以像以往那样以无知为支撑作出否定性回答。

---

① 拉塞尔·雅各比:《乌托邦之死——冷漠时代的政治与文化》,第一章注释 76,Basic Books,1999 年,第 188—189 页,该书中译本已经由笔者译出,于 2007 年由新星出版社出版。

正如雅格比指出的那样，"马克思本人更多地是因为社会主义者①无法理解如何能够达到未来而不是因为他们对未来的希望而谴责他们"，因为"他们并不理解政治活动取代了乌托邦蓝图"。这就是说，在马克思看来，时代已经使问题发生了转向，在他所处的那个时代，光有乌托邦蓝图是不够的，还必须有"政治活动"。在马克思看来，政治活动与乌托邦蓝图是并行不悖的。就某种意义而言，在他那个时代，政治活动比单纯的乌托邦蓝图来得更加紧迫，在某种意义上前者甚至取代了后者，但是后者的合理内核，也就是乌托邦蓝图的合法性与真理性，却内蕴于马克思所理解并倡导的政治活动中。"马克思的目的不是摧毁，而是实现各种远景。"

由此看来，马克思与乌托邦之间并不是截然对立的。但是，历史形成的误解却让我们一直在犯着"以讹传讹"的错误。

进入20世纪以来，最晚从20世纪30年代开始，对乌托邦的批评与审判就成为了以赛亚·伯林、卡尔·波普尔、汉娜·阿伦特、雅格布·塔尔蒙这些自由主义思想家乐此不疲的中心目标。

与此同时，我们也注意到，来自马克思主义阵营的批评家们对于将乌托邦与马克思主义联系起来的做法所持的批评态度，丝毫不比自由主义思想家对于马克思主义的批评逊色。

如果否认马克思主义同乌托邦的关系，如果否认共产主义同乌托邦的关系，那就不是一个真正的马克思主义者。一个简单的理由在于，如果没有了理想主义的色彩，共产主义的旗帜不会如此令人神往！

基于以上的理由，我们必须从源头出发，厘清马克思主义同乌托邦之间的关系。

马克思的反乌托邦主义的标准来源是弗雷德里希·恩格斯：《乌托邦社会主义和科学社会主义》②。这本书将乌托邦观念仅仅视为在历史中缺乏真实基础的"杂烩"而快速了断。对其德文标题的更加准确的翻译，即《社会主义从乌托邦到科学》，更好地抓住了恩格斯的论点。恩格斯赞成"科学的"社会主义，将其视为对"乌托邦的"社会主义的驱逐，因为它无法理解历史的矢量与工人阶级的向量。在《马克思主义名称辞典》（经典版本）中，"乌托邦的"一词，意思是无事实根据的、模糊不清的以及转移注意力的。但是马克思本人更多地是因为社会主义者无法理解如何能够达到未来而不是因为他们对未来的希望而

---

① 即"理想社会主义者"。
② 恩格斯：《乌托邦社会主义和科学社会主义》，北京：外文出版社，1975年。

谴责他们；他们并不理解政治活动取代了乌托邦蓝图。马克思的目的不是摧毁，而是实现各种远景。在其对巴黎共产主义小组的讲话中，他就已经指出过，工人阶级没有"现成的乌托邦可以推广……尽管他们没有要实现的理想，但是他们可以解放新社会的要素，这正是充满着正在垮塌的资产阶级社会本身所孕育的东西"。在那次讲话的一份草稿中，马克思说得更加精确、更加详细：尽管所有的乌托邦社会主义者"在他们对现存社会的批判中都清晰地描绘出了社会运动的目的"，但是他们不能理解手段，这主要是因为工人阶级本身没有获得充足的发展。乌托邦主义者"竭力通过关于新社会的异想天开的图画和蓝图想方设法补偿这种运动的历史条件，在新社会的宣传中，他们看到了拯救的真正手段"。他继续说道，"从工人的阶级运动变成真正空想的乌托邦这一刻起，它就渐渐消失了——不仅仅是因为工人阶级业已放弃了这些乌托邦主义者所针对的目的，而且因为他们已经找到了真正实现它们的手段"。①

即便是粗糙的列宁的现实主义偶尔也具有乌托邦主义的味道。在《国家与革命》②中，他坚定地主张，"我们不是乌托邦主义者"，但是没有多少页之后，他又为马克思主义者的乌托邦主义进行辩护，反对资产阶级的庸人习气。在其对《怎么办？》（*What Is to Be Done?*）的实践指南中，列宁督促自己要对高涨的革命有热情的洞察，在结论中这样指出，这就是"我们应该梦想的东西"。他然后嘲笑了清醒的马克思主义者对其感情充沛的洞察："'我们应该梦想！'我写下了这些话，然后吓了一跳。"他详细阐述了一位郁郁寡欢的同志的反对意见："我问道，马克思主义者根本没有任何权利梦想吗？按照马克思的观点，他知道人总是为其自身设定可以完成的任务，策略则是方法……这是同党一起成长起来的吗？"列宁通过援引小说家皮萨列夫（Pisarev）来对此予以回应，皮萨列夫断言，如果没有梦想，就没有人会将他或她自身献给政治或艺术或科学。列宁补偿说，"非常不幸的是，如今在我们的运动中，这种梦想太少了。那些对此负有最多责任的人就是那些自我夸耀其清醒的观点，即他们对'具体'的'接近'"。③

---

① 卡尔·马克思、弗雷德里希·恩格斯：《论巴黎共产主义小组》，莫斯科：进步出版社，1971年，第76、166页。另外也可参看文森特·杰奥戈根：《乌托邦主义与马克思主义》，伦敦：梅修恩（London: Methuen），1987年。

② 列宁：《国家与革命》，北京：外文出版社，1976年，第60、117—118、121页。

③ 列宁：《怎么办？》，纽约：国际出版社，1943年，第158—159页。

结论：正视马克思主义与乌托邦之间的关系

把马克思主义同乌托邦联系起来，决不是丢脸或背叛的事情，称马克思主义者为乌托邦主义者，决不意味着批判与否定！相反，在一定意义范围内，马克思主义者可以而且应该自豪地宣传，我们就是乌托邦主义者！共产主义理想就具有乌托邦的成分。这一点，在马克思本人的著述中，在马克思主义思想体系和整个学说中，都有其坚实的基础。

说到底，马克思和恩格斯为人类所描绘的共产主义远景，就具有乌托邦，尤其是经典乌托邦的诸多特征：比如没有阶级、国家消亡、"按需分配，各取所需"、"劳动成为人的需要，而不是手段"、"人们可以早上工作，中午休息，下午娱乐或者游戏"……凡此种种，都是传统的蓝图派乌托邦的典型特征。与传统蓝图派乌托邦不同的是，马克思和恩格斯尽量遏制了这种描绘未来的冲动。这种遏制，一方面来自马克思主义创始人的洞见与理性，另一方面也来自于马克思自身的民族文化传承。作为犹太人出身的杰出思想家，马克思同许多犹太人一样，都深深地秉承着犹太禁止偶像的传统。所不同的是，到了马克思这里，这种偶像禁律发生了非常有意思的变形，他把原本具有浓郁宗教底蕴的偶像禁律带入了自己的哲学与政治学思考中，马克思拒绝替未来勾画完整清晰的图像，更不用说具体而微的细节了。从这种考虑来看，马克思的确是伟大而卓越的，他对于"不可说的"东西，就尽量保持沉默！在某种意义上看来，"不可说的"也就是"不可命名的"、"不可描绘的"！凡"不可说的"、"不可命名的"、"不可描绘的"都具有神秘性，我们也必须同它们合作，维护其神秘性！

在内心，在思想的最幽深处，马克思是否曾经体察到了某种无助、无奈呢？对此我们不得而知，我们唯一可以肯定的是，马克思没有对未来作更多的推测式描绘，只能证明他的伟大！

他绝不缺乏描绘未来的才华，更不缺生描绘未来的辞藻。他所缺少的是"无知者无畏"的那种不知遮羞布为何物的"勇气"。他以自己的敬畏捍卫了自己以及马克思主义本身的尊严。

（本文责任编辑：任天）

How on Earth Is Marxism Related with Utopia?

Yao Jianbin

Abstract: If you examine the relation between Marxism and Utopia at its origin, you will find that the two are not diametrically opposite to each other. Even the primitive socialism advocated by Lenin contains some elements of Utopianism. It is by no means shame or betrayal to relate Marxism with Utopia. It is certainly not suspicion or negation to call Marxists Utopians. In fact, under certain circumstances, Marxists can and should proudly call themselves Utopians since communism contains some Utopian elements.

文化研究与文化领导权

——20 世纪英国文化研究中的"葛兰西转向"问题

段吉方[*]

(华南师范大学文学院)

【内容摘要】 "葛兰西转向"是 20 世纪英国文化研究与葛兰西思想发生深刻的理论融通的结果,具有重要的理论启发。"葛兰西转向"产生了一种"葛兰西式的文化研究",它既是一种理论范式的转折,又是一个重要的理论问题,体现了不同理论模式间的丰富的思想张力和实践影响,是英国文化研究理论在新的文化语境中的更新与重生。

在 20 世纪英国文化研究中,葛兰西的文化领导权理论具有不可轻视的理论影响与启发,它在与雷蒙·威廉斯、斯图亚特·霍尔、E. P. 汤普森等理论家的思想发生深刻的理论融通中促发了 20 世纪 70 年代英国文化研究中的"葛兰西转向"。"葛兰西转向"对 20 世纪英国文化研究的发展道路有着长期的重要影响,英国学者托尼·本尼特认为,在英国文化研究理论中,"葛兰西转向"超越了其他领域的理论联合,为一个重要工程即英国文化研究理论范式的转折提供了思想基础。[①] 约翰·斯道雷则提出,葛兰西的文化领导权理论从来没有像在英国文化研究中那样自由地发挥作用,它不但影响了后来整个的英国文化研究的理论进程,更是英国文化研究所包含的问题形式中最重要的内容之一。[②]

---

[*] 段吉方,文学博士,华南师范大学文学院教授,从事文学理论、马克思主义美学研究。
[①] [英] 托尼·本尼特:《本尼特:文化与社会》,王杰等译,桂林:广西师范大学出版社,2007年,第19页。
[②] [英] 约翰·斯道雷:《斯道雷:记忆与欲望的耦合——英国文化研究中的文化与权力》,徐德林译,桂林:广西师范大学出版社,2007年,第1页。

在文化研究的视野中,"葛兰西转向"既体现了葛兰西思想广泛的理论渗透力,同时也体现了 20 世纪英国文化研究的理论接受能力与思想重组能力,本文试图从发生学的角度探讨 20 世纪英国文化研究的"葛兰西转向"问题,以期对 20 世纪英国文化研究的理论发展提供一种阐释和理解的思想路径。

一、文化左派的危机与葛兰西思想在英国的接受

在 20 世纪西方马克思主义理论视野中,意大利思想家安东尼奥·葛兰西的文化领导权思想是一个里程碑式的理论迈进,佩里·安德森认为,葛兰西的《狱中札记》"是整个西方马克思主义传统中最伟大的作品",[①] "在葛兰西以后,西欧再也没有其他一位马克思主义者达到过同样的造诣"。[②] 这不但是因为葛兰西提出的"文化霸权"、"市民社会"、"有机知识分子"等一系列有鲜明针对性的理论观念和思想导致了西方马克思主义美学对传统马克思主义的一次集体性的理论重读,而且,在葛兰西之后,西方马克思主义美学在基础/上层建筑理论模式之外开始"用自己的密码式的语言来说话了"。[③] 葛兰西思想有着广泛的理论影响力,这种影响不仅仅是学理层面上的,更主要的是,葛兰西思想在不断融入当代西方社会和文化现实的过程中强化了 20 世纪以来的文化研究理论的批判性和现实性,从而使文化研究在"文化与社会"的张力中展现出了深刻的理论反思能力和理论建构能力,这其中就包括它在 20 世纪英国文化研究中的卓越影响。

一直以来,20 世纪英国文化研究因其拥有深刻的大众文化研究传统和面向现实文化经验的实践特色而赢得了广泛的关注,但拥有理查德·霍加特、雷蒙·威廉斯、斯图亚特·霍尔、E.P.汤普森等理论家的 20 世纪英国文化研究并非一种自足的理论传统,这个传统并非完全没有受到其他外来思想的影响。澳大利亚学者格拉姆·特纳在《英国文化研究导论》中曾经指出,在一般情况下,人们谈论文化研究往往无法抛开由理查德·霍加特、斯图亚特·霍尔、雷蒙·威廉斯、E.P.汤普森等人奠定的"英国传统",但"在文化研究中仍旧存在着其他重要的、非英国的传统","文化研究的英国传统所具有的明确性与实

---

① [英]佩里·安德森:《西方马克思主义探讨》,高铦等译,北京:人民出版社,1981 年,第 71 页。
② 同上,第 61 页。
③ 同上,第 44 页。

用性,正是来自于将欧洲理论模式相当恰如其分地应用于英国特定的文化形构"。① 意大利思想家葛兰西的文化领导权理论无疑就是这种文化形构中的重要力量。葛兰西思想在英国文化研究理论发展的关键时刻起到了非常重要的作用,"葛兰西转向"正是二者之间理论融通的结果和表现。

葛兰西的思想是在20世纪70年代被引入英国文化研究的,它的引入离不开两方面因素的促发与推动:一是英国以及西欧社会文化发展的特殊现实与历史情势对哲学、美学与思想理论模式的选择与批判,二是雷蒙·威廉斯、斯图亚特·霍尔、E.P.汤普森等对葛兰西思想的自觉接受与思想叙写。20世纪70年代,在葛兰西思想被介绍到英伦三岛的时刻,世界范围内的政治格局、文化格局以及理论格局正发生着巨大的变化,特别是西方左派文化正经受着复杂而严峻的考验。在当时,1968年革命失败的情绪仍然严重地笼罩着文化左派的心理,西方左派一直以来为之努力的激进思想遭受了沉重的打击,在这种情形下,西方思想界的文化左派不得不重新反思以前的革命策略和革命方式。在左派文化高潮的60年代,法国哲学家路易·阿尔都塞的思想曾经在欧洲文化理论界有着显著的影响,英国文化研究理论与阿尔都塞思想有着密切的关系,雷蒙·威廉斯、斯图亚特·霍尔、特里·伊格尔顿等都曾经受阿尔都塞思想的影响。但是,在历史推进到了20世纪70年代的时候,社会现实发生了新的变化,"西方左派知识分子或是被迫地向右转,或是玩世不恭地痛恨早年幼稚的理想主义,更有一小撮知识分子在最微弱的希望中继续探测革命的未来"。② 正是在这样一种特殊的时刻,西方思想界开始不同程度地对阿尔都塞理论产生怀疑甚至批判,阿尔都塞倡导的反人道的马克思主义在1968年革命的高潮阶段曾经起到了思想旗帜的作用,但现在,一度繁荣的左派运动几乎停业,先锋变成了残部,激进的理想也已经掺杂了复杂的悲观主义情绪,在这种情形下,"葛兰西而非阿尔都塞,是被左翼知识分子最热烈讨论的马克思主义理论家"。③

在广泛的左派危机的背景下,雷蒙·威廉斯、E.P.汤普森、斯图亚特·霍尔、特里·伊格尔顿等纷纷发表意见,在他们看来,阿尔都塞思想是一种伴随着理想主义的政治耗损和断裂而出现的文化理论,伊格尔顿提出,阿尔都塞是

---

① [澳]格雷姆·特纳:《英国文化研究导论·导言》,唐维敏译,台北:亚太图书出版社,2000年,第5页。
② [英]特里·伊格尔顿:《后现代主义的幻象》,华明译,北京:商务印书馆,2000年,第28页。
③ [美]丹尼斯·德沃金:《文化马克思主义在战后英国》,李凤丹译,北京:人民出版社,2008年,第320页。

在"非马克思主义状态中思考马克思主义"。① E. P. 汤普森更是发表了长达200多页的论文《理论的贫困》,严肃地批判阿尔都塞思想,并引发了"英国左翼学术界之中的最激动和剧烈的辩论"。② 葛兰西思想正是在现实政治格局和文化理论的巨大变革中被引入英国文化研究的,葛兰西思想的引入使英国文化研究理论在与域外理论思潮的理论融通中实现了理论的更新与思想的掘进,"葛兰西转向"也正是发生在这种思想接受与理论融通的过程之中,它促使20世纪英国文化研究开始迈向新的理论高峰。

二、"葛兰西转向"与20世纪英国文化研究的理论更新

20世纪70年代,雷蒙·威廉斯、斯图亚特·霍尔、E. P. 汤普森等不但深刻地批判阿尔都塞思想,而且积极从葛兰西的思想中重新汲取理论的能量,他们是促使英国文化研究发生"葛兰西转向"的关键力量。雷蒙·威廉斯与葛兰西有非常密切的理论关系,在《马克思主义与文学》和《马克思主义文化理论中的基础和上层建筑》等论著中,威廉斯曾专门讨论过葛兰西的文化领导权思想。威廉斯提出,葛兰西的文化领导权思想对文化理论的作用是显而易见的,它既涵盖又超越了此前两个重要的概念——一个是作为"整体的社会过程"的"文化";另一个就是"意识形态",它让人们更加清晰地认识到具有决定性意义的不仅是观念、信仰的意识体系,而且还有构成主导意义和价值的活生生的整体社会过程。③ "文化"和"意识形态"是威廉斯的文化理论的关键概念,在写作《马克思主义与文学》之前,威廉斯不但在《漫长的革命》等著作中对"文化"的概念做过系统分析,而且他对意识形态理论也有着独到理解,并因此提出了"作为一种整体生活方式"的文化概念,但在《马克思主义与文学》中,面对葛兰西思想,显然威廉斯的理论视野更加丰富了,同时明显表现出了一定的理论修正和补充。威廉斯看重的是葛兰西的文化领导权理论对作为社会整体生活方式的文化概念的经验性影响,更看到了它对意识形态概念的来自生活世界的实践性丰富,也正是在这个意义上,威廉斯更多地从葛兰西思想中摄取了理论的实践性和经验性成分,在更为细致的理论研究中将葛兰西思想有效

---

① Terry Eagleton, *Against the Grain*, London: Verso, 1986, 5—6.
② [美] 丹尼斯·德沃金:《文化马克思主义在战后英国》,李凤丹译,北京:人民出版社,2008年,第310页。
③ [英] 雷蒙·威廉斯:《马克思主义与文学》,王尔勃等译,开封:河南大学出版社,2008年,第116页。

地融入了文化和意识形态研究之中。

除了 1977 年的《马克思主义与文学》，雷蒙·威廉斯稍早时期的论文《马克思主义文化理论中的基础和上层建筑》（1973 年）也是受葛兰西思想影响的结果。在这篇被称为最早的"威廉斯与西方马克思主义的遭遇"以及"后来的《马克思主义与文学》的理论基础"①的文章中，威廉斯最引人注目的理论突破就是没有重复传统马克思主义的观念，而是坚持从"文化"的整体性范畴切入基础/上层建筑的二元逻辑，坚持以基础、文化、上层建筑的三元关系代替基础/上层建筑的二元模式。威廉斯指出，"任何对马克思主义文化理论的现代理解都必须从考察关于决定性的基础和被决定的上层建筑的命题开始"。② 但他反对将基础/上层建筑理论模式抽象化，主张在"文化"的物质性和生产性意义上打破基础/上层建筑理论模式的封闭性。在这里，威廉斯的理论调整展现出了重要的理论变革态势，他试图从文化的历史性与文化的经验性上打破"经济基础决定上层建筑"的理论限定，所找到的理论切入点正是葛兰西的文化领导权思想所提供的不同阶层文化经验的协商建构特性，从而超越了英国大众文化与意识形态研究单纯强调阶级性与对抗性的理论路径。英国学者约翰·斯道雷认为，威廉斯正是在拥抱葛兰西的文化领导权理论时，才改变了把文化理解为一种被实现的表意系统的方法，并最终"把文化与权力设置为英国文化研究的研究对象"。③ 这也正指出了威廉斯与葛兰西思想的微妙关系。

20 世纪 70 年代，E. P. 汤普森发表了他的著名的《理论的贫困》与《英国工人阶级的形成》。在《理论的贫困》中，汤普森指出，阿尔都塞的理论实践是唯心主义的，阿尔都塞的经验主义意识形态和经验主义思维方式把历史看作是一系列抽象化的理论范畴，它剔除了具体历史事件的实践过程，确立的是机械理性的社会结构概念。④ 而在著名的《英国工人阶级的形成》中，汤普森强调了工人阶级文化研究的历史学方法，通过对工人阶级文化经验的分析，汤普森试图说明英国工人阶级的形成并非是工业革命等社会现代发展的结果，而是工人阶级在现代英国社会发展中不断形成稳定的阶级意识与文化经验的结果。

---

① ［美］丹尼斯·德沃金：《文化马克思主义在战后英国》，第 207 页。
② ［英］雷蒙·威廉斯：《马克思主义文化理论中的基础和上层建筑》，许娇娜译，见《马克思主义美学研究》第 2 辑，桂林：广西师范大学出版社，1998 年，第 327 页。
③ ［英］约翰·斯道雷：《斯道雷：记忆与欲望的耦合——英国文化研究中的文化与权力》，徐德林译，桂林：广西师范大学出版社，2007 年，第 7 页。
④ Edward P. Thompson, *The Poverty of Theory and Other Essays*, New York: Monthly Review Press, 1978, 12.

正是工人阶级的文化经验所培育的集体的自我意识和自由精神，才对工业革命时代的伟大创举起到了重要的推动作用。《理论的贫困》和《英国工人阶级的形成》这两部作品尽管阐释重心与内容有很大差别，但都强调充分的社会实践，它们没有采用阿尔都塞结构主义的抽象的理论范畴和理论化的科学方法，而是更加接近20世纪英国文化研究的经验分析方法，它们是汤普森将葛兰西文化领导权理论的经验性特征引入文化研究的典范作品，在对文化与意识形态研究中充分呼应了"回到葛兰西"的理论策动。

英国文化理论家斯图亚特·霍尔曾受阿尔都塞理论的影响，但在20世纪70年代，他与雷蒙·威廉斯和E. P. 汤普森一样接受了葛兰西思想，并以"新葛兰西学派"的理论姿态取得了重要的理论成绩。这主要体现在两个方面：一个是他的"编码/解码"思想，另一个则是他独特的"耦合"概念。1973年，霍尔发表了重要论文《电视话语中的编码与解码》，霍尔提出，传统上的大众传播研究已经在"发送者——信息——接受者"的线性特征上将信息流通与传播过程概念化了，但在新的历史语境下，信息与话语流通必须经过转译或改造成社会实践的环节，必须经过"赋予意义"的产品分配检验，"不赋予'意义'，就不会有'消费'"，① 因此，"必须认识到信息的话语形式在传播交流（从流通的角度看）中占有一个特殊的位置，要认识到'编码'和'解码'的诸多环节是确定的环节，尽管二者与作为整体的传播过程相比仅仅是'相对自治的'。"② 从这种观念出发，霍尔更加重视编码/解码过程是如何在有效融入社会文化结构中展现信息接受对图像符码意义的结构性拓展的。他提出的问题是，观众如何在主导—霸权、协调符码以及对抗性符码等不同地位上从媒体信息中获取图像符码的意义，并根据信息编码的参照符码完成解码过程。在这种思考中，霍尔引入葛兰西的文化领导权思想，强调受众在对信息符码的生产、流通、使用以及再生产过程中以多种方式介入文化与权力的运作过程，从而剔除了电视话语意义接受中约定俗成的成分，并充分考虑到了主导—霸权符码在解码过程中的个体和组织性的作用，由此体现出了他对现代传播理论的深刻拓展。

"耦合"（articulation）则是霍尔在文化研究中提出的一个独特概念。"耦合"原初的意义来自于某种特殊联动装置的链接形式，就好比一种链接式卡车的驾驶室和拖车之间的链接部分，它所承载的意义既是确定的又是隐喻的。霍

---

① ［英］斯图亚特·霍尔：《编码，解码》，见罗钢、刘象愚主编：《文化研究读本》，北京：中国社会科学出版社，2000年，第346页。

② 同上。

尔将这个概念的隐喻含义充分应用于英国文化实践领域，在霍尔那里，"耦合"指向了一种特殊的文化表意实践行动，指的是社会文化以及语言系统中各种组成要素在某种链动机制的影响下是如何把那些个别性的文化表意符码再现为文化实践活动的，它代表的是一种话语和符号的总体性统一，也是文化与经验的结构性关联，是一种将社会文化系统中的经验与意识形态经过某种接合机制充分实践化的过程。霍尔在文化研究实践中得以充分应用"耦合"概念，是与他对葛兰西文化领导权思想的理论改造分不开的。在葛兰西思想中，处于社会主导位置的社会集团建构它的文化领导权并非意味着统治阶级意识形态的全面控制，也并非意味着统治阶级价值观念的自上而下的传播，文化领导权的构建过程融合了文化与权力机制中主导阶层与从属阶层的经验互动。正是在这个意义上，文化领导权包含了社会主导阶级与从属阶级文化价值观的"耦合"过程，霍尔也正是在将"耦合"概念广泛应用于文化研究中，开始了"从对反抗力量的赞扬转移到对'霸权'活动的包容"。①

就20世纪英国文化研究的发展进程来看，在经历了50年代文化主义的理论开拓，到60年代的阿尔都塞思想的拓展以及后来所面临的理论阻力，英国文化研究如何在自身的文化传统中突破理论与经验的矛盾是一个重要的问题，雷蒙·威廉斯、E.P.汤普森、斯图亚特·霍尔等正是在融会葛兰西思想的基础上解决了这个矛盾，从而为20世纪英国文化研究带来了新的理论元素。在葛兰西的启发下，英国文化研究在文化的经验性立场上更加重视一定社会的权力组合关系，认识到在占优势的权力阶层与从属阶级的价值观念之间不仅仅是冲突、对抗与持久的矛盾的关系，更存在着协商、再现与更新的理论联系，从属阶级的文化理想在某种程度上会成为文化领导权建构的主要浸淫形式。正是在这样的理论视界中，英国文化研究不断调整理论路向，并由此上升为对文化与意识形态理论的新的思考。

三、"葛兰西转向"与20世纪英国文化研究的理论转折

"葛兰西转向"既是英国文化研究在理论发展关键阶段呈现出的理论创新，同时更带来了理论范式的转折。在葛兰西思想引入之前，英国文化研究已经形成了文化主义与结构主义的理论范式。文化主义得力于20世纪50年代和60年

---

① [美]丹尼斯·德沃金：《文化马克思主义在战后英国》，第217页。

代的理查德·霍加特、E. P. 汤普森、雷蒙·威廉斯等人的理论建构，扎根于英国大众文化研究的广阔土壤。在英国文化研究中，文化主义不但重构了一种传统，而且在对文化与社会的深入阐释中形成了一种分析社会具体文化经验的理论范式。从20世纪50年代开始，在雷蒙·威廉斯、理查德·霍加特、E. P. 汤普森等人的努力下，文化主义的文化研究范式在英国取得了重要的进展，特别是随着工人阶级与大众文化的发展，英国文化研究在关于大众文化的生成、传播、接受与价值分析的过程中，展现出了深刻的实践性特征。结构主义的文化研究范式是受阿尔都塞思想影响的结果。20世纪的60年代，在阿尔都塞的影响下，英国文化研究者认识到，社会文化的构成不仅仅是社会生产组织中的各种文化要素以及社会个体的自觉建构，文化研究在面对个体经验的过程中其实也面临着社会整体结构建构的现实，因为个体不仅仅是意识形态的构成物，而且是社会意识形态的表征，经验、文化都是意识形态生产的结果，体现了社会意识形态的编码/解码过程。20世纪60年代风靡欧洲的阿尔都塞思想曾为当时的英国文化研究提供了一种关键性的理论导向，也让英国文化研究找到了新的方向，但是在20世纪70年代，随着阿尔都塞思想旗帜的动摇，结构主义的理论范式也逐渐淡出了英国文化研究的过程，"葛兰西转向"正是在承续阿尔都塞思想落潮的趋势中推动了英国文化研究的理论转折。

霍尔提出，到了20世纪70年代，"无论'文化主义'还是'结构主义'都不足以将文化研究构造成一个有明确概念和充分理论根据的领域"。[1] 在这种情形下，结构主义和文化主义的理论分歧是明显的。英国文化理论家托尼·本尼特曾经形象地说明："在结构主义的视野中，大众文化经常被视为一种'意识形态机器'，其炮制俨如法律的规则，专横通知大众的思想，一如索绪尔为结构主义提供组构范式的纲领"，"文化主义恰恰相反，经常是不作辨别地一味浪漫，赞扬大众文化是真实表达了社会受集团或阶级支配的兴趣和价值观"。[2] 他进而说到："更糟的是，仿佛根据某人的兴趣领域，我们不得不要么就是结构主义者，要么就是文化主义者——如果我们研究电影、电视剧或通俗文学，就是先者；如果我们的兴趣在于诸如体育、青年亚文化一类，就是后者。差不多好像文化天地给分隔成两个不相干的半球，各自展示着一种不同的逻辑。"[3] 文化

---

[1] [英]斯图亚特·霍尔：《文化研究：两种范式》，见罗钢、刘象愚主编：《文化研究读本》，北京：中国社会科学出版社，2000年，第61页。
[2] [英]托尼·本尼特：《大众文化与"转向葛兰西"》，第61页。
[3] 同上，第62页。

主义的范式和结构主义的范式都围绕着文化与意识形态问题展开研究，但按托尼·本尼特的说法，结构主义和文化主义"维持在两个对立的文化与意识形态阵营中间：资产阶级与工人阶级，两者锁定在一场零和游戏之中，一方有所得，另一方必有所失，游戏的最终目标是一方消灭另一方，从而胜利者得以占据被征服一方的地盘"。①正是由于文化主义和结构主义各自在理论发展与迈进中走向了非此即彼的选择，20世纪70年代英国文化研究的理论突破遇到了重要的困难，雷蒙·威廉斯、E. P. 汤普森、斯图亚特·霍尔等人也正是在英国文化研究理论发展最严峻的危急时刻接受了葛兰西思想。但是，无论是雷蒙·威廉斯、E. P. 汤普森还是斯图亚特·霍尔，他们在接受葛兰西的文化领导权理论时，没有完全走向纯理论化的建构，而是充分扬弃了葛兰西思想中的理论化的成分，积极将文化与意识形态分析与社会生产组织以及社会个体的文化从属形式联系起来，并在这个过程中走向了文化与权力机制中主导阶层与从属阶层的经验分析，从而不仅引发了明显的理论变化，而且还带来了20世纪英国文化研究的一种新的理论范式，这个范式用约翰·斯道雷的话说就是"葛兰西式的文化研究"②。

"葛兰西式的文化研究"有什么样的特征？约翰·斯道雷指出，"葛兰西式的文化研究"即是受到文化领导权理论启发的文化研究，它的特征是："大众文化既不是一种本真的工人阶级文化，也不是一种由文化产业强加的文化，而是葛兰西所谓的二者间的一种折中平衡，一个底层力量和上层力量的矛盾混合体；它既是商业性的，也是本真的，既有抵制的特征，也有融合的特征，既是结构，也是能动的。"③从文化研究的方法来看，这种"葛兰西式的文化研究"强调的是社会文本的被铭写过程以及意义与阐释间的复杂联系，并且始终坚持生产与消费、意义与阐释、文本与铭写的辩证关系，即霍尔说的"表达的耦合"与"连接的耦合"，它不主张从抵抗的角度去理解文化与意识形态，而强调更包容地预想各种社会阶层之间的文化联系，目的是获得文化领导权这个极具生产力的隐喻。相比文化主义与结构主义的理论范式，"葛兰西式的文化研究"具有明显的理论反思特征，更包含鲜明的实践性，这也是"为整个的马克

---

① [英] 托尼·本尼特：《大众文化与"转向葛兰西"》，第63—64页。
② [英] 约翰·斯道雷：《斯道雷：记忆与欲望的耦合——英国文化研究中的文化与权力》，徐德林译，桂林：广西师范大学出版社，2007年，第111页。
③ 同上，第108页。

思主义的传统引入了一种深刻的革新"① 的葛兰西思想的理论精髓所在。"葛兰西式的文化研究"不但促使了英国文化研究理论重心的转移，而且引发了理论范式的变革，在这个变革中，英国文化研究开始走出文化主义与结构主义的分化和矛盾过程，并对马克思主义理论传统进行了深刻的反思，开始将研究重心转向文化的意识形态属性以及文化与社会权力的组合关系上来，强调文化与社会意识形态的关系网络以及特定的实践方式，从而在文化、权力、政治、意识形态、历史等因素的复杂关系中开拓了新的理论空间。

四、"葛兰西转向"的问题形式及其美学意义

在 20 世纪英国文化研究中，"葛兰西转向"不仅仅是不同理论融通和对话所产生的新的理论范式和实践形式，同时也是西方文化研究不可忽视的理论内容，一直以来处于文化研究的理论核心位置。"葛兰西转向"凸显了大众文化研究的意义，推动了马克思主义美学研究的理论进步，既突出了葛兰西作为一个西方马克思主义理论家的影响，同时也证明了作为一个问题形式的"葛兰西转向"的美学意义。

20 世纪英国文化研究吸收了葛兰西思想，同时也以本土文化与理论精神丰富了葛兰西思想，但正像有的研究者指出的那样，英国文化研究吸收葛兰西的思想丝毫没有否认自身的理论传统，而是对英国文化研究的本土经验起到了扩展和更新的作用。② 从这个角度看，"葛兰西转向"既成为了葛兰西思想发展与播撒的重要阶段，同时也是 20 世纪英国文化研究的重要的理论篇章。

在 20 世纪英国文化研究理论的内部，斯图亚特·霍尔、托尼·本尼特与约翰·斯道雷等都曾经深入总结"葛兰西转向"后英国文化研究的新的理论收获。在霍尔看来，葛兰西思想为英国文化研究"在讨论'复杂的结构与上层建筑、独特的形式与时代之间的关系'中指出了一种道路"。③ 约翰·斯道雷则指出，"葛兰西转向"在英国文化研究中是通过两种方式体现出其鲜明的理论价值的，首先它引发了对大众文化的政治性重新思考，大众文化生产被视为霸权生产和再生产的一个关键场域，在这种新的构型中，大众文化被理解成一个

---

① [意大利] 萨尔沃·马斯泰罗内：《对〈狱中札记〉的历时性解读》，见萨尔沃·马斯泰罗内编：《一个未完成的政治思索：葛兰西的〈狱中札记〉》，黄华光等译，北京：社会科学文献出版社，2000 年，第 2 页。
② [美] 丹尼斯·德沃金：《文化马克思主义在战后英国》，第 8—9 页。
③ [英] 斯图亚特·霍尔：《文化研究：两种范式》，第 64—65 页。

斗争和谈判的场域，即统治集团和从属集团之间的斗争与谈判、统治集团利益的强加和从属集团利益的抵制之间的斗争和谈判；其次，在"葛兰西转向"中，文化领导权思想被引入文化研究，又引发了对大众文化概念的重新思考，这种重新思考把以前彼此对立的大众文化研究方式带入了积极的关系之中。①托尼·本尼特则向我们指出，"葛兰西转向"的理论价值在于它提供了一个整合框架，"对于文化和意识形态斗争的认知，它带来了完全不同的方法观念。"②"葛兰西转向"使英国文化研究理论发生了本质的变化，首先一个明显的表现就是在"葛兰西转向"中，英国文化研究在文化与意识形态研究中调整了非此即彼的理论路向，避免了结构主义和文化主义的二元对立，并将马克思主义理论引入了一个新的高度，在促成"文化马克思主义"的诞生与深入发展过程中，标志着英国文化研究新的理论高潮的出现。

其次，"葛兰西转向"不是单从理论的层面上发生的，而是葛兰西思想有效融入大众文化经验分析的结果，它对20世纪英国文化研究审美实践空间的开拓具有重要的意义。葛兰西的文化领导权理论强调从社会实践的复杂关系中发现文化与意识形态发展与运作的隐蔽机制，坚持从不同社会文化集团相互协商的文化实践中争取文化的领导权，所以，在"葛兰西转向"中其实存在着大众文化研究的另一种思想空间，这种思想空间不是文化主义的研究范式所强调的阶级性和异己性的力量对抗所构成的，也不是结构主义的主导意识形态的理论建构所形成的，而是市民社会中的具体文化经验与文化实践所构成的，20世纪英国文化研究有效地发展了这一思想，既完成了文化领导权理论的续写，同时也以自己的文化实践实现了自我的理论更新，这也正是"葛兰西转向"的美学价值所在。

最后，美国学者丹尼斯·德沃金曾指出，葛兰西的文化领导权理论提出了另一个重要的问题，这个问题就是："在发达的资本主义西方国家，工人阶级为什么不能以东方的俄国革命那样的规模来反叛。"③葛兰西在理论上提出了这个问题，英国文化研究则在转向葛兰西的过程中回答了这个问题。葛兰西的文化领导权理论提出，文化领导权的获得，并非是理论阐释和分析的结果，也远非

---

① ［英］约翰·斯道雷：《斯道雷：记忆与欲望的耦合——英国文化研究中的文化与权力》，第107页。
② ［英］托尼·本尼特：《大众文化与"转向葛兰西"》，见陆扬、王毅选编：《大众文化研究》，上海：上海三联书店，2001年，第64页。
③ ［英］约翰·斯道雷：《斯道雷：记忆与欲望的耦合——英国文化研究中的文化与权力》，第1页。

资产阶级文化批判能够自动实现，而是不同阶级力量在文化与意识形态中的协商与联系，这其中虽然也存在斗争与对抗，但争夺文化领导权的过程已经不完全是那种异己力量的直接争夺，而是文化与意识形态机制的建构与市民社会的培养。欧洲工人阶级的革命实践与东方的俄国革命的形式有非常大的差别，它不仅仅强调革命本身的实践力量，更关注市民社会的文化体验，20世纪英国文化研究正是在工人阶级与大众文化经验的研究中深刻地呼应了市民社会生活中的文化体经验问题，并采取了自下而上的方式重构文化与权力的生产与运作机制。正是以这样的方式，20世纪英国文化研究中的"葛兰西转向"超越了英国文化研究传统的理论范式所具有的思想能量，推进了英国文化研究的实践进程，所收获的是理论与实践的双重拓展。一直到今天，它的美学价值仍然值得我们作出认真的理论总结。

（本文责任编辑：任天）

Cultural Studies and Cultural Leadership: On the Issue of "Turn to Gramsci" in the 20th Century British Cultural Studies

Duan Jifang

Abstract: "Turn to Gramsci" is the consequence of cultural studies integrating with Gramsci Thoughts in the 20th century Britain, and it is theoretically inspirational. "Turn to Gramsci" brought about "Gramscian cultural studies", which not only marks a turn of theoretic paradigm but also poses a big theoretic issue. This phenomenon reflects the extension of thoughts and its influence on practice, and it marks the renewal and revival of British theoretical studies in the new cultural context.

论东欧新马克思主义对反映论美学模式的批判

傅其林[*]

(四川大学文学与新闻学院)

【内容摘要】 东欧新马克思主义对正统的马克思主义哲学及其美学思想进行深入的反思,从现象学和存在主义的知识模式出发,推动着从认识论美学向建构论美学转型。这种转型的重要维度之一则体现为对反映论美学模式的批判与超越,重新确立了文学艺术的人道主义的真理性意义,这对丰富和深化中国马克思主义文艺反映论的研究有所启示。

【关键词】 东欧新马克思主义;反映论;美学

20世纪60年代从东欧社会主义国家中涌现的一大批新马克思主义思想家,面对社会主义思想文化制度化的历史状况,以"马克思主义复兴"为旨归,对正统的马克思主义哲学与美学进行深入的反思与批判,不断从认识论向人类本体论、现象学、存在论进行范式转型。这种转型过程中的一个重要命题则是反映论美学范式的问题。本论文试图从东欧新马克思主义对列宁反映论模式和卢卡奇反映模仿论的批判以及对新艺术观念的建构的探讨,思考反映论美学的历史意义及其局限性。

一、对列宁反映论模式及其制度化之质疑

反映论虽然由来已久,但是作为重要的理论话语,首先是在列宁的马克思

---

[*] 傅其林,1973年生,男,四川岳池人,文学博士,四川大学文学与新闻学院教授,博士生导师。本文系国家社科基金重点项目"国外马克思主义文论的本土化研究——以东欧马克思主义文论为重点"(项目编号:12AZD091)阶段性成果。

主义哲学认识论框架中确立的,其《唯物主义与经验批判主义》无疑是马克思主义反映论哲学与美学的基本文献。① 东欧新马克思主义不仅揭示了列宁反映论的局限性,而且从社会政治的视角剖析了其被斯大林主义制度化而带来的问题。对此,波兰和南斯拉夫的新马克思主义者的批判具有代表性。

波兰著名的新马克思主义者科拉科夫斯基在其影响深远的代表著作《马克思主义的主潮》中分析了列宁的反映论模式的问题。他指出《唯物主义与经验批判主义》作为对马赫、阿芬那留斯、波格丹诺夫等人的唯心主义认识论的尖锐批判,极有偏见性地提出了唯物主义认识论哲学,这种哲学的基本部分是反映论或图像论,也就是认为"感受、抽象理念以及人类认识的所有其他方面,都是物质世界的事实性在我们头脑中的反映"。② 列宁从恩格斯关于物及其在思想上的模写或反映等观点的基础上提出反映论,把物质世界、客观现实视为不以人的意志为转移的客观存在,人通过感官对其加以复制、反映和摄影。他基于认识论的反映论试图解决人类认识的普遍问题,尤其契合自然科学的命题,"唯物主义和自然科学完全一致,认为物质是第一性的东西,意识、思维、感觉是第二性的东西。"③ "任何科学的思想体系(例如不同于宗教的思想体系)都和客观真理、绝对自然相符合,这是无条件的。"④ 列宁反复强调"复制",认为我们的感受是事物的图像,不纯粹是效果或者象征符号,其本质就是拒绝相对主义,追求传统的作为与现实一致性的真理观念。在科拉科夫斯基看来,列宁的反映论思想既存在着内在的不一致,又缺乏原创性的哲学思想,是对前-德谟克利特对图像信赖的思想的天真的重复。更为重要的是,没有人能够在物自身与其纯主观的图像之间找到类似性,无法弄清楚复制品与原本事物之间的比较方式。因而列宁不仅没有思考图像与现实相关的机制问题,更没有认识到主体意识、创造性意义,也没有达到维特根斯坦的语言图像理论的逻辑深度,列宁的认识论的逻辑性问题局限于古典的形式逻辑的思维框架之中。科拉科夫斯基还进一步揭示了列宁反映论的制度化的生成机制,主要是作为国家领袖的斯大林的政治权力话语的建构的结果,"《唯物主义与经验批判主义》在十月革

---

① 见苏联学者对列宁的反映论的文艺学、美学建构的代表性论文,如博列夫的《列宁的反映论与围绕形象思维认识论问题的斗争》、谢尔宾纳的《列宁的反映论与现代派的唯心主义文艺观》、安德列耶夫的《从列宁的反映论看社会主义现实主义形成的若干问题》等,见董立武、张耳编:《列宁文艺思想论集》,北京:中国社会科学出版社,1986年。
② Leszek Kolakowski, *Main Currents of Marxism*, Vol. II. Oxford University Press, 1978, p.453.
③ 《列宁专题文集·论辩证唯物主义和历史唯物主义》,北京:人民出版社,2009年,第10页。
④ 同上,第42页。

命前后一段时间没有产生特别的影响（尽管1920年发行了第二版）。后来，它被斯大林宣布为马克思主义哲学的基本轮廓，它和斯大林自己的一本小册子在大约15年的时间里成为苏联哲学学习的主要资源。"① 南斯拉夫实践派成员弗兰尼茨基在梳理马克思主义历史过程中，同样涉及到对列宁反映论及其形成机制的批判。他认为，列宁是从古典的关于主体和客体的关系出发来思考物质和意识的关系，并把自己的观点即"感觉、思想、意识是按特殊方式组成的物质的高级产物"视为马克思和恩格斯的观点，这是对马克思思想的简化，所以《唯物主义与经验批判主义》根本没有达到马克思的《巴黎手稿》和《关于费尔巴哈的提纲》的高度。虽然列宁在此书中涉及到实践，但它是认识论意义的具有功利性和客观真理特征的实践，没有顾及到人的存在的根本问题，而是证实唯一的、最终的客观真理，"认识只有在它反映不以人为转移的客观真理时，才能成为生物学上有用的认识，成为对人的实践、生命的保存、种的保存有用的认识。在唯物主义者看来，人类实践的'成功'证明着我们的表象同我们所感知的事物的客观本性相符合。"② 俄国马克思主义者在斯大林主义的笼罩下则把列宁简化的具有浓厚的自然科学色彩的反映论进一步制度化、绝对化，"他们把一般唯物主义的认识论观点宣布为马克思主义特有的观点，其次又把实践的范畴片面地理解为仅仅是认识论的范畴，同时在认识论内部把它片面地理解为真理的标准。"③ 这些马克思主义者局限在"主观反映客观"的一般原理之上，结果"'反映'的问题和原理，由于种种原因，已被现代马克思主义者，特别是斯大林主义化了的马克思主义者弄得声誉扫地。"④ 弗兰尼茨基在批判巴甫洛夫的心理学著作《反映论》时指出，"主观反映客观"的一般反映论公式不能解决具体的反映问题，认为应当对"反映"的不同阶段进行唯物主义的分析，要明确区别不同的反映形式，应该对颜色的感觉、形式的感知、颜色或声音的感知、逻辑概念形式的反映以及文艺作品或者整个意识形态的反映进行特殊的分析和说明，"而这种分析和说明却是一般公式无法作出的。苏联的思想家们、巴甫洛夫以及与他们相似的人的错误正在于此。"⑤ 事实上，南斯拉夫实践派对列宁的反映论模式进行了激烈的批判，正如贾泽林所总结的，"'实践派'极力

---

① Leszek Kolakowski, *Main Currents of Marxism*, Vol. II. Oxford University Press, 1978, p.458.
② 《列宁专题文集·论辩证唯物主义和历史唯物主义》，第46页。
③ ［南］普·弗兰尼茨基：《马克思主义史》上册，北京：生活·读书·新知三联书店，1963年，第305页。
④ 同上，第62页。
⑤ ［南］普·弗兰尼茨基：《马克思主义史》上册，第77页。

想从马克思主义哲学中排除'反映'这一范畴，从而取消整个马克思列宁主义的反映论。"①

东欧新马克思主义对列宁反映论模式的批判主要集中于《唯物主义与经验批判主义》及其制度化，这不仅涉及到反映论尚未解决的认识论问题，而且关涉到政治制度化所带来的思想文化枯竭现象的揭露。这种理论模式以"科学真理""普遍确定性""唯一标准"等话语规范着文艺反映的客观性，以自然科学的客观真理忽视人文社会科学的复杂意义，人的创造性和意识的主体性屈居于次要地位，反映话语成为政治话语的有机部分。譬如，虽然对艺术形式进行过细致的关注的卢那察尔斯基，在1932年的《列宁与文艺学》一文中高度肯定了列宁的《唯物主义与经验批判主义》，认为"不仔仔细细钻研这本书，就不能成为一个有教养的马克思主义者"，"由列宁论证过的马克思主义一般哲学原则，对无产阶级科学的一个支脉的文艺学自然也有着奠基的意义。"② 他把列宁的反映论运用于文学，认为"反映论所注意的，与其说是作家隶属的家系，不如说是他对社会变动的反映，与其说是作家主观上的依附性和他同某个社会环境的联系，不如说是他对于这种或那种历史局势的客观代表性。"③ 不过，东欧新马克思主义对列宁《哲学笔记》中关于反映论的复杂性、扭曲性的观点是持有一定的肯定态度的，认为虽然此书也被共产党作为讨伐机械唯物主义的支持性著作，但是它与《唯物主义与经验批判主义》是相矛盾的，在某种程度上切合了东欧新马克思主义的真理的多元性思想。更进一步说，虽然《哲学笔记》提出了人的意识的主动性、能动性的观点，遵循黑格尔所言"人的意识不仅反映客观世界，并且创造客观世界"④，但是其认识论和反映论仍然局限在对客观真理的认识框架中，主体性问题处于沉默或边缘地位。即使在20世纪50年代开始的苏联美学大讨论中对艺术本质的深入辨析，对艺术的主体性、个性甚至符号结构的理解，仍然没有摆脱审美意识形态的认识论框架，譬如波斯彼洛夫提出的"作为对于社会生活规律之反映的艺术"观点⑤以及赫拉普琴科立足于列宁反映论而提出的"反映世界上和人们生活中发生的过程"的"综合艺术形

---

① 贾泽林：《南斯拉夫当代哲学》，北京：中国社会科学出版社，1982年，第117页。
② 卢那察尔斯基：《论文学》，蒋路译，北京：人民出版社，1983年，第4—5页。
③ 同上，第6页。
④ 《列宁专题文集·论辩证唯物主义和历史唯物主义》，第138页。
⑤ [苏联] 格·尼·波斯彼洛夫：《论美和艺术》，刘宾雁译，上海：上海译文出版社，1981年，第298页。

象"理论。①

二、对卢卡奇反映模仿论的反思

东欧新马克思主义对反映论美学模式的批判通过对卢卡奇的反映论及其现实主义文学观念的反思更鲜明地透视出来。他们对卢卡奇的反映模仿论的反思是较为复杂的。一方面，他们在很大程度上是在卢卡奇开创的西方马克思主义的知识视野中成长起来的，其对反映论的批判深受卢卡奇的启发，"卢卡奇在二十年代就曾积极反对过反映论，'实践派'在六十年代反对反映论，想要以'实践'为核心创造一种新的哲学体系，显然是同卢卡奇一脉相承的。"② 这比较切合弗兰尼茨基的分析，他认为卢卡奇的《历史与阶级意识》"对反映论作了很尖锐的批评，在他看来，反映论和柏拉图的感觉论一样，也是一种神话理论。"③ 他指出，卢卡奇与科尔施一样都正确地看到"过去对反映的种种解释以及列宁在《唯物主义和经验批判主义》中所做的解释，实际上都是马克思以前的唯物主义"。④ 卢卡奇在此书中明确提出以现实的生成性论点来讨论思维与存在的哲学难题，这一难题通过人的思维意识与现实的相互生成的现象学视角得到了解决，从而超越了反映论，"当生成的真理就是那个被创造但还没有出世的将来，即正在（依靠我们自觉的帮助）变为现实的倾向中的新东西时，思维是否为反映的问题就显得毫无意义了"，"思维与存在都是同一的，就不是说它们是否'相符'，互相'反映'，它们是互相'平衡'或者互相'叠合'的。"⑤ 另一方面，尽管东欧新马克思主义对反映论的批判源于卢卡奇的基本思路，但是他们并没有袒护他，而是对他的反映模仿论美学进行深刻的反思。

科拉科夫斯基从"总体性"和"中介"范畴切入卢卡奇的艺术反映论，认为他以这些范畴作为传统反映论的批判，以建构马克思主义的唯物辩证的反映论。科拉科夫斯基颇为重视卢卡奇的作为审美范畴的模仿理论建构，也就是《审美特性》（又称为《美学》）的模仿理论。艺术是对现实的模仿，这是立足

---

① 《赫拉普琴科文学论文集》，张捷等译，北京：人民出版社，1997年，第244页。
② 贾泽林：《南斯拉夫当代哲学》，第113页。
③ [南] 普·弗兰尼茨基：《马克思主义史》下册，北京：生活·读书·新知三联书店，1963年，第361页。
④ 同上，第378页。
⑤ [匈] 卢卡奇：《历史与阶级意识——关于马克思主义辩证法的研究》，杜章智等译，北京：商务印书馆，1992年，第299页。

于特有形式的模仿之上的,因此只有现实主义才称得上艺术之名。在科拉科夫斯基看来,卢卡奇的模仿具有描述性和规范性的意义。就描述意义而言,任何小说或戏剧在某种程度上反映世界、社会条件和冲突,每件艺术作品在社会学意义上都是完成了的;在规范的意义上,"模仿"是作品的质性,这种质性"正确地"模仿现实,呈现时代的问题如"真正"的那样,这部作品的作者就是站在"正确"或进步一边的,这是卢卡奇最频繁使用的模仿意义。这种作为模仿的反映涉及到社会生活的总体性,联系着所有人类事件,更关涉到社会主义艺术所追求的理想。但是它还必须根据个体的图像,艺术不仅从属于总体性原则,而且从属于特殊性原则,这就是艺术的中介部分。按照科拉科夫斯基的理解,"卢卡奇的特殊性可以被视为作家借以把个体经验转变为普遍有效的类型或者图像的过程。"① 这样,卢卡奇以总体性、中介、模仿三个核心范畴重建了艺术反映论或者审美反映论,可以说为马克思主义审美反映论做出了独特贡献。但是,在科拉科夫斯基看来这种反映论是立足于现实主义基础上的反映论,是质疑现代主义的,因为现代主义的问题是不能领会总体性、贯彻中介的行为,它不是对艺术的丰富而是对艺术的否定。所以,虽然卢卡奇的反映论美学超越了列宁的《唯物主义与经验批判主义》的反映论模式,但它还是局限于斯大林主义的制度化藩篱之内,"卢卡奇的美学,至少就其独特的马克思主义特征,特别是就社会主义的和批判的现实主义以及先锋派文学而言,是斯大林文化政策的完美的理论论证。"② 卢卡奇铸就了文化专制主义的理性工具,虽然他批判了斯大林主义,但是并没有走出斯大林主义的阴影,可以说就是科拉科夫斯基论卢卡奇的标题所标明的"卢卡奇:服务于教条的理性"。南斯拉夫实践派成员苏佩克尖锐地指出总体性观念带来的文化集权主义后果以及文化批评的贫困,认为这个概念本身陷入本体论现实主义或者本体论唯名主义的矛盾和偏见之中,本体论现实主义的一个最核心的观念就是反映论。他指出,通过类似于主体对"客体"的反映,反映论设想文化上层建筑仅仅是社会的物质基础的反映,整个"社会现实"就价值而言被认为是更为真实更为重要的东西,文化创造始终是对现实的反映,这个理论是"客观现实"的柏拉图式的理想化,认为文化必然落后于现实。结果,"文化创造,以及整个美学领域就本体论意义而言仅仅是

---

① Leszek Kolakowski, *Main Currents of Marxism*, Vol. III. Oxford University Press, 1978, p. 291.
② Ibid., p. 305.

物质现实的副现象"。① 当然,这种激进的批判包含着武断的成分。

作为匈牙利最著名的新马克思主义的布达佩斯学派,对卢卡奇的反映模仿论美学进行了更为具体、深入,也更为复杂的批判性反思。此学派的主要成员赫勒、费赫尔、马尔库斯、瓦伊达等一致认为,虽然他们从来没有激进地拒绝自己的老师卢卡奇,但是他们"拒绝认识论(甚至在面向现实的认识论进行尝试的框架)的反映论。这可以从赫勒和费赫尔在20世纪60年代写作的关于卢卡奇的《美学》和具体的美学问题的许多著作中看到,我们已经长期扩展并转变了这个概念。"② 费赫尔剖析了卢卡奇中年的文学批评中的反映论模式,认为他在《现实主义辩》等文学批评中把现实主义的文学观念和古典主义结合起来,排斥现代主义艺术。这种古典主义模式的现实主义是贵族式的、本质主义的,内含着反映论的机制,"一种特有的认识论机制即卢卡奇的反映论连接着这种本质主义的观念。"③ 这种反映论对费赫尔来说是根本站不住脚的,其基本概念经不起分析和批判,"我们必须询问,反映的主体和合适的器官是什么?如果我们认为创造性的大脑是这种器官,那么我们就面临着众多认识论-方法论的困窘。"④ 费赫尔揭示了卢卡奇文学批评的内在的古典现实主义模式与伦理民主的矛盾,前者就是理性主义和普遍主义的认识论与反映论,问题丛丛,而后者是支持多元主义的民主自由观念,这也是费赫尔所认同的。也正是后者的民主观念使得卢卡奇在《审美特性》中以"模仿"取代"反映"概念,从而具有重大的意义,"从现实主义和反映向模仿的术语转移对卢卡奇的整个理论具有决定性的影响"。⑤《审美特性》使得卢卡奇摆脱了贵族式特征,积极走向伦理民主的人类物种的确认,审美活动把创作者和接受者从整体的人提升到人的整体,这种由模仿带来的物种特性向每一个人敞开。因此在费赫尔看来,《审美特性》为20世纪30年代和40年代的文学批评中勾勒的伦理民主的多元主义提供了普遍的哲学基础。卢卡奇从反映向模仿的转移也受到赫勒的关注。在赫勒看来,卢卡奇来自马克思的本体论立场所理解的反映观念在本质上突破了18世纪的反

---

① Rudi Supek, "Freedom and Polydeterminism in Cultural Criticism", in Erich Fromm ed., *Socialist Humanism: An International Symposium*, Garden City, NY: Doubleday, 1965. pp. 280—298.

② Ferenc Fehér, Agnes Heller, Gyrgy Márkus, Mihály Vajda, "Notes on Lukács' Ontology", in Agnes Heller ed. *Lukács Reappraised*. New York: Columbia University Press, 1983. p. 134.

③ Agnes Heller and Ferenc Feher, *The Grandeur and Twilight of Radical Universalism*, New Brunswick, NJ: Transaction, 1990, p. 264.

④ Ibid., p. 262.

⑤ Ibid., p. 272.

映论解释及其反映论在20世纪的庸俗化,"它主要不是认识论的范畴,更准确地说,卢卡奇探究的不是其认识论维度,而是本体事实的表达。"① 卢卡奇不是立足于自文艺复兴时期以来的对自然的模仿观念,而是回到亚里士多德对"民族精神的模仿"②,建构起"本体论-人类学基础"。③ 具有本体论-人类学意义的模仿是普遍的社会现象,在日常生活、科学等领域发挥重要作用,但是只有在艺术领域才得到最经典的表达。模仿作为掌握现实的积极形式,具有激发的特征,因为在模仿中形式始终是实质性的,必然联系着并引起情感与震惊的激发的效果,这种情感激发性与模仿形式使得艺术区别于科学,并建构起人类物种的价值领域,诚如席勒所言,实现对人类的审美教育,走向个体的自我完善的总体性。

事实上,布达佩斯学派对卢卡奇的反映模仿论的批判性分析把他的美学导向了对个体的存在的完善的看重,这恰恰符合东欧新马克思主义的个体性理论,这意味着反映论的转型,也透视出传统反映论的危机。虽然东欧新马克思主义在一定程度上肯定以模仿代替反映论或者对反映论进行拓展,但还是逐渐抛却了卢卡奇的反映模仿论,"在美学方面,我们尽力用模仿概念取代反映概念(卢卡奇的著作事实上沿着这条路线提供了一些启示),但是我们最终还是发现这个范畴也是无用的。"④

三、新艺术观念的崛起与反映论的式微

东欧新马克思主义对列宁反映论和卢卡奇的反映模仿论的反思与批判以"马克思主义复兴"为旨趣,主要是以青年马克思的著作尤其是《巴黎手稿》的哲学美学思想的创造性理解为基础。虽然他们的批判在20世纪60年代遭遇到马克思主义内部的反批判,但是在其美学思想中不同程度地昭示了反映论模式的式微,其哲学美学范式不断从认识论话语体系向实践存在论、后马克思主

---

① Agnes Heller, "The Aesthetics of Gyorgy Lukacs", in *The New Hungarian Quarterly*, no. 7 (1966), pp. 84—89.

② Agnes Heller, *Renaissance Man*, Trans. Richard E. Allen. London, Boston, Henley: Routledge and Kegan Paul, 1978, p. 409.

③ Agnes Heller, "The Aesthetics of Gyorgy Lukacs", in *The New Hungarian Quarterly*, no. 7 (1966), pp. 84—89.

④ Ferenc Fehér, Agnes Heller, Gyrgy Márkus, Mihály Vajda, "Notes on Lukács' Ontology". in Agnes Heller ed. *Lukacs Reappraised*, New York: Columbia University Press, 1983, p. 134.

义、后现代主义等话语与思维模式转型，焕发出马克思主义美学的当代活力与阐释效力，彰显出复杂而多元的人道主义美学特征。

第一，作为"能动阐释的反映论"（an activistically interpreted theory of reflection）。虽然在一些东欧新马克思主义的著作中仍然保留着反映的概念，但是这个概念的意蕴开始发生巨大的转变。波兰的新马克思主义者沙夫对反映论的独特性的重建则是有价值的尝试。他通过对认识过程的模式的理解和客观真理的批判提出了"能动阐释的反映论"，他在批判作为对客体的模写的机械唯物主义反映论和作为主体性建构的唯心主义认识论的基础上，重新确立主体与客体的交互关系即"彼此互动"（mutual interaction）的反映论模式，"主体和客体具有客观和真实的存在，同时彼此互动"。① 如此，人类个体作为反映的主体就不是被动的、接受的，而是创造的、能动的，在认识过程中具有重要的不可或缺的意义，阐释的差异性、个体性、多样性也就成为必然。沙夫的反映论深化了列宁反映论模式，其追求的真理也不是客观的真理而是作为过程的历史真理，因为客观真理是要求与现实一致，内在地联系着古典的机械唯物主义反映论，而历史真理是主体和客体相互建构的"作为过程的真理"，"毕竟，一个既定的客体的认识绝非只产生一个单一的判断；相反，当它提供对客体的不同侧面、维度和发展阶段的反映时，它是由许多判断构成的；它是一个过程"。② 可以说，沙夫的反映论建构融合了主客体交互作用的现象学理解和语言哲学的思路，超越了纯粹认识论意义的反映论范式。

第二，作为实践的艺术观念。实践范畴是东欧新马克思主义最为重要的一个范畴，它主要不是从认识论反映论意义上来理解的，而是被视为人作为人的存在的本体论意义，"人在本质上是一种实践的存在，即一种能够从事自由的创造活动，并通过这种活动改造世界、实现其特殊的潜能、满足其他人的需要的存在。"③ 因而，实践把自由和自我实现的规范意义作为内在的属性，区别了可以异化的劳动与功利性的实践活动，这种实践的界定本身包含着审美的维度，也是艺术活动的基础。捷克的新马克思主义者科西克明确地提出，真实世界是人类实践的世界，是生产和产品、主观和客观、起源发生和建构的统一体。他从现象学和存在主义的视角重新阐释了物的概念，转变了不以人的意志为转移

---

① Adam Achaff, *History and Truth*, Oxford: Pergamon Press, 1976, p. 51.
② Ibid., p. 71.
③ ［南］马尔科维奇、彼德洛维奇编：《南斯拉夫"实践派"的历史和理论》，郑一明等译，重庆：重庆出版社，1994年。第23页。

的纯粹客观的物的概念，认为物的结构即物自身不能直接地也不能通过沉思或纯粹的反思或者反映加以掌握，而只能借助于某种活动才能掌握。这些活动是人类掌握世界的不同类型或者方式，艺术也是人类掌握世界的方式之一。科西克认为，这里主要不是唯物主义认识论的问题，而是唯物主义现象学[①]的意向性的问题："现象学诸如'面向物的意向性'、走向物的意义的'意图'或多种感知模式的描述所阐述的问题已经被马克思在唯物主义基础上被理解为人类掌握世界的不同类型。"[②] 物、现实、社会结构都不能脱离人的意识而存在，不能脱离实践而存在。实践建立了主体与客体的交互关系，都具有两重性，既是一种反映，又是一种投射，既是反映又是预测，既是接受的又是积极的。在科西克看来，实践是主体和客体交互的生成过程的自由的活动，本身就属于艺术活动或是说艺术就是实践，"艺术始终被认为是一种出类拔萃的人类活动和人类作为区别于劳动的自由创造，"[③] 是一种自由的实践。这种艺术实践是本体建构的过程，也是本体论的可能性的基础。如此理解，寻求与现实一致性的真理观念的反映论不再处于核心地位。

第三，作为创造现实的艺术观念。东欧新马克思主义强调个体性、自由创造的实践，避免了反映论对主体性的漠视，形成了艺术的创造性与建构力量的观念。科西克通过社会现实的实践建构性的探讨，摆脱了现实主义与非现实主义长期纠缠的困境，重新阐发了社会意识与社会存在之间的复杂的动态的过程，尤其注意到意识对具体主体生产与再生产社会现实的动态过程，也就是如阿尔都塞所说的意识形态建构经济基础的过程。这样，意识本身就成为实践的一部分，本身就是现实，艺术也可以说是一种现实，"诗不是一种比经济学低级的现实。它同样是人类现实，虽然是不同类型和形式的现实，带有不同使命和意义。"[④] 艺术现实不是客观的现实，而是创造出来的现实，而且会构建出新的现实，具有构形现实的力量。中世纪的大教堂建筑是封建世界的图像，同时也是这个世界的构成性元素，它不仅是艺术性地复制中世纪的现实，也是艺术性地生产这个现实，"每一部艺术作品具有不可分割的二重性特征。它表现现实但也

[①] 里夫希茨提出了"唯物主义现象学"概念，"在马克思主义经典作家的著作中包含着一种关于社会存在和意识的唯物主义现象学——这就是哲学，同时也是政治学。"见里夫希茨：《马克思论艺术和社会理想》，吴元迈等译，北京：人民出版社，1983 年，第 12 页。

[②] Karel Kosik, *Dialectics of the concrete*, D. Reid Publishing Company, 1976, p. 10.

[③] Ibid., p. 124.

[④] Ibid., p. 67.

形成现实。"① 完美的艺术作品所形成的现实超越了各自时代的历史性现实，这就是艺术作品的建构性、创造性。因此，虽然艺术是社会决定的，但是艺术作品是现实的有机的建构因素。科西克对作为建构性、创造性的艺术作品的理解超越了社会决定论的反映论模式，因为社会决定论意味着把作品视为是外在于作品的现实所决定的，作品是次要的、被推论出来的、被反映出来的，把真理视为作品之外的东西，这无疑无视了艺术作品的创造性和建构力量，无视了艺术作品作为人类自由创造的本体论意义。弗兰尼茨基也肯定艺术的创造性本质，人类杰出的思想与艺术作品是思维创造的结果，"人的想象并非只是反映，它本质上是创造"，"哲学以及艺术是有独立见解的独立的和创造性的个体的创作。"②

布达佩斯学派成员瓦伊达从绘画美学角度通过探讨再现与装饰的关系，消解了幻觉主义的反映论，确立了作为创造的艺术观念。他并不认同卢卡奇把抽象的形式作为装饰以及把艺术作品的再现对象视为不可脱离现实的环境存在的做法，认为卢卡奇关于再现与装饰的区分设置了装饰艺术与再现艺术的对立，最终转变为装饰与艺术之间的根本区别。瓦伊达敏锐地看到，在卢卡奇的美学思想中实际上隐藏着一种特有的审美概念，也就是把绘画视为是再现世界的任务，这也是卢卡奇的《美学》的起点，"艺术是认识，而不是对世界的创造——更准确地说，创造从属于复制。"③ 这种美学观念正是文艺复兴时期兴起的资产阶级幻觉主义绘画时代的理想，因此卢卡奇关于再现与装饰的区分不是建立在客观的区分的基础之上的，而是一开始就隐藏着关于视觉艺术的特有的审美立场，因为再现的尝试只是一个有限时期的绘画追求。具体地说，只有欧洲文明才成功地达到了幻觉主义绘画的"顶峰"，并且只有这种绘画才能够在可能性的框架内最充分地复制可见世界，而二十世纪的绘画之梦不再是复制可见世界。瓦伊达通过揭示幻觉主义的再现艺术观念与中产阶级的世界观的关联，借助于20世纪兴起的现代主义绘画，突破了卢卡奇的认识论意义的艺术观念，主张具有存在主义色彩的艺术创造论思想。他说："我的明确观点是，艺术（包括绘画）不是认识（即不是对外在于艺术的某物的复制），而是生产、建构，或者如海德格尔所说，是'世界的建基'。复制的元素作为一个次要的关键词始终出现在生产中，在这并不重要。艺术作品之所以是艺术作品，在于它始终是从虚

---

① Karel Kosik, *Dialectics of the concrete*, D. Reid Publishing Company, 1976, p. 71.
② [南]普·弗兰尼茨基：《马克思主义多样化意味着什么》，见衣俊卿、陈树林主编：《当代学者视野中的马克思主义哲学·东欧和苏联学者卷》，北京：北京师范大学出版社，2008年，第378、384页。
③ Mihály Vajda, "Aesthetic Judgement and the World-View in Painting", in *Reconstructing Aesthetics*, eds. Agnes Heller and F. Feher, Oxford: Basil Blackwell, 1986, p. 125.

无中创造,即便某些元素(材料、母题)在它之前就呈现了出来。毕竟,一旦这些元素是艺术作品的构成'部分',它们就不再是之前的东西了。"①

此外,赫勒提出的作为自为对象化的艺术、作为个体性尊严的艺术、作为历史性意识的表达的艺术、作为交往互惠性的艺术、作为内在于人类喜剧性存在的艺术观念等等,也代表了东欧新马克思主义艺术观念的新方向。②

总之,东欧新马克思主义以"重构美学"为名的新的艺术观念逐步摆脱了反映论美学模式,走向了建构论、存在论、实践论。虽然他们还在一定程度上保留着反映概念,认识论的思维与话语体系仍不时闪现,但是不再处于核心角色,新的阐释性符码诸如存在、实践、自由、公正、对话、话语、创造、建构、异化、人类条件、个性、个体性、多元主义、自律、现代性、历史性、后现代性、偶然性、多元决定、意义等关键性范畴的喷涌,逐步淡化了唯物唯心、进步与反动、认识、客观性、图像、再现、复制、反映、普遍性、理性、物质、绝对真理、客观真理、谬误等范畴。东欧新马克思主义对反映论美学的批判性反思不仅意味着话语模式与艺术观念从宏大叙事模式向微观话语模式的变化,透视出从真理的证明与推演模式向意义的阐释模式的转型,从制度化规训向独立思考的位移,而且彰显其意识形态、政治哲学、伦理价值的嬗变。不过,他们的反思和批判存在不少对马克思主义反映论的误解,没有历史地评价反映论的历史价值、复杂形态与诸多探索性的建构,尤其是对苏联一些重要的反映论美学的新思想没有认真对待③,有的激进地拒绝马克思主义认识论美学模式,从批判的马克思主义或者马克思主义复兴走向后马克思主义,甚至脱离了马克思主义的基本范式,这是我们应当加以仔细辨析的。

(本文责任编辑:尹庆红)

---

① Mihály Vajda , "Aesthetic Judgement and the World-View in Painting", in *Reconstructing Aesthetics*, eds. Agnes Heller and F. Feher, Oxford: Basil Blackwell, 1986, p. 148.

② 参见傅其林:《宏大叙事批判与多元美学建构——布达佩斯学派重构美学思想研究》,哈尔滨:黑龙江大学出版社,2011年。

③ 虽然科普宁在1966年的《马克思主义认识论》一书中坚持列宁的反映论,但是认为形象反映既是复制,又不是复制,"艺术家在复制大师们的绘画时,力求做到使复制品与原作丝毫无差。认识的形象反映对象,在这个意义上才是复制,然而它的反映是创造性的,根据主体的要求,综合客观现实的内容,在这方面认识就不同于复制。"见衣俊卿、陈树林主编:《当代学者视野中的马克思主义哲学·东欧和苏联学者卷》,北京:北京师范大学出版社,2008年,第332页。弗里德连杰夫则解释了列宁反映论中关于意识的创造性,"意识本身在创造世界,它是积极的改造力量。艺术意识在创造艺术世界,这样或那样地反映现实,并在一定方面影响现实。"见程正民、邱运华、王志耕、张冰:《20世纪俄国马克思主义文艺理论研究》,北京:北京大学出版社,2012年,第120页。

On Eastern European Neo-Marxist Critique of Aesthetics of Reflection Paradigm

Fu Qilin

(Chinese Department, Sichuan University, Chengdu 610064, China)

Abstract: Eastern European Neo-Marxists reflect on the traditional Marxist philosophy and aesthetics, and attempt to transform from aesthetics of epistemology to constructivist aesthetics from points of view of mode of knowledge based on phenomenology and existentialism. One important dimension of its transformation is critique and transcendence of aesthetics of reflection as a classic paradigm, and new identification art with humanist significance, which could advance some insights into the rich and profound research for the theory of reflection in Chinese Marxist literary and artistic theory.

马克思主义美学可以再度成为公共话语吗?

王 杰[*]

(上海交通大学人文学院《马克思主义美学研究》编辑部)

【内容摘要】在当代中国,马克思主义美学重新成为公共话语不仅是可能的,而且是必要的。这需要美学回答现实所提出的一系列问题,诸如,在艺术和时尚相结合成为主要潮流的情况下,审美活动还有没有独立性和批判性?审美的动因与经济相结合,审美经验中的乌托邦因素是否仍然存在?审美经验中的快感和具有超越性品质的"艺术之韵"之间的区别是否不再存在了呢?如果这种区别仍然存在,那么,在今天的文化中,什么东西仍然在表征着与"被审美化了的日常生活"所不同的"另一种存在"呢?这是当代美学必须回答的问题,也是美学要重新成为公共话语的前提。而能否对当代文化和艺术现象作出具有公信度的解释,是马克思主义美学是否重新成为公共话语的关键。

马克思主义与新世纪中国美学的关系问题,无疑是当代中国美学乃至人文学科都应该重新思考和面对的一个十分重要的命题,也是中国美学进一步发展的重要基础。在中国社会和经济迅速发展的条件下,中国的社会责任、中国文化和中华文明在与世界其他文明对话中的学理依据,当代中国自身的意识形态建构和核心价值建构等等问题,在我看来,都不仅需要马克思主义与中国美学的积极参与,而且需要一种新的美学即马克思主义美学的积极介入。当代中国的社会发展,特别是在全球化的语境下,思考中国社会和文化的进一步发展,或者说,思考"中国社会和文化有没有未来?如果有,是一种什么样的未来?"这样一些重大的问题时,事实上,美学是一个重要的角度,而马克思主义美学

---

[*] 王杰,上海交通大学人文学院院长、教授、博士生导师,《马克思主义美学研究》主编。

则是一种较为切实的理论资源，而且很可能是找到"'真实'的希望"最重要的理论资源。

自鸦片战争以来，中国社会和文化走上了一条十分艰难的现代化道路。中国的现代化，如果说有自己的经验和道路的话，那么，美学在其中的作用应该是十分重要的。令人遗憾的是这一点并没有得到充分的认识，特别是没有得到美学之外的知识分子和社会的充分认识。为此，我们已经付出而且正在付出某种沉重的代价。从文化与社会关系的角度看，美学和文化批评一直为中国社会的现代化发展提供最重要的思想资源和文化资源。中国社会的现代化发展有两个重要的阶段，一个是从五四运动到1949年新中国成立，再一个是1978年三中全会到现在的中国社会和经济发展奇迹。从思想史的角度看，从"五四"到"左联"时期的新文化运动，以及20世纪80年代的美学大讨论，事实上都成为中国社会迅速发展和推进现代化进程的思想前提和文化基础。也许可以这样说，没有"五四"到"左联"时期的左翼文艺思潮和思想启蒙运动，就没有抗日战争和解放战争的胜利；没有80年代的新启蒙运动和美学大讨论，就没有近30年中国社会和经济的持续快速发展，这是从思想史和社会学的角度都可以证明的。

事实上，从"五四"到新中国成立这几十年的新文化运动中，左翼思想特别是马克思主义美学和文化理论的相关思想发挥了十分重要而且关键的作用，80年代的美学大讨论亦是如此。值得特别注意的是，自1992年开始的改革开放运动，美学，特别是中国的马克思主义美学出现了十分复杂的局面，马克思主义美学陷入低潮，出现了"西马化的马克思主义美学"、"没有马克思的马克思主义美学"以及以文化理论形式出现的美学和马克思主义美学的多样化局面。传统意义上的马克思主义美学不再担任第一小提琴，也不再演奏"主旋律"。我们面对的情况是：马克思主义美学面临十分艰难而且百感交集的复杂局面，马克思主义美学似乎丧失了文化发展的内在驱动力，丧失了表征和描述"未来"的能力。另一方面，传统中国美学在"国学热"的风潮中被某种民粹主义倾向的声音所遮蔽，也丧失了话语的公共性，或者说逐渐退出实践型[①]知识分子的论域。因此，马克思主义美学，特别是中国的马克思主义美学在当代可以重新成为公共话语吗？这就成为我们今天面临的一个问题，一个具有现实性的理论问题。

---

① 参见托尼·本尼特：《本尼特：文化与社会》，王杰、强东红等译，桂林：广西师范大学出版社，2007年。

在我看来，在当代中国，马克思主义美学重新成为公共话语不仅是可能的，而且是必要的。作为一种全球性现象，美学正在当代学术语境中重返公共学术话语的中心位置。丹尼尔·贝尔在他的《资本主义文化矛盾》一书中早就指出，审美动因是资本主义社会最基本的文化动因之一。在资本主义发展的很长一个历史阶段，经济的动因和审美的动因在社会中是互相矛盾的。大约在21世纪初，在西方社会和文化结构中，这种情况发生了重要的变化：审美的动因成为当代西方经济增长的动力！这个现象其实也是我们在日常生活中已经感受到的。大约是受浪漫主义美学影响太深的缘故，我们一直把审美和艺术看作抵抗经济中心主义和异化现象的基本依托。因此，在市场经济发展的过程中，特别是在全球化的社会生活条件下，美学的立场和理论基础变得混乱而模糊。但是，在文化全球化的条件下，资本主义或者现代化进程发展到一个被命名为"审美资本主义"[①]的阶段，美学怎样回答现实所提出的一系列问题，诸如，在艺术和时尚相结合成为主要潮流的情况下，审美活动还有没有独立性和批判性？审美的动因与经济相结合，审美经验中的乌托邦因素是否仍然存在？审美经验中的快感和具有超越性品质的"艺术之韵"之间的区别是否不再存在了呢？如果这种区别仍然存在，那么，在今天的文化中，什么东西仍然在表征着与"被审美化了的日常生活"所不同的"另一种存在"呢？这是当代美学必须回答的问题，也是美学要重新成为公共话语的前提。

从学理上说，康德在启蒙主义时代所提出和试图回答的问题与当代美学面临的问题已经完全不同了。审美自由不是在主体的内部通过精神的纯粹化就可以实现和完成的。审美自由实际上是人性在现实经验中的某种表述，是现实中的乌托邦存在，是主体在现实的悲剧性冲突中呈现和闪现出来的人的特殊气质和生存境界。审美自由是一种崇高而不是优美，是现实的某种存在状态而不是某种心理形式，是现实性的、世俗性的，而不是虚构的和彼岸世界的幻象。文学和艺术是人类勇敢"直面"现实的方式，虽然在形式上是想象性的和感性的，但在实际上是"真实"的和形而上的。在对现实生活的意义等当代文化的关键问题上，美学无疑比经济学、社会学具有更多的"公共性"和理论上的正义性。康德式的美学，或者浪漫主义美学没有能力解释当代文化和艺术，更不可能为当代社会生活赋予意义。马克思主义美学是一种发展中的理论，因为马克思以及马克思的后继者们并没有在理论上一劳永逸地建立起"马克思主义美

[①] 参见奥利维耶·阿苏利：《审美资本主义》，黄琰译，上海：华东师范大学出版社，2013年。

学"这样一种理论或者这样一个学科。但是，作为一种不同于"康德式"的美学，不同于浪漫主义美学的美学思想和美学范式无疑又是存在的。自1932年乔治·卢卡奇发表《历史和阶级意识》以来，西方马克思主义理论家发展起了形态多样的"马克思主义美学理论"，从法兰克福学派的"批判理论的美学"，到法国的"阿尔都塞学派的美学理论"，到英国雷蒙·威廉斯创立的"文化唯物主义"等等。马克思主义美学事实上一直在发展并且具有极强的生命力和对现代文化的解释能力。应该说，在西方学术界，马克思主义美学一直是一种公共话语，只是它以文化激进主义的形式存在罢了。对于当代中国马克思主义美学而言，能否对当代文化和艺术现象作出具有公信度的解释，是马克思主义美学是否重新成为公共话语的关键。

坦率地说，中国马克思主义美学的现状并不让人乐观。以我自己的经验为例，我是全国马列文论研究会的副会长。早在研究生时期我就参加这个学会的年会暨学术研讨会，学会当时汇聚了一大批美学界和文艺理论界的精英人才，学术活动办得有声有色，所提出的问题在社会上引起广泛讨论。但是，近几年来，学会在学术界的影响力，对中青年优秀学者的吸引力都在逐渐下降。关于这种情况，原因是复杂而深刻的，与中国社会的发展，与全球化的进程都直接相关。面对这种情况，在《马克思主义美学研究》杂志的编辑方针上，我们作了适当的调整。主要是加大力度介绍和引进国外马克思主义美学研究的研究成果，开展中国学者与国外学者的交流和对话，刊物才得以逐渐提升其质量和影响力。中国马克思主义美学面临的艰难局面与当代中国意识形态问题的复杂性直接相关，随着改革开放的进一步发展，随着全球化进程的进一步推进，社会对当代中国文化和美学问题的理论要求就越高，这一基本趋势为马克思主义美学成为一种公共话语提供了可能性和巨大的理论空间。特别是随着中国特色社会主义的发展和不断实践，国外马克思主义者对中国的美学和文学艺术的兴趣迅速上升，这就为中国学者与国外马克思主义美学及批判理论的各种观点交流与对话提供了良好的基础。另一方面，中国改革开放的实践，中国特色社会主义的美学经验也需要得到理论的概括和总结。

如果用比较宽泛的观点来定义马克思主义美学，应该看到，中国马克思主义美学发展已呈现出多样化甚至多元化的趋势，实践美学、后实践美学、审美意识形态论、文艺美学、存在论美学、审美人类学和文学人类学、生态美学等不同的理论都在积极的发展中，初步形成一种百花齐放的新局面。目前，理论上的发展和探索主要局限在学术的领域内，一些重要的论域正在形成，但还没有成为公共话语。我个人认为,随着中国马克思主义美学的进一步发展,随着不同的理论在对现实重大问题的深入研究中得到进一步发展和系统化,特别是随着马克思主义美学面对当代社会价值危机提出建设性的思路,对当代文化低俗化现象(审美资本主义的伴生现象)的批判和理论解释能力的提高,随着马克思主义美学自身的进一步学理化,中国马克思主义美学就能够重新成为公共话语,从而担当起批判现实和改变世界的历史责任。

(本文责任编辑:任天)

Will Marxist Aesthetics Become Public Discourse Again?

Wang Jie

Abstract: In contemporary China, it is not only possible but also necessary for Marxist aesthetics to become public discourse. For that purpose, aesthetics must cope with a series of questions: Can aesthetic action maintain its independence and criticalness when arts and fashion combine to make up the mainstream of the society? Does aesthetic experience still contain its Utopian features when the motive of aesthetics becomes economic? Is the pleasure in aesthetic experience still separable from the transcendental "artistic taste"? If that separation still exists, what symbolizes the "other being" as is different from the "aestheticized daily life"? Those questions challenge contemporary aesthetics and form the prerequisite for aesthetics to become public discourse. The critical point is that there must be a persuasive interpretation of contemporary culture and arts.

马克思主义与中国美学的未来

陈伯海[*]

（上海社会科学院文学研究所）

【内容摘要】20世纪中国美学以西学、马学与中学三大板块分立并峙的总体格局，迄今未变。但中国美学决不能停留于板块拼接的状态，自当有其表里完整、前后贯通的理论体系，它要求我们在不同传统之间进行综合会通，以生成真正属于中国未来的新的思路和新的理念。其中，马克思主义对于未来中国的美学构建仍会保持重大影响，它将以其巨大的前瞻性和包容性，促使马克思主义从革命、批判的思想武器转化为极富于魅力的建设指针。用好这一指针，让它为中国美学的未来建设广开道路。

美学在中国的发展经历了百年的行程，这并不意味着百年前的中国人不懂得审美，只是其丰富的审美经验多散见于诗论、文论、书论、画论、乐论、剧论乃至山水园林和其他日常生活的审美观感之中，未能构成专门的学问。故具有独立形态的美学学科实乃上个世纪之初从域外移植过来的，最先引进的是西方古代与近现代的美学，30年代起大力弘扬以俄苏为中转站的马克思主义美学，而后更借助这些既有的美学理念来观照和整理中国传统的美学思想，由此形成20世纪中国美学以西学、马学与中学三大板块分立并峙的总体格局，迄今未变。这一三足鼎立的局面是否将永久延续下去呢？应该承认，中、西、马三大板块的建立有其历史的渊源，今后若要从思想史的角度来梳理其演化的脉络，仍离不开就各自的承传关系分别立论。但作为未来中国学界可供选择的某种原理性建构，则中国美学自当有

---

[*] 陈伯海，上海社会科学院文学所研究员，上海师范大学特聘教授。

其表里完整、前后贯通的理论体系，决不能停留于板块拼接的状态，于是要求我们在不同传统之间进行综合会通，以生成真正属于中国未来的新的思路和新的理念。这将是新世纪赋予广大美学工作者和爱好者们的严峻课题，需要我们认真对待。

然则，在这一综合创新的过程之中，马克思主义又将扮演什么样的角色呢？作为一种具有强大生命力的观念形态，且在20世纪中国美学的进程中打下深刻印记的思想流派，马克思主义对于未来中国的美学构建仍会保持重大影响，是毫无疑义的，不过它的具体职能或将有适度的调整。众所周知，产生于19世纪中叶的马克思主义，是充当强有力的革命、批判的精神武器登上历史舞台的。它批判资本主义，批判私有制文明，批判各种专制政治与虚假的意识形态，批判一切扭曲人性的丑恶现象，锋芒锐利，所向披靡。这一革命、批判的功能在20世纪中国美学和文艺学领域内也曾有过出色的表现，起到了对形形色色的反动思潮与错误思想的催陷廓清的作用，今后仍当继续发挥。与此同时，亦应注意到，马克思主义的作用不尽在于批判，它还有一个建设的维度。批判旧世界，目的是为了构建新世界，是要指向未来。正是这一建设人类未来文明的信念，促使马克思本人从前人创造的精神财富中广泛吸取各种有用的成分以构建自己的思想理念，并努力保持自身理论的开放性以应对未来。这样一种立足建设、开阔视野、兼容并包、勇对未来的取向，当是21世纪中国学界的马克思主义思潮所须采取的积极的姿态，不这样，就不会有中、西、马三大板块的综合会通，也就不可能构建成具有崭新格局的中国美学的未来。

其实，马克思本人的著述中即含有大量极具前瞻性与包容性的论题，有待后人去精心开发。比如说，在其早年撰写的《关于费尔巴哈的提纲》里，他鲜明地揭示出旧唯物主义的一个根本性缺点，是只从客观存在上去理解世界，而未能从"人的感性活动"即"实践"的角度来把握世界，从而丢失了事物发展的能动的一面。恩格斯将这篇文献称之为"包含着新世界观的天才萌芽的第一个文件"（见《费尔巴哈和德国古典哲学的终结》），且在他自己后来写成的《劳动在从猿到人转变过程中的作用》一文中，将马克思的上述观点推演为"劳动创造了世界，也创造了人本身"这样一种说法，成为历史唯物主义的一个基本的观念。这个观点的重大革命意义在于扬弃了两千多年来传统哲学一力将世界本原归结为某种实体的做法，而认定创造活动才是本原，正是由于人的创造性劳动和各种社会实践活动的结果，才有了属人的世界和人自身的存在形态,这确是一种崭新的看待世界的方式。拿这个观点应用到美学领域中来,我们当能承认,审美也是一种创造活动,是有别于物质生产劳动的精神创造活动。它固然不能像物质生产劳动那样直接创造社会物质财富,却可以也必然会创造出某种精神财富,那就是美的世界。恰如同整个属人世界连带人自身归根结底是人类劳动的产物,各种审美的现象(美、丑、崇高、滑稽等美学属性)连同审美的人(指人的审美观念、情趣、需求与能力等),亦皆是由审美活动过程所孕育、生成并不断得到发展、演化的;那种脱离审美活动性能的考察,先验地设定审美客体和审美主体的做法,注定不会有结果。当然,审美活动并非孤立的存在,它必然要植根于人的总体生存与实践活动的基础之上,审美的需求与能力也必然要同人的多方面需求与能力相协调,故而从"人学"的角度,也就是从人的总体生存与实践活动的角度切入审美研究,确有其合理性。但有如马克思所指出,"对世界的艺术的掌握"(即审美观照),并不同于哲学的、宗教的或实践—精神的掌握方式(见《〈政治经济学批判〉导言》),这又提醒我们不能单纯停留在实践层面的探讨,要努力寻求从"人学"进入美学的通道。而不管这一寻求还将遭遇怎样的曲折,由马克思所开启的"活动本原"之说,终将一劳永逸地结束西方美学自柏拉图以来苦苦追索那虚无缥缈的"美本身"的命运,将关注点转移到现实的人的审美活动上来。与此同时,也就相应地打开了马克思主义与现代西方现象学、解释学、存在主义、生命哲学诸流派之间对话、交流的渠道,并使中国传统美学思想中的许多精华有可能获得重新提炼与整合的机会,反过来亦有助于拓宽马克思主义自身的视野,使美学创新落到实处。

再举个例子。大家都知道,马克思的"人学"关怀有个终极目标,叫作"一切人的自由发展成为每个人的自由发展的条件",通俗的说法即"全人类解放"。不过后者多用于社会学和政治学的涵义,指劳动者打碎了私有制的枷锁,从剥削和压迫下解脱出来,真正成为自己劳动的主人,而前者除了这层含义外,另具有一个精神世界得以自由解放的向度,亦便是人们常说的"个性的全面发展"了。马克思本人在其《资本论》第3卷里将这两层含义界析得甚为分明,他说:"事实上,自由王国只是在由必需和外在目的规定要做的劳动终止的地方才开始;因而按照事物的本性来说,它存在于真正物质生产领域的彼岸。"他还进一步申说道:"这个领域(按指物质生产领域)内的自由只能是:社会化的人,联合起来的生产者,将合理地调节他们和自然之间的物质变换,把它置于他们的共同控制之下,而不让它作为盲目的力量来统治自己；靠消耗最小的力量，在最无愧于和最适合于他们的人类本性的条件下来进行这种物质变换。但是不管怎样，这个领域始终是一个必然王国。在这个必然王国的彼岸，作为目的本身的人类能力的发展，真正的自由王国，就开始了。但是，这个自由王国只有建立在必然王国的基础上，才能繁荣起来。工作日的缩短是根本条件。"① 这段话语里明确区分了两种不同性质的"自由"：一种是"必然王国"里的"自由"，指人们在其社会实践活动中掌握规律以驾驭并改造对象世界的能动作用；另一种则是"自由王国"里的"自由"，意味着超越实际需求的范围以谋取人自身精神生活日趋丰富与发展的追求。在其未发表的手稿里，马克思更将这后一种"自由"的实现，归结为社会必要劳动减少到最低限度以使个人自由时间内得以充分享受艺术与科学教育活动。由此看来，审美（包括艺术活动）在马克思的心目中当属于那种超越必然的心灵开发需求，跟实践活动中掌握必然以改造世界的规划并不处在同一层面之上；人也只有摆脱了自身紧迫的实用功利计较，方有可能悉心领会美的熏陶。这也便是马克思为什么要发出"忧心忡忡的穷人甚至对最美丽的景色都无动于衷；贩卖矿物的商人只看到矿物的商业价值，而看不到矿物的美和特性"这样的感慨，进而主张扬弃私有财产，转变那种"对物的直接的、片面的享受"，以达致一切属于人的感觉和特性的彻底解放②。整个地说，马克思在"人的自由发展"的两重关系上的思考是十分深刻且辩证的，既看到了审美之类精神超越的需求不同于实用功利的需求，"个性的全面发展"应包含两种"自由"的相互协调与相互促进，同时承认超越性的精神追求终当以人的现实的生存与实践活动为依托，而心灵世界的彻底解放更离不开物质生产力的高度发达和社会机制变革的大前提。西方美学史上长期争议不休的有关"审美"与"功利"关系的话题，以及当下中国美学界在"实践美学"与"后实践美学"之间的反复驳难，是否有可能从这一天才的提示中找到某种相互沟通与整合的渠道呢？

以上举了两个简单的例子，用以说明马克思主义确具有巨大的前瞻性和包容性，也正是这一无可置疑的前瞻性与包容性，促使马克思主义从革命、批判的思想武器转化为极富于魅力的建设指针。用好这一指针，让它为中国美学的未来建设广开道路，让它继续生气勃勃地从古今中外人们创造的一切精神财富中汲取养料以推陈出新，我们的事业才会大有希望，理论研究亦才能精益求精。

---

① 引自《马克思恩格斯全集》第46卷，北京：人民出版社，2003年，第928—929页。
② 参见《1844年经济学—哲学手稿》，北京：人民出版社，1979年，第77—80页。

那种拘执于经典作家的某些言辞，斤斤于划分"马克思主义"与"非马克思主义"之间界限的做法，恰恰起到了封闭和禁锢马克思主义的不良作用，是理论建设工作中所当极力避忌的。

（本文责任编辑：任天）

Marxism and the Future of Chinese Aesthetics
Chen Bohai

Abstract: The 20th century Chinese aesthetics had been characterized by the tripartite formation of Western theories, Marxist theories and Chinese theories, and the formation still persists today. However, Chinese aesthetics should not rest on that fragmentation, but should on a consistent and complete system. We must coordinate between different traditions and develop new systems and thoughts in accordance with the future of China. In that process, Marxism must continue its influence on the construction of Chinese aesthetics in the future. With its brilliant foresight and inclusiveness, it must transform itself from a revolutionary critical weapon into a persuasive constructive guide. We should properly employ that guide in paving the way for the construction of the future of Chinese aesthetics.

发掘和继承马克思美学思想的批判性，建设中国现代美学

杨春时*

（厦门大学中文系）

【内容摘要】 中国美学要实现现代发展，必须摆脱对马克思美学思想的古典阐释，进行现代阐释，发掘和继承马克思美学思想的超越性和批判性。成熟期的马克思认为，审美与劳动实践分属于彼岸与此岸两个不同的世界。审美不肯定现实，哪怕是理想的现实，而是以自由精神超越现实、批判现实，使人获得自觉性。这样，马克思美学以其批判性而具有了现代性，成为现代美学思想的发源地之一。审美不再是理性（以及它制约下的感性）的显现，不再是现实生存的完善，不再是主体性的实现，而是超越理性和感性、批判现实生存、克服主客对立的自由生存方式。这一转变使中国美学与世界现代美学同步发展，并且适应了中国社会现代发展的需要。

马克思主义美学是不同历史时期、不同学派对马克思美学思想进行阐释的产物，因此并不是一个固定的美学思想体系。最初对马克思美学思想的阐释是依据"辩证唯物主义"而形成的"唯物主义美学"（蔡仪为代表），它认为美是客观的物的自然属性，美感是对美的反映。这一阐释否定了马克思美学思想的主体性和社会性。后来崛起的实践美学（李泽厚为代表），依据"历史唯物主义"和实践哲学，对马克思美学进行了新的阐释，它认为美是客观的社会属性，是实践的产物，是人的本质的对象化。这一阐释肯定了审美的主体性、社会性，在20世纪80年代的新启蒙运动中成为主流学派。但无论是"唯物主义美学"

---

* 杨春时，厦门大学中文系教授，博士生导师。

还是"实践美学",都是肯定的美学,如蔡仪认为美是物种的典型;而李泽厚认为美是人化自然的产物,是人的本质的实现,他们都认为审美具有现实性,审美是肯定性的。这些阐释都忽视了马克思美学思想的超越性、批判性,从而使其丧失了现代意义。古典美学与现代美学的分界,就在于古典美学以理性肯定现实,把审美当作理性的胜利,人性的实现;而现代美学则以审美超越理性,批判现实。西方马克思主义美学就发掘了马克思美学思想的批判性,提出了"否定的美学",对资本主义和现代性展开了审美批判。中国美学要实现现代发展,必须摆脱对马克思美学思想的古典阐释,进行现代阐释,发掘和继承马克思美学思想的超越性和批判性。

马克思美学是在特定历史阶段形成的,特别是在青年时期的著作《1844年经济学—哲学手稿》中得到系统的建构,同时又在后期有所发展。马克思美学思想体系包含着丰富的、多元的思想内涵,既有古典的、肯定性的美学思想,又有现代的、批判性的美学思想。因此,它为后来的阐释留下了广阔的空间,也为其现代发展提供了可能。我们先对马克思美学基本思想进行描述,从而展示其发展和内在的矛盾。

马克思美学思想是马克思主义哲学的组成部分,而马克思哲学在实践论的基础上继承和改造了黑格尔的辩证法,确立了人的自由本质(逻辑规定)——异化(历史行程)——人的本质复归(共产主义或审美)的逻辑—历史叙述。马克思首先进行了逻辑的规定,就是人的本质是自由自觉的活动,包括生产劳动以及精神活动在内。它既是人自然的本质,又是人的社会本质。他认为人与自然的统一,人的本质的对象化是通过劳动实现的,是人的本质的确证。他说:"而生产生活也就是类的生活。这是创造生命的生活。生命活动的性质包含着一个物种的全部特性、它的类的特性,而自由自觉的活动恰恰就是人的类的特性。"①"实际创造一个对象世界,改造无机的自然界,这是人作为有意识的类的存在物(亦即这样一种存在物,它把类当作自己的本质来对待,或者说把自己本身当作类的存在物来对待)的自我确证。"② 审美与劳动一样同属于人的自由自觉活动,是人的本质的确证。这一逻辑规定确定了审美就是人的本质——自由自觉性的实现。但是,它毕竟是一种逻辑规定,而不是现实的规定。因此,我们还要考察马克思关于劳动异化的论述。

马克思从逻辑进入到历史,于是发生了逻辑与历史的对立,从而提出了劳

---

① 马克思:《1844年经济学—哲学手稿》,刘丕坤译,北京:人民出版社,1979年,第50页。
② 同上,第50页。

动异化的思想。他认为，由于私有制度，劳动由自由自觉的活动变成了异化劳动，异化劳动是出卖体力和智力的片面活动，丧失了人类活动的丰富性，它不能确证人的本质，反而使人与人对立、人与自然分离，人的本质沦落。因此，在现实社会，劳动使人与自己的产品对立，人不能在对象世界"直观自身"，于是审美活动成为不可能。这就是说，劳动不能创造美，而成为非人的活动。马克思说，由于私有制以及劳动异化，造成了"劳动者和资本家的不道德、退化、愚钝"，于是劳动者丧失了审美的需求和能力："忧心忡忡的穷人甚至对最美的景色也无动于衷"；而富人也同样成为非审美的人："贩卖矿物的商人只看到矿物的商业价值，而看不到矿物的美和特性"①。可以看出，马克思在这里对私有制进行了人道主义的批判，并且否定了现实活动（包括实践劳动）与审美的一致性。

马克思在对现实进行批判的基础上，让逻辑回归历史，实现逻辑与历史的统一。他认为，实践劳动虽然是异化的，但也为其本质的回归开辟了道路。资本主义生产方式发展到顶点，就将自我否定，废弃私有制，而实现共产主义。在这个历史条件下，劳动异化将被克服，回归人的自由自觉本性，从而实现人与人、人与自然的统一，人类也终将获得解放和全面发展。在新的社会中，人的感觉获得解放，审美成为普遍的感觉世界的方式。他乐观地预言："因此，私有财产的废除，意味着一切属人的感觉和特性的彻底解放。"②"因此，人不仅在思维中，而且以全部感觉在对象世界中肯定自己。"③ 他认为，"不仅是五官的感觉，而且所谓的精神感觉、实践感觉（意志、爱等等）"都是属人的感觉，其中也包括审美的感觉。由于废除了"囿于粗陋的实际需要的感觉"，才使包括"即感受音乐的耳朵、感受形式美的眼睛"等"那些能感受人的快乐和确证自己是属人的本质力量的感觉，才或者发展起来，或者产生出来"。④ 由此可知，虽然马克思提出了劳动创造了美的命题，但这只是逻辑的设定，而不是历史的认定。他认为审美并不是劳动直接创造的，因为有史以来的劳动都是私有制度下的异化劳动，不具有自由自觉的性质；只有共产主义社会的实践活动包括劳动才具有自由自觉的性质，才能创造美。当代实践美学的错误就在于直接把实践肯定为自由自觉的活动，认为劳动创造了美，而否定了实践劳动的异化

---

① 马克思：《1844年经济学—哲学手稿》，第80页。
② 同上，第78页。
③ 同上，第79页。
④ 同上，第79页。

性质，从而把自由的审美降格到实践活动的水平。

马克思美学思想具有古典性和现代性双重品格。它的古典性在于其肯定性。青年马克思继承了费尔巴哈的人本主义，肯定人的感性本质，并且把它建立在实践活动的基础上。虽然他不肯定资本主义和一切私有制的现实，但毕竟认为劳动和审美可以在历史的最高阶段成为自由自觉的活动，于是现实活动与审美活动没有对立，人的本质可以得到实现，人与自然可以和谐，理性与感性可以得到统一，从而建立了一个社会的乌托邦。这一肯定性的美学思想带有古典哲学的印记，表达了一种启蒙主义的乐观精神。现代哲学打破了这种对人、理性、历史的乐观信念，揭示了现实生存的缺陷，这意味着即使历史在进步，但人永远不能克服与世界（社会、自然）的对立，不能实现感性与理性的同一，不能把实践活动变成自由自觉的活动，不能在现实中实现自由，从而也不能与审美同一。现代社会的现实证明了这一理论，结束了乌托邦的想象。于是现代哲学肯定存在的超越性，从而具有了鲜明的批判性。而现代美学也在这个哲学基础上强调了审美的超越性，对现实展开了审美批判。

马克思美学思想又具有现代性，蕴涵着现代哲学的批判精神。马克思以人本主义理想否定了有史以来的一切社会存在，特别是批判了资本主义的异化劳动，这是其美学思想的价值所在。马克思美学思想也体现了对资本主义现实的批判性。但这种批判精神为其他人本主义思想家所共有，并非马克思的独家创造。马克思美学思想的批判性另有所在，这要从其哲学体系中寻找、发掘。马克思认为人的本质是自由自觉的活动，它不容于异化劳动，只是在消灭私有制的社会中才得到实现，而审美是其中的一种。那么，如马克思所揭示，私有制下人与世界对立，审美的感觉丧失，就不可能存在审美活动，只有在共产主义中才会有审美。但历史事实是自从有文明以来，就发生了审美活动，并且在文学艺术领域结出了丰硕的果实。马克思也论述了资本主义异化劳动与审美的对立。如何解释这一现象呢？这就要诉诸审美的超越性。审美虽然发源于人的实践活动，但不等同于实践活动，实践活动是异化的，而审美是自由的。这就是说审美本源于存在，它具有超越性，即超越现实生存，包括超越物质生产实践，超越主客对立，超越理性与感性的分裂，从而达到了自由的领域。这一审美超越性思想，是马克思美学思想的合理推断，也是其必然发展。马克思美学思想也沿着这一逻辑线索发展着。首先，马克思改变了早期对实践劳动的浪漫主义肯定，不再认为只要消灭私有制就可以使人的一切活动都成为自由自觉的活动，不再认为可以在物质生产领域和实际生活领域创造出一个自由王国。他说：

事实上，自由王国只是在由必需和外在目的规定要做的劳动终止的地方才开始；因而按照事物的本性来说，它存在于真正物质生产领域的彼岸。象野蛮人为了满足自己的需要，为了维持和再生产自己的生命，必须与自然进行斗争一样，文明人也必须这样做；而且在一切社会形态中，在一切可能的生产方式中，他都必须这样做。这个自然必然性的王国会随着人的发展而扩大，因为需要会扩大；但是，满足这种需要的生产力同时也会扩大。这个领域内的自由只能是：社会化的人，联合起来的生产者，将合理地调节他们和自然之间的物质变换，把它置于他们的共同控制之下，而不让它作为盲目的力量来统治自己；靠消耗最小的力量，在最无愧于和最适合于他们的人类本性的条件下来进行这种物质变换。但是不管怎样，这个领域始终是一个必然王国。在这个必然王国的彼岸，作为目的本身的人类能力的发展，真正的自由王国，就开始了。但是，这个自由王国只有建立在必然王国的基础上，才能繁荣起来。工作日的缩短是根本条件。①

在这里成熟期的马克思修正了早期的思想：第一，实践劳动不再是自由自觉的活动，而只是一种生存的手段，属于必然王国。第二，自由不再是实践劳动的直接创造物，不能在现实世界实现，而只存在于物质生产领域的彼岸。第三，包括审美的自由活动要在实践劳动之外才能实现，因此要缩短工作日。共产主义之所以理想，不在于生产力的发展和物质消费的丰富，而在于工作日的缩短，剩余时间的增加，人们可以充分地从事包括审美、艺术活动在内的自由活动，从而得到自由、全面的发展。这一论述确认了现实与审美、必然与自由、物质生产与精神活动、此岸与彼岸的分别将永远存在，只是社会的发展为精神的、审美的超越创造了更充分的条件，从而开辟了自由的可能，而不是建立一个地上天堂。此外，成熟期的马克思还把艺术生产规定为"自由的精神生产"，以区别于意识形态等不自由的精神生产。这样，马克思美学思想就肯定了审美的自由性和超越性，从而更为彻底地具有了批判性。《手稿》中马克思对实践劳动与审美的敌对仅仅限制于私有制社会，而认为在共产主义社会审美与实践劳动之间的差距将得到消除。而在后来的发展中，他认为审美与劳动实践分属于彼岸与此岸两个不同的世界。审美不肯定现实，哪怕是理想的现实，而是以自由精神超越现实、批判现实，使人获得自觉性。这样，马克思美学以其批判

---

① 《马克思恩格斯全集》第25卷下，北京：人民出版社，1975年，第925—927页。

性而具有了现代性，成为现代美学思想的发源地之一。

中国当代美学正在经历着由古典到现代的转型，主要体现为超越理性主义，由肯定性向批判性的转变。这就是说，审美不再是理性（以及它制约下的感性）的显现，不再是现实生存的完善，不再是主体性的实现，而是超越理性和感性、批判现实生存、克服主客对立的自由生存方式。这一转变使中国美学与世界现代美学同步发展，并且适应了中国社会现代发展的需要。当前中国已经迈上了现代社会的门槛，现代性压抑加强，个体精神自由成为突出的问题，需要审美的批判和解脱，而古典美学对理性的信仰、对现实的肯定不能解决这个问题，只有具有超越性和批判精神的现代美学才能适应这一历史时期人的精神需求。马克思美学思想无疑成为这一转变的重要思想资源，但目前主流马克思主义学派实践美学仅仅保留了其古典性，而排斥了其现代性。它肯定实践与审美的一致性，不能批判市场经济的异化现实；它肯定主体性和理性精神，阻碍了审美现代性的实现。我们的任务是，超越实践美学对马克思美学思想的古典阐释，从现代哲学的高度，从历史发展的角度重新阐释马克思美学思想，发掘和继承其批判性精神，使其成为中国现代美学建设的积极因素。

（本文责任编辑：任天）

Explore and Retain the Critical Spirit of Marxist Aesthetics and Construct Modern Chinese Aesthetics

Yang Chunshi

Abstract: In order for Chinese aesthetics to achieve its modern advancement, it must give up its classical interpretation of Marxist aesthetics and strive for a modern interpretation. That is, it must explore and retain the transcendental and critical spirit of Marxist aesthetics. Marx, in his mature stage, believed that aesthetic perception and physical labor belong to the two sides of the world. Aesthetics does not approve of reality, not even idealistic reality. Instead, in its liberal spirit, it transcends and criticizes reality so that man achieves autonomy. Therefore, criticalness quips Marxist aesthetics with modernity, rendering Marxist aesthetics into a cradle of modern aesthetics. Aesthetic perception is no longer the embodiment of sense, the perfection of actual being, and the realization of subjectivity. Instead, it transcends sense and sensibility, criticizes actual being, and breaks down the opposition of the subjective and the objective. This change allows Chinese aesthetics to synchronize its advancement with international modern aesthetics. This serves the needs of modern Chinese development.

反思 20 世纪马克思主义美学的"主流现象"
——兼谈马克思主义美学与中国传统美学精神的关系

夏锦乾*

(上海交通大学人文学院)

【内容摘要】 反思 20 世纪中国马克思主义美学的"主流现象",拨开外在政治的和内在开放性的特点,人们看到,马克思主义美学与中国传统美学有深刻联结。马克思主义美学作为外来的美学思想如果不能在最基本的美学精神上与中国数千年来的美学精神相契合,就很难在中国长期"主流"下去的。这个最根本的美学精神,就是两者都强调了人对美的创造的能动性。然而,20 世纪中国马克思主义美学的"主流"现象留给当代人的课题是,马克思主义美学与中国传统美学的两个"人"在表面相同底下,却有巨大的差距。前者指的是个体存在的人,而后者是以家族血缘为基础的群体的人,20 世纪中国学人对马克思主义美学的接受,常以中国之"人"理解马克思之"人",这不能不说是 20 世纪中国的马克思主义美学"主流现象"的一个重要特征。从群体"人"向个体"人"的祛魅和转化,重塑中国"人"的形象,这就是新的现代中国美学的根本任务。

马克思主义美学是马克思主义整体的一个有机部分。随着马克思主义在 20 世纪初传入中国,马克思主义美学也随之在中国落地生根。从那时至今的百余年间,尽管传入到中国来的美学理论、美学思潮琳琅满目,但它们大多能落地却不能生根,能生根却不能发芽结果。唯有马克思主义美学却以不可阻挡之势,在中国土地上蓬蓬勃勃地生长,它毫无争议地成为以往百余年中国美学的主流。

---

* 夏锦乾,上海交通大学人文学院兼职教授,《学术月刊》编审。

我们把这一现象称为中国美学的"主流现象"。

面对新世纪的中国美学，这一中国现代美学史上的"主流现象"值得反思，这将涉及新世纪中国美学走向的重大问题。其中包含以下两大问题：其一，为什么马克思主义美学不同于其他美学思潮，有如此强盛的生命力？其二，新世纪中国美学仍然会这样"主流"下去吗？

对于第一个问题，人们往往认为主要出于以下两个原因。一是政治的原因。马克思主义一经传入中国，首先是作为民族解放的"行动指南"，政治斗争的锐利武器，因此，无论是在新中国建立之前还是之后，马克思主义都与现实的政治斗争紧密相联，马克思主义美学也因此表现出最鲜明的"党性"立场。在新中国建立之前，马克思主义美学就从认识论美学的角度，对文艺现象作反映论的解释，并最终确立了文艺的阶级性、本质观和现实主义创作原则。从而把文艺纳入政治斗争的领域；新中国建立之后，随着马克思主义成为国家的主导意识形态，马克思主义美学因此获得更加广阔的发展空间，其主流地位也就更加稳固——50年代虽然出现美学大讨论，但是论争的四派（主观派、客观派、主客观统一派和实践派）都以马克思主义美学为自身的依据，就是一个明证。二是马克思主义美学的开放性特征。马克思主义美学最可贵的理论品质便是面向现实，一切从实际出发，而不谨守于既有的教条。这样，发展了的现实不断地改造着、丰富着马克思主义美学的理论。正因为这个原因，从认识论的马克思主义美学到实践论的马克思主义美学，以及生态论的、存在论的马克思主义美学，其理论形态虽发生了重大的变化，但马克思主义美学的主流地位没有改变。也正因为如此，马克思主义美学打通了向其他"非马"的美学思潮、理论的交流和对话的渠道。心理主义的、现象学的乃至结构主义—符号主义的、解构主义和解释学的美学理论，作为独立的美学理论，它们在中国美学舞台上都曾走红过一时，但常常又时过境迁，没有持久的影响，但一旦与马克思主义美学结合起来，其理论精粹被马克思主义美学所吸收，情况就大为不同，如朱立元先生的实践存在论美学，便是在实践论美学基础上对存在论精华的摄入，它代表了实践论的马克思主义美学在新时代的新的发展。总之，马克思主义美学的主流地位并没有因各种思潮的蜂起而改变。

以上两个方面都有一定道理，但我认为，除此之外还有更深层、更持久的第三个原因。这就是中国传统美学精神的因素。马克思主义美学作为外来的美学思想如果不能在最基本的美学精神上与中国数千年来的美学精神相契合，就很难在中国长期"主流"下去；同样，马克思主义美学中国化，也并不简单地等同于国内学者对它的接受和实际运用，只有在某一根本点上和中国固有的审美精神真正地结合起来，并且以中国的审美精神形式阐释马克思主义美学精神，这才是货真价实的"中国化"。那么，真有这样的根本点吗？如果有，这一根本点是什么？它代表了怎样的美学精神？这些问题以前很少有人提及，所以不妨多展开几句。

首先我认为，这一根本点是有的，它就是人对于美的能动性创造。马克思主义的"实践"，就是马克思"从主体方面去理解"世界的概念，它显示的是人有意识、有目的的活动。按照马克思的观点，人与动物的区别在于，动物分不清自己和自己的生命活动，两者是直接等同的；而人把两者区别开来，从而"使自己的生命活动本身变成自己意志的和自己意识的对象"。①这种区分使得人的生命活动（即实践）获得了巨大的自由，诚如马克思所说，他既可以"按照任何一个种的尺度来进行生产"，也可以把自己"固有的尺度运用于对象"。②人的这种自由的生命活动（即实践）的一切成果，从某种意义上，都可以说是人的意志和意识的对象化，亦即"人的本质力量的对象化"。美的创造离不开这种"对象化"，它使人"在他所创造的世界中直观自身"，③它的过程成为人的审美活动的过程。可见马克思主义美学中极为重视"人的意志和意识"的能动作用（当然这与唯心论片面抬高意志和意识的作用完全不同），正是这一点，深得中国传统美学的呼应。

一提到中国传统美学，人们立即就会想到儒、道、墨各家的美学思想，历来它们被看作中国传统美学精神当然不二的代表。但是我要说，这些美学思想对于中国传统美学精神来说，都只能像庄子在《天下篇》中所说的是"一曲之学"，"寡能备于天地之美"。而真正的代表应该是以《易经》为标志的大易之美。儒、道、墨的美学精神都是对大易之美的不同发展。不错，《易经》原本只是一本巫卜之书，但在实际的历史过程中，随着巫术通过"绝地天通"的巫术革命，走上政治前台与家族血缘制权力相互结合，在中国创造了自颛顼至夏商周三代长达2000年灿烂辉煌的巫术文化，以此为基础，《易经》超越了巫卜之书的局限，成为2000年巫术文化的积淀和提升，成为中华民族的智慧精华，同时也成为此后中国文化和美学的精神渊源。按照当代人类学对巫术的定义，

---

① 《马克思恩格斯文集》第 1 卷，北京：人民出版社，2009 年，第 162 页。
② 同上，第 163 页。
③ 同上。

巫术是一种人类早期对于环境的控制术，是一种伪科学，伪技艺。它的背后是人类早期幼稚的意志崇拜。正如涂尔干所说："只要人类还不知道事物的秩序是不可改变和不可松动的，只要他们把它看作是反复无常的意志作用，那么他们很自然就会认为这些或那些意志可以随心所欲地改变事物"，① 巫术的意志崇拜不但如涂尔干所说相信"意志可以随心所欲地改变事物"，而且坚信这个意志就是巫者（巫师）自我，巫师可以通过某种法术（祈祷、念咒、模仿、交感）控制环境。所以《易经》所显现的巫术智慧说到底正是关于控制的智慧，而大易之美即是在巫术意志控制之下环境（世界、自然）所呈现的中庸、平衡、稳定、适度的美，这是巫术控制的最高理想和最高境界，它千变万化、生生不息，是一种动态中所显现的秩序，差别中产生的均匀。它们处处都打上了巫术意志的印记。所以大易之美就是意志控制之美，说白了是巫术意志的外在化，套用马克思的概念，也就是巫术意志的对象化。

所以，中国传统美学精神在本质上也凸显了人对美的创造的能动性，这并非是无稽之谈。在《易经》中，这种能动性虽然有别于科学技术，它是通过一系列法术和仪式，在原始思维的支配下，通过对环境施加想象性的干预来实现的，但是它却把这种想象性当作真实，变成马克思在《德意志意识形态》中所说的一种"真实地想象"的东西，从而在镜幻般的"真实"中体验人的本质力量，体验人之性与天地之性的调谐（"协于天地之性"），即得"道"的"惚兮恍兮"的境界。这就是巫术的能动性的创美原理。这一原理使得中国的先哲们在历史的源头就对人的崇高地位有了深刻的认识。《老子》早就说过："域中有四大：道大、天大、地大、人亦大"；《孝经》则说："天地之性人为贵"，《荀子》也说过："人有气、有生、有知、有义，故最为天下贵"；《中庸》则提出人"可以赞天地之化育"，"与天地参"的思想。他们都把人提高到了与天地并列的地位，直接参与了天地创生万物的进程。这种巫性的人的能动性创造观念可以说是中国传统美学精神的根本理念，也是它与马克思主义美学思想相交流、相契合的基本点。正因此，20世纪初期马克思主义的现实主义文学思潮能轻松地击败同样来自西方的主张以照相式实录生活的自然主义文学思潮，后者取消人在文学中的创造性的倾向，无疑在深层次上得不到中国作家的共鸣。而所有强调文学的倾向性直至文学的政治立场和党性原则的文学理论，至少部分也因为这个原因而畅行无阻。进入20世

---

① 涂尔干：《宗教生活的基本形式》，渠东、汲喆译，上海：上海人民出版社，2006年，第24页。

纪下半叶，实践论美学的崛起同样可以从它与中国传统美学精神的这种默契来加以阐释，而此后它受到后实践美学的批评，恰恰也出于同样的原因——许多批评都集中在实践论美学借社会历史的理性积淀代替人的感性创造。这些批评无疑从另一个角度表明了，20世纪以来马克思主义美学的"主流现象"，时刻受到中国传统美学精神的关联。

然而面对新世纪，这种关联还会存在吗？进而是，马克思主义美学的"主流现象"还会继续吗？这些之所以被作为问题提出，正是基于进入新世纪以来中国经济、文化和社会的发展，对于人的观念的深化。应该看到，说马克思主义美学与中国传统美学精神的契合，其实包含着很大的误读成分。两者虽都强调人的因素，但只要稍一深入就会发现，两者所说的人的含义是不同的。中国传统美学中的"人"虽然强大，能与天地并生，但是他不是指具体的血肉鲜活的个体的人（这样的人叫做"民"），而是指家族血缘的群体，群体的存在先于个体，群体的利益高于个体，个体为它而生，也为它而死。这样的人越强大，越完美，现实的人就越渺小，越丑陋。根本的原因就是中国传统社会是一个群体与个体尖锐对立，群体严重压制个体，从而虽有个体却没有个体意识的家族血缘社会。而马克思主义本质上是西方个体主义社会的产物。马克思的所有理论的出发点便是个体的实际存在的人，他坚持认为："全部人类历史的第一个前提，无疑是有生命的个人的存在。"① 而马克思理论的最终目标就是建立"自由人的联合体"，即共产主义社会，在他看来，这是一个个体人的全面发展的社会，"每个人的自由发展是一切人的自由发展的前提"。②同样，马克思高度重视的"实践"，也是建立在"现实的、肉体的、站在坚实的呈圆形的地球上呼出和吸入一切自然力的人"的基础之上。马克思主义美学与中国传统美学的两个"人"在表面相同底下，却有如此巨大的差距！而更重要的是，当马克思主义美学传入中国，中国学人对它的接受，常以中国之"人"理解马克思之"人"，这不能不说是20世纪中国的马克思主义美学"主流现象"的一个重要特征，而20世纪末实践论美学之遭诟病，大多也与两"人"之混杂有关。因此新世纪马克思主义美学和中国美学的一个艰巨任务，便是站在时代的高度对于两个"人"的清理。这就是说，对于马克思主义美学而言，应该悬搁百年来我们加诸它之上的解读，重新从马克思的出发点出发，建立起真正以个体的感性存在为基础的、以人的全面发展和自由为目的的马克思主义美学；对中国美学而言，

---

① 《马克思恩格斯选集》第1卷，北京：人民出版社，1972年，第24页。
② 同上，第273页。

则面临着将群体"人"向个体"人"的祛魅和转化,以百年来特别是近一二十年来中国现代化和市场经济中"人"的解放为基础,重塑中国"人"的形象,建立新的现代的中国美学。

(本文责任编辑:任天)

A Reflection on the "Maitstream Phenomenon" of Marxist Aesthetics of the 20th Century: Relation between Marxist Aesthetics and Traditional Chinese Aesthetics

Xia Jinqian

Abstract: By reflecting on the "mainstream phenomenon" of Marxist aesthetics of the 20th century China, and by recognizing the external politicalness and internal openness, one can perceive the strong connection between Marxist aesthetics and traditional Chinese aesthetics. As an exported theory, Marxist aesthetics must tally at its fundamental level with traditional Chinese aesthetics in order to remain "mainstream" in China. At it fundamental level, both Marxist aesthetics and traditional Chinese aesthetics acknowledge man's active creation of beauty. However, the "mainstream phenomenon" leads us to a discovery that the "man" in Marxist aesthetics discourse is not the same as that in traditional Chinese aesthetic discourse, the former being the individual subject while the latter being the collective subject bound by blood and familial ties. One of the characteristics of the "mainstream phenomenon" of Marxist aesthetics of the 20th century China is that Chinese scholars view the "man" in Marxist aesthetic discourse from the perspective of the "man" in traditional Chinese aesthetics. It is the primary task for modern Chinese aesthetics that the collective "man" must convert into the individual "man".

巫性美学：中国美学研究新路向

王振复*

（复旦大学中文系）

【内容摘要】 真正中国"特质"的美学研究所面临的重要课题之一，便是首先从文化人类学、文化哲学进入关于中国美学原始人文根因与根性问题的研究。迄今为止的人类美学，为神学美学与人学美学两大类，前者属神本主义，后者为人本主义。而中国美学走的是除此之外的"第三条路"。它介于神与人、神性与人性、神学与人学之际的一种巫性的审美形态，巫性作为处于神、人之际的一种"人文间性"，也是文化哲学意义的一种"主体间性"。对中国美学而言，巫与巫性便是其最原始的人文根因、根性。

与现实偕行的马克思主义及其关于美学的理念与方法，为中国美学的发展和创新提供了广阔空间。充分依凭中国当下与未来审美文化，以及密切联系于当下与未来之中国美学资源和传统的学术实际，力求达到学术之理念与实证、逻辑与历史相统一，无疑可为"打造具有中国特色、中国风格、中国气派的哲学社会科学学术话语体系"，以及为中国美学研究力求"自创一格"之学术目标的实现，打开通往学术真理之途。一种称为"中国巫性美学"的新美学，可望成为中国美学研究的新路向之一。

就此而言，对于以往一个多世纪以来的中国美学研究，重新进行有理据的总结与反思，是必要的。尽管自王国维至今的中国美学研究，已经获得巨大成就，然而有些学术现象与倾向，依然值得做进一步的讨论和省思。

其一，一些文本研究，固然不乏"美"、"审美"与"美学"等字眼的表

---

* 王振复，复旦大学中文系教授，博士生导师。

述，而实际仅仅是中国艺术论甚或文论而已，一般欠缺美学的哲学或文化哲学之学术理念及其论证、分析。其未能自觉意识到，美学的哲学之魂与哲学的美学意蕴之同构性的理念，对于中国美学研究而言，是何等重要。文学艺术固然是美学研究的主要对象，但文学艺术之审美现象及其理论形态，不是美学本身。如果离弃关于审美的哲学或文化哲学理念的统驭与分析，那么，这样的"美学"究竟还能剩下什么？而如将学术视野仅限于文学艺术领域且抽去美学所必需的哲学或文化哲学之魂魄，那么，那些大量存有、发展与非文学艺术领域如宗教、巫术、伦理、科技、自然环境与生活习俗等之中的美学问题，甚或哲学、文化哲学本身的美学意蕴等，究竟还能不能、要不要成为中国美学研究的题中应有之义？

其二，与此相反，是将美学等同于哲学或文化哲学。以为抓住了哲学，便抓住了关于美学的根本，而"天生"便成中国美学或中国文化美学。于是有些研究，又在脱离诸如人的感觉、感性、情绪、情感、欲望、想象、意象和信仰等诗性现象的情况下，展开不免空疏而不着美学之真际的哲学或文化哲学分析，踏入所谓"哲学即美学"的误区。

大凡为学，澄清前提且划定界限，是首要之事。这便是康德所谓学术"批判"之本义。中国美学研究的前提之一，无疑是关于一切审美现象与思想、理论形态相应的哲学或文化哲学；其学术界限，这里仅从对象而言，又是一定哲学、文化哲学理念"关怀"下以艺术审美为主的一切审美文化。

然而，由于众所周知的中国文化的特殊性，具有真正"中国"特质之中国美学研究所面临的重要课题之一，便是首先从文化人类学、文化哲学进入关于中国美学原始人文根因与根性问题的研究。这也便是如德国著名学者、国际美学协会主席海因茨·佩茨沃德所言"作为文化哲学的美学"。海因茨指出，"我们应该对美学进行反思，以置之于人类文化更为宏大的语境之中"[①]。此言极是。

从文化人类学、文化哲学角度审视，一般以为，迄今为止的人类美学，为神学美学与人学美学两大类，相应便有神性美学和人性美学。前者属神本主义，后者为人本主义。由于中国文化"淡于宗教"这一人文特质，此以梁漱溟所

---

① 海因茨·佩茨沃德：《符号、文化、城市：文化批评五题》，邓文华译，成都：四川人民出版社，2008年，第46页。

言，即所谓"中国文化在这方面的情形很与印度不同，就是于宗教太微淡"①。故迄今为止的中国美学研究，西方学术意义上的神学美学、神性美学，一直不甚发达是情有可原的。以西方眼光，中国学者关于中国佛教、道教与基督教等的美学研究，由于其研究对象所属各宗教门类文化要么被中国化、要么土生土长，故其神学、神性的特点不够也无法充分，使其难以成为西方那般典型的神学与神性美学。相比倒是中国的人学美学、人性美学，如火如荼、风起云涌。它们一般属于人学与人性、人格学这一大范畴。其中比如科学美学，以求真与审美之关系为研究对象而一般地排拒神性，故也可大致归于人学这一范畴和主题。但是，由于中国美学的原始人文根因、根性及其哲学之魂，本比由希伯来、古希腊文化传统所哺育、发展的西方美学的人文根底有别，因而，中国的人学美学、人性美学，实际与西方同类美学，不可同日而语，自当也不同于埃及、印度与伊朗等。

由此不难见出，必须找到一条真正属于"中国"的中国美学研究之路而力求有所发现、推进。当20世纪80年代中叶始，笔者尝试运用文化人类学、文化哲学关于巫学的理念、方法，研习真正堪称"中华第一国学"即易学及易文化美学时，体会到，原来人类文化及其哲学与美学之思，并非仅在于神与人、神性与人性、神学与人学二维。它其实是三维的。万类既一分为二又合二而一。这合二而一，即第三维。故人类文化及其哲学、美学等，应是"一分为三"的。中国文化与其哲学、美学，应走向与源自上古原始神话、原始图腾相系且以原始巫术文化为主导又以巫、巫性为主的"第三条路"。介于神与人、神性与人性、神学与人学之际的一种学术研究思维与思想，可称为关于巫、巫性文化的第三品类即巫学。其中，巫性是其中心范畴。因此，以文化哲学的理念与方法研究的中国美学，称为"中国巫性美学"。巫性美学是一种新的"作为文化哲学的美学"。笔者浅陋，而数十年间所思所写，大凡与此有关。

所谓巫性，拙著《周易的美学智慧》曾指出："从人之角度看，巫是神化的人，他假借神的旨意，施行巫术，以达到人的目的；从神之角度看，巫是人化的神，他为了达到人的目的，通过巫术，将自己抬高到神的高度。巫是人与神之间的一个中介和模糊状态，具有非黑非白、又黑又白的文化灰色。"②巫，既是"神化的人"又是"人化的神"。巫性，确是一种两栖于人、神之际之

---

① 梁漱溟：《东西文化及其哲学》，《梁漱溟全集》第1卷，济南：山东人民出版社，1989年，第441页。

② 王振复：《周易的美学智慧》，长沙：湖南出版社，1991年，第375页。

"灰调子"而属"第三维"的文化属性。

这里,人为现实世界之本在,而神为虚拟。虚拟之神究竟如何可能又是为何、应何?不妨可将神,看作关乎人的、人所预设又对应于人的另一"主体"。故巫性作为处于神、人之际的一种"人文间性",也是文化哲学意义的一种"主体间性"。由此可见,对于中国美学而言,倘说其原始人文根因、根性在于巫与巫性,那么,与"主体间性"相系的神性与人性,便成为一种"他者"的文化属性。而且这个巫性,又是关乎人之"命运"的一个范畴。"这里,命,可称为神性时间;运,则指人性时间。《周易》巫筮文化的时间意识,处于神、人即神性时间与人性时间之际,笔者将其称为巫性时间"①。中国人、中国文化最讲"命运",某种意义而言,中国文化是一种关乎"命运"的文化。"命运"是一种巫学范畴。

巫性这一范畴的设立,具有充分理据。这里,且不说殷之占卜与周之易筮文化源远流长,其历史、人文影响深巨;且不说《汉书·艺文志》所言"数术"即巫术六大类"天文、历谱、五行、蓍龟、杂占、形法",几乎无不施行于中华古人生命、生活的一切领域;也不说,诸如北京周口店龙骨山"山顶洞人"遗址(距今约18000年)、河南舞阳贾湖遗址(约8000年)、安徽含山凌家滩遗址(约5000年)与河南濮阳西水坡45号墓遗址(约4000年)等关于属巫的风水方位意识、理念与迄今所知最早占卜之具的考古发现,可证中国巫术文化之悠久的文化之源。这里,仅从《论语》所录关于鬼神意识和人对之态度的片言只语,如"敬鬼神而远之,可谓知矣"、"祭如在。祭神如神在"可证,所谓对于鬼神的且"敬"且"远",正是巫性意义之中国人的人生智慧、策略和"自由"处境。在这属巫的文化心灵中,神灵可"敬"可"远"。这其实是说,神灵对人而言,它们好像"在",又好像不"在"。而归根结底,纯然宗教意义之绝对权威的神尤其主神,毕竟不"在场"。中国先秦文化本无像样的宗教主神。先秦时代那个神性之"天"(天帝),终于未能达到宗教至上神格的高度,而终于被历史化为祖神的象征。在中国人心目中,神是被"祭"出来的。如果不"祭",神就不"在"了。可见,如异族上帝、梵天那般崇高、伟大的宗教主神,并未真正能够为中国哲学、中国美学提供本原、本体意义上的思维与思想资源。这也因中国文化基因,主要并非宗教"拜神",而是巫术"降神"之故。"降神"者,固然有对于神的适度的尊敬与信仰,这里有与宗教崇拜相

---

① 王振复:《周易时间问题的现象学探问》,《学术月刊》2007年第11期。

通之处。但巫在神灵面前只是跪倒了一条腿，而非宗教那般向神全人格地跪拜。巫，借助神灵之力，通过他自己的"作法"，使神灵"降"临且召唤神灵来为人类服务。

从中国上古原始神话、原始图腾与巫术三大原古文化形态的简略比较可见，如弗雷泽所言"万物有灵"意识与理念，确是此三者的共同文化成因。但三者在文化机制、功能、地位及对于中国哲学、美学思维与思想的建构方面，是有区别的。如果说，原始神话是先民向世界的一种"发言"文化方式，它主要发展了先民的原始想象，那么原始图腾文化的主旨，在于先民"倒错"地寻找其虚构的"生身之父"（历史真实之"父"其实不"在场"），它于自然崇拜与祖神崇拜的原始结合中，生成、发展了团结族群之前生命意识，而原始巫术文化，则是先民的一种生活、生命活动的常态和常式。哪里有难以克服的生存和人生难题，哪里便可能有巫术的施行。偏偏先民的生产力十分低下，而其主观上，又盲目迷信自己可以通过巫术克服一切困难。于是，在衣食住行、生老病死以及战争、政治等一切领域，几乎到处是巫术这一"倒错"的"伪技艺"（马林诺夫斯基语）的"用武之地"。

尽管中国原始神话、图腾与巫术在先秦春秋战国时期均不同程度地走向了"史"，但是三者在"史文化"的文化指向与地位有别。比如，关于原始神话中的伏羲和黄帝，在后代几乎被彻底地历史化了，《史记》就曾将黄帝作为真实的历史人物为其立传。又如原始图腾之主角的龙，也被历史化而给所谓"龙的传人"这一文化命题，赋予更多的历史意义。另一方面，凡此巨大的原始意象，一般也并未在后代被哲学而美学化，成为其本原与本体。相比之下，比如中国巫术文化中的"气"，原先作为巫术"灵验"的根由，却发育成为中国哲学和美学的一个十分重要的本原范畴。原始巫术讲"趋吉避凶"。吉、凶在巫文化中是一对偶性范畴。这在原始文化思维中，应是后代哲学、美学一系列对偶性概念、范畴的文化先导。尽管迄今甲骨文中只检出一个"吉"字而无"凶"字，但有与"吉凶"相对应的如"祸福"、"休咎"等属巫的对偶性范畴，这无疑为后代阴阳哲学与美学之"阴阳"的对偶性思维，提供了文化资源。从巫文化看，"吉凶"，是后世"真假"、"善恶"与"美丑"之文化意义的前期表达。其他再如原始巫筮之意象的四维转换，与艺术意象的四维转换，具有"异质同构"关系。

（本文责任编辑：任天）

Witchery Aesthetics: A New Direction of Chinese Aesthetic Studies

Wang Zhenfu

Abstract: One of the major tasks facing the aesthetic studies with real Chinese characteristics is that we should first of all start with the studies of cultural anthropology and cultural philosophy and then move on into the studies of the primary cause and character of Chinese aesthetics. So far the aesthetics of human beings can be classified into two types: theological aesthetics and humanist aesthetics, the former being theo-centered and the latter being human-centered. Chinese aesthetics takes the third route, that between deity and man, divinity and humanity, theology and anthropology. It is witchery aesthetics—interhumanity and intersubjectivity in the sense of cultural philosophy. Witch and witchery are the primary cause and character of Chinese aesthetics.

论中国美学研究的当下性

朱志荣[*]

(华东师范大学中文系)

【内容摘要】 当下的中国美学的研究,要在借鉴西方美学、继承中国传统美学思想的基础上,建构体现当下性特点和要求的美学理论体系,进一步加强多学科的融合,尤其要重视实验心理学的研究成果,重视审美鉴赏力的研究与培养,从而建构起中国特色的美学理论体系。这就要建设有中国特色的美学理论体系,将中国美学用世界可接受的方式向世界传播,既为中国当下的审美实际服务,又对世界作出自己独特的美学理论贡献。要发自美学家的内心,体现当下的实际和要求的肺腑之言;要关注和总结从古到今的审美意识,尤其是当下的审美意识,关注从古至今的审美意象的艺术实践和理论探索,关注马恩美学思想与中国审美实际相结合,协调本土美学理论与外来美学理论之间的相互关系,以进一步在中、西文化交流中互通有无,形成文化互补。

每个学科在自己的发展历程中,不同的阶段有自己不同的任务。美学学科也是如此。从一百多年前的引进和译介,乃至对中国古代的美学思想进行比附研究,到 80 年代开始逐步走向成熟的实践美学等等,中国美学在每个时期都有自己的任务。而当下中国美学研究的任务,则是在借鉴西方美学、继承中国传统美学思想的基础上,建构体现当下特点和要求的美学理论体系,进一步加强多学科的融合,重视美学学科与其他学科的交叉拓展,尤其要重视实验心理学的研究成果,重视审美鉴赏力的研究与培养,从而建构起中国特色的美学理论

---

[*] 朱志荣,华东师范大学中文系教授,博士生导师。

体系。这是当下美学理论研究的重要内涵。

中国美学的理论创新是美学学科发展历程中提出的必然要求，应当体现出美学学科发展和学理发展的必然规律，同时要顺应时代的要求。当前，中国作为世界重要的审美实践场，应当建构与之相适应的美学理论，对中国当下的审美实践进行归纳和总结，并起着指导作用，并在全球化时代对世界美学有自己的贡献。这主要包括两个方面，一是将中国传统的美学思想用世界可接受的方式向世界传播。中国自古以来在审美意识和美学思想方面做出过突出的贡献，如何从当下全球化视野出发，向世界展示中国美学的宝贵财富，与世界共享，是当下美学工作者的一项重要任务。二是建设有中国特色的美学理论体系，既为中国当下的审美实际服务，又要对世界作出自己独特的美学理论贡献。而对于系统美学理论体系的追求正是中国美学研究当下性的体现。中国现代美学经过多年的发展，系统美学理论体系的追求是瓜熟蒂落的事。

在具体美学理论体系的建构中，中国美学如何回应现实？如何实现创新？正是中国美学研究当下的主要任务。中国美学的理论建设要发自美学家的内心，体现当下的实际和要求的肺腑之言，而不是故作奇谈怪论，或人云亦云。中国美学研究要面对当下，关注日常生活与艺术的发展。中国美学界要提振当下美学研究的信心，使美学研究走出低谷，焕发生机，充满活力。每一位审美活动的主体都生活在当下，创造在当下。要关注现实问题，关注现实人生，关注身心健康前提下人们的精神生活，尤其是心灵的安宁。个体心灵的平和，自然生态的平衡，社会环境的和谐，都是中国美学研究要关注的当下新景观，新样态，要回应审美实践中的问题与挑战。

继承中国传统在中国当下美学研究中具有重要的价值和意义。厘清源流，重视古代的典籍和文献，重视美学和艺术的感性实践成果，对中国古代美学范畴的学理源流进行考察和辨析，归纳和概括中国美学范畴的发展史；注重整合研究，对古代美学范畴的元范畴、重点范畴和范畴群进行整合研究，揭示其内在学理联系和整体存在特征、价值意义；对不同时期美学范畴史研究中的问题，参照西方美学范畴史，从切合中国美学范畴的实际，进行发掘性研究，在凸显传统美学的主体脉络基础上，努力挖掘崭新的学理资源；同时对中国美学范畴史发展的关键内容进行梳理整合，并与西方美学范畴史的比较研究，衡量、审视中国传统美学范畴的当下理论价值，进而对重要范畴进行重点阐释，体现出其理论构成的文化有机性，探讨其现代转换的可能性，以揭示中国古代美学范畴古今绵延、变化和更新的理论意义。

中国当下的美学研究，还应当关注和总结从古到今的审美意识，尤其是当下的审美意识。历代的艺术创造和日常生活中不仅有精湛的艺术技巧和丰富的生活经验，更体现了人们审美理想和审美趣味，我们应当对它们进行自觉的理论概括和总结。中国古代虽然也有不少艺术创造和日常生活观念的概括和总结，但与当下的现实要求相比还远远不够。我们在充分学习西方美学的知识和规范、继承古代的美学思想的基础上，有条件、有能力从审美意识中总结和概括出美学理论，指导今后的审美实践，为世界美学理论作出自己的贡献。

中国当下的美学研究，应当关注从古至今的审美意象的艺术实践和理论探索。中国古代的审美意象范畴是经得起历史的检验，并且适应当下美学研究的重要范畴。意象从《易经》中开始萌芽，在《易传》中得到了具体的阐明，又在老庄思想中获得了更进一步的阐述，后世的艺术和文学理论多角度、多方位立体地阐释了意象理论，绵延数千年，使意象思想不断得以推进和深化。而从史前开始的工艺实践，则给我们留下了极为丰富的审美意象创构的物化形态，是我们当下理论研究与创新的重要基础。更为重要的是，20世纪初的庞德等人从诗歌创作和欣赏的角度将其借鉴到英美等国，为审美意象理论走向世界做出了有益的实践，值得我们概括、继承和总结。

20世纪以来对中国古典美学所做出的新的改造的历程和经验教训，值得我们加以总结。其中的宝贵经验值得我们在当下加以继承和发扬光大。与此同时，我们还要重点梳理和总结马克思主义哲学和美学思想在哲学基础、思维模式、方法论等层面对中国古典美学研究带来的帮助和局限，研究90年代以来实践论美学反思或创新阶段出现的中国古典美学现代转换的新动向，特别要结合马克思主义中国化这一现实问题，探索马克思主义美学思想如何更好地与中国传统美学相结合的问题，探索如何更好地建设有中国特色的当代美学体系的新的观点，从而发掘出马克思主义对中国美学的价值和启示。

在马恩美学思想与中国审美实际相结合方面，中国学者已经作出了积极的探索，尤其在马克思主义的抽象继承等方面，取得了一定的成效。当然，无论是一百多年前的马恩美学思想，还是古今西方其他美学思想，乃至中国古代和现代的美学思想，都不能被当作教条，不能以现在的教条来取代过去的教条，而应当从当下审美实际出发，切实解决中国当下审美现实中的重大问题。当下中国美学应当是时代精神状况在美学中的一种体现。

中国美学研究要面对中国实际，要在尊重民众审美趣味的基础上，对审美的实践进行积极的引导。中国美学要面对新的文化环境，面对中国的现实问题。

中国美学研究的当下性应该对审美实际起着积极的引导作用。这是一个不断变革，价值取向和审美取向变迁的时代，日常生活中的审美现象尤其显得丰富多彩。其发展的迅速，难免会出现鱼龙混杂、泥沙俱下的情形。如何对审美现实作出判断，如何对审美实际做出良莠之分并且加以积极引导，是中国美学界当下艰巨而光荣的任务。

新世纪以来，世界经济进入全球化，文化多元化问题越来越引起人们的注意。如何协调本土美学理论与外来美学理论之间的相互关系，以进一步在中西文化交流中互通有无，形成文化互补，就更有其新的深层意义。我们曾经批评美学研究的狭隘的功利性倾向。但是，每个时代的美学研究都应当有自己的特色，解决时代所提出的具体问题。特别是在这全球化时代，中国美学研究处于时代文化发展和繁荣的时代，中国美学研究必须有自己的当下性。一方面，我们不能以狭隘的民族主义观念抱残守缺，阻挡当下中国美学的不断进步。另一方面，我们要合理借鉴和消化西方美学理论，真正实现中西美学的对话，既不盲目引进、简单照搬，又不盲目排斥、简单批判。中国美学发展到今天，应当超越西方美学在中国的形态，而不能用现成的西方美学来生搬硬套和肢解中国审美实际。我们要在当年朱光潜等人"移花接木"的基础上将中国美学有力地向前推进。这是中国美学研究的历史要求，也是美学研究真正进入当下的应有姿态。西方美学只是我们学习借鉴的对象，不是我们简单移植的对象。

总之，中国美学研究的当下性，要正确地认识中国美学理论发展到今天的学理现实，要对前辈学人的理论"接着讲"，要水到渠成地把中国的美学理论继续向前推进；还要切实关注当下的艺术实践和日常生活中的审美问题，总结当下的审美趣味和审美理想的实际；同时，中国美学研究还要对当下的审美趣味和审美思潮起到积极的引导作用。中国现代形态的美学已经走过了百余年的风雨历程，经过几代人的努力，中国美学已经从单纯学习西方的时代进入到同时可以为世界作出自己理论贡献的时代。在全球化的今天，中国美学要特别重视对世界美学作出自己更大的贡献，中国美学界当前有能力、也有义务为世界作出更大的贡献，以自己独到的、富于创新的美学理论为世界的审美实践提供理论支持。

（本文责任编辑：任天）

The Present of Chinese Aesthetics Research

Zhu Zhirong

Abstract: The research on Chinese aesthetics at present should create the aesthetic system embodying the character and requirement of the day which is based on borrowing western aesthetics and carrying forward Chinese traditional aesthetics. Meanwhile, the research should further strengthen the multidisciplinary integration, especially taking the research findings of experimental psychology and aesthetic appreciation seriously, to create the aesthetic system with Chinese characteristics. This demands to spread Chinese aesthetics in the ways which can be accepted by the world to make a contribution to Chinese aesthetics of the day and the aesthetics of other nations in the world. This requires words from the bottom of the heart of aesthetes, the attention to aesthetic sense from the ancient to the day, the combination of Marxism aesthetics and Chinese aesthetics and the harmony of local aesthetics and alien ones in order to complement each other in the Sino-western cultural exchanges.

审美权利和审美伤害

——马克思主义美学研究的一个新视阈

徐碧辉[*]

(中国社会科学院哲学所)

【内容摘要】 本文试图探讨都市化生存中负审美的一些表现方式、它们的深层理论原因,并尝试提出一个新的概念:审美权利。以此概念为核心,以实践美学的情本体理论为基础探索一条解决都市化生存中负面审美问题的途径。

马克思主义美学作为一种关注人的"自由而全面地发展"的美学,不仅是抽象地谈论人性、人的审美存在,而且还要具体研究人的审美化存在如何在社会中得到具体的落实。人的幸福到今天的已不再仅仅让人填饱肚子,穿上衣服,不仅仅能够让人"活着",而且要让人活得有尊严,有诗意,有滋味,有光彩。这里的"尊严"、"诗意"、"滋味"、"光彩"在很大程度上便是关乎人的审美化生存问题。

今天的人的生存方式越来越向都市化靠拢。在一定程度上可以说都市化是今天人类的主要生存方式和生存遇境。无论是外在的行为、起居,还是内在的情感、感知,都受到都市化的决定、制约、规范。美学上升为都市化生存的显在性层面。都市里审美有着与传统社会建立在土地之上的田园风光、小桥流水、平沙荒漠、千里草原等等不同的诗情画意。都市里以人类设计建造/创造为核心的美是流光溢彩的,是由建筑、道路、桥梁、隧道、公园、绿地、广场、博物馆、音乐厅、美术馆等人为设施构筑的。它的美是人工的,炫耀的,壮丽的,光

---

[*] 徐碧辉,中国社会科学院哲学所研究员。

彩夺目的，气势恢弘的。然而，正因如此，失范的建筑、低劣的设计、凌乱的布局、拥挤的楼房等只能带来负面审美效果的都市构架便会对人的感知和心理造成加倍的伤害。城市是在一个有限的空间里容纳尽可能多元和复杂的元素。巨大的都市、庞大的建筑物和个人生活空间的狭小形成鲜明的对照，这对于生活在其中的人本来就会形成压迫感。因而负面的审美对人的伤害便不是无关紧要的，而是真实的，深切的，长久的。它戕害审美感官，凌辱审美知觉，降低审美趣味。它把人不是如席勒所言朝上拉升，而是向下扯拽，甚至使人性扭曲，道德失范。

这些负面的影响，阿诺德·伯林特称之为"负审美"（negative aesthetic），包括审美侵害（aesthetic offence）、审美疼痛（aesthetic pain）/审美伤痛（aesthetic hart）、审美剥夺（aesthetic deprivation）等等。

本文试图探讨现代化都市化生存中负审美的一些表现方式、它们的深层理论原因，并尝试提出一个新的概念：审美权利（aesthetic right）。以此概念为核心，以实践美学的情本体理论为基础探索一条解决都市化生存中负面审美问题的途径。

一、审美权利、审美剥夺和审美侵害

审美剥夺这一概念包含一个假设：人人都有审美的需求并且人人都有审美的权利。由于某种原因，某些人的审美需求被压抑了，剥夺了。

正如启蒙学者的假设人有天生的自由权利，我们假设人都有审美需求——这种假设基于人类的历史文化根源和自然生物基础。从自然性（生物性）根基来看，大量研究所发现的各种动物从鸟类到陆上爬行动物到深海鱼类，都有审美化趋向。那些色泽艳丽、声音婉转的鸟儿更能吸引异性并得到更多的交配机会。众所周知，雄性狮子之所以有一头漂亮的鬃毛，正是因为雄狮在求偶时要展示它那美丽的鬃毛以显示其"美"与"力"。这类例子不胜枚举。但这里我们更愿意强调的是，审美需求更是人类的本性，是人类在生物性基础之上发展起来的实践—历史和文化特性。世界各民族从它的早期起源就开始了审美的历程，人类审美的历史与人类本身的历史一样长久。对于个体来说，爱美、求美、审美、享美，也是人的天性。

遗憾的是，人的这种天性往往被剥夺，被压抑，有时候被扭曲，被畸形化。对于大多数还在为基本的生存而挣扎的平民来说，审美的需求往往被忽视，被压抑，被剥夺，被遮蔽，被扭曲。这种剥夺、压抑、忽视、遮蔽、扭曲有时候是有意识的，有时候是无意识的。有时候，一种荒唐的政治可以把全国百姓的审美需求剥夺掉，像管理军队一样管理百姓。甚至吃什么饭（"闲时吃稀，忙时吃干"）、穿什么衣服、梳什么发型等极其具体的生活细节都作出明确的规定。对于那些胆敢违反规定的人，穿件花衣服、烫个头发什么的，便冠以"生活作风问题"的罪名，轻则办"学习班"（实则是剥夺人生自由），重则游斗、收监。如今，这种明显荒唐的政治性审美剥夺没有了，但实际的审美剥夺仍然每天都在发生。表面上看，人们可以随自己的心愿选择自己的生活方式，自己的衣着、发型、娱乐方式。但是，对于大多数在仍在生存线上挣扎的平民来说，对于在高房价压力下求生的都市工薪阶层来说，对于那些甚至连本来微薄的薪酬都需要去讨要，还往往讨不到，往往因此被毒打、被迫害的农民工来说，他们的审美需求同样也是被遮蔽、被剥夺了的。马克思曾希望在未来社会，人们可以为了兴趣而工作，可以随着自己的兴趣选择自己的生活方式。但至少现在，对于大多数人来说，工作就是工作，就是谋生，很难把工作与审美结合起来，把工作变成一种审美。

从短时间看，剥夺一个人的审美需求似乎并没有像剥夺他的粮食和清水那么严重，那么致命。但是，从长远来看，从人身心的健全发展和整个社会的和谐这种深层次需求来看，这种审美剥夺的后果同样是严重的。人需要用两条腿走路。可是被剥夺了审美机会和审美权利的人，等于是被锯掉了一条腿——使人成为人的精神之支撑，成为跛脚。不但变得难看，行走不便，而且他的生命形成了巨大的缺陷。有某些境界他永远无法达到。他永远失去了进入某些高层次生命境界的权利。由于被剥夺精神性生存层面，他的生命只剩下了动物性，从人退化为动物。

如果说审美剥夺是人的审美权利的一种缺位和丧失，则审美侵害便是对审美权利的一种扭曲与侵犯；如果说审美剥夺是审美的一种"被空缺"，则审美侵害是审美的一种"被扭曲"、"被降低"。正如有的低劣的教育是对智商的侮辱，低劣的审美设计、环境或艺术也是对审美感知的凌辱。审美剥夺导致感性枯竭，生命萎缩；审美伤害和审美疼痛导致精神疾病和心理的扭曲变形。

生活中人们都有过类似的经历：当你来到都市的某一公共场所，比如购物中心或广场、公园，你只想买点东西，或是放松一下心情。但当你一进入这个场所，便听到阵阵强烈的音乐声。那是商家为了吸引顾客而放的CD，或是公园里某些人在跳舞、唱歌。质量低劣的音响、内容低俗的乐曲、高分贝的声响让你感到难以忍受。你那对音乐十分敏感的听觉感到极不舒服，你被那强烈的声波震得心跳加快，血流加速。你早餐吃的东西被震得一阵阵往上翻。你购物的兴致荡然无存；你休闲放松的心情完全被毁掉。而且，你无处逃避，无法逃避。

因为声音是一种具有侵犯性的元素,是一种包围着你的"环境"。它无处不在,无孔不入。你避无可避,退无可退,逃无可逃。这,便是审美侵害。实际上,这也是一种审美暴力。它虐待的是你的身体与心灵二者。也就是说,你的感官受到伤害,精神受到凌辱。

都市化生存中,审美侵害是全面的,不仅仅是听觉,而且包括视、听、味、触,所有感知。

拿视觉来说。都市里林立的高楼极大地升高了"视平线"——视线可触之线际。而且,这些年,中国所有的城市——不仅像北京、上海这些大城市,甚至一些中小城市也一样——楼房越盖越高,越盖越古怪,从高度、体积到形状均给人以巨大的压力。生活在都市里的人们一般说来再也无法看见地平线,甚至无法把视线稍微往远处延伸一点。视野可触之地,四面八方均是巨大的现代化建筑材料构成的各种建筑。行走在都市里,人犹如现代化时代的新的井底之蛙,再也跳不出都市这个"巨人怪兽"之"井"。同时,那些密集而体积庞大的建筑给人的心理压力和审美侮辱也是巨大的。建筑师们为了张扬个性,不惜拿都市里的公共建筑和住宅建筑作为自己的"艺术"理念的实验品;而决策机制的缺陷,长官意志垄断,也使得一些低劣的建筑或公共设施设计堂而皇之、理不直而气壮地在各城市登场亮相,一再考验人们的视觉神经,污染人们的视线。一些形状奇怪的建筑如雨后春笋,在各个城市、各个角落纷纷冒出。它们成为都市的"新地标"——有时候,却是可笑的、粗鄙的、丑陋的"地标"。典型的如央视的"大裤衩"。

光侵害可能是都市化生存中审美侵害最明显的。实际上,光侵害首先是对视觉的实际损伤,同时也是对视知觉的侵害,最后,是对视觉审美的凌辱。当巨大的反光建筑材料矗立在面前,任何角度都无法逃避其庞大的身影时,都市人的眼睛便只能被笼罩在这种光源之下。强烈的反光刺痛眼膜,眼睛对颜色的反应被降低。长时间的这种强刺激也导致大脑的损伤,因为光刺激通过视觉神经传导到大脑。当大脑长久处于这种强烈的信号之下,它对光与影、色与线的敏感都将大为降低。于是,人作为审美主体的审美知觉力逐渐下降,慢慢地,对于那些纤细和暗淡的色彩失去感知,对于大自然和艺术中极为丰富多彩的色调失去判断。只有那些强烈、粗犷的色与线才能唤起其感知。人们的世界变得粗糙、生硬、丑陋。

现代都市里的审美伤害远远不止视觉与听觉。严重的空气污染对于嗅觉的伤损,坚硬的水泥地面和高跟鞋对于脚的伤害,有害气体对于健康的侵蚀,在某种意义上说,都是对审美知觉的一种消减和伤害,也是对审美权利的侵犯。

"虽然污染由于其对健康和环境的有害后果(adverse effects on health and well-being)而在伦理学上受到了谴责,但值得注意的是,所有形式的污染也包括对知觉的戕害(perceptual insult)并导致审美损伤(aesthetic damage)。尖锐的声音,有害的空气,过度的光线刺激,拥挤的人群都导致审美和身体的双重损伤(aesthetically as well as physically damaging)。"[1]

二、审美权利和审美知觉

审美权利问题看起来是个社会美学问题,因为它涉及"权利"(right),而任何权利问题都是在某种关系域中(人与自然、人与人、人与社会)发生的。单独的个体不存在权利问题。上面所谈到的审美侵害(aesthetic offence)也主要是从人所生存的社会环境对人的身体和精神两方面的影响来谈的。但事实上,审美权利不仅涉及人所生存的社会环境,还涉及审美知觉和审美心理。因为任何审美活动都是通过审美知觉来进行的,无论是积极审美(positive aesthetic)还是消极审美(negative aesthetic)。

这里的积极审美和消极审美为阿诺德·伯林特提出的概念。前者指传统意义的审美活动,它导致的审美的正价值,如美丽、善良、勇敢、坚强、乐观等,它通常被与道德概念联系在一起,认为审美导致道德的提高,如康德所言,美是道德的象征。但是,在现代化生活中,审美并不常常导致正面的结果,产生正价值。它也有可能产生负价值。比如,前述审美侵害(aesthetic offence)和审美伤痛(aesthetic hart)便是一种负的审美价值。它也是一种"审美活动",却只会对审美知觉产生负面影响。比如,现代都市常见的一种景象,在污染的空气下,落日会变得又红又大,显得很是"好看"。人们赞赏:"哇,好美!"但其实,此时之"美"并非真正的美,它是非自然的,病态的,负面的。当人长久地习惯于欣赏这样的"美"时,人们的审美知觉力会被引向一种不健康的方向。人们会对此产生"美感",会从内心里欣赏这样的美。但这正是审美知觉受到伤害的表现。当人们习惯"欣赏"这类病态之"美"后,被损伤、被扭曲、被误导的知觉便不再有能力去接受、理解、欣赏、享受那些积极的、正面的审美价值。正如一个人,当他习惯于欣赏那些低俗的"艺术品"(某些流行音乐、通俗绘画、通俗小报上的"文学作品"、冗长的肥皂剧,等等),他的感

---

[1] Arnold Berleant, *Sensibility and Sense—The Aesthetic Transformation of The Human World*, Exeter, Imprint Academic, 2010, U. K. , pp. 162—163.

知/鉴赏力便将停留在这个层面，无法上升到更高一级，无法欣赏那些真正经典、深刻的艺术品，那些需要调动全部的知觉力与理解力、投入全部的身体与心灵的真正的艺术品。当一个人习惯于那些粗制滥造的儿童漫画或动画时，他对绘画的感知便以那些粗糙的线条和色块为限，那些古典的艺术杰作不再能唤起他的愉悦与欣赏。一个听惯流行音乐的耳朵往往也会排斥交响乐或歌剧。这时候，人的审美知觉是被遮蔽、被损伤、被降低、甚至被扭曲的，人类精神上的某些领域他再也无法进入；生命中的某些境界他无法达到；心理上的某些体验他根本无法得到。这些领域、境界与经验可能是他根本无法想象的。这便是审美知觉的损伤与剥夺。因此，审美剥夺与审美伤害最终其实是对人的审美知觉的毁损。

从社会层面来讲，审美权利是一个历史和实践概念，是在现代社会和文明社会里才变得突出的一个问题。当基本的生存权尚未得到保障时，审美权利是不可能真正受重视的，也不可能被现实地讨论。只有当大多数人的基本生存得到保障，社会的主要问题从解决生存问题上升到解决生存质量层面，即从"如何活"上升到"活得怎样"之后，审美权利才会被提出来。另一方面，审美权利也只有在都市化的生存方式下才变成一个现实问题。当人们从广袤的乡村汇集到高楼密集的都市之后，人们的生存空间变得狭小、窄逼。生存空间的变化产生了许多前所未有的问题。其中之一就是促逼的空间对审美知觉的侵蚀、磨损与消耗。如前所述，在拥挤不堪、建筑密集、机动车川流不息、废气包围的都市里，无论是视觉、听觉还是其他感知，都受到侵蚀、消损，产生审美侵害、审美伤痛和审美剥夺。审美侵害和伤痛导致审美知觉的损伤或扭曲，审美剥夺导致审美知觉的短缺。因此，在一个处处充满审美伤害和审美剥夺的社会里，审美权利应该成为美学研究的一个新领域。

如果要更加细化审美权利，则可以从外部和内部两个方面来说。从内在方面来说，审美权利体现在通过教育建构审美心理和审美知觉。从外部来说，则体现在建构一个有利于发展审美知觉的生存环境。

心理结构本是一个复杂的问题，有先天性的生物和遗传基础，有社会—历史和人文环境的浸染熏陶，更有教育、训练、培养的作用。实践美学强调审美心理是历史—文化—实践的结果，强调"经验变先验"，通过社会历史实践和教育来建构、培养、塑造个体的心理本体。其中，通过艺术创作和欣赏培养审美知觉是关键。审美知觉正是在对艺术的阅读、理解、欣赏、接受的过程中建构的。因此，审美教育和艺术教育对于审美知觉的构成是关键因素，也是审美权利的一种体现。

心理本体具体说来就是情本体。情本体是内在自然人化和人的自然化相互作用的结果。是在人类历史实践走向后现代社会，"经验变先验"、"心理成本体"的具体体现。情本体作为一种美学——伦理学概念，同样也可以有向外和向内两个维度。向外，它奠定人际间、人与社会间、人与自然间的爱与敬畏；向内，则是通过审美教育和艺术教育培养审美知觉力和艺术鉴赏力，提高审美知觉的敏感性。① 因此，审美权利概念内在地包括在实践美学的情本体概念之中。审美权利的落实，从个体层面来说，在于心理本体（情本体）的塑造与确立；从社会层面来说，在于改造城市的审美设计和空间布局，构建起美的都市，提供审美的生存环境。

通过内外两个方面，拒绝审美剥夺，反抗审美侵害，由此，真正落实每个人的诗意而审美的生存、自由而全面的发展的理想。

（本文责任编辑：任天）

Aesthetic Rights and Aesthetic Injury: A New Horizon of the Studies of Marxist Aesthetics

Xu Bihui

Abstract: This article proposes a new concept—aesthetic rights on the basis of a discussion of the expressions of and deep-level theoretic reasons for the negative aesthetics present in urbanized living. Based on this concept and emotionalism in practical aesthetics, this article also aims at finding out a solution to the negative aesthetics in urbanized living.

---

① 关于情本体，可参见李泽厚《实用理性和乐感文化》"情本体"一节；同时，徐碧辉在《和谐社会的美学解读》（《马克思主义美学研究》2008年第11期）、《情本体——实践美学的个体生存论维度》（《学术月刊》2007年第2期；人大复印资料2007年第4期）、《从工具本体到情本体——一种实践论的审美形而上学生存观》（《沈阳工程学院学报》[人文社会科学版] 2007年第3卷第1期）等文章中也有具体论述。

真实与现实：齐泽克式的一个考察

于 琦[*]

（上海交通大学人文学院）

【内容摘要】真实是齐泽克哲学中的核心概念，它源自拉康。在拉康看来，真实是符号化难以克服的硬核，它标示出象征秩序结构性的缺失，蕴含着刺破象征的激进性。齐泽克对真实进一步发展和推进，阐发了一种否定性和建构性兼具的真实观。他一方面认可拉康的基本解释，同时为避免使主体陷入无能为力的困境，并没有单纯强调真实的否定性。经过这一发挥，真实呈现出更丰富的层次和更多的理解角度，还被广泛应用于文化和社会政治批判。与拉康重视临床实践不同，齐泽克更看重如何改变现实。为此，他强调真实的激进性，并结合马克思理论改造世界的主张，力求通过行动重建批判当代全球资本主义的主体，以最终达成更美好的现实。

一、真实的基本内涵

真实（reel, Real）是拉康式精神分析学中的重要概念之一，象征（Symbolic）、想象（Imaginary）与真实三元组合构成了拉康理论大厦的基石。真实的涵义丰富而又复杂，很难用简洁的定义来进行描述。但被齐泽克沿用并做了个性发挥，"在某种意义上说，齐泽克的全部著作即是围绕真实而展开的。"[②] 拉康曾明确指出其术语有纯粹的数学符号功能，因此真实具有多层含

---

[*] 于琦，男，1974年生，山东菏泽人，文学博士，上海交通大学人文学院博士后，广西师范大学国际文化教育学院副教授。

[②] Sarah Kay, *Žižek: A Critical Introduction*, Cambridge: Polity Press, 2003, p. 3.

义，能够进行不同解释，它既具有专有名词的功能，可视为一种秩序（order）、一个阶段（phase）或一个辖域（register），同时也可以作形容词，意指理论上的真实，当然还包括社会现实中说某物是真实的等含义。也就是说，这一概念既可在拉康特定的意义上使用，有时又仅具有一般意义，齐泽克在运用这一概念时也是如此，对首字母的大小写和意义层次并没有进行明确区分。

在拉康的理论视野中，象征、想象与真实是一个用来表征人的身体关系以及一般自然界关系的三元图式。三者之间既非先后关系也非简单的线形发展，而是呈现出极其复杂的互动关系，大致说来，想象是个体脱离母亲身体来到世界时最初的整一感，它"代表与母亲形象的整一性相关的前意识领域"①；象征则是由语言等符号体系组成的规则系统或专横的意义系统，它把人的身体塑造成社会化存在，并在人们进入语言后发挥其影响，世界也被切割为前存在的实体与人们生活的世界两部分。真实则是原初性的，是先于存在的未被符号化的现实，象征即以它为基础建构而成，但这一建构又总是不完全的，其未完成性即由真实标示出来。真实刺破象征的整体性，对它形成破坏，因为总是有某物逃逸出来，表明象征中存在一些剩余物。在此意义上拉康称"真实总是拒绝被符号化的"。② 它代表着符号化难以克服的硬核和现实中不能被符号化的剩余。

当然，拉康的真实概念格外晦涩，飘忽不定又难以捉摸，自然不易理解。1954 年拉康首个研讨班就奠定了这一基调。他这样描述语言与象征、真实二者的关系，"要想理解语言，就只能把它视为一个网络，一个建立在事物整体性和真实整体性之上的网络。语言对真实层面的铭写是通过对象征层面的铭写进行的。"③ 由此可见真实与意义（signification）并不在同一个层面，无法用意义范畴加以描述。之后，他又提出真实逃避我们的掌握和理解，而精神分析学旨在分析这种"带有躲避我们的真实的"④ 始终被错过的遭遇。也惟有在精神分析学能够记录真实的不可能性的意义上，才可以理解"存在着某种可到达的真实"。⑤ 真实神秘又变幻莫测，似乎只有上帝才可能拥有到达真实的途径，如果

---

① Jill Scott, "Fantasies of Repressed Empire in Schnitzler's Traumnovelle", *Modern Austrian Literature*, Vol. 39, Issue 1, 2006, p. 59, note 6.

② Tony Meyers, *Slavoj Žižek*, London and New York: Routledge, 2003, p. 25.

③ Jacques Lacan, *Freud's Papers on Technique* 1953—4 (Seminar 1), translated by John Forrester, Cambridge: Cambridge University Press, 1988, p. 262.

④ Jacques Lacan, *The Four Fundamental Concepts of Psycho-analysis* (Seminar 11), translated by Alan Sheridan, Harmondsworth: Penguin, 1979, p. 53.

⑤ Jacques Lacan, *On Feminine Sexuality, the Limits of Love and Knowledge* (Seminar 20), Translated by Bruce Fink, New York: Norton, 1998, p. 22.

确实存在上帝的话,而且他也将是真实的组成部分。人们永远无法直接面对它,哪怕在梦中也不可能。为了描述真实不可知的神秘特性,拉康求助于数学公式,认为"数学独立自足,是一个不自我宣称表征世界的符号系统"。① 但"它能够导致登月成功,标志着思想成为真实之表现的见证者"。② 这样,真实既是环绕我们的事物,又是使我们得以存在的条件。

以上解释不免显得抽象,从真实与象征关系讨论或可提供更清晰的理解线索。简单地说,真实可视为优先于象征的一个领域。因为依据拉康式结构主义语言学,人对世界的全部认知均以语言为中介,语言充当了沟通人与世界不可或缺的桥梁。原因是人们并不具有直接认识世界和把握现实的能力,必须借助语言方式,通过语言与世界建立联系。在这种意义上,语言刻入之前的前符号化的世界就是真实。以一棵树为例,人们无法直接掌握什么是这棵树,只能用迂回的方法,通过描述"它的根扎在土里","它枝头上有几只松鼠",或者"它背后是一片蓝天"来使我们对"树"产生一种认识和理解。在此,真实是存在论意义上的"树",它自身没有意义,也不能被直接认知。我们所能掌握的则是已经符号化的"树"。真实是与象征相对立的一极,是一种不可能,具有神秘不可知又令人恐怖的特征。它超出了主体能承受或忍耐的范围,是主体始终无法坦然面对的一个领域。与它遭遇就意味着面对创伤(trauma,源于希腊语词 τράυμα)。"遭遇真实意味着到达这样的临界点,个体的一致性被打断,并且对其同一性的象征性支撑开始瓦解。"③ 它显而易见是否定性的。

此外,真实还与母亲相联系,因为在出生时我们被迫从母亲身体中分离出来,出生这一事实没有协商的余地,或者说与我们的主体性无关,而且这一分离过程也不可逆转,此后不论是否愿意,我们都必须面对现实或复杂的象征世界。母亲的身体在某种意义上也就具有了律法的功能,成了遥不可及的地平线,我们既无法复归,也不能违越。个体从母体中脱离的创伤性时刻或许可视为与真实遭遇的短暂瞬间。

由此,世界被分为前存在的、未被符号化的原初世界(真实)与人们所生活其中的现实世界。现实是经由符号化(象征)和形象的特定形式(想象)而传达出来的,它经过了系统的符号编码,可借用语言等媒介来体验和理解;真

---

① Catherine Belsey, *Culture and the Real: Theorizing Cultural Criticism*, London: Routledge, 2005, p. 50.
② Jacques Lacan, *Television*, ed. by Joan Copjec, New York: Norton, 1990, p. 36.
③ Jacques Lacan, *The Seminar of Jacques Lacan, XI: The Four Fundamental Concepts of Psycho-analysis*, 1963—1964, edited by Jacques-Alain Miller, translated by Alan Sheridan, London: Vintage, 1998, p. 55.

实则是在符号开始总体化工程之前的原初状态，也是人们进入象征秩序后所失去的部分，真实是原始的、整体的和完全的，每一种象征—想象都是关于真实的某种历史性的回答。由于真实既充当了象征的基础，又意味着对符号化的彻底否定，标示出符号化过程中结构性的、不可避免的不彻底或不足。或者反过来说，象征永远倾向于保持连续和整体性，但真实标示出象征结构性的缺失，指明了其永存的空缺和裂缝，导致象征始终无法彻底完成这一总体编码的过程。真实所蕴含的激进的否定性正肇因于此。

由以上梳理可以看出，真实与通常意义上所称的"现实"全然不同，二者并不在同一层面。现实在拉康理论中基本上属于象征领域，它是一个符号化的世界，一旦编码完成即可被人们感知和理解。真实则是一个原初状态，它是前存在的、超出人的认知和感受之外，是一个不能被直接掌握的令人恐怖又神秘莫测的领域。"真实是言说的身体的神秘性，是无意识的神秘性。"① 然而无意识并非真实，也不是真实的资源库，而只是真实缺失的结果。在拉康那里，主体尽管受现实驱使，并由现实的文化构形（culturally constructed images）所组成，但最终却仍只是空缺的。这就为齐泽克等后来者重塑主体的理论主张埋下了伏笔。

二、否定与建构：真实与现实的辩证关系

从拉康对真实概念的解释来看，真实是否定性的，它总是与限度相关，并表征着语言的局限，或者说"真实只在凸显与现实的对比差异时存在"②，但由于拉康的阐发格外艰深晦涩以及由于过分注重临床实践而忽视社会批判等原因，真实激进的否定性仍远未被彰显到彻底的程度。在此方面真正做了充分发挥和重要推进的当属齐泽克。他既在一定程度上沿袭了拉康的思路，同时又做了极具创造性的阐发，他逐步摆脱了拉康本人的结构主义语言学的影响，把真实应用于广义的文化批评实践，极大地拓展了真实的批评领域，并最终在社会政治批判方面超出了拉康的理论视野。

真实在齐泽克理论中仍旧晦涩难懂，而且在前后不同著作中的阐发也并不一致，甚至彼此矛盾。因此必须小心翼翼地细加辨别和分析。但可以明确的是，

---

① Jacques Lacan, *On Feminine Sexuality, the Limits of Love and Knowledge* (Seminar 20), translated by Bruce Fink, New York: Norton, p. 131.

② Sarah Kay, *Žižek: A Critical Introduction*, Cambridge: Polity Press, 2003, p. 168.

齐泽克对真实的理解和运用从一开始就带有明显的个人特征。他 1989 年问世的首部英文著作、也是让他在欧美学术界暴得大名的《意识形态的崇高对象》即是一例，书中对真实做了较多阐发，但把拉康真实的身体属性彻底清除出去。齐泽克认为真实是一个结构性的空缺、一个空白，最终空无一物。这比拉康把真实仅视为能指层面的缺失更加彻底，在拉康看来，真实是不可否认的。而齐泽克则坚持认为，真实只在其产生的功效是可见的这一基础之上被预先假定出来，它"只不过是一个不可能性"①，无论怎样也不可能被铭刻在象征秩序之中。"真实自身算不了什么，它只是一个空缺，一个处在象征结构中标示其不可能性的缺失。"② "作为真实或不可能的大写物的这一领域是纯粹类似的存在。"③ 它充其量是自我复制品，尽管真实的表现就在社会现实之中，但它并非自外于社会现实的存在。真实就成了象征中的一个无法被占据的位置，是克服象征的另一种存在。两者间相对立的紧张关系被高度凸显出来。

真实是超越和对抗符号化的硬核（hard core），只存在于象征之前或者未被象征化的剩余物中，约略可视为语言的限度或人们成为说话的动物时所失去的东西。同时它又是创伤性的，"真实类似于一台疯狂的机器和令人恐怖的惰性"④，人们无法直接与之面对，而"必须以扭曲的与移位的方式，通过一系列的结果来感知"。⑤ 换句话说，只能以曲折迂回的方式对它加以认识和了解。真实显得神秘莫测、难以捉摸，同时它又是不容忽视也无法回避的巨大存在，"真实总是在某种程度上被偶然遇见同时又不可避免"。⑥ 原因在于如下悖论：一个人头昂得越高，双脚就越离不开大地。真实扭曲和移位的压力总是要通过一系列对象体现出来。真实就基本而言是一个裂缝（gap），一个在主体性和社会核心中的空缺（void），它是一个不可能性的瞬间，抢先阻止了主体的同一和社会的凝聚。真实一方面极易消失（evasive），同时对象征而言又具有闯入性的物质特性。"真实因此是坚硬的也是不可穿透的内核，是拒绝象征化和纯粹的不真实的实体，自身没有本体的连续性，它是阻止任何象征化企图的巨石，是在全部

---

① Slavoj Žižek, *The Sublime Object of Ideology*, London and New York: Verso, 1989, p. 173.

② Ibid., p. 173.

③ Slavoj Žižek, *The Ticklish Subject: The Absent Centre of Political Ontology*, London: Verso, 1999, p. 302.

④ Sarah Kay, *Žižek: A Critical Introduction*, Cambridge: Polity Press, 2003, p. 4.

⑤ Slavoj Žižek, *The Sublime Object of Ideology*, London and New York: Verso, 1989, p. 163.

⑥ Steffen Böhm and Christian De Cock, "Everything You Wanted to Know about Organization Theory… But were afraid to ask Slavoj Žižek", *Sociological Review Monograph*, Vol. 53, Issue 2, 2005, p. 288.

可能世界（象征化的世界）中保持不变的坚硬的内核；不过与此同时，它的地位是彻底不稳固的，它是某种总意味着失败的或在阴影中错过的东西，在我们即将牢牢掌握其特性的时刻，它就自我消散了。"① 齐泽克坚持认为，真实作为纯粹的心理现象是逆向产生出来的。它出现的创伤性时刻是以死亡驱力的到来为标志的，投射到外部即呈现为激烈的社会对抗。"这一敌对性导向可憎人物或意识形态的崇高对象，正是借助它们无法忍受的真实的缺席和快感的不可能性得以成形。"② 换言之，象征的作用就是不断阻止创伤的恐怖条件的产生，而真实的出现则意味着缺失或创伤得以发生或实现。"存在于无意识当中的真实的创伤性内核拒斥被同化到象征秩序中，并且中断意义链条的平滑流动。"③ 格林·戴里对此做了相当准确的总结，"真实在象征之前建构了一个实体性的（substantial）坚硬的内核，它拒斥符号化，同时还标示出符号化的残余物，这是由象征自身安排或由它产生的。说真实在象征之前，是在这一意义上的，即任何象征秩序都必须令人困惑地开辟一系列的可能性，这些可能性将颠覆那一象征秩序本身。"④ 这就明确了真实的否定性质，它完全拒斥符号化。反过来说，属于象征秩序的现实则是为抵抗他者性的无限威胁而建构出来的。

总体来看，真实是与现实对立的一极，是"现实潜在的令人恶心的阴暗面"⑤，人们无法立足于真实，原因是我们的心灵被设想为高雅的，只能生活在体面的、可理解的世界，而真实恐怖的创伤性的特性与之格格不入，一旦置身于真实就会崩溃，就会在绝望中逃离。对真实而言，其激进性与创伤性正是一枚硬币的两面，或者换言之，真实彻底的激进性恰恰潜藏在这一创伤性维度之中。

不过，拉康本人阐发的真实不但艰深难解而且非常模糊，如齐泽克所指出的，"然而，拉康式真实的角色是彻底含混性的：它确实以创伤性复归的形式突然爆发，使我们的日常生活脱离常规，然而同时它也具有支撑日常生活维护其

---

① Slavoj Žižek, *The Sublime Object of Ideology*, London and New York: Verso, 1989, p. 169.
② Catherine Belsey, *Culture and the Real: Theorizing Cultural Criticism*, London and New York: Routledge, 2005, p. 54.
③ Slavoj Žižek, *Enjoy Your Symptom: Jacques Lacan in Hollywood and Out*, New York: Routledge, 2002, p. 23.
④ Glyn Daly, "Politics and the Impossible", *Theory, Culture & Society*, Vol. 16, Issue 4, August 1999, p. 75.
⑤ Sarah Kay, *Žižek: A Critical Introduction*, Cambridge: Polity Press, 2003, p. 4.

平衡的作用。"① 而且拉康的精神分析实践具有浓郁的临床诊断性质，使得其真实概念摆脱不了身体性和器官性，"真实正是不依赖我关于它的观念的东西"。② 为了用于临床把真实解释成超观念甚至是非观念性的，这也是拉康继承弗洛伊德思想的一个重要方面，而只有到了齐泽克阶段，才基本放弃了临床实践，把精神分析学概念广泛应用到社会文化批判尤其是政治领域。他不满足于使真实停留在纯粹的精神分析理论内部，而是主张把这一基本概念应用于复杂的社会现实，"齐泽克对真实的探寻使他与注重由性别差异导致的语言中的裂缝这一拉康式主张渐行渐远。"③ 他致力于将拉康理论潜在的激进性与马克思主义改造或变革社会现实的基本主张结合起来，极大地发挥了真实对象征秩序的彻底否定性力量，并应用于批判当代全球资本主义的理论实践，用真实洞穿资本主义的意识形态矩阵，彻底粉碎其整一性，以达到真正改变世界的目的。至此，真实的激进性被齐泽克推到了极致。

然而真实对现实而言，绝非单纯进行否定，它对后者还具有建构作用。其建构性表现在，它提供了一种不可能、一个障碍或创伤，使得现实得以围之展开。借用齐泽克形象化的说法，真实是"现实当中的黑洞"④，它似乎空无一物，但实际上现实正是环绕它而催生出来的。以甜甜圈这种常见食品为例，真实就像甜甜圈正当中的空洞，整个甜甜圈正是持续环绕这个空洞塑造成形的。尽管空洞实际上不包括任何物质，甚至什么都不是，只是一个"无"，但它具有使甜甜圈成其自身的功能。反过来说，如果缺失这个空洞，甜甜圈也就不可能存在。真实与现实的关系亦然。在某种意义上，真实就相当于现实之中的那一空洞，一方面它不属于现实，被现实排除，同时在另一方面，也正是它塑造了我们感知现实的方式。换用更理论化的表述，真实正是"能够使某物得以产生的那一空无"。⑤

因此可以这么理解，真实与象征是一种悖论性的关系，对象征而言，真实既是使之不可能的首要条件，与它根本对立；同时也是使其产生可能性的首要

---

① Slavoj Žižek, *Looking Ary: An Introduction to Jacques Lacan through Popular Culture*, Cambridge, MA: the MIT Press, p. 29.

② Bruce Fink, *The Lacanian Subject: Between Language and Jouissance*, Princeton, NJ: Princeton University Press, 1995, p. 142.

③ Sarah Kay, *Žižek: A Critical Introduction*, Cambridge: Polity Press, 2003, p. 168.

④ Slavoj Žižek, *Looking Ary: An Introduction to Jacques Lacan through Popular Culture*, Cambridge, MA: the MIT Press, p. 8.

⑤ Ibid.

条件，真实是"一个终极的所指，围绕它建构全部意义（signification），同时也发现自身的限度和不可避免的失败"。① 正如马路中央有一个大坑，过往的行人都竭力避开它，这样，坑就对路人的表现和行为模式成功加以塑形。可以说象征秩序正是围绕着缺失或空白建立起来的。用更学理化方式的表述，"真实以如下方式实现其功能，它运用否定的限度对意义秩序施加影响，而且通过这类限度的影响本身它同时也建构了这一秩序"。② 真实既是否定意义的不可超越的终极地平线，又是使意义系统成为可能的条件本身。因为影响象征秩序的恰恰就是真实与象征之间的裂缝，"这一裂缝作为这一秩序的内在限度发挥作用。象征被'阻隔'，意义链条是内在非连续'非一全部的'，围绕着一个空洞而被建构。"③ 这一内在的、不能被符号化的礁石维持着真实与象征之间的裂缝，正是它阻止了象征向真实下坠的进程。在这种意义上，真实就成了"在某物之中又超出此物本身"之物。它既严格地内在于象征又标示出象征的剩余。或许出于这一原因，齐泽克明确认为真实是模糊性和双重性的，它既能打破象征同时对象征而言又具有建构功能。

三、从真实到新的现实

齐泽克一方面继承了拉康强调真实之否定性和不可能性的做法，但同时也意识到，如果过度强调真实的创伤性和不可到达，把这一否定维度推到极限，就会导致主体陷入无能为力的境地，最终无法把真实的激进性应用于社会批判实践。为此，他并没有拘泥于对这一术语的标准理解，而是对拉康的原初理论进行高度政治性的解读，并最终大胆突破了拉康的理论视域，在《论信仰》与《因为他们并不知道他们所做的》第2版"前言"中作了发挥，把真实概念推进到了一个新阶段，发展为真实的真实，想象的真实，象征的真实。

《意识形态的崇高对象》中对真实的讨论，所突出的只是其否定性的一面，对于其在社会政治领域中的能动性则没能充分展开，这被齐泽克本人视为哲学上的缺陷："对拉康进行准先验的解读，认为真实是不可能实现的物自体（Thing-In-Itself），就意味着歌颂失败，即认为每一种行动都会以失败告终；勇

---

① Glyn Daly, "Žižek: A Primer", available at http://lacan.com/zizek-primer.htm, accessed on August 15, 2009.
② Slavoj Žižek and Glyn Daly, *Conversations with Žižek*, Cambridge: Polity Press, 2004, p. 7.
③ Slavoj Žižek, *The Metastases of Enjoyment: Six Essays on Women and Casuality*, London and New York: Verso, 2nd edition, 2005, p. 30.

于接受失败是值得赞颂的正确道德姿态。"①齐泽克坦然承认未处理好真实—想象—象征之间相互交织的复杂关系，而这三者当中每一个都具有三位一体的特征。于是接下来他做了更详细的划分，指出真实具有三种样态：其一是"真实的真实"（the real Real），如令人望而生畏的大写物、原始对象、异形等；第二种是"象征的真实"（the symbolic Real），指具有连贯性的真实体（the real）蜕变成无意义的能指，如量子物理学公式那样，永远无法再解释生活世界的日常体验，也不能与之产生联系；第三种则是"想象的真实"（the imaginary Real）如"我什么都不知道"（je ne sais quoi）之类的神秘话语，或者超凡特性借以通过普通对象表现出来的高深莫测的"某物"等。根据这种新解释，真实就成了实际并存的三个向度，是破坏每个连贯结构的深渊性漩涡（abyssal vortex），是现实被简化成数学公式的极其脆弱的纯粹现象。

这一新的多层次多角度的认识有助于我们理解真实否定性之外的另一维度。齐泽克没有把真实的不可能性提升到绝对化程度，因为一旦这样就意味着主体在行动中将陷入消极状态，无法有效地介入文化实践和社会政治。为了采取行动，必须打开通向真实的一条窄缝。于是他在保留了真实之不可能的同时，又把它视为可以到达的领域，这体现出一种在不可能的基础之上开出新可能的努力。格林·戴里指出，"认为齐泽克在社会存在中、和/或试图解决现实中的激进的非连续性中，仅仅局限于分析真实的'不可解读的内核'，是必须避免的一种看法。"②原因在于，真实的彻底否定性使它不能被直接表征，但能够以象征功能失效的方式被感知。在符号化失败时，真实即可通过创伤、打扰、非确定或令人恶心之物等被暗示出来，通过符号化失败的那些点达到真实是可能的。"齐泽克的中心观点是，通过激进地假定与真实的创伤性遭遇，根本的改变能够也确实正在实现。"③象征化的失败正标志着真实是无法被表征的实践，它超出语言等一切符号限制，不受社会关系的制约，在"能指的律法"之外享有极大的自由。这传达出一个信息：真实绝非单纯否定性的，同时也蕴含着无限可能，这使它可被应用于社会文化和政治领域，促成全新的社会样态出现。也正是在这一意义上，戴里指出，"真实这一问题不仅是精神分析学的，而且是马克思主

---

① Slavoj Žižek, *For They Know Not What They Do: Enjoyment as a Political Factor*, London and New York: Verso, 2nd edition, 2002, p. 2.

② Glyn Daly, "Žižek: A Primer", available at http://lacan.com/zizek-primer.htm, accessed on August 15, 2009.

③ Glyn Daly, "Žižek: A Primer", available at http://lacan.com/zizek-primer.htm, accessed on August 15, 2009.

义的"。① 他认为齐泽克的真实的伦理姿态是真正激进的开创姿态,是足以冲破意识形态牢笼的越界性的姿态。通过大胆地与真实遭遇,在实践中与真实的创伤—症候遭遇,以挑战不可能的彻底激进性不断展开批判,努力冲破现实世界的罗网,持续不断地推出新的开端,最终实现新事物对旧事物的置换,推出前所未有的新的社会类型。正是在理论改造世界的意义上,齐泽克与马克思主义紧密联系起来。

在齐泽克那里,真实不仅被用于狭义的文化研究,更被扩展到社会政治批判领域。他把真实与全球资本主义的潜在逻辑联系起来并坚持不懈地进行批判。在反思近年来的生态危机时,他指出:"这一悲剧给了我们的时代的真实一个实体:资本主义的要点是无情地漠视并摧毁个人的/特殊的生命-世界,威胁人性的幸存部分。"② 之后又批判了漫无边际的相对主义和历史主义,并不无争议地把资本视为真实,齐泽克反复声称,"今天建立了再意指限度的真实的正是资本:资本的平稳的功能在于,它在不受限制的争取霸权的斗争中,总是保持同一种状态,'总是回到自身的位置'。"③ 资本何以成为我们现时代的真实?齐泽克的思路是,任何改变都必须与某个不可改变的限度相对而言才能成立,而正是资本充当了当今的这一限度。"资本在其运行过程中,中立于其产生的社会影响之外。正是资本充当了幽灵般的驱力、隐藏在实际经验背后的系统结构以及游荡在社会性冲动之中的邪恶形式。"④ 说资本的逻辑是无可辩驳的真实是在拉康的数学公式是真实的这一意义上的。之后他又提到,"显而易见的是,资本的动力是关键因素,它正过度决定我们的整个社会生活,还支配着人类和自然之间的交换。"⑤ 在他看来,资本主义已形成了一个强大的象征秩序,一个严密的意识形态矩阵。要打破和穿透这一整体,就必须借助真实彻底的否定维度,发展出一种真正激进的批判力量。齐泽克把资本视为真实仍显得不易理解,但用真实批判资本主义的关键点在于,它导致象征性权威的解体并把主体削减为某种对象。其方式是通过把真实还原成现实的内在束缚,使之在其虚象和幽灵之

---

① Glyn Daly, "Politics and the Impossible", *Theory, Culture & Society*, Vol. 16, Issue 4, August 1999, p. 75.

② Slavoj Žižek, *The Ticklish Subject: The Absent Centre of Political Ontology*, London and New York: Verso, 2nd edition 2008, p. xxvii.

③ Judith Butler, Ernesto Laclau and Slavoj Žižek, *Contingency, Hegemony, Universality: Contemporary Dialogues on the Left*, London and New York: Verso, 2000, p. 223.

④ Slavoj Žižek, *The Fragile Absolute, or Why is the Christian Legacy worth Fighting For?* London and New York: Verso, 2000, p. 15.

⑤ Slavoj Žižek, "Cover Story: Who Rules the World?", *The Observer*, September 30, 2007.

下威胁现实并最终使现实瓦解。

齐泽克对黑格尔辩证法的坚持使他认为,正是真实构建出了个体无法描绘的单一性,他沿着黑格尔的思路,把真实视为可激发出"具体的普遍性"的要素。辩证法的观念可以使我们能够做如下理解,当前社会系统中的被排斥者(如底层阶级等)正是新的具体普遍性得以产生的生长点。而普遍性是我们反对资本主义全球化唯一的可求助对象。原因在于,资本全球化把一切事物都依照霸权性的资产阶级的利益加以商品化,只有重回普遍性维度才能对此形成有力的矫正和反拨。而且这种反拨不能仅仅停留在理论层面,更重要的还在于实践,如马克思曾经明确的,最终必须促成社会现实的彻底改变。或许正是在此意义上,莎拉·凯伊指出,"黑格尔事实上被他(齐泽克)解读成了新的马克思"。[1] 如何实现这一过程?那就要在发挥真实最激进的批判性基础上,通过"行动"(the Act)来完成。

行动在齐泽克理论中尽管在意义广狭和影响方面多有变化,但始终被当作"一个关键原则"。[2] 它与真实一样既显得高度抽象,同时在现实政治中又具有广阔应用空间。一方面,它与通常意义上的"行为"(activity)很不相同,行动具有暂时消灭并重塑主体的作用。"行动与一种积极的干涉(行为)不同,行动彻底地转换它的行为者:行动并不是我简单地'完成'某件事情——在行动之后,严格说来,我已经'不再是原来的我'。在这种意义上,我们可以说主体'遭受'(undergoes)行动,而不是完成它。主体被彻底消灭并随之再生(或再生失败)。也就是说,行动涉及到主体某种暂时的消失和性机能丧失恐怖(aphanisis)。"[3]行动明显更加激进,它不仅可以转换行动的对象,而且还可以彻底转换行动的主体,使之消失并进而浴火重生。行动导致主体暂时消失可与黑格尔的"世界之夜"联系起来。按照齐泽克的理解,"世界之夜"可被视为主体性的创建姿态,行动则是朝着那一姿态的回归,以重复对主体进行创建的时刻。行动是疯狂的,因为从世界中抽身而退无疑是一种冒险,不仅可能失去回归的可能,也有可能失去回归的目标。然而在齐泽克看来,冒险是必不可少的,因为希望、自由和行为者都只有通过疯狂才能产生出来,而正是这种疯狂为主体的重生打开了广阔空间。

---

[1] Sarah Kay, *Žižek: A Critical Introduction*, Cambridge: Polity Press, 2003, p. 47.

[2] Sarah Goldingay, "Plagiarising Theory: Performance and Religion?", *Studies in Theatre and Performance*. Vol. 29, Issue 1, 2009, p. 10.

[3] Slavoj Žižek, *Enjoy Your Symptom! Lacan in Hollywood and Out*, London: Routledge. 1992, p. 44.

另一方面，行动就其现实政治意义来说，又是这样一个过程，其行为主体能够打破支撑资本主义的机械主义，也就是齐泽克所称的象征秩序。行动能够带来彻底的改变，一般的政治行为则对此力不能及。所以与其置身于象征秩序的整体性之外获得那种不可能性，不如投入到真正的颠覆性的行动中来，后者显然更加有效。齐泽克经常讨论法国大革命，视之为一个真正的行动，他尤其看重其具有历史意义的恐怖，"每一个真正的行动中都内在包含恐怖之物。"[①] 大革命彻底改变了世界，从此一切大不相同。再以基督教为例，使徒保罗的"无条件挚爱"（agape），是基督教神学话语中存在着真正的行动的标志。这个术语的含义是牺牲自己以拯救他人之爱，它是纯粹的，不带任何附丽。"无条件挚爱的观念，通过忽略对资本主义交换行为的规避，通过绝对付出而不求任何回报，就可以动摇当前的晚期资本主义中的金融交换的力量根基。"[②] 简言之，借助真正的行动，象征秩序就能被打破，其支撑力量会被彻底瓦解。

如果说弗洛伊德的无意识理论肯定了能指的自治化，那齐泽克的重点则在于行动的自治化，通过真实阐明一种能打破既存结构或意义循环的基本的能力。"如果现实是一种结构性扭曲，那么精神分析的终极教训就是我们要为社会再生产负责。奇迹能够出现也终会出现，我们有能力通过付诸真正的行动，给与现实一个新的肌理和方向。行动反映出存在秩序中的缝隙、或自由的深渊。"[③] 齐泽克的看法由于对本体论的潜在追求而充满活力，他要通过真正的介入而获得"不可能"的本体潜能来得到支撑和力量。

在这一意义上，就可以认为齐泽克的真实同时包含了一个内在限度和一个开放空间，既阐明了政治的彻底否定维度，又论证了一种从无到有的条件。或者说，他阐发的是一种正面的、肯定的否定性和不可能，并试图以此开出无限新的可能。这也是齐泽克的真实观念极富张力之处。他提出了一个新视角，应该追求一种真实的政治。因为所有政治的次生形态都离不开真实的维度，目前此类政治次生形态都不是政治性的，需要加以再政治化（re-politicize）。他近年来提出的激进政治方案就是立足于真实彻底的否定性，以最彻底的激进姿态整体挑战资本主义，用真实刺破或洞穿社会现实的力量来开创新的政治可能性。

[①] Slavoj Žižek, *The Ticklish Subject: The Absent Centre of Political Ontology*, London and New York: Verso, 1999, p. 377.

[②] Sarah Goldingay, "Plagiarising Theory: Performance and Religion?", *Studies in Theatre and Performance*. Vol. 29, Issue 1, 2009, p. 11.

[③] Glyn Daly, "Žižek: A Primer", available at http://lacan.com/zizek-primer.htm, accessed on August 15, 2009.

由此可见，齐泽克努力倡导的激进性，并不是一种中立性的冷眼旁观，更重要的方面还在于其实践态度。早在160多年前，马克思在关于费尔巴哈的第十一条论纲中就已明确指出，"哲学家们只是用不同的方式解释世界，而问题在于改变世界。"① 近年来日益向马克思主义回归的齐泽克对此自然非常清楚，因此，他理论思考的重点不仅包含了真实的激进性，也包含政治行动的实践性，他致力于解决如何使批判性主体能够介入，如何得以付诸行动的问题，因为只有通过完成激进性的批判与实践，才能最终达成更美好的社会新秩序。

（本文责任编辑：任天）

A Žižekian Study on the Real and Reality

Yu Qi

Abstract: This article discusses the Real which is from Lacan and now has become the main coordinate in Žižek's political philosophy. Basically, the Real is the hard core of symbolization, and it indicates the possibility to break out of the Symbolic. Žižek, however; does not follow Lacan all the way down on the negativity, on the contrary, his central point is that radical change can and will occur by means of assuming the traumatic encounter with the Real itself. He argues there are in fact three orders of the Real: the real Real, the symbolic Real and the imaginary Real. What he aims at is developing a more radical approach to politics, a politics of the Real, by means of the Act. Žižek's ultimate goal is to call for a better social reality. He hitherto attacks global capitalism and tries to make radical change possible.

---

① 卡尔·马克思《马克思论费尔巴哈》，《马克思恩格斯选集》第1卷，北京：人民出版社1995年版，第61页。

左翼电影与马克思主义中国化

邵瑜莲[*]

(上海交通大学人文学院)

【内容摘要】 20世纪初期,阶级斗争学说是马克思主义原理中最受中国知识分子欢迎的理论。深受左翼文学影响的左翼电影在对马克思主义阶级斗争学说的运用中,逐渐摆脱了左翼教条化、极端化的倾向,不是绝对地以阶级斗争来进行理念的传达,而是把阶级斗争和人性、道德、人道主义等问题结合起来,极大地表现了阶级斗争的复杂性和人性的复杂性;另外,左翼电影把阶级对立处理成贫富对立,这种改写表面上是词语的更换,实则是摆脱了马克思主义阶级理论的话语困境,实现了马克思主义阶级斗争理论和中国农村风俗习惯、现实状况的完美融合,也即实现了马克思主义中国化的转变。在马克思主义中国化的历史进程中,左翼电影对马克思主义中国化做出了巨大的贡献,也产生过诸多问题。

马克思主义自从进入中国国门,便开始了马克思主义中国化的伟大历程。马克思主义中国化是马克思主义原理与中国具体实践相结合的过程,是抽象和具体、一般与个别的统一。在马克思主义中国化的过程中,也曾出现过对马克思主义原理简化、误解甚至曲解的地方。受国际无产阶级文学运动而兴起的左翼文学与马克思主义文艺思想相结合,迅速形成中国式的马克思主义文艺理论,而左翼电影直接受影响于当时的左翼文学,其政治服务性同样也不例外,而且因电影视觉的直观性、受众的广泛性、传播的快捷性,其工具性、武器性更明

---

[*] 邵瑜莲,1972年生,女,山东成武人,文学博士,上海交通大学人文学院博士后,副教授。本文系教育部人文社会科学重点研究基地重大项目"马克思主义与中国20世纪文学理论的发展研究"(项目编号:2009JJD750009)阶段性成果。

显。在马克思主义中国化的历史进程中,左翼电影对马克思主义中国化做出了巨大的贡献,也产生过诸多问题。

一、早期马克思主义中国化

社会文化语境提供了马克思主义传播的文化场域,十月革命胜利以后,新成立的共产党或工人党达 40 多个,各国共产党积极地把马克思列宁主义作为自己改造社会的思想武器。正如 E.布洛赫所说,"由于战争,日益增强的各种政治现象一目了然,这种现象或多或少必然导致了马克思主义"。① 近代中国,实验主义、功利主义、改良主义、无政府主义、空想社会主义、进化论等各种思潮涌入国门,但正如冯契先生所说,西方哲学传到中国来,真正发生了重大影响的是两种哲学:旧民主主义革命阶段的进化论和新民主主义阶段的马克思主义哲学。②

"马克思主义中国化"这个命题,最早是由毛泽东 1938 年在中共六届六中全会上正式提出的,他说:"没有抽象的马克思主义,只有具体的马克思主义。所谓具体的马克思主义,就是通过民族形式的马克思主义,就是把马克思主义应用到中国具体环境的具体斗争中去,而不是抽象地应用它。成为伟大中华民族之一部分而与这个民族血肉相连的共产党员,离开中国特点来谈马克思主义,只是抽象的空洞的马克思主义。因此,马克思主义的中国化,使之在其每一表现中带着中国的特性,即是说,按照中国的特点去应用它,成为全党亟待了解并亟须解决的问题。"③ 这个命题虽然在 1938 年才提出,但在此之前,中国先进知识分子、中国最早的马克思主义者,在对马克思主义的吸收和运用上就已经和中国具体的实际相结合,而实质上开始了马克思主义的中国化历程。可以说,我国对马克思主义思想的选择一开始就是与我国具体的社会问题相联系的,中国最早的马克思主义者李大钊、陈独秀、瞿秋白、蔡和森等都在译介马克思主义的过程中对马克思主义进行了中国化的努力。马克思主义在被译介进中国时,中国先进知识分子并不是全盘吸收马克思主义。因为,第一,对马克思主义的译介本身就是一个不断丰富的过程。第二,中国知识分子在理解、介绍马

---

① [德] E.布洛赫:《一个马克思主义者无权成为悲观主义者——与 J-M.帕米尔的谈话》,《世界哲学》,2007 年第 4 期,第 13 页。
② 冯契:《中国近代哲学的革命进程》,上海:上海人民出版社,1999 年。
③ 毛泽东:《论新阶段》,《中共中央文件选集》(第 11 卷),北京:中共中央党校出版社,1991 年,第 658—659 页。

克思主义思想时，对马克思主义的唯物史观、剩余价值学说、阶级斗争学说等是根据中国国情而有所选择并重点推荐的，其中特别引起他们注意的是马克思主义的"阶级斗争"学说。正如李泽厚所说，"真正极大地打动、影响、渗透到我们心灵和头脑中，并直接决定或支配其实际行动的，更多的是马克思主义的唯物史观。其中，又特别是阶级斗争学说。"[①] 这种选择性吸收本身就开启了马克思主义中国化的进程。马克思主义认为，阶级斗争是社会基本矛盾在阶级社会中的表现，是阶级对立社会发展的直接动力。在马克思主义诸多思想中，中国先进分子迅速地抓住了阶级斗争的武器。

而在电影方面，马克思主义中国化的努力可以说是从左翼电影开始的。左翼电影之前中国电影一般都是社会伦理片、滑稽片、武侠片、古装片、神怪片、喜剧片等，宣扬中国传统伦理甚至一些封建迷信的东西，尤其是古装、神怪片在 20 世纪 20 年代末大有市场，充满着淫秽妖艳、怪异迷信等低级趣味，这种情形引起了国民政府的注意，并制定了《电影检查法》以禁拍这类影片，电影市场因之一片萎缩而呈空白之势，左翼电影就是在这种情形下，迅速取代这种旧市民电影而登上历史舞台。左翼电影是时代和历史共同的产物，是左翼人士利用电影这个武器，运用马克思主义的方法论，进行救国救民的奋斗和抗争。电影因其通俗性和大众化的要求，相对其他艺术甚至政治本身对马克思主义的选择更加需要本土化，因此，左翼电影在马克思主义中国化的道路上可以说更加复杂和多元。

左翼电影的话语语境是内忧外患，一方面，帝国主义的炮火已打开了中国的大门，另一方面，国民党最初的不抵抗政策又使左翼电影深受国民党政府检查机关的控制，在这种情形下，左翼电影与马克思主义阶级斗争理论相遇，就像找到了救世的良药。但是，当时中国的语境和国际上公开张扬无产阶级运动的大语境又有所不同，当时中国的资本主义才刚刚起步，无产阶级的力量还十分薄弱，因此，左翼电影对马克思主义理论的应用必须结合中国实际而有所选择。左翼电影的产生和当时的左翼文化有着密切的关系，其中，左翼电影人士有很多都是左翼剧联的人员，但与深受苏联影响的左翼文学不同，这些曾是左翼剧联的中坚人物在进行电影剧本的创作和影评分析时，考虑最多的是如何用电影这个武器来影响大众，使观众愿意接受他们电影的理念。因此，电影不能照搬已显僵化的苏联模式，也不能直接把马克思主义阶级斗争学说的原理直白

[①] 李泽厚：《试谈马克思主义在中国》，《中国思想史论》（下），北京：东方出版社，1987 年，第 967 页。

地告诉观众，而是在具体创作实践中与中国社会的具体国情以及市场需求、观众的接受心理及接受喜好相接合，在电影实践领域产生了中国式的马克思主义。

二、左翼电影如何与马克思主义相结合

（一）左倾思想的问题：把阶级斗争简化为经济阶级斗争

马克思主义思想传入之初，中国最早的一些马克思主义者在接受马克思主义思想时是在简单理解甚至曲解与误解中进行的。马克思在提出阶级斗争理论之时，认为阶级斗争的根源在于各敌对阶级经济利益和政治要求的根本对立，但是中国最早在接受马克思主义的阶级斗争理论时，把阶级斗争直接简化为经济阶级的斗争，直接用经济地位决定政治态度。这种简化突出了矛盾重点，但另一方面也带来了问题，即没有考虑到阶级斗争的复杂性。例如，中国最早的马克思主义者李大钊就认为，经济原因是引发经济利益相反的不同阶级进行阶级斗争的深层动因。① 毛泽东在1925年根据马克思主义的经济基础决定上层建筑的原理，运用马克思主义的阶级分析方法，写出《中国社会各阶级分析》一文，全面系统地分析了中国社会的阶级状况。毛泽东指出，"一切勾结帝国主义的军阀、官僚、买办阶级、大地主阶级以及附属于他们的一部分反动知识界，是我们的敌人。工业无产阶级是我们革命的领导力量。一切半无产阶级、小资产阶级，是我们最接近的朋友。那动摇不定的中产阶级，其右翼可能是我们的敌人，其左翼可能是我们的朋友——但我们要时常提防他们，不要让他们扰乱了我们的阵线。"这种分析是建立在经济地位决定政治态度这一马克思主义唯物史观基础之上的，毛泽东对当时右倾机会主义及左倾机会主义进行批评，指出他们没有分清谁是真正的敌人，谁是真正的朋友。这一分析在当时的历史情况下起到了团结工人阶级的同盟——绝大多数农民的积极作用。但是这种分析显然是一种简化的唯物史观。运用辩证唯物主义的观点，不同的阶级之间也可能产生相同的政治要求，而同一阶级之间政治要求未必完全一致。毛泽东在当时的情况下为了团结大多数的农民，而没有考虑这种阶级的复杂性。无论李大钊还是毛泽东，中国共产党人早期在寻找阶级斗争的对象时，都是从经济地位入手的。这显然是一种简化了的阶级斗争。这种思想在左翼人士中间广为接受，深刻影响了当时的文艺理论与电影创作和电影批评。

---

① 李大钊：《李大钊文集》（上，下），北京：人民出版社，1984年。

（二）左翼电影对左倾思想的修正及其对阶级理论的中国化处理

中国式被简化的阶级理论，在很多激进色彩浓厚的左翼电影里广为流传，但是在一些优秀的左翼电影里恰恰得到了修补和匡正，不能不说是左翼电影对马克思主义阶级斗争学说中国化的一个最好的诠释，也可以说是马克思主义中国化的一个奇迹。

在优秀的左翼电影里，不是绝对地以阶级斗争来进行理念的传达，而是把阶级斗争和人性、道德、人道主义等问题结合起来，极大地表现了阶级斗争的复杂性和人性的复杂性。如广受欢迎的《姊妹花》（郑正秋，1933）、《渔光曲》（蔡楚生，1934）等都突破了简单的以经济地位决定阶级斗争的模式。《姊妹花》本来是按着阶级对立的套路来安排的，孪生姊妹大宝二宝失散，因为命运的安排，一个成了佣人，一个成了军阀的姨太太。影片有着鲜明的左翼色彩，如大宝向主人二宝（不相识的妹妹）借钱，二宝不给，大宝说，"难道我们穷人的性命不要紧，你们富人的面子要紧？""你不借还罢了，还给我一嘴巴！"大宝这种声讨式的语言和后来不得已的偷窃行为都是左翼反抗斗争思想的产物。影片开始对这种阶级对立表现得很是充分，但是影片打动人的不是这种阶级的对立，而是姐妹相认后血肉亲情战胜了阶级性的伦理观念。影片放映后，受到观众的热烈欢迎，连映60天，但是影片却受到当时"前进批评家"的批评，说它反映的是"小市民的世界观"，抓住的是"广大的小市民的观众"。这种批评现在看来过于偏激，"抓住小市民"现在不但不是缺点，反而是优点，因为"大众化正是马克思主义中国化的一个实现条件"，① 它不但真正体现了大众的需求，也是把抽象的阶级理论和我们普遍的人性相结合的一个最好的例证。

《渔光曲》则更前进一步，影片首先打破了阶级对立。佃农家的孩子小猴和小猫与大船户家的少爷何子英，他们不再是阶级斗争的两极，而是童年的好朋友。如果说这种友情更多的是儿童的天性的话，那么成年后的子英学成归来，仍然帮助、同情受苦受难的小猴小猫，就不能再说是天性，而应该是人性了。在这里，人性显然大于阶级性。影片放映以后，反响热烈，甚至打破了《姊妹花》的连映纪录，但在当时也同样受到极左人士所谓"小市民电影"的批评。对于诸多责难，蔡楚生也深感痛苦，但不改其志，因为他意识到，强硬灌输阶级斗争观念："必然地最少会减去一半观众，你又能说这不是一种损失吗？不过，这'方式'应用得不好时，就很容易出乱子——因为这是违背艺术原理的

---

① 王晓云、时永松：《大众化是马克思主义中国化的实现条件》，《江汉论坛》2008年第4期。

做法。"①

这种打破阶级对立的做法在优秀的左翼电影里得到了广泛的应用,如《野玫瑰》(孙瑜,1932)、《小玩意》(孙瑜,1933)、《风云儿女》(许幸之,1935)、《浪涛沙》(吴永刚,1936)、《青年进行曲》(史东山,1937)等,它们在当时都或多或少地遭到过一些激进派的粗暴批评,但是优秀的左翼电影人,一方面要注意到理念的引导,另一方面他们也知道,电影必须受艺术规律的制约,不能单单是口号和理念的影子。因此,他们可以不顾压力而坚持做下去。

其实,把马克思主义阶级理论和人道主义、道德、人性相结合的理念并不是只左翼电影的新发明,而是马克思主义阶级理论的本意。这一点,在李大钊早期的引介过程中已反复强调,"他(马克思,作者注)并不是承认人类的全历史,通过去未来都是阶级竞争的历史。他是确信人类真历史的第一页当与互助的经济组织同时肇始。……这最后的阶级竞争,是改造社会组织的手段。这互助原理是改造人类精神的信条。我们主张物心两面的改造,灵肉一致的改造。"② 这种阶级斗争和人道主义互助原则的结合,李大钊在早期的马克思主义阶级斗争学说中已经辩证地进行了理解和引介,但可惜的是,左翼人士大多强调的只是阶级斗争,对人性、道德、人道主义这一面有意无意地忽略了,甚至以阶级斗争理论来压倒人性论。左翼电影在这一方面,结合电影市场和观众的欣赏接受心理进行了有效的修正,但仍然遭到了同时代极左人士的恶劣对待。由此可见,真正理解和运用马克思主义并使之中国化路途是多么曲折、艰难。

其次,优秀的左翼电影善于以艺术的方式将阶级对立处理为穷人与富人的冲突戏剧。影片里很少有无产阶级、资产阶级一类的词语出现,而常常代之穷人和富人的说法。这就把马克思主义的书面化和正规化的理论转化成广大观众易于理解和接受的日常口语,极大地增强了影片与大众的亲合性。这种改写表面上是把马克思主义的阶级对立说成了贫富对立,实则是摆脱了马克思主义阶级理论的话语困境,实现了马克思主义阶级斗争理论和中国农村风俗习惯、现实状况的完美融合,也即实现了马克思主义中国化的转变。中国的广大农村是没有阶级意识的,"中国农村的居民是按照群落和亲族关系(如宗族成员、邻居和村落),而不是按照被剥削阶级和剥削阶级来看待他们自己的"。③ 如果电

---

① 蔡楚生:《会客室中》,《电影·戏剧》1936年第1卷第2、3期。
② 李大钊:《阶级竞争与互助》,《李大钊选集》,北京:人民出版社,1978年,第222—224页。
③ 弗里德曼、毕克伟、赛尔登:《中国乡村,社会主义国家》,陶鹤山译,北京:社会科学文献出版社,2002年,第124页。

影照搬马克思主义的阶级理论，一定会引起观众接受的生硬和隔膜，但是现在转化成富人和穷人的说法（中国人从一出生就知道自己是富人还是穷人，贫富对立模式在中国已有上千年的历史），观众以为影片主人公的生活就是自己的生活，就是自己的命运。正如胡克所说，左翼电影"在理论论述中对于马克思主义的阐释其实并未严格遵照原著，而是根据个人的理解加以发挥，根据社会条件和个人的思想发展，结合了很多民主主义观念，他们的阶级论主要不是论述资产阶级与无产阶级的阶级斗争，而是主要论述贫富对立，甚至认为，只要是推动社会进步，即使不写贫富对立，也应鼓励"。[1] 因此，这种把阶级斗争转化成穷人和富人之间的斗争的说法得到了观众的肯定，在左翼电影的创作中也成了一条黄金定律。

三、左翼电影中马克思主义中国化的根本特性

政治性：左翼电影的政治性首先是由左翼电影人士的双重身份决定的。左翼电影人的核心成员大都有着双重身份，他们首先是革命工作者，然后才是电影工作者。1932年，在瞿秋白的直接领导下，成立了中共的电影小组，由夏衍负责，以"左翼剧联"盟员为主的许多新文艺工作者，陆续介绍到"明星"、"联华"、"艺华"等影片公司，1935年，还建立了左翼自己的电影阵地"电通"公司。党派到各民营公司的电影工作人员夏衍、郑伯奇、田汉、洪深等，他们身兼数任，既是革命工作者，又是电影创作人员；既是文艺理论家，又是电影剧作家；既是电影理论家，又是影评人士。他们把电影当作革命事业，有着崇高的使命感，他们为完成使命而迅速地学习电影的各种理论和实践知识，正如夏衍所说："我对电影是外行，只因当时为了革命，为了搞左翼文艺运动，为了要让一些新文艺工作者打进电影界去，运用电影来为斗争服务，才逼着我们去学习一些业务，去摸索和探求。我们不是'为电影而电影'，我们搞电影有一个鲜明的目的性。"[2] 这个目的性就是政治性，即以电影为阶级斗争的武器，救亡图存。正如胡克所说："中国共产党作为政治力量参与电影创作和理论批评是不公开的，其根本的政治目的与军事手段一致，是要推翻国民党政权，因而必然带有鲜明的政治性"。[3] 可以说，政治性是左翼电影的合法要求，是其

---

[1] 胡克：《中国电影理论史评》，北京：中国电影出版社，2005年，第93页
[2] 夏衍：《写电影剧本的几个问题》，上海：复旦大学出版社，2004年，第6页。
[3] 胡克：《中国电影理论史评》，第90页。

顺应历史、肩负时代重任的一种必然选择。

其次，左翼电影的创作和批评都带有鲜明的政治性，这种政治性有时会显得非常突兀，这一点亦成为当时"软性电影"的鼓吹者刘呐欧、黄嘉谟、穆时英等批判的焦点，他们认为，左翼电影是"内容偏重主义"的"畸形儿"，是"暴露报告"，是"红色素"，是"不自然的浅薄的宣传品"，"充满着干燥而生硬的说教"。① 抛开软性电影对左翼电影诬蔑、打击的成分，左翼电影在当时的历史条件下的确存在着明显的说教、组织、宣传的成分，这与它鲜明的政治性是分不开的。夏衍回忆说："常常有这样的事情，一个剧本已经定了，快开始拍了，或者已开拍了，导演找我们商量，或者我们主动地向导演提出建议，给他们改动一些情节，修润几句对话，我们就抓住这种机会，想尽办法在这个既定的故事里面加上一点'意识'的作料，使这部影片多多少少能有一点宣传教育的意义。这当然是不足为法的创作办法，但是我们至今还引以为慰的是，我们终于经过这种方法，转弯抹角、点点滴滴地在资本家经营的电影商品中间，加进了一些进步思想，而执拗地把电影引向到为政治服务的方向。"② 为时代服务，为民族解放服务，决定了左翼电影本身鲜明的政治性，这与当时内忧外患的时局及艰难的创作环境有很大关系。

但是，有一点需要明确的是，左翼电影虽然有着强烈的政治目的，但是其政治性却是隐蔽的。尽管共产党领导的左翼人士的最终目的是要推翻国民党，但是因为电影的发行放映还必须要受到国民政府的检查，因此左翼电影不能像共产党、左翼思想家的政治要求那样公开地要推翻国民政府，甚至他们工作的身份都不能暴露，他们常常以笔名的形式出现在剧本创作和影评里，引导并践行着左翼电影的创作和批评。因此，"左翼电影理论公开提出的口号是反对帝国主义和封建主义，有时也加上反对大资产阶级，而把要推翻国民党政权这个根本目的隐蔽和悬置起来。……由于其中很少涉及无产阶级领导地位、武装夺取政权等概念和理论，因此可以说是高度策略性的新民主主义的阶级论。"③ 这种策略把左翼的政治性巧妙地隐蔽起来，而隐蔽的政治性相对于共产党人对马克思主义暴力革命阶级斗争学说的直接引用而言具有更大的弹性，因而也使马克思主义更加中国化，在国民党检查机关之下，慢慢培育出反对其政党的强大的力量，这种培育不得不归功于左翼电影隐蔽的政治性。

---

① 程季华主编：《中国电影发展史》第 1 卷，北京：中国电影出版社，1998 年，第 396—397 页。
② 夏衍：《中国电影的历史与党的领导》，《中国电影》1957 年 11、12 月合刊号。
③ 胡克：《中国电影理论史评》，第 91 页。

阶级性：左翼电影阶级性的一个首要表现是：通过暴露社会问题，反映阶级（贫富）对立。左翼电影最基本的策略就是暴露社会问题，从阶级对立的角度引导民众观察社会现实，而这种暴露问题的策略是得到革命文艺工作者、左翼文学家的倡导的，他们在电影理论中提倡、鼓励暴露社会问题并在创作中付诸实践。如席耐芳（即郑伯奇）所说："赤裸裸地把现实的矛盾不合理，摆在观众面前，使他们深刻地感觉社会变革的必要，使他们迫切地寻找自己的出路。"① 于是日寇灭绝人性的暴行，农民的苦难无告，小市民的悲哀呻吟、工厂的怒吼、各种天灾人祸都成了暴露的对象，并且运用阶级分析的观点来引导观众发现这些社会问题产生的根本原因。

暴露问题是一个方面，把问题暴露给谁看又是一个方面。在对"把问题暴露给谁看"这个问题上，左翼电影人士仍然运用阶级分析的方法，而且是以经济形态来划分阶级性质，这一点与恰恰是中国式马克思主义的阶级分析方法在左翼电影中的表现，如席耐芳说："在中国现在的经济状况之下，小市民层是电影观众的中坚。……整个的旧社会在加速度地崩溃。帝国主义更加强了瓜分和侵略。就是惯好白日做梦的小市民也渐渐不得不对冷酷的现实凝视。这时候，我们正可以把赤裸裸的社会现实暴露出来给他看。再不用瞻前顾后拿甜美的幻梦去迎合他了。"② 暴露问题给小市民看，教育这些在阶级斗争中最摇摆不定的人，也是电影市场上最大的观众群，就最大限度地团结了一切可以团结的民众。

民族性：左翼电影最打动观众的是它的民族性。安德森认为，"民族总是被设想为一种深刻的、平等的同志的爱。最终，正是这种友爱关系在过去两个世纪中，驱使数以万计的人们甘愿为民族——这个有限的想象——去屠杀或从容赴死。"③ 左翼电影之所以会在武打神怪片之后异峰突起，最关键的原因还是在于它契合了当时社会的抗日文化心理，也就是说"全民抗战，共赴国难"的文化心理。究其原因，是因为日本的侵略激发出了人们的民族情感，左翼电影在民族存亡的生死关头率先以自己为武器为民族的生存开出一条血路，这一点不但赢得了广大观众的赞赏，而且连国民党当局即使在早期与日本没有宣战的时刻，也是默许的，否则，无论当时的电影怎样隐晦寓意，怎样把日本鬼子写成狼和匪，电影检查局如果真的反对，也是不会允许这些左翼电影面世的。但是

---

① 席耐芳：《电影罪言》，《明星》1933 年第 1 卷第 1 期。
② 同上。
③ [美]本尼迪克特·安德森：《想象的共同体：民族主义的起源与散布》，吴叡人译，上海：上海人民出版社，2005 年，第 7 页。

左翼电影以曲折隐晦的方式与观众见面，国民党检查局之所以放行，首先是对国民有一个交代，表明他们也是抗日爱国的；而对日本方面，因为当时中日还没有正式宣战，这种曲折隐晦也好委婉托辞。从这一点来看，抗日时局激发出了所有中国人的民族情感，正如徐迅所言，"从激发民族主义情绪的功用而言，中华民族符号系统里还没有超过抗日战争的"。① 而左翼电影正是在这种民族的情感里召唤出了人们为国捐躯的热忱，人们愿意为它抛头颅、洒热血。即使不能亲临战场，看着同胞们上战场也是非常快意的事。因此左翼电影大量抗日影片受到观众的普遍欢迎，也极大地发动了广大群众团结一致，坚决抗日的决心。

马克思主义强调的是人类的一般规律，是阶级斗争和剩余价值，并不强调民族主义，正如安德森所说，"马克思主义和自由主义都不怎么关心死亡和不朽。然而，民族主义的想象却如此关切死亡与不朽，这正暗示了它和宗教的想象之间有着密不可分的关系。"② 左翼电影里描摹各种各样的死亡，战场上士兵的死亡，乡亲避难时的死亡，时局艰辛贫病死亡，这些都强烈地激起了人们的民族情感，左翼电影正是有效地疏导并凝聚了人们的民族情感，以开拓电影市场开启了人们的心灵。

民主性：左翼电影的民主性表现在三个方面，一是在电影批评向国民政府和上海租界争取拍摄自由的呼吁上，一是在电影理论上呼吁电影的大众化，一是在电影的创作方面输入民主、平等、自由的观念。

左翼电影人常常为争取影片的创作、拍摄自由而不断斗争与发声。20世纪30年代的抗战影片因为当局奉行不抵抗政策，受到了种种审查与限制。阿英为此呼吁：认为"日本帝国主义上了银幕，便成了'狼国'，便成了'匪'，而不能直接指出是'日本帝国主义'；反对日本帝国主义的片子，反对其他帝国主义的片子，义勇军的片子，在租界上绝对不能公演；以及所有的片子只能在条件限制下的可能的暴露，不能涉及广大民众的出路，这样，中国的电影运动如何能开展呢？为着整个的电影文化运动的前途，必须坚强的和一切不合理的压迫抗斗，必须坚决的争取思想言论上的一切自由，特别是反对帝国主义的自由。"③ 尘无（王尘无）也公开指出："要中国电影业产生反帝反封建的影片，首先非用群众的力量争取摄制放映的绝对自由不可。"④ 一边同现实的不合理审

---

① 徐迅：《民族主义》，北京：中国社会科学出版社，1998年，第142页。
② ［美］本尼迪克特·安德森：《想象的共同体：民族主义的起源与散布》，第9页。
③ 凤吾：《论中国电影文化运动》，《明星》1933年第1卷第1期。
④ 尘无：《中国电影之路》，《明星》1933年第1卷第1—2期。

查作斗争，一边运用影片进行反帝反封的爱国宣传，这在左翼电影界达成了共识，也是左翼人士奋斗的目标。

左翼时期无论是电影理论家还是电影批评家甚至电影创作人员本身都非常注意的一个问题就是电影大众化的问题。电影的大众化，是民主思想的一个结果，也是民主思想传播的一条根本途径。尘无认为，"要尽量的把电影大众化"，那么，"电影的内容，非尽量的引用大众的真生活和拿大众每天接触的人物做主角不可。至于形式上，也应该非常明快的展开，多动作，少对白，千万不要运用一切倒叙回忆等只有知识分子，或则看惯电影的人，才懂得的手法。就是暗示，也应该拿大家们每人看得懂为限。象征的手法，是不必要的，只有如此，反帝反封的影片，才能够为大众爱好了解。"① 郑正秋也指出："电影是大众的，不是一个公司或少数人所得而私的。"② 大众化的导向一直影响到国防电影的拍摄。如史东山在拍摄《保卫我们的土地》时的基本理念是，"剧情要简单而有力，内心表现不能太复杂"，"叙述剧情务须周详，表演的速度，Tempo 勿须稍慢。"③ 其目的就是要为广大民众服务，要让民众看得懂。左翼电影大众化的观念上承 20 世纪 20 年代电影理论电影平民化的观念，下启国防电影大众化的理念，影响深远。

电影民主化的诉求最直接的就是在电影创作方面输入民主、平等、自由的观念。优秀的左翼电影常常从个体命运出发，引发观众对自身命运的思考。如《青年进行曲》里，资产阶级阔少王伯麟和工人阶级出身的金弟之间的爱情，与其说是打破阶级性，追求进步使然，不如说是对爱情采取一种民主的立场，每个人有选择自己爱情的权利，哪怕是一个工人，爱上一个资产阶级阔少，那也不是她的错，爱情是自由的，是民主的。"爱上了一个人，就没有了法子。"这是金弟对爱情既幸福又痛苦的感言。在王伯麟这一边，尽管王伯麟之父百般阻挠，他对金弟的爱情依然不变。这是影片传达给观众的理念，爱情自由，爱情民主，王父不应该剥夺金弟爱情的权利。

左翼电影在对马克思主义思想的吸收和利用时，不是照搬马克思主义理论，不是如当时很多激进分子那样把马克思主义教条化和本本化，而是有机地结合了中国的实际，实现了马克思主义的中国化。正如胡克所说："左翼电影理论家把马克思主义与民主主义、民族主义融合，表面看起来没有坚持纯粹的马克思

---

① 尘无：《中国电影之路》，《明星》1933 年第 1 卷第 1—2 期。
② 郑正秋：《如何走上前进之路》，《明星月报》，1933 年第 1 卷第 1 期。
③ 史东山：《关于〈保卫我们的土地〉》，《抗战电影》，1938 年第 1 期。

主义和苏联的社会主义观念，但是却更符合当时中国社会实际。他们把马克思主义作为信仰和指导思想，而不是行动路线，在创作和理论批评实践中，以突出民族主义和民主主义的思想为主线。"① 左翼电影正是在实践中智慧地进行了马克思主义中国化的处理，只可惜，这些处理，没有引起人们足够的重视。但任何事情的发展都不是一蹴而就的，左翼电影在其发展过程中，也不是完美无瑕，它自身也不可能跳出历史文化的局限。

四、左翼电影马克思主义中国化所存在的问题

左翼电影最突出的特点就是政治性和阶级性，它所重视与创造的，究其实，是政治话语，而非艺术话语。因此，可以说，政治性和阶级性是左翼电影的特点，也是它的问题所在。左翼电影思潮直接受影响于当时的左翼文学，左翼文学与马克思主义文艺思想相结合，迅速形成中国式的马克思主义文艺理论，在中国模式的马克思主义文学艺术里，文艺的功能是："文学艺术是作为一种为社会变迁、社会变革服务的上层建筑的力量而非作为社会对立面的批评性力量而存在"，② 因此这就不可避免地会带来一些问题。电影同样也不例外，这种强烈的政治性和阶级性必然带来创作和影评上的一系列问题。

（一）阶级问题、政治问题道德化

左翼电影被人诟病为幼稚的一个问题就是阶级问题、政治问题道德化。阶级出身决定一个人的道德品质，阶级出身决定人物的革命性与先进性，以出身定先进，以出身定好坏。正面人物一般都是出身无产阶级（工人阶级），反面人物一定是地主阶级、资产阶级或知识分子，中间人物也是资产阶级阔少或小姐或软弱的知识分子，他们会经过党的教育而弃暗投明。如《壮志凌云》里顺儿和黑妞都是出身贫苦阶级，其阶级身份无可挑剔，它就像一道护身符一样给人物罩上了一层光辉的标签：顺儿自发地拥有斗争性、坚定性和政治正确性，天生拥有领导能力，而且长相俊美（也是天生的），是女人心中的白马王子，最可喜的是他情感纯洁，从不玩弄女人的情感。而黑妞更是貌美如花、淳朴端庄、勤劳勇敢。一个阶级出身便决定了一切的美好，仿佛与生俱来就是如此。这便使人物掉进阶级决定论的窠臼，人物可爱是可爱了，但却失之简单，这也

---

① 胡克：《中国电影理论史评》，第132页。
② 王杰主编：《马克思主义文艺理论》，北京：高等教育出版社，2011年，第237页。

是左翼电影耐不住咀嚼的原因之一。

这种阶级决定论模式一直延续到建国十七年乃至文革时期,这是一种异化了的马克思主义美学。马克思主义文艺批评的美学原则是"美学的和历史的观点"。"美学的和历史的观点"最早是恩格斯在19世纪40年代针对当时激进的小资产阶级评论家、"真正的社会主义"诗人和小说家卡尔□□格律恩等人评价歌德的错误倾向时提出来的。恩格斯在明确指出:"我们决不是从道德的、党派的观点来责备歌德,而只是从美学的和历史的观点来责备他;我们并不是用道德的、政治的、或'人的'尺度来衡量他"① 从"美学的历史的观点"来评价文学是马克思主义文艺批评的标准,也是马克思主义哲学观"历史唯物主义和辩证唯物主义"在文学观上的体现,但是左翼电影乃至整个左翼文学都是以阶级定出身:贫穷阶级的人,一定是善良、勤劳、正义、勇敢,而地主阶级和资产阶级的人,则懒惰、骄横、贪婪、无耻、奸诈、阴险。在这一点上,可以说左翼电影和当时的左翼思潮一致,曲解甚至违背了了马克思主义思想的本义,与马克思主义真正的美学观点渐行渐远。

(二) 阶级出身决定爱情的选择对象

"革命+爱情"是左翼文学的一个法宝,也是左翼电影的一条定律。在这种模式中,爱情的选择一定是革命生涯在现实生活中的投射,赢得爱情,便是赢得了人生,赢得了一切,包括革命。《青年进行曲》里资产阶级阔少王伯麟和两个女人之间的爱情,一个是工人阶级出身的金弟,一个是资产阶级出身的梁小姐,虽然梁小姐漂亮、时尚、有品味,而且温柔贤惠(至少在王伯麟面前如此),是王梁两家势力联盟的最好姻缘,王伯麟虽然不讨厌梁小姐,但他的爱情只给了金弟。他的朋友兼革命导师沈元中被敌伪暗杀,临终前对他说:"我希望你能够常常跟她接近,当然更希望你能够爱她,能够像她一样的感觉,也像她一样的想,我相信最后你不会叫我们失望的。"这句话成了时时提醒王伯麟的座右铭。这种嘱托仿佛是在建议他对爱情的选择,实际却是敦促他坚强地走革命的道路。这里有一种等价转换关系:选择女工金弟=选择革命=选择进步;选择资产阶级梁小姐=选择不革命=选择倒退。因此,影片没有一点显示过王伯麟有所犹豫,他一直处于对金弟的热恋之中。倒是金弟的情感表现的非常丰满,在表现她的思念、悲痛上她几乎与林黛玉没有什么不同,最后也是吐血而死,这个无产阶级女工倒是有点像资产阶级小姐了。其实,这里与阶级无关,

---

① 《马克思恩格斯全集》第4卷,北京:人民出版社,1972年,第257页。

是少女青春最真实的情感，它不只隶属于哪一个阶级。类似的例子如《野玫瑰》中画家江波对贫家女小凤的爱怜、《风云儿女》诗人辛白华舍弃贵妇而追求贫女阿凤、《小玩意》大学生袁璞对小手艺人叶大嫂的爱怜等都是一样为了寻求真理而寻求爱情。左翼电影和左翼文学一样，"革命＋爱情"的公式是演绎在阶级符号里同一件事情的两面。

其实爱情的复杂性远远大于阶级的单纯性。这种以阶级来决定爱情观念与封建的门第婚姻观念虽然是一个大大的进步，但是毕竟流于表面而难以令人信服。而且，人物形象因此显得扁平，失去了丰富性和复杂性。

（三）影评也以阶级观点进行权威式批评

凡是以阶级观点斗争形式出现的影片，即使形式粗糙，也会受到赞扬；凡是不符合阶级观点的影片都会遭到群起攻之的命运。但随着时间的流逝，我们发现在狭隘的阶级观点之下遭受批评的影片，今天恰恰是我们认为具有魅力与经典性的作品。如曾经遭受猛烈批评的《浪涛沙》，今天已经获得正名："《浪涛沙》的超越性价值取向和横向批判立场，既是编导吴永刚个人的'哲理观念'，也是以罗明佑为代表的、相当大一部分中国知识分子，对国内政治军事格局所发出警醒呼吁，更是'联华'一向激进、独立的左翼传统，和建立在电影市场基础上价值观念和艺术立场的体现。"[①] 这种批评价值观的转变，可以说是历史的产物，也是历史的必然。

左翼电影在马克思主义中国化的具体实践中进行了大胆的尝试，也做出了巨大的贡献，但是，因为历史的局限也存在着对马克思主义思想曲解甚至误读的地方。对其错误的历史教训，应该引以为戒，对其优秀的历史经验，则应继续发扬。

（本文责任编辑：任天）

[①] 袁庆丰：《黑白胶片的文化时态》，上海：上海三联书店，2009年，第334页。

Left-wing Film and Sinicization of Marxism

Shao Yulian

(School of Humanities, Shanghai Jiao Tong University)

Abstract: In the early 20th century, the class fight theory is one of the most popular theory in Marxist principles for Chinese intellectuals. Left-wing film affected by left-wing literature in the use of Marxist theory of class fight, gradually gets rid of the leftist folk, the polarizing tendency, not absolutely by class struggle, but combining the class fight with human nature, moral, humanitarian and other issues, greatly shows the complexity and the complexity of class fight and human nature. Moreover, left-wing film processed the class antagonism into a confrontation between the rich and the poor. This adaptation is words change on the surface, but actually to get rid of the predicament discourse of Marxist class theory. It has perfectly combined the marxist class fight theory and China's rural customs and the reality, which has realized the change of the sinicization of Marxism. In the historical process of sinicization of Marxism, the left-wing film made great contributions to Marxist sinicization, also produced many problems.

论特里·伊格尔顿美学批评的伦理学维度

贾 洁[*]

(上海交通大学人文学院)

【内容摘要】 对于如何实现共产主义社会下的伦理准则,伊格尔顿结合其美学批评所作出的思考大致可以归结为以下四个方面。首先,他认为马克思主义者应对社会抱持一种悲剧人文主义的关怀。其次,他明确主张"政治之爱",寻找超越资本主义社会的希望之源。再次,他指出马克思主义者无须拒绝"罪恶"这一概念,因为它有可能推动人类社会制度的进步。最后,伊格尔顿批判了康德一脉的伦理观,着力建构一种唯物主义的伦理学。

每个人的自由发展是一切人的自由发展的条件,这是马克思和恩格斯所设想的共产主义社会下的伦理准则。这一伦理目标在现实中如何得以实现呢?研究思考英国著名马克思主义美学批评家特里·伊格尔顿的著作,特别是其近五年来的新著,可以发掘他对该问题的独到见解。伊格尔顿对伦理问题的关注由来已久,在其出版于1990年的《美学意识形态》中,虽然他认为美学在这个时代替代了伦理学和政治学的话语功能,但另一方面他在该书中又对爱与恶等伦理问题十分重视。在出版于1997年的《马克思与自由》这本小书中,他则根据美学来描述马克思的伦理学。近些年,他出版了《人生的意义》、《陌生人的麻烦》、《理性、信仰与革命》、《论罪恶》、《马克思为什么是对的》等书,开始系统性地阐述其马克思主义的伦理学思想,当然,他的伦理观与其美学思想之

---

[*] 贾洁,女,江苏如东人,1981年10月生,南京大学文学博士,美国杜克大学访问学者,上海交通大学人文学院博士后与助教。主要从事西方马克思主义美学研究。本文系第53批中国博士后科学基金资助项目(2103BSH53W03)阶段性成果。

间仍然存在着密切的联系，本文即从以下四个方面予以阐述。

一、悲剧人文主义者的关怀

马克思主义理论不仅仅是对世界的评论，也是一个可以用来改变世界的工具。伊格尔顿认为，要实现共产主义只会遭遇更多的问题和争论，但人类没有理由不为着这个目标奋斗，因为没有人能找出比共产主义社会更有益、更有价值的生活方式。这样一来，大众的文化解放就显得尤为重要："就这个意义而言，理性、知识和自由之间存在着密切关系。某些知识对于人类的自由和幸福是至关重要的。当人们按照这些知识行事时，他们就会更深入地掌握它，进而更有效地依据知识展开行动。"①

那些矢志不渝地投身于大众文化解放事业②的马克思主义知识分子，在伊格尔顿看来，是出于对当代社会的一种悲剧人文主义者（tragic humanist）的关怀。何谓悲剧人文主义？伊格尔顿阐释如下：

> 从悲剧观的角度来说，救赎只在迫于我们自己遭遇必死的命运时才产生。这就是我一直提的悲剧人文主义，而不是自由人文主义。自由人文主义不理解一个道理，用叶芝的话讲就是，任何东西不开裂，单独或整体都算不上。对自由人文主义而言，我们身在何处与我们前往何处之间有本质上的连续性。对悲剧人文主义而言，这两者之间存在着巨大的断裂，而新奇的事物便从裂缝中生成了。在政治生活中，这就是革命。基督教有专门的术语形容这个断裂，即皈依（conversion）。在某些思想家看来，悲剧和乌托邦是对立的。在我看来，它们总是互相牵涉。③

伊格尔顿在《理性、信仰与革命》中通过分析托马斯·曼的小说《魔山》详细论证了这个问题。自由人文主义者塞特姆布里尼体现着资产阶级的现代精神，他赞美生命，但实际上处在死亡门口，他的世界主义是狭隘的欧洲中心主

---

① ［英］特里·伊格尔顿：《马克思为什么是对的》，李杨等译，北京：新星出版社，2011年，第146页。
② 详见本人的另一篇文章《批评家的任务——论特里·伊格尔顿》，《文艺理论与批评》2012年第2期。
③ Terry Eagleton and Matthew Beaumont, *The Task of the Critic: Terry Eagleton in Dialogue*, London: Verso, 2009, p. 279.

义,作为小说背景的第一次世界大战意味着他心中19世纪自由人文主义理想的破灭。而小说的主人公汉斯·卡斯托普逐渐认识到一种生中之死(death-in-life),这涉及确认人的卑微、认识到人的脆弱性和必死性。"这种悲剧人文主义拥抱死亡的破坏性……人必须尊重美、理想主义、渴望进步,同时以马克思主义或尼采式的方式承认在它们的根源存在着许多鲜血和苦难。"①

资本主义在文化、政治、经济方面耍出的伎俩,目的只有一个,就是要让人们相信资本主义的制度可以延续到无限之久远。尽管如此,许多以大唱反调的面目示人的激进思想家,如希钦斯和道金斯等人,也都难以摆脱这种思想的制约。无神论者希钦斯和道金斯出版了多本反宗教的书籍《上帝的错觉》、《上帝不伟大:宗教如何毒害了一切》,等等,将宗教定位为"万恶之源"。他们欢呼人性万岁,以为简单地丢弃掉许多压制性的障碍——传统、宗教、迷信,等等,我们就可以开足马力顺利实现社会主义和人类的解放。伊格尔顿毫不客气地批评道:"希钦斯、道金斯和像我这样的人的区别最终在于自由人文主义和悲剧人文主义的差别。他们觉得如果我们能消除神话和迷信等有毒遗产,我们就能获得自由。在我看来这样的愿望本身就是一个神话,虽然是精神可嘉的神话。悲剧人文主义和自由人文主义一样期望人类的自由繁荣,但是认为只有通过直面人性最糟糕的部分,才有可能实现这个目标。对人性最终值得拥有的惟一的确认,是要像对宗教改革幻灭的弥尔顿那样认真地质疑人性最开始到底值不值得拯救,理解斯威夫特笔下巨人国国王所言的人类是可憎的害虫。"② 一个人只有直面最坏的方面,才有能力瞥见更美好的方面。当马克思借由人性的彻底改进来谈论人性的彻底泯灭时,他是一位悲剧人文主义者,没有人能如此深刻地体会到人类的不幸,如果不对人类怀有同样深厚的期望的话。换句话说就是,悲剧人文主义者能够把难以抗拒的悲剧性的影响转变为一种正向的伦理。

在《陌生人的麻烦》中,伊格尔顿把社会主义描述成一项"悲剧性的工程"。社会主义的变革不是不可能达成,但一定是悲剧性的过程。伊格尔顿指出,威廉斯《现代悲剧》中论悲剧与革命的一章,从人性的角度最为精要地证明了进行社会主义的变革确实是一项悲剧性的工程。如威廉斯所言,马克思主义产生于怜悯和恐惧,摆在它面前的状况是社会中的一部分人泯灭了人性,真实的人的现实苦难随即而来:堕落、残忍、恐惧、嫉妒和仇恨。既然马克思主

---

① Terry Eagleton and Matthew Beaumont, *The Task of the Critic: Terry Eagleton in Dialogue*, London: Verso, 2009, pp. 163—164.
② Ibid., pp. 168—169.

义"这一理论的起源是悲剧性的,那么,它的行动同样是悲剧性的"。① 这种悲剧性行动的名称就是革命。"悲剧人文主义者不管是社会主义者、基督徒,还是心理分析师都相信只有通过自我放逐的过程和激进的重新制造,才能重生。"② 在此值得一提的是,伊格尔顿坚信,马克思的支持者中不乏宗教教徒,并且用马克思主义的观点判断,他们都是货真价实的唯物主义者③。这显然受益于阿冈本、巴丢、齐泽克等人的研究理论。

二、主张"政治之爱"

神学家汉斯·昆认为,对人的生命意义的提问是最高层次上的政治事件④,伊格尔顿所著《人生的意义》一书即是从伦理意义上拓展了马克思主义的政治概念。美国学者厄内斯特·德姆西在评论该书时说,该书给予人们的最宝贵的建议是:要使自己的人生有意义,你就必须把积极的价值当作目的本身。实践美好价值观是终极目的,没有任何意义能超越它。⑤ 那么,对马克思主义者来说,美好的价值观是什么呢?在《陌生人的麻烦》中,伊格尔顿明确主张"政治之爱"⑥:"爱,有的人认为它主要指性欲、爱情、性行为或暧昧关系,一旦我们将这个重大的概念援救出此类狭隘与贫瘠的理解,便可发现它是一种互惠关系,各方互为对方自我实现的依据。政治上的这种爱的相互关系可以按照《共产党宣言》中我先前也引用的那句话来理解,每个人的自由发展是一切人的自由发展的条件。"⑦ 自由主义者和保守主义者倾向于把爱看作是私人的事情,与政治无碍,在伊格尔顿看来,这个观点是现代性的一个灾难性的失利。

伊格尔顿提出"政治之爱"与其天主教神学思想脱不了干系。基督教文化的核心概念就是"爱",从整体上倡扬不分等级尊卑的博爱精神。不过,伊格

---

① [英]雷蒙·威廉斯:《现代悲剧》,丁尔苏译,南京:译林出版社,2007年,第69页。
② Terry Eagleton, *Reason, Faith, and Revolution: Reflections on the God Debate*, New Haven: Yale University Press, 2009, p.169.
③ [英]特里·伊格尔顿:《马克思为什么是对的》,李杨等译,北京:新星出版社,2011年,第159页。
④ 汉斯·昆:《艺术与意义问题》,徐菲译,载《神学与当代文艺思想》,上海:上海三联书店,1995年,第15—16页。
⑤ Ernest Dempsey, "Review: The Meaning of Life", in *Philosophy Now*, Vol. 78, 2010, p.39.
⑥ Terry Eagleton, *Trouble with Strangers: A Study of Ethics*, Oxford: Blackwell, 2008, p.59.
⑦ Terry Eagleton and Matthew Beaumont, *The Task of the Critic: Terry Eagleton in Dialogue*, London: Verso, 2009, pp.302—302.

尔顿却对这种博爱思想进行了批判,"西方哲学传统中的一大堆麻烦是在面对'爱'时引起的,它们总把爱看作是盈余无疆的圣爱或普遍的仁慈。"① 比如拉康的"无限之爱"(limitless love)的观念,恐怕只有耶稣才能做到。伊格尔顿特别强调"政治之爱"是一种互惠性的、交相利的爱。并在多处指出,人一旦意识到自身的局限——必死性,也就意识到了我们与其他人互相依赖、互相束缚的生存方式。"要是我们真的把死亡放在心上,几乎可以肯定我们现在的品行会更高尚。要是我们始终时刻面临死亡,我们想必会更容易宽恕敌人,修复关系"②,"如果别人也和我们采取同样的做法的话,结果将形成互惠互利的局面,为每一个人的充分发展提供环境。这种互惠互利的传统名称叫做'爱'。"③ 倘若有朝一日,政治之爱成为大众社会的普遍状况,共产主义社会便真正到来了。伊格尔顿的革命主张至此彰明较著,虽然他不完全排斥暴力革命,但更期望通过伦理道德意识与政治发生关系,从而转变政权结构和社会结构。当然,这成功与否,与大众文化解放事业息息相关。

其次,伊格尔顿提出"政治之爱"也是受到了精神分析学的影响。二战后,法兰克福学派的代表人物马尔库塞致力于把弗洛伊德的精神分析理论与马克思的学说结合起来。《爱欲与文明》是其努力的一大成果,但他仅从心理学分析的角度去窥视人类社会、分析人与自然的危机,不可避免地将人与自然的统一纳入到性欲的扩展和爱欲的解放中。这种解决人类危机的途径,并没有什么可取之处。正如齐泽克在分析巴丢时所言,"精神分析一直被限定在知识领域之内,不能达到真理过程的真正实证性维度。以爱为例,精神分析把它还原成性欲的升华表达。以科学和艺术为例,精神分析只能谈论科学发现或艺术工作的主观的力比多条件——譬如一位艺术家或一位科学家如何被其自身的俄狄浦斯情结或潜在的同性恋意识所驱使,等等。这些条件与这种工作的真理维度根本无关。以政治为例,精神分析只能构想一种集体状态以对抗《图腾与禁忌》或《摩西与一神教》背景下的原始罪过,因此精神分析不能想象一个激进的'革命性的'集体,它不被恋父恋母情结所约束,而是被爱的肯定力量所解放。"④ 这跟伊格尔顿之所见有相通之处。伊格尔顿研究伦理学的专著《陌生人的麻烦》大肆运用了拉康理论,那是因为他发现拉康对想象界、象征界和真实

---

① Terry Eagleton, *Trouble with Strangers: A Study of Ethics*, Oxford: Blackwell, 2008, p.59.
② [英]特里·伊格尔顿:《理论之后》,商正译,北京:商务印书馆,2009年,第202页。
③ [英]特里·伊格尔顿:《人生的意义》,朱新伟译,南京:译林出版社,2012年,第90页。
④ Slavoj Žižek, "Psychoanalysis in Post-Marxism: The Case of Alain Badiou", in *The South Atlantic Quarterly*, Spring, 1998, p.256.

界的思考，提供了一个特别有用的思考伦理的框架。

雅克·拉康采用结构主义的方法论对弗洛伊德的理论进行了重新解读，拉康本人声称，自己的目的是要"将从头至尾都浸润着文化意蕴的弗洛伊德思想从其坚守的生物学领域转移到文化领域"[1]。"对拉康来说，想象界就是我们进行认同的意象领域，但恰恰是这一行为导致我们误察和误认我们的自我。儿童在成长中会继续进行这种在想象中与客体的认同，他的自我就是这样逐步建立起来的。在拉康看来，自我只不过是一种自恋过程：藉此，我们通过发现世界中某一我们可以认同的客体，以支撑起一个虚构的统一的自我感。"[2] 拉康认为，每每有新的意象出现，我们都会试图重回其所称的"匮乏"之前的状态，也即真实界，我们设法从他者身上找到自我，但每一次努力都不可能成功。尤其在进入语言之后，真实界的完整性便一去不复返了，我们再也无法实现真实界中的那种纯粹的自我同一性和自我完满。

作为信仰共产主义的马克思主义者，伊格尔顿经研究开出了疗方——"政治之爱"。怎样才有可能做到这种政治之爱呢？因为，譬如不会有谁爱陌生人胜过爱自己的父母和孩子。伊格尔顿写道：

> 克瓦米·安东尼·阿皮亚提醒我们，"说我们要对陌生人尽义务，不是说像对待我们最亲近的人那样对待他们"，并不是简单地要我们像对待邻人那样对待陌生人，而是要我们把自己当作陌生人看待——承认人的存在是不可改变的累人的事实，最终是难以捉摸的，这是人类主体超越镜像的正确依据。黑格尔称之为精神（Geist），精神分析称之为真实界，犹太-基督教称之为上帝的爱。[3]

伊格尔顿是一位现实的马克思主义者，在他看来，完满的自我是不存在的，这就如同共产主义社会也不会完美无暇一样。共产主义要求给每个人自我实现的条件，但即便是在物质条件极大丰富的社会中，自我实现的程度也必须受到限制。这是每个人都必须认清的现实，惟其如此，才不会迷失于想象界。

---

[1] Jacques Lacan, *Four Fundamental Concepts in Psychoanalysis*, New York: Norton, 1989, p. 116.

[2] [英] 伊格尔顿：《二十世纪西方文学理论》，伍晓明译，西安：陕西师范大学出版社，1987年，第181页。

[3] Terry Eagleton, *Trouble with Strangers: A Study of Ethics*, Oxford: Blackwell, 2008, pp. 59—60.

三、论"罪恶"

在马克思看来,共产主义意味着物质匮乏的消除,以及大多数压迫性劳动的终结。但是必须认清楚一点,人类不会在物质极大丰富的世界中一下子变成纯洁的天使。对于作为传统哲学范畴的人性之恶,中西方多位哲学家都有阐述。伊格尔顿在论述悲剧为何能带来快感时说:"这个问题的一个答案也许可以是,因为我们都是施虐的浑蛋。根据大卫·休谟,我们难过地目睹了他人的不幸,同时他们也让我们感到高兴,主要因为他们使我们感受到一种优越感。悲剧就像崇高,允许我们沉浸在引发共鸣的死亡本能的愉悦中,并欣慰地得知自己不会真正受到伤害。"[1] 悲剧满足我们的正义感以及对现存秩序的愤怒,但它同时也迎合了我们的施虐倾向、死亡本能或受虐倾向。我们想看别人受难,这样,通过伴随他们一起受难,我们可以尽情享受受虐,但维持这种受虐意味着要让他们继续受难,这是一种施虐行为。可见,人的骨子里就存有邪恶的意识,但这尚不能算是罪恶之事。

在《论罪恶》中,伊格尔顿认为,"罪恶完完全全是关于死亡的——作恶者的死亡与受害者的死亡"。[2] 当然,这里的"死亡"不能被简单地理解成剥夺个体的生命。伊格尔顿常在其书中提到"恶魔般的"(demonic)一词,此词的使用实际上区分了两种罪恶:"这个词指的是一种状态,即人们被困于生与死之间,在现实中死不了,从摧毁他人或摧毁自己的、让人想到死亡的快感中获取某种可怕的伪存在感。只有凭借这种罪恶的破坏,他们才能够说服自己,自己还活着。跟恶魔对立的状态是死中之生(life–in–death),在该状态下,通过一种舍己为人的死亡,能获得真实的存在感。这就是为什么圣人和罪人在单纯的人看来往往很相似的原因。……恶魔是那些受制于死亡本能的人,病态地附着于极度快感(jouissance),以致把自己推入了错位的生存状态。"[3] 亚里士多德曾言,"自制的特点是能靠理性来抑制朝向低级的感官快乐的冲动欲望,能控

---

[1] Terry Eagleton and Matthew Beaumont, *The Task of the Critic: Terry Eagleton in Dialogue*, London: Verso, 2009, pp. 279—280.

[2] Terry Eagleton, *On Evil*, New Haven: Yale University Press, 2010, p. 18.

[3] Terry Eagleton and Matthew Beaumont, *The Task of the Critic: Terry Eagleton in Dialogue*, London: Verso, 2009, pp. 285—286.

制和忍受基于自然的需求和痛苦。"① 伊格尔顿形容的这种恶魔在犯罪时是完全无法自制的,这类病理上的罪恶暂不列入本文的讨论范围,本文要讨论的是非病理性的罪恶。

通俗地说,罪恶包括剥削、压迫、奸淫、战争、屠杀等。"罪恶"具有推动历史发展的作用的观点古已有之,近代以来的西方历史哲学对罪恶在历史上的作用有不少深刻的思想。从维柯、康德到黑格尔、马克思和恩格斯,均有阐述。譬如,马克思在1853年写了《不列颠在印度的统治》和《不列颠在印度统治的未来结果》两篇文章,在这两篇文章中,他认为西方殖民主义者虽然在东方犯下滔天罪行,但另一方面又推动了落后的东方社会的进步,非常鲜明地体现了马克思关于罪恶在历史发展中可以起积极作用的思想。为此,伊格尔顿明确指出,"马克思主义者无须拒绝'罪恶'的概念"②。在《论罪恶》中,他这样评述恐怖主义:"恐怖主义现在已经有了它自己的致命的动力。要注意,悔恨失去的和解机会与将对手当作是无理性的可被动摇的乌合之众来对待是两码事。对于后一种观点的拥护者来说,解决恐怖主义暴力的唯一方法是更多的暴力。"③ 在这段话中,伊格尔顿一并批评了近年来在西方发达资本主义国家愈演愈烈的反恐战争,美、英、法等国采取的以暴制暴的行动、肆意践踏其他主权国的行为上演的正是动物界弱肉强食的生存法则。

人性的完美不是一件指日可待的事情,"人从本性上来说就是政治的动物——这不仅因为我们是群居动物,更因为我们需要某种机制来管理我们的物质生活。……需要一种政治制度来控制剥削和不平等带来的冲突。"④ 伊格尔顿的意思是,恐怖主义连同反恐战争犯下的罪恶是时候让人类审视自己的社会制度了,由此,"罪恶"有可能推动人类社会制度再上一个台阶:

> 如果战争、饥荒、屠杀都源自人性的堕落,那我们就根本没有理由相信我们会有更加美好的未来。但如果这些都在某些程度上是不公正的社会制度造成的结果,而人类最多不过是这个制度的棋子,那么我们就有理由

---

① 亚里士多德:《论善与恶》,徐开来译,载《亚里士多德全集》第8卷,苗力田主编,北京:中国人民大学出版社,1992年,第461页。
② Terry Eagleton, *On Evil*, New Haven: Yale University Press, 2010, p. 14.
③ Ibid., pp. 158—159.
④ [英]特里·伊格尔顿:《马克思为什么是对的》,李杨等译,北京:新星出版社,2011年,第86页。

相信，改变这个制度就能带来一个更好的世界。①

人们按照自己的欲望采取各自的行动是一回事，而他们身在的社会秩序则是另一回事。制度的变革会对人们的态度产生重要的影响。虽然制度的一个重要特征是它们天生就带有保守性，人类历史上几乎每一次开明的改革在实施之初都受到强烈的抵制，但一旦做到了，就可以改变人们看待事物的方式。如果说在社会主义条件下，每个人都能最大限度地参与社会生活，那么人与人之间的冲突和争论显然只会增加，不会减少。共产主义不能消灭争端，只有真正的历史终结才可以。共产主义制度下也有敌对性的伤害，但不会像在资本主义社会下那样产生大规模的屠杀。"这并不是因为有了更高尚的人类美德，而是因为体制发生了变化。"② 在伊格尔顿看来，共产主义是某一套制度的设立，从而使我们最大限度地接近一种几乎不可能发生的状态——每个人的自由发展是一切人的自由发展的条件。

四、构建一种唯物主义的伦理学

当今政府把它的长手伸到经济领域，它也扩展到社会—文化系统，为的是保护政府继续统治下去的价值和已被习惯的团体理性。政府能力在社会事务中膨胀，用哈贝马斯的话来说，公共生活"重新封建化"③ 了。资本主义的伦理——将私人之间的相互帮助建立在利益的基础之上，不仅无益于现状的改善，反而起到了推波助澜的作用。20世纪90年代中期，德里达出版了《友爱的政治学》一书。他试图在国家、民族、地域性等界限约束之外重新理解政治，阐明政治的非政治维度。在书中，德里达着重解构了施米特的"敌友之分的政治概念"，呼唤一种承认无限的异质性、尊重无限的差异、承担无限的责任的"到来的民主"。

按照伊格尔顿的看法，德里达复兴的是康德一脉的伦理思想，这一脉可以用糟糕透顶来形容，因为"它是相当反政治的，它主要根据职责、义务、责任等来理解伦理"④，有以伦理取代政治的倾向。除了德里达，像巴丢、拉康、齐泽克等这些先锋的哲学家也都属于这一路。伊格尔顿想指出的是，"由于康德一

---

① ［英］特里·伊格尔顿：《马克思为什么是对的》，李杨等译，北京：新星出版社，2011年，第102页。
② 同上，第93页。
③ ［德］哈贝马斯：《公共领域的结构转型》，曹卫东等译，上海：学林出版社，1999年，第230页。
④ Terry Eagleton and Matthew Beaumont, *The Task of the Critic: Terry Eagleton in Dialogue*, London: Verso, 2009, p. 299.

脉危害极大的世系,另一脉从亚里士多德和阿奎那到黑格尔、马克思和尼采的世系举步维艰,在这一脉人看来,伦理是关于生活的丰富性、多彩多样的自我实现、权力、乐趣、能力的财富等等的"。① 伊格尔顿认为,与犹太教传统相一致,马克思是一位不屈不挠的道德思想家。虽然马克思经常谴责道德规范。然而,他所谴责的是那种忽略物质因素,赞成道德因素的历史探究。"严格地讲,马克思谴责的不是道德,而是道德主义。道德主义把某种被称为'道德价值'的事物从整个历史语境中剥离,将其抽象化,并由此得出一种绝对的道德判断。与之相反,真正的道德探究则会调查人类处境的所有方面。它拒绝把人的价值观、行为、关系和性格特征跟塑造它们的社会及历史力量割裂开来。因此,它能将道德判断与科学分析相结合,从而避免了道德主义的错误。真正的道德判断需要尽可能缜密地审视所有的相关因素。"②

关于道德主义,仍可以举个德里达的例子。德里达曾主张宽恕那些不可宽恕的事情。当你宽恕不可能获得宽恕的事情时,你必须做出一个绝对"不可能的"宽恕的姿态。"无条件的宽恕似乎是件不可能的事,因为宽恕那些不容饶恕的行为是一种不可能的宽恕。但宽恕尽力把不可能变成可能,去宽恕那些不容宽恕的行为。因此,宽恕那些不容宽恕的行为是人类理智的升华,或至少是将理智的原则具体化,这是一种人类心胸宽广的标志。宽恕就意味着自我超越。"③ 这种宽恕的品德正是一种超历史的、普遍的、永恒的道德主义。在德里达眼中,当代政治、宗教和文化舞台上频繁上演的所谓宽恕这一剧情,滥用了悔过和宽恕,那种与交易中的算计相联系的宽恕,仅是以居高临下的权力剥夺了牺牲者说话的权力。为此,德里达力求提供一个具有批判尺度的宽恕概念,但这个尺度无疑带有一种纯粹的、乌托邦式的超越性。伊格尔顿指出,"伦理和政治的关系不依照爱与管理、无限与有限、近与远、熟人与陌生人、或者对称与不对称的对比而定,这二者之间的关系不像精神之于物质、内部之于外部、个人之于社会、或单一之于普遍。对他者的责任,请列维纳斯和德里达原谅,不是绝对和无限,而必须通过公正、审慎和现实主义来调和。这不是说伦理处理与邻人的关系,政治处理与陌生人的关系。伦理不是简单的对他者的坦诚,

---

① Terry Eagleton and Matthew Beaumont, *The Task of the Critic: Terry Eagleton in Dialogue*, London: Verso, 2009, p.299.
② [英]特里·伊格尔顿:《马克思为什么是对的》,李杨等译,北京:新星出版社,2011年,第161页。
③ [法]雅克·德里达、伊丽莎白·卢迪内斯库:《明天会怎样——雅克·德里达与伊丽莎白·卢迪内斯库对话录》,苏旭译,北京:中信出版社,2003年,第212页。

而是规划对广告业或杀婴犯的政策的问题,因为被他们侵害的对象都不懂自己被侵害了。"① 伦理道德并非意味着某种绝对律令或守则,而是如何以最自由、最完整、最能实现自我的方式去生活的问题。对于马克思主义者来说,道德的终极内涵在于如何享受自我。但终究没有人能够孤立地生活,道德也因此不可避免地要涉及政治。这就是一种唯物主义的伦理学。

依伊格尔顿之见:

> 伦理和政治既不能被分开,也不能被混为一谈。伦理处理的是诸如人的价值、目标、关系、操行素质、行为动机之类的问题,而政治提出的问题是,为了确保养成特定的价值观和素质,我们需要什么样的物质条件、权力关系和社会机构。②

这正是伊格尔顿意义上的唯物主义伦理学与一般伦理学的不同。一般认为,伦理学是形而上的道德哲学,与政治无关。然而一旦过于抬高伦理学的重要性,就很可能像德里达那样犯下用伦理取代政治的错误。在《美学意识形态》一书中,伊格尔顿以"爱情"阐释了唯物主义伦理学的意义。爱人与被爱是人身体里的欲望,爱情则是一种互惠性的自我实现,就许多人的一生而言,无疑在"爱情"这种生活方式上表达了最高的人类价值。"唯物主义伦理学坚持认为,当我们达到这种最高价值的时候,我们正表现出我们本质中最好的可能性"③,然而我们的政治却没有看到从整个社会生活中扩大这种价值的需要、方法和可能性。这或许就是伊格尔顿明确主张"政治之爱"的原因所在。而对马克思主义知识分子而言,一种唯物主义的伦理学,在笔者看来,具体可表现为投身于大众的文化解放事业,这是马克思主义知识分子的一种自我实现。

综上,伊格尔顿结合美学理论对伦理学问题作出的思考是对马克思主义伦理学的必要补充和发展,是对马克思和恩格斯所设想的共产主义社会下的伦理准则"每个人的自由发展是一切人的自由发展的条件"的进一步阐发和论证。

(本文责任编辑:任天)

---

① Terry Eagleton, *Trouble with Strangers: A Study of Ethics*, Oxford: Blackwell, 2008, p. 324.
② Terry Eagleton and Matthew Beaumont, *The Task of the Critic: Terry Eagleton in Dialogue*, London: Verso, 2009, pp. 299—300.
③ [英]特里·伊格尔顿:《审美意识形态》,王杰等译,桂林:广西师范大学出版社,1997年,第410页。

On Ethics of Terry Eagleton's Aesthetic Criticism

Jia Jie

Abstract: This paper puts forward aesthetician Terry Eagleton's correlative solutions as to how to implement the ethical principle of Communist society. First of all, he pointed out that the Marxists should take a kind of tragic humanist care to the society. Secondly, he proposed a necessary moral quality — "political love", which can be the challenge to capitalism. Thirdly, he suggested that the Marxists do not have to refuse the idea of "evil", because it may advance social system for humanity. Finally, he criticized the ethics that descends from Kant, and consolidated and extended his commitment to constructing a materialist ethics.

什么样的生产主义

高建平*

(中国社会科学院文学研究所)

【内容摘要】现代文明的一个重要标志,就是时间观念的变化,能按时上下班,把工作与休息时间区分开。消费社会来临,带来日常生活审美化,推动了一种艺术走向生活的倾向,包括两个方面的内容:一是产业的艺术化,二是艺术的产业化。"生产主义"是说,"消费"发展了,走向泛滥,从而"为消费而消费",并且有了"主义"时,才提出回到"生产"上来,这才有了"生产主义"。人的理想不应该是不劳动,或者少劳动,而应该是劳动的性质发生变化,不再从事奴隶式的劳动。劳动的解放,生产的快乐,都体现在这一点上。

方喜要写一本书,在"消费主义"时代坚持谈一个话题:"生产主义"。对此,我很赞成,也常与方喜和研究室里的同事们在一道就相关的问题讨论。他让我把所说所想写出来,也许能与他作一个呼应,于是,就有了下面这段文字。

一

谈"生产主义",要从"时间"说起。方喜的这本书在最后一章谈"时间",我倒是认为,这个问题可以放到前面来谈。我碰到这个问题,是 20 多年前,当时我在瑞典留学。瑞典人称自己是一个"社会主义"国家。每到"五

---

* 高建平,男,1955 年生,中国社会科学院文学研究所研究员、国际美学协会(International Association of Aesthetics)主席,主要从事美学研究。

一",就有大规模的游行。参加游行的人按照约定到一个公园,党的社区支部书记自驾私车,运来一捆旗帜标语,分发给接到通知应约而来的本社区的同志,然后大家排队。每个社区一支队伍,依次出发,前面是军乐队开道,乐队奏《国际歌》和其他一些歌曲。最大最长的游行队伍是社会民主党的。许多人手持玫瑰花,那是他们党的标志。从鲜红变为玫瑰红,这是这个党"修正"的象征。社会民主党时而在台上,时而在台下。在台上时,游行更有气势;在台下时,游行更有激情。除此以外,还有许多别的党也在游行,甚至有秘鲁的"光辉的道路",举着毛主席戴红领章红帽徽的木刻像。各党都打各自的标语,代表着各自的政纲。我最感到好奇的是瑞典共产党,"苏东事变"改名左翼党。他们打出的口号,是"六小时工作制"。当时,中国还没有实行每周双休制,假期也不多,每年大约要工作300天。到了瑞典,发现他们每周只工作五天,再加上各种节假日和带薪休假,每年工作200天就够了。在我当时的感觉中,这已经够超前的了。如果再实行"六小时工作制",那经济怎么办?问题的关键还不在这里,是工作时间越短越好吗?到了共产主义,每天应该工作几个小时?我总觉得,这个思路有问题,此后许多年,我一直在回想。"六小时工作制"只是口号而已,20年过去了,也没有实行,看来也行不通。其实,即使实行了,是不是就到了应该提出"四小时工作制"的时候了。下一步是不是就"两小时工作制"?这样下去,结果是什么呢?

　　工作的时间少了,供自由支配的时间就多了。在现今的社会中,这的确能成为一个理想。上班是无奈的。不挣钱,怎么生活?不多挣钱,怎么付得起那些能体现自己的价值和品味的高档消费?下班是自由的。下班后是自己的时间,不归老板管,只要不触犯法律,干什么都行。理想的生活,是少上班,多挣钱。如果能意外发一笔财,就可以不上班了。但是,这似乎又不对。钱很多,一辈子也用不完的人,似乎也照样上班,而且还很认真地工作。对于他们来说,似乎还有人生追求。

　　如果我们放在一个较长时段考察,就会发现,上班是一个现代现象。在古代社会,农民无所谓上班下班,按照自然的节律,播种、插秧、除草、收获,日出而作,日落而息,自由地享受着劳动及其果实。手工业工人也无所谓上班,想做就做,累了就休息,对手艺精益求精,生活在对自己手艺的自豪感之中。

　　大工厂、公司出现了,于是就有了上班现象。上班不能迟到,更不能缺席。现代文明的一个重要标志,就是时间观念的变化。能按时上下班,把工作与休息时间区分开,这是一种文明素质。如果一个民族还不习惯准时上下班,比方说，让工人八点钟上班，他们不认为十点钟来就是一个错误，这个民族的经济就不可以发达。这需要经过一个文明化的过程。常听企业主抱怨，到有些经济落后的国家和地区投资很困难。尽管那里劳动力价格不高，但劳动力质量有问题。工人上班不守时，劳动纪律不好，劳资对立很厉害。尽管如此，我不认为这要从民族或文化上找根源，更不能从基因上找原因。现代文明之犁或迟或早会把全世界都深耕一遍，使全世界各民族都变成守时的民族，变成劳动纪律好的民族，上班好好干，下班好好玩的民族。这是由不可阻挡的经济规律决定的。

上班与下班的对立，造成了工作与娱乐的对立。上班时玩是不对的，下班时工作是可笑的。上班工作，成为下班后娱乐和享受所必须忍受的痛苦。上班时间属于老板的，下班时间才能属于自己的。老板发工资，把时间买去了，就属老板所有。如果老板要求工人加班，就应该再付钱来买，给加班工资。如果节假日还要加班，工资就得加倍。

现代社会还有一种发明，这就是打卡机，上下班要打卡，不是老板站在那里看着你是否迟到，而是机器监督你，用机器把你的上下班时间区分开来。这种非个人化的机器，避免了雇主与工人的直接冲突，使工作与业余的对立变得像自然规律一样不可抗拒。

在这种情况下，工作中的愉悦被忽略不计了。上班不是去找乐的：以上班为乐的心态要纠正，理由是，这样会从兴趣出发，而不是从工作需要出发来工作。在上班时找乐是不对的：上班是件严肃的事，负有重大责任的人在上班时，开不得半点玩笑，弄得不好事情会办砸；在危险岗位上工作的人更不能有玩笑的态度，稍有差错，人命关天。过分爱开玩笑，拿正经的事、重要的事开玩笑，是缺点而不是优点。

于是，既然上班，就得能吃苦耐劳，把事情做好。要寻欢作乐，下班以后再说。上班要拼命干，下班再拼命玩。这样，随着机械化、自动化、电子化的发展，生产效率提高了，不需要那么多工作时间了，当然就得缩短工作时间。

这种主张，是建立在工作与业余对立的基础上的。工作时，人是机器，业余时，人才还原为人。工作时间是人生必须忍受的时间，业余时间才是人作为人对时间的享受。

二

再来谈消费。过去的三十年，我们经历了从消费可耻到消费光荣的变化。

在我们这一代人的童年时代,消费是一件可耻的事。

只消费而不生产的人是社会的寄生虫,消费城市是寄生的城市。我家乡在扬州,又生长在重视"生产"的年代,从小就听了很多对旧扬州的批判。从小学到中学,老师都对我们说,解放前,扬州是一个消费城市,全城只有两家半工厂,休闲业很发达。扬州人过的是"早上皮包水"(上茶馆喝茶),"晚上水包皮"(上浴室泡澡)的生活。老师们又说,解放后,经过一些年的发展,扬州建成了一个工业城市,我们有了许多家的工厂,甚至都能造拖拉机和水泥船了。有一段时间,市里还想建钢铁厂,后来中央没有批准。老师说,账要算在刘少奇身上。大跃进时扬州就大炼钢铁,照那个方向发展,早就建成钢铁厂了,可惜后来砍掉了。砍掉后再建,就困难了。在那个年代,中国所有的城市,都是生产城市,能生产什么,就生产什么。社会不容寄生虫存在,一个人不能生产,他活着还有什么用呢?扬州城的西南角有一个湖,叫荷花池。文化革命时斗走资派,当时的扬州市长有一个大罪状,就是妄图把这个湖变成一个公园。我们当时也觉得该斗。当上了市长,还不想想多办几家工厂,建什么公园?

这些年,情况变了,消费变得光荣起来。"早上皮包水,晚上水包皮"成了介绍扬州的导游词,诱惑全国人民,都来包一包。荷花池真的成了公园,每天的早晨和晚上,都有很多老人聚在那里,唱歌、跳舞、做操、抖空竹。发展旅游产业,发展休闲产业,甚至发展养老产业,也能使一个城市繁荣发达。全国各大军区都在扬州有干部休养所,让有功勋的老军人在扬州安度晚年。现在占据着市领导的注意力的,是建成卫生城市,宜居城市,生态城市。这太好了,扬州人很以此为荣。

从重视"生产"向重视"消费"发展,这似乎符合经济发展的必然规律。物资匮乏时,有一个想象,如果物资丰富就好了。但等到物资丰富了,又有了新的烦恼,东西卖不出去怎么办?物质财富充分涌流了,反而带来了经济危机。

经济为什么会有危机,西方的一些政治家都会说,原因是消费信心不足,人们不敢花钱。消费信心是经济状况的一个指标。

我们现在也这么说。通过刺激消费来发展经济,这是常用的办法。让人们放心花钱。人们买商品,于是商品销出去了,制造业就发展了。人们买服务,于是服务业也发展了。

记得有人曾说,中国经济有一个很大的问题,就是老百姓不敢花钱。有钱总是往银行里存,留着养老、子女教育、治病,主要原因是社会福利不好。西方一些福利国家就不一样,人家不怕。养老、教育、医疗都有保障。无后顾之忧，就可放心消费，甚至贷款消费。

听了这个故事，我总是在头脑里浮上一个镜头：澳门赌场。有一年去澳门，参观赌场。那时，赌场的主要还是香港客光顾。里面供应便餐，以节省赌客时间。赌场还免费送一张回香港的船票，赌客不必留路费。赌场周围有很多的当铺，都取名为"必胜押"、"常胜押"等吉利的名字。在当铺里可以用随身的手表、珠宝等抵押借款，并可以在香港的连锁店赎回，不必再为赎当回一趟澳门。这样，赌客身上所有的钱都可拿出，所有值钱的东西都可以当掉。为你服务到家，服务你到家，你也就有了消费信心。到家之后如何，那就是你的事了。

是不是我们发展经济也要这么做。让人们没有后顾之忧，有钱就花。人们总喜欢说一个故事：一对中国夫妇攒了一辈子的钱，终于买到房子，住进去没有几天就死了；一对美国夫妇贷款买房，然后住进去，边还贷款边享受。可见美国夫妇多么聪明。

但是，这个故事已经过时了。更好的刺激消费的办法，是让消费成为时尚。对奢侈品的追求，原本是社会上的富裕阶层所特有的特征。早在原始社会，就有了各种装饰品的存在，如冠、笄、项链、金玉饰品等等。这种少数人对奢侈品拥有的现象，在以皇权和贵族特权为中心的传统社会，被发展到了极致。从曾侯乙墓到明定陵，挖出了大量东西供今天的人饱眼福，对墓主人的奢华生活发挥最充分的想象。到了当代，消费社会的特点，是奢侈品的普及化。人们在各种奢侈品的使用上，进行着激烈的攀比竞赛：汽车高档、衣服靓丽、手表名贵、提包入时、手机新潮，都成了身份的象征。

奢侈品成了经济发展的新的引擎。而这种消费具有无限性。一个古老的理想似乎行不通了。我们曾相信，物质财富"充分涌流"时，就可"按需分配"了。但现在，消费不再是有限的，吃饭、穿衣、住房，这些消费具有有限性，但现在，人的无限贪婪和无限的对奢侈品的追求，开启了经济发展的新的大门。在即使"充分涌流"也仍是有限的物质财富面前，人们有着无限的需求，"按需分配"仍是不可能的。因此，还是要多挣多花，仍是要鼓励人们能挣会花。这就进入了一个无休止的循环之中。

消费光荣，消费水平代表着品味，代表着档次，我消费故我在，消费成了人的新的存在方式。

三

审美、艺术和享受，原本是联系在一起的。农民看着绿油油、黄灿灿的庄稼地，牧民看着风吹草地见牛羊的美景，总是充满着喜悦。手工艺人，也具有半艺术家的性质。他们制作物品，在制作中充满着愉悦，对自己的制成品欣赏。在现代艺术观念形成以前，一件作品并没有由于被认定为艺术品而得到欣赏。制作者在制作时愉悦，接受者也分享这种快感，这就够了，与它是否被认定为艺术无关。

机器和资本，以及由此而形成的大规模生产剥夺了这种生产的愉悦，形成了生产、创造和审美三者的分离。对生产效率的追求，使得生产过程的愉悦被牺牲了。人成了生产机器中的齿轮和螺丝钉，只是有时比铁制的齿轮和螺丝钉更有效而已。赤裸裸的功利性追求，原本总是有一点忌讳，这时明白地提了出来。资本的运作，消除了原本笼罩在一些职业上的灵光，"它把医生、律师、教士、诗人和学者变成了它出钱招雇的雇佣劳动者"（马克思恩格斯《共产党宣言》语）。不仅如此，它将所有劳动者对他们劳动过程和成果的享受都剥夺了。对于一位劳动者来说，重要的不再是他的生产过程和他所生产的东西使他感到快乐，而是他的劳动的成果所换来的金钱使他有可能去购买快乐。

出现于18世纪的现代美学和现代艺术观念，就是在这种情况下形成的。现代美学的一个核心概念，是审美无利害。从世纪之初的夏夫茨伯里，经鲍姆加登，到世纪之末康德，这种思想逐渐成熟，成为一种现代美学体系的基石。在功利主义盛行的时代，辟出一个领域，给心灵一个住所，这是美学形成的一个理由。几乎与此同时，现代艺术体系和现代艺术观念也出现了。现代艺术体系，指18世纪中叶夏尔·巴图所提出的将诗、绘画、音乐、雕塑和舞蹈包括进来形成一个"美的艺术"的体系。夏尔·巴图的体系在经过修正后，被《科学、艺术和工艺详解百科合书》采来作为所依据的概念框架的一部分，后来在康德的《判断力批判》中，与美、崇高等概念结合起来，成为美学体系的一部分。现代艺术概念，从夏尔·巴图将这些艺术门类归结为单一的原理，即"摹仿"以后，被人们不断修正，形成了对艺术本质的共同追求。由此，艺术与工艺被明确地区分开来。这样就确定了，一些人制作的物品是艺术，而不是工艺或其他工业制成品，确定了一些人的活动是艺术活动，而不是生产活动，也确定了一些人是艺术家，他们是与普通人不一样的一个特殊人群，他们依据着与普通人不一样的原则而生活，对他们也要依据与日常生活不一样的原则来看待和欣赏，并以别的原则来与他们交往。

当艺术生产与工业和手工业生产的界限被明确分开来，艺术依赖于一系列相关的体制而得以确立的时候，在社会生活中同时发生的，是劳动与享受、工作与业余、上班与下班的分离。在这种情况下，艺术就成了工作之外的时间的填充。艺术要提升业余生活的品味，用美来克服庸俗，成为宗教消退时代的宗教，感情缺失时代的感情的寻找和制造者。这是一个巨大的社会设计的组成部分。艺术不是生活的一部分，但生活又需要艺术，这时，艺术就成了生活的滋补营养品，让生活的片面化得以缓解。人没有艺术也是可以活的，但有了艺术，就会活得更好。

消费社会来临，带来日常生活审美化，推动了一种艺术走向生活的倾向。这里包括两个方面的内容：一是产业的艺术化，即产品不再只是满足生活需要，而且以其外观满足审美的需要。通过时尚产品的制作，使消费符号化，成为财富和品味的象征。二是艺术的产业化，通过大规模生产，廉价的复制，利用新媒介的广泛传播，就使艺术改变了过去的性质，造成了制作者和接受者的脱离。

在这种情况下，迫使原来意义上的艺术面临两个选择，一是消亡，二是成为生活的救赎。在一个"产业艺术化，艺术产业化"的时代，实际上消除了美与日常生活的距离。这时，如果艺术还想在社会生活中起某种作用的话，只有一种办法，这就是宣布艺术化的产业只是产业，产业化的艺术不是艺术。艺术要别有一种追求，要针对生活的现状发言。这里，艺术与美分离了，艺术是生活的救赎，是解毒剂。它不再是滋补的营养品，而是医治社会之病的药品。

四

生产主义（producerism）是从消费主义（consumerism）而来的。并不是说，原来就有一种主义，叫"生产主义"，后来经济转型了，出现了"消费主义"。事实恰恰相反，在经济生活以"生产"为中心时，人们并没有提出一个"生产主义"。"生产"就是"生产"，无所谓"主义"。当然，认为生产关系的问题解决了，主要的力量应该放在发展生产力上，也是一种"主义"。但是，那与这里所谈的"生产主义"，不属于一个层面。"生产主义"是说，"消费"发展了，走向泛滥，从而"为消费而消费"，即"我消费故我在"，并且有了"主义"时，才提出回到"生产"上来，这才有了"生产主义"。

消费主义有多种理解。对消费主义，有人理解得很具体，即主张从消费者的角度看待商业行为，如保护消费者，反对包装、广告、价格和质量等方面的欺诈，推动包括"消费者日"在内的各种活动，保护消费者的权益。还有，意识到消费者的力量，并适当地使用这种力量，如抵制某商家或厂家的商品，抵制某国某地区的商品，以此作为政治的手段。另外，还有一些反消费主义者，他们从自然保护、环保、反对少数人的特权，等等角度，对种种社会现象提出质疑、批判和抗议。"生产主义"也是如此。在西方，一些"生产主义"者反对通过增税来增加非生产者的福利，还有一些人反对外来移民，要来保护本国劳工的就业机会。一般说来，在国外，生产主义的提法，都涉及具体的经济话题，与一部分人的权益有关，这种对权益的维护，有时还很狭隘。但是，"生产主义"也可以有积极的解读。

劳动本身，并非只是谋生的手段。劳动本身有着快乐。我们在生活中会看到大量的从劳作过程中汲取快感的例子。母亲对孩子的无微不至的照顾，其过程本身是充满着快感的，她不会计算单位劳动时间的产值。从手业者对手艺本身的爱好，从科学家对研究工作本身的痴迷，从运动员对比赛的享受，从艺术家在创作时的全身心投入，我们都可以看到一种劳动的快乐。这种快乐，是由人的智力和体力的自由运用所形成的，是由人的"知解力"与"想象力"的和谐运用所产生的，同时，也是自我实现的内在冲动得以体现出来时所产生的。从这个意义上讲，工作决非只是用来购买快乐所需要忍受的辛劳，上班与下班的对立可以化解，生产劳动本身，可以具有审美的性质。

最后，让我们再次回到这个话题：那么，理想的生活是什么呢？不是工作时间越短越好，挣的钱越多越好，不是"睡觉睡到自然醒，数钱数到手抽筋"就好，而是将"最喜欢的事做得尽善尽美"才好。人的理想不应该是不劳动，或者少劳动，而应该是劳动的性质发生变化，不再从事奴隶式的劳动。劳动的解放，生产的快乐，都体现在这一点上。人的全面发展，使兴趣与生产结合起来，使每个儿童的聪明才智通过教育得以发展，社会又能使这种聪明才智得到充分发挥的机会，应该成为我们的理想。孔夫子一生最大的感叹，是"不吾知也"。他的希望，是有人能用他，让他发挥自己的作用，但这个愿望在当时不能实现。未来社会的理想，当然不只是让某一个人发挥作用，而是让所有的人的聪明才智都得到发挥。一个自由、自觉、自为的社会，当全部力量被发挥出来时，它所能达到的成就，是不可限量的。

人类社会的发展，是一个从自然王国向自由王国的过渡过程。这个过程不能理解成从强迫劳动到不劳而获的过程，而应该理解成从劳动被奴役到解除这种奴役的过程。写到这里，打开电视等待一个重要信息。这些天电视上有一个主题：幸福。电视上打出了一个标题：幸福要靠创造性劳动。这当然是对的，但同时，我想强调另一点：幸福就是创造性劳动，或者说幸福包含了创造性劳动。幸福与劳动的对立消除了,奴隶式的劳动被取消了,人的全面发展才成为可能。

(本文责任编辑:张永禄)

What Kind of Productivism

Gao Jianping

(CASS Institute of Literature)

Abstract: An important symbol of modern civilization, is the change on the concept of time, to work on time, meaning the distinction between work and rest. The advent of the consumer society, brings aesthetics of daily life, and promotes an art tendency toward life, including two aspects: First, industrial art, the second is the art of industrialization. "Production doctrine" is to say, "consumption" has developed, to spread, thus "as consumption spending," and have a "doctrine" only when the proposed return to the "production" of up, this has been "production doctrine." Should not be the ideal person does not work, or work less, but should be changes in the nature of labor, no longer engaged in slave-like labor. The liberation of labor and the production of happiness are reflected at this point.

大众文化的另一种解读

陆 扬[*]

（复旦大学中文系）

【内容摘要】 大众文化长久被视为工业社会大批量制作的低质量文化产品，它有没有可能被定义为自下而上名至实归的大众的文化？大众文化的流行模态和趋势受制于社会和时代的制约，但是它的大众社会基础本身是在不断酝酿着时代风尚。坎托和沃思曼以古希腊作为起点的《大众文化史》，因此值得充分重视。无论是希腊的奥运会，抑或19世纪这个小说的黄金时代，其背后的大众文化底蕴，应是清晰可辨的。

一、大众文化的历史

大众文化的一个广为流行的传统定义，是后工业社会主导意识形态联手垄断资本，自上而下、唯利是图，大批量炮制的低质量文化产品。这个以阿多诺"文化工业"批判理论为其原型的大众文化认知，迄至今日广有影响，甚至可以名之为大众文化主流意识形态。由是观之，大众文化的历史，充其量不过是一百年间的故事。但是，假如我们将这一段历史上溯两千五百年，那又怎样？

美国史学家诺曼·坎托和米切尔·沃思曼1968年出版两人主编的《大众文化史》，收集各个时代的文化叙述文献，便将大众文化的历史上溯到古代希腊。该书按照历史的线索，将大众文化的发展阶段，分为七个时期。第一个时期是

---

[*] 陆扬，1953年生，男，复旦大学中文系教授，博士生导师，主要从事文艺学、文化研究。本文为国家社科基金重大项目"当代中国大众文化的价值观研究"（项目号：11&ZD022）阶段性成果。

从古希腊体育和戏剧到公元 450 年，以罗马帝国的灭亡为标志，这是古典时期。罗马也有自己的大众文化，比如让人欲罢不能的斗兽场、澡堂和宴饮的文化。第二个时期是中世纪，从 450 年到 1350 年。中世纪未必是"黑暗世纪"，这一时期的宗教生活，包括后来十字架东征的社会基础和对哥特式教堂的痴迷，以及亚瑟王一类传奇的流布，甚至，大学生活，都可以见到一种"大众文化"的基础。第三个时期是早期现代，1350 年至 1700 年。这是文艺复兴的辉煌时期，宫廷生活、贵族生活、政治生活，以及新兴资产阶级们的日常生活，都成为大众文化的考究对象。与此同时，艺术趣味则历经了从文艺复兴到巴洛克的转变。第四个时期名之为启蒙与革命，1700 年至 1815 年。这个时期的娱乐是暴力和死亡，酗酒和赌博也畅行其道，俱乐部、咖啡馆和沙龙这些最初的"公共领域"，正是在此一时期破土而出。第五个时期见证了工业社会的形成，1815 年至 1914 年整整一百年。假如把大众文化定义为工业社会最有代表性的文化产品，那么这一时期当仁不让就是大众文化实至名归的"经典化"时期。这个时期人心不古、世风日下的道德沦落，被小说家揭露得淋漓尽致，文学在普及的层面上第一次成为名副其实的大众文化。波西米亚亚文化一路走红的同时，体育成为大众的鸦片。针对人性和风化的堕落，鼓吹古道热肠、修身立命的大众传媒开始现身。与此同时，国家主义和帝国主义的狂热甚嚣尘上。第六个时期谓之现代世界，1914 年至 1955 年。这是一个被汽车改变了生活方式的时代，更是爆发两次世界大战的时代，女权主义开始觉醒，高等教育也迅猛发展。在大众娱乐方面，读书会、卡通热望尘莫及一马当先的电影，它很快就确立了大众文化的霸权。第七也是最后一个时期是当代世界，从 1955 年到该书面世的 1968 年。此一时期生活质量的提高为人瞩目，在这个大众消费社会中，文化消费与日俱增，旅游和休闲产业羽翼渐丰，足球成为体育家族的新贵。电视异军突起，开始分享电影的市场。当然，性革命也是一个绕不过去的话题。

由上所见，坎托和沃思曼所框架的大众文化史，毋宁说就是一部跨越两千五百年的城市风俗文化史。用两位编者的话说，他们这部大众文化史选文材料来源是严肃的社会史研究，主要史学家和社会学的著作，以及但凡以人文行为和人类社会性质为其对象的随笔和批评文章。无怪言及什么是大众文化，两人引了美国哲学家乔治·桑塔耶那一段语录，谓人类为外部力量所迫，殚精竭虑避免痛苦和死亡，不得任何自由快乐的时候，无疑就是自然和强权的奴隶。工作和游戏由此可以对应人类的奴役和自由两种状态。工作这里不是泛指人类一切有用的劳作，而是专指迫于生计的不情愿劳动。游戏则不再考虑有用无用，它是人类一切自然而然，以自身为其目的的活动，不论它有或没有一个最终目的。两人进而给他们笔下的大众文化作了一个充满诗意的表述：

> 大众文化可视为人类所有这些活动，以及所有因其自身目的而被创造出来的人工制品，这一切都使他的身心得到解放，离开了生活的悲惨重负。大众文化确实就是人们非工作状态中的活动；人类由此在追求娱乐、兴奋、美和满足感。[1]

这很难说是大众文化的一个定义。假如我们把它看作一个定义，那么很显然《大众文化史》的两位编者就是在编织大众文化的乌托邦愿景。它似乎是把大众文化定位在艺术创造上面，同时又顺应民主潮流，解构艺术的精英姿态，把它看作每一个人的天赋权利。但是实际上，如上所见，大众文化即便被理解为充满创造性的城市民间文化，它的含义很显然也远不限于哲学家多会以此同游戏对举的艺术。

在坎托和沃思曼看来，大众文化首先是多元化的而且兼容并包的，其中并没有哪一种文化形式高居霸权地位，颐指气使统治所有的其他文化形态。同样没有哪一种普世公理，说明文化首先是特权和富人阶级的专利，然后降尊纡贵，下放到黎民百姓头上。比如中世纪流行骑士风，但那是贵族圈子里的时尚，对于普通农民的消遣和娱乐，就关系不大。反过来下层阶级的趣味标准，也有可能一路上升，最终进入顶层阶级的生活方式。还有一种情况是，一个时代仅见于藏污纳垢之地的某些趣味，通过社会系统的过滤，可以流行不衰成为后代时尚的风向标，将社会名流、演艺人员、工人阶级，以及对此种时尚的来源懵然不知的年轻人一并俘获过来。如20世纪中叶高中女生的衣着打扮，在18世纪整个儿就是荡女范儿。

进一步看，坎托和沃思曼同样注意到，大众文化的流行模态和趋势总是受制于社会和时代的制约。当一个社会的大多数成员都是文盲，其生活也圈定在有限的地理空间里时，文化信息的传播必然有限的，跨文化的交际应无从谈起。反之，随着印刷术、铁路、轮船、广播和电视的发明，使人类及其思想的交通变得异常方便，不同背景的人们分享相同的文化经验，也从梦想变成现实。今天我们已经处在互联网的时代，天涯若比邻固不待言，文化自觉的意识应尤胜

---

[1] César Graña, "Bohemian Subculture," Norman F. Cantor and Michael W. Werthman ed. *The History of Popular Culture*, New York: The Macmillan Company, 1968, p. xxxvi.

过分享"相同的文化经验"。但假如说这一切使我们的好生活欲望层层加码无止境增长,那么大众文化毋宁说就是给我们对娱乐、休闲和刺激的追求,提供了一个合法的框架和组织结构。盖言之,成人的游戏白日梦,可望在大众文化的宣泄中得到无害的释放。很显然,这说到底还是用原始艺术的本能冲动,来解释大众文化。

二、希腊奥运的大众基础

基于以上视野,我们可以来看西方最早的大众文化之一,奥林匹克运动会这个古希腊体育和竞技文化最为典范的游戏仪式。古希腊物质出产并不丰富,战争倒是家常便饭,波希战争打了 43 年,伯罗奔尼撒战争打了 28 年,医学条件和卫生状态也简陋粗鄙,人的寿命大都短暂。是以尼采《悲剧的诞生》中以日神阿波罗冲动象征的造型艺术梦境,来给古代希腊人生披上一块如梦似幻的面纱,谓可使人忘却苦难,感觉人生尚可为继的说法,当非空穴来风,或者纯属他的异想天开。但坎托和沃思曼认为,古代世界虽然物质条件匮乏,战乱频仍,但是惟其如此,希腊人对于游戏的期盼,尤有一种如饥似渴的热诚。"进而视之,当社会的复杂程度还不足以提供作为生活特殊方面的专门娱乐,文明的最基础成分,就成了大众文化的材料。"[①]

《大众文化史》中第一篇选入的就是著名古代体育史学者伽迪纳(E. Norman Gardiner)的《希腊人的游戏》一文。19 世纪英国诗人和文学批评家马修·阿诺德在他的名著《文化与无政府状态》中,提出过"两希文化"的概念。据阿诺德说,希腊文化的最高理念,是如其本然看世界。希伯来文化的最高理念,则是行动和服从。所以希腊人孜孜不倦同身体和欲望作斗争,因为它们阻碍了正确的思想。同样希伯来文化也搏击身体和欲望,因为它们妨碍了正确的行动。所以希腊文化热爱理性,讲究人性的自然发展;希伯来文化,则是钟爱神性,讲究人性的约束与兑制。这个分析当然是有道理的。但是诚如一切宏大理论都会有以偏概全的弊端,我们发现奥运会这个希腊最典型的大众文化形式,推举起来,其实里面也不乏阿诺德所说的希伯来文化的成分。比如,首先它标举行动,而不是坐在书斋和画廊里沉思。其次,它推举神性,是希伯来文化特有的那种宗教的迷狂。但是奥运会说到底是希腊的传统,就像哲学、

[①] Norman F. Cantor and Michael W. Werthman ed. *The History of Popular Culture*, New York: The Macmillan Company, 1968, p. 1.

悲剧、民主这些希腊文化的独特遗产，它的原始面貌又当何论？或者说，我们从中可以见出一种大众文化的精神来吗？

回答是肯定的。我们先看奥运会的神性。事实上体育和祭祀庆典，可视为奥运会世俗和神圣的两个起源。古希腊的祭祀节庆层出不穷，但奥运会无疑是最大的盛会。竞技和体育取悦死而复生的神祇，又展现了胜利的荣光。而这一切辉煌，都是在主神宙斯的监护下，从容展开。可以说，正是古代奥运会的这一浸润在宗教迷狂和虔诚中的神性，使它有可能使全希腊所有城邦的代表相聚一堂，在同一规则下展开竞赛。换言之，它是大众的而不是贵族的游戏。但显而易见，奥运绝不仅仅是游戏。游戏作为体育的起源之一，足以显示体育是朝气勃发，而不是暮气沉沉的运动，但问题是，游戏又不同于奥运会的体育竞技。游戏是娱乐，竞技是拼搏。游戏疲乏了可以罢休，竞技即便精疲力竭，也决不能罢休，它要克服一切体能上的障碍，拼搏一往无前，甚至突破身体的极限。故而无论是业余还是专业的运动员，都要经过艰苦的训练，它是违背自然的快乐之道，以痛苦为快乐的。

所以荷马史诗写到拳击和摔跤，都使用了"忧伤的"这个形容词，这也是荷马用来形容战争的语词。但是诚如荷马笔下的英雄们都热衷此道，这是为什么？竞技的拼搏不似动物捕食，有猎物以为报偿。奥运会从它的原始形态开始，最高的嘉奖就是精神而不是物质。固然，胜出的运动员可以得到一头牛、一个女人、一张桌子，抑或一个奖杯，但是最高的奖励给的一个花冠，它是最高荣光的体现。就此而言，骄奢淫逸、萎靡不振的国度与奥运精神无缘，物质条件太为贫瘠，为内忧外患焦头烂额的国度，同样无以奢望奥运的荣光。积贫积弱的旧中国之长久隔离于奥运会，恐怕就是辛酸的后例。奥运的最初项目是跳、跑、投掷、搏击，它们充满阳刚之气，推崇体力和武力，这正是荷马的传统。说到底，古希腊的奥运会，是给希腊城邦的所有选手，提供了无须面对死亡，而得极尽荣耀的绝好机会。这个机会同样是给予大众而不是少数特权阶级的。

大众的权利意味着它应是平等的权利。在种族、阶级和性别这当今文化研究的三个焦点之中，奥运的平等精神至少涵盖了种族和阶级两端。运动员至少早在奥运会开幕前一个月，就来到圣地埃利斯，投身最后的强化训练。观众则不分等级阶层和肤色地区，四面八方蜂拥而至。无论是农夫、渔夫抑或王公贵胄，所有人享有同等权利，没有保留席位。赛场之外，举目望去，俨然就是一个大集市，毗邻一个野营大基地。但见演说家滔滔不绝比试口才，诗人充满激情朗诵荷马，雕塑家跃跃欲试寻找新的素材，政客和兵士、农民和艺术家、贵族和庶民,在这里的身份差异难得是消弭模糊了。参赛的运动员诚然是清一色的男性,妇女被禁止参赛,但是观众之中并非没有女性的影子。已婚妇女不允许出席奥运,但是未婚女孩可以到场观看,而且,很可能其中一些女孩是瞒过家长,擅自跑过来看热闹的。希腊文化是男性的文化,曾经作为法国大革命三大标识之一的"博爱",在古希腊语境中指的是男性之间的友谊,同女性没有关系。

古希腊奥运会上最激动人心的比赛项目今已不存。这个项目应是典型的精英竞技,它是四驾战车的比赛。因为装备价值不菲,非贵族的经济实力,无以染指。虽然古奥运的赛车场今已渺无踪影,但是从古代作家的文字里,我们知道战车是一字儿排开在起跑线上,通常是轻巧的两轮车厢,前方和左右各围有一栏,其间仅容车手一人站立。中间两匹马驾辕,边上两匹拉套,车手一袭白色长袍,右手持马鞭,左手拉缰绳。一旦号角吹响,快马加鞭,风驰电掣奋力向前。索福克勒斯《厄拉克特拉》里,描述过 10 辆战车并驾齐驱的壮观,而实际上,同时上场参赛的战车,最高可以达到 40 辆。40 辆战车在这方寸之地横冲直撞,惊心动魄可想而知。将近 9 英里的赛程中,事故频出是意料中事,每每是能够顺利通过 23 个弯道的战车,最有希望得胜。得胜的是车手,更是战车的主人。荷马时代主人亲自驾车,但是到奥运会鼎盛时期的公元前 5 世纪,王公贵族雇佣职业车手来参赛,已成惯例。最高的嘉奖同样是从宙斯神庙后面野生橄榄树上采摘下来的橄榄枝冠,置于黄金和象牙镶嵌的桌子上。裁判在欢声雷动中,高声宣读得胜者的名字、他的父亲、他的国家。这就是希腊文化的荣光,它足以让后代一切急功近利的辉煌,相形见绌。而正是欢声雷动的希腊大众的参与,最终传承了希腊奥运的荣光。

三、文学与大众文化

文学似乎历来与大众文化格格不入。它属于高雅文化,同大众社会的普及性娱乐自不可同日而语。按照英国批评家 F. R. 利维斯《大众文明与少数人文化》一书中的说法,文学集中承载了一个民族最优秀的文化传统,只有少数人能够品味但丁和莎士比亚的精致,所以此等少数精英的趣味是黄金,而"大众文明"即电影、广播、流行出版物为代表的大众文化,不过是无度发行的纸币罢了。这个后来被叫做"利维斯主义"的文学梦,虽然见证了伯明翰文化研究怎样同它分道扬镳,但是近来在《西方正典》等一系列著作中东山再起,试图在文学被日益边缘化的今天，力挽狂澜于既倒。如哈罗德·布鲁姆的《西方正典》，就同样是呼吁回归以莎士比亚为中心的西方文学经典，以专业化的文学批评，驱逐不着边际、专门同欧洲白种男人过不去的文化研究。

但是这个以莎士比亚为一切经典之经典的不怠经典情结，不足以作为排斥大众文化的依据。因为一个显见的事实是，莎士比亚能在伊丽莎白时代各路戏剧豪杰中脱颖而出，让专业意识明确得多的"大学才子"们望尘莫及顾影自怜，恰恰是缘因这位天才诗人出于生计本能的大众路线。莎士比亚去世后，他的同时代剧作家本·琼生作诗悼念说，我不想把你葬在乔叟或斯宾塞身边，再不叫博蒙躺过去点，给你挪出一块地方；因为你是一座无须墓地的丰碑。这可见，莎士比亚在他谢世之日，已经在同道当中多有影响。可是即便如此，当时的西敏寺也还是没有理会本·琼生的呼吁。今天在西敏寺诗人角里占据主位的莎士比亚雕像，是诗人辞世一个多世纪之后，迎入其中的。甚至享有"英国文学之父"美誉的乔叟，1400年去世给葬入西敏寺，还是因了他的近邻身份，正好又有个朋友在寺里当差。直到1556年，乔叟的尸骸在寺里搬家，挪进一个更要华丽的墓穴，这才有了"诗人角"的历史。这段历史假如不能说明别的，那么它或许可以说明，文学经典当其流行之初，本身毋宁说就是地道的大众文化。

19世纪是小说的时代。从司汤达到巴尔扎克到福楼拜和左拉，从萨克雷、狄更斯到勃朗特姐妹，不但精彩展现了工业化时代波澜壮阔的风俗画卷，而且以良知和情感深入人类心灵最深邃的部分。但是坎托和沃思曼的《大众文化史》同样表明，19世纪的小说之花，也还是盛开在大众文化的沃土之中。该书选了法国社会学家C.格雷纳（César Graña）《波西米亚与布尔乔亚：十九世纪法国社会》一书中的一个章节。作者以巴黎为法国文化的象征，指出它不但拥有令人叹为观止的博物馆、植物园、历史纪念碑，还有多不胜数的作家和科学家的沙龙，和培育出著名文学同人圈子的咖啡馆，以及27家剧院。而人口倍于巴黎的伦敦，只有八家剧院。街头的景观同样出彩，摩洛哥舞女、暹罗孪生子、机械人等等叫人目不暇给，满足了大众如火如荼的廉价猎奇心理。巴黎更是文学的天下。关于是时如雨后春笋般迭出不穷的文学期刊，大仲马对其来由作过这样一个比喻：一个没有书读的文人，遇到一个没有病人的医生，以及一个没有客户的律师，餐桌上大家都得掏空腰包付账的时候，那怎么办，很简单，办杂志吧。而且文学说到底是年轻人的梦想。有作家坚信巴黎有六千个年轻人愿意为艺术献身。这在其他欧洲城市无见其匹。巴黎的文学从业者，也位居世界之冠。大仲马曾经讽刺文学是最不可救药的青年流行病。每一个孩子都会在五年级的时候开始投身一场古典悲剧，到七年级的时候梦醒过来。即便在职业阶层和商界人士当中，也多有人在悄悄重温当年校园里未竟的文学大梦。格雷纳引 19 世纪 40 年代一位作家的文字，道是哪一个编辑要是头脑发热一至于刊出广告，欢迎来稿，那他准定就是死到临头了。因为铺天盖地滚滚而来的，只能是文学青年的习作、全职太太们的哀怨以及外省书记员和税收员们的业余遐想：

> 每日里他的邮箱满当当吐出稿件的洪流，它成了一场灾难。要想逃离也是徒劳无功的……门铃响了，那是文稿。他离家出走，门前台阶上是一部文稿。他掉转头进屋避开正门，后门口又是一包稿件。①

这位编辑如此成为文化大生产的牺牲品。19 世纪是文学替代哲学、小说家替代牧师，担当人类精神导师的文学世纪。文学在以它的悲天悯人情怀给苦难人生编织梦境，由此成为文化经国济世宏大叙事第一载体的时候，在它的基础结构里，我们看到了大众文化的支撑。这个时代我们是熟悉的，但是它已经一去不复返了。

之所以一去不复返了，是说大众对于文学的热诚渐行渐远。今天的文学生涯经济上早已是捉襟见肘，难以自保，遑论像巴尔扎克、大仲马、杰克·伦敦这样依凭超级写作能力，换来挥金如土生活。今天即便是专业作家，投诚影视亦为不二选择。政治上文学虽然不至于无端蒙上利用小说反党这类莫须有罪名，可是也别再指望祭出人文大纛，引领时代风尚，基本上它是处在自生自灭的无政府状态。在阅读终端由纸质文本向电脑，再向手机转移的大趋势下，一方面传统定义的纯文学作品在变得支离破碎的阅读经验中维持着它们的体面市场，一方面便是传统被叫做大众文化的那些作品不但畅行其道，而且无度泛滥。这类作品用雷蒙·威廉斯的说法，是为一个新的文类，可以名之为大众文学。如他的《关键词》一书中所言："一个新的范畴'大众文学'或者说'次文学'被制定出来，用来描述可能是虚构性的，但未必是想象性和创造性的作品，故此它们是缺乏审美趣味，不是艺术。"②

威廉斯收集相关文化与社会的 110 个语词，分别予以阐解的《关键词》发

---

① See César Graña, "Bohemian Subculture," Norman F. Cantor and Michael W. Werthman ed. *The History of Popular Culture*, New York: The Macmillan Company, 1968, p. 433.

② Reymond Williams, *Key Words: A vocabulary of culture and society*, New York: Oxford University Press, 1983, p. 186.

表在 1976 年。1983 年该书再版,作者又增补了"无政府主义"、"生态"、"性"等 21 个新词。这是大众文化已成气候,至少不再被简单视为乌合之众文化的时代。但是即便如此,我们发现,文学的门槛依然是清晰的。比如武侠小说、色情小说、侦探小说、科幻小说、恐怖小说一类,都会被挡在"纯文学"的门外,给发落到上述威廉斯所说的"大众文学"一类。虽然随着新媒体的不断发展,以经典来界定文学的传统也显得时过境迁、恍若隔世,可是文学依然在浸润我们时日太久的集体无意识中维护着它的尊严。比如虽然今日金庸的武侠小说不但登堂入室成为文学的正统,而且已经几被视为经典,琼瑶的言情小说很显然仍然还是在文学的边缘上徘徊。但是说到底,即便是具有充分想象性和创造性特点的纯文学即威廉斯所谓的"艺术",最终也将在市场之中得到完成,诚如莱斯利·费德勒在其《文学是什么?》一书中所言:

> 诚如所有的作家心知肚明的,这意味着即便我们大多数人,包括我自己羞于承认,文学和文学作品,都是只有在从书桌走到市场之后,才告完成。这是说,在被包装、宣传、广告和卖出之前,文学都是不完整的。不仅如此,作家们同样明白,他们自己好比尴尬的处女,朝着世界高喊:"爱我吧!爱我吧!"直到诚如这个行当的术语所言,"销出了她们的初夜"。[①]

莱斯利·费德勒是 20 世纪美国的异数批评家,以鼓吹"大众批评"蜚声。值得注意的是,《文学是什么?》这个书名中的"是",作者使用的是过去式 was,意思是文学过去是什么?今天我们还有叫做文学的这个东西吗?这自然是种过激之言。

大众文化有没有可能被定义为自下而上实至名归的大众的文化?答案应是肯定的。就文学而言,它的魅力早已经深深潜入我们的集体无意识,即便它陷入鱼龙混杂、偷梁换柱的市场漩涡,一时被人冷落,我们愿意相信它假以适当契机,时刻可以重振雄风。费德勒这本书有一个反讽语式的副标题:《高雅文化与大众社会》,这是典型的英国传统,从马修·阿诺德的《文化与无政府状态》,到 F. R. 利维斯的《大众文明与少数人文化》,都是判定一方面有居高临下,只有少数人能够解其精妙的高雅文学,一方面则是一盘散沙处于无政府状态,有待启蒙的大众社会。问题是,离开大众社会的大众文化,功成名就的经

[①] 莱斯利·费德勒:《文学是什么?》,陆扬译,南京:译林出版社,2011 年,第 16 页。

典文学，会不会变成无本之木？或许莫言的粗鄙情节和狂野想象终而获得诺贝尔奖的垂青，是再雄辩不过显示了经典是怎样在大众文化中炼成的。

（本文责任编辑：贾洁）

Another Interpretation of Mass Culture

Lu Yang

(The department of Chinese language and literature, Fudan University)

Abstract: The mass culture has been seen as a kind of cultural products of low quality in the industrial society. But could it be defined as a real bottom-up processing culture of the masses? The popular mode and the trend of mass culture are subject to the society and the times, however its public social basis is the developing fashion of times. Encyclopedia of popular culture, which was written by Cantor and Werthman, was beginning with the culture of Greek. We can find the profound mass cultural background from Greek Olympic or the novels in 19th century.

肩起马克思主义美学理论的时代使命

——第三届中英马克思主义美学双边论坛会议综述

杨荔斌[*]

(上海交通大学人文学院)

2013年4月6日至8日,由上海交通大学人文学院和英国曼彻斯特大学艺术、历史与文化学院联合举办的第三届中英马克思主义美学双边论坛在上海交通大学成功举行。本次论坛围绕"马克思主义与未来"这一主题,在马克思主义与中西美学的历史传统与现实境遇的结合点上思考马克思主义在未来社会建设中的作用与地位,以及美学在这种可能性面前面临的问题、挑战与任务。来自伦敦大学、比利时鲁汶大学、美国杜克大学、瑞士欧洲研究院、俄罗斯圣彼得堡大学、澳大利亚莫纳什大学、英国利兹大学、英国曼彻斯特大学等17所海外高校及北京大学、复旦大学、浙江大学、吉林大学、厦门大学、武汉大学、山东大学、中国传媒大学等20多所国内高校的近百位专家学者参加。会议在上海交通大学闵行校区的人文学院报告厅举行,副校长徐飞教授出席论坛并致辞,他高度评价了双边论坛的学术交流形式对促进马克思主义理论研究和发展的意义,以及促进上海交大国际学术交流的价值。上海交通大学人文学院院长王杰教授在大会的致辞中说,本届论坛的主题是基于对马克思主义,尤其是马克思主义美学如何在当代社会生活中发挥积极作用以应对当前深刻的世界危机的考虑而提出的。他指出在全球性的价值危机、伦理危机和社会矛盾复杂化的情况下,马克思主义与未来是一个充满挑战性、也包含着无限理论空间的重大问题。他进一步呼吁,我们正处在比马克思当年更为复杂的世界,但马克思对资本主

---

[*] 杨荔斌,女,1980年生,广西玉林市人,上海交通大学人文学院在读博士生,主要研究方向为审美人类学。

义的批判和对未来理想社会的展望仍然是 19 世纪留给我们最重要的思想资源，因而全世界的马克思主义者应该加强交流与合作，坚持对社会现实的批判性思考，共同迎接时代的挑战。该论坛的发起人之一、英国曼彻斯特大学教授 David Alderson 在致辞中也提及了以论坛的形式在学者之间展开批判性辩论，有助于我们进一步认清新自由主义所坚持的以主张私有化来反对国家干预的做法，它无法提供解决资本主义社会经济危机的良方，而如何在反思权力系统和市场之间的矛盾关系的过程中找准我们的视角和定位便显得尤为重要，当我们试图不断探索答案之时，实际上也在逐步接近对马克思主义与未来的关系的揭示。会议采取大会主题演讲、分会场讨论与论文交流的形式，就马克思主义与乌托邦、马克思主义与美学的革命、真实问题的美学意义、悲剧观念及其理论意义、审美资本主义批判和中国马克思主义美学与文学批评等若干当代理论的重大问题交流意见和开展讨论，同时对中国作家莫言的小说《酒国》和詹明信的新书《辩证法之价》之关于乌托邦的章节进行了专题性的深入探讨。

一、面向未来之"人"的立足点：西方的"人"与东方的"仁"

来自美国加州大学著名的马克思主义者 Kevin Anderson 教授做了题为《结构主义与后结构主义之后的社会主义人道主义：重构之例》的主题演讲。他认为，人道主义在社会主义人道主义者的意识中遭受了过多的轻视和污蔑，例如阿尔都塞和福柯。诚如恩格斯所认为的黑格尔的人道主义思想是马克思思考人的本质问题的重要思想来源，到了阿尔都塞这里，他却视黑格尔的影响为幽灵，并以结构主义之法对马克思在 1845 年之前（尤其是 1844 年《手稿》）的理论阐释作出了存在着"认识论断裂"的判定之后，宣称马克思主义在理论上是反人道主义的，号召为了捍卫马克思主义的科学性和严密性而以驱魔人的身份将黑格尔的幽灵驱逐出去。他的论争最终由于对人道主义马克思主义的矫枉过正而被戏谑为一种开放的反马克思主义，而在其此路不通之处则预见性地促成了后结构主义对这种简单地视马克思为黑格尔式的人道主义者的做法进行扬弃。Kevin Anderson 因而称阿尔都塞的理论为一条走不通的反人道主义马克思主义道路。而福柯的反人道主义体现在，受其老师阿尔都塞的影响，福柯也一度认为马克思是反人道主义者，而且更强有力地攻击人道主义，他嘲弄人道主义对"人"的执著、对一般人性的执著。在他看来，人类所具有的差异性是人道主义框架所无法捕捉到的，由此他在《词与物》这本书的结尾写道："启蒙使人性得以显现的同时也使人道主义时代接近了它的终结","人将被抹去,如同大海边沙地上的一张脸"。同时他对中央集权国家和现代性的敌意也促使他不加批判地包容了类似伊朗伊斯兰教主义运动那样的宗教内容。他的反马克思主义则体现在,福柯不仅在选取批判的切入点与马克思有所不同,即偏重于选取偏离中心的权力机构为批判对象,而不再以商品为中心,而且当他把一般人性连根拔掉,也导致了阶级性的荡然无存,福柯眼中的工人阶级已是被整合进了资本主义体系的一部分,能对权力进行抵抗的群体只有那些被边缘化了的人,如精神病患者、囚犯、性欲者、宗教的原教旨主义者。他对权力的抵抗所展现出的宽泛视野也是与阿尔都塞、布尔迪厄所不同的,而且他对宗教的怀旧也有别于阿尔都塞对宗教的鄙视。于是,当不少人提倡回归黑格尔及其辩证法之时,Kevin Anderson 提出了回归马克思主义人道主义的呼吁——不仅要回归见于 1844 年《手稿》、《政治经济学批判大纲》、《资本论》之中的马克思的人道主义,而且要回归第二次世界大战之后西方社会主义人道主义者的著作,如萨特、弗洛姆和杜娜叶夫斯卡娅;东欧持不同观点的马克思主义人道主义者,如科西克;以及非洲社会主义人道主义者,如法农。而在这些人的理论中,Kevin Anderson 尤为看重法农和杜娜叶夫斯卡娅的理论观点。他认为当多数社会主义和马克思主义的人道主义总是停留在对抽象的普遍价值的探索之时,只有法农和杜娜叶夫斯卡娅在发展社会主义人道主义的形式方面取得了成功,他们的成功在于接受了诸如种族主义和殖民主义的论述,以同时兼顾实现普遍化和认知差异性来实现对现实的回归。而所有这些马克思主义人道主义的左派则开启了某种挑战 1968 年之后以反马克思主义(特别是人道主义阵营中的马克思主义)为征貌的福柯主义和后结构主义的类型。值得强调的是,尽管这一反拨的形势日益强劲,我们仍需对像杜娜叶夫斯卡娅、法农、科西克他们所建构的以显示差异性为目的的整体性进行深刻的理解,同时,也需要从近几十年来后结构主义社会批判中关涉语言、监狱、帝国主义的文化遗留问题,乃至性别和性的论述中吸取合理的成分,从而形成 21 世纪马克思人道主义的深刻洞见。

与 Kevin Anderson 立足于西方社会的"人"进行阐述截然不同,来自北京大学高等人文研究院的杜维明教授则从儒家思想出发、以题为《修身、社会实践与信赖社群》的主题演讲论述了东方社会的"仁"。杜教授指出,作为东方社会思想典型代表的儒家学说要在新的历史环境中获得进一步发展,必须接受三种重要的西方思想的考验:以犹太教和基督教为代表的一元教的形而上学思想,以社会主义(特别是马克思主义)为代表的着重社会层面的理论思想,以弗洛伊德、弗洛姆等为代表的深度心理学思想。他认为，关注儒家思想与马克思主义之间的辩难和对话一直是当代儒学研究的主调，且至今仍是自身努力的方向。他具体从五个方面进行了论述。（一）对启蒙心态的批判。他指出，现代西方启蒙运动因孕育了社会主义、资本主义并结出现代社会价值和结构之硕果而成为人类历史上最大的意识形态，但同时也具有强烈的人类中心主义、工具理性、浮士德式宰制欲、男性中心主义、极端个人主义、欧洲主义等弊端。（二）儒家人道主义的再现。儒家人道主义作为精神性人道主义的复兴，在东亚创造了不同于现代西方的生活方式和思想方式。现代化传统及过程预设了多元文化形态，日本、亚洲四小龙、越南、中国大陆可为代表。儒家民主可想见、可实践，多元现代化而非现代化多侧面是未来的潮流，文明间真正的对话即将来临。（三）人类繁荣与修身。精神性转向与哲学上的认知论、语言学转向有着同等的重要性。在诸如印度教、中国哲学的非西方哲学传统中，将智慧、精神放在与知识同等的高度。因而轴心文明间的比较，科学与宗教、理由与信仰之间对话不可避免且令人期待。（四）培育文明间对话的社会实践。从"历史的终结"、"文明冲突"到文明间的对话等，对话成为了新的双边社会实践，在国际关系中，国与国间真正意义上的对话仍极少得到实践。以在多元伦理、文化、宗教团体间的交流所具有的深远意义而言，对话涉及在行动、态度、信念方面培养宽容的态度，应广泛认识到作为社会实践形式的对话在提升聆听、扩大知识视野、拓展、深化自我意识方面的作用。（五）精神性人道主义的文明对话。"亲如兄弟"是马克思主义者对人道主义的理解；它意识到我们同住"地球村"或同居"地球船"。在现实政治关系中，全球公民理念却仍是一个乌托邦。儒家人道主义所认同的生态自然不是客体的集合而是交流的主体。公众知识分子应肩负着伦理的责任，去想象和实践在我们日常生活中一个包涵一切"我们"的存在。

对中国传统哲学特别关注的比利时根特大学的 Bart Dessein 教授作了题为《马克思主义与新儒教的崛起》的发言，对马克思主义与中国传统哲学的关系进行了阐述。他用了马克斯·韦伯关于民族-国家的理论来看待传统中国是如何变成现代中国的，他指出在中国的现代化进程中，中国知识分子对儒家思想的质疑自受到欧洲帝国主义的欺凌始一直延续至新中国成立。忠实于家族社群的儒家思想如何与强调阶级斗争的马克思主义思想获得协调与融合？这不仅是中国面对由改革开放带动经济飞跃发展而引发一系列社会不平等的矛盾所应该深入思考的问题，也是面对如何抗争现代性所要作出的回应。

二、导向未来之基：现实的种种发问

与会学者们对未来的关注，既有对马克思主义理论本身的思考，也有对现实社会问题的反思。

对马克思主义理论本身的思考主要聚焦在马克思主义何去何从的问题之上。比利时鲁汶大学的 Ortwin de Graef 教授倾向于以语言学家的身份而不是作为哲学家或者政治科学家去探讨这样的问题。德里达于 20 世纪 90 年代初所作的题为《马克思的幽灵》的报告被视为一个在纪念马克思主义的出现方面前所未有的事件，Ortwin de Graef 认为应该继承德里达的做法，在他的题为《幽灵无序：神经马克思主义和灵魂之国》的发言中，他在解读诸如雪莱诗歌的文学文本以及这些文学文本所继承和传递的历史的基础上，对集体主义式的代理的表征和同情的意识形态进行了说明。他的结论是，马克思曾经宣称通过用一种非宗教的、彻底的国际主义的哲学科学方式对人类的具体存在进行阐释来建构国家，这近似于所谓的正义。马克思的精神之一是寻找这个世界所期待的，以及描绘出助长人类非人性特征出现的异化力量。另一点则是，以对人类特性观念和使用价值的适用性的质疑形成对 21 世纪人类生存的挑战。这种质疑虽认同神经科学对人类特性的发现，却没有将其视为解决问题的途径，而是作为由于人类没有履行移情规则而产生的问题呈现。他因而呼吁让神经马克思主义成为这种科学研究的代名词。上海社会科学院许明研究员从比较视野对当代马克思主义研究的话题进行了审视和反思。他认为，中国当代马克思主义研究经过三十多年的努力，已基本了解和掌握了西方马克思主义者研究的思路、思考的问题和见解。这更使我们看清，我们通常研究的马克思主义，似乎只是西方马克思主义研究者的话题的翻版，如存在主义、虚无、主体间性、异化、东方主义等等。其实中国还存在一种不被译介、不被知识界认同的，实践着的马克思主义，其话题之前沿、务实、新颖，是西方学者所不得不关注，并与之对话的。马克思主义的活的生命力就在于解释实践而不是别的。吉林大学文学院李志宏教授的发言，以《马克思主义美学的科学化维度——"知觉模式说"概论》为题，他主张在马克思主义世界观和方法论的基础上借助现代科学成果来重新解释事物的审美属性及审美价值，与 Ortwin de Graef 不约而同地对科学维度在马克思主义理论中的介入充满了期待。

在对现实问题的反思方面主要集中于对生产主义、性别身份意识和文化研究的关注。中国社会科学院文学研究所高建平教授的主题发言是"消费主义时代的生产主义"。他认为谈"生产主义"要从"时间"谈起。大规模机器生产模式的出现使工作时间成为人生必须忍受的时间，业余时间才是人作为人对时间的享受。随着生产水平的快速提高，物质财富不断增长，刺激消费便成为了化解物质财富充分涌流所带来的经济危机的常用办法。于是，消费成了人的新的存在方式，并且出现了为消费而消费的泛滥趋势。这一趋势虽然使原本基于机器和资本以及由此而形成的大规模生产造成生产、创造和审美三者分离而催生的审美无利害观念与区别于手工业生产的艺术生产逐渐消除了与日常生活的距离，带来了日常生活审美化，然而，却也迫使艺术放弃了对审美的追求，而沦落为以产业化的形式成为医治社会问题的解毒剂。在此过度消费的背景下提出回到对生产和劳动本身所具有的意义的关注，便成为了"生产主义"的重要生成来源和价值导向。英国曼彻斯特大学 David Alderson 教授则以《真人秀节目，性别自我意识和资本形式》的主题发言，从电视真人秀节目中涌现出的对男同性恋者不涉及女性化性征描述的创新表达，追溯了其中关涉日益增长的性别的社会自我意识所具有的重要意义，这种重要意义不仅在于体现了对传统保守社会需要树立多种衡量标准的诉求，在某些方面还可能是被新自由主义所推动的对后现代性别意识类别的批判。而针对文化研究，来自澳大利亚莫纳什大学的 Justin O'Connor 教授作了《什么样的唯物主义是新的唯物主义，或者新自由资本主义的文化逻辑》的发言。他通过对文化研究中的物质性转向及其对某种进步政治的含蓄表达的思考，试图解答这种转变所产生的问题。文化研究中的物质转向是指由原来被英国文化研究奉为基本信条的物质实践回归到物质或唯物主义。这种回归在 Justin O'Connor 看来，意味着在全球经济、环境和文化流动的背景下，在解释物质和物质性、人与非人性方面出现了多种不同以往的方式，但基于物质性的研究方法的有用性却仍未得到很好的证明，由此他认为，新唯物主义所体现的只是其自身的存在性，失去了对如何获得历史意义的解说能力，因而是反历史的。而这样一种阐释路径恰恰暗合了全球资本主义运作方式下那种不需要理想就可以生存的现状。华南师范大学文学院的段吉方教授，则以《文化研究与文化领导权：20世纪英国文化研究中的"葛兰西转向"问题》为题对"葛兰西式的文化研究模式"作了深刻探讨。他认为"葛兰西转向"是20世纪英国文化研究与葛兰西思想发生深刻的理论融通的结果，具有重要的理论启发。"葛兰西转向"产生了一种"葛兰西式的文化研究"，它既是一种理论范式的转折，又是一个重要的理论问题，体现了不同理论模式间的丰富的思想张力和实践影响,是英国文化研究理论在新的文化语境中的更新与重生。有别于 Justin O'Connor 教授和段吉方教授在文化研究理论上的探讨,复旦大学中文系的陆扬教授以"大众文化的另一种解读"为题的发言,侧重于对大众文化的历史及定义范畴的重新划归。他通过对坎托和沃思曼主编的《大众文化史》的研究和解读,认为该书以古希腊为起点,对诸如希腊奥运会和 19 世纪小说的黄金时代所蕴藏着的大众文化底蕴进行了清晰可辨的揭示,这使我们有理由相信,大众文化是有可能被定义为自下而上名至实归的大众的文化,而不仅仅局限于被视为工业社会大批量制作的低质量文化产品。

三、走向未来的跨越:政治与艺术的关系

政治与艺术的关系自古以来就是人们争论不休的话题。无论是认同艺术是政治的附属品,还是坚持艺术的完全独立以规避任何的政治影响,都符合传统马克思主义对两者关系的判断——政治与艺术由于同为建立在经济基础之上的上层建筑,且对人同样具有重大影响,因而不可阻隔地具有密切的联系。对两者关系的考虑是否能对以往的观点有所突破?这无疑是对构想未来的一种跨越式努力。

世界美学学会前任主席、斯洛文尼亚科学与艺术研究院的阿列西教授以题为"单刀直入:红锤破白岛"的主题发言,从法国大革命之后的艺术运动,尤其是先锋派艺术剖析了政治与艺术的关系。他认为,像 19 世纪巴黎公社时期的艺术家库尔贝那样,其画作的风格和技巧都不能显示先锋派艺术所彰显的独立自主的特点,因而不具有真正艺术意义上的革命色彩,换言之,他只是一个表现为艺术与政治交叠的艺术家兼革命家的典型代表。因此,对"先锋派"的界定便成为了处理政治与艺术的关系的一个富有代表性的领域。在大多数西方的美学先锋派看来,要判定一位艺术家是否属于先锋派,就要看其作品是否显示了人性走向何方以及人的命运究竟为何的命题。这就意味着以是否赋予了艺术作品以理论、哲学、意识形态以及世界观等精神烙印为条件来判定艺术家是否在政治意义上具有进步倾向、革命倾向或先锋派倾向。这样,对于未来的印象而言,不管是天堂的印象,还是共产主义的印象,或者永远革命的印象,每一种意识形态都是基于市场的商品和政治宣传之间的本质差异来对未来进行描摹的。前者是指市场本身的意向性透过隐匿于传播过程中的暗中操作性而存在,后者则以权力的意识形态最终也总是一种视野的权力来决定艺术只要服务于任

何一个政治或宗教的意识形态，也终将服务于艺术自身。但是尽管如此，阿列西认为这样的观点也仅仅适用于西方世界的艺术事件。以俄罗斯的建构主义为例，大多数西方学者认为，建构主义已经成为十月革命历史中不可或缺的一部分，而且是被作为一种新的政治秩序成果来欣赏。这样的结论似乎印证了建构主义艺术家将消除艺术的地位视为对人类历史上过时的资产阶级社会的抛弃和终结，因为艺术作为资本主义的一种发明创造的痕迹不是革命共产主义社会所需要的表达手段。同时也似乎印证了，在完全弥漫着政治意识形态思潮的20世纪20年代的俄罗斯社会，不存在艺术市场，而艺术要在政治上起作用只在那种超越了艺术市场范围之外的政治宣传语境之下才得以具备，且艺术成为一种政治宣传手段的同时也树立了一种新的艺术范式，这种艺术范式不可避免地与政治目的相联系。这样的艺术在原苏联国家不断地被加以复制。然而阿列西通过红锤破白岛的典型意象说明了，俄罗斯先锋派艺术家们的实际意图是要实现或积极参与双重革命，通过重新定义革命艺术实践，从而成为革命社会实践。艺术社会先锋派的雄心壮志是要弥合那些产生于假想与实践的接壤之处的分散行为之间的鸿沟。正是基于对蕴含在先锋派艺术中的政治与艺术的关系的解读，阿列西也向我们展示出了东西方在理解现代主义上所存在的巨大分歧。

伦敦大学戈德斯密斯学院 David Margolies 教授作了题为《辩证批判与具体分析》的主题发言。发言以英国在20世纪30年代和60年代末两个阶段，对马克思理论与实践、抽象与具体辩证统一观点的严重扭曲并产生了不良后果为背景，主要体现在：前一阶段恰如考德威尔所宣称的文学鼓励改变的力量来源于情感的重构而不是理性的政治争论所展现的，受西班牙内战影响，先是把对法西斯或支持、或反对的理性政治态度作为评价标准应用于各个领域，继而促成了左翼批评者直接将外在的政治视角作为首要的批评标准，原因在于法西斯主义在欧洲的崛起使人们开始看重共产主义整体的政治和文化观，同时共产党人还保留了强烈的阶级对抗态度，然而却最终导致了对美学、文学情感内涵的低估。但30年代英国激进派的批评视野所遭受的抽象之苦不如1968年以后那么明显。"五月风暴"之后，建立在语言学和电影研究基础上的法国理论以一种有关人类互动的复杂视角提供了一种无关乎苏维埃的马克思主义，并展示出令人瞩目的与英语传统相背离的勇气，这对英国的学院产生了巨大的影响。新的激进学者们认为，意识形态在其最狭隘的意义上是虚假的意识，而学生群体的情绪也被煽动起来，例如文学专业的学生就感觉自己被欺骗了，迫使他们要向假的道德低头，而且要对文学所具有的批判功能保持持续的忽略。文学不再被当作一种礼貌的愉悦，而成为了学者兑现自身使命感的工具和实现社会目的的载体。这样，1968 年激进的一代所得出的结论是，对文学文本的教授，从根本上来讲是错误的，对文学的学习也是具有腐蚀性的。这种影响促使了对文学的研究和教学于 1968 年以后完全转向了理论。毕竟理论不存在文本的危险，相反从理论本身而言又具有对文本的纠正性，而且通过理论的解构作用还能达到解除资本主义意识形态武装威胁的目的。为了达到此次发言的主旨，即以实际的文学文本分析来说明如何使马克思主义原理从抽象到具体化的实践，David Margolies 通过对两组无产阶级小说的分析——刘易斯·琼斯的《金丝雀》、《我们生活》和沃尔特·布赖尔利的《手段测试人》、《夹心人》，充分说明了理性与情感、具体与抽象之间的区别，揭露了深藏在英国教育体制当中对抽象的成见是与根深蒂固的阶级态度相联系的，重申了他对马克思主义理论的理解：马克思在《政治经济学批判导言》中提出的社会存在决定社会意识，为马克思主义改变世界提供了解释的语境和维度，是马克思主义者理解文化的基础。但是曾经的解释历史文化的典型并不等同于永恒不变的公式。在现实世界中对变化的要求显示了，对文化产品的批判不能只关注客体的政治联盟之事实，还应关注主体和情感的建构。忽视这种复杂的建构过程而对文学进行政治性要求，只能使最终的结果逐渐流于粗俗化。

在对诺贝尔文学奖获得者、中国作家莫言的长篇小说《酒国》所进行的专题讨论中，与会学者们再次就具体的文学文本探讨了政治与文学的关系。上海交通大学人文学院的何言宏教授指出，在马克思主义、未来与中国梦三者相关联的当下语境中解读莫言的《酒国》具有重要的时代意义。他的解读主要有三个方面：第一，关于"他的国"，即莫言的"国"。对"国"的想象和叙述是晚清以来现代文学的基本主题，莫言的《酒国》就将五四时期的启蒙主义和鲁迅的基本主题（例如"吃人"），融入到了对"国"的阐释和描绘之中，使作品渗透着对国民的理解，继承了五四以来的批判传统。第二，关于"国民"。莫言对国民的吃人本性及强大的同化力所进行的批判性书写，呈现了莫言对五四以来批判吃人之国民性的主题的继续，且表现了更加强烈的忧愤意识。第三，关于"国民文学"。文本中的互文和对话具有互相辩驳反讽的关系，莫言以此呼吁对五四以来的自我审判的继承。在以上三方面认识的基础上，他认为《酒国》的叙述可以为对马克思主义、未来与中国梦的理解提供某些经验和精神资源，即如何在对未来的规划中寻找自身的精神传统和精神起点。中国社会科学院文学研究所的吴子林教授发言的题目是《"重回叙拉古？"——论文学"超轶政治"之可能》。他借助柏拉图三赴西西里的叙拉古城邦,规劝其僭主戴奥尼素父子用哲学和正义治国,结果铩羽而归的典故,以莫言小说创作中对政治事件和尺度的把握来谈论文学与政治的关系,以及对知识分子如何批评与介入政治进行某种可能性的设想。他的结论是,莫言的文学选择不是"规避政治",而是"超轶政治",在既努力维护文学的自主性,又不至于妄图根据文学或审美的逻辑来塑造政治的创作中保持一种正确对待政治要求的心态和胸怀。上海交通大学人文学院博士研究生杨荔斌的题为《〈酒国〉之"酒"的叙事原点》的发言,则将对《酒国》的讽喻实质纳入了中国传统文化的视域中进行深入剖析,从小说的叙事场景、人物性征、叙事事件三方面展开了对小说叙事原点的解答。

四、建构未来之纬:关于乌托邦

英国伦敦大学 Matthew Beaumont 教授作了题为《乌托邦的幽灵》的发言。他认为将乌托邦比喻为鬼魂是恰当的,因为乌托邦主义如同鬼魂一般具有某种揭露社会不和谐因素的合理性,以及对消除各种不公正现象的希冀,这也深深触动了现代主义的神经。尤其在与过度消费相联系之时将乌托邦比喻成鬼魂,这实则有助于我们形象地理解乌托邦。鬼魂的使用一方面突出了辩证法之模棱两可的特性,另一方面则突出了乌托邦介于理想与真实之间、物质与精神之间的特质。假如鬼魂能够侵入被历史局限性和意识形态所压抑的现实,那么乌托邦则能够侵入因受压抑而导致缺失所指示的未来。乌托邦的闹鬼行为实际上借鉴了德里达《马克思的幽灵》一文中的阐释,展示一种存在于不存在之中的中间状态,但仍可见出乌托邦成为某种参与性政治的意义。因而未来社会的轮廓总是可以从现代获得,或者说未来可以从现代的内部进行建构。然而,基于审视现代社会所形成的"花瓶效应",并由此产生对乌托邦的期待,使现代变得异化而出现了诸多不稳定的现象,这究竟是社会主义还是野蛮主义?对此仍然是值得探讨的。

北京师范大学文学院姚建彬副教授作了题为《马克思主义同乌托邦究竟是什么关系?——关于'空想社会主义'译名的检讨及其他》的发言。他认为国内对于涉及马克思主义思想三大来源之一的"空想社会主义"的认识和理解仍然存在不能忽视的误区,主要表现在:为了强调马克思主义体系中的社会主义思想的科学性、正统性和权威性,自五四以来以对民主和科学的偏重造成了对乌托邦等重要外来思想范畴的轻视，甚至无视马克思对于乌托邦所做的具体而具有直接针对性的批评，将所有乌托邦思想都予以了批判和否定。这就形成了马克思主义等同于科学，而不可能同乌托邦有任何关系的有失偏颇之论。这显然违背了马克思主义的原旨，因为马克思恩格斯为人类所描绘的共产主义远景就具有经典乌托邦的诸多特征。因此，必须正视马克思主义与乌托邦之间的关系。

香港科技大学人文学部陈建华教授作了题为《1920年代上海/海上的反/乌托邦小说——文学城市空间的'情感结构'及辩证诠释》的发言。这是他读了詹明信关于"乌托邦"作为"方法的"的论说之后所产生的想法。主要是回顾晚清至1920年代上海这一"冒险家的乐园"所产生的乌托邦与反乌托邦的文学建构，以两篇短篇小说——周瘦鹃1921年《留声机片》和茅盾1929年《创造》——为例。在解读城市与乌托邦不同空间交互作用的文学表现时，试图运用雷蒙·威廉斯所说的"情感结构"（the structure of feeling）的理论，旨在揭示政治现实、社会机制与意识形态如何透过文学语言、风格及美学程式显示特定时代、集体与个人经验的印记。这一文学乌托邦的历史经验或许能在当下全球境遇中提供某种资源。

上海政法学院应用社会科学研究院祁志祥教授作了题为《从空想共产主义到马克思的共产主义》的发言。他回顾了历史上各种空想共产主义学说，由此剖析了马克思描绘的共产主义社会的基本特征以及中国改革开放新时期以来对它的变革与发展，以此呼吁对空想共产主义与马克思的共产主义两者的异同要有客观认识，并用科学的实事求是的态度对待马克思的共产主义学说。

五、探讨未来的中国话语：美学与文学

在对未来的探讨中发出中国话语的声音，这是马克思主义中国化努力的方向。与会的多位中国学者对此提出了许多富有创见性的见解。

在美学理论方面，上海交通大学人文学院王杰教授作了题为《中国悲剧观念：马克思主义美学与未来》的发言。他认为马克思主义美学要想重返公共话语空间，就要在历史悲剧的理论框架下对现代性悲剧存在作出反思。作为一种外来的理论模式，马克思主义悲剧美学必须在中国文化传统和现实审美经验之间找到内在的精神契合点。中国文化的悲剧观念和马克思主义美学的关于"日常生活悲剧"的理论以及当代艺术中"尘世的崇高"等美学特征是相通的。作

为中国文化传统与中国现代化过程中的悲剧性现象相结合的结果，中国悲剧观念已成为中国式审美现代性的核心概念之一。在审美现代性、悲剧观念、世俗性崇高等成为全球性现象和全球性问题的条件下，马克思主义美学有可能对这种陷于深刻伦理危机和价值危机的现象作出理论的阐释，并将获得自身理论的进一步发展。复旦大学中文系朱立元教授作了题为《马克思实践的唯物主义与现代美学革命》的发言。他认为马克思实践的唯物主义是绝对唯心主义和直观唯物主义的双重扬弃和超越。它颠覆了近代西方形而上学的传统，在哲学史上掀起了一场革命：确立了现代存在论的根基，超越了主客二分的认识思维模式；打破了形而上学的现成论，形成了动态生成的世界观；在"实践"的基础上建立了新的人本主义思想，关注人的本质的全面实现。这场深刻的哲学革命也为现代美学带来了革命性的转变，启发了现代美学在研究对象、研究内容和研究方式等方面进行学科建构的变革，同时也为当代中国美学走向中西融合、古今传承的历史性发展提供了多种可能。上海交通大学人文学院夏锦乾教授作了题为《反思20世纪马克思主义美学的"主流现象"——兼论马克思主义美学与中国传统美学精神的关系》的发言。他指出，反思马克思主义美学成为中国现代美学的主流需要对两大问题进行拷问：其一，为什么马克思主义美学不同于其他美学思潮，有如此强盛的生命力？其二，新世纪中国美学仍然会这样"主流"下去吗？对于第一个问题，除了政治原因和马克思主义美学本身的开放性特征外，还有中国传统美学精神的作用因素，即被视为中国传统美学精神之根本理念的巫术的能动性创造观念是与马克思主义美学思想相交流、相契合的基本点，因而能够在历史的进程中不断地与中国作家取得深层次的共鸣，继而占据主流地位。对于第二个问题，则需要站在时代的高度对马克思主义美学中的"人"和中国美学中的"人"加以阐释上的清理，由此重读马克思主义美学，重建中国美学。此外，华东师范大学中文系的朱志荣教授提出了对中国美学研究的当下性的认识，云南大学文学院的向丽副教授提出了对马克思的人类学思想及其美学意义的探讨，湖北黄冈师范学院文学院舒开智副教授从审美自由的维度展开了浪漫主义与马克思主义的比较研究。同时，还有对宗白华、朱光潜等人的美学思想的研究。

在文学研究与文艺理论方面，浙江大学中文系王元骧教授作了题为《对我国马克思主义文艺理论研究的哲学反思》的发言。他就以往我国马克思主义文艺理论研究中所存在的直观论、纯认识论和教条主义倾向作了简略的评论，并认为造成这些倾向的思想根源从哲学上来看，是由于把"思维与存在的关系"

混同于"精神与物质的关系",因而简单地以唯心和唯物来划分马克思主义与非马克思主义之故。上海交通大学人文学院叶舒宪教授则在题为《玉石之路:河西走廊与华夏文明的资源依赖》的发言中,通过对河西走廊之文明史意义的深刻发掘,以生动的个案示例了如何通过人类的历史经验去找出驱动一个文明的核心动力要素,如何实证性地说明马克思主义所认同的物质与精神的相互作用。华中师范大学文学院孙文宪教授的发言题目是《马克思主义批判对文学思想内涵的诉求》。他指出反思和批判"资本现代性"对文学活动、审美活动乃至整个精神生产的影响,构成了马克思文学批评的思想基础和主要对象,并由此形成了马克思主义文学批评的"问题域",形成了不同于一般文学理论的、马克思主义文学批评范式特有的问题意识、研究对象和理论范畴,这些内在规定,最终决定了马克思主义批评对文学思想内涵的诉求。上海交通大学人文学院张蕴艳博士作了题为《二十世纪中国的民族主义、世界主义及共同体价值——未来中国马克思主义文艺理论建设的一种视角》的发言。她认为,20世纪中国文学理论在文化与政治双重方向上思考民族主义、世界主义与马克思主义的关系问题,为马克思主义文学理论中国化提供了深刻的启示与教训。因此,在民族主义与世界主义的论域里构想未来中国的文学理论建设,必须考虑包括民族主义在内的政治文化共同体的价值,以期实现世界主义的某种乌托邦理想。此外,华东师范大学王峰教授对作为文学的伴随因素的"真实"作了论述,湘潭大学刘中望副教授以思想资源与政治语境的对接为切入对瞿秋白与列宁文艺理论的关系进行了阐述,河北大学文学院刘洁则对李长之在中国文艺美学的现代建构上开展的许多开拓性工作及其文艺美学思想进行了评述。

(本文责任编辑:任天)

马克思主义与中西美学的未来

——第三届"中英马克思主义美学双边论坛"综述

张蕴艳[*]

(上海交通大学人文学院)

未来既是对已经过去的历史和即将演变为历史的现在的回应,也暗示着过去与现在的变化、流逝、风险与不确定,将马克思主义文艺美学与未来的命题相连接,既是对马克思主义文艺美学的过去的历史书写,也是对马克思主义文艺美学的现状的反思考察,同时还是对马克思主义文艺美学的未来命运在消极与积极两方面的警醒、预测或希望。

有鉴于此,2013年4月6—8日,由上海交通大学人文学院、曼彻斯特大学艺术、语言与文化学院共同主办的第三届"中英马克思主义美学双边论坛"在上海交大人文学院顺利召开,本届论坛将主题确定为"马克思主义与未来"。论坛由上海交大人文学院、美学与文化理论研究所、《马克思主义美学研究》编辑部承办,《探索与争鸣》杂志社、鲁迅文化基金会学术部协办,受津辉人文基金赞助。本届论坛吸引了来自美国加利福尼亚大学圣芭芭拉分校、伦敦大学、斯洛文尼亚科学与艺术研究院、比利时鲁汶大学、比利时根特大学、美国杜克大学、瑞士欧洲研究院、俄罗斯圣彼得堡大学、韩国庆尚国立大学、英国切尔西艺术学会、英国奥斯顿大学、澳大利亚莫纳什大学、英国利兹大学、英国曼彻斯特大学等共17所国外高校与研究机构参会。来自香港科技大学、中国社会科学院、上海社会科学院、上海交通大学、北京大学、华中师范大学、复旦大学、华东师范大学、浙江大学、吉林大学、厦门大学、武汉大学、山东大

---

[*] 张蕴艳,1972年生,女,浙江温岭人,文艺学博士,上海交通大学人文学院讲师。

学、中国传媒大学、上海大学、上海师范大学、中央编译出版社、鲁迅纪念馆、《文艺报》、《社会科学报》、《文汇报》、《文汇读书周报》、《学术月刊》、《社会科学家》、《马克思主义美学研究》等 50 多所国内高校、科研院所、学术机构及新闻媒体的 80 多位专家学者参加了本次论坛。上海交通大学徐飞副校长、人文学院王杰院长、曼彻斯特大学大卫·奥尔德森教授在开幕式上致辞。上海交大文科建设处处长蒋宏主持了开幕式。徐飞副校长在致辞中高度评价了双边论坛的学术交流形式对促进马克思主义理论研究和发展的意义，以及促进上海交大国际化学术交流的价值。在开幕式上，一并举行了上海交通大学左翼文化研究中心的揭牌仪式，鲁迅文化基金会秘书长周令飞先生出席了揭牌仪式。

本届论坛的会议形式分大会主题演讲、专题讨论与论文交流三部分。在开幕式后的大会主题演讲中，一些有国际影响的教授作了主题发言，如美国加州大学著名的社会学、政治学和马克思主义、列宁哲学研究专家凯文·安德森（Kevin Anderson）教授、北京大学高等人文研究院杜维明教授、斯洛文尼亚科学与艺术研究院阿列西·艾尔雅维奇（Aleš Erjavec）教授、伦敦大学戈德斯密斯学院大卫·马格列斯（David Margolies）教授、曼彻斯特大学大卫·奥尔德森（David Alderson）教授、中国社会科学院文研所高建平教授等。大会专题讨论部分依托的是两个文本的细读，詹姆逊 2009 年出的新书 Valences of the Dialectic 和莫言的《酒国》。论文交流部分的论文是由大会秘书处在收到的 80 多篇论文的基础上遴选的。与会学者围绕"马克思主义与未来"这一主题，展开了深入热烈的讨论。如何以对"马克思主义与未来"的探讨为契机，在马克思主义与中西美学的历史传统与现实境遇的结合点上，思考马克思主义在未来社会建设中的地位与作用，以及美学在这种可能性面前面临的问题、危机、挑战与任务，是本届论坛的焦点所在。

一、乌托邦、现实与未来

在"历史终结论"、"美学终结论"、"末世论"等世纪末语境下，危机、风险、革命、希望与拯救成为马克思主义美学在新世纪初的关键词。其中，乌托邦再次成为一个聚焦的话题。正如马克思主义乌托邦哲学家布洛赫所言，希望不是与现实相联系，而是与未知的未来事实相联系。在"积极的意义上，希望却是乌托邦的基本原理，作为想象的形而上学，希望照明未来视域、纵览全体，构成各种未来思想的理论基础"。"希望能够作为乌托邦动因激励人们立足当下，回首流逝的过去，展望即将到来的未来。"从柏拉图《理想国》到近代托马斯·莫尔《乌托邦》、康帕内拉《太阳城》直到布洛赫《希望的原理》，作为乌托邦动因的希望理念，可谓是一个贯穿西方思想史的哲学主题。而马克思主义的乌托邦理念，是一种布洛赫意义上的"已知的希望"，它超越了以往许多乌托邦主义者是"做白日梦的人和不切实际的浪漫主义者"的藩篱，它以唯物辩证法为方法论，通过理论联系实际，让人类以积极投身社会变革和政治变革的本质力量去创造世界的未来前景。伦敦大学的 Matthew Beaumont《乌托邦的政治光谱》即通过探讨乌托邦思想这个概念在欧洲和北美的哲学和政治影响，探讨了塑造乌托邦思想史的辩证法的可能性和实用性。英国切尔西艺术学会的约翰·鲍尔温（John Baldwin）将"乌托邦"比喻为"鬼魂"（ghost），强调辩证地理解乌托邦在未来的多重可能。来自韩国庆尚国立大学的 JEONG Seongjin 则基于马克思对未来社会的概念，尤其是"共产主义"、"社团"和"计划"等概念，以客观地对 21 世纪各种模式的社会主义或共产主义作评述的方式回应乌托邦问题。北师大姚建彬教授则指出，在马克思看来，政治活动与乌托邦蓝图是并行不悖的。甚至在某种意义上，政治活动比单纯的乌托邦蓝图来得更加紧迫，但是后者的合理内核，也就是乌托邦蓝图的合法性与真理性，却内蕴于马克思所理解并倡导的政治活动中。说到底，马克思和恩格斯为人类所描绘的共产主义远景，就具有经典乌托邦的诸多特征：比如没有阶级、国家消亡、"按需分配，各取所需"、"劳动成为人的需要，而不是手段"，等等。但与传统蓝图派乌托邦不同的是，马克思和恩格斯尽量遏制了这种描绘未来的冲动，由此体现出其辩证色彩。来自上海交大的陈建华教授则认为，清末以来世界上各种政体与社会模式引起不同的中国想象和实践。20 世纪中国的乌托邦文学再现极其丰富，为未来中提供了多元的资源。"马克思主义与未来"需要回顾现代中国的历史，也包括对于马克思主义的中国理论与实践的反思。而在半殖民"第三世界"的中国，无论都市大众文化与"无产阶级"革命文化都表现出自身的特点，从它们所谓的文化整体来思考或许是我们的基本任务。因而他以周瘦鹃 1921 年《留声机片》和茅盾 1929 年《创造》两篇短篇小说为例，具体而微地回顾了晚清至 20 世纪 20 年代上海这一"冒险家的乐园"所产生的乌托邦与反乌托邦的文学建构。将对乌托邦的讨论落实到中国当代的现实中，论坛选取了莫言的《酒国》为契入点。上海交大何言宏教授主持了该场专题讨论并作了开场白。指出要将《酒国》置入 20 世纪初民族国家建构与五四启蒙的历史场景中，并在今天对中国梦的描画的长时段中来探讨《酒国》与民族国家乌托邦憧憬的关系。中国社会科学院文研所吴子林教授从《酒国》开始,全面考察概况了莫言创作的总体特征,指出莫言的文学选择不是"规避政治",而是"超轶政治";莫言是一个正确对待政治要求的小说家,他洞悉这一要求的限度所在;他努力维护文学的自主性,又不至于妄图根据文学或审美的逻辑来塑造政治。莫言所实践的是迥异于宏大叙事、侧重于伦理原则的"元政治",即捷克思想家哈维尔精辟地称之为"反政治的政治"。

二、人道主义、辩证法与未来

人道主义是第二届中英马克思主义美学双边论坛的主题,加州大学圣芭芭拉分校的凯文·安德森教授延续了上一届对人道主义的讨论,在本届论坛上以《结构主义和后结构主义之后的社会主义人道主义》为题,以系谱学方法回顾了从结构主义到后结构主义之后的人道主义的历史,反思了从萨特、阿尔都塞、布尔迪厄、福柯到弗洛姆、弗朗茨·法农、卡莱尔·科西克和拉亚·杜纳耶夫斯卡娅对人道主义的理解、批判与再创新的阐释,他特别从拉亚·杜纳耶夫斯卡娅及东欧马克思主义人道主义者的解放普世性中借鉴大量观点,认为需要特别密切关注那些社会主义的人道主义形式,比如杜纳耶夫斯卡娅、法农、科西克,因为他们的社会主义的人道主义允许将普世性进行特殊化,同时,需要批判性地将后结构主义社会批判家的一些见解运用到 21 世纪马克思主义人道主义中,为全球资本主义的批判提供一种新的内涵,它指向的是一个新的自由的社会,在那里,女人和男人能以一种既是社会的又是个体的方式行使他们的自决权。

在总结马克思主义人道主义的发展历程时,凯文·安德森教授也同时对辩证法的方法论在结构主义到后结构主义发展的框架里结合其与人道主义的关系进行了回顾。他指出无论是在像阿尔都塞这样的结构主义者或像福柯一类的后结构主义者影响下,都有从人道主义、从黑格尔以及从 20 世纪 70 与 80 年代更普遍的辩证法转移的倾向。在这些背景下,黑格尔已然变成反动的、赞成帝国主义的思想家,而马克思则变成欧洲中心主义的思想家。最近有些学者已经开始提倡回归黑格尔和辩证法,但是少有人正在回归社会主义和马克思主义的人道主义。在 21 世纪的背景下,他呼吁一种回归——不仅接受《1844 年经济学哲学手稿》、《政治经济学批判大纲》和《资本论》中所展现的马克思式的人道主义——也接受第二次世界大战后西方社会主义人道主义者的观点。对辩证法的探讨，也是大卫·马格列斯的发言主题。他指出马克思在他的《政治经济学批判导言》中宣称，社会存在决定意识，这是马克思主义者理解文化的一个基本原则，但它不是公式，它只是提供了解释的背景或语境。虽然它已经典型地运用于解释历史文化，但是就像它的建立者已经明确的，马克思主义也能改造这个世界。改造真实世界的要求意味着对文化产品的批判，必须不仅注意到客观的政治联盟的问题，也有主体性和情绪的建设的问题。忽略了这个复杂的过程的批评而将政治要求施加于文学将导致严厉专断的评判。他以29岁时在西班牙内战中被杀害的英国马克思主义者克里斯托弗·考德威尔为例，表明文学的鼓动变化的力量主要来自情感的重组而不是来自理性的政治争论，因而个体的情感体验必须是具体的，要求马克思主义文学批评必须加入这个具体性。浙江大学的王元骧教授也是针对唯物辩证法的具体性为中心，对以往中国马克思主义文艺理论研究中所存在的直观论、纯认识论和教条主义倾向作了简略的评论，并认为造成这些倾向的思想根源从哲学上来看，是由于把"思维与存在的关系"混同于"精神与物质的关系"，并简单地以唯心和唯物来划分马克思主义与非马克思主义之故，主张在马克思主义哲学包括文艺理论中，应将观点与方法统一起来。在学习马克思主义时，就不能仅仅只看它的结论，还应该关注这结论是怎样答出的，还应该同时把它当作是一种认识问题、分析问题和解决问题的方法来进行学习。这样我们对于问题的理解才能避免抽象而会有具体的领会。华中师大孙文宪教授呼应了对马克思主义研究方法讨论，指出马克思主义的研究方法是从属于马克思主义理论体系的，把方法从理论体系中剥离出来，无视理论系统对批评方法和批评对象的规定性，会从根本上模糊马克思主义批评的特质，忽略马克思主义文学理论特有的问题意识。马克思主义文学批评之所以是一种自成系统的文学研究范式，首先是因为马克思主义的理论体系是对其批评方法的规定性。对马克思主义美学方法系统的强调，可谓是与会学者对未来马克思主义美学的一种期待与研究的一个方向。

三、悲剧、美学革命与未来

从亚里士多德对悲剧的古典定义到20世纪现代悲剧的产生，尽管悲剧在西方的演进和发展也经历了重大的变化，但是悲剧对人的精神的高贵性的强调却从未改变。本届论坛的分议题之一是探讨"当代悲剧观念与马克思主义的阐释"。就此话题与会学者各抒己见。上海交大王杰教授认为雷蒙·威廉斯最大的贡献在于提出"革命悲剧"的理念，从而将那种被视为是真理系统和永恒抽象的神学或悲剧哲学推至具体的历史文化变迁的"情感结构"之中，并将之拉平至日常生活活生生的经验层面。在雷蒙·威廉斯看来，首先，悲剧意义总是受到文化和历史的双重限定，因而悲剧是一种我们每一个人都正感受和经历着的"经验形式"。其次，任何"革命"，无论是资产阶级革命，还是社会主义革命，都是"深层的悲剧性无序状况必不可少的运动"。马克思主义美学要想重返公共话语空间，就要在历史悲剧的理论框架下对现代性悲剧存在做出反思。作为一种外来的理论模式，马克思主义悲剧美学必须在中国文化传统和现实审美经验之间找到内在的精神契合点。中国文化的悲剧观念和马克思主义美学的关于"日常生活悲剧"的理论以及当代艺术中"尘世的崇高"等美学特征是相通的。思考马克思主义美学的未来，其一是从伦理精神的维度，对悲剧信仰的强调。马克思主义美学的批判不是高屋建瓴的道德批判，而是人伦意义上的"尘世"的悲悯，因为悲剧的苦难与超越是历史人群中每一个人的恶与善。其二，从发展的角度，马克思主义悲剧观提供了未来的价值指向。它表明历史不是某种抽象，而是可以经由主体的实践不断改变的过程。无独有偶，肯尼斯·苏林的《雷蒙·威廉斯的悲剧与革命》也是从雷蒙·威廉斯的书《现代悲剧》着手来阐释马克思主义对悲剧的理解的。苏林认为《现代悲剧》是重要的但被忽视了的一本书。在书中威廉姆斯试图在"情感结构"的方面赋予"悲剧性"概念以新的内容和意义，来适应20世纪的一个核心经验，即政治革命。雷蒙·威廉斯认为早期的悲剧规范理论，以一个高贵和有威望的角色遭受的痛苦来定义悲剧本质，从而将普通人排除在悲剧之外。而苏林认为《现代悲剧》中最重要的是威廉斯试图将革命的经验囊括到悲剧概念中，从而扩大西方古典悲剧的概念。在《现代悲剧》的写作（1962年）和修订版出版（1979年）这17年间，有一个重要的变化，即那17年里发生了许多社会和政治动乱。威廉斯的书是在反思包括古巴革命、越南战争、第三世界国家的独立斗争、1968年的布拉格之春和20世纪60年代的激进的学生运动基础上完成的。他认为现在可以寻找在我们自己的文化中的悲剧结构，重要的悲剧存在于旧与新的分解期与转化期的张力关系中。他认为马克思是让历史和悲剧进入意识关系中，威廉斯将自己与马克思看齐，提出将悲剧看作是在我们的时代"应对社会障碍"的一种深刻的"意识形态"。苏林指出在悲剧的缺席的情况下，不能没有悲剧。

马克思主义的悲剧观可谓是最具美学革命特征的艺术形式之一，来自斯洛文尼亚科学与艺术研究院的阿列西·艾尔雅维奇教授则在更广泛的先锋艺术层面探讨"美学革命"这一现代艺术与政治的关系。他的演讲题目《"红锤破白党"》追溯了十月革命后左翼的构成主义艺术，各种用于政治宣传的纪念碑、纪念塔、街头海报等。阿列西指出这样一些艺术形式和图像是有明显的政治教育和国家宣传的意识形态政治。来自复旦大学的朱立元教授、章文颖博士的论文《马克思实践的唯物主义与现代美学革命》则阐释了马克思实践的唯物主义这场哲学革命为现代美学带来的革命性意义。美学革命在中国语境同样回避不了文学与政治的关系。华中师大胡亚敏教授指出，马克思主义文学批评在中国当代形态的文学与政治新关系下，需要做相应的新的调整：一是要关注个体生命和日常生活中的政治；二是要揭示文学作品中的隐形政治；三是要注重政治与审美、经济的融合。除与政治的关系之外，美学革命在当代中国的另一方面是处理好美学与"生产"和"消费"的关系。中国社会科学院文研所高建平教授指出，从重视"生产"向重视"消费"发展，这似乎符合经济发展的必然规律，但由此而形成的大规模生产剥夺了这种生产的愉悦，形成了生产、创造和审美三者的分离，对生产效率的追求，使得生产过程的愉悦被牺牲了，这又是一个问题。如何解决人成了生产机器中的齿轮和螺丝钉的问题，让幸福包含创造性的劳动，消除幸福与劳动的对立，未来人的全面发展才成为可能。俄罗斯圣彼得堡大学的彼得罗夫（Alexander V. Petrov）也是在这一维度考虑分析在当代社会和经济条件下环境伦理学的矛盾发展的。他的报告讨论了环境伦理问题的可持续发展。他指出可持续发展的概念意味着经济社会发展与自然的和谐。为了保护未来几代人的生存，这种类型的社会和经济发展需要有效使用有限的资源，包括维护自然环境。他认为环境伦理已成为现代政治话语和社会科学不可分割的一部分，同时环境伦理已成为一个时尚的意识形态。来自曼彻斯特大学的戴维·安德森则从性别角度回应了彼得罗夫在环境问题上对新自由主义的批判。他的《扮演直男：电视真人秀、性别自我意识和资本的形式》一文，以电视系列剧《男人猜猜猜》为例，着眼于"直男扮演"这个术语在增加社会性别自我意识上的意义，认为虽然"直男扮演"被视为社会保守派在吸引各种性取向的人群，但在某些方面它可能也可被视为是在新自由主义的条件下某种"后现代"性别意识的提升，即"直男扮演"这一概念不应该被本质化，而是在社会性别和生理性别之间进行的进一步的互换。

四、保守与激进、传统与未来的共识建构

在本届论坛上，除了主题发言、专题讨论与论文交流之外，还穿插播放了

瑞士导演杰森·巴克的纪录片《重新加载马克思：没有选择的革命》，并请他进行了视频对话。杰森·巴克首先交代了这部电影拍摄的背景，通过几年来的观察他发现，马克思与我们"息息相关的"的想法已经被广泛的传播，甚至在马克思的"反对者"或至少在那些从不敢自称是马克思主义者的人们中间也是如此。在这种背景下，他开始编撰和导演纪录片《重新加载马克思：没有选择的革命》，这个片子于 2010 年拍摄，2011 年 4 月首次在文化电视台播放。这部电影的名称是 2009 年 3 月在伦敦伯克贝克学院齐泽克组织的研讨会上命名的。第二个研讨会于 2010 年 7 月在柏林召开，同样由齐泽克组织，其中部分内容出现在电影中。他将电影标题定为"重新加载马克思"是因为齐泽克认为今天的马克思主义面临的问题不再是马克思经典的剥削理论问题，剩余价值不再是来自劳动而是来自因信息革命导致的比尔·盖茨意义上个人订制的基本服务。这部电影是为了解决这一新形势下所谓的"共产主义的理念"这一"文化现象"，即在什么程度上这个"共产主义的理念"使我们能够更好地理解"大萧条"时代？或者说，在全球资本主义和共产主义的理念之间存在着什么样的可能的关系，因为一方面，全球资本主义看似存在着地方性和内在的危机；而另一方面，如何看待共产主义的理念，是将之当作资本主义的一个可能的"解决方案"，或还是将之当作资本主义之外的某种"选择"：一种哲学的、政治的或社会的选择？杰森·巴克认为事实上我们需要自问的不是"资本主义没有别的选择了吗？"而是"共产主义没有别的选择了吗？"，或"革命没有选择了吗？"。因此实际上，杰森·巴克开出的药方是颇为激进的。他将保守主义与激进主义之争比喻为选择"蓝色药丸"还是"红色药丸"，他认为面临今天残酷的全球经济和金融危机，简单地在两种药丸之间进行选择是无效的。而共产主义是一种自由平等选择，它选择的药丸始终是"红色"的。这就是他所说的"革命没有替代品"的意思。通过重新加载马克思，回归马克思的传统，他让我们后人看到资本主义是一种历史现象，它是作为社会的一部分和继续适应它而演变的，共产主义在未来政治中并未过时。

保守与激进之争也暗含着对待传统的态度。上海交大教授、《马克思主义美学研究》副主编夏锦乾反思了 20 世纪马克思主义美学的"主流现象"，马克思主义美学作为马克思主义整体的一个有机部分，是涉及新世纪中国美学走向的重大问题。他提出其中包含以下两大问题：其一，为什么马克思主义美学不同于其他美学思潮，有如此强盛的生命力？其二，新世纪中国美学仍然会这样"主流"下去吗？马克思主义美学作为外来的美学思想如果不能在最基本的美学精神上与中国数千年来的美学精神相契合，就很难在中国长期"主流"下去；同样，马克思主义美学中国化，也并不简单地等同于国内学者对它的接受和实际运用，只有在某一根本点上和中国固有的审美精神真正地结合起来，并且以中国的审美精神形式阐释马克思主义美学精神，这才是货真价实的"中国化"。上海交大叶舒宪教授则以《玉石之路》具体地诠释了这种结合。上海社科院许明教授指出，在马克思主义中国化的过程中，中国在马克思主义思想界没有自己的声音，因此，他强调要在中国与西方、在传统文化模式与马克思主义思想之间开展对话。从"主流"的角度说，儒学是不可忽略的中国文化传统。Bart Dessein 教授的《马克思主义与新儒家的兴起》一文指出，19 世纪末 20 世纪初之后，中国知识分子在反抗欧洲帝国主义同时也质疑传统儒家的价值，中华人民共和国的建立意味着中国儒家思想被中国官方意识形态马列主义所取代。他指出当代中国的典型特征即是"为现代化而奋斗"。针对这种情形，他评价了传统和当代中国政治参与的状况和问题。与之相反，北京大学高等人文研究院杜维明教授则认为，在新的历史条件下，马克思主义与儒学之间的交流与对话，是形成一种建设性力量的新尝试。一方面，马克思人文主义与儒家人文主义的相互配合，可以开拓一个崭新的人文视域，更好地指导现世中的人通过社会实践去改变世界；另一方面，在儒家传统根深蒂固的中国社会中，"马克思主义中国化"既是需要我们重新了解、辩证分析的一个命题，同时也是一个未完成的过程，即回到轴心文明、恢复中国最深厚的传统文化并实现中华民族自我救赎的过程。没有历史记忆就没有自由，在对自己的民族、文化与人性进行反思的过程中，一个健康的历史尤为重要。王杰教授回应了他的观点，认为马克思主义批判精神在当代社会的重新焕发，无疑有助于我们理性地辩难与思考问题，从而树立起悲剧意识。这是一种深刻的、中国式的悲剧意识，与我们的日常生活相联系。面对中国现代化的现实，对于悲剧观念的关注可以使我们更好地反省现实，进而找到伦理、正义以及经验的合理性。在浓厚的历史记忆的积淀之下，儒家传统文化中的每一个主体人都有一个丰富而悲剧的人生，具有一种"舍我其谁"的担当，最终目的则是为了人类全体而奋斗，这也就将个体人上升到具有普遍意义的人类全体。因此，马克思主义与儒家的交流与对话，不仅是文化上的终极关怀，同时也在精神世界中塑造个人与民族的方向，它面向的是未来，并关系到我们拥有怎样的未来。王杰教授进一步指出：马克思主义美学在当下正处于一种十分艰难而且百般交集的复杂局面，在当代中国，马克思主义美学重新成为公共话语不仅是可能的，而且是必要的。随着不同的理论在对现实重大问题的深入研究中得到进一步发展和系统化,特别是随着马克思主义美学面对当代社会价值危机不断提出建设性的思路,以及马克思主义理论批判能力和解释能力的提高,中国马克思主义美学就能够重新成为公共话语,从而在未来担当起批判现实和改变世界的历史责任。

  会议结束后,中英双方约定,第四届中英马克思主义美学双边论坛将于2014年4月21—23日在英国切斯特大学召开,会议主题确定为"宗教与现代美学"。

(本文责任编辑:任天)

图书在版编目(CIP)数据

马克思主义与未来:第三届中英马克思主义美学双边论坛论文集/王杰,(英)斯宾塞(Spencer,R.)主编. —北京:中央编译出版社,2013.11
ISBN 978-7-5117-1826-6

Ⅰ.①马…
Ⅱ.①王…②斯…
Ⅲ.①马克思主义美学-国际学术会议-文集
Ⅳ.①B83-53

中国版本图书馆 CIP 数据核字(2013)第 247983 号

马克思主义与未来:第三届中英马克思主义美学双边论坛论文集

出 版 人	刘明清
出版统筹	薛晓源
策 划 人	西　畴
责任编辑	王忠波
责任印制	尹　珺
出版发行	中央编译出版社
地　　址	北京西城区车公庄大街乙5号鸿儒大厦B座(100044)
电　　话	(010)52612345(总编室)　(010)52612339(编辑室)
	(010)66161011(团购部)　(010)52612332(网络销售)
	(010)66130345(发行部)　(010)66509618(读者服务部)
网　　址	www.cctphome.com
经　　销	全国新华书店
印　　刷	北京瑞哲印刷厂
开　　本	787毫米×1092毫米　1/16
字　　数	460千字
印　　张	26.5
版　　次	2013年11月第1版第1次印刷
定　　价	89.00元

本社常年法律顾问:北京市吴栾赵阎律师事务所律师　闫军　梁勤
凡有印装质量问题,本社负责调换。电话:(010)66509618